A TRUE ACCOUNT OF MY LIFE
AND SELECTED MEDITATIONS

The Other Voice in Early Modern Europe:
The Toronto Series, 87

FOUNDING EDITORS
Margaret L. King
Albert Rabil, Jr.

SENIOR EDITOR
Margaret L. King

SERIES EDITORS
Vanda Anastácio
Jaime Goodrich
Elizabeth H. Hageman
Sarah E. Owens
Deanna Shemek
Colette H. Winn

EDITORIAL BOARD
Anne Cruz
Margaret Ezell
Anne Larsen
Elissa Weaver

ANNE, LADY HALKETT

A True Account of My Life
and Selected Meditations

∽

Edited by
SUZANNE TRILL

Iter Press
NEW YORK | TORONTO

2022

© Iter Inc. 2022
New York and Toronto
IterPress.org
All rights reserved
Printed in the United States of America

978-1-64959-024-4 (paper)
978-1-64959-025-1 (pdf)
978-1-64959-038-1 (epub)

Library of Congress Cataloging-in-Publication Data

Names: Halkett, Anne, Lady, 1622-1699. | Trill, Suzanne, editor.
Title: A true account of my life and selected meditations / Anne, Lady Halkett ; edited by Suzanne Trill.
Description: New York : Iter Press, 2022. | Series: The other voice in early modern Europe: the Toronto series; 87 | Includes bibliographical references and index. | Summary: "Born in the early 1620s to parents of Scottish descent who were servants in Charles I's household, Anne, Lady Halkett (née Murray), grew up on fringes of the English court during a period of increasing political tension. From 1644 to 1699, Halkett recorded her personal and political experiences in both England and Scotland in a series of manuscript meditations and an autobiographical narrative (A True Account of My Life). Royalism, romance, and contemporary religious debates are central to Halkett's vivid portrayal of her life as a single woman, wife, mother, and widow: collectively, the materials edited here offer the opportunity to explore how Halkett's meditational practice informed her life writing in the only version of her writings to date available in a fully modernized edition"-- Provided by publisher.
Identifiers: LCCN 2021047483 (print) | LCCN 2021047484 (ebook) | ISBN 9781649590244 (paperback) | ISBN 9781649590251 (pdf) | ISBN 9781649590381 (epub)
Subjects: LCSH: Halkett, Anne, Lady, 1622-1699. | Great Britain--History--Charles II, 1660-1685--Sources. | Great Britain--Social life and customs--17th century. | Nobility--Great Britain--Biography. | Christian women--Religious life--Scotland. | Women--Scotland--History--17th century--Sources. | Women--Scotland--Intellectual life--17th century. | Meditations.
Classification: LCC DA447.H35 A3 2022 (print) | LCC DA447.H35 (ebook) | DDC 942.06/092 [B]--dc23/eng/20211001
LC record available at https://lccn.loc.gov/2021047483
LC ebook record available at https://lccn.loc.gov/2021047484

Cover Illustration

An Old Woman Reading, Probably the Prophetess Hannah, 1631 (oil on wood panel). Harmenszoon van Rijn, Rembrandt (1606–1669). Rijksmuseum, Amsterdam, The Netherlands. Bridgeman Images XOS1109214. Reproduced with permission.

Cover Design

Maureen Morin, Library Communications, University of Toronto Libraries.

Contents

Acknowledgments	vii
Illustrations	ix
Abbreviations	xi
INTRODUCTION	1
A TRUE ACCOUNT OF MY LIFE (1677–1678)	59
SELECTED *MEDITATIONS*	173
A Short Expostulation about Prayer, Meditations, and the Mother's Will to Her Unborn Child (1653–1657)	173
Occasional Meditations (1658/9–1660)	185
Occasional Meditations, Meditations and Prayers on Every Several Day Ordained to Be Kept Holy in the Church of England (1660, 1663)	197
Occasional and Select Meditations, including Instructions to My Son (1667–1670)	214
The Widow's Mite and Occasional Meditations (1673–1674/5)	237
The Art of Divine Chemistry and Select Meditations (1676–1678)	258
Meditations on St. Peter, the Passion, and Occasional Meditations (1686/7–1688)	266
Meditations on Moses and Samuel (1688–1689/90)	273
Occasional Meditations, Meditations upon Nehemiah, and Observations of Several Good Women Mentioned in Scripture (1690–1692)	276
Of Watchfulness, Select, and Occasional Meditations (1693/4–1695)	286
Select and Occasional Meditations (1696–1697)	298
Select and Occasional Meditations (1697–1698/9)	313
APPENDIX 1: Anne, Lady Halkett, "Letter to the Earl of Lauderdale" (n.d.)	327
APPENDIX 2: Anne, Lady Halkett, "Letter to Her Stepson, Sir Charles Halkett" (n.d.)	329
APPENDIX 3: Anne, Lady Halkett, "An Information of What Was Left Me by My Mother" (n.d.)	333
APPENDIX 4: Items from Simon Couper, *The Life of the Lady Halket* (1701)	337
1. "Experiences in Fyvie."	337
2. "Books by the Lady Halket."	339
3. Biblical References in the "Books by the Lady Halket."	350
Bibliography	359
Index of Names and Subjects	385
Index of Biblical References	405

Acknowledgments

This edition has taken an unexpectedly long time to make it to publication stage, and were it not for Professor Elizabeth H. Hageman's patience, support, and belief in this project, it might never have done so. For this, as well as for inviting me to produce this volume in the first place, I am enormously grateful.

Whereas my initial work on Halkett arose out of a period of research leave funded by the Leverhulme Trust and my previous edition for Ashgate was completed during a period of AHRB (now AHRC) funded research leave, this edition has been obstructed by a combination of complicated personal circumstances, and the demands associated with holding local and national leadership positions within the University and Colleges Union (UCU). Consequently, the bulk of the research for this edition has been two periods of institutional research leave (July–December 2015, and July–December 2018); without these breaks from day-to-day commitments, this edition could not have been completed. Although this used to be an integral part of a UK academic's contract, such support can no longer be taken for granted; while I am glad that my own institution, the University of Edinburgh, retains this practice, it with sadness I realize it is becoming a privilege that is not shared across the board.

I would also like to thank the many students who have elected to study "Shakespeare's Sister: Archival Research and the Politics of the Canon" and "Her Own Life: The Politics of Religion and the Emergence of the Female Subject 1650–1700" in recent years. Their enthusiasm for early modern women's writing in general and Anne, Lady Halkett specifically has been a significant source of inspiration, and I hope that my annotations are more reader friendly as a result of their comments and suggestions. Colleagues and friends too, whether based at the University of Edinburgh or elsewhere, have helped me to hone my ideas through both general discussion and specific feedback on different drafts. Among the latter, I would especially like to thank Raymond Anselment who revealed to me that he was the anonymous reader for the press. I am sad to say that Ray died in April 2022: his work on early modern women's writing will be deeply missed by all in the field and I mourn the loss of such a supportive colleague and friend. The other reader who provided detailed feedback was Julian Goodare: his and Ray's careful, close reading of the manuscript helped me to avoid many mistakes; however, whatever factual errors remain are most certainly my own responsibility. Although I have taken as much care as possible to avoid any inaccuracies in the preparation of this volume, oversights may remain. Nevertheless, it is important to me that this edition rectifies an earlier error; thus, in contrast to the misinformed designation of my previous edition, here my subject is more accurately referred to as "Anne, Lady Halkett."

I am immensely grateful for the financial assistance provided by the School of Literatures, Languages, and Cultures that enabled me to obtain the images and secure the permissions for the illustrations, most of which have been kindly provided by the British Library and the National Library of Scotland. Currently, there are no reliable portraits of Anne, Lady Halkett, so I would also like to thank Margaret English-Haskin for helping me find the cover image for this edition (Rembrandt, *An Old Woman Reading, Probably the Prophetess Hannah*, 1631) and to the Bridgeman Art Library for its use. While the Old Testament figure of Hannah is considered to be a prophetess for her song of thanksgiving (1 Samuel 2:1–10), according to the Rijksmuseum, Rembrandt's portrait is of Anna, the prophetess and widow of the New Testament (Luke 2:36–38) with whom Halkett identifies in "Upon My Deplorable Being a Widow." This connection, and the fact that the concept of herself as a "prophetess" is a recurring motif within Halkett's writing, seemed to me to make it an appropriate choice for this volume.

Without the support of family and friends, I doubt I would have seen this book through to completion; in particular, I would like to thank Cordelia Beattie, Fiona Brown, Celeste-Marie Bernier, Kate Burningham, Kate Chedgzoy, Sarah Dunnigan, Lynn Hyams, Carole Jones, Angi Lamb, and Carey Osborne for their love, support, and continual belief in me (especially when my belief in myself has wavered). In addition to their ongoing love and support, I am indebted to my mum (Valerie Trill) and Pat Bradley for going well beyond the call of duty by reading initial drafts (and asking awkward questions that I hope I have addressed in the notes). Andrew Bradley has been my rock since 2012, and has changed my life for the better with his calming presence and enduring love (as well as his willingness to assist in researching Halkett's connections with Barbados, and uncovering scientific evidence supporting her claim to have experienced an earthquake while at Naworth Castle). Finally, this edition is dedicated to the loving memory of Melanie Hansen/Osborne (1962–2013), without whom I would never have become an academic in the first place and whose absence remains keenly felt to this day.

Illustrations

Cover. *An Old Woman Reading, Probably the Prophetess Hannah,* 1631 (oil on wood panel). Harmenszoon van Rijn, Rembrandt (1606–1669). Rijksmuseum, Amsterdam, The Netherlands. Bridgeman Images XOS1109214. Reproduced with permission.

Figure 1. John Speed, *The Kingdome of Scotland* (London: Roger Rea, 1662). © National Library of Scotland, EMS.s.9B. Reproduced with permission. — 31

Figure 2. Title Page of Anne, Lady Halkett, *Meditations upon the Seven Gifts of the Holy Spirit, Mentioned Isaiah 11:2–3. As Also, Meditations upon Jabez His Request, 1 Chron. 4:10. Together with Sacramental Meditations on the Lord's Supper; and Prayers, Pious Reflections, and Observations,* edited by Simon Couper (Edinburgh: Andrew Symson, 1702). © National Library of Scotland, Ry.1.6.286, 4(19). Reproduced with permission. — 51

Figure 3. From Anne, Lady Halkett, *A True Account of My Life* (1677–1678). © British Library, BL, MS Add. 32,376, fol.1v. Reproduced with permission. — 62

Figure 4. From a 1654 map of Fife, showing Southern Fife and the Firth of Forth. From James Gordon and Joan Blaeu, *Fifae Vicecomitatus, The Sherifdome of Fyfe* (Amsterdam: Blaeu, 1654). © National Library of Scotland, EMW.X.015 (formerly WD.3B). Reproduced with permission. — 121

Figure 5. 1647 map of Edinburgh. From James Gordon, *Plan de la Ville d'Edenbourg, Capitale d'Ecosse* (Leiden: P. van der Aa, ca. 1729). © National Library of Scotland, EMS.s.53. Reproduced with permission. — 138

Figure 6. From Anne, Lady Halkett, *A Short Expostulation about Prayer, Meditations, and the Mother's Will to Her Unborn Child* (1653–1657). © National Library of Scotland, NLS, MS 6489, p. 7. Reproduced with permission. — 175

Figure 7. From Anne, Lady Halkett, *Occasional Meditations* (1658/9–1660). © National Library of Scotland, NLS, MS 6490, p. 132. Reproduced with permission. — 186

x Illustrations

Figure 8. From Anne, Lady Halkett, *Occasional Meditations, Meditations and Prayers on Every Several Day Ordained to Be Kept Holy in the Church of England* (1660, 1663). © National Library of Scotland, NLS, MS 6491, p. 19. Reproduced with permission. 199

Figure 9. Contents page for "Select Contemplations," from Anne, Lady Halkett, *Occasional and Select Meditations, including Instructions to My Son* (1667–1670). © National Library of Scotland, NLS, MS 6492, pp. i–ii. Reproduced with permission. 215

Figure 10. Contents page for "Occasional Meditations," from Anne, Lady Halkett, *Occasional and Select Meditations, including Instructions to My Son* (1667–1670). © National Library of Scotland, NLS, MS 6492, pp. iii–iv. Reproduced with permission. 216

Figure 11. Seal from Anne, Lady Halkett's "Letter to the Laird of Sauchie," (ca. 1673), in Pitfirrane Papers: Correspondence. © National Library of Scotland, NLS, MS 6407, fol.145v. Reproduced with permission. 239

Figure 12. From Anne, Lady Halkett, *The Art of Divine Chemistry and Select Meditations* (1676–1678). © National Library of Scotland, NLS, MS 6494, p. 2. Reproduced with permission. 260

Figure 13. From Anne, Lady Halkett, *Meditations on St. Peter, the Passion, and Occasional Meditations* (1686/7–1688). © National Library of Scotland, NLS, MS 6497, p. 329. Reproduced with permission. 268

Figure 14. Contents page for "Occasional Meditations," from Anne, Lady Halkett, *Occasional Meditations, Meditations upon Nehemiah, and Observations of Several Good Women Mentioned in Scripture* (1690–1692). © National Library of Scotland, NLS, MS 6499, p. i. Reproduced with permission. 277

Figure 15. "The Table," from Anne, Lady Halkett, *Of Watchfulness, Select, and Occasional Meditations* (1693/4–1695). © National Library of Scotland, NLS, MS 6500, pp. ii–iii. Reproduced with permission. 288

Figure 16. From Anne, Lady Halkett, *Select and Occasional Meditations* (1696–1697). © National Library of Scotland, NLS, MS 6501, p. 110. Reproduced with permission. 305

Figure 17. From Anne, Lady Halkett, *Select and Occasional Meditations* (1697–1698/9). © National Library of Scotland, NLS, MS 6502, p. 314. Reproduced with permission. 324

Abbreviations

Acc.	Accession.
Add.	Additional.
BCP	*The Book of Common Prayer: The Texts of 1549, 1559, and 1662*, edited by Brian Cummings (Oxford: Oxford University Press, 2011).
BHO	*British History Online*.
BL	British Library, London.
BP	*Burke's Peerage, Baronetage, & Knightage*, edited by Charles Mosley. 107th ed. 3 vols. (Wilmington, DE: Burke's Peerage, 2003).
CB	*Complete Baronetage*, edited by George E. Cokayne. 6 vols. (Exeter: W. Pollard & Co., 1900–1909).
CSP(Dom)	*Calendar of State Papers (Domestic)* (online version).
DSL	*Dictionary of the Scots Language/Dictionar o the Scots Leid* (online version).
ESTC	English Short Title Catalogue (online version).
FES	*Fasti Ecclesiae Scoticanæ: The Succession of Ministers in the Church of Scotland from the Reformation*, edited by Hew Scott. 7 vols. (Edinburgh: Oliver and Boyd, 1915–1928).
fol.	folio.
KJV	*King James Bible* (online version).
MS	Manuscript.
MSS	Manuscripts.
NLS	National Library of Scotland, Edinburgh.
NRS	National Registers of Scotland, Edinburgh.
ODNB	*Oxford Dictionary of National Biography* (online version).
OED	*Oxford English Dictionary* (online version).
r	recto.
RPS	*The Records of the Parliaments of Scotland to 1707* (online version).
sig.	signature.
SP	*State Papers* (online version).
TCP	*The Complete Peerage of England, Scotland, Ireland, Great Britain, and the United Kingdom, Extant, Extinct, or Dormant*, edited by George E. Cokayne. 13 vols. (London: St. Catherine, 1825–1911).
TNA	The National Archives, Kew.
TSP	*The Scots Peerage Founded on Wood's Edition of Sir Robert Douglas's Peerage of Scotland*, compiled and edited by Sir James Balfour. 9 vols. (Edinburgh: David Douglas, 1904–1914).
v	verso.

Introduction

The Other Voice

In this edition, for the first time, the autobiographical narrative of Anne, Lady Halkett (1621/3–1699) appears in print under the title that she herself gave it, *A True Account of My Life*,[1] which clearly confirms that Halkett wrote to justify herself and that she had an "Other" tale to tell.

The "otherness" of her story is multifaceted: it is the tale of a female Royalist of gentry status who is actively involved in political conspiracy; an orphaned youngest daughter facing continual financial insecurity; a woman accused of illicit sexual relations, not once but on many occasions; a stepmother, "which always hath a prejudice attending it, and none hath found it more than I";[2] and an Englishwoman living in Scotland who resolutely—indeed, defiantly—supported the liturgy of the Church of England in the land of the Covenanters.[3] Insofar as this means she existed on the edge of several social groups or cultures, Halkett's life could easily be defined as marginal. Simultaneously, however, her familial connections aligned her with figures who had—or came to have—enormous contemporary political power and influence throughout the seventeenth century.[4] In

---

1. Halkett's narrative was first edited by John G. Nichols as *The Autobiography of Anne Lady Halkett* (London: Camden Society, 1875), and then by John C. Loftis as *The Memoirs of Anne, Lady Halkett and Anne, Lady Fanshawe* (Oxford: Clarendon Press, 1979). Following the title provided in the BL catalogue, I referred to it as "The Autobiography of Anne, Lady Halkett" in Suzanne Trill, ed., *Lady Anne Halkett: Selected Self-Writings* (Aldershot, UK: Ashgate, 2007). During my research for the Ashgate edition, I discovered that Halkett referred to this narrative as *A True Account of My Life*, see "Introduction," xxxvi–xxxvii. See also "Meditations upon Psalm 106:4–5, Begun Monday, April 22, 1678" and "Saturday, February 19, 1697/8," 264–65, 318–21. Properly speaking, Halkett should be styled "Anne, Lady Halkett," which this edition follows throughout; consequently, subsequent references to my previous edition are abbreviated to "Trill, ed., *Halkett*." Subsequent references to *A True Account of My Life* are abbreviated to "*True Account*."

2. See "Upon the Death of My Dearest Sir James Halkett," 221. As Sara Mendelson and Patricia Crawford note, this was a difficult role that was often viewed negatively: furthermore, "wet nurses, stepmothers, and barren women were marginal figures" at risk of being accused of witchcraft. See Mendelson and Crawford, *Women in Early Modern England* (Oxford: Clarendon Press, 1998), 164.

3. There is a vast literature on the history of the Covenanters. A helpful place to start is David Stevenson, *The Covenanters: The National Covenant and Scotland* (Edinburgh: Saltire Society, 1988). For a more recent discussion, including an updated bibliography, see Sharon Adams and Julian Goodare, eds., *Scotland in the Age of Two Revolutions* (Woodbridge, UK: Boydell Press, 2014).

4. Among them Sir Robert Moray, the Earl of Tweeddale, and the Earl, later Duke, of Lauderdale. David Allan, "Moray, Sir Robert (1608/9?–1673)," in *Oxford Dictionary of National Biography* (hereafter *ODNB*), ed. Lawrence Goldman (Oxford: Oxford University Press, 2004–). Article published October 2007, accessed December 14, 2015, http://www.oxforddnb.com. All subsequent references to

1

this and so many other ways, Halkett is something of a paradoxical figure who resists categorization.[5]

Take, for example, the extant portion of her *True Account*: it focuses on the twelve years of her life from 1644 to 1656; is missing pages at crucial junctures; and ends in midsentence, making it incontrovertibly incomplete. Even the portion that now survives went unnoticed for nearly two hundred years, during which time our knowledge of her life and writing was based entirely on the selections from her manuscripts that her eighteenth-century biographer and editor, Simon Couper, published in 1701–1702 with his own political agenda very much in the forefront.[6] More recently, it has been established that Halkett wrote the *True Account* over the course of the seven months between September 1677 and April 1678.[7] Written after the Restoration, recalling the disruptions of the Wars of the Three Kingdoms, partially published in the eighteenth century, and only fully available in print from the mid-nineteenth and twentieth centuries, the *True Account* traverses several traditional periods of both literary and sociopolitical history. This presents challenges but also offers a unique opportunity to reassess our received categories, whether literary, historical, national, or theological.

As she remains most famous for her part in helping the then Duke of York, later James VII/II, to escape from St. James's Palace, Halkett's Royalist credentials appear unassailable; however, elisions in her narrative and the complexity of Royalist allegiances, especially in Scotland, mean that Halkett's life and writing offer an unparalleled opportunity to explore the nuances of what it meant to be a female "Royalist" over the course of the seventeenth century.[8] Previously read

---

the *ODNB* are to the online edition; John R. Young, "Hay, John, First Marquess of Tweeddale (1626–1697)," *ODNB*; Ronald Hutton, "Maitland, John, Duke of Lauderdale (1616–1682)," *ODNB*.

5. Suzanne Trill, "Critical Categories: Toward an Archaeology of Anne, Lady Halkett's Archive," in *Editing Early Modern Women*, ed. Sarah C. E. Ross and Paul Salzman (Cambridge: Cambridge University Press, 2016), 97–120.

6. Simon Couper, *The Life of the Lady Halket* [sic] (Edinburgh: Andrew Symson and Henry Knox, 1701). ESTC T72803. See "'Living Monuments of Praise': The Afterlife of Halkett's 'Books,'" 42–54. See also Margaret J. M. Ezell, "The Posthumous Publication of Women's Manuscripts and the History of Authorship," in *Women's Writing and the Circulation of Ideas: Manuscript Publication in England, 1550–1800*, ed. George L. Justice and Nathan Tinker (Cambridge: Cambridge University Press, 2002), 121–36.

7. Victoria Burke, "Bibliographic Data for BL, Add. MS 32376," Perdita Manuscripts. Adam Matthew Digital: 2007, accessed July 10, 2018, http://www.perditamanuscripts.amdigital.co.uk.

8. Halkett's life and writing can therefore add to the debates articulated in Jason McElligott and David L. Smith, eds., *Royalists and Royalism during the English Civil Wars* (Cambridge: Cambridge University Press, 2007), and the companion volume *Royalists and Royalism during the Interregnum* (Manchester, UK: Manchester University Press, 2010). See also Suzanne Trill, "Royalism and Resistance: The Personal and the Political in Anne, Lady Halkett's *Meditations*, 1660–1699" in *Worldmaking Women: New Perspectives on the Centrality of Women in Sixteenth- and Seventeenth-Century Culture*, edited by Pamela Hammons & Brandie Siegfried (Cambridge: Cambridge University Press, 2021), 153–67.

predominantly as a "romance," more recent criticism insists on the intersection of the sacred and the secular within her narrative. As Mary Ellen Lamb shrewdly observes, Halkett's *True Account* is shaped "as a series of cases of conscience," and its prefatory materials provide "a specifically sacramental context for her autobiography as a mode of self-examination undertaken in preparation for receiving the eucharist," and she remarks that this frame "is consistent with the prolific devotional writing she produced after her husband's death."[9] However, Halkett was also producing prolific devotional materials at the same time as writing her *True Account* and had been doing so for many years previously. As I have argued elsewhere, that text "is but 'a node within a network' of Halkett's extensive 'archive,'" and to understand her "'lives' and 'works'" more deeply we need to consider it within that wider corpus.[10]

Internal evidence suggests that the *True Account* was based on the *Meditations* she wrote at the time, many of which are no longer available to us.[11] However, the extant volumes augment that narrative in several significant ways: in some instances, they fill in hiatuses (for example, "The Great Conquest, or the Power of Faith" was written at the point Halkett learned that Bampfield's wife was definitely alive); they revisit and reconsider people, places, and events recorded there (including Charles I's execution, Charles II's coronation and Restoration, and James VII/II's escape from St. James's Palace); and, as those examples suggest, they prove her ongoing engagement with the political sphere throughout her long life. This, I hope, finally discredits the notion that Halkett's political activities ceased after marriage and that her *True Account* was simply shaped by her romantic liaisons. After all, the truncated narrative does not end with the curtain of marriage, but with Halkett interceding for her husband with Lord Broghill, Lord President of the council in Edinburgh, to prevent him being appointed as a Justice

---

9. Mary Ellen Lamb, "Merging the Secular and the Spiritual in Lady Anne Halkett's Memoirs," in *Genre and Women's Life Writing in Early Modern England*, ed. Michelle M. Dowd and Julie A. Eckerle (Aldershot, UK: Ashgate, 2007), 84, 83. For an overview of critical approaches to Halkett, see Suzanne Trill, "Beyond Romance? Re-Reading the 'Lives' of Anne, Lady Halkett (1621/2?-1699)," *Literature Compass* 6, no. 2 (2009): 446–59. See also Julie A. Eckerle, *Romancing the Self in Early Modern Englishwomen's Life Writing* (Aldershot, UK: Ashgate, 2013), and Sharon Seelig, "Romance and Respectability: The Autobiography of Anne Halkett," in *Autobiography and Gender in Early Modern Literature: Reading Women's Lives, 1600-1690*, 110–30 (Cambridge: Cambridge University Press, 2006).

10. Trill, "Critical Categories," 119.

11. See "Appendix 4.2," 339–49. Throughout this volume, when capitalized and italicized, "*Meditations*" refers to the entire corpus of Halkett's meditational writings (both select and occasional, print and manuscript). Both Halkett and Couper refer to her individual volumes of meditations as "books," and Halkett gave each volume a distinctive title, so when I refer to individual volumes their titles are italicized. See also "Select and Occasional Meditations," 41–42.

of the Peace. Halkett's extant narrative ends, then, with her assisting her husband in a political "case of conscience" of his own.

Halkett's *True Account* is an extended attempt to prove that, however people may judge her outward actions, her inward intentions were honorable, or "true" to her conscience.[12] In this she most certainly reflects contemporary casuistical thinking, which saw a rise in popularity during a period in which people had to choose a side and where what was "honorable" was not always straightforward.[13] We have perhaps been misled by the apparent "modernism" of Halkett's narrative. Even in its truncated, extant form, it is probably closer to the "standard" generic expectations of autobiography than any other such text written by a British woman in the seventeenth century: it is, after all, "a retrospective prose narrative produced by a real person, focusing on [her] individual life, in particular the story of [her] personality."[14] It is also now generally accepted that she wrote both the *True Account* and her *Meditations* with the expectation of an audience.[15] But nomenclature is significant: for Halkett, this was *A True Account of My Life*. In its early modern context, Halkett is signaling an engagement with contemporary conventions of life writing associated with "True Relations" and "Accounts." Frances E. Dolan has recently explored the former, and Adam Smyth points out that the latter offered "a paradigm for the writing of a life" in the early modern

---

12. "It was the oft-repeated counsel of the casuists that it is inward honesty and upright intention that ultimately matters"; see Andrew Lacey, "Texts to Be Read: Charles I and the *Eikon Basilike*," *Prose Studies* 29, no. 1 (2007): 11.

13. As Edward Vallance succinctly explains, casuistry is "the branch of moral theology devoted to resolving ethical dilemmas in particular cases"; see Vallance, "The Kingdom's Case: The Use of Casuistry as a Political Language, 1640–1692," *Albion* 34, no. 4 (2002): 557–83.

14. Philippe Lejeune, "The Autobiographical Pact," in *On Autobiography*, ed. Paul John Eakin, trans. Katherine M. Leary (Minneapolis: University of Minnesota Press, 1989), 4. The appropriateness of the term "autobiography" to early modern texts has been the subject of much debate. Although sympathetic to the arguments put forward by Smyth and Lynch, my preference is to use the term "life-writing." Adam Smyth, *Autobiography in Early Modern England* (Cambridge: Cambridge University Press, 2010); Kathleen Lynch, *Protestant Autobiography in the Seventeenth-Century Anglophone World* (Oxford: Oxford University Press, 2012); Suzanne Trill, "Life-writing: Encountering Selves," in *Handbook of English Renaissance Literature*, ed. Ingo Berensmeyer (Berlin; Boston: De Gruyter, 2019), 108–35. See also Adam Smyth, ed., *A History of English Autobiography* (Cambridge: Cambridge University Press, 2016); Ronald Bedford, Lloyd Davis, and Philippa Kelly, eds., *Early Modern Autobiography: Theories, Genres, Practices* (Ann Arbor: University of Michigan Press, 2006); Effie Botonaki, *Seventeenth-Century English Women's Autobiographical Writing: Disclosing Enclosures* (Lewiston, NY: Edwin Mellen Press, 2004); Elspeth Graham, "Women's Writing and the Self," in *Women and Literature in Britain, 1500–1700*, ed. Helen Wilcox (Cambridge: Cambridge University Press, 1996), 209–33; Michelle M. Dowd and Julie A. Eckerle, eds., *Genre and Women's Life Writing in Early Modern England* (Aldershot: Ashgate, 2007); Alan Stewart, *Early Modern*, vol. 2: *The Oxford History of Life-Writing* (Oxford: Oxford University Press, 2018).

15. Trill, "Beyond Romance," 450.

period.[16] While Halkett's writing certainly exhibits the overlap in terminology between the discourses associated with both the economic and the "affective or social" sphere (e.g., "trust, bond, credit, debit, and interest"), her primary focus is the final "Account" or reckoning that all will be called upon to deliver before Almighty God on Judgment Day.[17]

The *True Account* was made possible by her habitual self-examination and daily devotions, and it needs to be read as part of a continuum with her select and occasional meditations. Although the former is the most definitively "autobiographical," all of her writing constitutes "autobiographical acts."[18] The *Meditations* are part of her daily accounting for her life. Broadly speaking, the select meditations record how she spent her devotional time (that is, the hours she dedicates to reading specific biblical and theological texts), and the occasional entries explore daily experience, which frequently requires her to resolve current "cases of conscience." She also has much to say on the sacramental nature of oaths, covenants, and vows, which lends an extra valency to her use of these terms within the *True Account*. With the *Meditations* too, however, generic expectations can be misleading and even the organization of her "books" demonstrates a development in practice that reinforces a sense of a "subject-in-process." Halkett's sense of self is highly relational: her writing centers on the people, places, institutions, and events to which she was connected. Above all, however, Halkett's texts reveal the omniscient workings of a benign and providential Deity.[19] In this, Halkett is an exemplar par excellence of an "earnest" seventeenth-century Protestant whose life and writings bear witness to a decidedly "providential imagination."[20]

---

16. Frances E. Dolan, *True Relations: Reading, Literature, and Evidence in Seventeenth-Century England* (Philadelphia: University of Pennsylvania Press, 2013); Adam Smyth, "Money, Accounting, and Life-Writing, 1600–1700: Balancing a Life," in *A History of English Autobiography*, ed. Adam Smyth (Cambridge: Cambridge University Press, 2016), 86.

17. Smyth, "Money, Accounting, and Life-Writing, 1600–1700," 91.

18. Following Elizabeth Bruss, Kathleen Lynch argues that "autobiography is an act, not a form," *Protestant Autobiography in the Seventeenth-Century Anglophone World*, 13. However, this debate is being reanimated in relation to social media; see Arnaud Schmitt, "From Autobiographical Act to Autobiography," *Life Writing* 15, no. 4 (2018): 469–86.

19. As a self-identified adherent of the Church of England, Halkett's writing supports Alexandra Walsham's proposition that "providentialism was . . . a cluster of presuppositions which enjoyed near universal acceptance." See Alexandra Walsham, *Providence in Early Modern England* (Oxford: Oxford University Press, 1999), 2.

20. As "'godliness'" has become "a word with too partisan a flavor," Alec Ryrie argues that the term "'earnestness'" is more appropriate to describe "any attempt to practice Protestantism, which is, or which appears to be, intended seriously"; Alec Ryrie, *Being Protestant in Reformation Britain* (Oxford: Oxford University Press, 2013), 9. Halkett's life and writing therefore represent a counterbalance to the "persecutory imagination" so vividly expounded by John Stachniewski in *The Persecutory Imagination: English Puritanism and the Literature of Religious Despair* (Oxford: Clarendon Press, 1991).

The Lives of Anne, Lady Halkett

Born sometime between 1621 and 1623, the then Anne Murray came of age during the turbulent years of the English Civil Wars/Wars of the Three Kingdoms and maintained a principled and personal loyalty to the Royalist cause.[21] As she lived until the ripe old age—for this period—of between seventy-six and seventy-eight, and wrote from 1644 until 1699, her life and writing are shaped by the shifting relations between and within the three kingdoms over the course of the seventeenth century. Born in the final years of James VI/I's reign, Halkett died while William of Orange occupied the English throne. Not only did she live through the Civil Wars, the execution of Charles I, the Republic/Commonwealth, the Protectorate, and the Restoration, but she also experienced the accession of James VII/II, the Glorious Revolution, the death of Queen Mary II, and the initial difficulties surrounding the Darien scheme, which would play its part in the eventual Union of Scotland and England in Queen Anne's reign.[22] Sadly, Halkett's extant writings have little to say about the prospective union of the two nations, although her writings were to play an unexpected role within this debate.[23]

Nevertheless, she remains best known for her daring involvement in the plot to assist the then Duke of York, later James VII/II, to escape from imprisonment at St. James's Palace in 1648. While this unusual attention to an early modern woman's political engagement is much to be welcomed, its effects have been double-edged insofar as it means Halkett is forever tied to Colonel Joseph Bampfield, whose deceptions haunted her for the rest of her life.[24] Yet, while modern audiences have responded primarily to Halkett's royalism and romance, her earlier reception was radically different. Until the reemergence of the *True Account* in the late nineteenth century, Halkett's life and works were accessible only via Simon Couper's editorial interventions. The difference between the images of Halkett produced by her *True Account* and Couper's *The Life of the Lady Halket* have been considered as conflictual as the spirited heroine of the former

---

21. The "Three Kingdoms" were England (which incorporated Wales), Scotland, and Ireland. As her father died in 1623, this is usually taken to be her year of birth; see, for example, David Stevenson, "Halkett [née Murray], Anne [Anna], Lady Halkett (1623–1699)," *ODNB*. See also R. Malcolm Smuts, "Murray, Thomas (1564–1623)," *ODNB*. However, by her own calculations, she was born on January 4, 1621/2; Trill, ed., *Halkett*, xix, n9."

22. The Town Council of Dunfermline subscribed £10 to the scheme in 1696; at this time, Sir Charles Halkett, Anne, Lady Halkett's stepson, was provost of Dunfermline. Ebenezer Henderson, *Annals of Dunfermline and Vicinity, from the Earliest Authentic Period to the Present Time, A.D. 1069–1878* (Glasgow: J. Tweed, 1879), 360–61.

23. See "'Living Monuments of Praise,'" 42–54.

24. Even in her penultimate volume, she refers to him; see "Friday, May 14, 1697," 311–12.

becomes a tediously pious widow.[25] These differences are in part explained by the motivation for writing them and their anticipated audience: Halkett wrote to justify herself primarily to God, her family, and others connected to her; Couper hoped her exemplary piety would persuade politicians in both Scotland and England to support Episcopalianism.[26] While there are certainly inconsistencies *between* these texts, there are also discrepancies *within* each of them. In both, those incongruities are most apparent in their representation of Halkett's closest relationships.

Although usually considered an English woman writer, which fits with her own self-definition, Halkett's relationship with Scotland is highly significant: her parents were both Scottish; she married a Scotsman; and she lived in Scotland for most of her adult life.[27] It seems likely that all the Murrays' surviving children were born in England; certainly, extant records confirm this for their two youngest children, William (b. 1617)—affectionately referred to as Will throughout the *True Account*—and Anne (b. ca. 1621-1623).[28] Although Halkett makes a brief reference to another elder brother, Charles, the siblings to whom she most frequently refers are Henry, Elizabeth, and Will. Her father died within a few months of her birth, so Anne was the youngest of a family of at least five children.

While much has been written about the difficulties of the younger sons, less has been said about their female counterparts. Halkett is, in many ways, the "poor cousin" of both her nuclear and extended family. Her beloved brother Will died in

---

25. Kim Walker, "'Divine Chymistry' and Dramatic Character: The Lives of Lady Anne Halkett," in *Women Writing, 1550-1750*, ed. Jo Wallwork and Paul Salzman (Bundoora, Australia: Meridian, 2001), 133-49; Eckerle, *Romancing the Self in Early Modern Englishwomen's Life Writing*, 126-27; and Trill, "Beyond Romance," 452.

26. Queen Anne "indicated sympathy for the toleration of Episcopalian worship in 1703." Karin Bowie, "'A Legal Limited Monarchy': Scottish Constitutionalism in the Union of the Crowns, 1603-1707," *Journal of Scottish Historical Studies* 35, no. 2 (2015): 148.

27. Halkett defines herself as "English" on several occasions. For more on her Scottish connections, see David Stevenson, "A Lady and Her Lovers: Anne, Lady Halkett," in *King or Covenant: Voices from Civil War* (East Linton, UK: Tuckwell, 1996), 191; and Trill, ed., *Halkett*, xviii-xxxiv. Here it is important to note that her surname should be pronounced "Hackett." For example, when referring to her by this title in his letters, Sir Robert Moray writes "Lady Hackett." David Stevenson, ed., *Letters of Sir Robert Moray to the Earl of Kincardine, 1657-73* (Aldershot, UK: Ashgate, 2007), 96, 107. That this was how her name was also pronounced in early modern England is attested to in the recording of the award of a grant of £500 "to Lady Ann Hacket, in consideration of her zeal and sufferings" (November 20, 1662). William A. Shaw, *Calendar of Treasury Books, 1660-1667*, 4 vols. (London: Mackie & Co., 1904), 1:452. Moray also refers to Anne, Lady Halkett as "Lady Pitfirrin" or "Lady Pitfirrine" [sic]. David Stevenson, ed., *Letters of Sir Robert Moray to the Earl of Kincardine, 1657-73*, 144, 218.

28. For the baptismal records of both William (July 17, 1617) and Anne (November 7, 1624), see *England, Births, and Christenings, 1538-1975*, cited by Ancestry®: Genealogy, Family Trees & Family History Records, accessed August 08, 2018, https://www.ancestry.co.uk.

1648/9, leaving her the only "unsupported" member of the family.[29] Her brother Henry had married Anne Bayning in 1635, and her sister Elizabeth married Sir Henry Newton in 1640.[30] While information about Henry Murray is relatively hazy, Elizabeth made something of an impression on the diarist John Evelyn and was clearly well thought of.[31] Anne was the youngest, unmarried daughter and, as the subject of much scandal, was most likely a source of embarrassment for her siblings, especially Henry, who is negatively compared with both Anne's sister and her brother-in-law, Sir Henry Newton.[32] In many ways then she was an "other" within her own family. However, there are indications to the contrary in her relationship with her mother. Although the *True Account* focuses on the ruptures to that bond occasioned by Anne's liaison with Thomas Howard, even that episode concludes in reconciliation: "And from that time, she received me again to her favor and ever after used me more like a friend than a child."[33] Evoking this painful incident toward the end of her life, Halkett recalls that "by patient continuing in all dutiful observance to her, I obtained the greatest testimony she could give me of her affection: before her death, saying she had greater contentment in me than in all her children."[34] While this establishes her need to feel important to her mother, in a later entry Halkett pays poignant testimony to her

---

29. See *True Account*, 92.

30. See *True Account*, 65nn33, 38. Henry Murray married Anne Bayning on November 26, 1635, *TCP* 2:35. When Elizabeth first married, her husband's surname was Newton; however, as "heir male" to his cousin Jane Puckering after she died in 1652, Henry "subsequently assumed the name of Puckering." Jan Broadway, "Puckering [Newton], Sir Henry, Third Baronet (bap. 1618, d. 1701)," *ODNB*. However, Halkett continues to refer to her sister and brother-in-law as "Newton" throughout her extant volumes.

31. The only records of Henry I have been able to trace relate to his marriage and children, *TCP* 2:35, 2:36; *CB* 3:121, 3:546, 3:291, 4:110. John Evelyn's letters to Elizabeth Newton, later Puckering, dated ca. 1655–1660, can be found in "Evelyn Papers. vol. CXXXI. Letters from Evelyn to Various Correspondents, 1644–1679." BL, Add. MS 78298, fols. 65v, 75r, 80r, 81v, 82v, 90v, 100v. These letters can also be found in *The Letterbooks of John Evelyn*, edited by Douglas D. C. Chambers and David Galbraith. 2 vols. (Toronto, ON: University of Toronto Press, 2014), 1:158–59, 187–89, 208, 214, 216–17, 241, 269. Elizabeth Newton, later Puckering, also left evidence of book ownership. David Mckitterick, "Women and Their Books in Seventeenth-Century England: The Case of Elizabeth Puckering," *The Library* 1, no. 4 (2000): 359–80. In this essay, McKitterick provides references for two letters from Elizabeth Newton, later Puckering, to John Evelyn (dated "October 30, 1654" and "December 11, 1658"). His citation provides references to the Evelyn Papers before they were catalogued as part of the Additional manuscripts at the British Library; unfortunately, the volume in which they are probably located (BL, Add. MS 78316) has not yet been catalogued to item level, and I have not yet been able to access them. I would like to thank Elizabeth H. Hageman, Heather Wolfe, and Suzanne Young for their assistance in locating these letters.

32. See *True Account*, 94, 159, 165.

33. See *True Account*, 77.

34. See "1 Corinthians 15:58," 317–18. Jean Drummond died on August 28, 1647; see Couper, *The Life of the Lady Halket*, 14.

mother's importance to her. Reflecting on the death of one of her stepdaughters, Halkett expresses concern for her step granddaughters and prays: "Lord preserve them from what I met with after my mother's death, from which I may date all my misfortunes."[35]

Halkett's emphasis on the maternal here is a striking contrast to modern critical discussions of her texts, which, understandably, focus primarily on her relationships with men. This focus needs to be counterbalanced by reminding ourselves of her strong, and sometimes tense, relationships with women.[36] Her mother is a strong presence, and her sister Elizabeth, while not uncritical, gives her emotional and financial support, as well as shelter at several key moments. Elizabeth also helps facilitate Anne's marriage to Sir James Halkett and, after Elizabeth's death, it is Elizabeth's husband, Sir Henry Newton, who offers Halkett much-needed financial assistance. Throughout the *True Account*, her most constant companion is "Crew," her maid, and she is frequently on good terms with other female "servants" such as the midwife and the two ladies' companion at Naworth Castle.[37] In the early part of her narrative, it is other women who serve as conduits for her relationship with Thomas Howard, including his sister Lady Anne Howard; and it is she who offers the then Anne Murray the opportunity to evade possible imprisonment by inviting her to stay with her family at Naworth Castle. While in Scotland, she benefits from the hospitality of the Countesses of Dunfermline, Tweeddale, and Roxburghe; the company of Lady Anne Campbell, Lady Anna Erskine, and Sir Robert Moray's wife, Sophia Lindsay; and the financial assistance of Anna Mackenzie, Lady Balcarres, and the Dowager Countess of Dunfermline. On her return to England, it is the generosity of the Countess of Devonshire, and her brother-in-law, Sir Henry Newton, that enables her to settle her finances enough to be able to marry Sir James Halkett.

For the young Anne Murray, the support of these women was a sign of God's providence; however, her reliance on them also underlines her peripatetic lifestyle. Until 1648, she seems to have moved between family residences in Berkhamsted, St. Martin's Lane (Covent Garden), Whitefriars, and Charlton.[38]

---

35. Anne, Lady Halkett, *Meditations on St. Peter, the Passion, and Occasional Meditations* (1686/7–1688), NLS, MS 6497, p. 335.

36. A similar point is made by Ellen Moody, "'Cast Out from Respectability a While': Anne Murray Halkett's Life in the Manuscripts, 2006," accessed August 8, 2017, http://www.jimandellen.org/halkett/CastOut.html.

37. See *True Account*, 95, 101, 135.

38. Halkett's parents leased Berkhamsted Place, Hertfordshire, from Prince Charles, later Charles II; as a widow, Halkett's mother leased a house in St. Martin's Lane, a fashionable street in what is now Covent Garden; Halkett's brother, Henry, had a residence in the Whitefriars district of London; and on her marriage to Sir Henry Newton, later Puckering, Anne's sister, Elizabeth, took up residence at Charlton House in what is now the Royal Borough of Greenwich. William Page, ed., "Berkhampsted St. Peter: Introduction, Honor, Manor, and Castle," in *A History of the County of Hertford*, 4 vols.

From 1648 to 1652, she was a guest at various aristocratic houses at Naworth, Dunfermline, and Fyvie; and from 1652 until her marriage to Sir James in 1656, she lived either in lodgings or in the Earl of Tweeddale's house. From 1656 to 1670, she resided primarily at Pitfirrane House, but with the death of her husband she moved to what is now Abbot House in Dunfermline.[39] Apart from a brief return to Pitfirrane while her stepson was involved in the third Anglo-Dutch War (1672–1674), Halkett resided at Abbot House until her death there, on April 22, 1699. It is perhaps telling that Halkett herself frequently states that she often found more assistance from "strangers" than friends. Although she has personal and/or kinship relations with many of those who assisted her, it is notable that she seems to have received little or no support from her cousins, the Murrays of Dysart.[40] Both her brother Will and Colonel Joseph Bampfield were associated with the first Earl of Dysart, who was part of King Charles II's entourage in Scotland in 1650/1. Indeed, this marginal connection to more prominent figures is something of a recurring motif in Halkett's life and writing; in this, Halkett has much to teach us about women's vulnerable position within a patrilineal patronage and kinship system. She has enough credit to borrow from various nobles but has little financial security of her own. Evident in the *True Account*, this lack of security affects her right until the end of her life.

Such vulnerability also has a lot to tell us about the complexities of allegiance between the 1640s and 1660s (and beyond). Halkett did not have much choice about where she resided; however, at least at the points she is with them, most of those with whom she lived were—broadly speaking—Royalists. A potentially significant exception to this is Thomas and Anne Howard's father, Edward Howard, first Baron Howard of Escrick, who aligned himself with the Parliamentarians and was an assiduous member of the Committee of Compounding in the 1640s.

(London: Westminster, 1908), 2:162–71, *BHO*; G. H. Gater and F. R. Hiorns, eds., "St. Martin's Lane," in *Survey of London: Volume 20, St Martin-in-The-Fields, Pt. III: Trafalgar Square and Neighborhood*, 53 vols. (London: London County Council, 1940), 20:115–22, *BHO*; Walter Thornbury, ed., "Whitefriars," in *Old and New London*, 6 vols. (London: Cassell, 1878), 1:182–99, *BHO*. For a digitized map of early modern London, see Janelle Jenstad, ed., "The Agas Map." *The Map of Early Modern London*, Edition 6.6, accessed June 30, 2021, https://mapoflondon.uvic.ca/edition/6.6/map.htm. For further information on Charlton House, see "Charlton House," Royal Greenwich Trust, accessed August 8, 2018, https://www.greenwichheritage.org/visit/charlton-house.

39. Unfortunately, Abbot House has been closed to the public since 2015; however, renovations are ongoing, and it is scheduled to reopen in 2022. See Abbot House—The Reawakening of Dunfermline's Oldest Building, accessed May 5, 2020, https://www.abbothouse.org/.

40. Anne and William's cousin, also named William, was the son of another William Murray, minister of Dysart and brother of Thomas Murray. Dysart's daughter inherited his title and later married the Earl of Lauderdale. R. Malcolm Smuts, "Murray, William, First Earl of Dysart (d. 1655)," *ODNB*. Rosalind K Marshall, "Murray [Married Names Tollemache, Maitland], Elizabeth, Duchess of Lauderdale and Suo Jure Countess of Dysart (bap. 1626, d. 1698)," *ODNB*.

In 1645, Lady Anne Howard married Sir Charles Howard, first Earl of Carlisle, who "was charged with having borne arms for the King, largely on the grounds of having resisted capture by a Parliamentarian force during the Civil War" in 1646.[41] However, by 1650 he had been appointed High Sheriff of Cumberland, and he later fought for the Parliamentarians at the Battle of Worcester. Thus, although their allegiance was more to the Royalist side when Halkett was staying with them, their loyalty is not unwavering. While Halkett has been hailed as a female Royalist heroine, her *True Account* and her extensive *Meditations* register an anxiety about this identity: not because she herself had any equivocation on this point but because of the changing allegiances of those with whom she was most closely connected. Hallett's *True Account* serves not only as a justification of her own life but also as a repositioning of those around her.

Ironically, this repositioning includes Colonel Joseph Bampfield. While much has been written about his marital infidelity, rather less attention has been paid to his political duplicity.[42] Although his relationship with Halkett is the most hotly debated aspect of her narrative, until recently surprisingly little has been written about this "mysterious and controversial figure . . . a man of multiple and short-lived allegiances."[43] Born in the West Country, probably Devon, in 1622, Bampfield began his military service in 1639 as an ensign during the First Bishops' War and by 1643 he had risen to the rank of colonel. Although his role as a commander of forces was relatively short-lived, he was employed by Charles I "as a courier, occasional advisor, and intelligence agent from late 1645 until access to the King's person was halted in 1648."[44] At this point, he was resolutely Royalist: by February 1642/3, he was married to Catherine Sydenham and "in the summer

---

41. Gordon Goodwin, "Howard, Charles, First Earl of Carlisle (1628–1685)," *ODNB*.

42. In *The Memoirs of Anne, Lady Halkett and Anne, Lady Fanshawe*, Loftis castigates Bampfield's personal behavior in his introduction and relegates comments about his political activities to footnotes; however, he, along with Paul Hardacre, later edited Bampfield's *Apology* and viewed him more favorably. This change of perception is noted by Ottway, who examines the "public" and "private" version of events in the two narratives. While Ottway distances herself from her title's connection with "contemporary spy fiction," Nadine Akkerman emphasizes Halkett's role as a "she-intelligencer." Loftis, ed., *The Memoirs of Anne, Lady Halkett and Anne, Lady Fanshawe*; John Loftis and Paul H. Hardacre, eds., *Colonel Joseph Bampfield's Apology: "Written By Himself and Printed at His Desire," 1685* (London: Associated University Presses, 1993); Sheila Ottway, "They Only Lived Twice: Public and Private Selfhood in the Autobiographies of Anne, Lady Halkett and Colonel Joseph Bampfield," in *Betraying Our Selves: Forms of Self-Representation in Early Modern English Texts*, ed. Henk Dragsta, Sheila Ottway, and Helen Wilcox (Basingstoke, UK: Macmillan, 2000), 136–47; Nadine Akkerman, *Invisible Agents: Women and Espionage in Seventeenth-Century Britain* (Oxford: Oxford University Press, 2018), 182–203.

43. Geoffrey Smith, *Royalist Agents, Conspirators, and Spies: Their Role in the British Civil Wars, 1640–1660* (Farnham, UK: Ashgate, 2011), 7.

44. Alan Marshall, "Bampfield, Joseph (1622–1685)," *ODNB*.

of 1645, [he] was in London, appearing as a penitent Delinquent Cavalier before the Committee for Compounding at Goldsmith's Hall to settle his composition fine."[45] According to his *Apology*, he carried out some successful services for the King circa November 1645–March 1646, which included carrying letters to "a great and wise lady who was in extraordinary credit and had much influence upon the transactions of those times."[46]

By this time, Bampfield was associated with both William Murray (later Earl of Dysart)[47] and Will Murray (Halkett's brother). While Dysart's Scottish connections explain his support for the Covenant and Presbyterianism, Bampfield's motivation for supporting the latter is unclear. Whatever the reason, by 1646 he had been dispatched to London by Charles I with two tasks: first, to communicate the King's position to "the conservative leaders of the 'negotiated peace at any price' party" and, second, to rescue the Duke of York. While the former failed, the latter—eventually—succeeded.[48] On September 26, 1646, Charles I wrote to Henrietta Maria to tell her that Bampfield had a plan to rescue James; however, the actual escape did not take place until April 21, 1648.[49] While Smith lauds Bampfield's "impressive efficiency" in organizing the Duke's escape, other people did most of the preparations, including Anne Murray, George Howard, and an unnamed citizen who provided the finances.[50]

While this was Bampfield's "opportunity to perform a really significant service to the Stuart cause," it also led to a decision that was to tarnish forever his reputation with the then Prince of Wales.[51] In May 1648, without seeking appropriate authority, Bampfield encouraged the Duke of York to take command of a fleet of defecting Parliamentarian ships and attempt to rescue his father. Not only did his "presumptuous behavior" antagonize other exiled Royalists, but "his subsequent comments that the King's children should have taken a lead in rescuing their father permanently lost him the friendship of the Prince of Wales."[52] In addition, rumors began to circulate that Bampfield and others (including Halkett's

---

45. Smith, *Royalist Agents, Conspirators, and Spies*, 85.

46. Loftis and Hardacre, eds., *Colonel Joseph Bampfield's Apology*, 46. Smith suggests that "'the great and wise lady' was probably that inveterate dabbler in intrigue Lucy, Countess of Carlisle"; Smith, *Royalist Agents, Conspirators, and Spies*, 86. See also Roy E. Schreiber, "Hay [née Percy], Lucy, Countess of Carlisle (1599–1660)," *ODNB*.

47. Smuts, "Murray, William," *ODNB*.

48. Smith, *Royalist Agents, Conspirators, and Spies*, 94.

49. Smith, *Royalist Agents, Conspirators, and Spies*, 94–95.

50. George Howard was one of the Earl of Suffolk's younger brothers. Smith, *Royalist Agents, Conspirators, and Spies*, 105; see *True Account*, 82, 82nn128–30.

51. Smith, *Royalist Agents, Conspirators, and Spies*, 105.

52. Loftis and Hardacre, eds., *Colonel Joseph Bampfield's Apology*, 128–29; Smith, *Royalist Agents, Conspirators, and Spies*, 107–8; Marshall, "Bampfield," *ODNB*.

brother Will Murray) intended to take James to Scotland to have him, rather than Charles, recognized as King. Not surprisingly, "from this time onwards Charles and some of his principal advisors, most notably Hyde, regarded Bampfield with unrelenting hostility."[53]

Although Prince Charles had discharged Bampfield from the Duke's service by the end of May 1648, "in consideration of what he had performed," the Duke "supplied his wants, as well as he was able ... till sometime after his Majesty's Restoration."[54] Nevertheless, Bampfield was apparently still trusted by Charles I, who sent for him during the negotiations around the Treaty of Newport.[55] Bampfield states that he "returned unobtrusively" to England and, after the death of the King, he "continued secretly and disguised in England in several places, not knowing well in the disgrace I was then plunged in, how to subsist elsewhere."[56] In his version of events, he remained in England until after he escaped from the Gatehouse in the manner described by Halkett below.[57] After his escape, apart from a brief sojourn in Scotland, Bampfield claims that he was in Holland for the next five years, which would mean circa 1650–1655; thus, he excises from the story of his life almost all of the activities that connected him to the then Anne Murray.[58]

However, her *True Account* attests to some of his activities circa 1650–1652/3, which confirms that he "retained some prominent supporters among the exiled Royalists."[59] Among those who defended him were the "'royal Presbyterians'" with whom Halkett became associated; they, in turn, were all in some way associated with the Marquis of Argyll, who was the first person to visit the then Anne Murray after her arrival in Edinburgh, June 1650.[60] While this is flattering in some respects, it is a complicated connection for a loyal Royalist like Halkett, as the Marquess of Argyll was eventually executed for treason on May 27,

---

53. Smith, *Royalist Agents, Conspirators, and Spies*, 108.

54. J. S. Clarke, ed., *The Life of James the Second, King of England, &c. Collected Out of Memoirs Writ of His Own Hand. Together with the King's Advice to His Son, and His Majesty's Will*. 2 vols. (London: Longman, 1816), 1:43–44.

55. September 18, 1648–November 27, 1648. Loftis and Hardacre, eds., *Colonel Joseph Bampfield's Apology*, 79–80.

56. Smith, *Royalist Agents, Conspirators, and Spies*, 109; Loftis and Hardacre, eds., *Colonel Joseph Bampfield's Apology*, 80.

57. See *True Account*, 97–98. See also Smith, *Royalist Agents, Conspirators, and Spies*, 126; Loftis and Hardacre, eds., *Colonel Joseph Bampfield's Apology*, 136–37; Marshall, "Bampfield, Joseph," *ODNB*.

58. As Ottway notes, "nowhere in his *Apology* does Bampfield mention the name of Anne Halkett"; Ottway, "They Only Lived Twice," 144.

59. Smith, *Royalist Agents, Conspirators, and Spies*, 108.

60. Smith, *Royalist Agents, Conspirators, and Spies*, 176. See *True Account*, 118.

1661.[61] Although she never explicitly comments on Argyll's position, the fact that she notes the difficulties caused for Sir James Halkett by his kinship with Argyll suggests she was not unaware of his problematic status.[62] In Halkett's version of events, both "cases" serve to exonerate Sir James; however, it does mean that—yet again—she is potentially connected to a man whose loyalties are not straightforward.[63] Another member of Halkett's circle who was connected to Argyll was Charles Seton, the second Earl of Dunfermline.[64] Importantly, it has been established that Bampfield and the Earl of Dunfermline were in regular contact by May 1647, at which point Charles I may have placed more trust in Bampfield than in the Earl.[65] Nevertheless, Dunfermline aligned himself with the Engagers in 1648, was subsequently "debarred by the Act of Classes from holding any office of public trust," and joined Charles II in exile after the execution of his father.[66]

Shifting allegiances were not unusual during this unstable period. In many ways, Halkett's connections to Bampfield, Dunfermline, Balcarres, Moray, Mackenzie of Tarbat, and Sir James Halkett offer an exceptional opportunity to explore the "rainbow coalition" of royalism in Scotland in the 1650s.[67] Even so, Bampfield's position as a possible double agent is pretty remarkable. It is difficult to ascertain at exactly what point he switched to the Parliamentarian side: in 1652, they issued a warrant for his arrest, but by 1653 Charles II wanted him apprehended. While Balcarres was certainly aware of the latter fact, there is no indication that he acted on it, either within Halkett's *True Account* or elsewhere. Although initially convinced of Bampfield's treachery in *The Memoirs of Anne, Lady Halkett and Anne, Lady Fanshawe*, Loftis later seeks to exonerate him by suggesting that rumors about his involvement with the Parliamentarians in 1653 were motivated by divisions within the Royalist camp, but he confirms that by September 26, 1654, Bampfield was definitely working for Thurloe.[68] Nevertheless, Halkett

61. David Stevenson, "Campbell, Archibald, Marquess of Argyll (1605x7–1661)," *ODNB*.

62. Sir James Halkett's first wife, Margaret Montgomery, was the Earl of Argyll's niece.

63. See "Upon the Death of My Dearest Sir James Halkett," 222.

64. T. F. Henderson, "Seton, Charles, Second Earl of Dunfermline (1615–1672)," *ODNB*.

65. Paul Christensen, "Charles Seton, Second Earl of Dunfermline: The Reluctant Rebel," *History Scotland* 17, no. 6 (Nov./Dec. 2017): 32–36. One letter from the King suggests some doubt about the Earl's secrecy, and another excludes Dunfermline from confidences shared between only the King and Bampfield.

66. Henderson, "Seton, Charles," *ODNB*.

67. Barbara Donagan, "Varieties of Royalism," in *Royalists and Royalism during the English Civil Wars*, ed. Jason McElligott and David L Smith (Cambridge: Cambridge University Press, 2007), 66–88. David Stevenson, "Lindsay, Alexander, First Earl of Balcarres (1618–1659)," *ODNB*; Allan, "Moray, Sir Robert (1608/9?–1673)," *ODNB*; Colin Kidd, "Mackenzie, George, First Earl of Cromarty (1630–1714)," *ODNB*. See also Akkerman, *Invisible Agents*, 196–98.

68. John Loftis, *Bampfield's Later Career: A Biographical Supplement* (London: Associated University Presses, 1993), esp. 158–72. See also Smith, *Royalist Agents, Conspirators, and Spies*, 165–67; Ottway,

"provides no hint that she knew he had treacherously deserted the Royalist cause" during their final meeting that December.[69] Either way, she was not the only person who was oblivious to his actions, as he still has the Earl of Balcarres's ear. In a letter dated January 8, 1654/5, Bampfield informs him of a discovery of a Royalist plot in which, of course, he omits his own role. Loftis notes that this letter ends with the instruction, "If you write to me, if your Lady directs your letter to Mrs. Murray, to whom I think her Ladyship has an address, she will send them me," and suggests this indicates that Bampfield knew she had lied to him about her marriage to Sir James Halkett.[70] Whether or not this is the case, it is discomforting to read that Bampfield also offers an alternative recipient by whom the reply "will come very safe and more speedily, by reason that Mrs. Murray is at this time three or four miles off at her brother Newton's."[71] Whatever she knew at the time, it is difficult to believe she did not know about his change of allegiance by the time she wrote the *True Account*; for example, she was at Court for the King's coronation when he was again imprisoned.[72] This raises the possibility that it was less the sexual scandal surrounding their relationship she was concerned with and more her need to assert her unequivocal royalism.

As indicated above, she was surrounded by Scotsmen, including her future husband, Sir James Halkett, whose ambitions for the restoration of the monarchy were not entirely in alignment with her own. Perhaps she betrays some anxiety on this point, as she suspects him of being a Cromwellian sympathizer when they first meet; also, like many Scots, Sir James favored a settlement that would make Charles II a "covenanted King."[73] Unlike his descendants, not much survives about Sir James Halkett in either local history or the family papers. His parents were Sir Robert Halkett of Pitfirrane and Margaret Murray, and he was the only son of three surviving children, the other two being Grizel and Anne.[74] His first wife, Margaret Montgomery, was the daughter of Sir Robert Montgomery of

---

"They Only Lived Twice," 140–42; Akkerman, *Invisible Agents*, 196–98.

69. Loftis, ed., *The Memoirs of Anne, Lady Halkett and Anne, Lady Fanshawe*, 206. See *True Account*, 163–64.

70. Loftis, *Bampfield's Later Career*, 172. He cites the letter from the *Thurloe State Papers*, 3:87–88.

71. I.e., she was at Charlton, which suggests Bampfield was keeping an eye on her movements. Colonel Bampfield, "Letter to Earl Balcarres," January 8/18, 1655. *A Collection of the State Papers of John Thurloe*, ed. Thomas Birch, vol. 3, *December 1654–August 1655* (London: Fletcher Gyles, 1742), 87, BHO.

72. Even Bampfield's companion Silius Titus, who claimed to have been duped by him, was informed of his treachery in 1656. Smith, *Royalist Agents, Conspirators, and Spies*, 167. On his imprisonment, see Smith, *Royalist Agents, Conspirators, and Spies*, 250, and Loftis, *Bampfield's Later Career*, 188.

73. Bowie, "'A Legal Limited Monarchy,'" 142–44.

74. His mother was the daughter of Sir John Murray of Blackbarony and Margaret Hamilton. Grizel married Sir Thomas Ker of Cavers circa 1638, while Anne married twice: first, Sir Robert Henderson of Fordel, and second, Thomas Myreton of Cambo, *TSP* 4:15. For a record that suggests Anne's second

Skelmorlie from his second marriage in 1617 to Lady Mary Campbell, third child and only daughter of Archibald Campbell, seventh Earl of Argyll.[75] Halkett and Montgomery had a large family, of whom nine are identifiable (Mary, Charles, Robert, James, Margaret, Thomas, Anne/Anna, John, and Jean), although only four seem to have survived to adulthood.[76] Their children's birth dates indicate that Margaret Montgomery gave birth annually or biennially. Although her death is unrecorded, the date of birth for her final child, Jean, is said to have been September 1650. When Halkett meets the then Anne Murray in 1652, he is apparently already widowed. By Christmas that year, his attentions to Anne are noticeable enough that a servant offers them a minced pie to share. By 1653, he has made his intentions clear, although it is not until March 1655/6 that the couple are legally married. Thus, when Anne met Sir James, he could not have been widowed for more than two years, and, if the dates of birth identified by Pitcairn are correct, at a minimum he had two teenagers (Mary, fourteen; Charles, thirteen), a ten-year-old boy, James, and a five-year-old daughter, Anna/Anne.[77] It is perhaps not surprising that Anne Murray thought he was in need of a wife, albeit she didn't intend it to be her.

While Halkett obviously had a good relationship with Sir James's daughters (they stay with her in Edinburgh and in later life Halkett records the support of Sir William Bruce of Kinross to whom Mary was married), her relationship with her stepsons is more fraught.[78] While James is less frequently referred to,

---

marriage produced a child called Euphemia, see *Scotland: Select Marriages, 1561–1910*, cited by Ancestry®, accessed August 08, 2018, https://www.ancestry.co.uk.

75. Argyll's wife was Lady Agnes Douglas. The precise date of Halkett and Montgomery's marriage is unrecorded; however in a bond dated June 11, 1638, Margaret is identified as Sir James's spouse. William Angus, ed., *Inventory of Pitfirrane Writs, 1230–1740* (Edinburgh: J. Skinner & Co., 1932), 41.

76. Of the four who survived into adulthood, two were boys (Charles and James, who succeeded their father) and the two were girls (Mary and Anne/Anna). Baptismal records survive for Mary (September 7, 1638), Charles (September 26, 1639), Robert (November 7, 1640), James (July 13, 1642), Margaret (July 18, 1643), Thomas (February 10, 1646), Anne/Anna (July 29, 1647), John (February 25, 1649) in *Scotland: Select Births and Baptisms, 1564–1950*, cited by Ancestry®, accessed August 08, 2018, https://www.ancestry.co.uk. Sheila Pitcairn suggests there was a ninth child, Jean, born October 10, 1650. See Pitcairn, "Descendants of Sir James Halkett." Unpublished genealogy, n.d., 5.

77. Halkett provides the day of the week on which she first met Sir James, Thursday, but does not specify the month or year; the context suggests that meeting occurred sometime in the late summer/early autumn of 1652. If Pitcairn's "Descendants of Sir James Halkett" is correct and all the children were still alive, there would also have been Robert, twelve; Margaret, nine; John, three or four; and Jean, only two.

78. According to Couper, Mary married Sir William Bruce of Kinross and Anne/Anna married Sir Andrew Ker of Cavers, *The Life of the Lady Halket*, 30. John Lowrey, "Bruce, Sir William, First Baronet (c. 1625–1710)," *ODNB*. Anna Halkett married Andrew Ker in Dunfermline, on April 25, 1667, *Scotland: Select Marriages, 1561–1910*, cited by Ancestry®, accessed August 08, 2018, https://www.ancestry.co.uk.

Halkett's relationship with the eldest son and heir, Sir Charles Halkett, is riven with conflict, which might be partly caused by his age at his mother's death and the relative swiftness with which she was replaced by Anne Murray in his father's affections. As the *True Account* explains, she and Sir James were married on Saturday, March 1, 1655/6, and they apparently wasted no time in consummating their marriage, as Anne gave birth to their first daughter, Elizabeth ("Betty"), on November 26, 1656. Clearly concerned about the math, Halkett notes that it was also on a Saturday that her "child first made me sensible that it was quickened." Her anxiety perhaps is registered by her insertion of a more precise date in the margin: "it being that day nineteen weeks that I was married."[79] In addition to Betty, Halkett gave birth to three other children, Henry/Harry, Robert/Robin, and Jane, and she refers to a miscarriage of twins. Only one of their offspring, Robert, affectionately referred to as "Robin," survived beyond the age of five; nevertheless, even he predeceases his mother.[80]

In later life, Halkett consistently refers to Sir James as "the best of husbands." One of the reasons for this is his diplomatic silence on the matter of her relationship with Bampfield; however, while her marriage seems to have offered her emotional security, her relationship with Sir James is also framed by financial concerns. Sir James helps her with her legal cases to attain her inheritance, but, although he had some success, Halkett's finances remained precarious throughout her life. The delays and difficulties in obtaining income are attested to in the letters reproduced in appendices 1 through 3. Although Halkett began her case in the

79. Anne, Lady Halkett, *A Short Expostulation about Prayer, Meditations, and the Mother's Will to Her Unborn Child* (1653–1657), NLS, MS 6489, p. 199.

80. Elizabeth/Betty, b. November 26, 1656; d. November 13, 1660; Henry/Harry, b. June 13, 1658; d. May 12, 1661; Robert/Robin, b. February 1, 1659/60; d. October 5, 1693; Jane, b. October 11, 1661; d. February 11, 1665/6. See, respectively: Halkett, *A Short Expostulation about Prayer*, p. 253, and Anne, Lady Halkett, "Upon the Death of My Dearest Child, Betty, who Died of the Small Pox, upon Tuesday, November 13, 1660 in Covent Garden and Buried in that Church" in *Occasional Meditations, Meditations and Prayers on Every Several Day* (1660, 1663), NLS, MS 6491, pp. 1–18; see also Trill, ed., *Halkett*, 15–19; Anne, Lady Halkett, "Upon the Death of My Dear Son, Harry, being May 12, 1661," who "had he lived one month longer he had been just three years," in *Occasional Meditations, Meditations and Prayers on Every Several Day*, pp. 52–56; Anne, Lady Halkett, "Upon the Birth of My Son, Robert, on February 1, 1659/60, being upon Wednesday betwixt Two and Three [in the] Afternoon," in *Occasional Meditations* (1658/9–1660), NLS, MS 6490, pp. 297–324; Anne, Lady Halkett, "Friday, October 5, 1694," in *Of Watchfulness, Select, and Occasional Meditations* (1693/4–1695), NLS, MS 6500, pp. 351–52; Couper, *The Life of the Lady Halket*, 30, and in "April 14, being Easter Eve, 1688," Halkett recalls "the most remarkable things in 1665/6 began sadly with myself, for February 11, my dear child Jane died," in Halkett, *Meditations on St. Peter*, pp. 376–79, see also Trill, ed., *Halkett*, 152; and Anne, Lady Halkett, "Upon My Miscarrying of Two Children, March 7, 1658/9," in *Occasional Meditations*, pp. 1–9. To date, Halkett's experience as a wife and a mother has received little attention; however, "A Mother's Will to Her Unborn Child," and "Instructions to My Son [Robert]" are discussed in some detail by Jennifer Heller in *The Mother's Legacy in Early Modern England* (Farnham, UK: Ashgate, 2011), esp. 141–51.

summer of 1652 and by 1655 there is a related "Copy resignation of a factory by Sir James Halkett of Pitfirrane,"[81] the letters suggest that even by circa 1672/3 the case has not been successfully resolved. Like many of her contemporaries, Halkett wrote to the Earl of Lauderdale, probably in the late 1660s, in the hope of receiving some recompense for her Royalist activities during the Wars of the Three Kingdoms and some assistance in recovering her inheritance. The letter to her stepson, which internal evidence suggests was written sometime in 1672/3, notes the former's lack of success, despite the fact that Lauderdale had recently become a Duke and was now married to Halkett's cousin, Elizabeth Murray, Countess of Dysart.[82] Among the claims listed in "An Information of What Was Left Me by My Mother" is a potential right to one of Archibald Hay's plantations in Barbados.[83]

Links between Scotland and Barbados were established from the early seventeenth century, as "the first proprietor of Barbados was James Hay, first Earl of Carlisle," and trading was recorded "as early as 1611 with the voyage of the Janet of Leith."[84] Before his death in 1636, Carlisle had given control of his proprietorship to Sir James and Archibald Hay, who held it in trust for his son, later James, second Earl of Carlisle.[85] However, the role of proprietary agent was given to another kinsman Peter Hay, who acted as such from 1636 to 1641 and remained in Barbados as a planter.[86] Another kinsman, William Powrie, became secretary of Barbados in 1640 and "was a planter at Spring Plantation where he died before 1663."[87] There was unrestricted "trade in indentured servants": Scots were in demand, and after "the Battles of Preston (1648), Dunbar (1650), and Worcester (1651), thousands of prisoners were sent by Oliver Cromwell into exile in the American colonies, including Barbados."[88] In the *True Account*, the *Meditations*, and her letters, Halkett suggests she never actually received any income from this bequest, even though there is a record of "Spring Plantation, Barbados, and all other plantations in Barbados and the Caribee Islands" being sold "to Sir James Halkett and John Powrie, natural son of the said William Powrie, 1663."[89] She

81. "Copy Resignation of a Factory by Sir James Halkett of Pitfirren [sic], Commissioner for Anna Murray before the Commissioners for the Administration of Justice in Scotland against Mr. Andrew Hay as Executor of Archibald Hay at the Instance of Anna Murray, Assignee of a Bond for £4000," dated April 27, 1655. NRS, GD34/843/3/23.

82. Hutton, "Maitland, John," *ODNB*.

83. See "Appendix 3," 333–35.

84. David Dobson, *Barbados and Scotland Links, 1627–1877* (Baltimore, MD: Clearfield, 2005), i.

85. Harry J. Bennett, "Peter Hay: Proprietary Agent in Barbados, 1636–1641," *Jamaican Historical Review* 5, no. 2 (1965): 9.

86. Bennett, "Peter Hay," 9–29.

87. David Dobson, *Scottish Emigration to Colonial America, 1607–1785* (Athens and London: University of Georgia Press, 1994), 67.

88. Dobson, *Barbados and Scotland Links*, i.

89. Dobson, *Barbados and Scotland Links*, x.

makes reference to this in her letter to her stepson, Sir Charles Halkett, but it would seem the issue is still unresolved in 1689, as, after her sister Elizabeth's death, Sir Henry Newton offers "to cancel her Bonds before witnesses, and to assign the Security he had on Barbados to any she thought fit because it might be of use to her."[90] Regardless of whether Halkett was ever fully granted this right, it offers a fragmentary insight into a seventeenth-century woman's involvement in emergent colonialism and, by extension, with the slave trade.

Accounting for My Life: *Casuistry and the Providential Imagination*

Those financial concerns should remind us of the dual meaning of "account" within Halkett's writing; she is accounting for herself both spiritually and financially. While the ultimate arbiter in both cases is God, Halkett's many intended audiences include her son, her ministers, and a possible wider public. While she explicitly wrote "Instructions to My Son" for Robert, she intended to leave him all of her books; thus, until his death, she must have been mindful that he would one day have the opportunity to read them. That option no longer being open to her, Halkett made her ministers her literary executors instead and gave them permission to publish what they deemed appropriate.[91] When taken in isolation, the *True Account* was assumed to be a purely private document, existing as it did in manuscript. However, my research, building on the work of Ezell and Wiseman, has demonstrated that Halkett had anticipated an audience since at least 1663.[92] Furthermore, the volume of meditations that Halkett interrupted to write the *True Account* provides further information about what prompted her to write this narrative at that particular time. In *The Art of Divine Chemistry*, Halkett notes that she completed her meditation on "The Rule for Words," September 10, 1677; accidentally turning over two leaves (into which she later copies a "memorial" she had initially written on a loose piece of paper on Saturday, September 30, 1677), she dates her next entry "Monday, April 22, 1678" where she explains that she had interrupted that volume to write her *True Account*.[93]

However, the organization of this volume suggests that it took repeated occurrences of scandalous aspersions being spread about her for Halkett finally to decide to defend herself in writing. A note on the inside flyleaf of the volume informs us that *The Art of Divine Chemistry* was "begun June 20, 1676."[94]

---

90. Couper, *The Life of the Lady Halket*, 48. McKitterick, "Women and Their Books in Seventeenth-Century England," 378.

91. See "Saturday, February 19, 1697/8," 318–21.

92. See "Headnote," 198.

93. Anne, Lady Halkett, *The Art of Divine Chemistry* (1676–1678), NLS, MS 6494, pp. 291, 294–95. See also "Meditations upon Psalm 106:4–5," 264–65.

94. Halkett, *The Art of Divine Chemistry*, p. i.

Characteristically, Halkett provides a prefatory prayer in which she explains that she has chosen this topic so that by "divine assistance," she may be able "to extract good out of all the cross occurrences I have met withal of late," of which she then provides examples: "The failings of a good man; a professed friend; a faithful servant; and the unkindness of many in a time when I expected and had need of consolation, being distempered with palsy and sickness."[95] Despite her resolutions, however, by Saturday, July 14, 1677, she has become the object of scandalous rumors against which she struggles to defend herself:

> Since I left at this last stop the Lord hath thought fit to give a great trial both to my faith and patience: for I heard myself accused, with all that could be of infamy or reproach. And when the little I offered to say in my own defense could not be heard, I lifted up my hands to heaven, and said, "O Lord, who knows my innocence in what I am accused of, vindicate me and convince them; for unto thee, do I refer my cause." With an assured confidence I uttered this, and do expect a return of my prayer, and the ground of my faith was upon this promise:[96] *ye shall not afflict any widow, or fatherless child. If thou afflict them in any wise, and they cry at all unto me, I will surely hear their cry.*[97]

Unable to make herself heard orally, Halkett selects the medium of the "word" to provide the space she needs for self-expression, in part for herself, but also with the intention that her words would outlive her and justify her actions to others.

While this context confirms that Halkett was most certainly writing a justification of her life through which she desired to set the record straight, for both her contemporaries and future readers, it also establishes that the context in which she did so was "devotional." Given the apparent lack of biblical allusion in the *True Account*, many readers have sought to discount the fragmentary remains of the opening paragraph, which is clearly devotional in nature. However, Halkett's own pagination of her text and her practice in the extant volumes of meditations make it reasonable to assume that the initial missing leaf would have contained a title, an explanation of her motivation for writing on this topic at this time, and a longer dedication of her endeavor to God, with an extended appeal to him to forgive her trespasses. While the *True Account* is more "secular" in focus than her

---

95. See Halkett, *The Art of Divine Chemistry*, 261.

96. Exodus 22:22–23: "Ye shall not afflict any widow, or fatherless child. If thou afflict them in any wise, and they cry at all unto me, I will surely hear their cry." The first verse is included as an interlineal insertion in the original MS.

97. Halkett, *The Art of Divine Chemistry*, p. 282.

Meditations (especially the select ones), it is closer to Halkett's other writings than critics usually admit.[98]

A True Account of My Life

Since the twentieth century, Halkett's *True Account* has been read as a series of romantic liaisons interwoven with Royalist politics.[99] While these are undoubtedly central features of her narrative, they are indelibly linked to her religious convictions; furthermore, if we focus simply on Halkett's romantic attachments (Howard, Bampfield, Halkett), we limit our understanding of both her personal connections and her field of vision. After all, in some sense, Halkett's representation of her life follows the conventions of an "exemplary" auto/biography of the period.[100] Following her dedication of her narrative to God, she turns first to her genealogy to establish the "virtue" of her family, in which she emphasizes her noble connections and how her parents served the Stewart/Stuart dynasty. She then establishes how her mother ensured that she and her sister gained firm foundations in the forms of education most suited to women and pointedly highlights that the most important element of her upbringing was daily reading of the Bible (alongside daily attendance at both morning and evening services in the Church of England). With this devotional context established, Halkett's narrative focuses on the cases of conscience she faced along the way and the providential resolutions that God provided.

The "cases of conscience" contained with Halkett's *True Account* vary enormously. They encompass everyday events, such as emphasizing that she went to the Spring Gardens "before it grew something scandalous by the abuse of some" and resolving to avoid being the subject of male complaints by initiating the practice of female friends going to the Playhouse "unaccompanied," except for a footman.[101] An important element of casuistry was equivocation. While this could be used as a highly political discourse, within the *True Account*, Halkett uses it mostly in

98. Mary Ellen Lamb is an important exception; Lamb, "Merging the Secular and the Spiritual in Lady Anne Halkett's Memoirs." See also Trill, "Beyond Romance," 451–54; Trill, ed., *Halkett*, xvii–xxxix; Margaret J. M. Ezell, "Ann Halkett's Morning Devotions: Posthumous Publication and the Culture of Writing in Late Seventeenth-Century Britain," in *Print, Manuscript, Performance: The Changing Relations of the Media in Early Modern England*, ed. Arthur Marotti and Michael D. Bristol (Columbus: Ohio State University Press, 2000), 215–31; Susan Wiseman, "Legitimizing Conspiracy: Anne Halkett, Rachel Russell, Aphra Behn," in *Conspiracy & Virtue: Women, Writing, and Politics in Seventeenth-Century England* (Oxford: Oxford University Press, 2006), 313–59.

99. For an overview, see Trill, "Beyond Romance," 448–51.

100. A recent reappraisal of how to read such exemplary materials is provided in Raymond A. Anselment, "Anthony Walker, Mary Rich, and Seventeenth-Century Funeral Sermons of Women," *Prose Studies* 37, no. 3 (2015): 200–24.

101. See *True Account*, 65.

interpersonal situations, predominantly—indeed almost exclusively—with men.[102] The first occasion she employs this method is when Thomas Howard threatens to become a Catholic if she doesn't agree to marry him. In her report of this conversation, Halkett is careful to distinguish between Howard's request that she "promise" to marry him and her response in which she says only that she will "not marry" before he does. Significantly, Howard does not recognize the nuanced answer she has provided, which allowed them both to part "well pleased" on the basis of completely different understandings of what has been "agreed."[103] While these are small, private moments of casuistical thinking, Halkett's *True Account* also gestures toward the political significance of this way of thinking, as epitomized in *Eikon Basilike: The Portraiture of His Sacred Majesty in His Solitudes and Sufferings* (1649). Not surprisingly, Halkett knew of this book and in a meditation dating from 1660/1 clearly saw it as "an autobiography of a soul in travail, one seeking to discern and obey God's will."[104] The structure of the *True Account* follows a very similar pattern to Charles I's particular "case of conscience" concerning the trial and death of the Earl of Strafford, which "takes us step by step through the process by which a Christian discerns the true operation of conscience."[105]

In addition to the model offered by *Eikon Basilike*, numerous other books examining "cases of conscience" were published in this period. While Lamb points to William Perkins, a more likely influence on Halkett is bishop Joseph Hall's *Resolutions and Decisions of Divers Practicall Cases of Conscience in Continuall Use amongst Men* (1649), which is divided into "four decades:" 1) "Cases of Profit and Traffic"; 2) "Cases of Life and Liberty"; 3) "Cases of Piety and Religion"; and 4) "Cases Matrimonial."[106] First, Halkett credits Hall as the figure who inspired her to write her *Meditations* in the first place;[107] second, Hall's book was first published in 1649, which is not only the year of Charles I's execution but the period during which Halkett first became aware that Bampfield's wife might be an issue in their relationship; third, over the course of the *True Account*, Halkett engages

102. Vallance, "The Kingdom's Case," 557–83. Butler suggests that, for Catholics in the early seventeenth century, "equivocation was not permitted in moments both mundane . . . and highly spiritual." Todd Butler, "Equivocation, Cognition, and Political Authority in Early Modern England," *Texas Studies in Literature and Language* 54, no. 1 (2012): 138. There is one instance where Halkett uses equivocation with her mother. See *True Account*, 70.

103. See *True Account*, 68.

104. "Upon the Fast which by Proclamation was kept, January 30, 1660/1," 203–5. Lacey, "Texts to Be Read," 5. See also Jim Daems and Holly Faith Nelson, eds., *Eikon Basilike with Selections from Eikonoklastes by John Milton* (Ontario: Broadview, 2006).

105. Lacey summarizes this process in "Texts to Be Read," 12–13.

106. Lamb, "Merging the Secular and the Spiritual in Lady Anne Halkett's Memoirs," 84. Joseph Hall, *Resolutions and Decisions of Divers Practicall Cases of Conscience in Continuall Use amongst Men, Very Necessary for Their Information and Direction: In Foure Decades* (London: M. F., 1649). ESTC R202349.

107. See "Upon Reading Mr. Boyle's *Occasional Reflections*," 218.

with at least half of the cases identified by Hall as "Cases Matrimonial";[108] and finally, throughout her writing, she also negotiates questions raised in "Cases of Piety and Religion."[109]

The Howard episode is the first "act of disobedience" that Halkett deems significant enough to recount—and account for—within the main body of her narrative, although it is certainly not the first time she is aware of transgressing, which raises the issue of why this episode and why at such length.[110] In terms of narrative space, the amount of words devoted to the Howard episode is second only to the Nicholls debacle recounted at Naworth Castle.[111] Yet, if the Howard narrative is noted by critics at all, it is generally only to draw attention to Halkett's famous use of a blindfold, which enables her to act equivocally; that is, she obeys the letter of her law as required by her mother's oath while simultaneously disobeying its spirit.[112] Her concern for the consequences of oaths is also affirmed by her refusal to relate the detail of "the solemn oaths" Thomas Howard made before he left, which would be to reiterate them at a point at which he has clearly violated them. These incidents have been viewed as oddities barely worth the retelling; however, the fact that Halkett chose to include them should instead alert us to a difference of perspective that is meaningful. Halkett is only too aware of the dangers of violating a vow. Dismissing these actions as youthful follies means that Halkett has been misunderstood; vows, oaths, and covenants are sacramental, and breaking them had implications not only for this life but also for the next. Indeed, the Howard narrative sets up several motifs that have gone unremarked upon.

108. Hall's "Cases," which pertain to Halkett's experiences are: 1) "whether the marriage of a son or daughter, without or against the consent of parents, may be accounted lawful"; 4) "whether the authority of a father may reach so far as to command or compel the child to dispose of himself in marriage where he shall appoint"; 6) "whether it be necessary or requisite there should be a witnessed contract, or espousals of the parties to be married, before the solemnization of the marriage"; 8) "whether it be necessary that marriages should be celebrated by a minister; and whether they may be valid, and lawful without him"; 9) "whether there be any necessity or use of thrice publishing the contract of marriage in the congregation before the celebration of it; and whether it be fit, that any dispensation should be granted for the forbearance of it"; 10) "whether marriages once made, may be annulled, and utterly voided; and in what cases this may be done," *Resolutions and Decisions of Diverse Practicall Cases of Conscience*, sig. A11r–12v. Broadly speaking, the Howard affair explores cases 1 and 4; the Bampfield incident elucidates cases 10 and 6; and Halkett, while primarily affected by case 10, also alludes to issues raised in cases 6, 8, and 9.

109. Hall, *Resolutions and Decisions of Diverse Practicall Cases of Conscience*, sig. A9r–11r. Of particular relevance is number four: "whether vows be not out of fashion now under the Gospel of what things they may be made; how far they may oblige us; and whether and how far they may be capable of release," sig. A9v–10r.

110. Both Halkett and Couper record her youthful transgression of biting her sister's hand. See "Friday, May 14, 1697," 311; Couper, *The Life of the Lady Halket*, 4.

111. The Howard episode reaches around 6,700 words: the Nicholls incident around 6,880.

112. See *True Account*, 74.

In addition to the use of intermediaries, the difficulty of knowing the truth of a particular event, and a concern with appropriate, civil behavior, the Howard narrative emphasizes Halkett's extreme aversion to marriage without parental consent. Not only does Halkett object to Howard's proposal that they do so (and particularly to his having already arranged a minister and a ring for this purpose), but the outcome of his eventual marriage to Elizabeth Mordaunt—undertaken without parental consent—serves as a cautionary tale to any considering doing likewise.[113] In spite of herself, Halkett was protected from an imprudent marriage by her mother's objections; the Howard incident thus serves to remind Halkett and her readers that one's parents should be obeyed.

After the missing leaf, the narrative resumes midsentence with Halkett introducing Colonel Joseph Bampfield as one who "professed to have great friendship for my brother Will" and with whom she shared an interest in piety, loyalty, and virtue.[114] Nevertheless, in the next paragraph, Halkett reproves Bampfield for being a bad husband for not having seen his wife in more than a year and thus immediately highlights the central point of conflict within their relationship: his wife, Catherine Sydenham. Bampfield excuses his absence on the apparently "reasonable" grounds that his wife's relations are Parliamentarians. However, as Sydenham's stepfather was a notorious Royalist, Bampfield's explanation is perhaps his own form of equivocation. By contrast, external evidence supports Halkett's claim that he received many letters from Charles I that instructed him to assist the Duke of York in escaping from St. James's Palace, and her account of the escape itself is also externally verified.[115] Here, and later in her narrative (particularly while in Edinburgh in the 1650s), Halkett is most definitely a "she-intelligencer."[116] While this was a daring political intervention, Halkett's narrative also bears witness to more personal connections, including giving the young Duke a hug and providing one of his favorite cakes to eat on his journey.[117]

Eliding the controversy over Bampfield's failed naval expedition, in Halkett's relation he returns from the Continent to resume his intelligence activities for the King. She clearly enjoys playing her part in these activities herself, even while she anticipates the opprobrium such actions would later bring upon her. It is during this unspecified period that Bampfield first tells Halkett that his wife is dead,

---

113. Hall states that "it is altogether unlawful for a child to sleight his parents' consent in the choice of his marriage" and confirms that "the child cannot without sin balk the parents' consent to his choice of marriage"; nevertheless, "though such marriages without, or against consent, be not lawfully made; ye once being made, they are valid," *Resolutions and Decisions of Diverse Practicall Cases of Conscience*, 385; 386; 386–87.

114. See *True Account*, 80.

115. See *True Account*, 81, 81n115, 82, 82n128.

116. Akkerman, *Invisible Agents*, 188.

117. See *True Account*, 84, 84n140.

and, "after a little time," he proposes marriage. Halkett is careful to note that she does not immediately accept but has to be "prevailed" upon before she eventually agrees and "resolved to marry him as soon as it appeared convenient."[118] There has been much speculation on whether or not Bampfield and the then Anne Murray were ever officially married.[119] Here, the lack of specificity on timing makes an awkward question even more difficult to resolve. While Halkett frequently provides very specific dates for events, at other points months, occasionally years, are passed over in a paragraph or page. In addition to timing, the other mystery is where such an event may have taken place. Couper's biography suggests that Halkett may have spent some time in Holland, which has led some to speculate that she and Bampfield got married there in the winter of 1648. This, however, seems unlikely, as despite how he presented himself to Anne Murray, Bampfield had been discharged from the Duke of York's service and was deeply distrusted by the then Prince of Wales. According to his own account, Bampfield returned to England in late 1648 and remained there until after his escape from the Gatehouse, on December 21, 1649.[120]

Nevertheless, the vagaries of chronology in both Bampfield's *Apology* and Halkett's *True Account* make it difficult to be certain. As Halkett makes use of prolepsis and flashback at various points, it is possible that she has altered the timing of some events. For example, while most historians suggest that the "seeds of jealousy" between the two Princes were being sown in the latter part of 1648, in her narration Halkett's brother Will returns in disgrace after the execution of Charles I, on January 30, 1649.[121] Despite the timing issues, the detailed exposition of her brother's situation accords with her general intention of justifying herself and those around by establishing the workings of God's providence in even the most difficult of circumstances. In Halkett's version of events, Will is exonerated and his death is exemplary. Unlike the misuse of vows and sacraments proposed by Bampfield and Nicholls, Will's sacramental preparations for death—including confession, taking communion, and disavowing worldly concerns—mirror Halkett's sacramental presentation of her *True Account*. He dies with a clear conscience; however, his endorsement of Bampfield's honor is arguably equivocal, and it is about this time that Bampfield announces that his wife may not be dead after all.

118. See *True Account*, 87.

119. See, for example, Loftis, ed., *The Memoirs of Anne, Lady Halkett and Anne, Lady Fanshawe*, xii, xiv; Ottway, "They Only Lived Twice," 145; Sandra Findley and Elaine Hobby, "Seventeenth Century Women's Autobiography," in *1642: Literature and Power in the Seventeenth Century*, ed. Francis Barker et al. (Essex: University of Essex, 1981), 15; Stevenson, "A Lady and Her Lovers," 194; Lamb, "Merging the Secular and the Spiritual in Lady Anne Halkett's Memoirs," 91–92.

120. Loftis and Hardacre, eds., *Colonel Joseph Bampfield's Apology*, 80.

121. Smith, *Royalist Agents, Conspirators, and Spies*, 107–8; Ronald Hutton, *Charles II: King of England, Scotland, and Ireland* (Oxford: Oxford University Press, 1989), 31; Loftis and Hardacre, eds., *Colonel Joseph Bampfield's Apology*, 135.

Once reassured that Catherine Sydenham is indeed deceased, Halkett reaffirms her resolution "to marry as soon as we could put our affairs in order to prevent sequestration."[122] If Bampfield and Murray were married, this must have taken place sometime between March 1648/9 and the end of August 1649. There is a lacuna in Halkett's narrative during that period that has not previously been noted. In her preface to *Meditations on Moses and Samuel* (1688-1689/90), she recalls that on "the evening of Monday, May 21, 1649 ... I was under the greatest trial that ever any now living I believe hath met with." The timing makes it tempting to assume a connection with Bampfield, especially as she often describes their relationship as a trial; however, she continues, "the particulars, and the person that occasioned it, I desire ever to conceal," which makes any such assumption problematic.[123] Furthermore, in "What Crosses and Difficulties I Have Met with Myself, and Deliverances out of Them, ever to Be Remembered with Thankfulness and Praise," as Halkett is comparing her sufferings with those of St. Paul, she claims to have "in perils of my life" been "once threatened to be killed with a sword; another time to be brained with a pair of tongs (being the readiest instrument that one in the rage of fury had to make use of); another time with a dirk."[124] In the same entry she notes that she weekly remembers the "deliverance I had from these trials ... every Monday, being the day on which in the evening two of them arrived to me."[125] In her final extant manuscript, Halkett revisits this incident again during her Saturday devotions of May 21, 1698: she "accidentally" remembers "what had like to have been a sad tragedy" and notes "the particular account of it I did then write in a parchment book in folio with green strings, which I desire never to forget."[126] From what she says about her books, it seems likely that this is the now missing second volume *Meditations, Contemplations, and the Soul's Remembrancer* (1649-1650).

Whatever happened that night, it being "noised abroad" that she was involved with the Duke of York's escape encourages Halkett to accept Lady Anne Howard's invitation to accompany her to Naworth Castle.[127] On arrival, the household appears to follow the prescriptions of contemporary conduct books to the letter, with the additional benefit of an excellent chaplain, later named as Mr. Nicholls. Halkett's description of him as a "tutelar angel" is, however, consciously ironic.[128] While the initial interruption to Halkett's peace of mind and

---

122. See *True Account*, 89.
123. See "Monday, May 21, 1688," 273.
124. "A kind of dagger or poniard: specifically, the dagger of a Highlander," *OED*.
125. See "What Crosses and Difficulties I Have Met with Myself," 307-11.
126. According to Couper's catalogue, volume 2, which contained "The Soul's Remembrancer," was written between 1649 and 1650. See "Appendix 4.2," 341-42.
127. Halkett records the exact date of their departure, September 10, 1649, 93.
128. Loftis, ed., *The Memoirs of Anne, Lady Halkett and Anne, Lady Fanshawe*, 198.

physical health is occasioned by external factors (specifically further rumors that Bampfield's wife is very much alive), her "misfortunes" at Naworth are primarily attributed to Mr. Nicholls's dubious behavior. While most critics simply pass over this episode without comment, it occupies a similar amount of narrative space to her experiences with Thomas Howard, which suggests that Halkett viewed it as something much more than "a storm in a teacup."[129] Significantly, in *The Art of Divine Chemistry*, Halkett indicates that she is prompted to write the *True Account* because another "pious man" has let her down and that her relationship with him has led to suspicions that she is "guilty of my breach of resolution ... of holy widowhood."[130] In both instances, the appropriateness of Halkett's sexual conduct is called into question.

For undisclosed reasons, Mr. Nicholls seeks to persuade Halkett that Lady Anne is jealous of Halkett's relationship with her husband, Sir Charles Howard, and persuades Lady Anne that she has reason to be jealous. Nicholls actively discourages the two from talking directly to each other, and their lack of communication creates a climate of suspicion and entangled emotions that reaches its zenith around May/June 1650. Quite what Mr. Nicholls thought he would gain from sowing seeds of jealousy between them is something of a mystery; however, there is perhaps an oblique explanation hinted at by Halkett's insertion of a tale concerning two other female guests in the household. Mr. Nicholls's actions there position him as a contemporary stereotype: "Chaplains 'if they come single it's a thousand to one but they will either be in love or married before they go away.'"[131] It is therefore perhaps more than coincidental that Nicholls's machinations call Halkett's marital morality into question, especially as Halkett decides to test his integrity by confiding in him that she is married to Colonel Bampfield. Relations with Lady Howard become increasingly strained, and Halkett finds herself in an impossible position. Her options are already limited, but if she were to be suspected—again—of improper sexual conduct, she would most definitely be "unwelcome anywhere."[132] In dire straits and with no one to turn to, Halkett pours out her distress to God in prayer and supplication and anticipates a providential response, which manifests itself through the arrival of some letters that Halkett uses as a pretext to talk to Lady Anne privately.

The two women finally communicate directly. Despite their long friendship, both are susceptible to Nicholls's negative representations of each other, and the social distinction between them demands that Anne Murray respectfully address

---

129. Paul Delany, *British Autobiography in the Seventeenth Century* (London: Routledge & Kegan Paul, 1969), 163.

130. See Halkett, *The Art of Divine Chemistry*, 262; Trill, "Critical Categories," 111–15.

131. Quotation from 1632, cited by William Gibson, *A Social History of the Domestic Chaplain, 1530–1840* (London: Leicester University Press, 1997), 50. See *True Account*, 101–4.

132. See *True Account*, 105.

Lady Anne as "Madam." Although they draw on their knowledge of each other's actions, the deciding factor is a letter "under [Nicholls's] own hand" that proves that he has a higher opinion of Halkett than he pretended to Lady Anne Howard. Having already narrated much of what had occurred, Halkett glosses over the established details and instead moves to a climactic exchange in which she offers to swear on the Bible before Sir Charles, as a Justice of the Peace, that what she has said is true, only to be met with Mr. Nicholls being willing to do the same thing. Halkett gives herself the last word, in which she cautions Mr. Nicholls on the need to take such an oath seriously, but it seems to have taken the intervention of the Howards to calm things down, with Halkett again calling on God to demonstrate her innocence. They separate, with Mr. Nicholls going off alone, and Anne Murray departing with the Howards, but it is only when Sir Charles finally steps in and says there is no grounds for such assertions that the matter is dropped.

For Halkett, however, the situation is not fully resolved, as indicated by her private discussion with Nicholls before receiving the Sacrament. Halkett is internally divided on what to do in these circumstances: she wants to take the Sacrament but is concerned about doing so in "bad faith." Although she goes there to make clear that her attendance does not mean she condones his previous actions, she ends up reaffirming her lack of faith in him as a minister. Nevertheless, she tells him she forgives him, while warning him of the consequences to his own soul if he is not appropriately penitent. Still uncomfortable in the Howard household, Halkett seeks God's direction in what to do next. This time God's providence is revealed through two reminders of Bampfield's existence. While the first is less welcome, insofar as Halkett learns that he has been involved in a duel with her brother-in-law, Sir Henry Newton, in Flanders,[133] the second provides an opportunity to move on as his letter brings an invitation to come to Scotland and stay with the Earl and Countess of Dunfermline. With the Howards' material support, Halkett plans to leave as soon as possible but cannot resist the opportunity for a final confrontation with Nicholls. Sarcastically congratulating him on succeeding in getting her out of the household, she reminds him that God will hold him responsible for whatever he says about her, even if he himself has no conscience about doing so. Slippery to the end, Nicholls suggests that his actions were not entirely within his own control and offers to provide her with a character witness, which Halkett "disdainful[ly]" declines before prophetically admonishing him not to treat anyone else as he has done her, with the warning that it could prove his comeuppance.[134] This section of the narrative concludes with Lady Howard's anxiety for her friend, and Halkett's brief appraisal of the power of friendship that has been tested "and yet continued

---

133. See *True Account*, 113–15. See also Loftis, ed., *The Memoirs of Anne, Lady Halkett and Anne, Lady Fanshawe*, 198–99.

134. See *True Account*, 117.

firm."[135] However, although Halkett plans to return to Naworth in the summer/autumn of 1652, she does not do so, and I have yet to find any later reference to her friend in her extant writings.

Halkett arrives in Edinburgh on Thursday, June 6, 1650, and despite desiring anonymity, she is almost immediately recognized by the boardinghouse's mistress. Although she had been invited to Scotland by the Earl of Dunfermline, the first visitor Halkett mentions is the Earl of Argyll.[136] Hearing that Charles II has landed in the north of Scotland, Halkett writes to one of his most trusted grooms of the bedchamber, Henry Seymour, seeking advice on whether she "should go to kiss the King's hand." This case of conscience is prompted by two dilemmas, both of which arise from her connection to Bampfield: first, because of the doubts about his first wife being dead; and second, because both he and her brother were out of the King's favor. While Halkett chooses to ask Seymour's advice because he had personally known another of her brothers, Charles, it is worth noting that he was directly involved in "the acrimonious debate" over who was to command the fleet that Bampfield had unadvisedly awarded to the Duke of York.[137] Satisfied by Seymour's reply, the opportunity to do so is providentially supplied by the Countess of Dunfermline's invitation to accompany her for this very purpose. Halkett is careful to emphasize her sense of favor, honor, and obligation at being given this opportunity, which puts her in the company of some of the most influential Scottish courtiers of the period. It also brings her into contact with one of her brother Will's enemies, and Halkett's account of her experience indicates that she is by no means fully integrated into this aristocratic circle. Disappointed by the King's lack of attention, she seeks advice from another of her brother Charles's connections, Mr. Harding: this pays off the next day when the King addresses her directly, lays his hands on hers, and allows her to kiss his hand.[138]

While clearly enjoying being part of the King's entourage, that pleasure was mitigated by the humiliating settlement imposed on the King, Cromwell's invasion of Scotland, and the decisive defeat at the Battle of Dunbar.[139] Here, again, Halkett's "providential imagination" comes to the fore as she interprets the initial confidence of victory being subsumed by defeat as a lesson to make "us see how little confidence should be placed in anything but God."[140] Providence of a different kind is at work when the Countess of Dunfermline invites Halkett to accompany her to the Seton estate of Fyvie, Aberdeenshire. Sensible to the honor and favor of this invitation, Halkett's strained finances require her to borrow money

---

135. See *True Account*, 117.
136. Stevenson, "Campbell, Archibald (1605x7–1661)," *ODNB*.
137. Smith, *Royalist Agents, Conspirators, and Spies*, 108.
138. See *True Account*, 123.
139. Hutton, *Charles II*, 50–56.
140. See *True Account*, 124.

from friends and family, which enables her to make preparations for the journey that presciently include medical supplies so that she has the capacity to help dress the injuries suffered by some of the Scots wounded at the Battle of Dunbar.

Her relative "tranquility" is once again disturbed by the reappearance of Colonel Bampfield. Once again, the timing here is vague; his visit is delayed, and "some considerable time" elapses before Bampfield finally arrives. In the intervening period, Halkett falls dangerously ill because of "the conflict betwixt love and honor" that she experiences.[141] While she is still recovering, Bampfield arrives and is discouraged to find she doubts his word; in a curious parallel with her brother Will, Bampfield offers to take the Sacrament to prove his innocence, which Halkett disapproves of and refuses to sanction.

Although riven with doubt, Halkett is not yet able confidently to dismiss Bampfield's claims and clearly retains some hope that he really is telling the truth. As with Thomas Howard, she treads a fine line by reaffirming her promise to marry him "whenever I found I might lawfully and conveniently make good what I had designed."[142]

It is perhaps telling that Halkett summarizes her time at Fyvie as "too tedious to relate" but claims "that in all my life I never was so long together so truly contented."[143] Tranquility makes monotonous reading, and Halkett is keenly aware of her audience's needs; however, it is interesting to note that she is most content when she is not involved in romantic liaisons. Instead, she is living in a predominantly female environment, primarily in the company of the pregnant Countess of Dunfermline and Lady Anna Erskine, where she practices her devotions without distraction except for the welcome diversion of offering medical assistance to those in need. In later life, she is frequently called upon to act as a midwife, so it is perhaps no accident that she does not leave Fyvie until after the Countess has given birth to her daughter, Henrietta.[144]

Although, like numerous other Royalists in this time, Halkett is effectively living a "retired" life, she still actively engages with political debate when the opportunity arises. When she occasionally treats English soldiers, she takes the opportunity to exhort them "to repent their sin of rebellion and become loyal," and she engagingly recounts her dexterous containment of marauding English soldiers.[145] However, the focal point of her time at Fyvie is clearly her political

---

141. See *True Account*, 128. Gabriele Rippl, "'The Conflict Betwixt Love and Honor': The Autobiography of Anne, Lady Halkett," in *Feminist Contributions to the Literary Canon: Setting Standards of Taste*, ed. Susanne Fendler (Lewiston, NY: Edwin Mellen Press, 1997), 7–29.

142. See *True Account*, 129.

143. See *True Account*, 129.

144. See *True Account*, 134.

145. See *True Account*, 129, 130–31.

Figure 1. John Speed, *The Kingdome of Scotland* (London: Roger Rea, 1662). © National Library of Scotland, EMS.s.9B. Reproduced with permission.[146]

146. A digital image of this map is available to view freely on the NLS website: https://maps.nls.uk/view/00000601.

debate with Colonel Robert Overton. Although that encounter commences with Halkett's catch-up with personal matters, the detail in which she records her discussion with Overton is unique within the extant narrative and quite extraordinary given the contemporary political climate. At this point, Cromwell's forces appeared unstoppable, and Overton was an influential Parliamentarian officer who had successfully led regiments in England before heading to Scotland to join the forces at Dunbar. He played a key role in establishing Cromwellian rule across Scotland, and by November 1651 he was governor of Aberdeen.[147] For Halkett to speak her mind as forthrightly as she does in this episode was, at the very least, courageous. Perhaps Halkett knew that Overton had a reputation for "civility" toward his opponents; either way, her representation of him reinforces the impression that Overton's political convictions did not make him intolerant.[148] This episode is also notable for its conclusion, where Overton's acknowledgment that if Halkett's words prove true, he "will say you are a prophetess" is, of course, vindicated. Halkett's prophecy proves her loyalty and her truthfulness, even when that truth appears inconceivable. While we associate prophecy with the radical sects, once again Halkett occupies a position that challenges conventional categorization.

As most of Scotland was under Cromwell's rule, Fyvie was no longer a place of retirement, so Halkett returns to Edinburgh. As elsewhere, she "resolves" to go to Edinburgh and we see her "providential imagination" at work; whereas her waiting woman is discouraged by her mistress's plans and weeps in distress, Halkett "resigns" herself to God and is confident that although everything seems bleak, God will provide, which he does, this time via the midwife, who fortuitously asks Halkett to deliver her wages to an appointed place in Edinburgh.[149] On her return, events conspire in such a way that she is offered rooms in the Earl of Tweeddale's house in Edinburgh, which places her at the center of Royalist intrigue circa 1652–1654/5 and introduces her to her future husband, Sir James Halkett. Their initial encounter is apparently inauspicious as she distrusts a "Scotch man with a sword";[150] however, rather than trusting her own judgment, an interruption occasioned by the arrival of Mr. David Dickson (who was later to play a prominent role in enabling her to solve the crucial "case of conscience" relating to Sir James's proposal of marriage) allows her to clarify her error.

---

147. Barbara Taft, "Overton, Robert (1608/9–1678/9)," *ODNB*.

148. It is possibly also an early indication that he was "disappointed with successive revolutionary governments, [but] served them as existent obstacles to monarchy." Taft, "Overton, Robert," *ODNB*.

149. See *True Account*, 135–36.

150. See *True Account*, 141.

It is at this point that Bampfield reemerges, but he is not immediately invited to join the "cabal" comprising the Earl of Dunfermline, the Earl of Balcarres,[151] Sir James Halkett, Sir George Mackenzie of Tarbat,[152] and Sir Robert Moray.[153] Quite what Halkett's role in this group is, apart from liaising with Bampfield and providing a plausible space for their meetings, is never really clarified. While she provides a useful insight into their operations, she is also silent on some major areas of contention, not the least being the question of whether the "cabal" received the King's instructions to place Bampfield under guard. She also draws attention to their foibles, without allocating blame: who, for example, was responsible for their using the well-known practice of using white ink to convey secret messages to the King? While Halkett reassures us all worked out well, this is one of the many occasions on which she is not explicit about timing.

As Sir James Halkett's first cousin, Sir Robert Moray was to become a close relation to Anne Murray/Halkett. Her sense of a strong connection to him is evidenced not only in her detailed description of his behavior at his wife's side on her death bed, but also in her recalling this memory when Sir Robert himself dies.[154] Clearly upset by Lady Moray's death, Halkett once more prepares to move lodgings, and Robert Moray's absence provides Sir James Halkett with the pretext he needs to pay constant attention to the then Anne Murray by taking care of her legal and financial business. Ever vigilant against perceived impropriety, she persuades him to find himself a wife and is delighted to be involved in that process. As one so adept in equivocation, it is fitting that Sir James also appears to be so, as he tells her he was now "determined upon one but was resolved I should be the first proposer of it."[155]

This plan is interrupted by the arrival of the news that Bampfield's wife is irrefutably alive. This event is very precisely dated as "Monday, March 21, 1652/3."[156] Halkett's *Meditations* reveal a compulsive interest in the days and dates of specific events: here both are of great significance because it is another terrible blow that befalls her on a Monday and on the twenty-first day of the month. As another leaf of the manuscript is missing, the *True Account* omits her response to this news; however, "The Great Conquest, or the Power of Faith" affords insight into her contemporaneous thought processes.[157] The language used there reflects that of the next two paragraphs of the extant *True Account*, which are self-condemnatory

151. Created Earl of Balcarres by Charles II on January 9, 1651. David Stevenson, "Lindsay, Alexander," *ODNB*.

152. Colin Kidd, "Mackenzie, George," *ODNB*.

153. See *True Account*, 153.

154. See "Upon the Death of Sir Robert Moray, who Died Suddenly in June 1673," 249–52.

155. See *True Account*, 149.

156. See *True Account*, 150.

157. See "The Great Conquest, or the Power of Faith," 176–84.

but submissive to God's will. Even at this most testing of times, her writing bears witness to her persistently "providential imagination."

Perhaps in part to distract her, the Earl of Dunfermline chooses this moment to employ Halkett in another Royalist "conspiracy" by sending her to warn the Earl and Countess of Balcarres of their imminent arrest. With incredible efficiency, Halkett makes the hazardous journey across the Firth of Forth in time to give the Earl and Countess many hours advance on the Cromwellian soldiers who arrive to arrest them. Working deep into the night, she and two servants pack up the Balcarres's extensive library, taking the time to write out a short inventory of each of the trunk's contents, and have them dispatched to various people. A combination of physical and emotional exertion results in Halkett, once again, falling gravely ill, which requires her to remain at Balcarres until her recovery and brings her the acquaintance of Lady Ardross and two ministers who had refused to read the 1650 Proclamation.[158]

On her return to Edinburgh, her first visitor is Sir James, whose attentions indicate that he still wishes to establish a more intimate relationship than Anne Murray is prepared to entertain. Her first line of defense is her "resolution never to marry," which she refrains from actively vowing only because she "questioned if such vows were lawful."[159] Sir James again demonstrates his own prowess at equivocation when, in response to her request that he "forbear ever to speak again of what you now mentioned," he answers, "it should be against [my] will to do anything to displease" her.[160] Nevertheless, she agrees to keep talking to him and moves lodgings again so that his two daughters can stay with her to access education in Edinburgh. Too proud to receive direct financial recompense for giving his daughters "board," Murray accepts his provision of food and, therefore, his company at mealtimes, which leads to a resumption of his suit. It is here that her relationship with another minister, David Dickson, plays an important role. Dickson wrote numerous commentaries on different books of the Bible, including three volumes on the Psalms that were published between 1653 and 1654.[161] At the time Dickson was counselling Anne Murray, he was also writing "his most important theological work ... *Therapeutica Sacra* (1656)," which is devoted to conscience and conversion.[162] Although not dealing with specific instances of

---

158. See *True Account*, 153.

159. See also "Upon Making Vows," 208–10.

160. Halkett uses almost the same phrase the then Anne Murray directed to her mother, see *True Account*, 70.

161. The first volume, David Dickson's *A Brief Explication of the First Fifty Psalms* (London: T. M., 1655), was dedicated to "my Lady Marquise of Argyle, and my Lady Anne Campbell her eldest daughter" (sig. A3r). ESTC R175951.

162. Holfelder, "Dickson, David (ca.1583–1662)," *ODNB*. David Dickson, *Therapeutica Sacra; Shewing Briefly the Method of Healing the Diseases of the Conscience, Concerning Regeneration: Written First in*

"Cases of Conscience," Dickson's general definition of a "sick conscience" includes some aspects that Halkett would certainly have recognized.[163]

Despite the prurient interest in establishing the exact nature of Murray and Bampfield's marital status, its legal status is ultimately irrelevant. Whatever the "facts" may have been, Halkett clearly viewed that relationship as binding. Her attitude to vows and covenants generally should make this apparent.[164] The point of conscience that vexed her most was "whether marriages once made may be annulled, and utterly voided; and in what cases this may be done."[165] Hall's general advice is very straightforward: "The indissoluble knot of marriage with a former still surviving husband or wife . . . frustrates and voideth any supervening matrimony"; for the avoidance of doubt, he reiterates that the second marriage is "null."[166] However, the principles of casuistry assert that in the end individuals are responsible for their own decisions. Halkett's apparent prevarication about marrying Sir James is part of a lengthy process she needs to go through to convince herself that this marriage would be acceptable to God. Importantly, her concern here is not just for herself but for another, as she is wary of bringing Sir James Halkett into disrepute by proxy, through scandal and financial difficulties.

Delays in her Scottish legal suit means that she does not leave Edinburgh until September 1654. Taking refuge in Whitefriars,[167] Halkett receives an unsolicited visit from Colonel Bampfield, who seeks to "vindicate himself," which Halkett interrupts by confronting him with the inescapable truth that his wife is still alive. Nevertheless, Bampfield queries Murray's own marital status, compelling her to make another casuistical equivocation before he disappears from her narrative.[168] Halkett reassures her reader that "from that time to this, I never saw from him nor heard from him."[169] However, this is immediately qualified with the exception of his returning proofs of her rights to her mother's inheritance, which he had apparently taken with him to Holland, perhaps in 1648/9. At the first opportunity,

---

Latin by David Dickson, Professor of Divinity in the Colledge of Edinburgh, and Thereafter Translated by Him (Edinburgh: Evan Tyler, 1664). ESTC R24294.

163. Dickson, *Therapeutica Sacra*, 8–9.

164. See "Upon Making Vows," 208–10.

165. Hall, *Resolutions and Decisions of Diverse Practicall Cases of Conscience*, 488.

166. Hall, *Resolutions and Decisions of Diverse Practicall Cases of Conscience*, 493–94; 495–96. Hall's advice makes it clear that Halkett was by no means alone in this dilemma: "many unhappy, and perplexed cases have we met withal in this kind; neither doth it seldom fall out, that the husband being confidently being reported for dead in the wars . . . the wife after some years stay, and diligent inquisition . . . bestows herself in a second marriage; not long after which, her only true revived husband returns, and challengeth his right," *Resolutions and Decisions of Diverse Practicall Cases of Conscience*, 494–95.

167. See "Introduction," 10n38.

168. See *True Account*, 163–64.

169. See *True Account*, 164.

she writes to Sir James about this encounter, and his calm acceptance of this news provides further evidence of his gentlemanly disposition and encourages her to complete her business so that they can finally be married.

Nevertheless, it is not without further internal debate that she "came at last to be determined to marry."[170] Even with the backing of God himself through providence, and the many reassurances she had received from Mr. Dickson, Halkett still feels the need to spend a full day in fasting and prayer to make absolutely sure she had correctly ascertained "the determined will of God."[171] Such preparations are similar to what she would do before taking the Sacrament, and it is therefore appropriate that she does so before entering into what is a most solemn sacrament: marriage. In the introduction to "The Form of Solemnization of Matrimony," the minister reminds all present that marriage is not to be "taken in hand unadvisedly, lightly, or wantonly," but rather "reverently, advisedly, soberly, and in the fear of God, duly considering the causes for which matrimony was ordained."[172] Begging God, "with the fervor of my soul," Halkett entirely resigns herself to God's will, whatever that may be, and reaffirms the accuracy of this account by reference to 2 Corinthians 11:31: "The God and Father of our Lord Jesus Christ, which is blessed for evermore, knoweth that I lie not."[173] Despite the prevarications of others' vows, and her own equivocations at specific points, here Halkett is extremely careful to stress the purity of the truth she has just told us (perhaps all the more necessary given how soon she gave birth to her beloved daughter Betty), and to note that she suffered no further doubts on this issue before, during, or after her marriage. Like the *True Account* as a whole, this specific event is prefaced with Sacramental preparations: for Halkett, this makes her marriage a matter of life or death.[174]

After Halkett's meticulous preparations, she and Sir James seem to have been married at least twice, possibly even three times. On the evening of Saturday, March 1, 1655/6, they were married twice: first, "after supper" in her brother-in-law's closet at Charlton House by the Countess of Devonshire's chaplain, who

---

170. See *True Account*, 166.

171. See *True Account*, 156–57, 166.

172. BCP, 434–35.

173. See *True Account*, 166.

174. Ryrie reminds us that "Protestant preachers of every stripe ... insisted that to receive communion was to take your life in your hands," and when "Christopher Sutton warned that God would strike dead those who received unworthily," the threat was not metaphorical, as it was scripturally based, *Being Protestant in Reformation Britain*, 338. 1 Corinthians 11:27–29: "wherefore whosoever shall eat this bread, and drink this cup of the Lord, unworthily, shall be guilty of the body and blood of the Lord. But let a man examine himself, and so let him eat of that bread, and drink of that cup. For he that eateth and drinketh unworthily, eateth and drinketh damnation to himself, not discerning the Lord's body." See also Jeremiah Dyke, *A Worthy Communicant; or, A Treatise, Showing the Due Order of Receiving the Sacrament of the Lord's Supper* (London: R. B[ishop], 1636). ESTC S100166.

probably used the outlawed service from the Book of Common Prayer as it is 1655/6; and second, "after the evening sermon," by Justice Elkonhead according to the rules set out in *A Directory for the Publicke Worship of God* (1645), the only legally recognized ceremony at this time.[175] Intriguingly, however, Halkett closes her narrative of their marriage with the comment, "but if it had not been done more solemnly afterwards by a minister, I should not have believed it lawfully done," which strongly suggests they were married again in church, presumably after the Restoration. Three services may seem something of an overcompensation for the dubious "marriage" to Bampfield, but perhaps lends further credence to the notion that the prior relationship was not formally solemnized.

Apparently intending to summarize their return journey as nonincidental, Halkett cannot contain herself from relating another "extraordinary providence": this time, the prevention of their deaths in a potential coach accident due to angelic intervention. After finally arriving safely and receiving "a very kind welcome from all Sir James' friends and neighbors," they return to Edinburgh to visit the Broghills and prevent Sir James from being appointed as a Justice of the Peace. Lord Broghill is immediately ready to do her whatever service might assist her and gives her his word that they "shall never hear of it more."[176] However, within a few days of returning to Pitfirrane, an order for Sir James to take up that role or go to Edinburgh Castle arrives; thus, the extant narrative concludes with Halkett's attempt to rectify this situation: her final relation, then, involves assisting Sir James in a political "case of conscience" of his own.

Select and Occasional Meditations

As Alec Ryrie observes, "'meditation' is a word with a long and distinct history in Christian piety" that refers to "a well-established but ill-defined genre of pious writing."[177] Nevertheless, Halkett largely follows the distinctions recommended by bishop Joseph Hall in *The Art of Divine Meditation* (1606), in which he identifies two main kinds of meditation, "extemporal and deliberate."[178] In Halkett's

---

175. Anon, *A Directory for the Publicke Worship of God throughout the Three Kingdoms of Scotland, England, and Ireland* (Edinburgh: Evan Tyler, 1645). ESTC R31329. See also "An Act Touching Marriages and the Registering Thereof; and Also Touching Births and Burials, August 1653," in C. H. Firth and R. S. Rait, eds., *Acts and Ordinances of the Interregnum, 1642–1660* (London: Her Majesty's Stationary Office, 1911), 715–18.

176. See *True Account*, 171.

177. Ryrie, *Being Protestant in Reformation Britain*, 109.

178. Frank Livingstone Huntley, *Bishop Joseph Hall and Protestant Meditation in Seventeenth-Century England: A Study, with the Texts of The Art of Divine Meditation (1606) and Occasional Meditations (1633)* (Binghamton, NY: Center for Medieval and Early Renaissance Studies, 1981), 72–76. Or, following Hall's son, Robert, she "makes the distinction between 'sudden thoughts' and 'fixed meditations.'" Huntley, *Bishop Joseph Hall and Protestant Meditation in Seventeenth-Century England*, 21.

case, the division is between meditations that concern daily events, thoughts, or activities (occasional) and those that focus on specific biblical passages or liturgical events (select).[179] While the majority of Halkett's volumes contain both kinds of meditations, this edition includes excerpts from several volumes that Halkett defines as containing select meditations only: *A Short Expostulation about Prayer, Meditations, and the Mother's Will to Her Unborn Child* (1653–1657), *The Art of Divine Chemistry* (1676–1678), and *Meditations on Moses and Samuel* (1688–1689/90). It also includes excerpts from the select meditations within *The Widow's Mite and Occasional Meditations* (1673–1674/5). As defined by Halkett, the rest of the materials edited for this volume are occasional. However, one of the many interesting aspects of Halkett's *Meditations* is how she develops her own style of writing, which is quite distinct from general practice.

While extemporary, or occasional, meditation is "triggered by daily sights and sounds," deliberate meditation occurs "when we self-consciously set ourselves to meditate without an external prompt."[180] Bishop Hall outlines an "eleven-step structure" for deliberate meditation; while he is careful not to be too prescriptive, according to Ryrie the striking aspect of this schema for a modern reader "is that the first ten of its eleven steps are to do with logical analysis," as the topic is examined from a series of perspectives, and only "in the final step, do we allow the findings of our analysis to bleed through to the affections," although the ultimate aim of meditation is, in Hall's words, "to affect the heart."[181] Halkett was by no means alone in emulating Hall: many writers followed his example and put their own occasional meditations into print.[182] He appealed to a range of writers, from Puritan, through moderate, to Laudian because of "his dynamic view of meditation. For him, it was neither a state nor a goal, but a purposeful intellectual

---

179. There are two instances where Halkett uses different terms to categorise her texts: on the contents page of *Occasional and Select Meditations, including Instructions to My Son* (1667–1670), where the select materials are classified as "contemplations," and on the contents page of *Select and Occasional Meditations* (1696–1697), where the select and occasional texts are referred to as both "observations" and "reflections."

180. Ryrie, *Being Protestant in Reformation Britain*, 115.

181. Ryrie, *Being Protestant in Reformation Britain*, 115.

182. Ryrie notes that Elizabeth Isham and Elizabeth Hastings, Countess of Huntingdon were avid readers of Hall's work; Ryrie, *Being Protestant in Reformation Britain*, 115. For more detailed discussions of the art of the occasional meditation and its practitioners, see: Marie-Louise Coolahan, "Redeeming Parcels of Time: Aesthetics and Practice of Occasional Meditation," *Seventeenth Century* 22, no. 1 (2007): 124–43; Raymond A. Anselment, "Feminine Self-Reflection and the Seventeenth-Century Occasional Meditation," *Seventeenth Century* 26, no. 1 (2011): 69–93; Raymond A. Anselment, ed., *The Occasional Meditations of Mary Rich, Countess of Warwick* (Tempe: Arizona Center for Medieval and Renaissance Studies, 2009); and Kate Narveson, "Godly Gentility as Spiritual Capital: The Appeal of Hall's Meditations in Early Stuart England," *Explorations in Renaissance Culture* 30, no. 2 (2004): 149–70.

process," in which resolution becomes a prelude to action, and action might be "inner and spiritual." Nevertheless, the relationship between meditation and prayer is complicated, as "although he believed that you should approach prayer through mediations, [Hall] also urged that meditation should begin with prayer and compared the two to inseparable twins"; "As prayer is our speech to God, so is each good meditation . . . God's speech to the heart. The heart must speak to God that God may speak to it. . . . Prayer maketh way for meditation; meditation giveth matter, strength, and life to our prayers."[183] Nevertheless, Ryrie concludes that while meditation and prayer "cannot be separated, it is also clearly important that contemporaries chose to use distinct words."[184] In this context, it is worth noting that the terms Halkett associates with meditation are "refreshment," "entertainment" and "employment."[185]

By these definitions, "The Great Conquest, or the Power of Faith" and "The Widow's Mite, Part of It Relating to the King," provide the fullest flavor of Halkett's deliberate meditative style within this edition.[186] Before beginning "The Great Conquest, or the Power of Faith," Halkett's first surviving volume opens with "Expostulations about Prayer," which concludes: "Lord, make this work fit for what I do intend it, which is to dedicate it unto thee, with myself and all that's mine, as being thine own, and so my God receive it and dispose of it according to thy will, amen."[187] Focusing on "the victory that overcommeth the world, even our faith," (1 John 5:4), Halkett draws upon Scripture to remind herself of God's promise as she struggles to overcome the world and ascertain whether she is among the "redeemed ones of Christ."[188] Like the epistle's initial audience, Halkett's faith needs strengthening, and in the main body of the meditation she seeks to understand what faith is, how it is attained, and what are the signs that she is among the faithful. At the beginning of the meditation, Halkett laments her inability to let go of the temptations of the world, even though she knows they are bad for her. That these temptations relate to Bampfield is suggested not only by the time of writing but also by her phraseology:

---

183. Huntley, *Bishop Joseph Hall and Protestant Meditation in Seventeenth-Century England*, 85.

184. Ryrie, *Being Protestant in Reformation Britain*, 116–18.

185. Suzanne Trill, "'Refreshment,' 'Intertainment,' and 'Imployment': Anne, Lady Halkett's *Meditations* and the Practice of Daily Devotion" (Paper presented for the London Renaissance Seminar, Birkbeck College, London, February 2002).

186. The extracts from "The Art of Divine Chemistry" and "What Crosses and Difficulties I Have Met with Myself" primarily focus on the "application" section of the text; that is, the parts in which Halkett draws parallels between her subject matter and her own life and experiences. The material reproduced from *Meditations on Moses and Samuel* constitutes the prefatory prayer rather than the main body of the text, 273–75.

187. Halkett, *A Short Expostulation about Prayer*, p. 5.

188. See "The Great Conquest, or the Power of Faith," 176–84.

> Thou seest, O Lord, the variety of troubles that I am encompassed round with, and if thou dost not help me, it is impossible for me to overcome them, and all I do desire is that thou wouldst keep me from sin. Let me not sin against thee, my God, in thinking any more of that which now I am assured of was unlawful.[189] Oh, for thy Son's sake pardon my transgressions, . . . but since thou hast shut me up in this straight that I cannot lawfully either [p. 24] satisfy myself or any other, teach me submission and keep me from repining at thy will.[190]

Reproaching herself for sin, Halkett reminds herself of God's forgiveness through Christ's sacrifice, and seeks, above all, to resign herself to God's will—or providence—regardless of what that might be.

Following Hall's recommendations, through the course of this meditation, Halkett bewails her "wants and untowardness," establishes her soul's "hearty wish . . . for what it complaineth to want," and makes an "earnest Petition for that which we confess to want," before moving to "a cheerful Confidence in obtaining what we have requested" and concluding with a "Recommendation of our soul and ways to God."[191] Although Hall outlines a number of elements that meditations should address, he is not prescriptive; instead, he requires "only a deep and firm consideration of the thing propounded."[192] Halkett's practice is more cyclical than linear, and she returns to the elements highlighted above at different points until her mind has been so bent to the will of God that she can conclude: "Strengthen me for this victory and make it perfect that, by faith, I may overcome all things that separate from thee. Amen."[193] Here, Halkett textually materializes her movement from separation to integration insofar as what began as God's word, italicized and separated from her "own" words, is now incorporated within her meditation: her words and God's have merged. In this she epitomizes the observation that "in Hall's meditative program the meditator does not move through various stages toward a goal; rather [s]he realizes with a new intensity where [s]he already is."[194]

Nevertheless, in its "application" section, "The Great Conquest, or the Power of Faith," includes material drawn from everyday experience. Rhetorically, Halkett asks: "Lord, shall I ever forget that object which thy providence did lead

---

189. I.e., her betrothal to Bampfield.

190. See "The Great Conquest, or the Power of Faith," 179–80. See also *True Account*, 151.

191. Huntley, *Bishop Joseph Hall and Protestant Meditation in Seventeenth-Century England*, 101, 102, 103, 105, 106.

192. Huntley, *Bishop Joseph Hall and Protestant Meditation in Seventeenth-Century England*, 88.

193. See "The Great Conquest, or the Power of Faith," 184.

194. Ronald J. Corthell, "Joseph Hall and Protestant Meditation," *Texas Studies in Literature and Language* 20, no. 3 (1978): 370.

me to behold (at Rossie when Sir Robert Montgomery was married), when I was in a sad, and despicable condition?"[195] And recalls how on seeing a sheep, isolated from its flock (which were feeding on the best pasture), apparently content to make do with thorns on a slippery bank, "I heard this whispered to my soul: if thou are a true sheep of Christ's own fold, thou wilt as little as this beast repine.... For as this sheep gets nourishment from this barren soil, so mayst thou receive virtue from the severest dispensation that God can send thee if thou be his own."[196] Its unusual placement within a "select" meditation is further enhanced by the rarity of this kind of subject matter within Halkett's oeuvre. My selection from *The Widow's Mite* is also notable for how Halkett moves from the "personal" to the "political." As the title suggests, this volume explores Luke 21:1–4; however, a large part of it is designated as "Relating to the King."[197] Although she is primarily reflecting on the current state of political affairs (ca. 1674), she draws upon the memory of Charles I's execution and Charles II's coronation to reassure herself that God's providence is at work even if she doesn't understand his logic. Thus, even within her select meditations, Halkett includes materials that are richly autobiographical.

As she achieves this within the more formal art of select meditation, it is perhaps not surprising that Halkett's occasional meditations are similarly full of self-reflection. Hall's and most other occasional meditations (either by men or women, in print or in manuscript) focus on the "Book of Creatures" (e.g., spiders, flies, birds, trees), everyday objects (e.g., mirrors, maps, glasses), or people and activities (e.g., walking, yawning, being drunk, and having disabilities). Although according to Couper's "catalogue," Halkett started writing in 1644 (which ties in neatly with the *True Account* insofar as nothing of note happens before that date), the earliest surviving examples of her occasional meditations were composed 1658/9–1660. Even then, Halkett had more to say about her daily life and political events than she did about candles, sugar, or mirrors.[198] Strictly speaking, it is primarily the use of "upon" in their titles and Halkett's industry in producing these texts that aligns these materials with the genre of occasional meditation; even so, as she discusses "riches," "poverty," and "imagination," their contents have much in common with Bacon's *Essays*.[199] Two other entries from this early volume stand out because their titles do not begin with "upon": "The Conviction upon 2

---

195. See "The Great Conquest, or the Power of Faith," 183.
196. See "The Great Conquest, or the Power of Faith," 183.
197. See "The Widow's Mite, Part of It Relating to the King," and "The Great Conquest, or the Power of Faith," 241–49, 184–85.
198. Trill, ed., *Halkett*, xxxvi.
199. Trill, "Critical Categories," 118. See also John Pitcher, ed., *Francis Bacon: The Essays* (Harmondsworth, UK: Penguin, 1985).

Chronicles 28:10" and "The Power of Faith, upon Mark 16:17–18."[200] Although she gives this volume the title *Occasional Meditations*, Halkett here appears to be acknowledging their difference from the other entries. Strictly speaking, as considerations of biblical texts, they are select rather than occasional forms, and Couper certainly redesignates them as such. However, what interests me is the slippage between genres and how they intermingle across Halkett's "books."

In the main body of her volumes, Halkett starts in 1660 to include the date at which an entry was written as well as its subject matter; by 1674/5, she intersperses entries with titles only, dates only, or a combination of the two; but by 1687, the occasional meditations are consistently identified by date only. Nevertheless, as I detail in the headnotes to the individual volumes below, there are various discrepancies between Halkett's practice at the time of writing and how she records them within her list of the volume's contents: there, she usually supplies topics or subjects for the entries she chooses to record. This, along with her stylistic revisions to their contents, points to the fact that, like many of her contemporaries, Halkett regularly reread her *Meditations*. Sometimes she explicitly identifies them as an *aide memoire*: on "Monday, May 21, 1688," her recollection of what happened that day forty-eight years earlier "is as fresh in my memory, with the help of a reflection that I writ the next day, as if it were but yesterday performed."[201] Sometimes she uses them to gauge her progress, or lack thereof, with regard to particular issues, especially her precarious financial situation. And in at least one instance, it was their existence that enabled her to write another narrative, her *True Account*. Sadly, however, the last entry in her final volume suggests that Halkett continued to battle against misrepresentation until the very end of her life, for there she reflects upon some discouraging circumstances that culminate in the receipt of "a long letter from an undiscreet man last night, who I had often obliged, and none could writ more unjust untruths of me."[202] Of course, at the time of writing, neither Halkett's *True Account* nor Couper's *The Life of the Lady Halket* had been published. Nevertheless, Halkett consciously crafted both her *True Account* and her *Meditations* as monuments of memorialization.

"Living Monuments of Praise":[203] The Afterlife of Halkett's "Books"

Hagiographical as Couper's *The Life of the Lady Halket* undoubtedly is, it provides an insight into the "religious" side of her personality that modern critics have

---

200. Halkett, *Occasional Meditations*, pp. 161–73. 2 Chronicles 28:10: "And now ye purpose to keep under the children of Judah and Jerusalem for bondmen and bondwomen unto you: but are there not with you, even with you, sins against the Lord your God?" See also "The Power of Faith, upon Mark 16:17–18," 189–93.

201. See "Monday, May 21, 1688," 273–75.

202. See "Saturday, November 26, 1698," 324–25.

203. See "Upon Reading Mr. Boyle's *Occasional Reflections*, January 25, 1668/9," 218.

mostly avoided. While the pious figure he draws there may be somewhat unpalatable to modern tastes, it is possible to trace much of what he writes to specific instances in Halkett's extant volumes; that is, he is drawing directly from her own words. For the most part, he summarizes her accounts, and strips them of much of their personal reflection; nevertheless, at times he provides important insights into Halkett's devotional life, including that her day was divided into devotion (five hours), "necessary refreshment" (ten hours), and business (nine hours). While her hours of devotion were set (5–7 am; 1–2 pm; 6–7 pm; and 9–10 pm), she was flexible when necessary.[204] He begins his narration of her "youth" with the declaration that she frequently rededicated herself to God by "renewing and confirming her baptismal vows," as evidenced most solemnly in her annual birthday reflections. He emphasizes how she chose to read God's word daily and became "a great proficient" in the art of meditation.[205] This is accompanied by its "twin," prayer, and "from the example of a devout lady" extends to the practice of fasting. This regular practice was enhanced when she prepares for the Lord's Supper, which he states she partook of "four times in the year";[206] however, Couper is careful to emphasize that this way of life was continual for her, rather than simply an act of preparation for the Sacrament, and he cites her writings liberally over the next three pages to prove his point.[207]

He notes her acts of charity, which include the extensive medical expertise for which physicians consulted her, but he carefully emphasizes her "modesty" in knowing that things worked only by God's will. This paragon of virtue had not, as yet, experienced the world's "calumny and malice"; however,

> This excellent lady had scarce well appeared on the stage of the world in a public place and critical age, when she found exercise enough for her virtue; and almost all sorts of trials to prove the constancy of her mind: being tossed, as it were, between waves and pursued with a constant series of difficulties and incumbrances for the space of fourteen years, both in England and Holland; until at length the one shipwrecked and bereaved of all comforts (except her virtue and integrity) she arrived at some settled state.[208]

This is an important passage, as it sets the scene for Couper's summary of the main events of Halkett's life as recorded in the *True Account*.[209] As Couper later

---

204. Couper, *The Life of the Lady Halket*, 55–56.
205. Couper, *The Life of the Lady Halket*, 7.
206. Couper, *The Life of the Lady Halket*, 7.
207. Couper, *The Life of the Lady Halket*, 8–11.
208. Couper, *The Life of the Lady Halket*, 13. Original emphasis.
209. Couper, *The Life of the Lady Halket*, 13–30.

indicates that the "settled state" was her marriage to Sir James Halkett in 1656, this suggests that her "various trials and temptations" began in 1642.[210] While the metaphor of shipwreck sits well with Halkett's own account, insofar as she identifies with St. Paul, this sentence opens up the possibility of a more literal sea journey, which has led to much speculation about whether or not she and Bampfield were married in Holland sometime in 1649.[211]

Nevertheless, Couper acknowledges his own need to truncate his explication of her life and begins his summary with the statement, "There were several proposals of marriage made, which came all to no effect."[212] Howard and Bampfield are thereby almost entirely erased from Halkett's history. As he wants to relate her involvement in the Duke of York's escape, Couper cannot avoid an allusion to Bampfield; however, he doesn't name him but instead describes him as "a gentleman, who was a trusty and faithful friend to [the King's] interest."[213] While Couper generally follows the narrative trajectory of the *True Account*, he also intersperses references to materials in other volumes, or perhaps from the unspecified "stitched books." Tantalizingly, this means he provides insights into the contents of some of the volumes that are now missing. For example, volume 1, *Meditations, Prayers, and Vows in Childbirth* (1644–1658), includes "Meditations upon One Verse of Every Psalm, Continued to the Fiftieth Psalm." In Couper's catalogue this is all the information we are given; however, *The Life of the Lady Halket* tells us that on September 12, 1648, which "happened not only to be the day of the week she had set apart for her private fasting, but also the day appointed for public humiliation for good success to the Treaty with the King at Newport," her chosen text was Psalm 7:9, which he cites as "O Let the wickedness of the ungodly come to an end, but guide thou the just."[214] By January 20, 1648/9, she has

---

210. Couper, *The Life of the Lady Halket*, 13.

211. 2 Corinthians 11:25: "Thrice was I beaten with rods, once was I stoned, thrice I suffered shipwreck, a night and a day I have been in the deep." See also Halkett, "What Crosses and Difficulties I Have Met with Myself," 307–11. On the question of marriage, see Lamb, "Merging the Secular and the Spiritual in Lady Anne Halkett's Memoirs," 91–92.

212. Couper, *The Life of the Lady Halket*, 13.

213. Couper, *The Life of the Lady Halket*, 16.

214. Psalm 7:9: "Oh let the wickedness of the wicked come to an end; but establish the just: for the righteous God trieth the hearts and reins." See England and Wales Parliament, "Die Sabbathi, 2 Septemb. 1648. Ordered by the Lords and Commons Assembled in Parliament, That Tuesday-Come-Seven-Night, the Twelfth [sic] of This Instant September, Be Appointed and Observed as a Day of Publique Humiliation, by the Members of Both Houses, and in All the Churches and Chappells within the Late Lines of Communication and Weekly Bills of Mortalitie, to Seeke God Earnestly for a Blessing upon the Treaty [of Newport]" (London: John Wright, 1648). ESTC R221344. This proclamation is also addressed in William Gouge, *The Right Way; or, A Direction for Obtaining Good Successe in a Weighty Enterprise. Set out in a Sermon Preached on the 12th of September 1648 before the Lords on a Day of Humiliation for a Blessing on a Treaty between His Majesties and the Parliaments Commissioners*

reached Psalm 24 and on "the day on which the King was brought to the infamous pageantry of a trial," she made the first verse the subject of her meditation: "The earth is the Lord's, and the fulness thereof; the world, and they that dwell therein."

After this, Couper summarizes the events as recounted in the *True Account* until the newlywed Halketts return to Scotland. He then rapidly abridges Halkett's fourteen years of marriage by reference to their children and her stepchildren and a precis of her attempts to regain her inheritance. Given how he has already spliced information from different sources to fill in some of the gaps in the *True Account*, it is impossible to tell where the original manuscript may have ended. What is clear, however, is that he continues to draw upon Halkett's own words for his narrative, as his description of Sir James Halkett's life and death, and her own sadness at becoming a widow draws directly from her meditations on those subjects reproduced below.[215] Nevertheless, he avoids mentioning her difficult relationship with her stepson, Sir Charles Halkett, and goes so far as to claim that "all affairs between the Lady and him were peaceably concluded with great kindness and condescension on both hands: both were so just and generous that there could not have been a more amicable agreement had she been his own mother."[216]

In his relation of Halkett's later life, he again draws on materials that are no longer extant, noting that "there was nothing of moment either in public affairs, or in more private occurrences which came to her notice which she did not make the subject of a serious meditation and reflection."[217] The examples Couper chooses include her "public" concern in early in 1672 about the proposed "Proclamation for Toleration and Liberty of Conscience" (which she "prayed God to divert them")[218] and her "private" care for her son, Robin, who she took to St. Andrews in February 1674 to enroll him at the University, leaving him under the protection of a regent, Mr. Skein, and a governor, Mr. Alexander Lundy: their good care of him is in part evidenced by his taking communion in August that year.[219] With Robin settled in St. Andrews, and Sir Charles, now married, having

---

(London: A. Miller, 1648), ESTC R202327; and Jean d'Espagne, *The Abridgement of a Sermon Preached on the Fast-Day Appointed to Be Held for the Good Successe of the Treatie That Was Shortly to Ensue between the King and the Parliament, September 12, 1648*, trans. William Umfrevile (London: Ruth Raworth, 1648). ESTC R20881.

215. Couper, *The Life of the Lady Halket*, 32–34. See "Upon the Death of My Dearest Sir James Halkett" and "Upon My Deplorable Being a Widow," 220–26, 226–32.

216. Couper, *The Life of the Lady Halket*, 36. See also Anne, Lady Halkett, "Letter to Mr. Thomas, December 27, 1670?" Pitfirrane Papers: Correspondence, NLS, MS 6407, fol. 26r–27v.

217. Couper, *The Life of the Lady Halket*, 39.

218. Couper, *The Life of the Lady Halket*, 37. Charles II, *His Majesties Declaration to All His Loving Subjects, March 15, 1672. Published by the Advice of His Privy Council* (Edinburgh: Evan Tyler, 1672). ESTC R171213.

219. Couper, *The Life of the Lady Halket*, 39. Mr. Skein became Dr. Skein, provost of the Old College; Couper, *The Life of the Lady Halket*, 42.

returned to Pitfirrane, Halkett moved back to Dunfermline.[220] Characteristically, Couper brushes over whatever scandal encouraged her to write both *The Art of Divine Chemistry* and her *True Account*, saying only: "About this time she was trysted with some troubles, occasioned by persons of whom she expected better things; upon which she applied herself to the study of extracting good out of all these cross occurrences."[221]

One of her difficulties is her precarious financial situation, exacerbated by her charitable assistance of the poor, which incurred large apothecary's bills and sometimes prevented her from paying off her creditors.[222] By 1683, things had gotten so bad that "she was resolving to break up her house and retire to England"; however, God's providence intervenes, and by the combination of taking in boarders and finally receiving a yearly pension of £100 from the King, she was able to survive.[223] Although she undoubtedly did instruct them in religion, those children were committed "to her care, partly with respect to her, and partly to the conveniency of their education at School": Dunfermline had had a Grammar School since 1625 that was a well-respected institution.[224] According to Couper, her family was "increased with the heirs of eight several families; all of them motherless, save one, who was fatherless."[225]

For Couper, Halkett's continued interest in public affairs is primarily directed by her concern for religion; while she is relieved at Monmouth's defeat, she is discouraged by the many conversions to Catholicism prompted by James VII/II's accession. Couper is at pains to reassure the reader that Halkett was a confirmed Williamite and that she doubted the legitimacy of James's son:[226] he suggests she was surprised by "so mischievous a design as to impose a spurious child on the three kingdoms," and his account suggests she believed this to be "provoking to God."[227] Yet within the surviving materials, Halkett celebrates his birth and says nothing about doubting his legitimacy; while she likely did want James VII/II to listen to the bishops, Couper is less than truthful when he suggests

---

220. They married August 5, 1675; Couper, *The Life of the Lady Halket*, 39. See also Angus, ed., *Inventory of Pitfirrane Writs, 1230–1740*, no. 628, 45.

221. Couper, *The Life of the Lady Halket*, 41.

222. Couper, *The Life of the Lady Halket*, 51.

223. Couper, *The Life of the Lady Halket*, 44, 45.

224. Couper, *The Life of the Lady Halket*, 45; Henderson, *The Annals of Dunfermline and Vicinity*, 290. See also Anne, Lady Halkett, *Instructions for Youth. Written by the Lady Halket, for the Use of Those Young Noblemen and Gentlemen, Whose Education Was Committed to Her Care*, ed. Simon Couper (Edinburgh: Andrew Symson, 1701). ESTC T72792.

225. Couper, *The Life of the Lady Halket*, 45. See Trill, ed., *Halkett*, xxvn52.

226. Edward Gregg, "James Francis Edward [James Francis Edward Stuart; Styled James; Known as Chevalier de St George, the Pretender, the Old Pretender] (1688–1766)," *ODNB*.

227. Couper, *The Life of the Lady Halket*, 46.

that on "reading the Prince of Orange's Declaration, she was fully satisfied of [his] legitimacy."[228] Time and again the extant volumes attest to her detestation of William of Orange and her disapproval of his wife's actions as well. The volumes that remain extant for this period do not include occasional meditations; however, Couper's account of Halkett's response to James VII/II's exile and William and Mary's accession strongly suggests that she wrote about these events in some detail.[229] This elision on Couper's part enables him to emphasize Halkett's anti-Catholic persuasion and downplay her support for the Jacobite cause. Similarly, in his account of her son, Robin, Couper omits to mention that the reason for his incarceration was fighting alongside James VII/II. Instead, he records Robin's return to Dunfermline on December 17, 1692; "it was no small comfort to her to see him, though much broken (as to the state of his health) by ill usage in prison and sickness which followed."[230] He goes abroad again, on September 20, 1693, and just a month later, Halkett receives the news that he died in Brielle after a sickness on the voyage over. Couper reproduces an excerpt from a meditation written at the time, which is no longer extant, in which she submits stoically to God's will.[231]

Couper returns to Halkett's piety by emphasizing her commitment to the Lord's Supper, despite its infrequent practice in Scotland, and noting her careful preparations for receiving the Sacrament. Tellingly, this is the point at which he draws attention to her grief at her ministers' deprivation.[232] About this time, Halkett stops taking in boarders, and through the assistance of "a friend and kinsman" she finally manages to put her worldly affairs into some kind of order. As he moves toward a description of her death, Couper reaffirms "her gratitude to all who had been helpful to her, especially the great obligations and respect she had to the family of Pitfirrane." In March 1699, Halkett "became feverish and much

228. Couper, *The Life of the Lady Halket*, 47. See Anon., *The Prince of Orange His Declaration: Shewing the Reasons Why He Invades England. With a Short Preface, and Some Modest Remarks on It* (London: Randall Taylor, 1688). ESTC R3225; King James VII/II, *By the King, a Declaration as We Cannot Consider This Invasion of Our Kingdoms by the Prince of Orange without Horror* (London: Charles Bill, Henry Hills, and Thomas Newcomb, 1688). ESTC R37010; King William III, *The Declaration of His Highnes William Henry, by the Grace of God Prince of Orange, &c. of the Reasons Inducing Him, to Appear in Armes in the Kingdome of England, for Preserving of the Protestant Religion, and for Restoring the Lawes and Liberties of England, Scotland, and Ireland* (The Hague: Arnold Leers, 1688). ESTC R187748; "April 11. A Proclamation, Declaring William and Mary King and Queen of England to Be King and Queen of Scotland" (London: G. Croom, 1689). ESTC R225323.

229. Couper, *The Life of the Lady Halket*, 47–49.

230. Couper, *The Life of the Lady Halket*, 48–49. He does not provide a specific date, but Halkett learns of his imprisonment on Monday, August 25, 1690. See Anne, Lady Halkett, *Occasional Meditations, Meditations upon Nehemiah, and Observations of Several Good Women Mentioned in Scripture* (1690–1692), NLS, MS 6499, pp. 15–16; see also Trill, ed., *Halkett*, 158–59.

231. Couper, *The Life of the Lady Halket*, 49–50.

232. Couper, *The Life of the Lady Halket*, 50.

troubled with rheum, which she presently took to be the harbinger of death."[233] In true *ars moriendi* style, Halkett has sorted out her worldly affairs, and though in great pain she continues to pray, albeit less frequently and more quietly than in the past. As she weakened, Couper assures us that she "was duly attended by the Lady Pitfirrane, her daughters and others."[234] The recipient of God's providence to the very end, Halkett died between seven and eight o'clock in the evening of Saturday, April 22, 1699:

> The day which for twenty nine years she had weekly set apart for abstinence, meditation, and preparation for death, on which she wished (if it might so please God) to die: and about the same time on which she used, on these days, to take refreshment to her body, her soul was called to the heavenly supper, and began its everlasting sabbath of rest. And her body was on the twenty fourth honorably convoyed and laid in the same grave in which her husband Sir James had been laid.[235]

While this is the conclusion of his biography, the next four pages provide an abridged overview of her life that serves as an elegiac encomium in which she is a "widow indeed" who "much delighted in God's house and the public worship and was a conscientious observer of the Lord's Day."[236] Obedient as she was to the requirements of public worship, she occupied a more ambivalent position within the household, insofar as her care "that all her family served the Lord" meant that "when she wanted a chaplain, [she] performed the offices of morning and evening worship herself."[237] As well as leading her family in public, household prayers, by example and exhortation she encouraged them in "private devotion; and for such as needed them, she composed forms of prayer for their use."[238] Outside the family, Couper represents her as "very moderate in her sentiments about disputable points." Couper notes her preference for the Church of England but claims "yet she complied with the customs and forms of the country where God had cast her lot, finding the essentials of religion the same in both."[239]

---

233. Couper, *The Life of the Lady Halket*, 53.
234. Couper, *The Life of the Lady Halket*, 54.
235. Couper, *The Life of the Lady Halket*, 54.
236. Couper, *The Life of the Lady Halket*, 55.
237. Couper, *The Life of the Lady Halket*, 55.
238. Couper, *The Life of the Lady Halket*, 55.
239. Couper, *The Life of the Lady Halket*, 55. For further details on the matters of debate, see Alasdair Raffe, "Presbyterians and Episcopalians: The Formation of Confessional Cultures in Scotland, 1660–1715," *English Historical Review* 125, no. 514 (2010): 570–98.

Her balanced nature extends to her combination of both contemplative and active Christianity. Noting that "contemplation had so spiritualized her mind that almost every object suggested pious thoughts to her,"[240] Couper provides a short list of the kinds of topics he means. His selections place Halkett's compositions firmly among the meditations of Hall, Boyle, Rich, and others, as they include reflections upon trees, sheep, and bees, as well as beating sugar, seeing a floating pitcher, and looking on a map. His final example holds out the tantalizing possibility that there is, somewhere, a picture of Halkett; for "looking on her own picture, drawn at large, with her sister as two shepherdesses, the postures in which she found herself drawn . . . represented to her the hieroglyphic of her life."[241] For Couper, this means representing Halkett as one who, though often in worldly difficulty, was so supported by God that nothing could truly shake her. He completes her character by reference to her "books," in which he emphasizes the secrecy with which she wrote.[242]

By contrast to his suggestion that Halkett was reluctant to enter the public sphere, on the reverse of the title page of *The Life of the Lady Halket* there is the following advertisement: "There will shortly be published her *Meditations on the Twenty-fifth Psalm.*"[243] Furthermore, that volume itself concludes with another "Advertisement" for further works by the Lady Halkett: "There is now in the press, and will be shortly published, *Select Meditations and Prayers upon the First Week; With Observations on Each Day's Creation; And Considerations on the Seven Capital Vices to Be Opposed: And Their Opposit Virtues to Be Studied and Practiced.*"[244] The final text to be published in 1701 was *Instructions for Youth.*[245] The first two volumes comprise select meditations upon specific biblical texts, Psalm 25 and Genesis 1 and 2:1–3; the third is a variation on the "Parental Advice" genre.

In its published form, *Meditations upon the Twentieth and Fifth Psalm* opens with a preface and extends to around twenty thousand words.[246] According to

---

240. Couper, *The Life of the Lady Halket*, 56.

241. Couper, *The Life of the Lady Halket*, 57–58.

242. Couper, *The Life of the Lady Halket*, 58. See also "Appendix 4.2," 339–49.

243. Couper, *The Life of the Lady Halket*, sig. ¶1v. First published as Anne, Lady Halkett, *Meditations upon the Twentieth and Fifth Psalm*, ed. Simon Couper (Edinburgh: Andrew Symson and Henry Knox, 1701). ESTC T72797.

244. Halkett, *Meditations upon the Twentieth and Fifth Psalm*, 48. Published as Anne, Lady Halkett, *Meditations and Prayers, upon the First Week; With Observations on Each Day's Creation: And Considerations on the Seven Capital Vices, to Be Opposed: And Their Opposit Virtues to Be Studied and Practiced*, ed. Simon Couper (Edinburgh: Andrew Symson, 1701), ESTC T72793.

245. Halkett, *Instructions for Youth*. ESTC T72792.

246. According to Couper, this folio volume contained only fifty-nine pages, "Appendix 4.2," 342. Another surviving folio, *True Account*, contains an approximate average of 366 words per leaf; by

David Dickson, "in this Psalm, the prophet, being in danger of his life by his enemies without and troubled with the sense of sin within, maketh prayer for relief from both, mixing meditation with prayer along the Psalm for strengthening of his faith."[247] In her distressed and isolated state in Fyvie, Halkett also draws interesting connections between David's distress and the story of Elkanah, Peninnah, and Hannah: Elkanah's "love was divided between two Wives, and loved one better than the other."[248] Thus, although Couper presents this text as "by one who had found how beneficial it was to have the soul continually placed upon divine objects," the subject matter veers beyond the simply spiritual.[249] The contents of *Meditations and Prayers, upon the First Week* are succinctly summarized by Couper, and with reference to *Instructions*, as Couper indicates, this (relatively short) publication positions Halkett as in loco parentis and provides general instructions for civil Christian behavior. Although her boarders included women, the *Instructions* are directed to a specifically male audience.

The next year, these were followed up by *Meditations upon the Seven Gifts of the Holy Spirit* and *Meditations upon Jabez His Request, 1 Chron. 4:10. Together with Sacramental Meditations on the Lord's Supper; and Prayers, Pious Reflections and Observations*.[250] While there is evidence that the first was published separately, most of the surviving copies are of the combined texts.[251] Here again, Couper appears to focus on publishing Halkett's select meditations; however, the actual contents of both the *Sacramental Meditations on the Lord's Supper* and *Prayers, Pious Reflections and Observations* are often drawn from sources that Halkett herself defined as occasional. Halkett regularly writes as part of her preparation for the Lord's Supper; while these are undoubtedly sacramental, extant volumes suggest that she viewed such preparations as appropriate for the particular occasion. Indeed, Couper's final excerpt is acknowledged to have been written on "the

---

comparison, this suggests that the *Meditations upon the Twentieth and Fifth Psalm* would have contained no more than twenty-two thousand words in total.

247. Dickson, *A Brief Explication of the First Fifty Psalms*, 139.

248. Halkett, *Meditations upon the Twentieth and Fifth Psalm*, 8; 1 Samuel 1; see also Susan Wiseman, "'The Most Considerable of My Troubles': Anne Halkett and the Writing of Civil War Conspiracy," in *Women Writing, 1550–1750*, ed. Jo Wallwork and Paul Salzman (Bundoora, Australia: Meridian, 2001), 37.

249. Halkett, *Meditations upon the Twentieth and Fifth Psalm*, title page.

250. Anne, Lady Halkett, *Meditations upon the Seven Gifts of the Holy Spirit, Mentioned Isaiah 11:2–3. As Also, Meditations upon Jabez His Request, 1 Chron. 4:10. Together with Sacramental Meditations on the Lord's Supper; and Prayers, Pious Reflections and Observations*, ed. Simon Couper (Edinburgh: Andrew Symson, 1702). ESTC N10709.

251. Anne, Lady Halkett, *Meditations upon the Seven Gifts of the Holy Spirit*, ed. Simon Couper (Edinburgh: Andrew Symson, 1702). ESTC T200617. Only two copies of this edition survive, whereas there are thirteen copies of the combined texts.

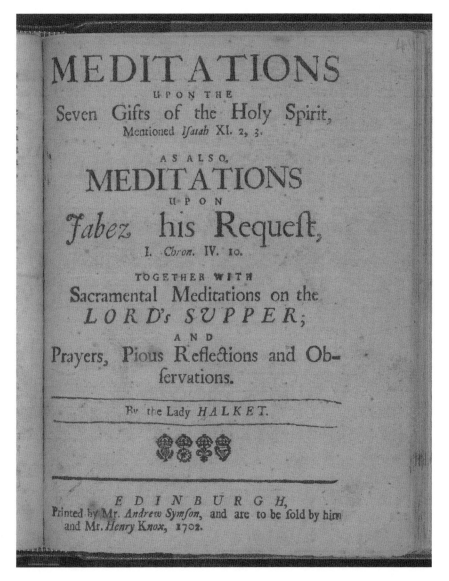

Figure 2. Title Page. *Meditations upon the Seven Gifts of the Holy Spirit. As Also, Meditations upon Jabez His Request, 1 Chron. 4:10. Together with Sacramental Meditations on the Lord's Supper; and Prayers, Pious Reflections, and Observations.* Edited by Simon Couper (Edinburgh: Andrew Symson and Henry Knox, 1702). © National Library of Scotland, Ry.1.6.286, 4(19).
Reproduced with permission.

last occasion she enjoyed of the Lord's Supper, August 11, 1695."[252] More precisely, this was the final time Halkett was physically able to partake of the Lord's Supper; due to the changes in Church organization in Scotland, from this date Halkett has to console herself with making personal preparations at dates she knows others will be celebrating the Sacrament in order to join with them in spirit. It is perhaps significant that Halkett makes this decision after discovering her practice of kneeling to receive the Sacrament was deterring others from participating; although she claims to look "upon that posture as a matter of decency and not essential," it is with difficulty that she forgoes her previous practice.[253]

The final selections made by Couper for printing, *Prayers, Pious Reflections, and Observations*, are actually collected under the titles "Prayers upon Several Occasions, by the Lady Halket [sic]" and "Pious Reflections and Observations, collected out of the Lady H's Occasional Meditations."[254] The first section contains seven "Prayers," only three of which are dated: the dates provided indicate that Couper's selections no longer survive in manuscript.[255] Of the rest, all are very brief, with two intended for "daily use in the family," one "for Sick Persons," and the last "A Prayer on Sermon Days."[256] Although they echo sentiments expressed elsewhere in Halkett's extant volumes, their format suggests to me that in most cases Couper has extracted these materials from longer entries. Furthermore, within the extant volumes, Halkett rarely designates her entries as "prayers,"[257] so that label is probably Couper's intervention. Similarly, the adjective "Pious" is likely his addition to the title of the final collection, as are his titles for individual entries. As discussed above, when Halkett provides titles for her occasional meditations, they invariably begin with "upon"; here, Couper consistently uses "of." This is perhaps a conscious attempt to differentiate Halkett's texts from those lampooned by Swift.[258] In the selected excerpts, there is no engagement with contemporary politics; instead, Couper presents Halkett as primarily concerned with devotion, marital status, debt, and being in good temper. Furthermore, the

---

252. Halkett, *Meditations upon the Seven Gifts of the Holy Spirit*, 57. ESTC N10709.

253. Halkett, *Meditations upon the Seven Gifts of the Holy Spirit*, 57. ESTC N10709. Whether one should kneel to receive the Sacrament was a controversial topic; see Margo Todd, *The Culture of Protestantism in Early Modern Scotland* (New Haven: Yale University Press, 2002), esp. 80, 102–4; and Trill, ed., *Halkett*, xxvi–xxvii.

254. Halkett, *Meditations upon the Seven Gifts of the Holy Spirit*, 68–75, 76–86. ESTC N10709.

255. "A Prayer for the Public, February 7, 1678/9," 68–72; "A Prayer in a Long-Continued Storm of Frost and Snow, January 24, 1684," 72–73; and "A Prayer for the Persecuted Protestants in France, December 15, 1685," 73. Halkett, *Meditations upon the Seven Gifts of the Holy Spirit*. ESTC N10709.

256. Halkett, *Meditations upon the Seven Gifts of the Holy Spirit*, 73–76. ESTC N10709.

257. For exceptions, see volumes 5 and 7, "Appendix 4.2," 342–44.

258. Coolahan, "Redeeming Parcels of Time," 136–37; Raymond A. Anselment, "Robert Boyle and the Art of Occasional Meditation," *Renaissance and Reformation* 32, no. 4 (2009): 73–92.

final three entries, although given contemplative titles, focus on sheep, sparrows, marlins, and larks; for Couper, Halkett's occasional meditations safely follow the examples provided by bishop Joseph Hall.

Despite, or perhaps because of, their "exemplary" nature, Couper's *The Life of the Lady Halket* and his editions of Halkett's writings were popular enough that they survive in multiple copies and were reprinted as a single volume collection in 1778.[259] Couper's Halkett is as uncontentious as possible, which perfectly suits his immediate political agenda. During the late seventeenth century, both the Episcopalians and the Presbyterians sought to defame their opponents as "ungodly" and to present their own faction as exemplary figures of Christian conduct. Couper thus utilizes Halkett's "life" as part of an attempt to prove the extent of Episcopalian piety. This political intention is further evidenced by the fact that Couper also published a series of treatises on the "true" order of the Church in the same period as he published Halkett's texts.[260] Additionally, his texts were published by Andrew Sympson and distributed by Henry Knox, who were both former Episcopalian ministers. The politics of printing was a complicated affair in seventeenth-century Scotland, and the kinds of texts that Couper published with them directly concerned "the government of the church," which, at this point, should only have been "published with permission"; the act of publication, and the choice of publishers, denotes a very specific "political allegiance."[261]

However, the dry nature of his selections has done much to maintain Halkett's marginal literary status and perhaps explains John Gough Nichols's surprise at how interesting her *Meditations* are.[262] Sadly Nichols died before completing his edition of Halkett's narrative, but the posthumous publication contains a short selection of nine of her *Meditations* as appendices.[263] Building on Nichols's

---

259. Anne, Lady Halkett, *Meditations upon the Twenty-Fifth Psalm. Also, Meditations and Prayers upon the First Week: With Observations on Each Day's Creation. Likewise, Instructions for Youth. By Lady Halket. To Which Is Prefixed, an Account of Her Life* (Edinburgh: Bayne and Mennons, 1778), ESTC T106403.

260. Couper's texts were published both singly and collectively between 1701 and 1705. See Couper, *Four Essays Concerning Church Government* (Edinburgh: Andrew Symson, 1705). ESTC T183203.

261. Ezell, "Ann Halkett's Morning Devotions," 226–28; Alastair J. Mann, *The Scottish Book Trade, 1500–1720: Print Commerce and Print Control in Early Modern Scotland* (East Linton, UK: Tuckwell, 2000), especially 139–48.

262. Trill, "Critical Categories," 117.

263. Nichols, *The Autobiography of Anne Lady Halkett*, "Appendix," 109–116. None of the meditations are reproduced in full, but the excerpts are from: "Upon the Fast which by Proclamation Was Kept January 30, 1660/1," see 203–5; Anne, Lady Halkett, "Upon the Death of My Dear Son Harry, May 12, 1661" in *Occasional Meditations, Meditations and Prayers on Every Several Day* (1660, 1663), NLS, MS 6491, pp. 52–56; "Upon Making Vows," see 208–10; "Upon the Disbanding of the Army," see 199–203; see also Trill, ed., *Halkett*, 19–22; Anne, Lady Halkett, "Upon the Meeting That Was to Determine Church Government, Tuesday, November 3, 1661," in *Occasional and Select Meditations*,

research, in 1979 John Loftis edited Halkett's work alongside that of Ann, Lady Fanshawe, and identified many of the figures originally only referred to by initials within Halkett's narrative. Loftis also supplied some much-needed information about Colonel Joseph Bampfield, although most of that material was relegated to footnotes. While he inveighs against Bampfield's duplicity there and labels him "an unconscionable opportunist," in the preface to his edition of Bampfield's *Apology*, Loftis moderates his opinion and instead asserts that "his changes of allegiance were forced on him."[264] Loftis's edition was highly influential in facilitating Halkett's entry into the canon of English literature; however, the separation of Halkett's *True Account* from the rest of her corpus, and the feminist impulse to recover early modern women's writing that mirrored twentieth-century concerns, alongside the majority of her volumes being deposited at the National Library of Scotland, combined to ensure the continued erasure of Halkett's *Meditations*. It was not until the twenty-first century that this material came back into view. My previous edition was intended to serve as a form of corrective to this imbalance and sought to reflect the new bibliographical interest in the materiality of her texts. While other editions of the *True Account* exist, this is the first fully modernized version, the first to give *A True Account of My Life* the title Halkett herself attributes to it, and the first to situate the *True Account* within selections from both her select and occasional meditations.[265]

A Note on the Text

The material that follows has been freshly edited from Halkett's autograph manuscripts. *A True Account of My Life* is based on BL, Add. MS 32376, which is catalogued as "The Autobiography of Anne, Lady Halkett." The selections from Halkett's *Meditations* are all based on the autograph manuscript volumes deposited at the National Library of Scotland (NLS, MSS 6489–6502). These are part of a broader collection, The Pitfirrane Papers, which chart the Halkett family's personal, political, and financial history (NLS, MSS 6406–6511), including

---

including *Instructions to My Son* (1667–1670), NLS, MS 6492, pp. 76–80; see also Trill, ed., *Halkett*, 23–24; although untitled by Nichols, the next excerpt is from "The Widow's Mite, Part of It Relating to the King," see 241–49; the final two excerpts ("Meditations and Resolutions upon Luke 2:36–38," and "Kneeling in Prayer") can be found in Anne, Lady Halkett, *The Widow's Mite* (1673/4–1675), NLS, MS 6493, pp. 51, 64–66, 78.

264. Loftis, ed., *The Memoirs of Anne, Lady Halkett and Anne, Lady Fanshawe*, xii; Loftis and Hardacre, eds., *Colonel Joseph Bampfield's Apology*, 13.

265. As Sharon C. Seelig noted, the Ashgate volume included only occasional entries, "Review of *Lady Anne Halkett: Selected Self-Writings*, and *Witchcraft, Exorcism and the Politics of Possession in a Seventeenth-Century Convent: 'How Sister Ursula Was Once Bewitched and Sister Margaret Twice,'" Renaissance Quarterly* 61, no. 2 (2008): 680–82.

the material reproduced in appendices 2 and 3.[266] For those with institutional or personal access, Halkett's *True Account* and her *Meditations* are available in digital form via Perdita Manuscripts.[267] The scholarly apparatus there includes full bibliographic information and physical descriptions of these volumes and their contents. While the majority of Halkett's volumes are bound quartos, the extant material includes two folios and one octavo.[268] While these volumes share many characteristics, each one has unique qualities that are explained in a headnote at the start of the selection from each of her "books." These headnotes contain detailed information about each volume's contents and organization. Halkett habitually paginated her volumes; however, due to later insertions, omissions, and human error, sometimes that pagination goes awry. For consistency and ease of reference for anyone wishing to compare the edited texts with the original manuscripts, I have used the library cataloguer's numbering in all cases, with a comment on the reason for any discrepancy in the headnote. Halkett generally defines her meditations as either select or occasional and usually places them in different sections of her books in chronological order. Here, again, there are exceptions, which are explained in the headnote; for consistency, the materials edited below are all presented in chronological order.

In producing this edition of Anne, Lady Halkett's *True Account* and a selection of her *Meditations*, my main aim has been to offer an accessible, standardized version of her text that is suitable for general reading and classroom discussion. The excerpts from the *Meditations* focus directly on people, places, and events described within the *True Account*. Nevertheless, my selection is by no means exhaustive. Certain issues recur throughout Halkett's volumes, which provide a valuable insight into the cyclical nature of her experience: for example, as an ardent Royalist, she annually fasts on January 30 and celebrates the monarch's birthday; and throughout her widowhood, she not only regularly marks the anniversary of her husband's death (September 24, 1670) but frequently remembers him on the day (Saturday) and date (24) of that event as well. It would be impossible to include every example, but for those interested in following up on these connections, I have provided references in footnotes. The select meditations range from a (relatively) short exposition of one biblical verse to an entire volume dedicated to a book of the Old Testament or biblical figure.[269] Consequently, although

---

266. "Appendix 1" is in a separate collection, see 327–28.

267. Perdita Manuscripts. Adam Matthew Digital, 2007. http://www.perditamanuscripts.amdigital.co.uk.

268. See "Appendix 4.2," 339–49.

269. Halkett's exegesis of one biblical verse can be extensive; for example, she spends forty pages on Hebrews 13:5 (compared with seven pages on Psalm 18:20) in *Occasional and Select Meditations*, pp. 141–81; 206–13. Extant volumes that focus on biblical figures predominantly concern Old Testament figures (Joseph, Jonah, Moses, and Samuel). Halkett's discussion of these figures undoubtedly has

all of the occasional meditations selected appear below in their entirety, her select meditations are represented by excerpts, with footnotes providing summaries of the omitted materials.

Readers who are interested in analyzing Halkett's texts linguistically, or who wish to gain a deeper sense of the materiality of her writing, may be referred to my 2007 edition *Lady Anne Halkett: Selected Self-Writings*, published by Ashgate. As part of the Other Voice series, the version of the text that follows has been regularized in both spelling and punctuation according to the conventions of standard twenty-first-century American practice. In early modern English, "u"/"v" and "i"/"j" were interchangeable; however, in this edition they are silently normalized. I have also silently substituted "s" for the old-style long "ſ." In common with her contemporaries, Halkett's spelling, even of the same word, can be inconsistent (for example, "address" appears as "adres," "addrese," "adrese"). To maintain consistency and avoid distraction by orthographic variation, Halkett's usage has been silently regularized according to modern conventions.

As is customary, I have expanded the numerous contractions Halkett employs that we no longer use: so "ye," "yt," and "ym" become "the," "that," and "them"; "wch" becomes "which"; and "&" becomes "and." Where Halkett uses the abbreviation "yn," I have replaced it with "then" or "than" as appropriate, and I have silently regularized her use of "then" to "than" where necessary. She also consistently condenses the conjunction "until" to "till," which my edition expands. However, as they remain current, I retain her use of abbreviations for peoples' titles: thus, "Mrs" is "Mrs.," "Mr" is "Mr.," "Sr" is "Sir," and "Dr" is "Dr." Also, Halkett frequently abbreviates "Lord" to "L" or "Ld" and "Lady" to "L" or "La," and "Duke," "Countess," and "Earl" appear respectively as "D," "C," and "E." In all such cases, I have replaced the abbreviation with its expanded modern equivalent and retain Halkett's capitalization as it conforms to current practice. Notably, especially within her *True Account*, Halkett identifies her protagonists primarily by their initials only. This practice was not unique to her: it is also characteristic of the contemporary emerging genres of the memoir and the novel.[270] However, for clarity and consistency, where identification is secure, in this edition names are given in full throughout in their standardized modern form; where names remain as initials, the individual has so far eluded identification. Like that of her contemporaries, Halkett's use of capitalization seems haphazard to a modern reader: I

---

typological resonance with contemporary religious and political events. See Kevin Killeen, "Chastising with Scorpions: Reading the Old Testament in Early Modern England," *Huntington Library Quarterly* 73, no. 3 (2010): 491–506. Other volumes include meditations on Christ, and Saint Peter, as well as "Observations of Several Good Women Mentioned in Scripture"; see "Appendix 4.2," 339–49.

270. Rachel Carnell, "Slipping from Secret History to Novel," *Eighteenth-Century Fiction* 28, no.1 (2015): 1–24; and Ian. P. Watt, "The Naming of Characters in Defoe, Richardson, and Fielding," *Review of English Studies* 25, no. 100 (1949): 322–38.

have regularized capitalization for proper names (e.g., "Christ," "Devil," "God," "Holy Spirit"), but I have used lowercase letters for terms such as "mercy," "grace," "sanctification," "sin," "reprobate," and "redemption." These terms had specific political and religious resonance in the seventeenth century, which is usually associated with the more radical Protestants (from Calvinists and Presbyterians to the Civil War sects). Halkett's religious identification is complicated; however, her insistence on her adherence to mainstream Church of England practice means that regularizing capitalization here might distort our perception of her position. The one exception is "Sacrament," which Halkett consistently capitalizes herself as a signal of respect for Holy Communion or the Lord's Supper.

Halkett's punctuation is limited to commas, colons, hyphens, and periods, although she does not always use these marks in the same way as we do today. While I have retained her own markings where possible, for the most part the punctuation here represents my attempt to clarify her meaning for a modern reader. Any semicolon, question mark, exclamation mark, or possessive apostrophe can be assumed to be my intervention. One aspect of Halkett's *True Account* that has generated critical discussion is her "dramatization" of certain incidents and her "novelistic" writing style. In particular, I hope that the addition of quotation marks to signify direct speech will facilitate further discussion on such points, for at various crucial moments Halkett uses a combination of direct speech, reported indirect speech, and first-person narration to great effect. Her syntax is controlled (and often compelling), but it is frequently convoluted and overextended for a modern reader. In common with her contemporaries, Halkett frequently begins a sentence with either "And" or "But"; indeed, these words are sometimes the only indication that a new sentence has started. Such practices are now generally frowned upon except when used for rhetorical effect, so I have tried to minimize their use; however, as they are signs of a natural break for Halkett, they appear more frequently than a modern reader might expect. As paper was at a premium, most early modern writers also used hyphens more often than we do today: in Halkett's manuscripts, any word that was not completed by the end of the line was marked with "-" or "=" and continued onto the next line. Here, however, all such marks are omitted, and the syllables are silently reconnected to form the whole word. Therefore, any remaining end-of-line hyphens in this edition are the result of modern typesetting requirements.

I have not attempted to reproduce Halkett's use of spacing between letters, words, or lines, the layout of her writing on the page, or her page breaks. Nor have I retained her paragraphing: while there are points at which she clearly signals a paragraph break, without intervention this would commonly mean six or seven pages of continuous prose without a break (which is not only difficult to read but may inhibit discussion by difficulty in identifying a passage). However, for ease of cross-reference, I have included the folio or page numbers assigned to the original text by the cataloguer in square brackets within the edited text. Where there are significant discrepancies between the cataloguer's numbering and Halkett's own pagination, this is explained in the relevant headnote. Although less frequent in her *True Account*, Halkett's *Meditations* include numerous biblical references that are most often placed in the left- or right-hand margin of her page: in this edition, where Halkett's original references are complete, they are included in the main text within brackets; however, where references are incomplete, or missing in the original, the necessary information is provided in a footnote. Intext citations use abbreviated forms of the titles of biblical books; the full title is provided in a footnote. On occasion, Halkett differentiates between her own words and someone else's by altering the size of her writing; in general, this is limited to letters in the *True Account* and biblical quotations in the *Meditations*: in these cases, the relevant text below is italicized.

Halkett's texts show many signs of rereading and/or revision, including crossings-out, inserted alterations or additions, and cross-references to other texts (of both her own writings and other, usually published, materials). The full extent of Halkett's revisions are recorded in my 2007 edition for Ashgate; here, only substantive alterations are documented and placed in footnotes. Halkett's texts are written in her own highly legible, italic hand. Nevertheless, usually due to damage to the manuscripts, there are some instances where my readings remain conjectural. In such cases my editorial additions are enclosed within square brackets.

Throughout her writing, Halkett maintains a dual dating system in which she regularly records her celebration of New Year on January 1 while consistently identifying the months of January through March as 1642/3, or 1698/9.[271] In common with her contemporaries when she refers to a specific hour, she writes "X a clocke," which I have silently altered to "X o'clock."

---

271. In an aside on the subject of God's creation of light in March, Halkett reaffirms her commitment to the English dating system: "And therefore, I the more approve of the custom of England, who never change the date of the year until the five and twentieth day of March, though they join with others in calling the first of January, New Year's Day." Anne, Lady Halkett, *Meditations on Moses and Samuel* (1688–1689/90), NLS, MS 6498, p. 82.

A True Account of My Life *(1677–1678)*

As figure 3 below demonstrates, the first leaf of the extant *True Account* is badly damaged. The manuscript begins midsentence; nevertheless, because Halkett habitually paginated her volumes, we know that she deemed that leaf to be pages 2 and 3. As her extant volumes demonstrate, there was usually at least one leaf (often more) containing prefatory material before she commenced her main text, so we cannot be sure how many pages preceded what has survived. Similarly, we cannot be sure how much longer the original manuscript was, as it too finishes midsentence. This is one of only two surviving folio volumes; the other, *A Short Expostulation about Prayer*, extends to 150 pages. Couper does not include the *True Account* in his list of Halkett's "books," and the length of the missing folio volumes range from 59 to 376 pages. According to Halkett's numbering, the extant manuscript concludes on page 126, which suggests that the possible parameters for the original were somewhere between another 24 and another 250 pages.[1] Indeed, Halkett's reference to the grant made to her on November 20, 1662, as well as her reference to the "Act of Indemnity" (1660), suggests that she intended to continue her narrative until at least the Restoration.[2] Furthermore, comments in the volume she interrupted to write this narrative suggest that it was prompted by another accusation of sexual impropriety, which may mean she intended to continue her narrative up to the date of writing (i.e., 1677–1678).[3] Until such time as the rest of the manuscript should serendipitously come to light, however, this will remain a mystery.

[*one leaf, two pages, missing from the manuscript*]

[fol. 1r] his word. And since we have an advocate with the father [of] Christ the righteous, he will plead for me wherein I am innocen[t] and pardon wherein I have been guilty (I John 2:1).[4] For God sent not his Son into the world to condemn the world, but that the world through him might be saved, in whom we have

---

1. Of the other fourteen volumes in the NLS, twelve are quartos. According to Couper's catalogue, Halkett's quartos ranged from 315 to 556 pages. His recording of extant volumes can be verified as being between 326 and 452 pages. See "Appendix 4.2," 339–49.
2. Trill, ed., *Halkett*, 140n220; Trill, "Beyond Romance," 457n28.
3. Trill, "Critical Categories," 113–15.
4. Damage to the page means the biblical reference here is incomplete and reads only "Jo[hn] 1"; the passage Halkett cites here is 1 John 2:1: "My little children, these things write I unto you, that ye sin not. And if any man sin, we have an advocate with the Father, Jesus Christ the righteous."

boldness and access with confidence by the faith of him (John 3:17; Eph. 3:12).[5] And that is the reason why I faint not under tribulation:[6] for there is no sin that ever I have been guilty of in my whole life but I repent with as much sincerity as I seek pardon. And I supplicate for grace to live uprightly here, with the same fervor that I seek for heaven hereafter. And, if the Lord sees fit to continue me still in the furnace of affliction (Isaiah 48:10), his blessed will be done so that I may be on[e of his] chosen.[7]

"This Manuscript written by Anne, daughter of Mr. Thomas Murray, Provost of Eton, and Preceptor of Charles 1st. –she was Lady of the Bedchamber to Queen Henrietta Maria, and married Sir James Halkett, Knight of Pitfirrane"[8]

For my Parents I need not say much since they w[ere]
    And I need not be ashamed to own [the]m
    was mentioned as my reproach that I was of
    ion, whereas he that now succeeds to that fa
    was once [xxx] was as good a gentleman as any
    tter. I shall ever be satisfied with what ca
    the advantage of that family, but some that
    to, both by father and mother would take it ill [xxx]

---

5. Damage to the page means the biblical reference here is incomplete and reads only "Joh[n] 17 and "ians 12"; the citations here are John 3:17: "For God sent not his Son into the world to condemn the world; but that the world through him might be saved"; and Ephesians 3:12: "In whom we have boldness and access with confidence by the faith of him."

6. An allusion to Ephesians 3:13: "Wherefore I desire that ye faint not at my tribulations for you, which is your glory."

7. Damage to the page means the biblical reference here is incomplete and reads only "Isa:" The full reference is Isaiah 48:10: "Behold, I have refined thee, but not with silver; I have chosen thee in the furnace of affliction."

8. This attribution is written in black ink, in a hand other than Halkett's. It is characteristic of Halkett's layout of her texts for there to be a space between the prefatory material and the main text. I have not found any supporting evidence for the claim that she was a lady of Henrietta Maria's bedchamber; however, her brothers Charles and Henry were grooms of Charles I's bedchamber; see Loftis, ed., *The Memoirs of Anne, Lady Halkett and Anne, Lady Fanshawe*, 193. According to Halkett's narrative, her brother William, who died in 1648, was also a member of the royal household; Murray's position is also confirmed by Bampfield; see Loftis and Hardacre, eds., *Colonel Joseph Bampfield's Apology*, 76. One "William Murry," son of Thomas Murray, was baptized on July 17, 1617, at St. Peter's church in Berkhamsted *England: Select Births and Christenings, 1538–1975*, cited in Ancestry®, accessed August 08, 2018, https://www.ancestry.co.uk. However, he must be distinguished from their cousin William Murray, who later became Earl of Dysart; see Smuts, "Murray, William," *ODNB*.

[th]ought gentlemen: for my father claimed [xxxxxxx] of being derived from the Earl of Tullibardine's family and my mother from the Earl of Perth's.[9]

He was thought a wise King[10] who made choice of my f[ather] to be tutor to the late King of blessed memory.[11] And what that excellent Prince learned in his youth kept him steadfast in his religion (though under all the temptations of Spain),[12] temperate in all the excesses that attend a court, virtuous and constant to the only lawful embraces of the Queen, and unmovable and undisturbed under all his unparalleled sufferings. For all recompense to my father's care in discharging his duty he was made Provost of Eton College[13] (where he [fol. 1v] [li]ved not long but died when I was but three months old). Yet it seems the short time he lived amongst those prebends[14] they were so well satisfied both with him and my mother that, after my father's death, they petitioned to have his place continued to my mother a year (which was never before granted to any woman, and during her time they all renewed their leases as a testimony of their respect and desire to give her that advantage).[15]

---

9. While I have not yet been able to trace the links claimed here, it seems likely that Thomas Murray was the son of Patrick Murray of Woodend and his wife, Elizabeth Murray, daughter of David Murray of Carsehead. If so, he was one of at least six siblings (Alexander, Thomas, William, Patrick, and Robert, with the possibility of two more [David and Christina]). His brother William was minster of Dysart, and it was his son who became the first Earl of Dysart. According to the same source, Halkett's mother, Jean Drummond, is descended from the Drummonds of Blair Drummond. "Families Database," Stirnet.com, accessed November 10, 2015, http://www.stirnet.com/genie/index.php; see also Smuts, "Murray, Thomas," *ODNB*.

10. I.e., James VI/I; see Jenny Wormald, "James VI and I (1566–1625)," *ODNB*.

11. I.e., Charles I; see Mark A. Kishlansky and John Morrill, "Charles I (1600–1649)," *ODNB*.

12. Here, Halkett alludes to the negotiations surrounding the possible marriage of Charles I to the Spanish Infanta Maria in the early 1620s; see Kishlansky and Morrill, "Charles I," *ODNB*.

13. Founded in the fifteenth century, Eton College, or Eton, is a prestigious independent boarding school for boys. The position of provost of Eton remains a Crown appointment; see H. C. Maxwell-Lyte, *A History of Eton College, 1440–1910* (London: Macmillan, 1911); Tim Card, *Eton Established: A History from 1440–1860* (London: John Murray, 2001).

14. A prebend was "the estate or portion of land from which a stipend is derived to support a canon of a cathedral or collegiate church, or a member of its chapter," *OED*. The "prebends" to whom Halkett is referring here are the fellows of Eton College.

15. While there is no record of such a petition, Thomas Murray died in April 1623, and competition for the position meant that Wotton did not officially take up the role until July 24, 1624; see Maxwell-Lyte, *A History of Eton College*, 206–12; Trill, ed., *Halkett*, xix, xixn13.

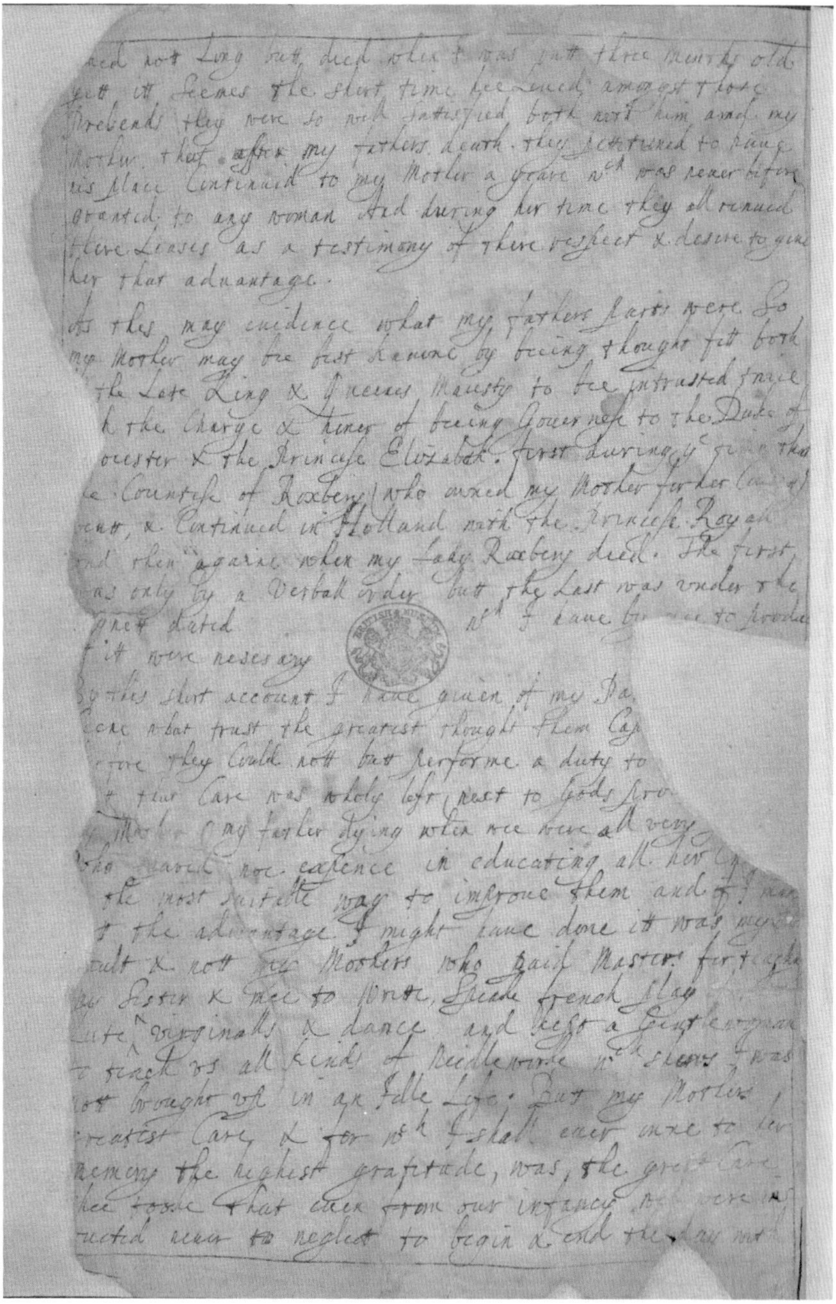

Figure 3. From Anne, Lady Halkett, *A True Account of My Life* (1677–1678). © British Library, BL, Add. MS 32376, fol. 1v. Reproduced with permission.

A True Account of My Life 63

As this may evidence what my father's parts[16] were, so my mother may be best known by being thought fit both [by] the late King and Queen's majesty to be entrusted twice [wit]h the charge and honor of being governess to the Duke of [Gl]oucester[17] and the Princess Elizabeth.[18] First during the time that [th]e Countess of Roxburghe (who owned my mother for her cousin)[19] went and continued in Holland with the Princess Royal,[20] and then again when my Lady Roxburghe died. The first was only by a verbal order but the last was under the [si]gnet dated _____[21] which I have by me to produce [i]f it were necessary.[22]

By this short account I have given of my pa[rents]
seen what trust the greatest thought them cap[able]
[th]erefore they could not but perform a duty to
tt that care was wholly left (next to God's prov[ision]
[to m]y mother (my father dying when we were all very y[oung]
who spared no expense in educating all her ch[ildren]
the most suitable way to improve them and, if I made
[no]t the advantage I might have done, it was my own [f]ault and not my mothers who paid masters for teachi[ng] my sister and me to write, speak French, play further the Lute and[23] virginals, and dance. And kept a gentlewoman to teach us all kinds of needlework, which shows I was not brought up in an idle life.

16. The plural of "part," which refers to "a personal quality or attribute, esp. of an intellectual kind; an ability, gift, or talent," *OED*.

17. Halkett's mother is not among those listed as caring for the Duke of Gloucester by Stuart Handley, "Henry, Prince, Duke of Gloucester (1640–1660)," *ODNB*.

18. Nor is she mentioned by Gordon Goodwin, "Elizabeth, Princess (1635–1650)," *ODNB*.

19. Jane [Jean] Ker[r], née Drummond, married Robert Ker, then Lord Roxburghe, in 1614 and became known as the Countess of Roxburghe. She was a Catholic confidante of Queen Henrietta Maria and became governess to Mary, the Princess Royal, in 1631; by 1641, she was also the governess of the Duke of Gloucester and Princess Elizabeth. Since she was sister-in-law to Alexander Seton, first Earl of Dunfermline, she was connected to Halkett's mother by both kinship and employment; see Helen Payne, "Ker [Kerr; née Drummond], Jane [Jean], Countess of Roxburghe (b. in or before 1585, d. 1643)," *ODNB*.

20. Mary, the Princess Royal, was married to William of Orange in 1641; their son, also named William, became King of England in 1688, see Marika Keblusek, "Mary, Princess Royal (1631–1660)," *ODNB*.

21. There is a blank space in the manuscript where the date of the signet should be provided. This claim is repeated by Simon Couper, but he provides no date either, *The Life of the Lady Halket*, 3. However, there are two relevant entries in the *CSP(Dom)*: "That the letter from the King appointing Mrs. Jane Murray to be governess of the King's children be reported to both Houses tomorrow. *[In margin*: 'Deferred till Tuesday']," June 8, 1645, *CSP(Dom)*, vol. 20: October 1644–July 1645, SP 21/8, fol.321; and "that the letter from his Majesty to Mrs. Murray be reported to both Houses. That this vote be recalled," June 11, 1645, *CSP(Dom)*, vol. 20: October 1644–July 1645, SP 21/8, fol.329.

22. Halkett's loyalty to the King is founded on a sense of personal connection; see also "The Widow's Mite, Part of It Relating to the King" and "Tuesday, June 24, 1690," 241–49, 278–79.

23. "And" is an interlineal insertion.

But my mother's [g]reatest care, and for which I shall ever own to her memory the highest gratitude, was the great care she took that even from our infancy we were ins[t]ructed never to neglect to begin and end the day with [fol. 2r] prayer; and orderly every morning to read the Bible; and ever to keep the church as often as there was occasion to meet there, either for prayers or preaching.[24] So that for many years together, I was seldom or never absent from divine service at five o'clock in the morning in the summer, and six o'clock in the winter, until the usurped[25] power put a restraint to that public worship so long owned and continued in the Church of England (where, I bless God, I had my education, and the example of a good mother, who kept constant to her own parish church [a]nd had always a great respect for the ministers under whose charge she was).[26]

What my childish actions were, I think I need not give account of here,[27] for I hope none will think they could be either vicious[28] or scandalous.[29] And from that time until the year 1644, I may truly say all my converse was so innocent that my own heart cannot challenge me with any immodesty (either in thought or behavior) or an act of disobedience to my mother (to whom I was so observant that, as long as she lived, I do not remember that I made a visit to the nearest neighbor or went anywhere without her liberty).[30] And so scrupulous I was of giving any occasion to speak of me (as I know they did of others) that, though I loved well to

---

24. For an in-depth exploration of the principles and practices associated with Protestantism in this period, see Ryrie, *Being Protestant in Reformation Britain*. In *The Widow's Mite*, Halkett confesses that "my prayers for many years was customary, and formal, and what proceeded more from sense of want or duty; so, in gratitude to my mother's memory, I ought to acknowledge her care in breeding me up from my infancy to pray, read the Holy Scriptures, and keep the church upon all occasions of public service," 68. Halkett later observes: "I esteem it the greatest honor I have, that I have been educated in the Church of England in the time in which it had greatest encouragements," "Thursday, January 8, 1690/1," 282.

25. "To intrude forcibly, illegally, or without just cause into (some dignified or important office, position, etc.); to assume or arrogate to oneself (political power, rule, authority, etc.) by force; to claim unjustly," *OED*. In 1645, the use of the *BCP* was prohibited; it was replaced by *A Directory for the Publicke Worship of God. BCP*, xli.

26. Halkett's representation of her mother differentiates her from "sermon gadding" Puritans. Andrew Cambers, *Godly Reading: Print, Manuscript, and Puritanism in England, 1580–1720* (Cambridge: Cambridge University Press, 2011), 14.

27. In later life, Halkett recalls an early transgression in which she bit her sister's hand until it bled. "Friday, May 14, 1697," 311.

28. "Of the nature of vice; contrary to moral principles; depraved, immoral, bad," *OED*.

29. "Of the nature of a scandal; grossly disgraceful. Also (now rarely) of a person: Guilty of grossly disgraceful conduct, infamous," *OED*.

30. "To give (a person) liberty to do something," *OED*: i.e., to give permission. Halkett reflects further on how she felt when her mother would not allow her to accompany her on visits in "Upon Reading Mr. Boyle's *Occasional Reflections*, January 25, 1668/9," 219.

see plays and to walk in the Spring Garden[31] sometimes (before it grew something scandalous by the abuse of some), yet I cannot remember three times that ever I went with any man besides my brother;[32] and if I did, my sisters or others better than myself was with me.[33] And I was the first that proposed and practiced it for three or four of us going together, without [fol. 2v] any man, and everyone paying for themselves (by giving the money to the footman who waited on us and he gave it in the playhouse). And this I did first upon hearing some gentlemen telling what ladies they had waited on to plays and how much it had cost them, upon which I resolved none should say the same of me.

In the year 1644, I confess I was guilty of an act of disobedience, for I gave way to the address of a person[34] whom my mother, at the first time that ever he had occasion to be conversant with me, had absolutely discharged[35] me ever to allow of. And though before ever I saw him severals[36] did tell me that there would be something more than ordinary betwixt him and me, which I believe they judged from the great friendship betwixt his sister[37] and me (for we were seldom asunder at London, and she and I were bedfellows when she came to my sister's house at Charlton[38] where for the most part she stayed while we continued in the country),

31. According to John Evelyn, the Spring Gardens, a little thoroughfare behind the southwest frontage to Charing Cross, which "had been the usual rendezvous for the ladies and gallants at this season," was "shut up and seized on" by "Cromwell and his partisans" by May 10, 1654, *Diary*, cited in "Spring Gardens," in *Survey of London*, ed. Gater and Hiorns, 20:58–65; see also Mary Thomas Crane, "Illicit Privacy and Outdoor Spaces in Early Modern England," *Journal for Early Modern Cultural Studies* 9, no. 1 (2009): 4–22.

32. Most likely Will, with whom Halkett was more closely connected than her other brothers.

33. Loftis suggests that as Halkett had only one sister, Elizabeth, the plural here "may also refer to her sister-in-law, Anne, daughter of Paul, Viscount Bayning of Sudbury." Loftis, ed., *The Memoirs of Anne, Lady Halkett and Anne, Lady Fanshawe*, 193. Anne married Halkett's brother Henry on November 26, 1635; the couple had three daughters, Elizabeth, Jane, and Mary, TCP 2:35, 2:36; TCB 3:121, 3:546, 3:291, 4:110. Her sister Elizabeth's library included a copy of Shakespeare's Second Folio, collected editions of works by Ben Jonson, Francis Beaumont, and John Fletcher, along with other plays by Philip Massinger, William Davenant, and Thomas Middleton. McKitterick, "Women and Their Books in Seventeenth-Century England," 376–77.

34. I.e., Thomas Howard (1625?–August 24, 1678), the son of Edward Howard, first Baron Howard of Escrick and Mary Boteler. He succeeded his father as second Baron in April 1675. Victor Stater, "Howard, Edward, First Baron Howard of Escrick (d. 1675)," *ODNB*.

35. "To forbid (a person, etc.) to do something; to ban from (of) doing; to prohibit (an action, practice, etc.)," *OED*.

36. "Several persons or things," *OED*.

37. I.e., Lady Anne Howard; in 1645, she married Sir Charles Howard and moved to Naworth Castle, where Halkett resided in 1649–1650, see *True Account*, 94–117. Goodwin, "Howard, Charles," *ODNB*.

38. Halkett's elder sister, Elizabeth, married Sir Henry Newton (later Puckering) around 1640, by which time he had inherited Charlton House. Broadway, "Puckering [Newton], Sir Henry," *ODNB*. In the seventeenth century, Charlton was in Kent; today, it is situated in the Royal Borough of Greenwich.

yet he was half a year in my company before I discovered anything of a particular inclination for me more than another. And, as I was civil to him both for his own merit and his sister's sake, so any particular civility I received from him I looked upon it as flowing from the affection he had to his sister and her kindness to me.

After that time, it seems he was not so much master of himself as to conceal it any longer. And having never any opportunity of being alone with me to speak himself, he employed a young gentleman (whose confidante he was in an *amour* betwixt him and my Lady Anne, his cousin German)[39] to tell me how much he had endeavored all this time to smother his passion, which he said began the first time that ever he [fol. 3r] saw me. And now was come to that height that, if I did not give him some hopes of favor, he was resolved to go back again into France (from whence he had come when I first saw him) and turn Capuchin.[40]

Though this discourse disturbed me, yet I was a week or ten days before I would be persuaded so much as to hear him speak of this subject. And desired his friend to represent several disadvantages that it would be to him to pursue such a design. And knowing[41] that his father had sent for him out of France with an intention to marry him to some rich match that might improve his fortune, it would be high ingratitude in me to do anything to hinder such a design (since his father had been so obliging to my mother and sister as to use his Lordship's interest with the Parliament to prevent the ruin of my brother's house, et cetera).[42] But when all I could say to him by his friend could not prevail, but that he grew so ill and discontented that all the house took notice, I did yield so far to comply with his desire as to give him liberty one day when I was walking in the gallery to[43] come there and speak to me. What he said was handsome and short, but much disordered; for he looked pale as death, and his hand trembled when he took mine to lead me, and with a great sigh said, "If I loved you less I could say more."

While alterations have been made to the building over the centuries, it retains many of its original Jacobean features; see Royal Greenwich Trust, "Charlton House," accessed August 8, 2018, https://www.greenwichheritage.org/visit/charlton-house.

39. Cousin German: "the son or daughter of (one's) uncle or aunt; (one's) first cousin," *OED*. So, this is Lady Anne Howard, daughter of the second Earl of Suffolk, who later married Colonel Thomas Walsingham. Victor Stater, "Howard, Theophilus, Second Earl of Suffolk (1584–1640)," *ODNB*; *BP* 3.3814.

40. I.e., become a Roman Catholic, specifically "a friar of the order of St Francis," *OED*.

41. "Ing" is an interlineal insertion.

42. In 1643, Parliament set up two committees to deal with Royalist estates; the "Sequestration Committee" and the "Committee for Compounding with Delinquents." As a member of the second, Edward Howard was able to advocate for Sir Henry Newton, whose name appears many times in the Calendar for 1646.

43. Here, "give him leave to" has been crossed out and replaced with the interlineal insertion of "come there and."

I told him I could not but think myself much obliged to him for his good opinion of me, but it would be a higher obligation to confirm his esteem of me by following my advice, which I should now give him myself since he would not receive it by his friend. I used many arguments to dissuade him from pursuing what he proposed, and in conclusion told [fol. 3v] him I was two or three years older than he, and were there no other objection yet that was of such weight with me as would never let me allow his further address.[44]

"Madam," said he, "what I love in you may well increase but I am sure it can never decay."

I left arguing, and told him I would advise him to consult with his own reason, and that would let him see I had more respect to him in denying than in granting what, with so much passion, he desired.

After that, he sought, and I shunned, all opportunities of private discourse with him, but one day, in the garden, his friend took his sister by the hand, and led[45] her into another walk, and left him and I together. And he, with very much seriousness, began to tell me that he had observed ever since he had discovered his affection to me that I was more reserved, and avoided all converse with him. And, therefore, since he had no hopes of my favor he was resolved to leave England since he could not be happy in it, and that whatever became of him might make him displease either his father or his friends, I was the occasion of it; for, if I would not give him hopes of marrying him, he was resolved to put himself out of a capacity of marrying any other, and go immediately into a convent,[46] and that he had taken order to have post horses ready against the next day.

I confess this discourse disturbed me (for though I had had no respect for him, his sister, or his family, yet religion was a tie upon me to endeavor the prevention of the hazard of his soul). I looked on this as a violent passion, which would not last long and perhaps might grow the more by being resisted, when as a seeming complaisance[47] might lessen it. I told him I was sorry to have him entertain such thoughts as could not but be a ruin to him and a great affliction to

---

44. Diana O'Hara points out that "although disparities in age may not have been uncommon in the early modern period, their acceptance remained questionable," *Courtship and Constraint: Rethinking the Making of Marriage in Tudor England* (Manchester: Manchester University Press, 2000), 159. Although individuals' ages at marriage varied widely, there appears to have been a general assumption that the woman should be around two years younger than her husband, and there was "contemporary disapproval of the implicit sexual appetite of women for younger men"; O'Hara, *Courtship and Constraint*, 162.

45. "Lead" in MS.

46. In early modern English, the term "convent" could refer to either male or female communities: "a company of men or women living together in the discipline of a religious order and under one superior; a body of monks, friars, or nuns forming one local community," *OED*.

47. "The action or habit of making oneself agreeable; desire and care to please; compliance with, or deference to, the wishes of others; obligingness, courtesy, politeness," *OED*.

all his relations, which I would willingly prevent if it were in my power. He said it was absolutely in my power: for, if I would promise to marry [fol. 4r] him, he should esteem himself the most happy man living, and he would wait whatever time I thought most convenient for it. I replied, I thought it was unreasonable to urge me to promise that which 'ere[48] long he might repent the asking, but this I would promise to satisfy him: that I would not marry until I saw him first married. He kissed my hand upon that with as much joy as if I had confirmed to him his greatest happiness, and said he could desire no more for he was secure I should never see nor hear of that until it was to myself. Upon this we parted both well pleased: for he thought he had gained much in what I promised, and I looked upon my promise as a cure to him but no inconvenience to myself (since I had no inclination to marry any and, though I had, a delay in it was the least return I could make to so deserving a person).

But I deceived myself by thinking this was the way to moderate his passion; for now, he gave way to it without any restraint and thought himself so secure of me as if there had been nothing to oppose it. (Though he managed it with that discretion that it was scarce visible to any within the house, not so much as either his sister or mine had the least suspicion of it; for I had enjoined[49] him not to let them or any other know what his designs were because I would not have them accessory whatever fault might be in the prosecution of it.)

Thus it continued until, towards winter, that his sister was to go home to her father again; and then, knowing he would want much of the opportunity he had to converse with me, he was then very importunate[50] to have me consent to marry him privately (which it seems he pleased[51] himself so[52] with the hopes of prevailing with me that he had provided a wedding ring and a minister to marry us).[53] I was much unsatisfied with his going that length, and, in short, told him he need never expect I would marry him without his father's and my mother's consent: if that could be obtained [fol. 4v] I should willingly give him the satisfaction he desired, but without that I could not expect God's blessing neither upon him nor me, and I would do nothing that was so certain a way to bring ruin upon us both. He used many arguments from the examples of others who had practiced the

---

48. I.e., before.

49. "To enjoin (a person) to a penalty, observance, etc.," OED.

50. "Of a person: persistent or pressing in making requests or offers, esp. to an irritating or distressing degree. Of a request, offer, etc.: made persistently or pressingly," OED.

51. After "pleased," "so" is an interlineal insertion that is also crossed out.

52. "So" is an interlineal insertion.

53. On secret or clandestine marriages and the protocols surrounding betrothals, weddings, and marriages, see David Cressy, *Birth, Marriage, and Death: Ritual, Religion, and the Life-Cycle in Tudor and Stuart England* (Oxford: Oxford University Press, 1997), esp. 316–36; Mendelson and Crawford, *Women in Early Modern England*, esp. 112–16, 124–28; and O'Hara, *Courtship and Constraint*.

same and was happy, both in their parents' favor and in one another, but finding me fixed beyond any persuasion, he resolved to acquaint my sister with it and to employ her to speak of it to his father and my mother.

She very unwillingly undertook it because she knew it would be a surprise to them and very unwelcome, but his importunity[54] prevailed. And she first acquainted my mother with it, who was so passionately offended with the proposal that (whereas his father might have been brought to have given his consent, having ever had a good opinion of me and very civil) she did so exasperate[55] him against it that nothing could satisfy her, but presently to put it to Mr. Howard's choice: either presently to marry a rich citizen's daughter that his father had designed for him or else to leave England. The reason I believe that made my mother the more incensed was, first, that it was what in the beginning of our acquaintance she had absolutely discharged[56] my having a thought of allowing such an address. And though in some respect his quality was above mine (and therefore better than any she could expect for me), yet my Lord Howard's fortune was such as had need of a more considerable portion than my mother could give me or else it must ruin his younger children.[57] And, therefore, my mother would not consent to it, though my Lord Howard did offer to do the utmost his condition would allow him if she would let me take my hazard with his son. But my mother would not be persuaded to it upon [fol. 5r] no consideration, lest any should have thought it was begun with her allowance. And to take away the suspicion of that did, I believe, make her the more violent in opposing it and the more severe to me.

My sister made choice of Sunday to speak of it first, because she thought that day might put them both in a calmer frame to hear her and confine their passion (since it would be the next day before they would determine anything). But finding, both by my mother and my Lord Howard, that they intended nothing but to part us so as never to meet again except it was as strangers, Mr. Howard was very importunate[58] to have an opportunity to speak with me that night, which I gave. My sister being only with me, we came down together to the room I appointed to meet with him. I confess I never saw those two passions of love and regret more truly represented, nor could any person express greater affection and resolution of constancy (which with many oaths he sealed) of never loving or marrying any but

---

54. I.e., persistence.

55. "To embitter, intensify (ill feeling, passion, wickedness) or "to irritate (a person); to provoke to anger; to enrage, incense," *OED*.

56. "To forbid (a person, etc.) to do something; to ban from doing; to prohibit (an action, practice, etc.)," *OED*.

57. In addition to Thomas and Anne, Howard had another son, William, who survived both his father and his brother. Richard L. Greaves, "Howard, William, Third Baron Howard of Escrick (ca. 1630–1694)," *ODNB*.

58. "Of a person: persistent or pressing in making requests or offers, esp. to an irritating or distressing degree. Of a request, offer, etc.: made persistently or pressingly," *OED*.

myself. I was not satisfied with his swearing to future performances, since, I said, both he and I might find it most convenient to retract, but this I did assure him, "as long as he was constant he should never find a change in me. For though duty did oblige me not to marry any without my mother's consent, yet it would not tie me to marry without my own."

My sister, at this, rises and said, "I did not think you would have engaged me to be a witness of both your resolutions to continue what I expected you would rather have laid aside, and therefore I will leave you."

"Oh Madam," said he, "can you imagine I love at that rate as to have it shaken with any storm? No, were I secure [fol. 5v] your sister would not suffer in my absence by her mother's severity, I would not care what misery I were exposed to, but to think I should be the occasion of trouble to the person in the earth that I love most is unsupportable."

And with that he fell down in a chair that was behind him but as one without all sense, which I must confess did so much move me that, laying aside all former distance I had kept him at, I sat down upon his knee, and laying my head near his, I suffered him to kiss me, which was a liberty I never gave before (nor had not then, had I not seen him so overcome with grief, which I endeavored to suppress with all the encouragement I could, but still pressing him to be obedient to his father either in going abroad or staying at home as he thought most convenient).

"No," says he, "since they will not allow me to converse with you, France will be more agreeable to me than England; nor will I go there, except I have liberty to come here again and take my leave of you."

To that I could not disagree if they thought fit to allow it, and so my sister and I left him, but she durst[59] not own to my mother where she had been.

The next morning early my Lord Howard went away, and took with him his son and daughter, and left me[60] to the severities of my offended mother, who nothing could pacify. After she had called for me (and said as many bitter things as passion could dictate upon such a subject), she discharged[61] me to see him, and did solemnly vow that if she should hear I did see Mr. Howard she would turn me out of her doors and never own me again. All I [fol. 6r] said to that part was, that it should be against my will if ever she heard of it.

Upon Tuesday, my Lord Howard writ[62] to my mother that he had determined to send his son[63] to France, and that upon Thursday after he was to begin his journey; but all he desired before he went was to have liberty to see me, which

---

59. Past tense of "dare."

60. "Me" is an interlineal insertion.

61. "To forbid (a person, etc.) to do something; to ban from doing; to prohibit (an action, practice, etc.)," *OED*.

62. I.e., "wrote."

63. After "son," "away" has been deleted.

he thought was a satisfaction could not be denied him; and therefore desired my mother's consent to it, which she gave (upon the condition that he should only come in and take his leave of me, but not to have any converse but what she should be a witness of herself). This would not at all please Mr. Howard, and therefore he[64] seemed to lay the desire of it aside. In the meantime, my chamber and liberty of lying alone was taken from me, and my sister's woman was to be my guardian, who watched sufficiently so that I had not the least opportunity—either day or night—to be without her. Upon Thursday morning early my mother sent a man of my sister's (whose name I must mention with the rest that at that [time] was in the family, for there was Moses, Aaron and Miriam[65] all at one time in it, and none either related or acquainted together until they met there); this[66] Moses was sent[67] to my Lord Howard with a letter to enquire if his son were gone.

I must here relate a little odd encounter which aggravated my misfortune. There came no return until night, and having got liberty to walk in the hall, my mother sent a child of my sister's and bid him walk with me and keep me company.[68] I had not been there a quarter of an hour but my maid, Miriam, came to me and told me [fol. 6v] she was walking at the back gate, and Mr. Howard came to her and sent her to desire me to come there and speak but two or three words with him; for he had sworn not to go away without seeing me, nor would he come in to see my mother (for he had left London that morning very early and had rid up and down that part of the country only until it was the gloom of the evening to have the more privacy in coming to see me). I bid her go back and tell him I durst[69] not see him because of my mother's oath and her discharge. While she was pressing me to run to the gate and I was near to take the start,[70] the child cried out, "O my Aunt is going," which stopped me, and I sent her[71] away to tell the reason why I could not come.

---

64. "He" is an interlineal insertion.

65. The servants' biblical names reinforce the notion that Halkett's sister's home was a holy and well-governed household. Books on household organization abounded in the seventeenth century, one of the most famous being John Dod and Robert Cleaver, *A Godly Form of Houshold Government, for the Ordering of Private Families, According to the Direction of God's Word* (London: Thomas Man, 1630). ESTC S117160. For a discussion of how this worked in practice, see R. C. Richardson, "Social Engineering in Early Modern England: Masters, Servants, and the Godly Discipline," *Clio* 33, no. 2 (2004): 163–87.

66. "This" is an interlineal insertion.

67. "Was sent" is an interlineal insertion.

68. Sir Charles Newton, later Puckering, and Elizabeth Murray had four sons, all of whom predeceased their father. Broadway, "Puckering [Newton], Sir Henry," *ODNB*.

69. Past tense of "dare."

70. "To decamp, run away," *OED*.

71. I.e., Miriam.

I still stayed walking in the hall until she returned, wondering she stayed so long. When she came, she was hardly able to speak, and with great disorder said, "I believe you are the most unfortunate person living, for I think Mr. Howard is killed." Anyone that hath ever known what gratitude was, may imagine how these words disordered me. But impatient to know how (I was resolved to hazard my mother's displeasure rather than not see him), she told me that while she was telling him my answer, there came a fellow with a great club behind him and struck him down dead, and others had seized upon Mr. Tindall (who formerly had been his governor and was now entrusted to see him safe on shipboard) and his man.[72] The reason of this was from what there was too many sad examples of at that time, when the division was betwixt the King and Parliament, for to betray a master or a friend [fol. 7r] was looked upon as doing God good service.

My brother-in-law, Sir Henry Newton,[73] had been long from home in attendance on the King, for whose service he had raised a troop of horse upon his own expense and had upon all occasions testified his loyalty (for which all his estate was sequestered, and, with much difficulty, my sister got liberty to live in her own house and had the fifth part to live upon, which was obtained with importunity).[74] There was one of my brother's tenants called Musgrove, who was a very great rogue, who farmed my brother's land of the Parliament and was employed by them as a spy to discover any of the Cavaliers[75] that should come within his knowledge. He, observing three gentlemen[76] upon good horse, scouting about all day and keeping at a distance from the highway, apprehends it was my brother who had come privately home to see my sister and resolves to watch when he came near the house. And had followed so close as to come behind and give Mr. Howard that stroke, thinking it had been my brother Newton, and seized upon his governor and servant (the post boy[77] being left at some distance with the horses). In the midst of this disorder, Moses came there, and, Miriam having told what the occasion of it was, he told Musgrove it was my Lord Howard's son he had used so. Upon which he and his accomplices went immediately away, and Moses and Mr. Howard's man carried him into an alehouse hard by, and laid him on a bed, where he lay sometime before he came to himself.

---

72. Identified as John F. Tindall, Thomas Howard's Tutor at Corpus Christi College, Cambridge. Loftis, ed., *The Memoirs of Anne, Lady Halkett and Anne, Lady Fanshawe*, 194.

73. Broadway, "Puckering [Newton], Sir Henry," *ODNB*.

74. Halkett has deleted "difficulty" and replaced it with "importunity," which is used here in the sense of "perseverance or persistence of action; determination, stubbornness," *OED*. Many Royalists had their lands sequestered during the Commonwealth and Protectorate.

75. "A name given to those who fought on the side of Charles I in the war between him and the Parliament; a seventeenth-century Royalist," *OED*.

76. Here, an interlineal insertion of "and a" has been deleted.

77. "A person who rides a posthorse, a post boy; (more generally) a courier, a swift messenger," *OED*.

So, hearing all was quiet again, and that he had no hurt only stonished[78] with the blow, I went into the room where I had left my mother and sister, which, being at a good distance[79] [fol. 7v] from the back gate, they had heard nothing of the tumult that had been there. A little after Moses came in and delivered a letter from my Lord Howard which, after my mother had read, she asked, "What news at London?" He answered, the greatest he could tell was that Mr. Howard went away that morning early post to Dieppe and was going to France, but he could not learn the reason of it. My mother and sister seemed to wonder of it, for none in the family (except my maid) knew anything that had fallen out or had any suspicion that I was concerned in it but my mother and sister.

After Moses went out, my mother asked me if I was not ashamed to think that it would be said my Lord Howard was forced to send away his son to secure him from me. I said I could not but regret whatever had occasioned her displeasure or his punishment, but I was guilty of no unhandsome[80] action to make me ashamed; and, therefore, whatever were my present misfortune, I was confident to evidence before I died that no child she had, had greater love and respect to her, or more obedience. To which she replied, "It seems you have a good opinion of yourself!"

My mother now believing Mr. Howard gone, I was not, as former nights, sent to my bed and the guard upon me that was usual. But I stayed in my mother's chamber until she and my sister (who lay together) was a-bed. In the meantime, Mr. Howard had sent for Moses and told him, whatever misfortune he might suffer by his stay there, he was fully determined not to go away without seeing me; and desired I would come to the banqueting house in the garden, and he would come to the window and speak to me, which he told me (and withal that Mr. Tindall, who was a very serious, good man, did earnestly entreat[81] [fol. 8r] me to condescend to his desire to prevent what might be more inconvenient to us both). I sent him word when my mother was a-bed I would contrive some way to satisfy him, but not where he proposed because it was within the view of my mother's chamber window.

After I had left my mother and sister in their bed, I went alone in the dark through my brother's closet to the chamber where I lay, and as I entered the room, I laid my hand upon my eyes, and with a sad sigh, said, "was ever creature so unfortunate and put to such a sad difficulty: either to make Mr. Howard forsworn if he sees me not, or if I do see him, my mother will be forsworn if she doth not expose me to the utmost rigor her anger can invent?" In the midst of this dispute with myself what I should do, my hand being still upon my eyes, it presently came

---

78. "To stun mentally, shock, or surprise," *OED*.
79. "Distance" in an insertion in the bottom right-hand margin.
80. "Unfitting, unbecoming, unseemly; discourteous, mean," *OED*.
81. "Entreat" is a subscript interlineal insertion, replacing the deletion of "desire."

in my mind: that if I blindfolded my eyes, that would secure me from seeing him, and so I did not transgress against my mother; and he might that way satisfy himself by speaking with me. I had as much joy in finding out this means to yield to him without disquiet to myself, as if it had been of more considerable consequence.[82] Immediately, I sent Moses to tell him upon what conditions I would speak with him: first, that he must allow me to have my eyes covered and that he should bring Mr. Tindall with him; and if thus he were satisfied, I ordered him to bring them in the back way into the cellar where I, with Miriam, would meet them the other way, which they did.

As soon as Mr. Howard saw me, he much importuned[83] the taking away the covert from my eyes, which I not suffering, he left disputing that to employ the little time he had in regretting my not yielding to his importunity to marry him [fol. 8v] before his affection was discovered to his father and my mother; for had it been once past their power to undo, they would been sooner satisfied, and we might have been happy together and not endured this sad separation. I told him I was sorry for being the occasion of his discontent, but I could not repent the doing my duty whatever ill success it had; for I ever looked upon marrying without consent of parents as the highest act of ingratitude and disobedience that children could commit, and I resolved never to be guilty of it. I found his greatest trouble was the fear he had that my mother, in his absence, would force me to marry M L (who was a gentleman of a good fortune who some people thought had a respect for me).[84] To this I gave him as much assurance as I could that neither he, nor any other person living, should lessen his interest until he gave me reason for it himself. It is unnecessary to repeat the solemn oaths he made never to love nor marry any other; for, as I did not approve of it then, so I will not now aggravate his crime by mentioning them (but there was nothing he left unsaid that could express a sincere, virtuous, true affection).

Mr. Tindall (who with Moses and Miriam had all this time been so civil to us both as to retire at such a distance as not to hear what we said) came and interrupted him, and desired him to take his leave lest longer stay might be prejudicial to us[85] all. I called for a bottle of wine, and giving Mr. Tindall thanks for his civility and care, drunk to him, wishing a good and happy journey to Mr. Howard. So,

---

82. "As Louis Potter has noted, the blindfold ploy was also employed in Cowley's *The Guardian* (1641) in which the female protagonist Lucia wears a veil to prevent her beloved Truman from breaking his oath, forced by his father, not to see him again"; Lamb, "Merging the Secular and the Spiritual in Lady Anne Halkett's Memoirs," 85. See also Louis Potter, *Secret Rites and Secret Writing: Royalist Literature, 1641–1660* (Cambridge: Cambridge University Press, 1989), 108.

83. "To ask or request something of (a person) persistently or pressingly; to accost with questions or requests; to beg, beseech," *OED*.

84. This is the only reference to this potential suitor in the *True Account*, and I have been unable to identify him or trace any further references to him in her other writings.

85. After "us," "both" has been deleted and replaced by "all."

taking a farewell of them both, I went up the [fol. 9r] way I came, and left them to Moses's care to conduct them out quietly, as he led them in. (This was upon Thursday night, October 10, 1644.)[86] This was not so secretly done but some of the house observed more noise than ordinarily used to be at that time of night, and, by satisfying their curiosity in looking out, discovered the occasion of it. But they were all so just as none of them ever acquainted my mother with it, though I did not conceal it from my sister the first opportunity I had to be alone with her.

I was in hopes, after some time that Mr. Howard was gone, my mother would have received me into her favor again, but the longer time she had to consider of my fault the more she did[87] aggravate[88] it. And though my Lord Howard (who returned shortly after with his daughter) and my sister did use all the arguments imaginable to persuade her to be reconciled to me, yet nothing would prevail: except I would solemnly promise never to think more of Mr. Howard, and that I would marry another whom she thought fit to propose. To which I begged her pardon, for until Mr. Howard was first married, I was fully determined to marry no person living. She asked me if I was such a fool as to believe he would be constant. I said I did, but if he were not, it should be his fault not mine, for I resolved not to make him guilty by example.

Many more were employed to speak to me: some used good words, some ill. But one that was most severe, after I had heard her with much patience rail[89] a long time, when she could say no more, I gave a true account how innocent I was from having any design upon Mr. Howard, and related what I have already mentioned of the progress of his affection; which [fol. 9v] when she heard, she sadly wept, and begged my pardon, and promised to do me all the service she could. And I believe she did, for she had much influence upon my Lord Howard (having been with his Lady[90] from a child), and did give so good a character of me and my proceedings in that affair with his son that he again made an offer to my mother to send for his son if she would consent to the marriage. But she would not hear it spoken of but said she rather I was buried than bring so much ruin to the family she honored.

---

86. The sentence in brackets is an insertion in the bottom margin of fol. 8v.
87. "Did" is an interlineal insertion.
88. "To increase the gravity or seriousness of (suffering, a problem, etc.), to make more grievous or burdensome; to make worse, intensify, exacerbate," OED.
89. "To rant at, harangue," OED.
90. Howard's wife, Mary Boetler, who was "the fifth daughter of Sir John (later first Baron) Boteler of Brantfield, and his wife, Elizabeth, who was Buckingham's sister," died in January 1633/4. Stater, "Howard, Edward," ODNB.

My mother's anger against me increased to that height that for fourteen[91] months she never gave me her blessing, nor never spoke to me but when it was to reproach me, and one day said, with much bitterness, she did hate to see me. That word I confess struck deeply to my heart and put me to my thoughts what way to dispose of myself to free my mother from such an object. After many debates with myself and enquiries what life I could take to that was most innocent, I resolved, and writ to Sir Patrick Drummond, a cousin of my mother's, who was conservator in Holland,[92] to do me the favor to inform me if it was true (that I had heard) that there was a nunnery in Holland for those of the Protestant religion. And that he would enquire upon what conditions they admitted any to their society, because if they were consistent with my religion, I did resolve upon his advertisement[93] immediately to go over, and desired him to hasten an answer, and not divulge to any what I had writ to him.

About a fortnight after, my mother sent for me one morning into her chamber and examined me what I had writ to Sir Patrick [fol. 10r] Drummond. I ingeniously[94] gave her an account and the reason of it; for, since I found nothing would please her that I could do, I was resolved to go where I could most please myself (which was in a solitary, retired life), and so free her from the sight she hated. And since it was upon that consideration, I did not doubt the obtaining her consent. It seems Sir Patrick Drummond, who was a wise and honest gentleman (apprehending discontent had made me take that resolution which I had writ to him about), instead of answering my letter, writes to my mother a very handsome, serious letter acquainting her with my intention, and concluded it could proceed from nothing but her severity, perhaps upon unjust grounds. And therefore, used many arguments to persuade her to return to that wonted[95] kindness which she had ever showed to all her children, and that he was sure I would deserve whatever opinion she had lately entertained to the contrary. This he pressed with so much of reason and earnestness that it prevailed more with my mother than whatever had been

---

91. In the original manuscript, it is possible to see that Halkett initially wrote "thirteene." There is an attempt in her own hand to overwrite "thir" with "four," as well as the interlineal insertion of the number "14." However, in her discussion of "1 Corinthians 15:58," she says it was "thirteen months," 317.

92. A "Conservator" was "an officer appointed to protect the rights and settle the disputes of Scottish merchants in foreign ports or places of trade," *OED*. Like Halkett's mother, Sir Patrick was descended from the Drummonds of Blair Drummond. He had been one of Charles I's ushers and was "then preferred to be Conservator for the Scots at the staple of Camphere, in the Low Countries, where he lived to a great age, in much credit and honor." William Drummond, *The Genealogy of the Most Noble and Ancient House of Drummond by the Honorable William Drummond* (Edinburgh: A Balfour & Co., 1831), 115.

93. "The action of informing or notifying," *OED*.

94. While this may appear to indicate some deception on Halkett's part, in early modern English the word meant "freedom from dissimulation; honesty, straightforwardness, sincerity," *OED*.

95. "Customary, or usual," *OED*.

said before. And from that time, she received me again to her favor and ever after used me more like a friend than a child.[96]

In the meantime, all care was used that might prevent Mr. Howard's correspondence and mine. But he found an excuse for sending home his man, believing him honest and faithful to him, and with him he writ and sent me a present; but instead of delivering them to me gave them to his father, who other ways disposed of them. Yet in requital I sent back with him a ring with five rubies, and gave him something for his pains when he came to me and endeavored to vindicate himself by protesting that, unexpectedly, he was searched as soon as ever he entered his Lord's house, and all was taken from him. But I found afterwards he was not so honest as I believed: for he never delivered my ring to his master, nor anything I entrusted him with.

At this time, my Lord Howard had a sister in France, who gloried much of her wit, and contrivance, and used to say she never designed anything but she accomplished it.[97] My Lord Howard thought she was the fittest [fol. 10v] person to divert his son from his *amour*, and to her, he writes and recommends it to her management: who was not negligent of what she was entrusted with, as appeared in the conclusion, though her carriage[98] was a great disappointment to Mr. Howard, for he expected by her mediation to have obtained what he desired, and that made him the more willing to comply with her (who designed her own advantage by this to oblige her brother, who might be the more useful to her in a projected marriage she had for her own son).[99]

Upon Thursday, February 13, 1645/6, word was brought to my mother that the Countess of Banbury was come out of France and Mr. Howard with her, which was a great surprise to her and all his relations. My mother examined me if I had sent for him or knew anything of his coming which I assured her I had not, and she said not much more. But I was as much disturbed as any: sometimes thinking he was come with an assurance from his aunt that she would accomplish what he had so passionately desired; or else that he had laid all thoughts of me aside and was come with a resolution to comply with his father's desires. The last opinion

---

96. Halkett revisits this episode in "1 Corinthians 15:58," 317.
97. Later named as the Countess of Banbury. Elizabeth (Howard) Knollys Vaux, countess of Banbury, the second wife of William Knollys, first Earl of Banbury, who was in France between 1643 and 1644. Victor Stater, "Knollys, William, First Earl of Banbury (ca. 1545–1632)," *ODNB*.
98. Used here in the now obsolete sense of "manner or way of conducting or managing (an affair)," *OED*.
99. The paternity of her sons, Edward and Nicholas, has been doubted because of the Countess's relationship with Edward Vaux, whom she married five weeks after her first husband's death. Although Edward was named second Earl of Banbury (1641), he was unmarried at the time of his murder in France sometime in June 1645. His brother, Nicholas, became the third Earl of Banbury, 1646. He married Lady Isabella Blount, whose mother, Anne Boteler, was sister to Edward Howard, first Baron Howard of Escrick's wife, Mary. Stater, "Knollys, William," *ODNB*; *TCP* 1:401–5.

I was a little confirmed in: having never received any word or letter from him in ten days after his return, and meeting him accidentally where I was walking, he crossed the way; and another time was in the room where I came in to visit some young ladies, and neither of these times took any notice of me more than of one I had never seen. I confess I was a little disordered at it but made no conclusions until I saw what time would produce.

Upon Tuesday, March 4, my Lady Anne Walsingham,[100] his cousin, came to my mother's, and having stayed a convenient time for a visit with my mother (for then it was not usual for mothers and daughters to be visited apart), I waited on her down. And taking me aside, she told me she was desired by her cousin (Thomas Howard) to present his most faithful service to me, and to desire me not [fol. 11r] to take it ill that he did not speak to me when he met me; for, finding his aunt not his friend as he expected, he seemed to comply with her desire only to have the opportunity of coming home with her, and had resolved for a time to forbear all converse with me, and to make love to all that came in his way.[101] But assured me it was only to make his friends think he had forgot me, and then he might with the less suspicion prosecute his design, which was never to love or marry any but me. "And this," she said, "he confirmed with all the solemn oaths imaginable."

In pursuance of this, he visited all the young ladies about the town. But an Earl's daughter[102] gave him the most particular welcome, whose mother, not allowing him to come as a pretender,[103] she made appointment with him and met him at her cousin's house frequently, which I knew and he made sport of. The summer being now advancing, my mother and her family[104] went with my sister to her house in the country,[105] which being not far from London we heard often how affairs went there; and, amongst other discourse, that it was reported Mr. Howard was in love with my Lady Elizabeth Mordaunt and she with him. At which, some smiled, and said: it might be her wit had taken him but certainly not

---

100. Lady Anne Walsingham (1631–1695), fourth daughter of Theophilus Howard, second Earl of Suffolk, and therefore niece to Thomas Howard's father, and wife to Colonel Thomas Walsingham. Loftis, ed., *The Memoirs of Anne, Lady Halkett and Anne, Lady Fanshawe*, 21, 193, 270. See also Stater, "Howard, Theophilus," *ODNB*.

101. "To pay amorous attention; to court, woo," *OED*.

102. Elizabeth Mordaunt, daughter of John Mordaunt, first Earl of Peterborough (1599–1643), and his wife, Elizabeth Howard, *BP* 2.2772.

103. While this term could be used for a genuine "suitor" or "wooer," in this context it also carries the suggestion that Howard might be pretending to court Mordaunt, and therefore be a "pretender" in the sense of "a person who lays claim to an ability, quality, skill, etc., esp. without adequate grounds or with intent to deceive; a charlatan; a dissembler," *OED*.

104. Used here in the early modern sense of referring to Drummond-Murray's "household," that is, those who lived with her (including her daughter Anne and her servants).

105. I.e., Charlton.

her beauty (for she had as little of that as myself). Though these reports put me upon my guard, yet I confess I did not believe he was real in his address there; neither did his sister, who was sometimes a witness of their converse and gave me account of it. But I approved not of his way, for I thought it could not but reflect upon himself, and injure either that Lady, or me.

But she took a way to secure herself; for upon the last Tuesday in July 1646, a little before supper, I received a letter from Mrs. H (a particular friend of mine)[106] who wrote me word that upon the Tuesday before Mr. Howard was privately married to my Lady Elizabeth Mordaunt, and the relations of both sides was unsatisfied.[107] I was alone in my sister's chamber when I read the letter, and flinging myself down [fol. 11v] upon her bed, I said, "Is this the man for whom I have suffered so much? Since he hath made himself unworthy my love, he is unworthy my anger or concern." And rising immediately, I went out into the next room to my supper as unconcernedly as if I had never had an interest in him, nor had never lost it.

A little after, my mother came to the knowledge of it from my Lord Howard, who was much discontented at his son's marriage and often wished he had had his former choice. Nothing troubled me more than my mother's laughing at me (and, perhaps, so did others), but all I said was I thought he had injured himself more than me, and that I much rather he had done it than I. And once I confess, in passion, being provoked by something I had heard, I said (with too much seriousness), "I pray God he may never die in peace until he confesses his fault and ask me forgiveness." But I acknowledge this as a fault and have a hundred times begged the Lord's pardon for it; for though in some respects it might be justified as wishing him repentance, yet many circumstances might make it impossible for me to be a witness of it. And God forbid that any should want peace for my passion.

When Miriam first heard he was married, she lifted up her hands, and said, "Give her, O Lord, dry breasts and a miscarrying womb,"[108] which I reproved her for. But it seems the Lord thought fit to grant her request, for that Lady miscarried of several children before she brought one to the full time, and that one died presently after it was born;[109] which may be a lesson to teach people to govern their wishes and their tongue (that neither may act to the prejudice of any lest it

---

106. It has not been possible to trace this individual.

107. The marriage took place on July 21, 1646, BP 2.2772.

108. Hosea 9:14: "Give them, O Lord: what wilt thou give? give them a miscarrying womb and dry breasts."

109. Howard and Mordaunt had at least four children: Henry, Francis, Lewis, and Frances. Francis and Frances survived to marriageable age. Despite the travails of childbirth, Elizabeth lived until August 9, 1716, and thus survived her husband, who died on August 24, 1678, BP 2.2772.

be placed on their account at the day of reckoning).[110] Not only was this couple unfortunate in the children but in one another, for it was too well known how short a time continued the satisfaction they had in one another. Nor did his aunt, the Countess of Banbury, who first put him upon . . .

One leaf (two pages) missing from the manuscript.[111]

[fol. 12 r] . . . time and not the worse that he[112] professed to have great friendship for my brother Will.

This gentleman[113] came to see me, sometimes in the company of ladies who had been my mother's neighbors in St. Martin's Lane, and sometimes alone. But whenever he came, his discourse was serious, handsome,[114] and tending to impress the advantages of piety, loyalty, and virtue; and these subjects were so agreeable to my own inclination that I could not but give them a good reception, especially from one that seemed to be so much an owner of them himself. After I had been used to freedom of discourse with him, I told him I approved[115] of his advice to others, but I thought his own practice contradicted much of his profession; for one of his acquaintance had told me, he had not seen his wife[116] in a twelve month, and it was impossible in my opinion for a good man to be an ill husband, and therefore he must defend himself from one before I could believe the other of him. He said it was not necessary to give everyone[117] that might condemn him

---

110. Matthew 12:36–37: "But I say unto you, that every idle word that men shall speak, they shall give account thereof in the day of Judgment. For by thy words thou shalt be justified, and by thy words thou shalt be condemned."

111. While we cannot know what Halkett wrote on these pages, it seems unlikely that she passed over her mother's death, August 28, 1647, without comment. Couper certainly suggests that she spent some time resolving "to walk more circumspectly"; *The Life of the Lady Halket*, 14–15. Reflecting on the death of one of her stepdaughters, she hopes that her daughters be preserved "from what I met with after my mother's death, from which I may date all my misfortunes"; "Saturday, November 26, 1687," Halkett, *Meditations on St. Peter*, p. 335. According to Couper, after her mother's death, Halkett lived with her brother Henry and his wife for about a year, but he does not clarify whether that was in Whitefriars or Kent, *The Life of the Lady Halket*, 15.

112. I.e., Colonel Joseph Bampfield. See Marshall, "Bampfield, Joseph," *ODNB*. See also Loftis and Hardacre, eds., *Colonel Joseph Bampfield's Apology*; Smith, *Royalist Agents, Conspirators, and Spies*, 14, 17; and "Introduction," 24–26.

113. I.e., Colonel Joseph Bampfield.

114. "Of action, speech, etc.: appropriate, fitting; deft, clever," *OED*.

115. After "approved," "much" has been deleted.

116. Bampfield's wife was Catherine Sydenham (1622–1657), daughter of John Sydenham (1589–1627) of Brympton, Somerset. They were married before February 1, 1642/3. Loftis and Hardacre, eds., *Colonel Joseph Bampfield's Apology*, 18, 250.

117. "One" is an interlineal correction.

the reason of his being so long from her; yet to satisfy me, he would tell me the truth, which was that (he being engaged in the King's service) he was obliged to be at London where it was not convenient for her to be with him (his stay in any place being uncertain). Besides, she lived amongst her friends, who though they were kind to her, yet were not so to him (for most of that country[118] had declared for the Parliament and were enemies to all that had, or did, serve the King); and therefore, his wife, he was sure, would not condemn him for what he did by her own consent. This seeming reasonable, I did insist no more upon that subject.

[fol. 12v] At this time he had frequent letters from the King[119] who employed him in several affairs, but that of the greatest concern which he was employed in was to contrive the Duke of York's[120] escape out of St. James's (where his Highness, and the Duke of Gloucester,[121] and the Princess Elizabeth[122] lived under the care of the Earl of Northumberland and his Lady).[123] The difficulties of it was represented by Colonel Bampfield, but his Majesty still pressed it. And I remember this expression was in one of the letters: "*I believe it will be difficult, and, if he miscarry in the attempt, it will be the greatest affliction that can arrive to me. But I look upon James's escape as Charles's preservation and nothing can content me more. Therefore, be careful what you do.*"[124]

---

118. I.e., the county of Somerset. In early modern usage, "country" could refer either to the nation or to "an area of land of defined extent characterized by its human occupants or boundaries; a district or administrative region, typically one smaller than a nation or state; esp. a county," *OED*.

119. I.e., Charles I; see Kishlansky, and Morrill, "Charles I," *ODNB*. Some of the letters are reproduced in Loftis and Hardacre, eds., *Colonel Joseph Bampfield's Apology*, 69–70. See also Smith, *Royalist Agents, Conspirators, and Spies*, 105.

120. The Duke of York (1633–1701), who later became James VII/II. W. A. Speck, "James II and VII (1633–1701), King of England, Scotland, and Ireland," *ODNB*.

121. The Duke of Gloucester was Charles I's third son, Henry (1639–1660), who was eventually allowed to go to the Continent. Soon after his return at the Restoration he died of smallpox. Handley, "Henry, Prince," *ODNB*. See also, "Upon the Fast which by Proclamation Was Kept, January 30, 1660/1," 203–5.

122. The Princess Elizabeth, Charles I's second daughter, was later imprisoned in Carisbrooke castle on the Isle of Wight and died there on September 8, 1650. Goodwin, "Elizabeth, Princess," *ODNB*.

123. The Earl of Northumberland was the tenth Earl, Algernon Percy, who was by this time married to his second wife, Lady Anne Howard, daughter of the second Earl of Suffolk. George A. Drake, "Percy, Algernon, Tenth Earl of Northumberland (1602–1668)," *ODNB*; Stater, "Howard, Theophilus," *ODNB*.

124. King Charles I had been planning his son's escape "as far back as . . . September 1646, and since that time there had been several abortive designs which had come to nothing. By early 1648 the need to rescue James had become urgent, as one of the possible solutions to the deadlock in negotiations that was being seriously considered by the army leaders was to depose Charles and put James in his place as a puppet king"; Smith, *Royalist Agents, Conspirators, and Spies*, 105. Bampfield reproduces several letters in his *Apologie* but not this one; Halkett refers to it again in her meditation upon "1 Corinthians 15:58," 318. Bampfield, *Colonel Joseph Bamfield's [sic]Apologie Written by Himself and Printed at His Desire* (The Hague? [s. n.], 1685). ESTC R16264.

This letter amongst others he showed me, and where the King approved of his choice of me to entrust with it for to get the Duke's clothes made, and[125] to dress him in his disguise. So now all Colonel Bampfield's business and care was how to manage this business of so important concern, which could not be performed without several persons' concurrence in it. For he being generally known as one whose stay[126] at London was in order to serve the King, few of those who were entrusted by the Parliament in public concerns durst[127] own converse or hardly civility to him (lest they should have been suspect by their party, which made it difficult for him to get access to the Duke). But to be short: having communicated the design to a gentleman attending his Highness,[128] who was full of honor and fidelity, by his means he had private access to the Duke; to whom he presented the King's letter by order to his Highness for consenting to act what Colonel Bampfield [fol. 13r] should contrive for his escape, which was so cheerfully entertained and so readily obeyed that, being once designed, there was nothing more to do than to prepare all things for the execution.[129]

I had desired him to take a ribbon with him and bring me the bigness of the Duke's waist and his length to have clothes made fit for him. In the meantime, Colonel Bampfield was to provide money for all necessary expense, which was furnished by an honest citizen.[130] When I gave the measure to my tailor to enquire how much mohair[131] would serve to make a petticoat and waistcoat to a young gentlewoman of that bigness and stature, he considered it a long time; and said he had made many gowns and suits, but he had never made any to such a person in

---

125. "And" is an interlineal insertion.

126. "Stay" is an interlineal insertion replacing the deletion of "being."

127. Past tense of "dare."

128. According to James VII/II's memoirs, this gentleman was "Mr. George Howard, brother to the Earl of Suffolk who at that time was his master of horse" and who communicated verbally with Bampfield, "which was all the part he had in the employment." Clarke, ed., *The Life of James the Second, King of England &c.*, 1:33–34. George Howard was therefore the brother of the third Earl of Suffolk, James Howard, who succeeded to the title in 1640. Richard Minta Dunn, "Howard, James, Third Earl of Suffolk (1619–1689)," *ODNB*. Howard's name, and position as master of the horse, is also mentioned in a letter from the King reproduced by Bampfield. See Loftis and Hardacre, eds., *Colonel Joseph Bampfield's Apology*, 70. See also Smith, *Royalist Agents, Conspirators, and Spies*, 105.

129. Bampfield's version of these events does not mention Halkett, although he does mention later that her brother Will acts as a messenger between him and the King. Loftis and Hardacre, eds., *Colonel Joseph Bampfield's Apology*, 69–70, 76, 79. While Bampfield's narrative includes many letters from the King, none of them contain the exact phrases Halkett recalls above.

130. The anonymous donor was very generous, for "there is a record of receipts for £20,000 and of disbursements for £19,559." Loftis, ed., *The Memoirs of Anne, Lady Halkett and Anne, Lady Fanshawe*, 196.

131. "Fabric or yarn made from the hair of the Angora goat, typically mixed with wool, cotton, etc.," *OED*.

his life. I thought he was in the right; but his meaning was, he had never seen any woman of so low a stature have so big a waist. However, he made it as exactly fit as if he had taken the measure himself. (It was a mixed mohair of a light hair color, and black, and the underpetticoat was scarlet.)

All things being now ready, upon April 20, 1648, in the evening was the time resolved on for the Duke's escape. And, in order to that, it was designed for a week before, every night as soon as the Duke had supped, he and those servants that attended his Highness (until the Earl of Northumberland and the rest of the house had supped) went to a play called "Hide and Seek." And sometimes he would hide himself so well that in half an hour's time they could not find him. His Highness had so used them to this, that when he went really away, they thought he was but at the usual sport. A little before the Duke went to supper that night, he called for the gardener (who [fol. 13v] only had a treble key besides that which the Duke had) and bid him give him that key until his own was mended, which he did. And after his Highness had supped, he immediately called to go to the play,[132] and went down the[133] privy[134] stairs into the garden, and opened the gate that goes into the park, treble locking all the doors behind him. And at the garden gate, Colonel Bampfield waited for his Highness, and (putting on a cloak and periwig)[135] hurried him away to the park gate where a coach waited that carried them to the waterside; and, taking the boat that was appointed for that service, they rowed to the stairs next the bridge (where I and Miriam waited in a private house hard by that Colonel Bampfield had prepared for dressing his Highness, where all things were in a readiness).

But I had many fears; for Colonel Bampfield had desired me—if they came not there precisely by ten o'clock—to shift[136] for myself, for then I might conclude they were discovered and so my stay there could do[137] no good but[138] prejudice myself. Yet this did not make me leave the house though ten o'clock did strike, and he that was entrusted often went to the landing place, and saw no boat coming was much discouraged, and asked me what I would do. I told him I came there with a resolution to serve his Highness, and I was fully determined not to leave that place until I was out of hopes of doing what I came there for and would take my hazard. He left me to go again to the waterside, and while I was fortifying myself against what might arrive to me, I heard a great noise of many (as I

---

132. The phrase "called to go to the play" is an interlineal insertion.
133. "The" is an interlineal insertion.
134. I.e., private.
135. A "highly stylized wig," *OED*.
136. "To provide for one's own safety, interests, or livelihood; to depend on one's own efforts," *OED*.
137. "Do" is an interlineal insertion.
138. Used here in the early modern sense of "only."

thought) coming upstairs, which I expected to be soldiers to take me. But it was a pleasing disappointment; for the first that came in was the Duke who, with much joy, I took in my arms and gave God thanks for his safe arrival.[139] [fol. 14r] His Highness called, "Quickly, quickly dress me," and putting off his clothes I dressed him in the women's habit that was prepared (which fitted his Highness very well and was very pretty in it).

After he had eaten something I made ready while I was idle, lest his Highness should be hungry, and having sent for a Wood Street cake[140] (which I knew he loved) to take in the barge, with as much haste as could be his Highness went across the bridge to the stairs where the barge lay (Colonel Bampfield leading him). And immediately the boatmen plied the oar so well that they were soon out of sight, having both wind and tide with them. But I afterwards heard the wind changed and was so contrary that Colonel Bampfield told me he was terribly afraid they should have been blown back again. And the Duke said, "Do anything with me rather than let me go back again," which put Colonel Bampfield to seek help where it was only to be had; and, after he had most fervently supplicated assistance from God, presently the wind blew fair and they came safely to their intended landing place. But I heard there was some difficulty before they got to the ship at Grave's End, which had like to have discovered them had not Colonel Washington's lady assisted them.[141]

After the Duke's barge was out of sight of the bridge, I and Miriam went where I appointed the coach to stay for me and made drive as fast as the coachman could to my brother's[142] house where I stayed. I met none in the way that gave me any apprehension that the design was discovered, nor was it noised[143] abroad

---

139. According to James's own account, he and Bampfield traveled in a hackney coach, driven by one Mr. Tripp, as far as Salisbury House, and then at Ivy-Lane took a boat "and landed again on the same side of the River close by the bridge. From thence they went into the house of one Loe a surgeon where they found Mrs. Murray, who had women's clothes in a readiness to disguise the Duke." Clarke, ed., *The Life of James the Second, King of England &c.*, 1:35. See also Smith, *Royalist Agents, Conspirators, and Spies*, 105–6.

140. "Wood Street Cake—[is] a lightly yeasted fruitcake with a rosewater icing originating in the City of London. Wood Street is just between Cheapside and Cripplegate, and, in the seventeenth century, was famous for its cakes." Erica Wagner, "The Greater British Bake-Off," *Financial Times*, November 29, 2013, accessed September 08, 2018, https://www.ft.com/content/68926c64-56f3-11e3-8cca-00144feabdc0. The article reproduces a 1675 recipe for Wood Street cake.

141. Loftis suggests that this is "probably Elizabeth, the wife of Colonel Henry Washington (1615–1664), who had served with distinction in the King's army during the Civil Wars." Loftis, ed., *The Memoirs of Anne, Lady Halkett and Anne, Lady Fanshawe*, 196.

142. I.e., her elder brother, Henry, who lived in the Whitefriars area. Couper confirms that he supplied rooms for his sister and her maid after their mother's death, *The Life of the Lady Halket*, 15.

143. "Rumored," *OED*.

until the next day.[144] For, as I related before, the Duke [fol. 14v] having used to play at hide and seek, and to conceal himself a long time, when they missed him at the same play, thought he would have discovered himself as formerly when they had given over seeking him. But a much longer time being past than usually was spent in that divertisment,[145] some began to apprehend that his Highness was gone in earnest past their finding, which made the Earl of Northumberland (to whose care he was committed)—after strict search made in the house of St. James and all thereabouts to no purpose—to send and acquaint the Speaker[146] of the House of Commons that the Duke was gone (but how or by what means he knew not, but desired that there might be orders sent to the Cinque Ports[147] for stopping all ships going out until the passengers were examined, and search made in all suspected places where his Highness might be concealed).

Though this was gone about with all the vigilancy[148] imaginable, yet it pleased God to disappoint them of their intention by so infatuating[149] those several persons who were employed for writing orders that none of them were able to writ one right, but ten or twelve of them were cast by before one was according to their mind. This account I had from Mr. Norfolk,[150] who was Macebearer to the Speaker at that time and a witness of it. This disorder of the clerks contributed much to the Duke's safety; for he was at sea before any of the orders came to the Ports and so was free from what was designed if they had taken his Highness. Though severals[151] were suspected for being accessory to the escape, yet they could not charge any with it but[152] the person who went away, and he, being out of their reach, they took no notice as either to examine or imprison others.

---

144. Isabella Twysden dates the escape to April 21, 1648. F. W. Bennitt, "The Diary of Isabella, Wife of Sir Roger Twysden, Baronet, of Roydon Hall, East Peckham, 1645–1651," *Archaeologia Cantiana* 51 (1939): 124. See also Suzanne Trill, "Re-Writing Revolution: Life-Writing in the Civil Wars," in *A History of English Autobiography*, ed. Adam Smyth (Cambridge: Cambridge University Press, 2016), 76; and Akkerman, *Invisible Agents*, 190–91.

145. "Diversion," *OED*.

146. The Speaker of the House of Commons was William Lenthall. Stephen K. Roberts, "Lenthall, William, Appointed Lord Lenthall under the Protectorate (1591–1662)," *ODNB*. Halkett returns to this event in "Monday, June 8, 1696," 299–302.

147. I.e., the five historic ports of Sandwich, Dover, New Romney, Hythe, and Hastings, which are located on the south coast of England in the counties of Kent and Sussex. The "Antient Towns" of Winchelsea and Rye are also affiliated with the Cinque Ports.

148. Obsolete form of "vigilance," *OED*.

149. "To confound, frustrate, bring to naught," *OED*.

150. In the *True Account*, Norfolk is identified only as "Mr. N." However, when recalling this incident later in life, Halkett provides his full name; see "Monday, June 8, 1696," 300.

151. "Several persons or things," *OED*.

152. I.e., "except."

After Colonel Bampfield had been so successful in serving the Duke, the Prince[153] employed him and commanded him back again to London (with several [fol. 15r] instructions that might have been serviceable to the King, had not God Almighty thought fit to blast all endeavors that might have conduced[154] to his Majesty's safety).[155] As soon as Colonel Bampfield landed beyond the Tower, he writ to desire I would do him the favor as to come to him, as being the only person who at that time he could trust; and, when he should acquaint me with the occasion of his coming, he doubted not but I would forgive him for the liberty he had taken. I, knowing he could come upon no account but in order to serve the King, I immediately sent for an honest hackney coachman (who I knew might be trusted), and taking Miriam with me, I went where he was. Who giving me a short information[156] of what he was employed about and how much secrecy was to be used (both as the King's interest and his own security), it is not to be doubted but I contributed what I could to both. And, taking him back in the coach with me, left him at a private lodging not very far from my brother's house that a servant of his had prepared for him.[157]

The earnest desire I had to serve the King made me omit no opportunity wherein I could be useful, and the zeal I had for his Majesty made me not see what inconveniencies[158] I exposed myself to; for my intentions being just and innocent made me not reflect what conclusions might be made for the private visits, which I could not but necessarily make to Colonel Bampfield[159] in order to the King's service. For whatever might relate to it that came within my knowledge I gave him account of, and he made such use of it as might most advance his design. As long as there was any possibility of conveying letters secretly to the King, he frequently writ and received very kind letters from his Majesty (with several instructions, and letters to persons of honor and loyalty); but, when all access was debarred by strict guard placed about the King, all he could then do was to keep warm those affections in such as he had influence until a seasonable opportunity to evidence their love and duty to his Majesty. Though Colonel Bampfield discovered himself to none but [fol. 15v] such as were of known integrity, yet many coming to that place where he lay made him think it convenient for his own safety to go sometime into the country and at his return to be more private.

---

153. I.e., the Prince of Wales, later Charles II.

154. "Contribute to," *OED*.

155. See "Introduction," 24.

156. "A fact or circumstance of which a person is told; a piece of news or intelligence; (in early use) an account or narrative (of something)," *OED*.

157. Her brother's house was somewhere in Whitefriars, see "Introduction," 9n38.

158. "Inconveniencies" is an interlineal insertion.

159. Here, Halkett has crossed out "him" and inserted Bampfield's initials.

One evening when I went to see him, I found him lying upon his bed, and asking if he were not well, he told me he was well enough, but had received a visit in the morning from a person that he wondered much how he found him out. He was a solicitor that was employed by all the gentlemen in the county[160] where he lived, which was hard by[161] where his wife dwelt, and he had brought him word she was dead, and named the day and place where she was buried. I confess I saw him not in much grief, and therefore I used not many words of consolation, but left him after I had given him account of the business I went for. I neither made my visits less nor more to him[162] for this news; for loyalty being the principle that first led me to a freedom of converse with him, so still I continued it as often as there was occasion to serve that interest. He put on mourning and told the reason of it to such as he conversed with but had desired the gentleman, who had first acquainted him with it, not to make it public (lest the fortune he had by his wife, and she enjoyed while she lived, should be sequestered).[163]

To be short: after a little time, he—one day when I was alone with him—began to tell me that now he was a free man, he would say that to me which I should have never known while he lived if it had been other ways; which was that he had had a great respect and honor for me since the first time he knew me, but had resolved it should die with him if he had not been in a condition to declare it without doing me prejudice. For he hoped, if he could gain an interest in my affection, it would not appear so unreasonable to marry him as others might represent it; for, if it pleased God to restore the King (of which he was not yet out of hopes) he had a promise of being one of his Majesty's bedchamber, and though that should fail yet what he and I had together would be about eight hundred pound sterling[164] a year, which (with [fol. 16r] the Lord's blessing) might be a competency to any contentment[165] minds. He so often insisted on this when I had occasion to be with him that—at last—he prevailed[166] with me, and I did consent to his proposal, and resolved to marry him as soon as it appeared convenient (but we delayed it until we saw how it pleased God to determine of the King's affairs).

I know I may be condemned as one that was too easily prevailed with, but this I must desire to be considered: he was one who I had been conversant with for

---

160. Both Bampfield's and his wife's families lived in the West Country, specifically Devon and Somerset.

161. "In close proximity to; very near to," *OED*. As the solicitor lives "hard by" Bampfield's wife, he must have lived in Gloucestershire, Wiltshire, or Dorset.

162. "To him" is an interlineal insertion.

163. Loftis and Hardacre suggest the "estate might have been in jeopardy even without passing to Bampfield"; Loftis and Hardacre, eds., *Colonel Joseph Bampfield's Apology*, 246.

164. "Sterling" is an interlineal insertion.

165. "The fact, condition, or quality of being contented," *OED*.

166. "To succeed in persuading, inducing, or influencing," *OED*.

several years before; one that professed a great friendship to my beloved[167] brother Will; he was unquestionably loyal, handsome, a good scholar (which gave him the advantage of writing and speaking well); and the chiefest[168] ornament he had was a devout life and conversation, at least he made it appear such to me. And whatever misfortune he brought upon me, I will do him that right as to acknowledge I learnt from him many excellent lessons of piety and virtue, and to abhor and detest all kind of vice. This being his constant dialect[169] made me think myself as secure from ill in his company as in a sanctuary. From the prejudice which[170] that opinion brought upon me, I shall advise all never to think a good intention can justify what may be scandalous; for though one's actions be never so innocent, yet they cannot blame them who suspect them guilty when there is appearance of their deserved reproach. And I confess I did justly suffer the scourge of the tongue[171] for exposing myself upon any consideration to what might make me liable to it, for which I condemn myself as much as my severest enemy.

The King's misfortune daily increasing, and his enemies' rage and malice, both were at last determined in that execrable murder never to be mentioned without horror and detestation.[172] This put such a damp upon all designs of the Royal party that they were for a time like those that dreamed,[173] but they quickly

---

167. "Beloved" is an interlineal insertion.

168. Archaic adverbial form of "chiefly, principally," *OED*.

169. "A manner of speech peculiar to, or characteristic of, a particular person, class or geographical area," *OED*. Here, Halkett is using the word in a manner closer to our modern notion of a "discourse"; that is, a form of expression relating to a specific field (in this case, religion).

170. "Which" is an interlineal insertion.

171. An allusion to Job 5:21: "Thou shalt be hid from the scourge of the tongue: neither shalt thou be afraid of destruction when it cometh."

172. Here, of course, Halkett refers to the execution of Charles I, January 30, 1649. While she makes only a brief mention of this momentous event, she evidently wrote about it at some length at the time. According to Couper, "she was so transported with grief and detestation, with horror and dread, at so bold a villainy, that (as she confesses with regret) she broke forth more in imprecations against the actors thereof than in prayers for him who suffered": it takes him almost two pages to summarize the full version of her response, *The Life of the Lady Halket*, 19–20. "Execrable" means to call "forth expressions of extreme disgust; of wretched quality, bad beyond description," *OED*. In this, and the phrase "like those that dream," Halkett echoes the language used in "A Proclamation, for Observation of the Thirtieth Day of January as a Day of Fast and Humiliation According to the Late Act of Parliament for That Purpose" (London: John Bill,1661). ESTC R226600. See also "Upon the Fast which by Proclamation Was Kept, January 30, 1660/1," and "The Widow's Mite," 203–5, 241–49. Halkett returns to this event on numerous occasions. To contextualize Halkett's response, see Marcus Nevitt, "Agency in Crisis: Women Write the Regicide," in *Women and the Pamphlet Culture of Revolutionary England* (Aldershot, UK: Ashgate, 2006), 49–84.

173. An allusion to Psalm 126:1: "When the Lord turned again the captivity of Zion, we were like them that dream."

roused up themselves and resolved to leave no means unassayed[174] that might evidence their loyalty. Many excellent designs were laid, but the Lord thought fit [fol. 16v] to disappoint them all (that his own power might be the more magnified by bringing home the King in peace when all hostile attempts failed).[175]

In the meantime, Colonel Bampfield was not idle—though unsuccessful—and still continued in or about London where he could be most secure. One day when I went to see him, I found him extraordinary melancholy, and having taken me by the hand, and led[176] me to a seat went from me to the other side of the room, which I wondered at because he usually sat by me when I was with him. With a deep sigh, he said, "You must not wonder at this distance; for I have had news since I saw you that, if it be true, my distance from you must be greater, and I must conclude myself the most unfortunate of men."

I was much troubled at the discourse, but it was increased when he told me the reason of it; for he said one had informed him that his wife was living. What a surprise that was to me none can imagine because I believe none ever met with such a trial.

He, seeing me in great disorder, said, "Pray be not discomposed until the truth be known; for upon the first intimation of it, I sent away my man (Ned. B.[177] who served me long and knows the country and persons where she lived) who will return within a fortnight. If it be false, I hope you will have no reason to change your thoughts and intentions; if it should be true, God is my witness, I am not guilty of the contrivance of the report of her being dead, nor had no design but what I thought justifiable."

I could not contradict what he said, and charity led me to believe him. I left him in great disturbance, but could conclude nothing until the return of his servant, who brought word that his wife died at the same time that he first got knowledge[178] of it, and that he[179] was at her grave where she was buried; which I believing, continued former resolutions and intended to marry as soon as we could put our affairs in such order as to prevent sequestration.

[fol. 17r] About this time my brother Will came home much discontented, as he had great reason: for some persons, who made it their business to sow the seed of jealousy betwixt the King[180] and Duke of York, in pursuit of that accused my brother that he kept a correspondence with Colonel Bampfield (who stayed at

---

174. "To try, test, prove or attempt," *OED*.

175. Halkett begins praying for the King in 1645, see "Upon a Dispute with Myself, New Year's Day, 1661," 210–11.

176. "Lead" in original MS.

177. Ned. B. remains unidentified. Loftis and Hardacre, eds., *Colonel Joseph Bampfield's Apology*, 249.

178. "Knowledge" is an interlineal insertion and replaces the deleted "news."

179. "He" is an interlineal insertion.

180. I.e., Charles II.

London to hold intelligence in Scotland) and their design was to have the Duke of York come there to be crowned King.[181] Though the King did not believe it (as he told my brother when he sent for him) yet such was his present condition that he must either banish him, or else disoblige those persons whose service was most useful to him. This his Majesty expressed with some trouble, "But Will," said he, "to show you I give no credit to this accusation, whenever you hear I am in Scotland (where I hope shortly to be) come to me and you shall have no doubt of my kindness."

My brother humbly entreated his Majesty to let him know his accusers, and put him to a trial, and if they could make good what they charged him with he would willingly die.

"No," says the King, "I will not tell you who they are, and if you have any suspicion of the persons, I charge you upon your allegiance, and as you expect my favor hereafter, not to challenge them upon it."

Thus, with great unjustice[182] and severity was my brother banished the three courts: the King's,[183] Queen Mother's[184] and the Princess Royal's.[185] When he came out from the King a gentleman took him in his arms, who expressed great kindness and much trouble for his ill usage, who he knew undoubtedly to be one of his greatest enemies. All he said to him was, "You know the King hath tied me up and therefore I will say no more." Had not duty and former obligations been a tie to all he was capable to perform it was but an ill requital for many years' faithful service and much hardship with hazard of his life. For none could brand him with disloyalty or cowardice, nor did he know how to refuse any employment that was serviceable to the King though never so dangerous to undertake.

[fol. 17v] But this injury contributed through the mercy of God to his eternal good. For he took ship immediately and landed near Cobham, where by the favor of the Duke and Duchess of Richmond he was well entertained.[186] But nothing could free him of the great melancholy he took; for, as a person of worth told me who was a witness of it, he would steal from the company, and going into the wood and lie many hours together upon the ground (where perhaps he catched[187]

---

181. Smith, *Royalist Agents, Conspirators, and Spies*, 108.

182. "Injustice; unfairness; unjust action or behavior," *OED*.

183. I.e., King Charles II; see Paul Seaward, "Charles II (1630–1685), King of England, Scotland, and Ireland," *ODNB*.

184. I.e., Henrietta Maria; see Caroline M. Hibbard, "Henrietta Maria [Princess Henrietta Maria of France] (1609–1669), Queen of England, Scotland, and Ireland, Consort of Charles I," *ODNB*.

185. See Keblusek, "Mary, Princess Royal," *ODNB*.

186. Cobham Hall in Kent was the family seat of James Stuart, Duke of Richmond and his wife, Lady Mary Villiers, to which he reputedly retired after the execution of King Charles 1. David L. Smith, "Stuart, James, Fourth Duke of Lennox and First Duke of Richmond (1612–1655)," *ODNB*.

187. "To receive, incur, or contract, through exposure," *OED*.

cold and that, mixing with discontented humors, turned to a fever whereof he died). But I bless God I had the satisfaction to see him die as a good Christian. For as soon as he found himself distempered[188] he writ to me to get him a private lodging near the waterside, which I did and he, coming there, immediately went to bed and never rise out of it.

After he had given me account of what I have now related, he told me he had heard Doctor Wild[189] preach at Cobham, and that he was extremely well pleased with his sermon. And desired me to enquire for him and entreat him to come to him, which he did willingly and[190] frequently, and they had both much satisfaction in one another. My brother being desirous to receive the communion, the Doctor appointed the next morning for the celebration. But before we were to communicate, my brother said, "I am now going to partake of that most holy Sacrament and shortly after to give an account to God Almighty for all my actions in this life. And I hope, Sir," said he, to Doctor Wild, "you will believe I durst[191] not speak an untruth to you now. And therefore, I take this time to assure you that I am not guilty of what they have accused me of to the King, and I desire you to vindicate me."

I asked him if he thought Colonel Bampfield had any hand in such a design: he said he thought he may say as much for him as for himself. So, having sometime composed himself after saying this, the usual prayers of the church being ended, my brother, weak as he was, put himself upon his knees in the bed and so received the[192] [fol. 18r] blessed Sacrament, and we that were with him. He had before expressed great charity in forgiving his enemies, and though he had[193] told me who (upon good grounds he had reason to believe) they were, yet he enjoined[194] me as I loved him to forgive them. For they had proved his best friends,

---

188. Used here in the combined sense of "disorder or disease," and "disturbed in humor, temper, or feelings," *OED*.

189. After the Restoration, Wild became Church of Ireland bishop of Derry. Although at the time William and Anne Murray knew him, he had been sequestered from his living in Biddenden, Kent, he "continued to officiate as a clergyman where he could." Later, in December 1655, he "'preached the funeral Sermon of preaching' in advance of the planned implementation of Cromwell's proclamation against the ministrations of Anglican clergy or the use of the prayer book." Richard Bagwell "Wild, George (1610–1665)," rev. Jason Mc Elligott, *ODNB*. This perhaps explains his willingness to administer communion in the manner of the Church of England despite Parliamentary opposition. As Loftis notes, "he had been chaplain to Archbishop Laud and had preached to Charles I at Oxford." Loftis, ed., *The Memoirs of Anne, Lady Halkett and Anne, Lady Fanshawe*, 197.

190. "And" is an interlineal insertion.

191. Past tense of "dare."

192. "And so received the" is an insertion in the bottom margin of the folio.

193. "Had" is an interlineal insertion.

194. "To impose (a penalty, task, duty, or obligation)," *OED*.

for by their means he came to see the vanity of the world, and to seek after the blessedness of that life which is unchangeable.[195]

While he lay sick Colonel Bampfield came once to see him, and but once because there was search made for him.[196] The constant attendance I gave my brother kept me from seeing Colonel Bampfield or sending often to him. But early one morning, one of his servants came and told me that, being sent early out, as they returned they saw an officer with some soldiers marching that way where he privately lay, and that he feared his master was betrayed. I then took my sister into the next room, and told her I must now communicate something to her that I had concealed as knowing she would not approve of my intention; but, all considerations being now laid aside, I must own the concern I had for Colonel Bampfield, and with tears begged of her, by all kindness she had for me or if ever she desired to contribute anything to my contentment, that she would make inquiry what was become of Colonel Bampfield and assist him to escape if it was possible. The trouble she saw me in prevailed so with her that it made her say little as to what I might expect of severity, and took a coach, and went immediately where she thought it most likely to do him service. And it proving but a false alarum[197] served only to make him the more circumspect, and did afterwards something justify[198] me that I, at that time, owned to my sister my resolution of marrying him.

My brother's fever increasing and his strength decaying, a few days put an end to his conflict, for as death was welcome to him so he came peaceably as a friend and not an enemy; for I believe never any died more composedly of a fever in the strength of their youth. He seldom or never raved nor expressed much of dissatisfaction at the usage he had met with, only once [fol. 18v] he said, "Were I to live a thousand years, I would never set my foot within a court again, for there is nothing in it but flattery and falsehood."

After my brother was buried in the Savoy church[199] near my father and mother, within [a] few days I went again to my brother Murray's where I stayed

---

195. The idea of the world being full of vanity is most closely associated with Ecclesiastes, especially 1:2 and 12:8: "Vanity of vanities, saith the preacher, vanity of vanities; all is vanity."

196. Smith notes that Bampfield's return to England "was a dangerous action at this time," as his "well-advertised role in the duke's escape and his connections with leading Presbyterians were quite enough for the authorities to take an interest in his reappearance in England," *Royalist Agents, Conspirators, and Spies*, 126. By December 1649, Bampfield was imprisoned, see *True Account*, 96–98, 114–15.

197. "A warning of danger, esp. one intended to startle or rouse the previously unwary into action," *OED*.

198. "To warrant, support or vindicate," *OED*.

199. Savoy church "now known as 'The Queen's Chapel of the Savoy' was built in the thirteenth century"; Loftis, ed., *The Memoirs of Anne, Lady Halkett and Anne, Lady Fanshawe*, 197. There are no burial records for the early period and the layout of the graveyard has been altered. According to Robert Somerville, "the most famous of all the preachers to use the pulpit at the Savoy was undoubtedly Thomas Fuller . . . [who] was a very popular preacher with people crowding around to hear

until the importunity[200] of my Lady Howard[201] prevailed with me to go home with her to the north. My brother and sister approved of it and Colonel Bampfield most willingly consented to it, resolving suddenly[202] to follow me, and then publicly to avow what we intended, and to live[203] with a gentleman (a friend of his that was a great Royalist) where he expected to be welcome until such time as we found it convenient for us to return where we had more interest. This being determined, I left all that concerned me in such hands as he advised with hopes of preventing sequestration, but it fell out unhappily (as many things else did) and occasioned greater inconvenience. One of the great motives that invited me to go north was that it began to be discoursed of amongst many Parliament men that I had been instrumental in the Duke's escape, and—knowing that several women were secured upon less ground—I thought it best to retire for a time out of the noise[204] of it. It was not without trouble that I left my brother and sister but finding it necessary made it the more easy.

We began our journey September 10, 1649,[205] and had nothing all the way to disturb us until we came to Henderskelf beyond York to a house of Sir Charles Howard (where his sisters lived).[206] There in one night both Sir Charles and his Lady fell so extremely ill, with vomiting and purging in so great violence, that nothing but death was expected to them both, and some were so ill natured as to say they were poisoned but it pleased God they recovered. And then their son took the small pox, who was about 3 years old.[207] His fever great and appearance of being extraordinary full and, by the advice of Sir Thomas Gower[208] (who stud-

---

him: in December 1642, his text was 'Blessed are the peacemakers'"; Robert Somerville, *The Savoy: Manor, Hospital, Chapel* (London: Chancellor and Council of the Duchy of Lancaster, 1960), 59. W. B. Patterson, "Fuller, Thomas (1607/8–1661)," *ODNB*.

200. "Persistent or pressing in making requests or offers," *OED*.

201. I.e., Lady Anne Howard, the sister of Thomas. In December 1645, she married Sir Charles Howard, see Goodwin, "Howard, Charles," *ODNB*.

202. "Without delay, forthwith, promptly, immediately, directly, at once," *OED*.

203. After "live," "private" has been deleted.

204. "Common talk, rumor, report" and "slander," *OED*.

205. "1649" is an interlineal insertion.

206. In the original manuscript, "Henderskelf" is referred to only by its initial "H." It was identified by Loftis, ed., *The Memoirs of Anne, Lady Halkett and Anne, Lady Fanshawe*, 198. There are no visible remains of the house that, from 1699, became the site of Castle Howard; see, "The Building of Castle Howard," Castle Howard, accessed July 19, 2016, https://www.castlehoward.co.uk/visit-us/the-house/history-of-castle-howard#.

207. Edward Howard, later second Earl of Carlisle, *TCP* 3:34–35.

208. Spelt "Gore" in the manuscript. Richard Wisker, "Gower, Sir Thomas, Second Baronet (1604/5–1672)," *ODNB*.

ied physic more for divertissement[209] than gain), he took a purge which carried away a great part of the humor, so that nature, as he said, would be able to master the [fol. 19r] rest. And it had so good success that he recovered perfectly well, without the least prejudice. I cannot but mention this from the extraordinariness of the cure.

As soon as his health would allow of travail,[210] we took journey and came to Naworth Castle,[211] where I was so obligingly entertained by Sir Charles and his Lady (and with so much respect from the whole family) that I could not but think myself very happy in so good a society: for they had an excellent governed family, having great affection for one another; all their servants civil and orderly; had an excellent preacher for their chaplain,[212] who preached twice every Sunday in the chapel and daily prayers morning and evening. He was a man of a good life, good conversation, and had in such veneration by all as if he had been their tutelar angel.[213] Thus we lived sometime together with so much peace and harmony as I thought nothing could have given an interruption to it.

But it was too great to last long. For the post, going by weekly, one day brought me sad letters. One from Colonel Bampfield, giving me account that (just the night before he intended to come north, having prepared all things for accomplishing what we had designed) he was taken, and secured in the gatehouse at Westminster, and could expect nothing but death.[214] With much difficulty he had got that conveyed out to me to let me know what condition he was in, and that he expected my prayers since nothing else I could do could be available[215] (for he had some reason to apprehend those I was concerned in and might have influence upon was his enemies, and therefore I might expect little assistance from them). Presently after, I received a letter from my brother Murray and another from my sister Newton (his very severe, hers more compassionate), but both representing Colonel Bampfield under that character of the most unworthy person living; that

---

209. "Diversion," *OED*.

210. "Bodily or mental labor or toil, especially of a painful or oppressive nature; exertion; trouble; hardship; suffering," *OED*.

211. In the original manuscript, the castle is identified only by its initial, "N"; Naworth Castle was Charles Howard's family seat. Images and information can be found at Naworth Castle, accessed 07 July 2018, http://www.naworth.co.uk.

212. Later named as Mr. Nicholls.

213. "An angelic deity with supernatural protective powers; a guardian or patron," *OED*. As Loftis notes, "Halkett's remarks about Mr. Nicholls are consciously ironic." Loftis, ed., *The Memoirs of Anne, Lady Halkett and Anne, Lady Fanshawe*, 198.

214. Bampfield records this event in his *Apologie*; see Loftis and Hardacre, eds., *Colonel Joseph Bampfield's Apology*, 80, 136. Smith notes that Bampfield was imprisoned in December 1649 "for holding correspondence with the enemy"; Smith, *Royalist Agents, Conspirators, and Spies*, 126.

215. "Of avail, effectual, efficacious," *OED*, i.e., the only way Halkett could assist Bampfield was to pray.

he had abused me in pretending his wife was dead, for she was alive; and that her uncle Sir Ralph Sydenham[216] had assured them both of it, which made not only them but all that ever had kindness for me so abhor him that[217] though he were now [fol. 19v] likely to die yet none pitied him.

Had the news of either of these come singly, it had been enough to have tried the strength of all the religion and virtue I had, but so to be surrounded with misfortunes conquered whatever could resist them, and I fell so extremely sick that none expected life for me. The care and concern of Sir Charles and his Lady was very great, who sent post to Newcastle for a physician but he, being sick, could not come but sent things which proved ineffectual. My distemper increased, and I grew so weak that I could hardly speak. Apprehending the approach of death, I desired my Lady Howard to vindicate me to my brother and sister, for as I was ignorant and innocent of the guilt they taxed me with, and so I believed Colonel Bampfield was; and therefore I earnestly entreated her to write to her father[218] to be his friend, and that malice might not be his ruin which she promised. And having taken my last leave (as I thought) of them all I desired Mr. Nicholls (the chaplain) to recommend me to the hands of my redeemer, and I lay waiting until my change should come, and all was weeping about me for that I expected as the greatest good.

But it seems the mercy of God would not then condemn me into hell nor his justice suffer me to go to heaven, and therefore continued me longer upon earth that I might know the infiniteness of his power that could support me under that load of calamities.[219] Having lain some hours speechless (how I employed that time may hereafter be known if the Lord think fit to make it useful unto any), I began to gape[220] many times one after another and I found sensibly[221] like a return of my spirits, which Mrs. Culcheth[222] seeing came to me and told me if I saw another in that condition I could prescribe what was fit for them, and therefore it were a neglect of duty if I did not use what means I thought might conduce[223] to my recovery. Her discourse [fol. 20r] made me recollect what I had by me that was proper for me. I called to Crew (who served me) for it, and with the use of some cordials I sensibly grew better to the satisfaction of all that was

216. Sir Ralph Sydenham married Ursula Hill, daughter of Robert Hill, *BP* 1.774.

217. "That" is an interlineal insertion.

218. I.e., Lord Edward Howard, first Baron Escrick; see Stater, "Howard, Edward," *ODNB*.

219. Psalm 57:1: "Be merciful unto me, O God, be merciful unto me: for my soul trusteth in thee: yea, in the shadow of thy wings will I make my refuge, until these calamities be overpast."

220. "To open the mouth wide" or "to gasp from pain," *OED*.

221. I.e., "in an appreciable degree," or "with self-consciousness, consciously," *OED*.

222. The wife of Sir Charles Howard's steward at Naworth Castle who had been Lady Howard's governess. See *True Account*, 99.

223. "Contribute to," *OED*.

about me.[224] I confess death at that time had been extremely welcome but, having entirely resigned myself up to the disposal of my gracious God, I could repine at nothing he thought fit to do with me; for I knew he could make either life or death for my advantage.

Though that was a great disturbance to me which my brother and sister had written to me concerning Colonel Bampfield's wife's being alive, yet I gave not the least credit to it because I thought their information might come from such as might report it out of malice or design. For none of her relations loved him because he was not of their principles,[225] and a considerable part of her portion being still in their hands I judged it might be still to keep that they raised that story, which had little influence upon me because I gave it no belief, only looked upon it as a just[226] punishment to have that thought true now which I once mentioned when I thought it not true only to conceal my intentions.

For my Lord Howard and my sister Murray[227] (having observed Colonel Bampfield come sometimes when he durst[228] steal abroad[229] to see me) said to me one night, "I lay a wager you will marry Colonel Bampfield."

I smiled and said, "Sure you would not have me marry another woman's husband."

They replied they knew not he had been married, upon which I told them whose niece she was (whom they both knew) that[230] was his wife but I did not say she was dead, though at that time I believed it. And therefore, now looked on[231] this as inflicted for my dissimulation (for God requires truth in the inward parts[232] and I have a thousand times begged his pardon for that failing).

Upon these grounds it was that I gave so little entertainment to that story, and all my trouble and fear was (after I began to recover) for Colonel Bampfield

224. This occurred on a Friday, see "What Crosses and Difficulties I Have Met with Myself," and "Friday, May 14, 1697," 308, 311.

225. Catherine Sydenham's stepfather, Sir Francis Dodington, had been a colonel in the Royalist army and had "gained a reputation for ruthlessness, bordering on barbarity"; however, by 1648/9, he was in exile in France, see Michael French, "Sir Francis Dodington (1604–1670): A Prominent Somerset Royalist in the English Civil War," *Somerset Archaeology and Natural History Proceedings* 156 (2013): 114, 119.

226. "Just" is an interlineal insertion.

227. Loftis suggests that the "sister Murray" referred to here is her brother Henry's wife, Anne; however, when Halkett uses the abbreviation "Lord H.," she is usually referring to Lord Howard (her friend Lady Anne Howard's husband).

228. Past tense of "dare."

229. Here, Halkett inserted "come" as an interlineal insertion and subsequently crossed it out.

230. "That" is an interlineal insertion.

231. "On" is an interlineal insertion.

232. See Psalm 51:6: "Behold, thou desires truth in the inward parts: and in the hidden part thou shalt make me to know wisdom."

lest the Parliament should condemn to die as they had many gallant gentlemen before. But I was much supported one day by reading what fell out [fol. 20v] to be part of my morning devotion, *"for he hath looked down from the height of his sanctuary,*[233] *from heaven did the Lord behold the earth to hear the groaning of the prisoner to loose those that are appointed to death"* (Psa. 102:19–20).[234] I cannot omit to mention this because it was so seasonable a promise and I was so assisted by faith to rely upon it that in a manner it overcame all my fears. To confirm it is not in vain to believe and expect promised mercies, within [a] few days there came several letters both to Sir Charles Howard, his Lady, and myself that Colonel Bampfield had made his escape out of the gatehouse just the night before he was to have been brought to his trial.[235]

None then could give account how or by what means he had got out. But afterwards, I was informed by the person he employed that, having with much dexterity conveyed into him a glass of aqua fortis,[236] he with that (and much pains) cut the iron bars of the window asunder, but let it stand (by a little hold) until the time was fit to make use of it. And then, having found means to appoint such as he relied upon to be under the window at such a time as the guards were past that tour, he took the ropes of the bed, and fastened them to some part by the window, and so went down by them (but his weight made them fail and he fell down not without hurt). But the next difficulty was a paling[237] that was about the verge of the window, but his assistants, by standing upon one another's shoulders, reached over to him and got him over the paling, and so escaped the fury of his enemies (which many was glad of, and more had joined with them if they had not been possessed with a prejudice against him for the injury they supposed he had done me in persuading me his wife was dead when she was alive). But he not being now in a capacity to vindicate himself, it was easy to lay upon him what guilt they pleased. But all that his enemies could allege never [fol. 21r] prevailed with me to lessen one grain of my concern for him, because all they could say was the report that she was living (but they never named the person that could testify it from their own knowledge except such as might be biased by what I have mentioned already). I cannot but acknowledge I had great satisfaction in the news of

---

233. "From the height of his sanctuary" is an interlineal insertion.

234. According to the table for reading the psalms in the *BCP*, this means that it was the twentieth day of the month. The appropriateness of this psalm to Halkett's present condition is evidenced by its subtitle: "A Prayer of the Afflicted, when He Is Overwhelmed, and Pours Out His Complaint before the Lord." Halkett's wording confirms that she used the King James Version of the Bible.

235. "Apparently, he escaped on the night of 20–21 December 1649: the Council of State resolved on 20 December that the examination of him would be 'the first business tomorrow,'" Loftis and Hardacre, eds., *Colonel Joseph Bampfield's Apology*, 136–37.

236. "Nitric Acid," *OED*. In the MS "aqua" is "itqua."

237. "A fence made of wooden pales or stakes," *OED*.

his escape, and though I was sometimes disturbed because I heard not from him where he was or how, yet I pleased myself with the hopes he was well and secure (and so the better dispensed with my want of letters since I knew he could not convey them without hazard of being discovered).

It is not to be imagined by any pious, virtuous person (whose charity leads them to judge of others by themselves) but that I looked upon it as an unparalleled misfortune (how innocent so ever I was) to have such an odium[238] cast upon me as that I designed to marry a man that had a wife, and I am sure none could detest me so much as I abhorred the thought of such a crime. I confess I looked upon it as the greatest of afflictions, but that I might not set limits to myself the Lord thought fit to show he could make me suffer greater, and yet support me under them.

The first Sunday that my health and strength would permit me to go out of my chamber, I went to the chapel in the morning (with the rest of the family) to offer up thanksgiving to my God who had raised me from the gates of death. And after dinner, retiring into my chamber as I usually did, the door being locked and I alone, I was reading a sermon with which I was very well pleased. But on a sudden[239] I was so disordered and in so great an agony that I thought it not fit to be alone, and (all the servants being at dinner and none within my call) I went immediately to Mr. Nicholls's chamber who was much surprised seeing me come in so much disordered. I freely told him every circumstance, imagining he was a person fit to [fol. 21v] entrust with any disorder of my soul, and desired his prayers, which the Lord blessed with so good success that I immediately left trembling and found a great serenity both of mind and body. Having given[240] him thanks for the great concern he showed for me, and had his promise to conceal what I had communicated to him, I left him to go and make myself ready for attending my Lady Howard to the chapel, thinking myself as secure of what I had said to him as if it had been within my own breast; where it should have been still if I had then been acquainted, as I have been often since, with the effects of melancholy vapors.[241] But having never known them before, in others or myself, made them appear the more dreadful, but those who have experience of them will, I hope, have the more charity for me when they consider what effects they have had upon themselves.

I am sorry I cannot relate my own misfortunes without reflecting upon those who was the occasion of them, especially being one of that profession that I have ever looked upon with great respect. I have already given a character of Mr.

---

238. "The reproach or shame attached to or incurred by a particular act of fact; disgrace. Also: an instance of this; a taint, slur," *OED*.

239. Archaic form of "suddenly."

240. "Given" is "giving" in the MS.

241. "A morbid condition supposed to be caused by the presence of such exhalations; depression of spirits, hypochondria, hysteria, or other nervous disorder," *OED*.

Nicholls's parts and practice, and how much he was valued by all the family and such as conversed with him. One day, he having preached at Carlisle at the meeting for the Assize,[242] when he came home, he came to my chamber, and told me he had left Sir Charles, and came home with Mr. Culcheth who had entertained him by the way with many variety of discourse.

"But amongst the rest," said he,[243] "he tells me that my Lady Howard is jealous of Sir Charles and you."

I was strangely surprised to hear that, and said, "Sure he was drunk for as I am sure I never gave her the least occasion, so I am confident she knows her own interest so great in Sir Charles that she need not fear being supplanted by any. And besides she knows all the concern I can have for any is already fixed, and that may secure her were there nothing else; but I am very far from entertaining the least thought that she can have any such suspicion."

[fol. 22r] "If I had it," said he, "from any other hand I would think so too, but no doubt he hath had it from his wife (who you know was governess to her before she was married and is still entrusted with all her concerns)."

He insisted much on this discourse, and used many arguments to confirm he had reason to believe it true, and withal that he had observed of late she was not so kind to me as formerly, and that he thought it a strange thing that she should use one so ill who had left all relations and friends to come to a remote place out of kindness to her.

I assured him I found nothing of alteration in her, and that I was resolved to tell her what I heard (though not the author), and expected from the long friendship betwixt us that ingenuity[244] as freely to own if she were guilty of the imperfection of jealousy, and that she might dispose of me how she pleased in order to her own satisfaction.

"Can you imagine," said he, "that she will own to you she is jealous? No, she hath too much pride for that."

"What will you then advise me to do?" I replied.

"The truth is she is of so odd a humor," said he, "that it is hard in such a case what to advise. I heartily pity Sir Charles who I look upon as one of the finest gentlemen in the nation, and had he had the good fortune to have had you to have been his wife, he had been the happiest man alive."

All I concluded[245] at that time was[246] that he should be free in telling me whatever he saw in my carriage that looked like giving ground for such a suspicion. With many serious protestations, he freed me for giving any occasion but

---

242. "A sitting or session of a consultative or legislative body," OED.

243. "Said he" is an interlineal insertion.

244. "Honesty, straightforwardness," OED.

245. After "concluded," "of was" has been deleted.

246. After "time," "was" is an interlineal insertion.

daily gave me account of the increase of it. To be as short as the circumstances will allow: he was never with me, but he magnified Sir Charles up to the skies, spoke much to his Lady's disadvantage, but what he said of me was so greatly [fol. 22v] allied to flattery that I should have abhorred it from any other that had not appeared as he did.

At last I began to observe my Lady Howard grow more reserved than usual, and the whole family abate[247] much of their respect, only Sir Charles continued as formerly to me. I used daily to be until five o'clock with my Lady Howard working,[248] or any other divertissement[249] that she employed herself in, and then retired to my chamber for half an hour. Then Sir Charles and his Lady came and stayed with me (until the time we went to the chapel) either playing on the guitar, or with the children that lay near me, or discoursing, and this was for a long time our constant practice. But on a sudden, I found an alteration for[250] my Lady Howard would come to the door with Sir Charles, but when he came in she went into the children's chamber, which I, observing, followed her and left Sir Charles in my chamber. One night as I was thus going out to follow his Lady, he pulled me back and would not let me go, and the more pressing he was to have me stay, the more earnest I was to go; but seeing he was resolute, I stayed.

He told me he had observed of late that I was grown very strange to him and that whenever he came in, I went out of my chamber. I said it was only to wait upon his Lady and therefore he could not take it ill. He saw me in great disorder[251] and was very urgent to know what the reason of it was. I confess the tears were in my eyes which[252] he, seeing,[253] vowed he would not go out of the room until I resolved him. I told him I would upon the condition he would promise not to speak of it to any person and that he would do what I should desire. He said he would if it were in his power and bid me be free with him.

I said, "Sir, I confess I have received much civility from you ever since I came into your family, and as I know you showed it as a testimony of your affection to your Lady because I had an interest in her favor, so I valued it upon that account and not as I believed I deserved it. But now I much desire you, as you respect yourself, as you love your Lady, or have any regard to me, retrench[254] your civility into more [fol. 23r] narrow bounds else you may prejudice yourself in the opinion of those who thinks me unworthy your converse."

247. "To lessen, diminish, or reduce," *OED*.
248. In this context, "working" suggests that the two women were sewing.
249. "Diversion," *OED*.
250. "I found an alteration for" is an interlineal insertion.
251. "To disturb the mind or feelings of; to agitate, discompose, disconcert," *OED*.
252. "Which" is an interlineal insertion.
253. "Seeing" is an interlineal insertion.
254. "To cut short, check, or repress," *OED*.

He grew angry and said he must know who those persons were. I said he must pardon me for that it was enough I had told him how he might prevent an inconvenience, and if he either divulged what I had said, or did not perform the condition in doing what I desired, I would go out of his house upon the first discovery.

I left him after I said this and went to his Lady (who sometimes would be free enough, another time so reserved as she would hardly speak to me, either at table or any other time, which made me then give the more credit to what Mr. Nicholls had told me of her).

But again, I was at a stand[255] when, being alone with her one day, she told me she knew not what to think of Mr. Nicholls, but she bid me be upon my guard when I conversed with him; for she assured me he was not my friend so much as I believed. I thanked her for her advice but knew not what to conclude (because he had possessed me with an opinion that she was lessened in her respect to him because he was so civil to me). But this I concealed from her knowing it was upon another ground, which may not be amiss to insert here.

There were two young ladies in the house who had been bred up Papists and by Sir Charles's example and care was turned Protestants.[256] These two Sir Charles recommended to Mr. Nicholls's care to instruct them in the principles of our Religion, and they daily went to his chamber (sometimes together, sometimes alone as their conveniency[257] led them). They being very young, and hugely virtuous, and innocent, and having Sir Charles's order for going frequently to his chamber thought the oftener they went, the better; and sometimes after supper would go and stay there an hour or two. They had a discreet woman attended them who I had recommended. She came to me one morning and told me she could not but acquaint me with something that she would seek [fol. 23v] my advice in. I said I should give it freely.

Says she, "You know I am entrusted with the care of these young ladies and that Sir Charles orders them to go frequently to Mr. Nicholls's chamber. But I have observed the eldest of them stay much longer than the other, and to go after supper, and sometimes stay there until midnight. And though I have gone several times to call her, yet she would not come with me."

I said I was sorry to hear that; for though I did believe she might as innocently converse with him as with her brother, yet it might give occasion of reflection upon them both, which I wished might be prevented (but without saying anything to Sir Charles or his Lady).

---

255. "A state of checked or arrested movement; a standstill; unable to proceed in thoughts, speech or action," *OED*.
256. I have not been able to identify these women, but their experience mirrors Sir Charles's own: he was raised a Catholic and subsequently converted. See Goodwin, "Howard, Charles," *ODNB*.
257. Archaic form of "convenience."

This fell out to be about the beginning of my Lady Howard's growing a little reserved to me, but whenever I had any opportunity of converse with her, I still brought in some discourse of love and friendship and jealousy, and that sometimes it might be where there was greatest intimacy. But if I could have a suspicion of any person that I thought worth my friendship, she should be the first person herself that I would declare it to: for if she were virtuous, there is nothing I could desire her to do that she would omit for my satisfaction; and if I believed her vicious,[258] she were not worthy my converse. I uttered this with more than an ordinary sense which I thought made some impression of her.

And I thought I was fully confirmed, when early one morning she came into my chamber before I was out of my bed, and lying down by me, she said, "I have so much confidence of your friendship and discretion, that I am come to seek your advice and assistance how to manage what I have of late discovered that, if not prevented, will make great disorder amongst us."

I took her in my arms with great joy and told her she might as freely [fol. 24r] communicate anything to me as to her own heart, for I should be just in concealing and active[259] doing whatever she pleased to entrust me with (being fully persuaded if she were guilty of that imperfection of jealousy, she was now come to acquaint me with it and to advise about a remedy).

But I was in a mistake.[260] For she told me she had of late made some little observation that Mrs. F (who was the eldest of the two sisters) was looked upon more kindly by Mr. Nicholls than was usual with his gravity, which gave her the curiosity the day before when she went out of the dining room after dinner (all the company being gone, and remembering she had left them two together), she turned back, and looking through the cranny of the door, she saw Mr. Nicholls pull her to him and with much kindness lay her head in his bosom.

I said that might be very innocently done, though I confessed it had been better undone, "For sure he can have no ill design, being I believe a very good man, and she is too much a child to think of marrying her, though there were nothing else to object."

She said she was not so much a child as her stature made her appear, and therefore had great apprehensions[261] that the respect Sir Charles had for him might encourage him to hope if he could gain her consent to obtain his. "But if he[262] should have the least ground to suspect what I fear, he would never suffer him in his sight. And if we wanted[263] him you know," says my Lady, "that in these

258. "Addicted to vice or immorality; of depraved habits; profligate, wicked," *OED*.
259. "Concealing and active" is an interlineal insertion.
260. "Under a misapprehension," *OED*.
261. "Fear as to what may happen; dread," *OED*.
262. I.e., Sir Charles Howard.
263. "To be deprived of, to lose," *OED*.

times we should find it difficult to get one in his place who could so well discharge his duty to our satisfaction,[264] and yet so discreet as not to give offence to those of a contrary judgment such as most are hereabout."[265]

I acknowledged it was true that her Ladyship said and, in my opinion, it would be best for me to speak [fol. 24v] (since her Ladyship would entrust none else with it) to him about it. And I thought he was so ingenious[266] a person, and had often professed to have[267] so great an opinion of me, that I thought he would not conceal his intention from me and I should freely give her Ladyship an account of his answer.

I made use of this opportunity to insist much upon the satisfaction I had in her long continued friendship, and that I hoped, whatever my present misfortune was, yet that she would make no conclusions to my prejudice without giving me leave to vindicate myself; which she promised, and left me having engaged[268] me to let none know what had passed betwixt us.

The first conveniency[269] I had, I told Mr. Nicholls that I was going to ask him a question, and that I desired and expected he would be ingenious in resolving me, because it was not to satisfy my own curiosity but out of an intent to serve him, which I could not do if he were reserved in his answer. He seemed to be surprised with this discourse but assured me he would be very ingenious.[270] I asked him then if he had any inclination for Mrs. F or any design to marry her. He protested

---

264. Chaplains were expected to administer divine services in accordance with the rites and rituals of the Church of England; they could be discharged from their posts for "unsatisfactory conduct." Kenneth Fincham, "The Roles and Influence of Household Chaplains, ca. 1600–ca. 1660," in *Chaplains in Early Modern England: Patronage, Literature, and Religion*, ed. Hugh Adlington, Tom Lockwood, and Gillian Wright (Manchester: Manchester University Press, 2013), 13.

265. The conflict between the Howards and their community is reflected in an appendix to the anonymous *Strange News from the North. Containing a True and Exact Relation of a Great and Terrible Earthquake in Cumberland and Westmoreland. With the Miraculous Apparition of Three Glorious Suns That Appeared at Once* (London: J. Clowes, 1650). ESTC R205789. In "The charge against Charles Howard Esquire, High Sherriff of the County of Cumberland, Exhibited to the Commissioners for Sequestration in Cumberland," Howard's allegiance to the King positions him as an enemy to the Commonwealth, as does his association with Catholicism, *Strange News from the North*, 4–6, 3. Nevertheless, by 1651, Howard was fighting on the Parliamentarian side at the Battle of Worcester; Goodwin, "Howard, Charles," ODNB. As Gibson notes in *A Social History of the Domestic Chaplain, 1530–1840*, "During the Civil War, chaplains often supported a family in politics as much as in religion," 92.

266. "Having or showing a noble disposition, high-minded; honest, candid, open, frank, ingenuous," OED.

267. "To have" is an interlineal insertion.

268. "To bind or secure by a pledge," OED.

269. Archaic form of "convenience."

270. Here, as elsewhere, "ingenious" is used as a synonym for "ingenuous."

with much seriousness he had not. I said I was very glad to hear it, for now with the more confidence I could suppress the suspicion which some had of it.

"But," said he,[271] "what would you have done if I had confessed, I had loved her?"

"Truly," I replied, "I would have represented to you the prejudice you would have brought upon yourself; for undoubtedly Sir Charles, who is now your great friend, would turn your professed enemy and make all others so that he had influence upon." Therefore, as his intentions was free from such a design, so I desired his converse might be suitable, and I would then endeavor to convince them of their error who apprehended what I had told him. I gave my Lady Howard an account of what discourse Mr. Nicholls and I had, which she was satisfied with.

But this was [fol. 25r] the ground upon which I knew my Lady Howard had not so good an opinion of Mr. Nicholls as formerly, and therefore I could not well know what to think when my Lady told me (as I have already mentioned) that he was not my friend so much as I believed nor so good[272] a secretary.[273] I had the same information from her woman too (a discreet person who until that time loved me well).[274] I thought I would take a trial of him.

And the first time he came into my chamber, he falling upon his usual discourse (regretting to see my Lady Howard so unkind to me), I said I confessed I could not but[275] look upon it as my greatest misfortune, and such as swallowed up my former trouble because, to anyone that should believe me guilty of such unworthiness as occasioned her unkindness, it could not but be a confirmation of the crime laid to my charge with Colonel Bampfield, and the more unpardonable because ignorance in this could be no excuse. I said I would communicate a secret to him if he would solemnly promise not to discover it to any person living, which he engaged with all the protestations that was fit for one of his profession. I told him I was married and, if he believed I understood what either love or duty tied me to, that was enough to secure my Lady Howard from her apprehensions[276] though I had never had a value for her friendship. (I confess I only told him this out of design to try if he would speak of it again and was indifferent whether it was believed true or false since I hoped a little time would make the discovery.) He seemed to be highly sensible of the injury she did me, and at my request undertook to tell her that he had observed her unkindness, and as much as was fit for him to press for the reason of it, which if she gave, then to assert my innocence and the wrong she did both to her husband and herself. And in this I thought he

---

271. "He" is an interlineal insertion.
272. "Good" is an interlineal insertion.
273. "One who is instructed with private or secret matters; a confidant," *OED*.
274. See also Lady Moray's advice, cited in "Upon the Death of Sir Robert Moray," 250.
275. "But" is an interlineal insertion.
276. "Fear as to what may happen; dread," *OED*.

would oblige both them as well as me:[277] [fol. 25v] this he promised, but how he performed it shall be after manifest.

I saw daily my Lady Howard grow now to that height of strangeness[278] that when I spoke to her she would give me no answer, or if she did it was with that slightness[279] that I could not but be very sensible[280] of it. And that which angered me most was that whenever Sir Charles came where I was, he was ten times more free in his converse than he had been before I had spoken to him. These two extremes, with my own present condition, was deplorable[281] (having spent all the money I brought with me, being in a strange place where I had neither friendship nor acquaintance with any). To London I durst[282] not go for fear of being secured[283] upon the account of the Duke's escape (and besides I knew I need not expect anything but unkindness from my brother and sister); and how to send to Colonel Bampfield to advise with him I knew not. To stay where I was, I had no manner of satisfaction. And if I had known whither[284] to go, to leave that family with such an odium[285] as was laid upon me could not but make me unwelcome anywhere. Thus, when I reflected upon my disconsolate condition, I could find content in nothing but resorting to the hearer of prayer, who never leaves nor forsakes those that trust in him.[286] To the God of mercy, I poured forth my complaint in the bitterness of my soul,[287] and with abundant tears presented my supplication to him that judgeth righteously and did know my innocence; and therefore I interceded for the merits of my redeemer that he would deliver me out of the trouble that encompassed me round,[288] and direct me how to dispose of myself in that sad exigent[289] that I was in. And having resigned myself wholly to the disposal

---

277. "As me" is an interlineal insertion.

278. "Absence of friendly feeling or relations; discouraging or uncomplying attitude towards others; coldness, aloofness," *OED*.

279. "A small amount; carelessness or indifference," *OED*.

280. "Liable to be quickly or acutely affected by (some object of sensation); sensitive to or of," *OED*.

281. "Was deplorable" is an interlineal insertion.

282. Past tense of "dare."

283. "To seize or confine; to keep or hold in custody; to imprison," *OED*.

284. "To what place," *OED*.

285. "The reproach or shame attached to or incurred by a particular act of fact; disgrace. Also: an instance of this; a taint, slur," *OED*.

286. Hebrews 13:5: "Let your conversation be without covetousness; and be content with such things as ye have: for he hath said, I will never leave thee, nor forsake thee."

287. Psalm 142:2: "I poured out my complaint before him; I shewed before him my trouble."

288. Luke 19:43: "For the days shall come upon thee, that thine enemies shall cast a trench about thee, and compass thee round, and keep thee in on every side."

289. "A state of pressing need; a time of extreme necessity; a critical occasion, or one that requires immediate action or aid; an emergency, an extremity," *OED*.

of his will, I did with confidence expect a deliverance because I knew him whom I trusted.[290]

By the way I cannot [fol. 26r] omit to mention what was remarkable the time I was in that family. One night, being fast asleep, I was suddenly wakened with the shaking of the bed, somewhat violent but of short continuance. In the morning I told Sir Charles and my Lady that I had heard of earthquakes, but I was confident I had felt one that night and related how it was. They laughed at me and said I had only dreamt of it. I could not convince them nor they me, but a little before dinner came in some gentlemen that lived within three or four mile, and Sir Charles asked them, "What news?" They replied the greatest they knew was that there had been an earthquake that night, and that several houses were shaken down with it. Then they believed what I had told them.[291]

Another day my Lady Howard and I was sitting together alone in my chamber, about an ell[292] or more[293] distant from one another, and suddenly the room did shake so that both our heads knocked together. She looked pale like death and I believe I did the same, and we were hardly well recovered from our fears when Sir Charles came in to see how we were. And told us he was walking in the gallery with Mr. Nicholls, and that they were so shaken they could scarce hold their feet and was forced to hold themselves on the sides of the house. These both happened in the year 1649.

But to return where I left. My Lady Howard's strangeness did not make me neglect anything that I usually did before. And one Sunday morning, I went to her chamber to wait upon her as formerly when she went to the chapel. I found the door shut but heard her talk to her women, so I knocked: one of them came to the door and asked who was there. When they [fol. 26v] knew it was I, they said they could not open the door for their Lady was busy. I thought this was a great alteration; however, I said nothing, but went up to walk in the gallery, which was the usual passage to the chapel until she was ready to go. I had not walked a turn, or two, but Sir Charles came to me. I was in disorder, which he seeing asked what

---

290. Psalm 22:8: "He trusted on the Lord that he would deliver him: let him deliver him, seeing he delighted in him."

291. Halkett's account is partially verified by the anonymous pamphlet, *Strange News from the North* (1650), which dates the event to about five o'clock in the evening on April 11, 1650, and claims, "In the Counties of Cumberland and Westmoreland, we had a general earthquake; the people were so frighted therewith, that they forsook their houses, and some houses were so shaken, that the chimneys fell down," 2–3. Both are cited by Roger M. W. Musson, who notes that "it is most probable that the second event was in fact the April 11, 1650 earthquake and the first a foreshock which may have occurred in 1649 or 1650, probably the latter"; Musson, "Early Seismicity of the Scottish Borders Region," *Annals of Geophysics* 47, no. 6 (2004), 1837.

292. "A measure of length varying in different countries. The English ell = 45 inches; the Scots = 37.2 inches; the Flemish = 27 inches," *OED*.

293. "Or more" is an interlineal insertion.

ailed me. I told him I found he had been unjust to me, and I should be so just to myself in keeping my promise as that I resolved the next day to leave his house (for I could not suffer to live in any place where I had not the favor of the owners).

"I know," says he, "that you take it ill to see my wife so strange to you, and she doth it a purpose[294] that you may enquire the reason of it from herself, and then she will resolve you."

I said that should not be long in doing, nor had it been so long undone, but that she had avoided all occasions that might give me opportunity of speaking to her. (Another reason, which I did not mention, was that Mr. Nicholls had used many arguments to dissuade me from taking notice of it to her, some of them not much to her advantage.)

We went all to the chapel together, and after sermon the post came with letters while we were at dinner (some to them and some to me). I made use of this when we rose from the table to tell my Lady Howard that I had received letters from London, and that there was something of concern I had to say to her Ladyship. And asked when I might have her alone. She told me she would come within a little while to my chamber, where I went, and within a little while she came there, and I, [fol. 27r] taking her in my arms, kissed her and welcomed her to my chamber as a great stranger. So, locking the door, we sat down.

"Madam," said I, "though I made a letter the pretense for seeking this favor to speak with you, yet there is nothing in that worth your Ladyship's knowledge. And the only thing I have to say is to beg of you, by all the friendship and kindness you ever had for me, to be free with me and let me know what I have done to make you of late so unkind?"

"Truly," said she, "I wondered you were so long enquiring, and resolved until you asked the question, I would never tell you. But now you have begun, let me ask you how you could have the vanity to believe Sir Charles was in love with you and I was jealous of you? And have the confidence to speak of it to Mr. Nicholls, and speak so unworthily of me as you have done to him this long time, as if I were the most contemptible creature living, and that you pitied Sir Charles for having such a wife? Was this done like a friend? Oh," said she, "if I had not had it from Mr. Nicholls, who is so good a man that I cannot but believe him, I should never have given faith to it from any other person."

I was, I confess, astonished to hear him given as the author of that accusation, being all his own words which he had often used to me as his opinion. But it seems he had represented them as mine. "Madam," said I, "I[295] cannot wonder at your strangeness if you believed this true, but rather how you could suffer such a one within your family?"

---

294. I.e., on purpose.

295. This "I" is an interlineal insertion.

"Had I followed Mr. Nicolls's advice," she replied, "I had sent you away long since; for he pressed it often, and when he could not prevail with me, he writ to my father from whom I received a very severe letter for letting you stay so long with me. This I now tell you plainly to confirm what I once told you before: that Mr. Nicholls was not your friend so much as you believed, nor I so unworthy as the character you gave of me."

"Madam," said I, [fol. 27v] "I must acknowledge I did believe him my friend and so excellent a man that I thought, as all your family did, that it was a blessing to have him in the house. But now so much the greater is my misfortune to have him for my accuser, who is so much respected by all and whose very profession would enforce belief. I love not retaliation and to return ill for ill,[296] but since I have no other way to assert my own innocency,[297] I must freely declare he was himself the only person that took pains to persuade me you were jealous of me. And when I resolved to vindicate myself from whatever might seem to give occasion for it, he dissuaded me, and said you had too much pride to own it, and that you would but laugh at me, and would expose me to your scorn. And what he related as my words were his own, which when at any time I contradicted he would say it was my partiality made me defend you and not my reason. This Madam is so great a truth that I will own it before him whenever you find it convenient. But pray, Madam," said I, "when he told you all these things to my disadvantage did it not lessen your belief of it, coming from a person who professed to have so great respect for me and yet performing acts so contrary to it? Did not this plead for me in your thoughts that he who could dissemble might be unjust and I innocent?"

"I confess," said my Lady, "it did prevail much on your side, and one day when he was railing against you, I said to him, 'how comes you are so civil to her and profess so great an esteem of her if you have so ill an opinion of her?' 'I, an esteem of her?' replied he, 'I could[298] not but be civil to her because I saw Sir Charles and your Ladyship respect her, but, God is my witness, I never [fol. 28r] looked upon her but as one of the airiest[299] things that ever I saw, and admired[300] what it was your Ladyship and Sir Charles saw in her to be so kind to her.'"

I smiled and said, "I wish I could as easily confirm he was the author of what he related of me as I can, under his own hand, that he had better thoughts of me than 'so airy a thing' as he then represented me."

---

296. Possibly an allusion to Christ's advice in the Sermon on the Mount, specifically Matthew 5:38–39: "Ye have heard that it hath been said, an eye for an eye, and a tooth for a tooth: But I say unto you, that ye resist not evil: but whosoever shall smite thee on thy right cheek, turn to him the other also."

297. Archaic form of "innocence."

298. Here, "can" has been deleted and replaced by the interlineal insertion of "could."

299. "Unsubstantial, thin, light; vain, empty (of character)," *OED*.

300. "To be surprised," *OED*.

She was desirous to see the letter, which I showed her with the copy of my own to which his was an answer. And was the first letter that ever I copied of my own and fell out well that I had it else his would not have been well understood. (The occasion of it was at the first notice I had of Colonel Bampfield's wife's being alive before it came to be publicly known. It is not to be imagined but it put me in great disorder, and, having none I would communicate it to, I writ a serious letter to him representing something of [the] disorder I was in and earnestly desired his prayers to which his letter answered.[301] And were it not too tedious I should insert them both here.)[302]

As soon as my Lady Howard read the letter she said, "I am afraid this man hath deceived us all and will prove a villain."[303]

While we were at this discourse Sir Charles knocked at the door. We let him in, and he, smiling, said, "I hope you understand one another." We gave him some short account of what had been betwixt us which he said did confirm what he had been of opinion of a pretty while. "But," said he, "I will enjoin you both, whatever passeth betwixt you when you are alone, let no person know but that you are still at the same distance you were before until my return; for I am immediately informed of some Moss Troopers[304] that are plundering in the country, and I and all my men are going to try if we can take them: therefore, you must pray for [fol. 28v] me, since I cannot go with you now to the chapel."

We both promised to follow his injunctions and parted. Though I did what I could to conceal anything of satisfaction, yet the joy I had to see some glimpse of light appear for my vindication put a visible change upon me. And my Lady Howard found it difficult to restrain her former kindness from appearing after she began to find she had been injured as well as I.

When Sir Charles returned, he was a witness of many debates betwixt us. When she considered what a person Mr. Nicholls was, she then condemned me guilty of all he accused me of, but when I urged the many years' experience she had had of my converse and whether she had ever known me do any unworthy act, then, when she reflected upon that, she condemned him. But, to be short, she concluded that it was fit to have her cleared from the aspersion of jealousy and the consequences of it, which one of us had taxed her with, and none had more reason to press that than I who suffered most by it. At last we resolved as the fairest way

---

301. "To which his letter answered" is an interlineal insertion.

302. Although several of Halkett's letters have survived, these are currently missing.

303. "Originally, a low-born base-minded rustic; a man of ignoble ideas or instincts; in later use, an unprincipled or depraved scoundrel; a man naturally disposed to base or criminal actions, or deeply involved in the commission of disgraceful crimes," *OED*.

304. "A member of any of the marauding gangs which, in the mid-seventeenth century, carried out raids across the 'mosses' of the Scottish Border," and by extension "a member of an undisciplined or renegade group," *OED*.

for me to go to Mr. Nicholls and tell him that I was resolved to vindicate myself, and therefore to[305] desire him not to take it ill if I brought him for a witness of my innocency,[306] who was the first and only[307] person that told me of my Lady's being jealous, and who had often assured me he saw nothing in my carriage that could give the least ground for it.

Sir Charles had left us to our contrivance. And[308] when we were determined, I left my Lady Howard and, appointing the garden to be our meeting place where I was to bring Mr. Nicholls, I went to his chamber but found him not there. I immediately went alone to the garden to the walk where my Lady Howard and I had [fol. 29r] designed to meet, and in the way to it I saw Sir Charles and Mr. Nicholls very serious together, in a close[309] walk. I took no notice I saw them but went on to the place appointed, and while I was walking there I began to consider that it fell out well I had not met with Mr. Nicholls alone; for he, that had already injured me so much, might possibly allege that I had prevailed with him to take that upon him he had never said only to conceal my guilt, and so I might still be thought what he first represented me. Therefore, I resolved to propose it to my Lady Howard, when she came, to go together where Sir Charles and he was walking and there speak of it before them. She approved of my reason and resolution, and said it was very likely he might make such a use of it. And that this way would be more satisfaction to her than the other.

So, we went together to the close walk where Sir Charles and he was walking together. (By the disorder I saw him in, I knew Sir Charles had given him some hint of what was amongst us, and the reason he gave his Lady, and I, afterwards was because he had not a mind to have him too much surprised and knew that that meeting would not be for his advantage.)

"Mr. Nicholls," said I, "you could not but have observed a great strangeness from[310] my Lady Howard to me a good while, and being no longer able to suffer it, I have pressed to know the reason and, being informed of it, I know it is in your power to make the reconciliation. And therefore, I expect it from you."

"Truly, Mrs. Murray," replied he, "I shall be very glad to be an instrument in so good a work."

Then said I, "Mr. Nicholls, do you not remember that day you came from Carlisle you told me of a person that informed you my Lady was jealous of me?"

"No, indeed," said he, "I remember no such thing."

---

305. "To" is an interlineal insertion.

306. Archaic form of "innocence."

307. "And only" is an interlineal insertion.

308. "And" is an interlineal insertion.

309. "Concealed," "secret," "private," or "secluded," *OED*.

310. After "strangeness," "betwixt" has been deleted and replaced by "from" in an interlineal insertion.

"It is impossible," I replied, "your memory can be so ill, [fol. 29v] but to make it better I will beg leave of Sir Charles and my Lady to whisper[311] the person in your ear that you named, because I desire not to disoblige him with this contest."[312] They both gave leave and I whispered softly, "Did not you tell me Mr. Culcheth told you, and you were sure he had it from his wife, and so you could not doubt the truth of it?"

"I remember indeed," said he, "that I told you your carriage was such that if you did not mend it you would give my Lady occasion to be jealous."

I lifted up my eyes and hands to heaven, and said, "Good God, hath this man the confidence to say this!"

I turned to Sir Charles and my Lady and then repeated several things already mentioned (wherein he had condemned my Lady and magnified me to a high degree of flattery).

"And" I said, "I confess it is a great disadvantage I have to contest with such a person whom there is much more reason should be believed than I. But, Sir, you are a Justice of the Peace and therefore may lawfully take my oath. And I will most solemnly give it upon the Bible[313] that he did say these things to me, and insisted often on them, and dissuaded me often when I was resolved to have justified myself to your Lady."

"And I," replied he, "will take my oath upon the same Bible that it is not true she says."

My admiration[314] was such to hear him speak at that rate that I was almost struck dumb, and all I said more was, very calmly, "Mr. Nicholls, you have made more use of the Bible than I have done, and therefore perhaps think you may be bolder with it, but I would not swear your oath to have Sir Charles's estate."

He would have insisted, but Sir Charles and his Lady interrupted him, and desired there might be no more of it. I said I could say no more than what I had offered, and I left my part to be made evident by the great and [fol. 30r] holy God, who knew how I was wronged, and to him I did refer myself, who I knew would do me right.

My Lady and I then went in, and Sir Charles followed us. And when we were together, everyone freely gave account what character he had given of us. My Lady and I, he had most equally balanced together; for whatever ill he had said of me to her, he had said as much of her Ladyship to me; and as he endeavored to possess me with the opinion of her being jealous, so he persuaded her that she had reason for it by my being desperately in love with Sir Charles.

---

311. In MS this reads "whispers."
312. "Dispute or conflict," *OED*.
313. "Upon the Bible" is an interlineal insertion.
314. "The action or an act of wondering or marveling; wonder, astonishment, surprise," *OED*.

Sir Charles laughed at this discourse and said, "He hath been so wise as not to have much of this to me, only once he said that he was sure you were in love with me and I could not but perceive it. And I told him, as I was an honest man, I had never seen anything like it."

"Well," said I, "then it seems in this he had something of justice, that he had a mind I should think as well of you in gratitude as he would have your thoughts been of me; for he gave you high commendations, and one of your excellent qualities was that you had a great value for me, which I did then and shall still acknowledge I have received much more civilities from you than I deserved: yet no more than I might expect from any civil[315] person in their own house who loved their Lady, and for her sake would oblige those she loved. It was, Sir," continued I, "upon this account that I both received and returned what you gave, and I paid. And now, before your Lady, I conjure[316] you, by all the hopes you have of happiness here or hereafter, and as you would avoid all the curses threatened to dissemblers, freely declare what I have ever done or said since I came within your family that might confirm you of Mr. Nicholls's opinion of me."

He most solemnly declared he never saw no ground for it, and that, that was the first thing which made him apprehend Mr. Nicholls not being what he should be [fol. 30v] (by the contradiction he saw in that). There was nothing more contributed to vindicate me than the disorder which from that day appeared in Mr. Nicholls; for it was visible to the meanest[317] in the house (though few knew the reason of it, because Sir Charles had a respect for him and desired all should respect him, and therefore did as much as could be to conceal what had been amongst us).

Sometime after this the Sacrament was to be celebrated in the chapel, and I had many debates with myself what to do. At last, being resolved, I sent for Mr. Nicholls to my chamber, and told him it was not without great disputes in my thoughts of the good and ill of partaking or leaving that holy mystery that had made me send for him. And though he had injured me beyond a possibility of being forgiven by any as a woman, yet as a Christian I forgave him. And though he had wronged me, yet I would not wrong myself by wanting the benefit which I hoped for and did expect in that blessed participation.

"This," said I, "I thought fit to tell you that you may not think I go for custom or formality, but with a sense of both my duty and advantage; and let not my charity make you think little of your fault, for without great repentance, great will be your judgment."

He approved much of my charity and would have said something to vindicate himself, but I interrupted him and desired him to consider what he was going

---

315. "Civil" is an interlineal insertion.

316. "To constrain by oath, to charge or appeal to solemnly," *OED*.

317. I.e., those of lowest social status.

about, and that it would aggravate[318] his guilt to think to justify himself since no excuse could be made. I instanced that particular that was an undeniable fault, which was his going immediately from me to tell[319] Lady Howard that I had as a secret told him I was married.

"How can I but suspect," said I, "the truth of all you speak out of the pulpit when you divulge that, after such solemn engagements of secrecy, which I only said for a trial of your fidelity?"

"Oh," replied he, "if you knew what temptation I had [fol. 31r] to make that discovery you would forgive me."

"It was only to tell you that," said I, "that[320] I sent for you. And, again I repeat it, that I do forgive you, and pray God to make you penitent for your sin that so you may obtain mercy, and that taking[321] the holy Sacrament may not be for your greater condemnation. And this is all I have to say to you." So, he left me.

After the solemn time of our devotion was over, I began seriously to think what way to dispose of myself; for though Sir Charles and his Lady were returned to their former kindness, yet I thought it not fit to stay where I had been so injuriously traduced.[322] Therefore,[323] to leave that family I was fully resolved, but where to go I could not determine.

In all this time I had never heard nothing of Colonel Bampfield, nor from him, which had been trouble enough to me had it not been overcome by the present trouble I was in, which made me unsensible[324] of what was at a greater distance. But no sooner was I delivered from the sadness and discontents occasioned by what I have now[325] related than a new misfortune arrives. When I was hardly well composed after one storm, another rises, which by the danger of others involved me by sympathy and gratitude in great disturbance.

My sister[326] writes me a long letter full of passion and discontent informing me that a cousin of her husband's, an heir to whom he was to succeed, was stolen away; and that after much enquiry he heard that the gentleman who had stolen her away had carried her to Flanders; and that she had fled to a monastery to

---

318. "To make (an offence) more heinous or offensive; to increase in offensiveness," OED.

319. After "to," "told" has been deleted and replaced with "tell" in an interlineal insertion.

320. "Said I, that" is an interlineal insertion.

321. "Taking" is an interlineal insertion.

322. "To speak ill of, esp. falsely or maliciously; to defame, malign, vilify, slander" and thereby "expose to contempt; to bring discredit upon; to dishonor, disgrace," OED.

323. "Therefore" is an interlineal insertion.

324. I.e., "insensible," or "unaware," OED.

325. "Now" is an insertion in the right-hand margin.

326. I.e., Elizabeth Newton, later Puckering.

secure herself until my brother could come there to relieve her.[327] And unhappily, in the same ship that he went over in, Colonel Bampfield was a passenger. And though he was disguised, yet my brother knew him, and as soon as they landed, he challenges him: they chose their seconds, fights, and my brother was wounded in the hand so dangerously that [fol. 31v] to lose the use of it was the least that was expected. How sadly this surprised me[328] is not to be imagined, for I should have been concerned in his misfortune though a stranger had occasioned it. But to think it was upon my account and done by one I was interested in, these considerations did highly aggravate my trouble and made me conclude the same that my sister did in her letter: that I was the most unhappy person living. For I had not only made myself so but brought misfortune upon all that related to me. Yet in the midst of all these disconsolations,[329] I cannot but acknowledge I had a satisfaction to know so worthy a person as my brother Newton owned a concern for me, which he would never have done (I was assured) if he had believed me vicious.[330]

Within a little while after, Colonel Bampfield sent an express[331] to me, who was one of the persons who had assisted him in his escape and could therefore give me a true account of it, and where he was concealed until that unhappy time of the encounter betwixt my brother Newton and him. Colonel Bampfield knew very well I could not but hear of[332] it and that it would very much afflict me, and therefore he writ a long letter in his own vindication. And lest I should have a doubt of what he said, he referred the confirmation of it to an enclosed letter (directed to me) written by the two seconds and subscribed by them both, who had been two colonels in the King's army. My brother's second I cannot for the

---

327. Identified as Jane Puckering. Loftis, ed., *The Memoirs of Anne, Lady Halkett and Anne, Lady Fanshawe*, 198. She was the daughter of Sir Thomas Puckering and Elizabeth Morely and was abducted by one Joseph Walsh on September 26, 1649. She was taken to France and Holland, where Walsh claimed they were married. Her case was heard by Parliament and led to "An Act Enabling the Lords Commissioners for Custody of the Great Seal of England, to Issue Commissions of Delegates in Cases of Pretended Marriages (January 1561)." C. H. Firth and R. S. Rait, eds., *Acts and Ordinances of the Interregnum, 1642-1660* (London: HMSO, 1911), 496–97, BHO. Puckering later married Sir John Bale, but she died in childbirth, January 27, 1651/2. Sir Henry Newton, who was Sir Thomas's nephew, inherited the estate (which included a house near Warwick) and took the name Puckering." On Sir Thomas Puckering, see N. G. Jones, "Puckering, Sir John (1543/4–1596)," *ODNB*.

328. "Me" is an interlineal insertion.

329. "The state or condition of being disconsolate; unhappiness, despondency," *OED*.

330. "Addicted to vice or immorality; of depraved habits; profligate, wicked," *OED*.

331. A messenger sent "specially, on purpose, for a particular end; hence (to go, send, etc.) with speed," *OED*.

332. After "of," "that" has been deleted and replaced with "it" in an interlineal insertion.

present remember his name, but Colonel Bampfield's second was Colonel Lowe (who afterwards came into Scotland with the King).[333]

The account they gave me was this. When they were all four in the place appointed and their doublets off, Colonel Bampfield, with his sword in his hand, came to my brother Newton and told him he [fol. 32r] was never engaged in any employment more contrary to his inclination than to make use of his sword against him who drew his in the defense of the person he loved beyond any living. That he knew not but what he was going now to say might be the last that ever he should speak, and therefore, as such, he desired to be believed. He said he did believe there was not[334] a more virtuous person in the world than I, nor did he know his wife was living, and as this was true, so[335] he desired the Lord to bless him in what he was going about. So, they fight and had several passes without advantage to either but, my brother receiving a wound in his hand and bleeding fast the seconds ran in and parted them.[336] Colonel Bampfield extremely regretting what he had done and my brother seeming to be satisfied that he had not got it unhandsomely.[337] This, in short, was the substance of their relation which they concluded with a great compliment to me. Though I never approved of duels, yet if my prayers were heard for my brother's recovery, I thought this would not be to my disadvantage.[338]

---

333. Identified as Colonel Hercules Lowe; Loftis, ed., *The Memoirs of Anne, Lady Halkett and Anne, Lady Fanshawe*, 198. Lowe's being entrusted to seize the King's goods—in order to return them to him—is recorded on May 26, 1660 in the *Journal of the House of Lords* 11, 1660–1666 (London: HMSO, 1767–1830), 42–43. BHO.

334. "Not" is an interlineal insertion.

335. "So" is an interlineal insertion.

336. "In June 1650, Newton, still in the Netherlands, wrote to his friend Sir Ralph Verney about the duel, saying that he had been 'seven weeks in the cure'"; Loftis and Hardacre, eds., *Colonel Joseph Bampfield's Apology*, 137.

337. "Discourteously, rudely; without due respect or consideration," OED.

338. As Anna Bryson observes, "dueling was a problematic aspect of the code of gentlemanly behavior for moralistic conduct writers, who were nevertheless committed to ideals of 'honor'"; Anna Bryson, *From Courtesy to Civility: Changing Codes of Conduct in Early Modern England* (Oxford: Oxford University Press, 1998), 248. In "A Mother's Will to Her Unborn Child," Halkett advises, "As I would not wish thee in the least degree to be a coward, so I should be as ill satisfied to have thee one of those who are justly termed foolhardy; for it is such as make 'a mock of sin,' as Solomon says (Proverbs 14.9). But a wise man will avoid all occasions that may make either his religion or his courage questioned, and certainly there is more true valor in overcoming our own imperfections than in subduing the greatest duelists." Halkett, *A Short Expostulation about Prayer*, pp. 221–22. Fortunately, the reported duel took place abroad and before Cromwell issued "An Ordinance against Challenges, Duels, and all Provocations Thereunto" (London: William du-Gard and Henry Hills, 1654); see Markku Peltonen, *The Duel in Early Modern England: Civility, Politeness, and Honor* (Cambridge: Cambridge University Press, 2003), 14.

But that which pleased me most was that Colonel Bampfield had met with my Lord Dunfermline[339] in Flanders (who with other Commissioners were sent from Scotland to invite his Majesty home); and acquainting his Lordship with what had been betwixt him and me, and justified himself as to what reports had been made to his disadvantage, to oblige both him and me, the Earl of Dunfermline writ very earnestly to desire me to come into Scotland where the King intended to be shortly. And therefore, he thought that would be the most convenient time for me to come, when I would have many friends to assist me for the recovery of my portion which was in Scotch hands. Colonel Bampfield seconded this with many arguments to persuade me to hasten my journey all that was possible while the [fol. 32v] road was clear (for there was reason to apprehend that Cromwell would soon march thither with the army when he heard the King was landed).

I showed my Lady Howard my letters and my resolution of obeying them, but my difficulty was how to undertake the journey, or live in a strange place, having little or no money. But as to that, my Lady Howard very generously said I need not trouble myself, for I should not want what money I desired, nor horses, and men to attend me to Edinburgh.[340] I was not then long determining of the day for my departure. And Sir Charles appointed an old gentleman, a kinsman of his own, with others to be ready to conduct me (and she that served me) at the time prefixed.

The night before I was to come away, I sent for Mr. Nicholls and told him he should now have his desire in seeing me out of the house, which was what he had used many unhandsome[341] ways to bring about. And had it not been for him, it is possible I had left that house with more regret. Now I was likely to be at a great distance from him, and therefore might expect he would be the more liberal[342] in his discourse of me when I could not vindicate myself.

"But," said I, "remember whenever you speak anything to my disadvantage you are heard by the Almighty God, who will plead for me, and your own conscience (if you have one) will condemn you: for you know I am innocent of those unworthy things you charged me with."

"I confess," replied he, "there hath some unhappy circumstances fallen out that may seem to give you reason for what you say, but I must suffer rather than vindicate myself to the prejudice [fol. 33r] of those under whose roof I dwell. But if ever I am so happy as to see you out of this family, I shall then let you see how

---

339. Henderson, "Seton, Charles," *ODNB*.

340. The household accounts state: "June 19. [1650] pd. Mrs. Murray at her going from Naworth, £44. 5s. 6d"; Loftis, ed., *The Memoirs of Anne, Lady Halkett and Anne, Lady Fanshawe*, 199.

341. "Unfitting, unbecoming, unseemly; discourteous, mean," *OED*.

342. In the sixteenth and seventeenth centuries, this term was often used pejoratively, meaning to be "unrestrained by prudence or decorum, or to be licentious," *OED*.

much you have been mistaken of me; and to evidence what my thoughts are of you, I will give it you under my hand that I do believe you as virtuous a person as lives."

I smiled at that and, with a disdainful look, told him my virtue would have but a weak support if I had nothing to uphold it but a testimony from him. "No," said I, "I have a better hand to rely upon to defend me, and such a one as will make you ashamed for what you have done, except you repent. The respect I have to your calling, and the benefit I have had by your preaching and prayer, shall keep me from divulging your faults; but as you expect the Lord's blessing upon your ministerial office, and would avoid the being a scandal to it, leave off the course you have begun with me, lest if you practice it on any other it may bring to remembrance the injury you have done me, and so aggravate your future crime." After I had said this, I left him, and gave my Lady Howard account of what I had said to him.

The next day I took my leave of my Lady and all the family, and Sir Charles, with a good attendance, went a part of the way. And none in the family but[343] gave some evidence of their concern in parting with me, except Mr. Nicholls who hardly went to the gate with me and for that was much censured by all (especially my Lady Howard who had great expressions of kindness to me, and said if that journey proved unhappy to me it would be a trouble to her as long as she lived because she was sure I had never undertaken[344] it so willingly if I had not been disobliged where I was). I could not contradict so great a truth, nor be insensible[345] of her very great friendship, which was the more to be valued because it had met with so strong a trial and yet continued firm.

[fol. 33v] The second night after I left Naworth Castle I came to Edinburgh (Thursday, June 6, 1650)[346] and lodged at Sanders Peers at the foot of the Canongate. I had discharged[347] all that were with me to tell my name to anyone until I could find out some that I had formerly known in England. That night at supper, the old gentleman being with me and the Mistress of the house sitting just against me, I could not but look earnestly upon her, and I said, "Mistress, I cannot but have a kindness for you because you have a very great resemblance of my Mother."

---

343. Here, Halkett's use of "but" creates a kind of double-negative: "And none... but," when contrasted with "except Mr Nicholls," means that everyone else in the household other than him displayed their sense of her importance to them at her departure.

344. In MS this reads "undertaking."

345. I.e., "insensible," or "unaware," *OED*.

346. The specific date here is a note in the left-hand margin.

347. "To forbid (a person, etc.) to do something; to ban from doing; to prohibit (an action, practice, etc.)," *OED*.

At that she clapped her hands and said, "Nay then, I will never enquire any more who you are, for I am sure you are Will Murray's sister, for he often told me the same." She then informed me of a kinsman of my mother's (who she made her executor) that had been at her house that day, and she knew he would be glad to see me. And I was well pleased to hear of him and sent for him to advise whether I should continue where I was or take a more private lodging. But he told me it was a very civil house and the best quality lay there that had not houses of their own. When the gentleman and those that came with me had rested some time and seen the town, they returned back again with all the acknowledgements I was capable to make to Sir Charles and his Lady for their great civility and kindness.

When I had been two or three days in the town I received a visit from the Earl of Argyll,[348] who invited me to his house and the next day sent his coach for me, which I made use of to wait upon his Lady.[349] When I came upstairs I was met in the outward room by my Lady Anne Campbell,[350] a sight that I must confess did so much surprise me that I could hardly believe I was in Scotland: for [fol. 34r] she was very handsome, extremely obliging, and her behavior, and dress was equal to any that I had seen in the court of England.[351] This gave me so good impressions of Scotland that I began to see it had been much injured by those who represented it under another character than what I found it. When I was brought in to my Lady Argyll, I saw then where her daughter had derived her beauty and civility (one was under some decay, but the other was so evident and so well-proportioned that while she gave to others she reserved what was due to herself).

---

348. In 1650, this was Archibald Campbell, eighth Earl, later Marquis, of Argyll. He was executed for treason on May 27, 1661, partly on the basis of rumors that he had agreed to the execution of Charles I during discussions with Oliver Cromwell in 1649. Stevenson, "Campbell, Archibald, Marquis," *ODNB*.

349. Lady Margaret Campbell, née Douglas, Countess of Argyll (1610–1678), daughter of William Douglas, seventh Earl of Morton and Lady Anne Keith (d. 1649); she married Archibald Campbell, eighth Earl of Argyll, on August 6/7, 1626. She was the sister of Mary, Countess of Dunfermline. Stevenson, "Campbell, Archibald, Marquis," *ODNB*.

350. Lady Anne Campbell was the eighth Earl of Argyll's daughter.

351. At about this date, there had been a suggestion that Lady Anne Campbell might marry Charles II. Smith, *Royalist Agents, Conspirators, and Spies*, 150. Maurice Ashley cites a letter proposing her as a bride for Charles II (The Hague, May 20, 1650), which describes her in very similar terms as "a gentlewoman of rare parts and education" and as "very handsome, extremely obliging and her behavior and dress equal to any seen in the Court of England"; Maurice Ashley, *Charles II: The Man and the Statesman* (St. Albans, UK: Panther, 1973), 51.

After I had stayed a convenient[352] time, I returned home to my lodging, where amongst several persons that visited me Sir James Douglas[353] came, and earnestly invited me to Aberdour to stay some time with his Lady. It was too obliging an offer to refuse. And upon June 15, I went with him and crossed at Leith to Burntisland:[354] as soon as I landed, Sir James Douglas had me by one hand, and the Laird of Mains[355] by the other, and they bid me welcome to Fife. And immediately I fell flat down upon the ground, and said, "I think I am going to take possession of it." They blamed one another for having had so little care of me. But what I thought then accidental, I have since looked upon as a presage of the future blessings I enjoyed in Fife (for which I shall forever bless my God, and the memory of that prostration shall raise in me praise to the Lord of bounty and mercy while I live).[356] When I came to Aberdour I was led in through the garden,[357] which was so fragrant and delightful that I thought I was still in England. I intended to have stayed there but two or three nights, but they would not part with me until June 22, and then I returned to Edinburgh but with a promise to be back again, which I made good the twenty seventh day.

About this time the news came that the King was landed in the north and was coming south.[358] [fol. 34v] I began to reflect upon my own misfortune in the unhappy report that was of Colonel Bampfield's wife's being alive and it was known to severals[359] about the Court what my concern in him was. This, with the unhandsome[360] and unjust character given both to him and my brother Will, made me apprehend might make me not be so well looked upon by the King

---

352. "Suitable to the conditions or circumstances; befitting the case; appropriate, proper, due," *OED*.

353. James, tenth Earl of Morton, who married Anne Hay, daughter of Sir James Hay and Sidney Massey, February 10, 1649, *TSP* 4:379–80.

354. Halkett originally wrote "Brun Island"; however, she means Burntisland, which is a royal burgh and parish on the south coast of Fife.

355. This was the tenth Laird, Sir Archibald Douglas, son of Alexander Douglas, ninth of Mains, and Grizel Henderson. "Archibald Douglas, Tenth Laird of Mains." Macfarlane Families and Connected Clans Genealogies, accessed September 08, 2018, https://www.clanmacfarlanegenealogy.info/genealogy/TNGWebsite/getperson.php?personID=I22363&tree=CC.

356. Halkett's jocular suggestion that she will become the owner of the land onto which she fell retrospectively appears prophetic as her husband, Sir James Halkett, owned the estate of Pitfirrane, Fife.

357. *Aberdour Castle* passed to the Douglas family in 1342, and the Earls of Morton resided there from 1546 to 1790. A brief description of the castle, its gardens, and its inhabitants, which cites Halkett's comments, can be found in M. R. Apted, *Aberdour Castle*, 2nd ed. (Edinburgh: Historic Scotland, 1985), 16.

358. Charles II landed at Garmouth on June 24, 1650, Seaward, *ODNB*.

359. "Several persons or things," *OED*.

360. "Unfitting, unbecoming, unseemly; discourteous, mean," *OED*.

as otherways I might expect. And therefore, to inform myself what reception I should get I sent an express to Mr. Seymour,[361] who was one of the Grooms of the bedchamber and[362] who had been fellow servant with my brother Charles. And to him I writ representing the disadvantages I lay under and that I expected his friendship in advising me whether I should go to kiss the King's hands or forbear; for I had much rather want the honor than receive it with a frown. To which this was his answer dated from Falkland,[363] July 17, 1650, "*Madam, I shall*[364] *have only time to tell you that his Majesty saith that you shall be very welcome to him when-so-ever you will give yourself that trouble, and that the world is too full of false rumors easily to engage his belief in anything that shall be to your prejudice. And I am very confident when you have spoken with him you will rest as assured of the esteem that he hath of you, as that I am upon all occasions, Madam,*[365] *your very humble servant, Henry Seymour.*" I was much satisfied with this letter and now my greatest concern was to find out a convenient time and place where to perform my duty.

But I was soon put out of that dispute by the Countess of Dunfermline[366] who came to Aberdour to see her brother and his Lady, and then told me she had received a letter from her Lord acquainting her what day the King had determined to be at Dunfermline (where his Lordship had invited his Majesty), and enjoined her [fol. 35r] to give me an invitation to be there that day, as knowing no place in Scotland I had more interest in nor fitter for me than there to attend the King. My Lady was pleased to second her Lord's desire, with so many obliging expressions, that I could not in civility have denied to obey her commands though it had been contrary to my inclination. But knowing it both my honor and advantage to be presented to the King in that noble family, I acknowledged the offer for a very great favor and promised to wait upon her Ladyship the day appointed (which I made good by the assistance of Sir James Douglas, who went along with me, and we came to Dunfermline some three hours before the King's arrival).

---

361. Henry Seymour had been "a page of honor to Queen Henrietta Maria and became a groom of the bedchamber to Prince Charles in May 1638." Although he accompanied the King to Scotland in 1650, he was deprived of his position during the Scottish committee's purging of the royal household. W. A. Shaw, "Seymour, Henry (bap. 1612, d. 1687)," rev. Ronald Clayton, *ODNB*. See also Smith, *Royalist Agents, Conspirators, and Spies*, 156.

362. "And" is an interlineal insertion.

363. I.e., Falkland Palace, Fife.

364. "Madam" and "shall" are interlineal insertions.

365. "Madam" is an interlineal insertion.

366. The Countess of Dunfermline was Lady Mary Seton, née Douglas, daughter of William Douglas, seventh Earl of Morton and Lady Anne Keith. In 1632, she married Sir Charles Seton, second Earl of Dunfermline. See J. R. M. Sizer, "Douglas, William, Seventh Earl of Morton (1582–1648)," *ODNB*.

A True Account of My Life 121

Figure 4. From a 1654 map of Fife, showing Southern Fife and the Firth of Forth. From James Gordon and Joan Blaeu, *Fifae Vicecomitatus, The Sherifdome of Fyfe* (Amsterdam: Blaeu, 1654). © National Library of Scotland, EMWX.015 (formerly WD.3B). Reproduced with permission.[367]

367. A digital image of this map is available to view freely on the NLS website: https://maps.nls.uk/view/00000444.

After his Majesty had been some time in the bedchamber reposing after the journey, I waited upon my Lady Dunfermline and my Lady Anna Erskine[368] to kiss the King's hand, being introduced by[369] my Lord Argyll and other persons of honor. And the first person I saw in the bedchamber was one of them who my brother Will had told me was his enemy. I cannot but acknowledge I was at first disordered when I saw him, and the more that he put a question to me to answer which I was obliged either to dissemble or say what was very unfit for the King to hear, but I avoided both with that reason, because I was so near, for the King heard my answer and smiled. When I recollected the promise I had made my brother to forgive that person and never to quarrel with him for the injury he had done him, I so far made it good that I had an opportunity that, with much ease and unknown, I could have had him put from the Court at that time when many were dismissed that had come home with the King. For a person who had great influence upon those who then governed enquired of me particularly concerning him, of whom I gave so favorable a character that he was continued to attend his Majesty.[370]

During the time the King continued at Dunfermline (which was eight or ten days,[371] being[372] royally entertained [fol. 35v] by the Earl of Dunfermline and all those who attended his Majesty), every day I waited upon my Lady and her niece when they went to attend the King either at dinner or supper. And though at those times he was pleased to look favorably upon me, yet it was no more than what he did to strangers. This did much trouble me. And therefore, the day before the King was to go from Dunfermline, I sent for Mr. Harding[373] in the morning to my chamber; and told him though my acquaintance with him was but of a short

---

368. Identified below as Lady Anna Erskine, the Earl of Dunfermline's niece. Charles Seton's sister, Anne, married Sir Alexander Erskine, Viscount Fentoun in April 1610; they had seven children, among them a daughter named Anna (who married William, Lord Forbes in 1668), *TCP* 3:50.

369. "Being introduced by" is an interlineal insertion.

370. On September 27, 1650, the committee of estates "ordered that the King's household be thoroughly and finally purged" of Malignants and Engagers. Maurice Lee, Jr., *The "Inevitable" Union and Other Essays on Early Modern Scotland* (East Linton, UK: Tuckwell, 2003), 214.

371. Other accounts give different information about the length of the King's visit: Henderson states only that the King visited in July, "Seton, Charles," *ODNB*; Sir James Balfour suggests that the King stayed only two days, July 24–25, 1650. Sir James Balfour, *The Historical Works of Sir James Balfour: Annals of the History of Scotland*, 4 vols. (Edinburgh: W. Aitchison, 1824), 4:82.

372. "Being" is an interlineal insertion.

373. Identified by Loftis as Richard Harding, an attendant of the King. Loftis, ed., *The Memoirs of Anne, Lady Halkett and Anne, Lady Fanshawe*, 200. Like Seymour, Harding was ejected from the royal household. Rev. W. Dunn Macray and Rev. H. O. Coxe, eds., *Calendar of the Clarendon State Papers Preserved in the Bodleian Library* (Oxford: Clarendon Press, 1872), 2:69.

date, yet for the friendship I heard he had for my brother Charles,[374] who was his fellow servant, I made choice of him (whose age and experience might make more sensible of what I could not but regret than those whose youth made them unconcerned in any trouble that was not their own).

I then vindicated my brother Will from the aspersing[375] he lay under (and[376] which I am confident occasioned his death) and represented my own misfortune, which possibly I might have avoided if I had not engaged in serving his Highness, the Duke of York, in his escape (many circumstances attending that having contributed to my present suffering both as to my fame and fortune). For being necessitate[377] to leave London for my own security, it was easy for the malicious to deprive me of both when I was not in a capacity[378] to speak in my own defense. "And after all this," said I, "it is an aggravation of my trouble to see the King never take notice of me, which may be a great discouragement to those persons of honor who have been very civil to me to continue so when they see me so little regarded by his Majesty." I could not utter this without tears, in which the good old gentlemen did keep me company, expressing a very great respect for me, and promised to speak to the King and give an account of what I had said.

The next day presently after the King had dined, when his Majesty had [fol. 36r] taken leave of my Lady Dunfermline and given her a compliment, and my Lady Anne Erskine (her Lord's niece), he came to me and said, "Mrs. Murray I am ashamed I have been so long speaking to you but it was because I could not say enough to you for the service you did my brother; but if ever I can command what I have right to as my own, there shall be nothing in my power I will not do for you."[379] And with that the King laid his hand upon both mine as they lay upon my breast. I humbly bowed down and kissed his Majesty's hand, and said I had done nothing but my duty, and had recompense enough if his Majesty[380] accepted of it as a service and allowed me his favor. After some other discourse which I have forgot, the King honored me with the farewell he had given the Ladies, and immediately went to horse.

---

374. Clarendon mentions a Charles Murray but only to note that he was "sent away from the King," February 28, 1646; Rev. O. Ogle and W. H. Bliss, eds., *Calendar of the Clarendon State Papers Preserved in the Bodleian Library* (Oxford: Clarendon Press, 1872), 1:364.

375. "The action of casting damaging imputations, false and injurious charges, or unjust insinuations; calumniation, defamation," *OED*.

376. "And" is an interlineal insertion.

377. "Obliged," *OED*.

378. "Position or condition," *OED*.

379. Unfortunately for Halkett, Charles II did not reward her as much as she might have expected, although she did later receive £500 from the exchequer, see *True Account*, 168.

380. "If his Majesty" is an interlineal insertion.

As soon as the King parted from me, there came two gentlemen to me: one took me by one hand, the other by the other, to lead me out to the court where all the ladies went to see the King take horse, with so many flattering expressions that I could not but with a little disdain tell them I thought they acted that part very well in *The Humorous Lieutenant*[381] (where a stranger coming to see a solemnity was hardly admitted to look on by those who afterwards troubled her with their civilities when they saw the King take notice of her). This answer put them both a little out and made them know I understood their humor.

To allay the joy that all the loyal party had for the King's return, there was two great occasions for disturbance, the one being strengthened by the other: Cromwell coming in with an army when there was so great divisions both in church and state, and such unsuitable things proposed for accommodation as I wish were buried in perpetual silence.[382] After the King had been invited to several places and entertained suitably to what could be expected, his Majesty returned [fol. 36v] again to Dunfermline, having ordered the forces to march. And one morning came letters from the army lying at Dunbar that they had so surrounded the enemy that there was no possibility for them to escape, which news gave great joy and much security. But the sad effects made us see how little confidence should be placed in anything but God, who in his justice thought fit to punish this kingdom and bring it under subjection to a Usurper because they paid not that subjection that was due to their lawful King.

The unexpected defeat which the King's army had at Dunbar[383] put everyone to new thoughts how to dispose of themselves, and none was more perplexed than I where to go or what to do. Again my Lady Dunfermline invited me to go north with her Ladyship, assuring me of much welcome and that I should fare as she did (though she could not promise anything but disorder from so sudden a removal to a house that had not of a long time had an inhabitant). I had much

---

381. Here, Halkett alludes to Fletcher's highly popular play, *The Humorous Lieutenant* (1618), which is "a fast-moving comedy of manners," Gordon McMullan, "Fletcher, John (1579–1625)," *ODNB*. In the opening scene, the central female character (Celia) is "[a]ttending an audience at the court of King Antigonous, [where she] is treated rudely until Prince Demetrius, her lover, kisses her. She then comments ironically on the abrupt change in demeanor of the company towards her." Loftis, ed., *The Memoirs of Anne, Lady Halkett and Anne, Lady Fanshawe*, 200. For further discussion of this connection, see Walker, "'Divine Chymistry' and Dramatic Character," 133–49.

382. Hutton summarizes these divisions in *Charles II*, 51–54; despite Halkett's wish for "silence," the eventual result was published at the insistence of the Commission of the Kirk as *A Declaration by the King's Majesty, to His Subjects of the Kingdoms of Scotland, England, and Ireland* (Edinburgh: [s.n.], 1650). ESTC R35923. According to Henderson, the document is also known as "The Dunfermline Declaration, August 16, 1650," *The Annals of Dunfermline and Vicinity*, 322–23.

383. David Plant, "The Battle of Dunbar, September 3, 1650." BCW Project: British Civil Wars, Commonwealth & Protectorate, 1638–1660, accessed September 08, 2018, http://bcw-project.org/military/third-civil-war/dunbar.

reason to accept of this offer with more than an ordinary sense of God's goodness; for there could not have been a more seasonable act of generosity than this[384] to a stranger[385] that was destitute of all means that should assist me in a retreat. I sent my woman over to Edinburgh, and writ to a lady who I had known from my infancy at London, and another letter to the gentleman who was my mother's executor, and from both I desired to borrow what money they could conveniently spare. I named the sum I desired from the Lady, which she very friendly sent upon the note of my hand; but my cousin[386] excused himself, because he had it not of his own, but said he had spoken to Sir G S who had promised to lend me £25 sterling upon my note, which he made good. And then I was the better satisfied to wait upon my Lady Dunfermline to the north, when I was [fol. 37r] provided so with money as that I should be the less troublesome to her Ladyship.

Upon Saturday, September 7, 1650,[387] we left Dunfermline and came that night to Kinross where we stayed until Monday. I cannot omit to insert here the opportunity I had of serving many poor wounded soldiers. For as we were riding to Kinross I saw two that looked desperately ill, who were so weak they were hardly able to go along the highway, and enquiring what ailed them, they told me they had been soldiers at Dunbar and were going towards Kinross if their wounds would suffer them. I bid them when they came there enquire for the Countess of Dunfermline's lodging and there would be one there would dress them. It was late, it seems, before they came, and so until the next morning I saw them not; but then they came, attended with twenty more. And betwixt that time and Monday that we left that place, I believe threescore[388] was the least that was dressed by me, and my woman, and Ar. Ro.,[389] who I employed to such as was unfit for me to dress. And besides the plasters or balsam[390] I applied, I gave every one of them as much with them as might dress them three or four times (for I had provided myself very well of things necessary for that employment, expecting they might be useful).

Amongst the many variety of wounds amongst them, two was extraordinary. One was a man whose head was cut so that the _____[391] was very visibly

---

384. "Than this" is an interlineal insertion.

385. "One who is not a native of, or who has not long resided in, a country, town, or place. Chiefly, a newcomer one who has not yet become well acquainted with the place, or one who is not yet well known," *OED*.

386. This cousin was probably William Murray, later Earl of Dysart, who was among the King's supporters in Scotland at this point. Smith, *Royalist Agents, Conspirators, and Spies*, 144, 156.

387. "1650" is an insertion in the right-hand margin of the manuscript.

388. A score is twenty, so Halkett suggests she assisted more than sixty soldiers injured at the Battle of Dunbar.

389. This person remains unidentified.

390. "Or balsam" is an interlineal insertion.

391. There is a gap in the manuscript, but presumably the missing word is "brain(s)."

seen and the water came bubbling up, which when Ar. Ro saw he cried out, "Lord have mercy upon thee, for thou art but a dead man!" I, seeing the man, who had courage enough before, begin to be much disheartened, I told him he need not be discouraged with what he that had no skill said; for if it pleased God to bless what I should give him, he might do well enough. And this I said more to hearten him up than otherways for I saw it a very dangerous wound, and yet it pleased God he recovered, as I heard afterwards, and went frankly[392] from dressing having given him something to refresh his spirits. The other was a youth about sixteen that had been run [fol. 37v] through the body with a tuke.[393] It went in under his right shoulder and came out under his left breast, and yet had little inconvenience by it. But his greatest prejudice was from so infinite a swarm of creatures[394] that it is incredible for any that were not eyewitnesses of it. I made a contribution, and brought him other clothes to put on him, and made the fire consume what else had been unpossible[395] to destroy.

Of all these poor soldiers there was few of them had ever been dressed from the time they received their wounds until they came to Kinross, and then it may be imagined they were very noisome;[396] but one particularly was in that degree, who was shot through the arm, that none was able to stay in the room, but all left me. Accidentally a gentleman came in, who seeing me (not without reluctancy) cutting[397] off the man's sleeve of his doublet which was hardly fit to be touched, he was so charitable as to take a knife and cut it off and fling in the fire.

When I had dressed all that came, my Lady Dunfermline was by this time ready to go away, and came to St. Johnston that night, where the King and court was. My Lady Anna Erskine and I waited upon my Lady into her sister, the Countess of Kinnoull,[398] and there my Lord Lorne[399] came to me and told me that my name was often before the Council that day. I was much surprised, which his

---

392. "Freely, openly; without restraint or reserve," *DSL*.

393. "A rapier," *OED*.

394. I.e., insects.

395. I.e., impossible.

396. "Harmful, injurious, noxious, especially in relation to the sense of smell; foul-smelling," *OED*.

397. Here, "ing" is an interlineal insertion.

398. The Countess of Kinnoull was Anne Hay, née Douglas, daughter of William Douglas, seventh Earl of Morton, and Lady Anne Keith. By the time Halkett met her, she was a widow, as her husband, George Hay, second Earl of Kinnoull, died in 1644. *TSP* 5:223–25.

399. Archibald Campbell, later ninth Earl of Argyll. His first wife, Mary Stuart, was the daughter of James Stuart, fourth Earl of Moray. They married on May 13, 1650, but she died in childbirth in May 1668. She and the Earl had six children who survived infancy. In 1670, he married Lady Anna Mackenzie, formerly Countess of Balcarres. David Stevenson, "Campbell, Archibald, Ninth Earl of Argyll (1629–1685)," *ODNB*. Rosalind K. Marshall, "Mackenzie, Anna [Known as Lady Anna Mackenzie], Countess of Balcarres and Countess of Argyll (ca. 1621–1707)," *ODNB*.

Lordship seeing kept me the longer in suspense. At last, he smiling told me there was a gentleman (which it seems was he that had cut off the man's sleeve) that had given the King and Council account of what he had seen and heard I had done to the poor soldiers; and representing the sad condition they had been in without that relief, there was presently an order made to appoint a place [fol. 38r] in several towns and chirugions[400] to have allowance for taking care of such wounded soldiers as should come to them. And the King was pleased to give me thanks for my charity. I have made this relation because it was the occasion of bringing me much of the divertissements[401] I had in a remoter place.[402]

Upon Thursday night, September 19, my Lady Dunfermline kissed the King's hands and took leave of all her relations in St. Johnston to go on her journey to Fyvie:[403] the first night, we lay at Glamis; the next two nights, at Brigton; upon Monday night, at Dunnottar; the next night, at Aberdeen where we stayed until Friday the twenty seventh;[404] and that night came to Fyvie, where I was entertained with so much respect and civility both by my Lady Dunfermline and my Lady Anna Erskine, and the whole family that I shall ever acknowledge it with all the gratitude imaginable.

After I had been there some time, the King came to Aberdeen,[405] and my Lord Dunfermline came home for a week to see his Lady and told me that Sir G S had desired his Lordship to let me know that some friends of his was to present the King with a purse with gold, and if I would employ any that I had interest in to speak to the King for me, he doubted not but his Majesty would give me part of the present. When my Lord returned I writ of it to Mr. Seymour, and at the first proposal the King was pleased to give order for sending fifty pieces to me. Half of it I paid to the gentleman that had formerly lent it me, who had found this way to secure himself and oblige me, and so I was free of that debt to my very great satisfaction.

I had not been long enjoying the tranquility of that retired condition I was in, when I received a letter from Colonel Bampfield that he was at Aberdeen, and desired to know if he might have liberty to come and see me at Fyvie. I was altogether averse to it and used many arguments to dissuade him from it, being

---

400. I.e., doctors.

401. "Diversion," *OED*.

402. I.e., for the two years that she stayed in Fyvie. Halkett continues to provide medical assistance to those around her throughout her life. See "Introduction" and "The Widows Mite," 30, 240.

403. The Earl of Dunfermline had an estate in Fyvie. A.M.W. Stirling, *Fyvie Castle: Its Lairds and Their Times* (London: John Murray, 1928). While there, Halkett wrote *Meditations upon the Twentieth and Fifth Psalm*, which was later published by Simon Couper. ESTC T72797.

404. Glamis is in Angus; Brigton and Dunnottar are in Kincardinshire; Fyvie is in Aberdeenshire.

405. After his coronation at Scone, January 1, 1651, Charles attempted to reunite the Scots under his rule; as part of this process, he visited Aberdeen in February 1651. Hutton, *Charles II*, 60–61.

positively determined not to see him until he could free himself of what he was taxed with: for though I did not believe it, and that he had so fully satisfied my Lord Dunfermline [fol. 38v] in Holland that his Lordship (as he often told me) had not the least doubt, yet I thought the safest way was to keep at a distance until it was past dispute. He so often importuned[406] me that at last he prevailed and, having acquainted my Lady Dunfermline with his desire and obtained her Ladyship's liberty, I gave my consent. But while the question was in debate the King returned towards Stirling,[407] and he, attending as the rest did, his Majesty, it took up a considerable time before my answer could come to him and he come to Fyvie.

But after I had dispatched his footboy, I began to have great debates with myself, and the conflict betwixt love and honor was so great and prevalent that neither would yield to other, and betwixt both I was brought into so great a distemper that I expected now an end to all my misfortunes. But it seems the Lord had some further use for me in the world and therefore thought fit then again to spare me. What the trials were that I met with under that sickness are known to some yet living, and the submission under them[408] was, I hope, acceptable to Him that gave it.[409]

Before I recovered so much strength as to be able to sit up, Colonel Bampfield came, whose satisfaction in seeing me was much abated to find me so weak, and for seeming so doubtful of the reports concerning him. And since what he had said to my brother Newton (when he thought it might have been the last moment of his life) did not satisfy me, he offered to take the most holy Sacrament upon it that he was innocent if it should be true that his wife was living, and gave so many reasons why it should not be true that I could not but acknowledge pleaded much for him. I altogether disallowed[410] of making use of that sacred institution for the end he proposed, since I did not think it warrantable,[411] nor could it convince me of the untruth of the report though it

---

406. "Of a person: persistent or pressing in making requests or offers, esp. to an irritating or distressing degree. Of a request, offer, etc.: made persistently or pressingly," OED.

407. Around April/May 1651, Hutton, *Charles II*, 62–63.

408. "Under them" is an interlineal insertion.

409. In Couper's catalogue of Halkett's "books," volume 4 is titled *Meditations on Death*; however, he dates that volume as being written in 1652. In "What Crosses and Difficulties I have Met with Myself," Halkett recalls God's assistance "at Fyvie, when I thought I was dying there," and that "the whole particular of this trial and deliverance is mentioned in the parchment book in folio, part written at Fyvie, in which that is writ, and many other things entitled *The Soul's Remembrancer*," 309. Although this volume is now missing, Couper dates it as having been written between 1649 and 1650.

410. "To refuse to approve or sanction; to disapprove of," OED.

411. "That may be guaranteed as good, true, genuine, or the like; of good warrant; praiseworthy, acceptable," OED.

might confirm he was innocent of it, and that charity inclined me to believe. For he could [fol. 39r] expect no advantage with me to countervail[412] the contrivance of so ill a design, and I thought no person could be so ill as do what's sinful merely because it is a sin; and therefore, I concluded either the report false or he miserably abused as well as I. After he had stayed two nights he took his leave of me, [I] having assured him ever to keep a due distance with him until the truth were evident beyond any one's contradiction, and if I found he had been injured he might be confident no other misfortune under heaven should separate me from him whenever I found I might lawfully and conveniently make good what I had designed.

It would be too tedious to relate here how I spent the time I was at Fyvie, which was near two years, but it was so agreeably that in all my life I never was so long together so truly contented. For the noble family I was in daily increased my obligation to them, and the Lord was pleased to bless what I gave to the help of the sick and wounded persons came to me. (Part of them from Kinross, and some English soldiers came to try my charity, which I did not deny to them, though they had it not without exhorting them to repent their sin of rebellion and become loyal.)

The variety of distempered persons that came to me was not only a divertissement,[413] but a help to instruct me how to submit under my own crosses by seeing how patient they were under theirs, and yet some of them intolerable by wanting a sense of faith which is the greatest support under afflictions. There was three most remarkable of any that came to me: one Isabel Stevenson who had been three year under a discomposed[414] spirit; the other was a young woman who had been very beautiful and her face became loathsomely deformed with a cancerous[415] humor that had overspread it (which deprived her of her nose, and one of her eyes, and had eaten much of her forehead and cheek away); the third was a man that had a horn on the left side of the hinder[416] part of his head betwixt four or five inches about and two inches long, and his wife told me she had cut the length of her finger off (as she usually did) two or three days before he [fol. 39v] came to me, because the weight of it was troublesome.[417] A further account of these may be had hereafter if it be necessary.

412. "To counterbalance, compensate, make up for," OED.

413. "Diversion," OED.

414. "Having lost one's self-possession; disturbed, agitated, unsettled," OED.

415. "Originally any of various types of non-healing sore or ulcer, esp. one that extends into surrounding tissue," OED.

416. "Situated behind, or at the back," OED.

417. Curious as this case may sound, Halkett's patient was not alone in suffering from this disease which is known today as a cutaneous horn. A similar case is described in *A Brief Narrative of a Strange and Wonderful Old Woman That Hath a Pair of Horns Growing upon Her Head* (London: T[homas]

The misfortune in the King's affairs gave his enemies the greater advantage, and was a discouragement to the loyal party to see how successful Cromwell's army was, who now marched where they pleased and gave laws to the whole kingdom.[418] The Earl of Dunfermline, being left behind the King (when his Majesty marched into England)[419] with others of the Council to order what was fit to be done in his Majesty's absence, they were soon put from acting anything and was forced to suffer what they could not prevent. But as long as they had any retreat, they still retired to be out of their enemies' hands, and my Lord Dunfermline came to Fyvie, and when the army came to Aberdeen he went to Moray[420] until he could make some capitulation[421] for himself; for when no resistance could be made, the next remedy was to make as good conditions as everyone could for themselves.

The army coming now towards Fyvie, some scattering[422] soldiers came in[423] there who had no officer but one they made amongst themselves and called him "Major." When they came into the house, they were very rude, beating all the men came in their way, and frighting[424] the women, and threatening to pistol[425] whoever did not give what they called for. My Lady Dunfermline, being then great with child, was much disordered with fear of their insolence, and with tears in her eyes, desired me to go and speak to them to see if I could prevail with them as being their countrywoman. "But," says she, I know not well how to desire it, because I hear they say they are informed there is an English woman in the house, and if they get her, they will be worse to her than any."

J[ohnson], 1676). ESTC R29132. For an earlier case, see also *A Myraculous, and Monstrous, but yet Most True, and Certayne Discourse, of a Woman (Now to Be Seene in London) of the Age of Threescore Yeares, or There Abouts, in the Midst of Whose Fore-Head (by the Wonderfull Worke of God) There Groweth out a Crooked Horne, of Foure Inches Long* (London: Thomas Orwin, 1588). ESTC S105391, cited Walsham, *Providence in Early Modern England*, 202. For a more recent case, Qin Zie, "Meet the 87-year-old Woman Who Has a Five Inch Horn Growing Out of Her Head," *MailOnline*, August 28, 2015, 8:42 a.m. BST, http://www.dailymail.co.uk/news/peoplesdaily/article-3212536/Meet-87-year-old-woman-five-inch-HORN-growing-head.html.

418. See David Plant, "Cromwell in Scotland, 1650–1651," BCW Project, accessed August 02, 2018, http://bcw-project.org/military/third-civil-war/cromwell-in-scotland.

419. The Battle of Worcester took place September 3, 1651, on the anniversary of the Battle of Dunbar, and was another decisive defeat for the Royalists. Smith, *Royal Agents, Conspirators, and Spies*, 156–58.

420. Originally "Murray," but this is a reference to the burgh of Moray.

421. "The making of terms, or of a bargain or agreement," *OED*.

422. "A sparse number or amount; a small proportion (of people) interspersed," *OED*.

423. "In" is an interlineal insertion.

424. "To affect with fright; to scare, terrify," *OED*.

425. I.e., to shoot.

"Madam," said [fol. 40r] I, "if my going to them can do your Ladyship service, I will take my hazard, and had gone to them before, but that[426] I thought it not fit for me (in your Ladyship's house) to take upon me to say anything to them until I had your Ladyship's command for it."

Then calling my woman, I went down where they were, and being instructed which was the "Major" (as they called him) who ordered the rest as he pleased (and I believe got that authority by humoring them in all they desired), I made my address first to him, believing if I prevailed with him the rest were soon gained.

As soon as I came amongst them, the first question they asked was if I were the English whore that came to meet the King? And all set their pistols fast[427] against me. (I had armed myself before by seeking assistance from him who only could protect me from their fury, and I did so much rely upon it that I had not the least fear, though naturally I am the greatest coward living.) I told them I owned myself to be an English woman and to honor the King, but for the name they gave me, I abhorred it. But my coming to them was not to dispute for myself, but to tell them I was sorry to hear that any of the English Nation, who was generally esteemed the most civil people in the world, should give so much occasion to be thought barbarously rude as they had done since their coming into the house (where they found none to resist them, but by the contrary, whatever they called for, either to themselves or horses, was ordered by my Lady to be given them).

"What advantage," said I,[428] "can you propose to yourselves to fright a person of honor who is great with child, and few but children and women in the house? And if by your disorder any misfortune happen to my Lady or any belonging to the family, you may expect to be called to an account for it, because I am very confident you have no allowance from your officers to be uncivil to any. And I am sure it is more your interest to oblige all you can than to disoblige them; [fol. 40v] for the[429] one will make you loved, the other hated, and judge which will be most for your advantage."

They heard me with much patience. And at last flinging down their pistols upon the table, the Major gave me his promise that neither he nor any with him should give the least disturbance to the meanest in the family, only desired meat, and drink, and what was necessary that they called for. And they did so keep their word that my Lady Dunfermline was by their staying in the house secured from many insolences that were practiced in other places.

---

426. "But that," means "except."

427. "Firmly, fixedly," *OED*.

428. "I" is an interlineal insertion.

429. "The" is an interlineal insertion.

A little after there came to Fyvie three regiments with their officers, being commanded by Colonel Lilburn, Colonel Fitch and Colonel Overton.[430] My Lady Dunfermline enquired of me, when she heard they were coming, if I knew any of those because she would desire me if I did to get a pass for my Lord Dunfermline to have liberty to return home. I said I had only seen Colonel Fitch when I was at Naworth Castle but had never spoken to him, and if he owned the knowledge of me I[431] would then endeavor to serve her Ladyship, but if not I would speak to those I had never seen rather than him. When they all came up to the dining room and saluted my Lady Dunfermline and my Lady Anna Erskine, when Colonel Fitch came to salute me, he lifted up his hands as being astonished to see me there, and came to me with the greatest joy he could express, and taking me by the hand said to my Lady Dunfermline, "Madam, I must beg liberty to speak with Mrs. Murray and give her account of her friends in England."

So, he and I sat down together at some distance from the rest, and he gave me a relation of all that had happened in Naworth Castle after my coming away. Some things that I was sorry for, even for Mr. Nicholls, who it seems had not followed my advice, but traducing[432] [fol. 41r] a person (who came there presently after I went away) who could not suffer it as I had done but took a revenge suitable enough to the fault (though unsuitable to one of his function). And I cannot omit to remark that it was performed in the garden, not far from the place where he so confidently denied a truth, which I hope being punished there made him reflect upon his sin and made him penitent for it. And I have reason not only to forgive him, but to thank him for the injury he did me since the Lord turned it to my advantage.

When I found Colonel Fitch thus free and civil, offering me any service in his power, I told him how much he would oblige my Lady Dunfermline, who was now near her time, if he would give a pass for my Lord to return, which he promised and made good when he came to Elgin[433] where my Lord was (for he went to him and prevented his Lordship's seeking anything by making offer of all he could desire).

---

430. For further details on these officers, see Barry Coward, "Lilburne, Robert (bap. 1614, d. 1665)," *ODNB*, and Barbara Taft, "Overton, Robert (1608/9–1678/9)," *ODNB*. Thomas Fitch "probably served in the northern forces"; he was governor of Carlisle 1649–1651, but by the end of 1651, "he suddenly appears in Scotland in command of a regiment marching to Garrison Inverness." Charles Firth and Godfrey Davies, *The Regimental History of Cromwell's Army*, 2 vols. (Oxford: Clarendon Press, 1940), 2:509–10. Overton became governor of Aberdeen in November 1651, and by February 1652 was heading further north, which indicates the time at which this discussion took place.

431. "I" is an interlineal insertion.

432. "To speak ill of, esp. (now always) falsely or maliciously; to defame, malign, vilify, slander; to blame, censure," *OED*.

433. Elgin: a parish in the neighboring burgh of Moray.

That day the officers went away, Colonel Overton, sitting by me at dinner, said to me[434] that God had wonderfully evidenced his power in the great things he had done. I replied, "No doubt but God would evidence his power still in the great things he designed to do."

I spoke this with more than ordinary earnestness,[435] which made him say, "You speak my words, but not, I think, to my sense."

"When I know that sense," said I then, "I will tell you whether it be mine or no."

"I speak," said he, "of the wonderful works that God hath done by his servants in the late times, that are beyond what any could have brought about without the immediate assistance of God and his direction."

"Sir," said I, "if you had not begun this discourse, I had said nothing to you, but since you have desired my opinion," which he did, "of the times, I shall very freely give it, upon the condition that, whatever I say, you may not make use of it to the[436] prejudice of the noble family I live in; for I can hold my tongue, but I cannot speak anything contrary to what I think. I cannot but confess you have had great success in all your undertakings, but that's no-good rule to justify ill actions. You pretend to great zeal in religion and obedience to God's words. If you can show me in all the Holy Scripture[437] a warrant for murdering your lawful King and banishing his posterity, I will then say [fol. 41v] all you have done is well and will be of your opinion. But as I am sure that cannot be done, so I must condemn that horrid act and whatever is done in prosecution of its vindication."

He replied that those who had writ upon the prophecy of Daniel[438] showed that he foretold the destruction of Monarchy many years since, and that it was a tyrannical government and therefore fit to be destroyed.

---

434. "To me" is an interlineal insertion.

435. "Vehemence, great ardor or passion," *OED*.

436. "The" is an interlineal insertion.

437. After "Scripture," there is an interlineal insertion of "show me," although the word "show" has been deleted. For sense, I have also deleted "me."

438. Mid-seventeenth-century radicals found justification of their actions in the biblical book of Daniel, and Cromwell cited it when he took on the role of Lord Protector in 1653. For some, especially the Fifth Monarchists, Cromwell did not go far enough, see Mary Cary, *The Little Horn's Doom and Downfall; or, A Scripture-prophesie of King James, and King Charles, and of this Present Parliament, Unfolded* (London: [s. n.], 1651), ESTC R210569, and Anna Trapnel, *The Cry of a Stone; or, A Relation of Something Spoken in Whitehall* (London: [s.n.], 1654), ESTC R203788, and *Strange and Wonderful Newes from White-Hall* (London: Robert Sele, 1654), ESTC R3949. For historical accounts, see Bernard Capp, *The Fifth Monarchy Men: A Study in Seventeenth-Century Millenarianism* (London: Faber, 1972); Christopher Hill, *The World Turned Upside Down: Radical Ideas during the English Revolution* (Harmondsworth, UK: Penguin, 1975); and James Holstun, *Ehud's Dagger: Class Struggle in the English Revolution* (London: Verso, 2000).

"How comes," said I, "you have taken the power from the Parliament and those successive interests that have governed since you wanted the King?"

"Because," said he, "we found after a little time they began to be as bad as he, and therefore we changed."

"And," said I, "so you will ever find reason to change whatever government you try, until you come to beg of the King to come home and govern you again; and this I am as confident of as I am speaking to you."[439]

"If I thought that would be true," replied he, "I would repent all that I have done."

"It will come to that, I dare assure you," said I, "and the greatest hindrance will be that you think your crimes have been such as is impossible he should forgive you; but to encourage you, I can assure you there was never any Prince more inclined to pardon nor more easy to be entreated to forgive."

"Well," says he, "if this should come to pass, I will say you are a prophetess."[440]

Here we broke off because we saw the rest of the table take notice of our seriousness. I found afterwards he was not unsatisfied with my discourse; for he came several times to see me when I came to Edinburgh and remembered many things I had said to him which I have now forgot.

When the whole kingdom[441] was now brought under the bondage of the Usurper,[442] and finding no remedy but to submit until the Lord thought fit to give them deliverance, everyone thought now of returning where their interest led them. And my Lord Dunfermline having been at [fol. 42r] Fyvie some time and stayed until his Lady was delivered of her daughter (my Lady Henrietta),[443] and mending again his Lordship resolved to go to Edinburgh about his affairs. And I thought it would be a convenient time for me to return then with his Lordship. But he, having first some occasion to go to Elgin, my curiosity to see that country made me prevail with my Lady Anna Erskine to go with her uncle and let me wait upon her to Moray. We went from Fyvie, Wednesday,[444] June 2, 1652, and crossed

---

439. See "Upon the Return of his Majesty after his Long Banishment and Variety of Other Troubles," 193–96.

440. See "The Widow's Mite, Part of It Relating to the King," 242.

441. I.e., Scotland.

442. I.e., Oliver Cromwell.

443. The Seton's only daughter, Henrietta, became Lady Henrietta Fleming, Countess of Wigtown and, later, Countess of Crawford. She married twice; first, on September 8, 1670, William Fleming, fifth Earl of Wigtown at Dalgety, with whom she had three children; second, as his second wife, William, eighteenth Earl of Crawford, ca. 1681. Henrietta died on April 8, 1681. Stirling, *Fyvie Castle*, 234–35; *TSP* 3:373–75.

444. "Wednesday" is an interlineal insertion.

the river Spey at the Bog;[445] upon Friday, came back again to Garmouth,[446] and crossed there the next day; and came home by Fordyce[447] to Fyvie.

Though I was resolved of my journey to Edinburgh, yet I was much troubled how to perform it; for my money was near spent and, having been so long a trouble to my Lady Dunfermline, I had not the confidence to seek to borrow any for carrying me south. Many difficulties in the way represented themselves to me, and what I might meet with at Edinburgh, and my woman was weeping by me (as being much discouraged with the inconveniences she apprehended I might be exposed to).[448] I smiled upon her and bid her have a good heart;[449] for though my present condition seemed very dark and cloudy, yet I was confident[450] I should see a sunshiny day; for though I was now encompassed round with misfortunes, yet I was very sure I should be as happy as I could desire, though I could not tell which way it would come to pass. And for my present supplies, I would rely upon God who had never yet left me in my greatest difficulties, and to his direction I resigned myself, being confidently assured he would provide some unexpected means to free me of my present trouble. And with that conclusion, I went to bed with as quiet repose as if I had had nothing to disturb me.

The next morning, early, the midwife (who had come from Dalkeith to my Lady Dunfermline) came into my chamber with her riding clothes [fol. 42v] on to take her leave of me, and said she had a request to me before she went, which was (hearing that I intended to be at Edinburgh shortly) that I would do her the favor to take the money she had got from my Lady Dunfermline and others[451] at the christening and bring it south with me, because she durst[452] take no more with her than her expenses by the way (because she apprehended being plundered by the soldiers). I told her if she thought it secure with me, I should do her that courtesy and deliver it where she would appoint at Edinburgh. So, I received it from her and gave her a note of my hand for it, being about ten-pound sterling, and she went away very well pleased, but little knew how much more reason she had given me to be so. For I looked not on it only as a present advantage, but as a

---

445. Most likely Bogmoor, near Garmouth.
446. Garmouth, in the parish of Urquhart, Moray.
447. Fordyce is a parish near the north coast of Aberdeenshire.
448. See "The Power of Faith, upon Mark 16:17–18," 191.
449. Psalm 27:14: "Wait on the Lord: be of good courage, and he shall strengthen thine heart: wait, I say, on the Lord"; Psalm 31:24: "Be of good courage, and he shall strengthen your heart, all ye that hope in the Lord."
450. "Was confident I" is an interlineal insertion.
451. "Others" is an interlineal insertion.
452. Past tense of "dare."

recompense for the reliance I had upon my most gracious God and an encouragement still to do so.[453]

It was no wonder if I had trouble to part with the noble family at Fyvie, where I had been near two year treated with all the kindness imaginable and where my satisfaction was so great that I could contentedly have spent the remainder of my life there (if it had been as convenient as it was pleasing).[454] But now it was time to free my Lady Dunfermline of the trouble I had given her so long, and necessary for me to go to Edinburgh to look after what was my concern and to begin a lawsuit for recovering the most considerable part of my portion.[455] So having taken[456] my leave of my Lady Dunfermline, and my Lady Anna Erskine, and all the family, not with dry eyes of either side (but the tears that moved me most was from that good old man, Mr. George Sharpe, minister of Fyvie, and his wife, to and from[457] whom I gave and received much respect).[458]

Upon Thursday, June 24, 1652, my Lord Dunfermline (with his nephew, the late Lord Lyon[459] and several other gentlemen) went from Fyvie, allowing me and my woman the honor of their company, and lay that night at my Lord Frazer's at Muchall;[460] the next night, at Northwater Bridge; and Saturday [fol. 43r] night at Balcarres, where we stayed until Tuesday; that night came to

---

453. See also "Upon Riches," 185–88.

454. She continues to recall their kindness in treating her "as a daughter of the family," see "Friday, April 5, 1695," 294.

455. See "Introduction," 17–19.

456. In MS this reads "taking."

457. "To and from" is an interlineal insertion.

458. Presented by Charles I, June 10, 1635, George Sharpe was minister at Fvyie from that date until at least 1653. Like Halkett, he had extended experience of debt, having petitioned Parliament about the nonpayment of his stipend, and "for the plundering of his goods by malignants and delinquents" in 1644. It was not until 1647 that he received "reparation for his losses amounting to eleven years' stipend." His wife was Elizabeth Anderson, whom he married on February 7, 1636, *FES* 6:256–57.

459. The title "Lord Lyon" is given to the sole King of Arms in Scotland who is head of the Heraldic Executive and the Judge of the Court of the Lord Lyon which has jurisdiction over all heraldic business in Scotland. The Society of Scottish Armigers, "The Lord Lyon Court of Arms," accessed August 03, 2016, http://www.scotarmigers.net/lordlyon.htm. Sir Charles Erskine of Cambo held this office in 1662 but died in September 1677 (during the period in which Halkett was writing her *True Account*). His mother was the Earl of Dunfermline's sister, Lady Anne Seton, who married Alexander Erskine, Viscount Fentoun, on April 6, 1610, *TSP* 5:86.

460. The Frasers of Muchall started building Castle Fraser in 1575, by the time of Halkett's visit was in the possession of Andrew, second Lord Fraser. "Fraser of Muchall," The Baronage (The Baronage Press Ltd and Pegasus Associated Ltd.), accessed August 3, 2016, http://www.baronage.co.uk/bphtm-03/fraser04.html.

Burntisland;[461] and Wednesday 30, to Edinburgh, where I went to my former lodging at Sanders Peers; and stayed there some time until Sir Robert Moray[462] and his Lady came to town, who lying at the Nether Bow[463] persuaded me to take a chamber near them (which was an advantage not to be refused, having also the conveniency[464] of being nearer the place where all my business chiefly lay). The lodging they chose[465] for me was up the stairs by John Meen's shop, belonging to a discreet old gentlewoman who had a back way up to the rooms she used herself.

I had not been there two or three nights when, my Lord Dunfermline and my Lord Balcarres[466] having supped with me and gone away about nine o'clock, I sat up later than ordinary to write letters to Fyvie with one going there the next morning, and before I had quite done there came soldiers to the chamber door and knocked very rudely. At first, I made them no answer, but they knocked with that violence that I thought they would have broke up the door. And then I enquired who they were, and what they would have: they told me they would come in and see who was with me or what I was doing. I told them I knew no warrant they had for that enquiry, yet to satisfy them I assured them there was none there but myself and my woman. They told me I lied, and that if I would not open the door they would break it open. I knew not what to say or do, but I bid Crew (which was my woman's name) go and desire the Mistress of the house to come down.

They, hearing the back door open, cried out, "She hath now let them out at the back door. Go and stop them!" And with that they forced up the door and run through the room, and some went upstairs and some down the stairs, but finding nobody they came in, in a great chafe.[467]

---

461. Originally "Mohall," "Northwater brig," "Balcaress," and "Brunt Island." Northwater Bridge is in the parish of Marykirk, just above Montrose; Balcarres, presumably Balcarres House, can be found in the parish of Kilconquhar in north east Fife, and is the family seat of the Earls of Crawford and Balcarres. Burntisland is a parish in Fife, situated on the shore of the Firth of Forth. In the seventeenth century, it was an important seaport, second only to the Port of Leith.

462. For an overview of Moray's life, see David Allan, "Moray, Sir Robert (1608/9?–1673)," *ODNB*. Sir Robert Moray married Sophia Lindsay (1624–1653), the daughter of David Lindsay, first Lord Balcarres, sometime in 1650. The marriage was short-lived, as she died while giving birth, on January 2, 1653. See also Frances Harris, "Lady Sophia's Visions: Sir Robert Moray, the Earl of Lauderdale, and the Restoration Government of Scotland," *Seventeenth Century* 24, no. 1 (2006): 129–55.

463. See figure 5, map of Edinburgh, 138.

464. Archaic form of "convenience."

465. In MS this reads "chused."

466. David Stevenson, "Lindsay, Alexander, First Earl of Balcarres (1618–1659)," *ODNB*.

467. "Passion or fury," *OED*.

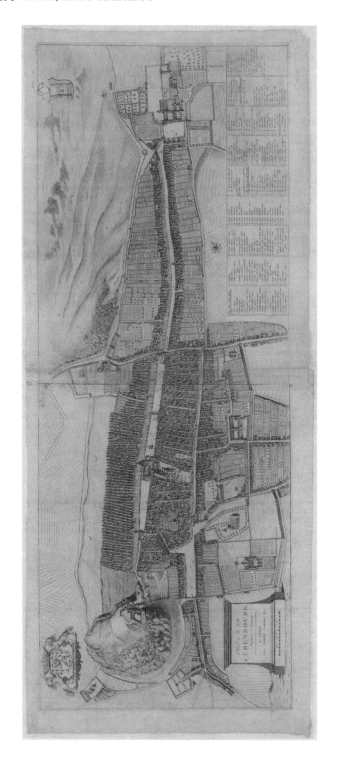

Figure 5. 1647 map of Edinburgh. From James Gordon, *Plan de la Ville d'Edenbourg, Capitale d'Ecosse* (Leiden: P. van der Aa, ca. 1729). © National Library of Scotland, EMS.s.53. Reproduced with permission.[468]

468. A digital image of this map is available to view freely on the NLS website: https://maps.nls.uk/towns/rec/2705.

I asked them if they had found those they went to seek. They said, no, for I had let them out. "Gentlemen," said I, "You may assure yourselves I will complain of you to your officers. For if I may not have liberty in my own lodging to sit up and burn a candle as long as I please without having such a disturbance, and upon such unworthy grounds as you would infer, I think few will hear of it that will not condemn your [fol. 43v] uncivil actions."

They seemed to justify themselves by an order they said they had to break up any doors where they saw lights after ten o'clock, and that they had been civil and expected I would give them something to drink. I told them when they deserved it they should have it, but sure they could not expect it from me having done as much as they could to bring a scandal upon me that was a stranger newly come there[469] and therefore might be the greater prejudice. They saw me very angry, and that they could not prevail[470] to get anything, and therefore left me in disorder enough to think what the neighbors about might think of me to hear what they said, and did, at my chamber door.

The next morning, I sent for William Murray of Hermiston,[471] who was very great with the English officers, and desired him to go to their Captain and complain, which he did, and their Captain sent down to refer to me their punishment (for they had no allowance for what they did). I soon remitted their punishment, conditionally that they did not practice the like again. The noise[472] of this came to as many persons' ears as I was acquainted with, and the disorder I was in by apprehending it might be usual to have such alarums as long as I lay there (having a great window to the street and none in the house but women), this made me think of changing my lodging. But where to fix I was undetermined when my Lord Tweeddale[473] and my Lady[474] very obligingly offered me the use of some rooms in his Lordship's house (they being then to go out of town and left only one room furnished and a porter to take care of the house).[475] I accepted of the offer with very great sense of the favor, but my next difficulty was where to borrow or hire furniture for my chamber and my woman's. That want was without my seeking

---

469. "Newly come there" is an interlineal insertion.

470. "To persuade or influence (a person); to induce to do something," OED.

471. This "may have been a Sir William Murray, a Royalist who served under the Duke of Hamilton"; Loftis, ed., *The Memoirs of Anne, Lady Halkett and Anne, Lady Fanshawe*, 201–2.

472. "Rumor or report," OED.

473. Young, "Hay, John," ODNB.

474. Hay's wife was Lady Jean Scott (1629–1688), second daughter of Walter Scott, first Earl of Buccleuch (d. 1633). Young, "Hay, John," ODNB.

475. See figure 5, map of Edinburgh, 138.

supplied by my Lady Balcarres,[476] who very civilly lent me all necessary accommodations; so, I removed my lodging into my Lord Tweeddale's house, which I had never had the offer of if the insolencey[477] of the soldiers had not given occasion for it, and so I had an advantage by the prejudice they intended me.

After I had been sometime settled I enquired for Mr. W. H.[478] who was the lawyer who (in my mother's lifetime had upon her assignation to me of the bond [fol. 44r] of £2,000 sterling with interest from 1647) began the suit in my name against Archibald Hay[479] who was caution for that sum with the Earl of Kinnoull.[480] Archibald Hay being now dead, I was to proceed against his executors. What the trouble and expense of that process was is too tedious to relate here, but in gratitude I shall ever acknowledge the obligation I had to my Lord Newbyth[481] and his father, who I could never persuade to take one penny of me, and yet they were as ready to assist me with their advice and attendance to solicit the judges as they who took most from me. The great disadvantage I had was that my antagonist was very favorably looked upon by the English judges as being inclined to their principles, and they looked upon me as a malignant.[482] And therefore they gave him all the advantage he could desire against me, which was by delays while he secured himself by fraudulent conveyances[483] of all the money in good hands, and then they gave me a Decreet[484] for recovering the rest. What I have now related in few words cost me some years' attendance.[485] But I shall leave what relates to that to mention some other particulars more to my satisfaction.

After I had been some time at my Lord Tweeddale's house, one Thursday my Lord Dunfermline came to see me and brought a gentleman with him who I had never seen before; and told me they had been both dining with my Lady

476. Marshall, "Mackenzie, Anna," *ODNB*. See also Mary McGrigor, *Anna, Countess of the Covenant* (Edinburgh: Birlinn, 2008), and "Saturday, June 23, 1694," 289–90.

477. I.e., "insolence: offensive contemptuousness of action or speech due to presumption; impertinently insulting behavior; sauciness," *OED*.

478. This person remains unidentified.

479. Identified as "Archibald Hay" in Couper, *The Life of the Lady Halket*, 27, and Halkett in "Appendix 3," 334. See also "Copy Resignation of a Factory by Sir James Halkett of Pitfirren [sic]," NRS GD34/843/3/23.

480. George Hay, third Earl of Kinnoull died in 1650, so the Earl to whom Halkett refers is probably his son, William, fourth Earl of Kinnoull, *TSP* 5:226–28.

481. Sir John Baird, Lord Newbyth, was a judge and son of the advocate, James Baird. Both father and son were Covenanters, and despite being "quickly reconciled to the Restoration after 1660," Newbyth was "excepted out of the Scottish Act of Indemnity in 1662, paying a fine of £2400." Stuart Handley, "Baird, Sir John, Lord Newbyth (bap. 1620, d. 1698)," *ODNB*.

482. I.e., a Royalist.

483. "Cunning management or contrivance; underhand dealing, jugglery, sleight of hand," *OED*.

484. "A judicial judgment or pronouncement; a decree of a court or competent judge or arbiter," *DSL*.

485. See also "Upon the Many Disappointments I have Met with in My Business at Court," 205–7.

Morton[486] (who was going to Sir John Gilmour's Lady's burial[487] and had promised to call them) and they had only so much time as to come in and ask how I liked my new lodging. I had scarce given an answer when one came in to tell me Mr. David Dickson[488] was without. I went to the door to bring him in, but chiefly to ask one of my Lord Dunfermline's servants what gentlemen that[489] was with his Lord, who told me it was Sir James Halkett. I said, "If he had not come with your Lord, I would not have been so civil as I am to him, because he hath a sword about him." For all the nobility and gentry had that mark of slavery upon them that none had liberty to wear a sword,[490] [fol. 44v] only such as served their interest and disowned the King, which made me hate to see a Scotch man with a sword.

Mr. Seaton,[491] who I was speaking to, smiled and said I was mistaken; for it was only a stick he held in his hand under his coat that stuck out like a sword, for he was too honest a gentleman to wear one now. Going in again and seeing my error made me change my thoughts of him.[492] Presently after, word came that my Lady Morton stayed in her coach for them at the door and they went away. This was the first time I saw Sir James Halkett, but before Saturday night I had five visits from him, every time making a several[493] pretense (either inquiring for Sir Robert Moray, or my Lord Dunfermline, or bringing some commissions to me from my Lady Morton). He was cousin German[494] with Sir Robert Moray, and much respected and very intimate[495] with the other,[496] and therefore I could not

486. The Countess of Morton was Anne Douglas, née Villiers (b. 1610, d. 1654). The daughter of Sir Edward Villiers and Barbara St. John, she had married Robert Douglas, eighth Earl of Morton, in April 1627; as he died in 1649, the Countess was a widow when the then Anne Murray met her, *TCP* 9:296.

487. Sir John Gilmour was married four times, but the name of his first wife is unknown. He was an advocate who favored the implementation of Royalist policies, and his "constant allegiance to the crown" earned him a knighthood in 1650 or 1651. J. A. Hamilton, "Gilmour, Sir John, of Craigmillar (bap. 1605, d. 1671)," rev. Gillian H MacIntosh, *ODNB*.

488. David Dickson was a Church of Scotland minister and theologian. Although initially supportive of the "Protesters," by 1651 he had shifted his allegiance toward the "Resolutioners." Holfelder, "Dickson, David," *ODNB*.

489. "That" is an interlineal insertion.

490. After "sword," "and" has been deleted.

491. Possibly Alexander Seton, first Viscount Kingston. See John J. Scally, "Seton, Alexander, First Viscount Kingston (1621–1691)," *ODNB*.

492. While Sir James Halkett may well have only been carrying a stick by this time, up until January 1651, he had been a Colonel in the Covenanting armies. His career can be traced in Edward M. Furgol, *A Regimental History of the Covenanting Armies, 1639–1651* (Edinburgh: John Donald, 1990), 222–23, 251, 313–15.

493. "Distinctive, particular," *OED*.

494. "The son or daughter of (one's) uncle or aunt; (one's) first cousin," *OED*.

495. Originally "intimately and"; "ly and" was deleted and "with" added as an interlineal insertion.

496. I.e., the Earl of Dunfermline.

but be very civil to him upon that account. And I saw no reason but that he might challenge[497] it upon his own.

After I had been some time at Edinburgh, I had a visit from one who had frequently been at my mother's and was much obliged to a near relation of mine. And to him[498] I told the difficulty I had to get any money out of England, and the few I had interest in to borrow of in Edinburgh, and he very civilly lent me what paid the money which the midwife trusted to my care and for other necessary occasions.

Being now settled, and put my affairs in such hands as would be careful of them in my absence, I resolved to go into England and see my Lady Howard, having the conveniency[499] of horses lent me by my Lord Dunfermline's mother[500] (who was extremely obliging to me and the more because she knew I was a faithful servant to all that owned the King's interest, for she was an extraordinary Royalist).

Being provided with all things for my journey, and [fol. 45r] intending to go first to the Floors[501] where I was invited by the Countess of Roxburghe,[502] to hasten my journey I received a letter from Colonel Bampfield, writ in cypher,[503] giving me account that after many hazards and difficulties he was come to the north of England, where he stayed privately until he could enquire where I was and that I could advise him where he might speak with Sir Robert Moray. I gave him an answer by the same way I received his, and acquainted him with my intention of going to Naworth Castle, and appointed a day that I intended to be at Alnwick,[504] where if he durst[505] venture to come, I should then let him know Sir

---

497. "To assert one's title to, lay claim to," OED.

498. In original, this reads "them."

499. Archaic form of "convenience."

500. Lady Margaret Hay (1592–1659), the sister of John Hay, first Earl of Tweeddale. Henderson, "Seton, Charles," ODNB.

501. "Fleurs" in MS.

502. The Dowager Countess of Roxburghe, Lady Isabel Douglas (d. 1672), daughter of William Douglas, fifth Earl of Morton, was the third wife of Robert Ker, first Earl of Roxburghe. She lived at Floors Castle, near Kelso. Alan R. MacDonald, "Ker, Robert, First Earl of Roxburghe (1569/70–1650)," ODNB.

503. "A secret or disguised manner of writing, whether by characters arbitrarily invented... or by an arbitrary use of letters or characters in other than their ordinary sense, by making single words stand for sentences or phrases, or by other conventional methods intelligible only to those possessing the key," OED.

504. Originally "Anwicke," but presumably this is modern-day Alnwick in Northumbria, where there is a castle owned by the Earls of Northumberland at which Halkett may have stayed. See Alnwick Castle website, accessed August 10, 2016, https://www.alnwickcastle.com.

505. Past tense of "dare."

Robert Moray's opinion of the fittest place for[506] to meet with him (for I had told Sir Robert my design and had his approbation).

When I was come to the Floors and stayed there two or three days, I went on my intended journey towards Naworth Castle but when I came to Alnwick, Colonel Bampfield dissuaded me from going there because there was some there that I was not desirous to see. And so I returned back again the next day, and came to the Floors where I stayed until Crew came back[507] (who I sent to Naworth Castle to bring my trunks and what I had left there for a want of conveniency[508] to bring them with myself when I came from thence).[509] The entertainment I had at the Floors was so agreeable that I had no reason to be weary the time I was there, nor was I unsatisfied to return to Edinburgh because Colonel Bampfield was uncertain how to dispose of himself until he heard again from me.

I gave Sir Robert Moray and my Lord Dunfermline an account of his designs, which was to wait all opportunities wherein he might serve the King, and if there were any probability of doing it in Scotland, he would then come there and hazard his life as far as any could propose it to be rational.[510] The advice they gave was to conceal himself where he was for some time, until they saw a fit opportunity to invite him to Edinburgh, where they believed he might be secure enough since he was known to very few there but such as was his friends. While he continued in the north of England, I heard frequently from him and still gave him account of what hopes[511] there was of acting anything[512] for the King, [fol. 45v] which I had the more opportunity to do because my chamber was the place where Sir Robert Moray most commonly met with such persons as were designing to serve the King.[513] Amongst the rest Sir James Halkett seldom missed to be one.

Sir Robert Moray's Lady,[514] being great with child and having no convenient lodging where she used to lie, desired some rooms in my Lord Tweeddale's house, which his Lordship readily granted to my very great satisfaction, for I could not desire the converse of any person more for my advantage; for she was devoutly

---

506. After "for," him has been deleted.

507. After "back," "again" has been deleted.

508. Archaic form of "convenience."

509. "When I came from thence" is an interlineal insertion.

510. "In accordance with reason; reasonable, sensible; not foolish, absurd, or extreme," *OED*.

511. After "hopes," "or fears" has been deleted.

512. Originally "something," Halkett deleted the "some" and replaced it with "any" in an interlineal insertion.

513. Smith, *Royalist Agents, Conspirators, and Spies*, 166.

514. Sir Robert Moray married Lady Sophia Lindsay (1624–1653), the daughter of David Lindsay, first Lord Balcarres, sometime in 1650. David Allan, "Sir Robert Moray, 1608/9–1673)," *ODNB*. Sadly, the marriage was short-lived; she died while giving birth to the child she was expecting here, on January 2, 1653, as Halkett records below and in "Upon the Death of Sir Robert Moray," 250–51.

good, without show or affectation, extremely pleasing in discourse, civil to all, and of a constant cheerful humor. We always ate together and seldom asunder any other part of the day, except for convenient[515] retirements, and though that house was the rendezvous of the best and most loyal when they came to town, yet none was so constantly there as Sir James Halkett. And though his relation to Sir Robert was ground enough for his frequent being there, yet any[516] that saw him in my company could not but take notice that he had a more than ordinary respect for me (which though I thought myself obliged to him for, yet it was a great trouble to me, since I was not in a capacity to give him such a return as he might expect or deserve).

And to prevent his declaring to me what was visible enough, I resolved to give him an opportunity of being in my chamber alone with me (which before I had much avoided) that I might put an end to his being further concerned in me. When he came in and was set down, after some general discourse I told him I had been very much obliged to his civility ever since I knew him, and I looked upon him as so worthy a person that I could not conceal from him the greatest concern I had, and my greatest misfortune: which was that when I had engaged myself to a person who I was fully determined [fol. 46r] to marry, my brother and sister (to dissuade me from it) found no motive so strong as to endeavor to persuade me that I was abused in believing his wife was dead, for she was alive; and because I did rather believe him than they, this[517] occasioned their unkindness.

"You may believe," said I, "such a report could not but make me think myself extremely unhappy. But those whose judgments I rely upon more than my own, as Sir Robert Moray and my Lord Dunfermline, who hath spoke with him and are fully convinced he is injured that they chide me when I seem to have the least doubt of it. Now Sir," said I, "this relation may confirm I have a great confidence of your friendship when I trust you with this and do intend when he comes here, which I shortly expect, to present him to you as one that I hope you will not believe unworthy your knowledge."

This discourse did strangely surprise him. But he endeavored to hide his disorder as well as he could, and said he was sorry for my brother's unkindness, and if he were near him he would endeavor to reconcile him again (for he was well acquainted with him when he was in Scotland).[518] And for Colonel Bampfield, whenever he came to town he would serve him to the utmost of his power, for he could not but believe he was deserving since he had my esteem. Presently after this he left me, and I expected he would have laid aside all concern for me. But I soon found my mistake, and that I was in an error when I believed he loved me at

---

515. "Suitable to the conditions or circumstances; befitting the case; appropriate, proper, due," OED.
516. After "yet," a repeated "yet" has been deleted and replaced by "any" as an interlineal insertion.
517. "This" is an interlineal insertion.
518. I have not been able to trace any records of Henry Murray in Scotland.

an ordinary rate; for it was never more visible than when he had least hopes of a recompense, and changed that affection to a virtuous friendship from[519] which at first he might have expected a lawful enjoyment.

Sometime after this, I was advised to write to Colonel Bampfield to come to Edinburgh, which he did as soon as was possible after the receipt of my letter, and had a lodging provided[520] for him and his man in a private house near my Lord Tweeddale's house, where he might come without being seen upon the street. Every night in the close of the evening he came in, and that was the time appointed where those persons met with him [fol. 46v] who were contriving some means to assert their loyalty and free their country from continuing enslaved. Those who most frequently met was Earl Dunfermline, Lord Balcarres, Sir James Halkett, and Sir George Mackenzie of Tarbat[521] (who Sir Robert Moray had a great opinion of, though he was then very young, and brought him into their cabal[522] as one[523] whose interest and parts might make him very useful to their designs). After they had formed it in the most probable way to be successful, they found it necessary to be armed with the King's authority for what they did; and therefore, sent to acquaint his Majesty with what they intended, and to desire commission for several persons nominate, and some blank for such as might afterwards be[524] found fit for the employment.

A few days after these letters were sent (the material part whereof was writ in white ink[525] and what was writ in ordinary ink was only to convey the other without suspicion), Sir George Mackenzie came into dinner to Sir Robert Moray and told him he had been in a stationer's shop, and taking up a book accidentally the first thing he saw in it was direction to write without being discovered, and there found the same way which they had been making use of in their address to the King, which put them in some disorder.[526] But Sir Robert Moray said the only

519. "From" is an interlineal insertion.
520. "Provided" is an interlineal insertion.
521. Kidd, "Mackenzie, George," *ODNB*.
522. "A small body of persons engaged in secret or private machination or intrigue; a coterie, a party, faction," *OED*. By the time Halkett was writing, the term had a specific political resonance, as it had been applied to Charles II's "Committee for Foreign Affairs which had the chief management of the course of government, and was the precursor of the modern cabinet," *OED*.
523. After "one," "that" has been deleted.
524. "Be" is an interlineal insertion.
525. I.e., a form of invisible ink.
526. This may have been J[ohn] W[ilkins], *Mercury: or, The Secret and Swift Messenger; Shewing, How a Man May with Privacy and Speed Communicate His Thoughts to a Friend at any Distance* (London: J. Norton, 1641), which advises "There is also a secret way of writing with two several inks. . . . Those letters that are described with milk or urine, or fat, or any other glutinous moisture, will not be legible unless dust be first scattered upon them, which by adhering to those places, will discover the writing," 42. ESTC R1665. Loftis, ed., *The Memoirs of Anne, Lady Halkett and Anne, Lady Fanshawe*, 203.

hopes he had was that, if that book came into the English[527] hands, they would not believe anything so common as to be in print would be made use of in any business of consequence. But not long after they received an account of their letters coming safe to his Majesty's hands, and a full complying with their desire in sending the commissions with a safe hand to the north of Scotland where those persons were to attend their arrival.

In the meantime, Sir George Mackenzie was preparing for his journey north, and Colonel Bampfield was to go with him under another name (for he needed no other disguise, being known to none in the kingdom but those persons I have mentioned, who was too much his friends and mine to have done him any [fol. 47r] prejudice). Amongst all his acquaintance none professed more friendship to him than Sir James Halkett and made it good in all circumstances wherein he could make it appear, giving him several presents useful for the employment he was going about and a fine horse durable for service. Colonel Bampfield understood very well upon what account it was that he received these testimonies of kindness, and did regret the misfortune of not having it in his power to oblige him; for he knew nothing could do it more than his resigning his interest in me and that was not possible for him to do (though he would often tell me if anything should arrive to deprive him of me, he thought in gratitude I was obliged to marry Sir James Halkett). I could not but own a very great sense of his civilities, but nothing could be more disagreeable to me than speaking either in jest or earnest of my marrying him; for nothing but the death of Colonel Bampfield could make me ever think of another (for what after fell out I had no belief of, and therefore could not apprehend it as a reason for my change). The day being come appointed for Sir George Mackenzie's and Colonel Bampfield's departure, some interruption intervened, and therefore it was delayed for a time.

Upon Christmas day, an English woman who had been a servant to my Lady Balcarres (Sir Robert Moray's Lady's mother),[528] according to the English custom had prepared (in her own house where she kept a change)[529] better fare than ordinary, and amongst the rest a dish of minced pies of which, when we were at dinner, she brought over two and said: one she intended for Sir Robert and his Lady, and the other for Sir James Halkett (who was then there) and me.[530] All the

527. "There" has been corrected to "the;" "English" is an interlineal insertion.

528. I.e., Lady Sophia Seton, daughter of Alexander Seton, first Earl of Dunfermline and Lilias Drummond, *TCP* 1:376.

529. "'A small inn or alehouse' (Jamieson). (Perhaps originally a wayside inn at which horses were or might be changed; in which sense it sometimes remains as a proper name on the old coachroads)," *OED*.

530. While serving mince pies was part of the "English Custom" at Christmas, Cromwell had banned the celebration of Christmas in England since 1647. This brought England in line with Scotland, which had, theoretically, stopped celebrating this festival since the 1560s. See Christopher Durston, "Lords of Misrule: The Puritan War on Christmas, 1642–60," *History Today* 35, no. 12 (1985): 7–14; and

table smiled at what she said, but I looked very gravely upon it, and rather wished it with him that had more interest in me.

All the company being in a better humor than ordinary, we were all extremely merry. A woman being in the house called Jane Hambleton, who they say had the second sight, observing all very well pleased, said to my Lady Moray's woman and mine, [fol. 47v] "There is a great deal of mirth in this house today but before this day eight days there will be as much sadness," which too truly fell out.

For within three or four days my Lady Moray took her pains, but they all struck up to her heart, and all means being unsuccessful she died with as much regret as any person could have. Though her patience was as great as was imaginable for any to have upon the rack,[531] and her love to[532] her husband great as her other qualifications were, yet she earnestly desired death many hours before it came; and Sir Robert sat constantly upon her bedside, feeling her pulse, and exhorting her cheerfully to endure those moments of pain which would soon be changed to everlasting pleasure. And though no doubt her death was the greatest misfortune could arrive to him, yet he did speak[533] so excellently to her as did exceed by far what the best ministers said who frequently came to her. And was so composed, both at and after her death, that neither action nor work could discover in him the least of[534] passion.[535] He immediately took care for transporting her body to Balcarres to be buried there with her child, which she carried with her to her grave being never separated. This was a sad loss to me; for besides the advantage I had in her obliging converse, I had the assistance of Sir Robert's advice in any difficulty in my business, and he went oft times to consultations with me and employed his interest as far as it could be useful to me. And when he went away, he very earnestly recommended me and my concerns to his cousin, Sir James Halkett, who was not ill pleased with the employment.

This for some time put a stop to[536] Sir George Mackenzie going north because Sir Robert had some thoughts [fol. 48r] of going with him, which he either did or followed soon after. Upon Monday, February 7, 1652/3, Sir George Mackenzie and Colonel Bampfield began their journey from Edinburgh. The

---

Margo Todd, "Profane Pastimes and the Reformed Community: The Persistence of Popular Festivities in Early Modern Scotland," *Journal of British Studies* 39, no. 2 (2000): 123–56. See "Christmas Day, Thursday, December 25, 1690," 280–81.

531. "Something which causes acute physical or mental suffering. Also: the result of this; intense pain or anguish," *OED*.

532. "To" is in interlineal insertion.

533. "Speak" is an interlineal insertion.

534. "Of" is an interlineal insertion.

535. Halkett recalls this in her occasional meditation "Upon the Death of Sir Robert Moray," 250–51. His stoicism during his wife's death is also noted by Allan, "Moray, Sir Robert," *ODNB*.

536. "To" is an insertion in the left-hand margin.

night before, the Earl of Dunfermline supped with him and me at my chamber, and then ordered the way of keeping correspondence, and what advice he thought fit for the action he was going about. It is not to be imagined but my trouble was great to part with him, considering the hazards he was exposing himself to; but I must confess it was increased by reflecting upon what Jane Hambleton had several times said to Crew: that she had observed a gentleman come privately to my chamber and said she knew that I and severals[537] looked upon him as one I intended to marry, but he should never be my husband. And remembering how truly, but sadly, fell out what she had foretold before made me the more apprehensive of this separation (though I was one that never allowed myself to enquire or believe those that pretended to know future events).

I had of late been so used to good company that I was the more sensible now[538] of the want of it, and finding it would be more for my advantage to be in some private house (where my meat might be dressed than to have it from the cooks, or keep one for that use), therefore I resolved to take another lodging. And having returned the furniture I borrowed, with my humble thanks for their use and the use of the house, I took two rooms in Mr. Hugh Wallace's house in the foot of Blackfriar's Wynd.[539]

But one remarkable passage I met with before I left the Earl of Tweeddale's house which I cannot but mention.[540] One evening, towards the close of daylight, there came a tall, proper[541] man into the room where I was and desired he might speak to me. I went towards him, and he told me he was one who had not been used to seek but was now reduced to that necessity that he was forced to ask my [fol. 48v] charity to keep him from starving. His looks were so suitable to his words that I could not but compassionate[542] his condition and regret my own; for all I had was but one poor shilling nor knew I where to borrow two pence. I thought to give him all I had might appear vanity if any should know it, and to give him less could not supply his want; and therefore, I resolved to give it him all and referred myself to His hands for whom I did it (concluding that perhaps some would lend me that would not give him). And I doubted not but God[543] would provide for me. So I gave him the shilling, which raised so great a joy in him that I could not but be highly pleased to be the instrument of that which brought such praises to the God of mercy, who left me not without a recompense; for the next

---

537. "Several persons or things," OED.

538. "Now" is an interlineal insertion.

539. See figure 5, map of Edinburgh, 138.

540. See "Upon Riches," 185–88.

541. One "of good character or standing; honest, respectable, worthy," OED.

542. "To regard or treat with compassion; to pity, commiserate (a person, or his distress, etc.)," OED.

543. "But God" is an interlineal insertion.

morning before I was ready, the Earl of Roxburghe[544] came to my chamber, who was newly come from London, and brought me a very kind letter from my sister and twenty pound sterling for a testimony of her affection which I received as a reward for my last night's charity.

To make good the promise Sir James Halkett made to Sir Robert Moray, he never came to town but I was the first person he visited, and was very solicitous in any of my concerns, and went with me when I had occasion to attend the judges. I found frequency of converse increased what I was sorry to find, and to divert it from myself I often persuaded him to marry. And used several arguments from what he had acquainted me with in his own condition that made me, by way of friendship to him and for preventing some inconveniences to his family, very seriously advise him to marry. And, I confess, I proposed it as a great satisfaction to myself to have his condition such as might make it utterly impossible for him to have any thoughts of me but what might be allowable to him in a married state. I, at last, prevailed so far with him that he acknowledged he was [fol. 49r] convinced it would be for his advantage to have a good discreet wife, and he had had several in his thoughts since I was so urgent with him; and now was determined upon one, but was resolved I should be the first proposer of it.[545] I was very well pleased to undertake the employment.

And the way he designed was by my recommending him by a letter to my Lord Balcarres, who had an interest in a handsome, young widow, and to desire his Lordship's assistance to obtain his design. This he did only to complement me, for his own interest with my Lord Balcarres was much more than any I could pretend to; for he had a great esteem for Sir James, and I remember once when I was at Balcarres (where I went frequently) my Lord was speaking something of Sir James, and I said, "Pray my Lord, give me leave to ask what the ground was that some people takes to speak with some reflection[546] upon him?"

"Truly," my Lord replied, "I believe never person was more injured nor worse requited for a gallant action. And he could not have desired a better witness to vindicate him than the King, for he was a witness all the time, standing upon the leads of my Lord's Belmerinoth's[547] house at Leith and saw the whole procedure; for if it had not been for Sir James and those he commanded, all the

---

544. Born William Drummond, the second Earl of Roxburghe, changed his name to Ker in 1650 when he took up that title. He was the son of John Drummond, second Earl of Perth, and Lady Jean Ker (daughter of Robert Ker, first Earl of Roxburghe), *TCP* 1:378. See also MacDonald, "Ker, Robert," *ODNB*.

545. See "Introduction," 33.

546. "Blame, censure, reproof; a remark casting some discredit on a person," *OED*.

547. John Elphinstone, third Lord Balmerino and second Lord Cupar (1623–1704), "received Charles II at his mansion in Leith on the King's visit to Scotland" in 1650. John Coffey, "Elphinstone, John, Second Lord Balmerino (d. 1649)," *ODNB*.

King's forces at that time at Musselburgh had been cut off, and he stood in the face of the enemy while the rest retreated and came handsomely off with very little disadvantage. And as I am a Christian," said my Lord, "this is true. And I have heard the King speak several times of it with great applause to Sir James and anger at those who traduced him in what was so eminently false."[548]

And upon that occasion he heard the King say, "Lord keep me from their malice, for I see they will spare none they have a prejudice against."

To confirm[549] that this humor did very much reign, I cannot but mention what I was a witness of myself. One day, Sir James [fol. 49v] came to see me and brought a gentleman with him, who he believed much his friend. And after several discourses of public affairs, the gentleman sat silent a little while, and then smiling said, "Sir James, now that I am convinced you are an honest man and love the King and his interest, I will make a confession to you. You were so great with my Lord Argyll[550] that I thought it impossible you could be honest. And therefore, I have lain in my bed in a morning inventing some ill story of you and reported it when I went abroad, and it was joy to me to have it believed; and now I see my error, I ask your pardon," which Sir James soon gave and passed it over as a jest.

But to return where I left. After Sir James was resolved to make address to that Lady, he intended to go upon Monday, March 21, 1652/3 to Balcarres and desired to have my letter ready, and in the morning, he would call for it. I was not long in writing and did recommend the design to my Lord Balcarres with as much earnestness as the greatest concern I could have. And had the letter ready against he came for it, which was punctually the time he appointed.

When he came into my chamber I saw something of joy on his face that I had not observed in a long time; and I said I was glad to see him look so well pleased, for had he sooner resolved to go a-wooing, I had sooner seen a change in him. Though I saw him well pleased, yet I saw him in disorder with it, and he stood still a pretty while without speaking a word.

---

548. "To speak ill of, esp. (now always) falsely or maliciously; to defame, malign, vilify, slander; to blame, censure," *OED*. As Loftis explains, Sir James Halkett had been accused of cowardice; Loftis, ed., *The Memoirs of Anne, Lady Halkett and Anne, Lady Fanshawe*, 204. Although the details are sketchy, Balfour provides some information: "The last of July Sir James Hackett received a great fright at a skirmish with the enemy; he should have seconded the Lieutenant General but turned and never loosed a pistol against the enemy but took him to the speed of his horse's heels." However, on August 3, 1650, Balfour reports that "Sir James Hackett and Colonel Scott, cleared by the committee, yet that did little salve their honor amongst honest men and soldiers of worth and reputation," *The Historical Works of Sir James Balfour*, 4:86–87, 88–89. This episode is also recounted in Furgol, *A Regimental History*, 315. Despite her defense of her husband here, in "Upon the Death of My Dearest Sir James Halkett," she intimates that he may not have been entirely loyal, 222.

549. "To confirm" is an interlineal insertion.

550. See Stevenson, "Campbell, Archibald, Marquess of Argyll," *ODNB*.

A True Account of My Life 151

At last he said, "I have heard news this morning, and though I know it will trouble you, yet I think it is fit you should be acquainted with it. Just as I was turning down Blackfriar Wynd," said he, "to come here, Colonel Hay[551] called to me and told me the post that came in yesterday morning had brought letters from London that undoubtedly Colonel Bampfield's wife was living and was now at London, where she came chiefly to undeceive[552] those who believed her dead."

"Oh," said I with a sad sigh, "is my misfortune so soon divulged . . .

[one leaf (two pages) missing from manuscript][553]

[fol. 50v] unworthy. And in what appeared so, none living could condemn me more than I did myself. But I had some circumstances to plead for me without which I had been unpardonable; and that was the concealing my intended marriage merely because he durst not without hazard of his life avowedly appear, and therefore it had been imprudence to publish what might have been (in those times) ruin to us both.

As soon as I could get myself composed so as to go abroad, I went where duty led me more than inclination; for I apprehended[554] everyone that saw me censured me, and that was no little trouble to me when I reflected on my misfortune that gave them but too just grounds. But that I was with patience to suffer, and whatever else my lord God thought fit to inflict, to whom I did entirely submit and could make nothing unwelcome from his hand (who had so wonderfully supported me in so unparalleled a trial).

In May, 1653, the Earl of Dunfermline[555] came to my chamber, and told me he had got certain information that there was a party of horse to be sent the next day[556] to Balcarres and take my Lord and bring him prisoner to Edinburgh, which he durst not writ nor communicate to any but me.[557] And desired I would go and

---

551. Colonel Hay remains unidentified.

552. "To free (a person) from deception or mistake; to deliver from an erroneous idea," *OED*.

553. For an indication of Halkett's response to this revelation, see "The Great Conquest, or the Power of Faith," 176–84.

554. "To anticipate with fear or dread; to be fearful concerning; to fear," *OED*.

555. This is the last time Halkett refers to the Earl of Dunfermline in her narrative; however, she later recalls the family's great kindnesses to her, as she commemorates the death of his son, "Friday, April 5, 1695," 293–94.

556. After "day," "to go" has been deleted.

557. Although Balcarres was loyal to the King, his commitment to Presbyterianism made him reluctant to serve under the Earl of Glencairn, whom the King had entrusted to lead an uprising. When intercepted letters revealed this, Balcarres "withdrew from the rising, traveling in disguise through England to France, to present the Presbyterian–Royalist case to the King. His wife, Anna, accompanied him, and 'through dearness of Affection, marched with him, and lay out of doors with him in the Mountains during his months in the highlands.'" Stevenson, "Lindsay, Alexander," *ODNB*.

let him know what was designed that he might escape, which I undertook and went early the next morning, taking only a man with me (for I was necessitate to leave my woman to look after some business then fell out). And the tide falling to be betwixt three and four in the morning and a very great wind so as few but the boatmen and myself ventured to go over, which contributed well for I landed safe and was at Balcarres before ten o'clock. And my Lord and Lady went away immediately; and had desired me to stay in the house with the children, and take down all the books and convey them away to several places in trunks to secure them (for my Lord had a very fine library, but they entrusted were not so just as they should have been, for many of them I heard afterwards were lost).[558]

[fol. 50v] I was very desirous to serve them faithfully in what I was entrusted, and as soon as my Lord and Lady were gone, I made lock up the gates. And with the help of ___[559] Logan, who served my Lord, and one of the women (both being very trusty), I took down all the book, and, putting them in trunks and chests, sent them all out of the house in the night to the places appointed by my Lord (taking a short way of inventory to know what sort of[560] books was sent to every person). And with the toil and want of sleep (for I went not to bed that night and had but little sleep the night before) that I took the suddenest[561] and the most violent bloody flux[562] that ever I believe any had in so short a time, which brought me so weak in ten days' time that none saw me that expected life for me.

But I forgot to tell that the things had not been two hours out of the house when the troop of horse came and asked for my Lord. Their officer came up to me, and I told him my Lord had been long sick, which was true enough, and finding it inconvenient to be so far from the physicians was gone to Edinburgh for his health. They searched all the house and seeing nothing in it but bare walls, and women, and children, they went away. I gave account by an express what I said, according to their order, and after some few days staying concealed at Edinburgh, my Lord and Lady went to the north and from thence went abroad.[563]

---

558. "Were lost" is an insertion in the bottom margin of the page. Later Anna Mackenzie, by that point Countess of Argyll, asks Halkett to give board to her grandson; see "Saturday, June 23, 1694," 289–90.

559. There is a blank space here in the manuscript.

560. "Sort of" is an interlineal insertion.

561. Originally "sodainest." While "sodaine" can be used adjectivally, the *OED* gives only one example of its use in the sense of "suddenness" (Gascoigne, 1575).

562. "Bloody diarrhea," or, more likely in this context, "bleeding from another part of the body, especially menstrual bleeding, when excessive or prolonged," *OED*.

563. According to Alexander, Lord Lindsay, master of Crawford and Balcarres, the estate was sequestered January 4, 1654, and their children were left in the care of Mr. David Forret, minister of Kilconquhar; Lindsay, *A Memoir of Lady Anna Mackenzie, Countess of Balcarres and afterwards of Argyll, 1621–1706* (Edinburgh: Edmonston and Douglas, 1868), 33–34.

I had sent for my woman, who came the next day after I fell sick, and pressed much my sending for a physician. But I knew none but Dr. Cunningham,[564] and I could not send for him because I knew he was with my Lord Balcarres, and those physicians who lived near Balcarres was not at home. So, I concluded that the Lord had determined now to put an end to all my troubles, and death was very welcome to me (only I begged some relief from the violent pain I had, which was in that extremity that I never felt anything exceed it).[565]

[fol. 51r] But it seems it was only sent for a trial and to let me find the experience of the renewed testimony of God's favor in raising me from the gates of death.[566] During my sickness, I was much obliged to the frequent visits of most of the Ladies thereabouts but particularly the Lady Ardross.[567] And Mr. David Forret and Mr. Henry Rymere seldom missed a day of being with me: they were both pious good men and their conversation was very agreeable to me.[568] As soon as I was able to go out and had been at the church, the Lady Ardross's importunity[569] prevailed with me to stay with her a week before I went to Edinburgh, which I did, and then having taken my leave of all those whose civility to me made it necessary, I returned to Edinburgh. Where I had not been long before Sir James Halkett came to see me (who had sent often to enquire after me when I was at Balcarres) and excused not coming himself, which he did refrain lest it should occasion discourse of that which he knew would displease me. I seemed not to understand what he meant, neither was I curious to be resolved, only thanked him for what

---

564. Cunningham was admitted as the King's physician in October 1650. Balfour, *The Historical Works of Sir James Balfour*, 4:128. According to Loftis, his first name was Robert and he "had fought in the King's army at the Battle of Worcester. After the Restoration, he became Charles II's physician in Scotland. In 1673, the year before his death, he was created a baronet"; Loftis, ed., *The Memoirs of Anne, Lady Halkett and Anne, Lady Fanshawe*, 205.

565. At least not until childbirth; in "Upon Seeing One Tormented with the Toothache," Halkett is horrified to hear a woman who "hath by sad experience known what the pains of childbed is, and yet she wishes to exchange one for the other, even for that which to me is the most frightful pain that is in this world"; Halkett, *Occasional Meditations*, pp. 112–13.

566. Psalm 9:13: "Have mercy upon me, O Lord; consider my trouble which I suffer of them that hate me, thou that liftest me up from the gates of death."

567. Probably Helen, eldest daughter of Sir Robert Lindsay; in 1634, she married Sir William Scott of Ardross. See Loftis, ed., *The Memoirs of Anne, Lady Halkett and Anne, Lady Fanshawe*, 205; *TSP* 5:401–2.

568. Mr. David Forret and Mr. Henry Rymere were among the ministers in Fife who refused to read a 1650 proclamation addressing "the causes of a solemn public humiliation upon the defeat of the army, to be kept throughout all the congregations of the Kirk in Scotland," possibly because two of its clauses advocate humbling the King (and accompanying "malignants") and purging the royal household. Balfour, *The Historical Works of Sir James Balfour*, 4:102–8; for further details, see *FES* 5:196, 203.

569. "Of a person: persistent or pressing in making requests or offers, esp. to an irritating or distressing degree. Of a request, offer, etc.: made persistently or pressingly," *OED*.

he had done, and what he left undone (for it was not reasonable for me to expect a visit from him at that distance).

From the first day of my acquaintance with him I discovered a particular respect he had for me, and I have already related what way I took to prevent the increase of that which could have no hope of a suitable return, and yet how obliging he was to that person who chiefly interrupted[570] it. Now that being, as he thought, removed, I found by many circumstances and indirect words that he pleased himself with what I never had a thought of (though I had been highly ingrate[571] if I had not had more than an ordinary value for him). But lest he should speak directly to me of what I knew too well and did regret, he seldom was with me that I did not mention my resolution never to marry, and that nothing kept me from vowing it but that I questioned if such vows were lawful.[572] The more he used arguments to dissuade me [fol. 51v] from that resolution, I urged the greater reasons I had to confirm me in it, and at this rate we conversed severals[573] months: he seeking, and I avoiding, all occasions of his discovering his affection to me.

At last one day, when he had been some time with me speaking of many variety of subjects, when I least expected it he told me he could no longer conceal the affection he had for me since the first visit he ever made me, and had resolved never to mention it had my condition been the same it was; but now, looking upon me as free from all obligation to another, he hoped he might now pretend to the more favor having formerly preferred my satisfaction above his own. I was much troubled at this discourse, which he could not but observe, for the tears came in my eyes.[574] I told him I was sensible that the civility I had received from him were not of an ordinary way of friendship, and that there was nothing in my power that I would not do to express my gratitude. But if he knew what disturbance any discourse like that gave me, he would never mention it again, "For as I never propose anything of happiness to myself in this World, so I will never make another unhappy, and in this denial, I intend to evidence my respect to you much more than if I entertained[575] your proposal. And therefore, I entreat you, if you love either yourself or me, let me never hear more of it."

"But" said he, "I hope you will not debar my conversing with you?"

"No," replied I, "I will not be so much my own enemy, and upon the condition you will forbear ever to speak again of what you now mentioned, no person

---

570. "To hinder, stop, prevent, thwart," *OED*.

571. "An ungrateful person; one who does not feel or show gratitude," *OED*.

572. See "Upon Making Vows," 208–10.

573. "As a vague numeral: of an indefinite (but not large) number exceeding two or three; more than two or three but not very many," *OED*.

574. See "Upon a Proposal," 256–57.

575. "To keep (a person, country, etc.) in a certain state or condition; to keep (a person) in a certain frame of mind," *OED*.

shall be welcomer to me, nor any will I be willinger to serve whenever I have opportunity."[576]

He said it should be against his will to do anything to displease me but he would make no promises.

A little after he desired me to let his two daughters[577] stay [fol. 52r] with me, for he designed to bring them to Edinburgh to learn what was to be taught there, and if I would let them stay with me he would think himself obliged to me. I told him I had formerly promised him any service that lay in my power and he need not doubt my performance; and if he or they could dispense[578] with what entertainment I could give them he needed not doubt of their being welcome, and it would be an advantage to me to have so good company. His youngest daughter was but a child, but his eldest was near a woman, and even then by more than ordinary discretion gave expectation of what since she hath made[579] good. The lodging I was then in not being convenient for more than myself, I removed up to Mrs. Glover's at the head of Blackfriar's Wynd, where they and their woman came and stayed with me. And we lived with very much quiet and content in our converse, Sir James coming often to see them and bringing many times their uncle and cousin, Sir Robert Montgomery[580] and Haslehead, who were both extremely civil to me,[581] and frequent in their visits.

It is so usual where single persons are often together to have people conclude a design for marriage that it was no wonder if many made the same upon Sir James and me, and the more that his daughters were with me. But I had no thoughts of what others concluded as done; for I thought I was obliged to do all I could to satisfy him, since I could not do what he chiefly desired. I often desired him to dine and supp with his daughters, which had been a neglect if I had omitted considering he was often sending provision from his own house to them (for he knew I was not of a humor to take board nor did he offer it, but made it that way equivalent, not without trouble to me for my inclination was ever[582] more to give than receive).

---

576. Here, Halkett uses adverbial superlatives.

577. Couper states that Sir James had two daughters by his first wife, Lady Margaret Montgomery: "Mary, married to Sir William Bruce of Kinross; and Anna, to Sir Andrew Ker of Kavers"; Couper, *The Life of the Lady Halket*, 30.

578. "To deal with indulgently; to manage with; to do with, put up with," *OED*.

579. "Made" is an interlineal insertion.

580. Sir Robert Montgomery was their maternal uncle. As Loftis notes, Halkett's syntax here is confusing, but there is a Robert Montgomery of Haslehead listed as having married Margaret Livingston on April 29, 1656. *Scotland: Select Births and Christenings, 1561–1910*, cited in Ancestry®, accessed August 08, 2018, https://www.ancestry.co.uk.

581. "To me" is an interlineal insertion.

582. "Ever" is an interlineal insertion.

Towards the winter he stayed most constantly at Edinburgh and then grew so importunate[583] with me, not only to allow his address but to give him hopes that it should be successful, that to put him past all further pursuit, I told him I looked upon it as an addition of my [fol. 52v] misfortune to have the affection of so worthy a person and could not[584] give him the return he deserved. For he knew I had that tie upon me to another that I could not dispose of myself to any other if I expected a blessing, and I had too much respect to him to comply with his desire in what might make him unhappy and myself by doing what would be a perpetual disquiet to me. He urged many things to convince me that I was in an error, and therefore that made it void. But when he saw nothing could prevail, he desired me for his satisfaction that I would propose it to Mr. David Dickson (who was one he knew I had a great esteem of his judgment) and rely upon his determination.[585] This I was content to do, not doubting but he would resolve the question on my side.

The first time Mr. Dickson came to me (which he usually did once in a week), being alone, I told him I was going to communicate something to him which hitherto I had concealed, but now would entrust him with it under promise of secrecy and being impartially ingenious[586] in giving me his opinion in what I was to acquaint him with; which he promising, I told him I did not doubt but he, and his wife, and many others in Edinburgh did believe Sir James Halkett's frequent visits to me was upon design of marriage. And I would avow to him that it was what he had oft with great importunity proposed, and had a long time evidenced so real an affection for me that I could not but acknowledge if any man alive could prevail with me it would be he. But I had been so far engaged to another that I could not think it lawful for me to marry another, and so told him all the story of my being unhappily deceived, and what length I had gone, and rather more than less.

He heard me very attentively and was much moved at the relation, which I could not [fol. 53r] make without tears. He replied he could not but say it was an unusual[587] trial I had met with and what he prayed the Lord to make useful to me. But withal, he added, that since what I did was supposing Colonel Bampfield a free person, he not proving so, though I had been publicly married to him and avowedly lived with him as his wife yet the ground of it failing, I was as free as if I had never seen him.[588] And this, he assured me, I might rely upon: that I might,

---

583. "Of a person: persistent or pressing in making requests or offers, esp. to an irritating or distressing degree. Of a request, offer, etc.: made persistently or pressingly," *OED*.

584. "Not" is an interlineal insertion.

585. See Holfelder, "Dickson, David," *ODNB*.

586. "Discerning, sensible," *OED*.

587. "Un" is an interlineal insertion.

588. See "Introduction," 34–37.

without offence either to the laws of God or man, marry any other person whenever I found it convenient, and that he thought I might be guilty of a fault if I did not when I had so good an offer. He used many arguments to confirm his opinion, which though I reverenced coming from him, yet I was not fully convinced but that it might be a sin in me to marry. But I was sure there was no sin in me to live unmarried.

I was very just to Sir James in giving him account what Mr. Dickson had said, though not until he urged to know it. And being determined on what he had often pleaded[589] for, he hoped now I would have nothing more to object. I told him though he had made it appear lawful to me, yet I could not think it convenient,[590] nor could I consent to his desire of marrying without doing him so great prejudice as would make me appear the most ungrate[591] person to him in the world. I acknowledged his respect had been such to me that were I owner of what I had just right to and had never had the least blemish in my reputation (which I could not but suffer in considering my late misfortune), I thought he deserved me with all the advantages was possible for me to bring him; but it would be an ill requital of his civilities, not only to bring him nothing but many inconveniencies by my being greatly in debt, which could not but be expected, having (except a hundred pound) never received a penny of what my mother left me, and had [fol. 53v] been long at law (both in England and Scotland) which was very expensive. And I gave him a particular account what I was owing. Yet all this did not in the least[592] discourage him, for he would have been content at that time to have married me with all the disadvantages I lay under. For he said, he looked upon me as a virtuous person and in that proposed more happiness to himself by enjoying me than in all the riches of the world.

Certainly, none can think but I had reason to have more than an ordinary esteem of such a person, whose eyes were so perceptible as to see and love injured virtue under so dark a cloud as encompassed me about. When I found he made use of all the arguments I used to lessen his affections as motives to raise it higher, I told him, since he had left caring for himself, I was obliged to have the more care of him, which I could evidence in nothing more than in hindering him from ruining himself. And therefore, told him I would be ingenious[593] with him and tell him my resolution was never to marry any person until I could first put my affairs in such a posture as that, if I brought no advantage where I married, at least I would bring no trouble. And whenever I could do that, if ever I did change my condition, I thought he was the only person that deserved an interest in me.

589. After "pleaded," "it" has been deleted.
590. "Morally or ethically suitable or becoming; proper," OED.
591. "An ungrateful person; an ingrate," OED.
592. "Least" is an insertion in the left-hand margin.
593. "Open, frank, candid," OED.

And this I was so fixed in that nothing could persuade me to alter, which gave him both trouble and satisfaction by delay and hopes. Many proposals he made wherein he designed to remove my objections, but though they were great expressions of his affection, yet I would not admit of them. But they had this effect as to make me the sooner project[594] the putting myself in a capacity to comply with his desires since I found they were unchangeable. And I did resolve as soon as the winter session was [fol. 54r] done, which I expected would put a close to my lawsuit here,[595] I would go to London and vindicate myself from the supposed guilt[596] I was charged with, and then try what I could persuade my brother[597] to do in order to the paying of what I owed. I acquainted Sir James with my intention, which he approved of since he could not persuade me to nothing else.

Presently after this, Sir James came and showed me a letter he had received from London from the Countess of Morton[598] who very earnestly desired him to come to her. For she had entrusted him with the oversight of her jointure[599] and it related to the settling of that and other things of concern that made her importunate[600] for his coming to her. He told me my Lady Morton was a person who had ever shown much respect to him and that he would willingly serve her Ladyship, but the chief thing that would make him now obey her commands was in hopes his being at London might be serviceable to me if I would employ him. I said, if his own conveniency[601] would allow of his journey and that he did incline to it, I would write with him to my sister who I would oblige to be civil to him upon my account (though he deserved it for his own). Within two days he went, and I gave my sister such a character of him as made his reception liker a brother than a stranger.[602] I referred much to him to say which was not convenient to write, and

594. I.e., actively devised a specific plan to do so.

595. "Here" is an interlineal insertion.

596. "A failure of duty, delinquency; offence, crime, sin," OED.

597. I.e., Henry.

598. Anne Douglas, née Villiers. Her letters to Sir James Halkett reveal that he frequently assisted in her financial affairs, especially after her husband Robert's death in 1649. Her daughter, Anne Douglas, continued the correspondence; see Pitfirrane Papers: Correspondence, NLS, MS 6409, nos. 19-26, 27-37. Anne became the second wife of William Keith, sixth Earl of Marischal, in April 1654, TSP 6:59, 378.

599. Originally, "the holding of property to the joint use of a husband and wife for life or in tail, as a provision for the latter, in the event of her widowhood." Hence, by extension, "a sole estate limited to the wife, being 'a competent livelihood of freehold for the wife of lands and tenements, to take effect upon the death of the husband for the life of the wife at least,'" OED.

600. "To ask for or obtain by persistent solicitation or entreaty," OED.

601. Archaic form of "convenience."

602. "One who is not a native of, or who has not long resided in, a country, town, or place. Chiefly, a newcomer, one who has not yet become well acquainted with the place, or one who is not yet well known," OED. Halkett's use of "liker" here means "more like."

desired her to speak to my brother and give me account what I might expect of his kindness in the proposal I have lately mentioned, of which I expected no answer until Sir James returned.[603]

About a week after he was gone, I fell into a feverish distemper which continued some time so that I found it necessary to send for Doctor Cunningham, which gave occasion to some people to say that I fell sick with heartbreak because Sir James Halkett was gone to London to marry my Lady Morton (which report went current amongst some, though not believed by any that was well acquainted with any of the three); but this [fol. 54v] acquainted me with the humor of some people that use to make conclusions of their own rather than seem ignorant of anything. By the speedy return Sir James made he convinced them of their folly who raised the report and brought much satisfaction to me by the assurance I had from my sister of being very welcome to her whenever it was convenient for me to come. And until then she thought it best to delay speaking of any particular to my brother, but for her husband[604] I might be secure of his kindness to be ever the same I had found it. At the same time, I also received several letters from them who had formerly had much friendship for me; by which I found it had no abatement by the late trial[605] I had met with, which did much encourage me to keep my resolution of going to London whenever the season of the year would admit of it. In the meantime, I endeavored the settling of my business so as it might receive no prejudice by my absence.

But got so many delays, yet daily hopes of being put to a close, that it was the beginning of September 1654 before I could take journey, which I was much assisted to perform by the kindness and favor of the old Countess of Dunfermline[606] who invited me to go with her to Pinkie[607] the Saturday before I was to go for London. And being very inquisitive how I was provided for my journey by my ingenuity[608] her Ladyship found I was not very certain of what was convenient. And upon the Monday when I was coming away, my Lady brought me ten pounds, and said if she had been better provided, she would have lent me more but she had borrowed it of her Lord. I gave her Ladyship many thanks, who unasked had

---

603. It was common practice to use the bearer of a letter to communicate further information verbally, especially if it was of a sensitive nature.

604. I.e., Sir Henry Newton, later Puckering.

605. "That which puts one to the test; esp. a painful test of one's endurance, patience, or faith; hence, affliction, trouble, misfortune," OED.

606. Here, Halkett presumably means Margaret Hay, wife of the deceased first Earl of Dunfermline (Alexander Seton), although she subsequently married James Livingston, first Earl of Callendar. David Stevenson, "Livingston, James, First Earl of Callendar (d. 1674)," ODNB.

607. One of the Earl of Dunfermline's mansions, Pinkie House is located in Musselburgh.

608. "Freedom from dissimulation; honesty, straightforwardness, sincerity; honorable or fair dealing; freedom from reserve, openness, candor, frankness," OED.

so civilly assisted me, and desired to know whether I should make the note of my hand (which I should send the next day) in my Lord's [fol. 55r] name or her Ladyship's; and she desired it might be in my Lord's name, which accordingly I did, and paid since I was a widow.[609]

The great civilities I received from all Sir James Halkett's relations made me without scruple go to his sister to the Cavers the first night, where he went with me and his eldest daughter who stayed there until my return.[610] (The youngest he left at school in Edinburgh.) Sir James went another day's journey with me and would have gone further, but I would not give him any further trouble, but urged his return and went on my journey to York (where I expected to meet the post coach but was disappointed and forced to ride another day's journey).

Sir James had an excellent footman who he had promised my sister and sent him along with me, who I gave money to pay for his diet[611] and lodging after we came to the coach because I thought it not reasonable to expect he could keep up with it. After we had gone half the first day's journey and the coachman driving at a great rate, I heard the coachman and postilion saying, "It cannot be a man, it is a devil; for he lets us come within sight of him and then runs faster than the six horses!" So, he stops the coach and enquires if any of us had a footman. I told him I had. "Then," said he[612] "pray make much of him, for I will be answerable he is the best in England." When I found he could hold out, as he did all the way, I made him run by the coach and he was very useful to all in it.

That journey brought me the acquaintance of Sir ___[613] Witherington and his nephew Mr. Arington, who had one man, and my woman and myself was all we had in the coach. I had discharged[614] my woman and the footman to tell my name to any but took a borrowed name. Sir ___[615] being a very civil person entertained me with many handsome variety of discourses, and related how he had designed to go for Flanders and all his things a-ship board, and while he was taking his leave [fol. 55v] the ship set sail from Newcastle; and so he was forced

---

609. As Sir James Halkett did not die until September 24, 1670, this means that the first Earl of Callendar had to wait more than sixteen years before being repaid.

610. Sir James Halkett's sister, Grizel, married James Ker of Cavers, Roxburghshire in 1638. "Families Database," Stirnet.com, accessed November 10, 2015, http://www.stirnet.com/genie/data/british/hh4aa/halkett1.php#da2. They had four daughters, the third of whom, also named Grizel, married Patrick Hume, Lord Polwarth, first Earl of Marchmont, in 1660. *TSP* 6:15.

611. Specifically, "an allowance or provision of food," *OED*. However, the reference to "lodging" suggests the more general sense of an "allowance for the expenses of living," *OED*.

612. "Said he" is an interlineal insertion.

613. There is a blank space in the original manuscript.

614. "To forbid (a person, etc.) to do something; to ban from doing; to prohibit (an action, practice, etc.)," *OED*.

615. There is a blank space in the original manuscript.

to go by land, which fell out well for me because I could not have met with civiler gentlemen, but I regretted to find they were Roman Catholics. And by my naming Mr. Fallowfield[616] as one that I had seen, they presently knew who I was and said they would enquire no further, for they had heard him speak of me as one he had so great respect for as that they would have the same. This Mr. Fallowfield was an old priest that used some time to come to Naworth Castle when I was there and had often writ letters to me for sick persons and highly complimented me upon their recovery. When I found they did know my name, I told them the reason why I concealed it was because I had been long absent from my friends, and there had been many changes since I left them, and therefore I resolved they should see me before they heard of me.

We came to High Gate[617] about two o'clock where I desired to be left, and writ a note in with the footman to an old servant of my mother's to take a lodging in some private place in London and to come to me the next morning with a coach, which accordingly he did. And I went to Whitefriars, where my brother Newton's lodging used to be and most of those who desired not to appear publicly.[618]

I then writ to my sister, who was then and her husband at Warwick,[619] by the footman Sir James Halkett had sent her, acquainting her where I was and that I intended to be known to very few until I heard what she advised me to do. For though I knew the power that then governed did (at that time) endeavor to secure themselves rather by obliging the loyal party than ruining them, yet it was chiefly to such who could do them most [fol. 57r] prejudice, and so that was no security to me. Besides, the debt I had was considerable, and therefore, until I was sure they to whom it was due would not attempt any unhandsome[620] action against me, I thought it was fit (upon both these considerations) to conceal where I was until I had some way secured myself from the inconvenience that I might suffer both upon a public and private account. My sister, within three of four days, returned

---

616. Sir Charles Howard's association with Mr. Fallowfield is also mentioned in *Strange News from the North*: "Our new Sheriff of Cumberland, the most powerful man of the County, we find he hath been in arms, both in the first and second war; and now hath for his agent and councilor, one lawyer Fallowfield, a professed Papist, and now said to be a priest; and the other day came from the Irish rebels (as I hear) in Ireland," 3.

617. High Gate, now a suburban area of north London at the north-eastern corner of Hampstead Heath, was then a distinct village (on the route of the main road to the north and Scotland).

618. Originally named after the Carmelite Priory established in the thirteenth century, by "the early years of the seventeenth century it began to attract a criminal population who wished to enjoy the right of sanctuary still possessed by the precinct." A royal charter of 1608 extended the right of sanctuary to debtors, "and the district became known as Alsatia"; L. W. Cowie, "Whitefriars in London," *History Today* 25, no. 6 (June 1975): 439.

619. The Priory, Warwick on the estate of Priory Park. The mansion was moved to Virginia after being bought by A. W. Weddell at a demolition sale in 1925.

620. "Unfitting, unbecoming, unseemly; discourteous, mean," *OED*.

back the footman to me again with a very kind letter and twenty pieces, promising to be with me as soon as she could and until then thought it best for me not to go anywhere abroad.

In the meantime, I employed my mother's old servant to enquire of some that he was acquainted with, who ruled much in those times, what their opinion was of my coming to London. But there had been so many changes among themselves (and some who they did much confide in who had left them, being convinced of their error) that they looked now the more favorable upon those who had never been on their side, and did more easily pardon what they acted against them. And this made me the more secure as to the public. And for my private troubles, there was not one who I was really owing anything to but they were as civil as I could desire, and as ready as ever to serve me in what they had that could be useful to me. Having thus far satisfied myself, I only stayed now until my sister came that my going first abroad[621] might be with her, which was shortly after. And having made some few visits to some particular persons, I went with her and her husband to Charlton, which was a house of theirs within five or six miles of London. My brother, who lived then in the country with his family,[622] came to see me and invited me to his house where I went and stayed some time, but my most constant residence was with my sister (where I knew I was most welcome to her and [fol. 56v] her husband).

But sometimes I went to London and had a lodging in Crew's[623] mother's house, where I stayed when I had any persons to meet with in order to settle what I came there for. One morning when I was there, they brought me word there was two gentlemen desired to speak with me who had brought a letter to me from the Earl of Callendar.[624] I sent for them up to my chamber and did something wonder to find the man tremble when he gave me the letter and his lips quiver that he could hardly speak. I took the letter and read it (concerning a business his Lordship had recommended to my care). I asked who brought it from Scotland? He was not well able to answer me, but pointing to the other man, he came and arrested me. I was strangely surprised, having never met with nothing like it, and asked at whose instance. He pointed to the other, who had given me the letter, and named him Mr. Maitland. I said, I thought it strange upon what account he could do it who I had never seen. He said it was for a debt my brother Will owed his

---

621. "Out of one's house or abode; outdoors; in the open; away from home," *OED*.

622. Halkett's brother was married to Anne Bayning, later Viscountess Bayning of Foxley, whose father had estates in Essex, *BP* 3.3814.

623. Crew was Halkett's maidservant. See *True Account*, 137.

624. James Livingston, created Earl of Callendar in 1641, had been Lieutenant General of the Scottish army that tried to rescue Charles I and was defeated at Preston in 1648. He was arrested in 1654, imprisoned in Edinburgh Castle and had his estates confiscated. His lands were restored when he went to London and "kissed the Lord Protector his hands" in 1655. Stevenson, "Livingston, James," *ODNB*.

wife and I promised to pay. I said it was very strange I should promise to pay what I never until then knew was owing, nor did I ever hear of that woman's name[625] until that time of my coming to London.

Yet though all this was true, I was forced to give bail and to answer at the Guildhall which I did by Attorney Allen.[626] And though they had hired a man of their own to come and swear that I had promised to pay the debt, yet he so far contradicted himself that it was visible it was a cheat and the bill was flung over the Bar;[627] which so exasperated that wicked woman that there was nothing imaginable that is ill she did not say of me publicly in the street, and [fol. 57r] the interest she had with the soldiers (who was daily drinking in her house at the Mews) made all people unwilling to meddle with her. But I need not insist upon this which cost me dear enough before I ended with her. But it hath cost her dearer since if she did not repent, and if she did, since the Lord hath forgiven her, I bless him for it[628] so did I (as I sent her word by her husband when I heard she was dying).

I heard constantly once in a fortnight from Sir James, with many renewed testimonies that neither time nor distance had power to change him. I had not been long at London when I heard Colonel Bampfield was come there, who sent to me several times to have leave to come once but to speak to me, which I as often positively denied as he earnestly asked it. But one Sunday night, December 10, 1654, after I had supped and was walking alone in my chamber, he came in which I confess strangely surprised me so that, at first, I was not able to speak a word to him. But a little being recollected, I said[629] I thought he had brought misfortune upon me enough already without adding more to it by giving new occasion of my being censured for conversing with him. He entreated me to give him leave but to sit down by me a little and he would immediately leave me, which I did, and he begun to vindicate himself as he had done often. But I interrupted him, and told him though my charity would induce me to believe him innocent yet that could be no argument why I should now allow him liberty to visit me, since he could not pretend[630] ignorance of that which made me think allowable once what were heinously criminal now.

He said he desired me only to resolve him one question which was whether or not I was married to Sir James Halkett. I asked why he enquired. He said

---

625. Maitland's wife is named below as Mrs. Cole.

626. Possibly Sir Thomas Allen, an English politician, Royalist, and lawyer. Eveline Cruickshanks, "Sir Thomas Allen (1603–1681)," in *The History of Parliament: The House of Commons 1660–1690*, ed. B. D. Henning (London: Boydell and Brewer, 1983), BHO.

627. I.e., the case was rejected.

628. After "it," "and" has been deleted.

629. After "said," "to him" has been deleted.

630. After "pretend," "now" has been deleted.

because if I was not, he would then propose something that he thought might be both for his advantage and mine, but if I were, he would wish me joy but never trouble me more. I said nothing a little while, for I hated lying [fol. 57v] and I saw there might be[631] some inconvenience to tell the truth. And Lord pardon the equivocation,[632] I said, "I am" out loud and secretly said, "not".

He immediately rose up and said, "I wish you and him much happiness together."

And taking his leave, from that time to this,[633] I never saw him nor heard from him, only when he had got my writings (of what concerned me left to me by my mother, which I had left with him when I went out of London and he had taken for security with him when he went first to Holland after his escape out of prison) that he sent them to me with a letter.

The liberty he took in coming out from his concealed lodging upon Sunday was upon an Act[634] made by the Usurper, which was that none upon any account (whatever was their crime) should be apprehended upon that day but should have liberty to go to any church they pleased or any other place, which showed a veneration he had for that day, though in other things he forgot obedience where it was due by the same authority that commanded that day to be kept holy. But when that hypocrite reigned the people were ensnared.[635]

The first post after Colonel Bampfield had been with me I gave Sir James an account of it, who was so far from being unsatisfied with it that he writ me word, if it were not that it might do me more prejudice in other people's thought than

---

631. "Be" is an interlineal insertion.

632. "The use of words or expressions that are susceptible of a double signification, with a view to mislead; esp. the expression of a virtual falsehood in the form of a proposition which (in order to satisfy the speaker's conscience) is verbally true," *OED*.

633. A partial, marginal reference is here obscured by the pasteboards. On close inspection of the original manuscript, this reads "Ja 8," which, given the dates she began and completed this volume, must mean January 8, 1677/8.

634. Probably the "Act for the Repeal of Several Clauses in Statutes Imposing Penalties for Not Coming to Church. September 1650," in Firth and Rait, eds., *Acts and Ordinances of the Interregnum, 1642–1660*, 423–25, BHO. Finding that "several Acts made in the times of former Kings and Queens of this nation, against Recusants not coming to Church" had resulted in "divers religious and peaceable people, well-affected to the prosperity of the Commonwealth" being "molested and imprisoned," Parliament repealed the Acts and associated penalties. However, "to the end that no prophane or licentious persons may take occasion by the Repealing of the said Laws (intended only for Relief of pious and peaceably minded people from the rigor of them) to neglect the performance of Religious Duties," the same Act required "all and every person and persons within this Commonwealth and the Territories thereof," to "diligently resort to some public place where the Service and Worship of God is exercised, or shall be present at some other place in the practice of some Religious Duty, either of Prayer, Preaching, Reading or Expounding the Scriptures, or conferring upon the same."

635. Job 34:30: "That the hypocrite reign not, lest the people be ensnared."

it would do in his, he would not care though I daily conversed with him, so little did he apprehend any unhandsome[636] action from me. And therefore, it had been the highest unworthiness and ingratitude to have been false to so great a trust as he reposed in me. I was above a twelve month endeavoring all I could so to settle my affairs that I might have given Sir James some encouragement to come to me, which he often designed to do but I dissuaded him from it until it might be with more satisfaction to himself. For I knew it would be but a trouble to him to stay long at London or return [fol. 58r] without me and the ill success I had (in my proposals to my brother) would make one of them necessary.

But Sir James's patience being long tried, he would not be hindered any[637] longer, but towards the latter end of the year 1655 he came to London (where I, at that time, had come for two or three days). And he returned with me to Charlton to my sister's house where he stayed for the most part while he continued at England. The constancy of his affection and the urgency of his desiring to marry made me now unite all the interest I had, either by relation or friendship, to get money (if not to pay all I owed, yet such as was most pressing) and to accommodate myself in some way suitable for what I designed.

I employed some again to try my brother who—though one of the best natured men living—could not be prevailed with either to lend or engage for one penny for me, but I did not blame him since the hindrance was from another hand.[638] And that disappointment came[639] to make me more highly value the kindness of my brother Newton, who voluntarily lent me three hundred pound and the Countess of Devonshire[640] two hundred (which was an obligation I shall

636. "Unfitting, unbecoming, unseemly; discourteous, mean," OED.

637. "Any" is an interlineal insertion.

638. I.e., by his wife, who was another Anne Murray; in this case, second daughter (b. April 23, 1619) of the first Viscount Bayning of Sudbury. She outlived Henry, who died before May 1, 1673. Her second marriage, to Sir John Baber (physician to Charles II), took place on August 1, 1674, TSP 2:35; 3:399; T. F. Henderson, "Baber, Sir John (1625–1704)," ODNB.

639. After "came," "from another" has been deleted.

640. At this date, the Countess of Devonshire was Elizabeth Cecil (1620–1689), daughter of William Cecil, Second Earl of Salisbury, who married William Cavendish, March 4, 1639. Although Cavendish supported the exiled court, he did not become involved in "active conspiracy"; Victor Stater, "Cavendish, William, Third Earl of Devonshire (1617–1684)," ODNB. By contrast, his mother, the Dowager Duchess of Devonshire, Christian(a) Cavendish, née Bruce, was an active Royalist plotter, who had become highly skilled at fighting—and winning—financial lawsuits. As a Bruce, she also had Scottish connections, which suggests she was the then Anne Murray's benefactress; Victor Stater, "Cavendish [née Bruce], Christian [Christiana], Countess of Devonshire (1595–1675)," ODNB. It was also she to whom Robert Gale was chaplain, see Daniel Lysons, "Putney," in *The Environs of London*, vol. 1, *County of Surrey* (London: T Cadell and W Davies, 1792), 404–35. BHO. It is Gale who marries Halkett to Sir James in her brother-in-law's closet, and it was listening to one of his sermons that convinced her it was "a necessary duty" to pray "for the establishment and preservation of the King in peace and safety"; "Upon a Dispute with Myself," 211.

never forget, nor what pains Mr. Neal took for me to persuade her Ladyship and was bound with me to her for the money). I wish I had as much power to requite as I have memory to retain the sense of those undeserved favors, and that my reflecting upon them may raise up my thoughts to the adoration and praise of him who is the fountain of mercy and from whom only all blessings are derived.

After this money was received, and paid where it was most necessary, and that I had satisfied all that I knew anything was due to, I went to London for some few days, where Sir James came to me in order to conclude our marriage, which I could not now in reason longer defer (since the greatest objections I had made against it was removed, and that I was fully [fol. 58v] convinced no man living could do more to deserve a wife than he had done to oblige me). And therefore, I intended to give him myself though I could secure him of nothing more, and that was my regret, that I could not bring him a fortune as great as his affection to recompense his long expectation.

It was not without many debates with myself that I came at last to be determined to marry. And the most prevalent argument that persuaded me to incline to it was the extraordinary way that Sir James took even in silence to speak what he thought necessary[641] to conceal until it appeared to be fit for avowing, and then not to be discouraged from all the inconveniences that threatened his pursuit was what I could not but look upon as ordered by the wise and good providence of the Almighty; whom to resist, or not make use of so good an opportunity as by his mercy was offered to me, I thought might be offensive to his divine Majesty, who in justice might deliver me up to the power of such sins as might be a punishment for not making use of the offer of grace to prevent them. And this consideration, being added to Sir James's worth, ended the controversy.

However, lest I might have been mistaken,[642] or Mr. David Dickson in his opinion who thought it lawful for me to marry, I entered not into that state without most solemn seeking the determined will of God; which by fasting and prayer I supplicated to be evidenced to me, either by hedging up my way with thorns that I might not offend him, or that he would make my way plain before his face and my paths righteous in his sight.[643] And as I begged this with the fervor of my soul, so it was with an entire resignation and resolution to be content with whatever way the Lord should dispose of me. To this I may add St. Paul's attestation, "*The God and Father of our Lord Jesus Christ, which is blessed for evermore, knoweth that I lie not*" (2 Corinthians 11:31).[644]

641. After "thought," "fit" has been deleted and replaced by the interlineal insertion "necessary."

642. In original, this reads "mistaking."

643. Hosea 2:6: "Therefore, behold, I will hedge up thy way with thorns, and make a wall, that she shall not find her paths"; Proverbs 15:19: "The way of the slothful man is as an hedge of thorns: but the way of the righteous is made plain."

644. Halkett's reference here is incomplete, as she does not provide the verse number.

[fol. 59r] After this day's devotion was over, everything that I could desire in order to my marriage did so pleasingly concur to the consummation of it, and my own mind was so undisturbed, and so freed of all kind of doubts that with thankfulness I received it as a testimony of the Lord's approbation, and a presage[645] of my future happiness. And blessed be his name, I was not disappointed of my hope.

Upon Saturday, March 1, 1655/6,[646] Sir James and I went to Charlton and took with us Mr. Gale,[647] who was chaplain to the Countess of Devonshire,[648] who preached (as he sometimes used to do) at the church the next day. And after supper, he married us in my brother Newton's closet, none knowing of it in the family or being present but my brother, and sister, and Mr. Neal. Though conform to the order of those that were then in power (who allowed of no marriage lawful but such as were married by one of their Justices of Peace) that they might object nothing against our marriage, after the evening sermon, my sister (pretending to go see Justice Elkonhead, who was not well, living at Woolwich)[649] took Sir James and me with her in the coach, and my brother and Mr. Neal went another way afoot[650] and met us there.

And the Justice performed what was usual for him at that time, which was only, holding the Directory[651] in his hand,[652] asked Sir James if he intended to marry me. He answered, "Yes." And asked if I intended to marry him, I said, "Yes." "Then," says he, "I pronounce you, man and wife."

So, calling for a glass of sack,[653] he drunk and wished much happiness to us, and we left him (having given his clerk money who gave, in parchment, the day and witnesses, [fol. 59v] and attested by the Justice that he had married us). But if

---

645. "A prediction, a prophecy, a prognostication," OED.

646. Here the year date is an interlineal insertion.

647. Robert Gale was chaplain to Christiana Cavendish, née Bruce, Countess of Devonshire. Lysons, "Putney," 404–35. Halkett refers to Mr. Gale twice again: first, when describing one of the reasons for changes in her devotional practice in "Upon a Dispute with Myself, New Year's Day, 1661," 210–11, and, second, when remembering her marriage in "Tuesday, March 2, 1697/8," 321.

648. Stater, "Cavendish, née Bruce, Christian[a]," ODNB.

649. Woolwich is a town in the royal borough of Greenwich, nearby to Charlton House (Halkett's sister's residence).

650. I.e., on foot.

651. That is, A Directory for the Publicke Worship of God compiled in 1644 by the Westminster Assembly, ratified by Parliament on January 4, 1645, and adopted by the Scottish General Assembly on February 6, 1645. See also, "An Act Touching Marriages and the Registering Thereof; and Also Touching Births and Burials, August 1653," in Firth and Rait, eds., Acts and Ordinances of the Interregnum, 715–18. BHO.

652. "Hand" is an interlineal insertion.

653. "A general name for a class of white wines formerly imported from Spain and the Canaries," OED.

it had not been done more solemnly afterwards by a minister, I should not believe it lawfully done.

After I was married, I stayed but a short while with my sister and concealed my marriage from all, except some particular persons that either relation or friendship made me have confidence of; for it was not a time for any that honored the King to have any public celebration; and another reason for performing it privately was that about ten days before I was married, Mrs. Cole, who was Maitland's wife, had arrested me again, and I was forced to give in new bail (who were such as I owned my intention of marrying and going immediately after for Scotland). And obliging myself to keep them harmless,[654] I left the management of it to him who before I had employed for my attorney, who was so confident she could never recover two pence of me, that he said he would be content to pay whatever should be determined by the Judges against me. For he said he could prove by very good witnesses that she said, when her former bill was cast over the Bar, "Well, I will have one that shall swear to the purpose, though I should give him ten pounds for his pains."

He, being an understanding, active[655] man and giving me such assurance, made me with the less disturbance leave London; for if I had had any apprehension of what after fell out, I might have easily prevented the prejudice she did me. For three years after my attorney died, and my bail being in the country, she got out a Judgment against me privately so that none ever heard of it that was concerned in me. And though it cost me a great deal of trouble and expense (which to this day I am owing for to Mr. Neal)[656] [fol. 60r] to have[657] that Judgment reduced, yet found it impossible (because it was confirmed by the Act of Indemnity made by the King when his Majesty first came home, which was much out of my way as well as[658] injurious to many others).[659] But that was my misfortune, which I had felt the weight of more heavily if, at the same time, the King had not been graciously pleased to grant me 500 pound out of the exchequer. But of this I shall have more occasion to speak hereafter.[660]

---

654. "Free from loss, free from liability to punishment, or to pay for loss or damage," *OED*.

655. "Practical," *OED*.

656. As Halkett wrote this text in 1677/8, Mr. Neal had already waited more than twenty years to be repaid. Here Halkett has deleted "yet the."

657. In original, this reads "had."

658. "As" is an interlineal insertion.

659. King, Charles II. "An Act of Free and Generall Pardon, Indempnity, and Oblivion, 1660," in *Statutes of the Realm: Volume 5, 1628–80*, ed. John Raithby (Great Britain Record Commission: s.l., 1819), 226–34, *BHO*. The Act's lack of provision for financial redress for Royalists led to it being known as "an Act of Indemnity for the King's enemies and oblivion for his friends"; Hutton, *Charles II*, 142.

660. The grant was made on November 20, 1662, "to Lady Ann Hacket, [sic] in consideration of her zeal and sufferings"; Shaw, *Calendar of Treasury Books, 1660–1667*, 1.452. Halkett's stated intention to

Sir James, and I, having taken leave of our friends, came safe without any ill accident (in the post coach) the length of Bow bridge within ___[661] mile of York.[662] And there we had so remarkable a deliverance that I cannot omit the relation of it. There was none in the coach but Sir James and I, his man and my woman, and a big, fat gentleman (whose name I forgot but he was one that had employment under the bishop of Durham).[663] About a quarter of a mile before we came to the bridge, that gentleman had lighted out to walk a little, and came in and sat on the side of the coach which was contrary to the place he was in before, which contributed much to our safety; for Sir James and he being on the one side of the coach, and his man in that boot,[664] Crew's weight and mine was the less considerable, who were next to the danger. But all of us had unevitable[665] been drowned and had our necks broke without an extraordinary providence.

For six horses being in the coach and the postilion not careful how he entered the bridge (which was but narrow without any ledges upon it, and built of the fashion of a bow from which it had the name), he driving carelessly, both the wheels of that side where I sat went over the bridge, which the coachman seeing, cried out, "We are all lost," and flung himself out of the coachbox; and to escape [fol. 60v] hurt his leg very ill, so that he could hardly get up to pull the horses to him, nor was there scarce room upon the bridge to give any assistance. But that[666] which was our preservation was some good angel, I think (sent by his master) who, seeing the danger we were in, held the coach behind all the way until it was off the bridge. It was so extraordinary a deliverance that we knew not how to be thankful enough to God Almighty, who had given it, but resolved to reward the man who had been instrumental in it. But when we all came out of the coach at the end of the bridge and enquired for the man, there was none to be seen. Nor had we all that day met or overtaken any traveler;[667] only that man was seen by Harry Macky and the Coachman to hold up the coach along the bridge, but they both declared they never saw him before nor after the danger; and that which made it appear the more strange was that he seemed to be but a poor man, and such doth not usually do any service without seeking a recompense. But whatever

---

explain this matter further supports my suggestion that her original narrative continued beyond the Restoration. See also "Appendix 3," 335.

661. There is a blank space in the manuscript where the distance should be provided.

662. There has been a bridge over the river Ouse since the medieval period; however, the bridge the Halketts crossed had been built in 1566. "Ouse Bridge," History of York, accessed August 8, 2016, http://www.historyofyork.org.uk/themes/tudor-stuart/ouse-bridge.

663. I have been unable to trace this gentleman.

664. "An uncovered space on or by the steps on each side, where attendants sat facing sideways," OED.

665. I.e., "inevitably."

666. "That" is an interlineal insertion.

667. After "any," "passenger" has been deleted and replaced with the interlineal insertion of "traveler."

he was, it was he the Lord made use of as a means of our safety, and the less we knew of his coming the more we had reason to be thankful to him who brought him there.

When we came to York and related what we had escaped, it was the admiration[668] of all that heard it. The coachman and postilion was very penitent for their fault, and therefore we forgave them, but would make no more use of them; for we hired another coach to Newcastle, where Sir James had appointed his own horses and servants to meet him because he intended to see his sisters as he went home, which he did. And we came safe without any other accident to the Cavers, where I was[669] received with much kindness by all, but most from Sir James's daughter, who I [fol. 61r] had left there and was very well pleased to return home with me which she did after some days stay at Cavers.

When we came to Edinburgh I sent my excuse for not being fit then to wait upon my Lady Broghill,[670] who was then there with her Lord who was President of the Council, but resolved to come there again only to pay that respect which I had for them both: not as they were then employed, but as I had long been intimately acquainted with them before, and knew that what they acted now was more out of a good design than an ill (as was evident by the civility they showed to all the Royalists).

After we came home and had received a very kind welcome from all Sir James's friends and neighbors, and that we were a little settled, he thought it convenient for us to go over as I promised to wait upon my Lady Broghill. And the reason which made Sir James the sooner do it was that several gentlemen, who had engaged to serve under the English power in public employment as Justices of Peace, had pressed to have Sir James one of that number; but he declining, they made his name be inserted in the list with this certification: that whoever refused to act in that station who was nominate should be sent to the Castle at Edinburgh.[671] This made us hasten our journey, and as soon as we came there, a gentleman (who I will not now name because I hope he repents what he then did) that had been very urgent with Sir James to accept the employment[672] came and

---

668. "The action or an act of wondering or marveling; wonder, astonishment, surprise," *OED*.

669. After "was," "very" has been deleted.

670. Roger Boyle, Lord Broghill, was lord president of the council in Edinburgh in March 1655–1656, making him the "head of civil government of Scotland." In 1654 and 1656, he was the Westminster Parliament representative for Cork, and in 1656 for Edinburgh as well. He married Lady Margaret Howard (1623–1689), daughter of Theophilus Howard, second Earl of Suffolk, on January 27, 1641. Toby Barnard, "Boyle, Roger, First Earl of Orrery (1621–1679)," *ODNB*.

671. For an explanation of the complexities of government in Scotland at this time, including the appointment of Justices of the Peace, see Patrick Little, *Lord Broghill and the Cromwellian Union with Ireland and Scotland* (Woodbridge, UK: Boydell, 2004), 91–123, especially 111–12.

672. "To accept the employment" is an interlineal insertion.

importunately[673] pressed him again. And to make me the better satisfied with the proposal told me many advantages he would receive by it and was very desirous that he might go with me to make my acquaintance with my Lady Broghill. I excused my going at such times as he mentioned only because I would not have him with [fol. 61v] me, nor did I take notice as if I had ever seen her. But as soon as I was free of him, I went presently after dinner.

They lay then in the Earl of Murray's house in the Canongate,[674] and just as I came in at the gate my Lord Broghill was going out, and with him a great attendance; and amongst the rest that gentleman who had been so forward to have Sir James put to be a Justice of Peace. He was a little surprised when he saw my Lord Broghill come, with so much freedom and kindness, and bid me welcome, and bringing me to the stairs asked if I had any service for him.

I said, "My Lord, though there hath been many sad changes since I saw your Lordship, yet I still look upon you as the same person you were, and therefore, in short, I am come to beg your Lordship's favor to Sir James, who I hear is in the list."

"Why," said he,[675] "hath he not a mind to be a Justice?"

"No, my Lord, so far from it that he will go to the Castle first."

"Well, my word for it," replied he, "you shall never hear of it more."

Being then in haste, going up to some committee, he left me with his Lady and engaged me to dine with them the next day, which I did; and had all the assurance I could desire that Sir James should be free from having anything imposed upon him that was contrary to the duty and loyalty that became a faithful subject.

After two or three days stay in Edinburgh, we returned home, and presently after came the order to Sir James either to join with the other Justices of Peace or go to the Castle. When I saw it, I confess, I was much disordered, and the more because I had such confidence of my Lord Broghill's word.[676] I desired Sir James to tell the messenger that the next week he would do one of them if desired, and immediately I writ a letter to my Lord Broghill telling how much I was surprised with that order, after I had his Lordship's promise to have . . .

---

673. "Of a person: persistent or pressing in making requests or offers, esp. to an irritating or distressing degree. Of a request, offer, etc.: made persistently or pressingly," *OED*.

674. See figure 5, map of Edinburgh, 138.

675. "Said he" is an interlineal insertion.

676. Little cites this incident as an affirmation of Broghill's broader friendship to the Scottish Royalists; sadly, however, he affirms that "we do not know whether Broghill's promises were finally put into action"; Little, *Lord Broghill and the Cromwellian Union with Ireland and Scotland*, 94.

Selected Meditations

A Short Expostulation about Prayer, Meditations, and the Mother's Will to Her Unborn Child *(1653–1657)*

This is the first volume in Couper's "catalogue," which remains extant; importantly, assuming Couper's dating is accurate, it is the only volume contemporaneous with the events narrated in *A True Account of My Life* that has survived.[1] The manuscript was rebound in the nineteenth century, so, unlike later volumes, it does not have its original covers (inside of which Halkett generally records the start and end date of a particular volume's composition). In this volume, she only provides dates for "The Mother's Will to Her Unborn Child" and an inserted account of a dream. In a different ink, Halkett has added the information that "The Mother's Will" was "writ at Pitfirrane when I was with child of my dear Betty, 1656."[2] The timing of the insertion of the dream is uncertain; however, its contents are dated precisely: "Finding here an empty place, I cannot but insert a dream which I found in a loose paper that I had writ the next day after. (The dream was upon August 19, 1651 that night.)"[3] There is, however, a list of the volume's contents in Halkett's own hand, and for once her version is identical to that produced by Couper.[4]

This volume comprises five "select" meditations, each of which has its own title and is separately paginated by Halkett. The material below is extracted from the second of these, which is titled "The Great Conquest, or the Power of Faith," an exegesis of 1 John 5:4: "This is the victory that overcommeth the world, even our faith" (7–39). In many ways, this entry is typical of Halkett's meditative style.[5] The text reproduced below represents almost half of the entire meditation: the missing sections are summarized in footnotes in more detail below but consist

---

1. In Couper's original list, the date range for this volume is 1653–1675; however, as Elizabeth (Betty) was born in November 26, 1656, and the final entry "A Thanksgiving after My Deliverance out of Childbed" is composed after her christening, it is more likely that the actual date range is 1653–1657. Halkett, *A Short Expostulation about Prayer*, p. 258. The transposition of numerals is not unique within Couper's catalogue, see "Appendix 4.2," 339–49.

2. "At Pitfirrane" is an interlineal insertion within the later addition. Halkett, *A Short Expostulation about Prayer*, p. 198.

3. In this dream, which Halkett explicitly compares with Job's experience, she seeks God's mercy and is visited by a man who first tests her and then reassures her of God's forgiveness, Job 33:6: "Behold, I am according to thy wish in God's stead: I also am formed out of the clay." Halkett, *A Short Expostulation about Prayer*, pp. 196–97.

4. Halkett, *A Short Expostulation about Prayer*, p. ii. This is volume 5 in Couper's catalogue.

5. See "Introduction," 39.

primarily of "Comparisons and Similitudes," and "Testimonies of Scripture."[6] While Halkett frequently references her own life within her exegetical texts, such allusions are generally sparse. By contrast, this entry contains an unusual amount of "self-application," which is perhaps suggestive of her state of mind in 1653; that is, around the time she was reliably informed by Sir James Halkett that Colonel Bampfield's wife was very definitely alive.

---

6. Huntley, ed., *Bishop Joseph Hall and Protestant Meditation in Seventeenth-Century England*, 96–98, 99–100.

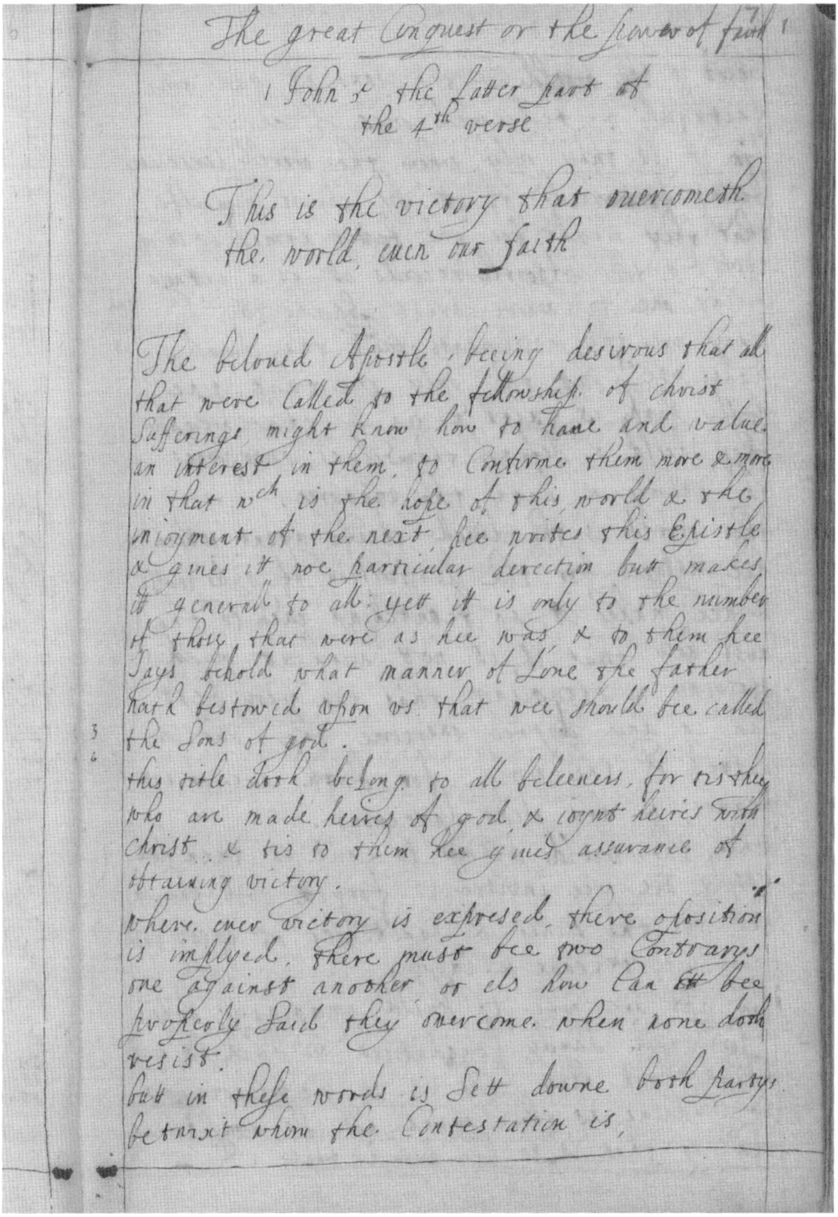

The great Conquest or the power of faith

1 John 5: the later part of
the 4th verse

This is the victory that overcometh
the world, even our faith

The beloued Apostle, beeing desirous that all
that were called to the fellowship of christ
Sufferings might know how to haue and value
an interest in them, & conferme them more & more
in that wch is the hope of this world & the
inioyment of the next, hee writes this Epistle
& giues it noe particular derection but makes
it generall to all; yet it is only to the number
of those, that were as hee was, & to them hee
says, behold what manner of Loue the father
hath bestowed vpon vs that wee should bee called
the Sons of god.
this title doth belong to all beleeuers, for tis they
who are made heires of god, & ioynt heires with
christ, & tis to them hee giues assurance of
obtaining victory.
where euer victory is expresed, there oposition
is implyed. there must bee two contrarys
one against another or els how can bee
properly said they ouercome, when none doth
resist.
but in these words is sett downe both partys
betwixt whom the contestation is,

Figure 6. From Anne, Lady Halkett, *A Short Expostulation about Prayer, Meditations, and the Mother's Will to Her Unborn Child (1653–1657)* © National Library of Scotland, NLS, MS 6489, p.7. Reproduced with permission.

The Great Conquest, or the Power of Faith.

[p. 7] *This is the victory that overcommeth the world, even our faith* (1 John 5:4).

The beloved Apostle—being desirous that all that were called to the fellowship of Christ's sufferings might know how to have and value an interest in them to confirm them more and more in that which is the hope of this world, and the enjoyment of the next—he writes this epistle and gives it no particular direction but makes it general to all.[7] Yet it is only to the number of those that were as he was, and to them he says: behold, what manner of love the Father hath bestowed upon us that we should be called the sons of God.[8]

This title doth belong to all believers, for it is they who are made heirs of God, and joint heirs with Christ,[9] and it is to them he gives assurance of obtaining victory.

Where-ever victory is expressed, there opposition is implied. There must be two contraries—one against another—or else how can it be properly said they overcome when none doth resist?

But in these words, is set down both parties betwixt whom the contestation is, [p. 8] which is the world and the sons of God, the faithful and redeemed ones of Christ.

For it is they only whom the world persecutes, being forewarned of it by Christ himself that they might be the better armed to encounter, and this Apostle records it as a witness, being one to whom Christ spake it (John 16:33).[10] Many are the instruments that the devil makes use of[11] but the only one that the godly hath is faith, and it is by that weapon they shield[12] and defend themselves, overcome the enemy, and hath victory.

The world is the Devil's chief agent which he employs for the destruction of God's people. And he makes it so bewitching, even to the most holy, that it is

---

7. "As 1 John has no formal greeting or conclusion, it may have been a circular for the building up of various churches in the vicinity of Ephesus," which aims primarily to "strengthen the faith of his readers" and "to combat a specific threat to his readers' faith: Gnosticism," *The King James Study Bible* (Nashville: Nelson, 1988), 1879.

8. 1 John 3:1: "Behold, what manner of love the Father hath bestowed upon us, that we should be called the sons of God: therefore, the world knoweth us not, because it knew him not."

9. Romans 8:17: "And if children, then heirs; heirs of God, and joint heirs with Christ; if so be that we suffer with him, that we may be also glorified together."

10. John 16:33: "These things I have spoken unto you, that in me ye might have peace. In the world ye shall have tribulation: but be of good cheer; I have overcome the world."

11. "Of" is an interlineal insertion.

12. Ephesians 6:16: "Above all, taking the shield of faith, wherewith ye shall be able to quench all the fiery darts of the wicked."

not without much striving and struggling that the very best can in any degree overcome the love or hatred of the world, for both are in extremes and are alike dangerous.

When the world seems to love us, then how easily are we invited to forget God, though he be the giver and sanctifier of every good thing we receive and enjoy?

How apt are we to build imaginary hopes upon these sandy foundations,[13] and such as we think will never fail us, and yet nothing so sudden as their ruin, nor so empty as the joy that is to be had in them?

[p. 9] What a strong snare is prosperity to that soul that is not truly acquainted with God, that hath not learned to esteem of the world and all things in it but as a perishing and fading creature.[14]

What was the world created for but to serve man and to teach him how to serve his God? And yet it is become the greatest cause of our forgetting to be thankful or obedient.

Oh, sinful man, how miserable art thou since thou hast brought that curse upon thyself, so as to make thy servant to become thy master and to rule over thee?

It is not much to see them that live without God in the world subject to the world, but it is sad to see they that have given themselves to God yet to be led away with many temptations of the world.

But the strangest of all is that those who hath never anything but the hatred of the world that yet they should love it.

This is my sad condition. I never knew what was good in the world but only to make me find the want of it more bitter, and yet I cannot hate it as I should, though sad and heavy hath the afflictions been with which it hath this long time persecuted me.

First, it held to me the promise of the greatest happiness it could allow to any. And when it made me constant to the expectation of it; now, I see [p. 10] sin the beginning, and shame the end as a most just reward.

Oh, my good God, if thou wert not beyond expressions merciful, what would become of me? Guilty I am before thy face: angels, and men, and devils, all must needs condemn me. And yet I will not despair of pardon because mercy doth belong to thee.

Had forgiveness of sin been put in any other hands but thine, I had never found the benefit of it because my infinite transgressions could never have been forgiven by any but by a God more infinite in goodness than I could be in sin. From this then comes my hope, being a branch of faith, which is the grace to which is promised victory over the world.

---

13. Matthew 7:26: "And everyone that heareth these sayings of mine, and doeth them not, shall be likened unto a foolish man, which built his house upon the sand."

14. "A created thing or being, a product of creative action; a creation," *OED*.

Now to consider rightly of faith we must look: first, what it is; secondly, how it is attainable; thirdly, particular and general fruits of faith . . .[15]

[p. 13] Had I not faith to uphold me in this sad time of my affliction what could I expect but the beginning of wrath here, and the continuance of it forever hereafter?

Without faith, what joy could any object give me. Nay rather[16] what grief, wailing, and astonishment? Am I not confirmed of that which must convince me of my former life being so sinful that it exceeds all that was ever known, and though my God doth know with innocence I have been ignorantly led to all that I have been guilty of, yet by the law I am condemned. For if a soul sin in committing anything which is forbidden to be done by the commandment of the Lord, though he wist[17] it not, yet he is guilty and shall bear his iniquity (Lev. 5:17) . . .[18]

[p. 21] Lord, thou seest what need I have of faith to overcome what now I have to encounter: want, and reproach, and injuries, and which is worst of all applying these afflictions as I ought to thy glory and my consolation; for the rod

---

15. Halkett addresses these issues in turn: she defines faith as "the substance of things hoped for, the evidence of things to come" (Hebrews 11:1) and then provides various biblical examples and her own aphorisms ("Faith makes the Devil silent, overcomes the world, and quiets the distempers of our own accusing consciences," p. 11); she then argues that faith is only attained by total reliance on Christ ("I am the vine, ye are the branches: He that abideth in me, and I in him, the same bringeth forth much fruit: for without me ye can do nothing," John 15:5), which requires constant intercessory prayer and a recognition that "whatsoever is not of faith is sin" (Romans 14:23), pp. 10–13.

16. "Rather" is an interlineal insertion.

17. "To know," OED.

18. Leviticus 5:17: "And if a soul sin and commit any of these things which are forbidden to be done by the commandments of the Lord; though he wist it not, yet is he guilty, and shall bear his iniquity." From here, Halkett explores what faith means by comparison; like the tree of life, it "bears several fruits and is good to heal the nations" (Revelation 22:2), and she spends most time exploring "the seven several promises made to seven particular churches," which are made to those who overcome by faith. Noting the parallel between the so-called seven deadly sins, Halkett suggests that the promises could help to overcome those sins: Church of Ephesus, Revelation 2:1–7; Smyrna, Revelation 2:8–11; Pergamos, Revelation 2:12–17; Thyatira, Revelation 2:18–29; Sardis, Revelation 3:1–6; Philadelphia, Revelation 3:7–13; Laodicea, Revelation 3:14–22: "The last is a general promise to all: he that over-commeth shall inherit all things, and I will be his God, and he shall be my son," Revelation 21:7. Halkett, *A Short Expostulation about Prayer*, p. 17. Although the promises are made to specific churches, Halkett reasons that they are also made to every particular member of the church; while others might suggest this includes only people already within the church, Halkett points out this would exclude future converts. She also notes that none of the seven churches were without sin, and that they all needed a combination of repentance, faith, and perseverance to be able to overcome. Even so, they only achieve this with God's assistance, which leads Halkett to praise God for his infinite goodness, *A Short Expostulation about Prayer*, pp. 13–21.

and reproof should give me wisdom (Prov. 29:15),[19] and teach me not to offend thee [p. 22] who in the greatest justice remembers mercy, and though I am like thy servant Paul, troubled on every side, yet not distressed[20] because still I find refuge under thy wings, oh, let my habitation be forever there.[21]

Mercy, I must acknowledge thou art pleased to show in[22] raising up any to assist and help me in all the wants and difficulties I meet with, but I beseech thee let it not become a snare unto me, rather hedge up my way with thorns before I should any more find out the paths of sin (Hosea 2:6).[23]

I confess, my God, I am in a great straight and know not what to do, but my eyes are upon thee: let me not like the house of Israel halt betwixt two opinions but in all things follow thee[24] who art both Lord and God (1 Kings 18:21).[25] Therefore, show thyself powerful, I beseech thee, in delivering me[26] from everything that is sinful that I may not in the least thought offend thee: so shall I have a great share in this victory if I can but overcome all my corruption.

And now, my Lord, with confidence I do address myself to thee, and hope with full assurance to be partaker of those mercies promised to those thy churches; for though there is degrees of sin, and mine exceeds all that can be registered, yet thy goodness is unlimited and can as easily extend to the pardon of a million as well as of a mite . . .[27]

[p. 23] Thou seest, O Lord, the variety of troubles that I am encompassed round with, and if thou dost not help me, it is impossible for me to overcome them, and all I do desire is that thou wouldst keep me from sin. Let me not sin against thee, my God, in thinking any more of that which now I am assured of

---

19. Proverbs 29:15: "The rod and reproof give wisdom: but a child left to himself bringeth his mother to shame."

20. 2 Corinthians 4:8: "We are troubled on every side, yet not distressed; we are perplexed, but not in despair."

21. Psalm 57:1: "Be merciful unto me, O God, be merciful unto me: for my soul trusteth in thee: yea, in the shadow of thy wings will I make my refuge, until these calamities be overpast"; 2 Chronicles 6:2: "But I have built an house of habitation for thee, and a place for thy dwelling forever."

22. After "in," "find" has been deleted.

23. Hosea 2:6: "Therefore, behold, I will hedge up thy way with thorns, and make a wall, that she shall not find her paths."

24. "Thee" is an interlineal insertion.

25. 1 Kings 18:21: "And Elijah came unto all the people, and said, how long halt ye between two opinions? If the Lord be God, follow him: but if Baal, then follow him. And the people answered him not a word."

26. "Me" is an interlineal insertion.

27. Halkett blesses God that he has given her the faith to make the prior application, considers again her unworthiness (by comparison with Job), and recognizes what Christ had to suffer for humanity's sins to be forgiven, pp. 22–23.

was unlawful.[28] Oh, for thy Son's sake pardon my transgressions, nor let me not do anything for human reason that is contrary to that light[29] with which thou hast illuminated my conscience, but since thou hast shut me up in this straight that I cannot lawfully either [p. 24] satisfy myself, or any other, teach me submission and keep me from repining at thy will.

I am almost brought to that, that I can see no way whereby I can preserve myself from great difficulties in my temporal condition; for thou hast removed all those from me that formerly I[30] relied on, as those I might expect much comfort from. But as long as thou dost not remove thyself, all other wants I can with joy bear with, because thy presence is to me more than my tongue can[31] speak . . .[32]

[p. 25] As circumcision tied a man to be a debtor to the whole law, so faith ties a man to the performance of every duty in the Gospel, and he serves God rightly in nothing that doth not endeavor to serve and obey him in all things. Christ must be the object to whom we direct all our prayers and requests, and we ought to look up to him first before we look upon any creature.[33]

Nay, all our actions are unholy that hath not the reflection of his goodness in them. My God, I will not then desire anything in reference to my present condition because I know not what to ask; but I will fix my heart and my affections upon thee, and for thy goodness' sake direct them, and me, to seek what thou thinkest best to grant and nothing more.

There is not anything that I could wish but [p. 26] I can see a way to have that which I could most desire, a cross in the enjoying, and a blessing in the want: why should I then seek anything but the sanctified use of ill things?

Give me thyself, my God, and I will never seek anything else.

No creature living ever hath transgressed like me, how dare I seek for grace then? Oh God, canst thou forgive that sin? Lord, I know it is not beyond mercy, though it deserves[34] the greatest justice; therefore, I will hope because thy mercies never fail. I will, like thy servant Habakkuk, tremble in myself that I may find rest in thee in this day of my calamity (Hab. 3:16).[35] I will hate and abhor myself, and love thee for destroying me for my iniquity. Do, my Lord, cast me off in they

---

28. I.e., her betrothal to Bampfield.

29. "Light" is an interlineal insertion.

30. "I" is an interlineal insertion.

31. After "can," "tell" has been deleted.

32. Halkett then advises that, as we cannot avoid what God has predetermined, we must be ready to accept all that God puts before us and place our trust in Christ's redemption, pp. 24–25.

33. "A created thing or being, a product of creative action; a creation," *OED*.

34. In MS reads "deserve."

35. Habakkuk 3:16: "When I heard, my belly trembled; my lips quivered at the voice: rottenness entered into my bones, and I trembled in myself, that I might rest in the day of trouble: when he cometh up unto the people, he will invade them with his troops."

displeasure: for there is such a body of sin about me, so much corruption in me, all of me so polluted, that every faculty of soul and body is a snare unto itself to pull down speedily destruction.

How can I murmur at any reproach I suffer? For though, O Lord, thou knowest my innocency[36] in some respect, yet I am guilty enough to deserve all that can be inflicted either by men or devils . . .[37]

[p. 31] Lord, do thou be pleased to subdue sin in us which is the occasion of all our differences amongst [p. 32] us, both in civil things and ecclesiastic; for[38] the Holy Spirit of God saith that for the transgression of a land many are the princes thereof.[39] And if our sins had not been so great as to pull down God's wrath so heavily upon us, He had never made our punishment thus pointing at our sin (which was our not being thankful for the blessing we had under one, and therefore God hath sent us many rulers which will still reign over us until we can learn to subdue ourselves and our corruptions).[40]

How can anyone say, this man, that faction, that design put to death an innocent King, and made his posterity pilgrims and strangers in a foreign land? No, no, it was thy sin and mine, and not his own which was his loss. And I fear his blood will be required at many a man and woman's hand that thinks themselves not guilty in a thought of it. But thus, we are all guilty: our prayers for him were[41] not so fervent and so full of faith as was required; for the Apostle exhorts Timothy, as the first thing that was to be done in relation to others, was that supplication,

---

36. Archaic form of "innocence."

37. Halkett implores God to take pity on her, and "give me grace as well as pardon" (p. 26), and reaffirms her faith in God and confidence in his grace, as past experience teaches her that God will not let her down, even though she has sinned so frequently. She reiterates her hope that this will be the case, which will help to steer her through this vale of misery. This leads her to reflect on how God's ordinances are currently abused, including the denial of childhood baptism and the permitting of anyone who claims to have God's spirit to be allowed to preach even "when they preach and practice that which is most contrary to the spirit of Truth." Halkett, *A Short Expostulation about Prayer*, pp. 29–30. Halkett notes "it is true St. Paul labored in his calling being a tent-maker (Acts 18:3), but can every tinker and cobbler that now preaches shew the same warrant, for the Lord declares himself of Paul that he was a chosen vessel to him (Acts 9: 15)." Halkett, *A Short Expostulation about Prayer*, p. 30. Acts 18:3: "And because he was of the same craft, he abode with them, and wrought: for by their occupation they were tentmakers." Acts 9:15: "But the Lord said unto him, Go they way: for he is a chosen vessel unto me, to bear my name before the Gentiles, and kings, and the children of Israel."

38. "For" is an interlineal insertion.

39. Proverbs 28:2: "For the transgression of a land many are the princes thereof: but by a man of understanding and knowledge the state thereof shall be prolonged."

40. In her discussion with Overton at Fyvie, Halkett alludes to the various changes in government, which continued until the Restoration of Charles II in 1660, see *True Account* and "Appendix 4.1," 133–34, 337–38.

41. In MS reads "was."

prayers, and intercession, and giving of thanks be made for the Kings, and them that be in authority (1 Tim. 2:1–2),[42] and this he advises as a thing acceptable in the sight of God our Savior.[43] How we have all been faulty in this our own consciences doth bear witness, and will testify how we have broke the Fifth Command [p. 33] which doth enjoin one precept for a duty, both to our parents and our prince.[44]

And if our days be not long and happy in the land it is because we have not given honor to whom honor was due (Rom.13:7).[45]

Lord, for thy mercy sake, pardon this transgression, and be thou first reconciled to us, and then we shall not want long reconciliation one with another . . .[46]

[p. 34] But, when I hear how vilely I am reproached by others, then, on the other side, my adversary is increasing of the load as if it were not supportable for myself, and intolerable for others to endure me; and therefore, as one without all hope of comfort in this world or the next, he tempts me to give over all thoughts or expectation of relief. Until my most gracious God sends me the faith and patience of the Saints (Rev. 13:10),[47] which doth enable me to wait and cheerfully go through many tribulations because I know it is through them that I must enter the kingdom of heaven (Acts 14:22).[48]

[p. 35] Thus continually I have a private war within, though there be never so much peace without, and by experience this I find: let anyone be watchful over their own heart and they shall find trouble enough from thence to keep them humble though there were nothing else from others to perplex[49] them . . .[50]

---

42. 1 Timothy 2:1–2: "I exhort therefore, that, first of all, supplications, prayers, intercessions, and giving of thanks, be made for all men; for kings, and for all that are in authority; that we may lead a quiet and peaceable life in all godliness and honesty."

43. 1 Timothy 2:3: "For this is good and acceptable in the sight of God our Savior."

44. The fifth commandment is "Honor thy father and thy mother: that thy days may be long upon the land which the Lord thy God giveth thee" (Exodus 20:12). The full list of the Ten Commandments can be found in Exodus 20:1–17 and Deuteronomy 5:6–22.

45. Romans 13:7: "Render therefore to all their dues: tribute to whom tribute is due; custom to whom custom; fear to whom fear; honor to whom honor."

46. Halkett provides the example of Nebuchadnezzar's being restored to his kingdom once he came to know God and expresses her hope that God will do something similar for England.

47. Revelation 13:10: "He that leadeth into captivity shall go into captivity: he that killeth with the sword must be killed with the sword. Here is the patience and the faith of the saints."

48. Acts 14:22: "Confirming the souls of the disciples, and exhorting them to continue in the faith, and that we must through much tribulation enter into the kingdom of God."

49. "To cause (a person) to feel troubled by deep uncertainty; to puzzle greatly; to baffle, confuse, bewilder," *OED*.

50. Now Halkett encourages herself to seek perfection; even if it is unattainable on this earth, we should still strive for it. Having shown herself what faith is, how to attain it, and what its fruits are, she moves to a conclusion in which this is made visible within her own life.

[p. 36] What need I then care for the opinion of this world, which at the best vanishes in a moment, when I consider that my Lord, my Judge, doth either know my innocence, or will accept of me as being so through his Son? What need want perplex[51] me when I remember that my heavenly Father careth for me, and knoweth better than myself what I have need of?

For in all things either necessary or useful the Lord can either give me what I want or take away the desire that I shall find no want of it, and either is alike satisfiable.

I do confess nothing can afflict me in this life but sin, for it is that takes from me peace of conscience. But when I consider there is not a sin I can be guilty of now but God's justice was satisfied for before it was committed; if it was not of power before to hinder the mercy of my God from electing me, it cannot now be of force[52] to hinder the mercy of my God from pardoning me, and this is only my consolement.[53]

Lord, shall I ever forget that object which thy providence did lead me to behold (at Rossie when Sir Robert Montgomery was married)[54] [p. 37] when I was in a sad, and despicable condition, with sense of sin for neglecting to keep that watch upon my heart which thou requirest, being perplexed[55] for it, and finding thy displeasure by the want of comfort in religious duties?

I walked solitarily abroad to seek him whom my soul loved, but still thou were as a stranger to me. But, returning home, I saw a flock of sheep feeding, and one amongst the rest far distant from his fellows upon a slippery bank, where nothing grew but thorns, which he made his food and seemed as contented with it as the rest with the best pasture. A long time I considered of the choice it made without an application, but before I was aware I heard this whispered to my soul: if thou are a true sheep of Christ's own fold, thou wilt as little as this beast repine when he doth suffer thee to go on slippery places, and give thee nothing but briars and thorns for to sustain thee. For as this sheep gets nourishment from this barren soil, so mayst thou receive virtue from the severest dispensation that God can send thee if thou be his own, even from his withdrawing of that grace that thou so earnestly dost seek.[56]

51. "To trouble, afflict, torment," *OED*.

52. After "force," "the" has been deleted.

53. "Consoling, consolation," *OED*.

54. The information in parenthesis is an insertion in the bottom margin of the page. "At Rossie" and "at Rossie" are also written in both the left- and right-hand margins of p. 37; the latter is obscured by an ink blot or attempt to eradicate, but the former is still visible. Probably the marriage of Sir Robert Montgomery, third Baronet of Skelmorlie (d. February 7, 1684), who married Anna/Antonia Scott, daughter/coheir of Sir James Scott of Rossie by Antonia Wilobie, *TCB*, 2:336.

55. I.e., troubled, afflicted, tormented.

56. Couper summarises this section as follows: "Observing a sheep, feeding pleasantly among thorns, at a distance from the flock, she thought it an emblem of her own state: a stranger in a strange land,

Oh, blessed be my God for this divine and pious contemplation, and for the comfort which from thee it gave me; for it shall teach me how to improve by every manifesting of thy attributes [p. 38] to me, either of justice or of mercy, thy omniscience and omnipotence.

For even my most secret thought to thee is visible; for I have felt thy correcting hand, even for those vain and idle thoughts that never could be possible to come to action.

And I have felt thy power in giving consolation to me when I have been as one without all help. Mayest thou be ever glorified therefore: for is it not infinite mercy that I should now be sensible of that which many years I was benumbed[57] in?

How many hundred Sabbaths have I misspent and never asked pardon for until of late? How little care had I either of words or actions to keep restraint upon them, so that they neither might be offensive unto thee, my God,[58] nor scandalous unto thy people?

Lord, how heinous hath my former life been, when I never thought of serving thee, if it be so wicked now when I endeavor all I can to do thy will? What I want in obedience, give me, O Lord, in humility, and what I want in repentance, give me in faith that so I may overcome the world, and that which gives the world a power over me, even my own corruption.

Then shall I live like one that hath an [p. 39] interest in this promise: that the gates of hell shall not prevail against me (Matt. 16:18).[59] Lord, make this promise true to me that sin may not prevail; for that, to me, is worse than hell. For I had much rather suffer punishment and be without sin,[60] if that were agreeable to thy justice, than sin without being punished. For I love thee for thy self, my God,[61] not for thy mercy. Oh, suffer me not then to sin against what I love above my soul, since thou art its joy, the consolation of my heart, and all that I desire: strengthen me for this victory, and make it perfect that, by faith, I may overcome all things that separate from thee.

Amen.

---

far from her nearest relatives, encompassed with difficulties, yet through the mercy of God finding a pleasant pasture, and enjoying a cheerful and undisturbed mind." Couper, *The Life of the Lady Halket*, 57.

57. "To render (the mental powers, the will, or the feelings) senseless or inert; to stupefy, deaden," *OED*.

58. "My God" is an interlineal insertion.

59. Matthew 16:18: "And I say also unto thee, that thou art Peter, and upon this rock I will build my church; and the gates of hell shall not prevail against it."

60. "Sin" is an interlineal insertion.

61. "My God" is an interlineal insertion.

Occasional Meditations *(1658/9–1660)*

This is the smallest of the surviving volumes, and the only one that, according to Halkett's classification, consists entirely of occasional meditations.[1] By contrast, as I have discussed elsewhere, Couper redefines several of its contents as "select" meditations.[2] Although it retains its original calfskin covers, this volume has been rebound and, as with the previous volume, there is no stated start or end date. Nevertheless, the opening meditation, the heartrending "Upon My Miscarrying of Two Children," is dated March 2, 1658/9, and the final entry, "Upon the Return of His Majesty after His Long Banishment and Variety of Other Troubles," must date from May/June 1660. Halkett does not provide a list of this volume's contents, nor does she paginate it; instead, each of the meditations is numbered, from one to thirty-five, and that number is used as a running header throughout the entry. As the opening and final titles suggest, the meditations address diverse personal and political events.[3] In contrast to the sad opening entry, meditation thirty-one records the birth of her only child to survive into adulthood: Robert, affectionately known as Robin ("Upon the Birth of My Son, Robert, on Wednesday, February 1, 1659/60, betwixt Two and Three o'clock in the Afternoon").[4] Although in generally good condition, the final pages show signs of extensive damage and, despite some conservation work, the text becomes increasingly illegible.

Upon Riches.[5]

[p.132] How many in the world hath plenty, and fullness, and in a manner choked with riches while others are in want, and care, and penury, and knows not at night where to get the next morsel to preserve them from famishing?

And yet perhaps they are more dear to God than the others who are heaped up with temporal benefits, [p. 133] so that, as Solomon says, no man knoweth either love or hatred by all that is before him (Eccles. 9:1).[6]

---

1. Halkett, *Occasional Meditations*, p. i. This is volume 6 in Couper's catalogue.
2. Trill, "Critical Categories," 106–7.
3. A full list of this volume's contents can be found in Trill, "Critical Categories," 119–20.
4. Halkett, *Occasional Meditations*, pp. 297–324.
5. This is the seventeenth meditation in this volume.
6. Ecclesiastes 9:1: "For all this I considered in my heart even to declare all this, that the righteous, and the wise, and their works, are in the hand of God: no man knoweth either love or hatred by all that is before them."

For all things come alike to all, and one event to the righteous and the wicked;[7] that is, while they are upon the earth many wicked men will enjoy those things that are promised as blessings to the righteous.

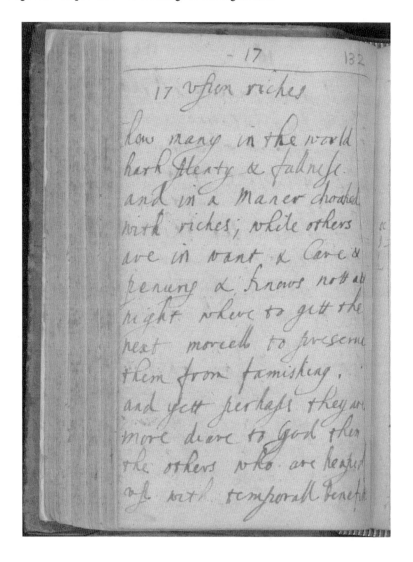

Figure 7. From Anne, Lady Halkett, *Occasional Meditations* (1658/9–1660)
© National Library of Scotland, NLS, MS 6490, p. 132.
Reproduced with permission.

7. Ecclesiastes 9:2: "All things come alike to all: there is one event to the righteous, and to the wicked; to the good and to the clean, and to the unclean; to him that sacrificeth, and to him that sacrificeth not: as is the good, so is the sinner; and he that sweareth, as he that feareth an oath."

And the righteous will suffer many crosses, and troubles, and afflictions which are as punishments threatened to the wicked.

[p. 134] Yet is not the Lord unjust in these dispensations[8] because he that made man best knows his frame,[9] and what suits everyone's temper.

So, perhaps the Lord sees that if I had abundance of the world it would take my heart altogether from himself, and therefore he deals sparingly with me, giving me supplies only for necessity, that so, like a child to a father, I may daily come and tell him [p. 135] all my wants and all my desires.

I am sometimes thinking with myself that if I had but what were sufficient for such and such things, it would free me much from that trouble and care which sometimes diverts me from serving of my God with that fervor that I ought to have. But how foolish am I in doing so, since I have often earnestly begged of God never to give me plenty in this world if it would make me [p. 136] lose[10] my love to him or his poor servants? For what advantage hath the rich more than the poor, if the Lord takes away their heart from making that use of it for which it is chiefly given (which is to try their love to God, and that is most visibly seen in being charitable in bestowing on the relief of the poor and the distressed)?

For several times I have found that recompensed [p. 137] when I was a stranger in this land which now the Lord hath graciously been pleased to make the lot of mine inheritance.[11]

I have seen some in very great want, and I have given them all the supply I had even when I knew not where to get money to buy my next meal. And this I did not out of ostentation but merely from compassion; for I knew the Lord could again provide for me, and [p. 138] had sent that person to me to try if I would so much rely upon him as to part with what I had to relieve another, and then I thought again many [a] one would lend me money which perhaps would not give them any.[12]

And never did I thus give but I had an unexpected supply.

How much may the remembrance of this check any murmuring or repining at [p. 139] what I want, since the least I have is infinitely more than I have right to? And it is not that the Lord wants power more now than formerly to help me

---

8. "Ordering, management; especially, the divine administration or conduct of the world; the ordering or arrangement of events by divine providence," *OED*.
9. Psalm 103:14: "For he knoweth our frame; he remembereth that we are dust."
10. "Lose" is an interlineal insertion.
11. Psalm 16:5: "The Lord is the portion of mine inheritance and of my cup: thou maintainest my lot."
12. See *True Account*, 148–49.

out of my difficulties, but that I have need of these trials to put me in mind from whence[13] every good and perfect gift comes.[14]

For riches are good in themselves, but to make them a perfect gift [p. 140] the use of them must be blessed and the enjoyment; for one may have riches but if the Lord doth not bless it, it will have wings and fly away, and as if it were put in a bag with holes it will fall away, and neither they nor any of their children shall ever be the better for it.[15] I bless the Lord I envy not the prosperity of any, [p. 141] nor do I wish part of what belongs to others, but if the Lord saw fit to give me what I have right to (to give others their own, and that I might see some provision made for the children[16] he hath blessed me with), it would be great ease to my mind, and contentment to my spirit that is some time overwhelmed with apprehensions of what may be, both to them and me.[17] But I will quiet myself [p. 142] with this: the Lord hath brought me out of as great troubles as any I can now imagine to fall upon me, and if he sees it for his glory, and the good of me and mine, he can yet manifest his power even in giving me what I desire (since he knows I desire it with submission, and chiefly to be just in rendering what is due to others). But if this I cannot [p. 143] obtain, give me thy self, O Lord, who art[18] the true riches, and be thou the portion of mine inheritance, and then place my heart and my affections entirely in heaven where my treasure is,[19] and then thy all sufficiency shall be my strength on which I shall rest both for myself and all that thou hast given me.

---

13. "From which source or origin (as a product); from which cause (as a result)," *OED*.

14. James 1:17: "Every good gift and every perfect gift is from above, and cometh down from the Father of lights, with whom is no variableness, neither shadow of turning."

15. Proverbs 23:5: "Wilt thou set thine eyes upon that which is not? for riches certainly make themselves wings; they fly away as an eagle toward heaven"; Haggai 1:6: "Ye have sown much, and bring in little; ye eat, but ye have not enough; ye drink, but ye are not filled with drink; ye clothe you, but there is none warm; and he that earneth wages earneth wages to put it into a bag with holes."

16. Betty and Henry (Robert was born after she wrote this entry).

17. See "Appendices 1–3," 327–35.

18. Archaic form of "are."

19. When asked for the secret to eternal life, Jesus replies "go and sell all that thou hast, and give to the poor, and thou shalt have treasure in heaven: and come and follow me." This story is found in all three of the synoptic Gospels and concludes with the suggestion that it "is easier for a camel to go through a needle's eye, than for a rich man to enter into the kingdom of God"; Matthew 19:16–24; Mark 10:17–25; Luke 18:18–25.

Selected Meditations 189

The Power of Faith, upon Mark 16:17–18.[20]

[p. 222] And these signs shall follow them that believe, in my name they shall cast out devils; they shall speak with new tongues; they shall take up serpents; and if they drink any deadly thing, it shall not hurt them; they shall lay hands on the sick, and they shall rejoice.

Our Lord, after he was risen, appeared several times before his diffident[21] disciples would believe his [p. 223] resurrection though he had foretold them of it even before his sufferings. And therefore, when the eleven are met together, he comes amongst them and upbraids them for their unbelief, then commissionates[22] them to preach the Gospel universally to all, but restricts the benefit of it to only such as believeth and is baptized:[23] for they only shall be saved.

And as that is promised to such as receive the Gospel, so there are promises made to them that dispense[24] [p. 224] the[25] Gospel, and these signs shall follow them that believe: first, in the name of Christ they shall cast out devils, which was made good by Paul on the woman that was possessed with the spirit of Pithon (Acts 16:16–18).[26]

Secondly, they should speak with new tongues, which was verified upon the whole company of the Apostles by the descending of the Holy Ghost who spake with other tongues as the spirit gave them utterance (Acts 2:4).[27]

[p. 225] Thirdly, they should take up serpents without hurt, and drinking that which was deadly to others should not hurt them. The proof of the serpent

---

20. This is the twenty-sixth meditation in this volume. "The power of faith" is an interlineal insertion. Mark 16:17–18: "And these signs shall follow them that believe; in my name shall they cast out devils; they shall speak with new tongues; they shall take up serpents; and if they drink any deadly thing, it shall not hurt them; they shall lay hands on the sick, and they shall recover." Although Halkett writes "rejoice" here, below she uses "recover," see 190n29.

21. "Lacking in trust or faith; full of or characterized by doubt or misgivings," *OED*.

22. An obsolete form of commission, "to empower, authorize, or charge (a person) (to do something); to assign or entrust with a duty, role, or task," *OED*.

23. Galatians 3:27: "For as many of you as have been baptized into Christ have put on Christ." The Baptism service opens with the minister asserting that "none can enter into the kingdom of God (except he be regenerate, and born a new of water, and the holy ghost)," *BCP*, 46.

24. "To administer (e.g. a sacrament)," *OED*.

25. "The" is an interlineal insertion.

26. Acts 16:16–18: "And it came to pass, as we went to prayer, a certain damsel possessed with a spirit of divination met us, which brought her masters much gain by soothsaying. The same followed Paul and us, and cried, saying, these men are the servants of the most high God, which shew unto us the way of salvation. And this did she many days. But Paul, being grieved, turned and said to the spirit, I command thee in the name of Jesus Christ to come out of her. And he came out the same hour."

27. Pentecost, as described in Acts 2:4: "And they were all filled with the Holy Ghost, and began to speak with other tongues, as the spirit gave them utterance."

was by the viper upon Paul's hand which he cast off without hurt.[28] And undoubtedly that promise of preservation against the drinking any deadly thing was to assure them of help, and to keep them from distrust of such enemies as might secretly practice their destruction.

[p. 226] Fourthly, they should lay hands on the sick, and they should recover.[29] And this was manifested both by Peter and Paul, who not only recovered the sick by laying on their hands but their shadow passing over the sick cured them, and the touch of their clothes as well as by their voice.[30] And further did their power extend [p. 227] of even to raise the dead (Acts 9:40).[31] Oh, the infinite advantages of faith!

What is the desolate condition that any can be in that hath true faith but[32] they may find comfort and consolation?

Under the greatest temporal pain, faith can give ease: in poverty and want it shows where riches is, and teaches how to wait; under reproach and injuries learns them contentation;[33] and, with Saint Paul, the hardest [p. 228] lesson, both how to abound as well as how to[34] want.[35] For though there is many temptations attend adversity, yet prosperity hath its snares as the most dangerous because for the most part men are then most secure when they are in a prosperous estate.

28. Acts 28:3–6: "And when Paul had gathered a bundle of sticks, and laid them on the fire, there came a viper out of the heat, and fastened on his hand. And when the barbarians saw the venomous beast hang on his hand, they said among themselves: No doubt this man is a murderer, whom, though he hath escaped the sea, yet vengeance suffereth not to live. And he shook off the beast into the fire and felt no harm. Howbeit they looked when he should have swollen or fallen down dead suddenly: but after they had looked a great while, and saw no harm come to him, they changed their minds, and said that he was a god."

29. Whereas the opening citation of the biblical verse ended with "rejoice," here Halkett follows the *KJV* with "recover."

30. Acts 5:15: "Insomuch that they brought forth the sick into the streets, and laid them on beds and couches, that at the least the shadow of Peter passing by might overshadow some of them." See also Acts 3:11 and 28:8.

31. Halkett cites Acts 9:40; however, the full version of Dorcas's resurrection is Acts 9:39–41: "Then Peter arose and went with them. When he was come, they brought him into the upper chamber: and all the widows stood by him weeping, and shewing the coats and garments which Dorcas made, while she was with them. But Peter put them all forth, and kneeled down, and prayed; and turning him to the body said, Tabitha, arise. And she opened her eyes: and when she saw Peter, she sat up. And he gave her her hand, and lifted her up, and when he had called the saints and widows, presented her alive."

32. Here used in the sense of "appending a statement which is not contrary to, but is not fully consonant with, or is contrasted with, that already made: Nevertheless, yet, however," *OED*.

33. "The contenting oneself or one's mind with what one has; acquiescence in or acceptance of the situation," *OED*.

34. "How to" is an interlineal insertion.

35. Philippians 4:12: "I know both how to be abased, and I know how to abound: everywhere and in all things I am instructed both to be full and to be hungry, both to abound and to suffer need."

Who more than I ought to exalt the infinite advantages of faith, [p. 229] and in that praise the Lord? Who made it the channel by which he was pleased to convey unexpected and unmerited mercies to my soul in the day of my calamity: when I was as a stranger amongst my own friends, the Lord made strangers friends unto me.[36] And now I find all the unkindness that I met with, and injustice from others, was but to bring about what was determined for [p. 230] my benefit and happiness (though for the present, while I was under the rod,[37] I thought there was almost an impossibility of being ever delivered). Such was sometime the weight of my afflictions, and like waves they came one tumbling upon another, and had undoubtedly overwhelmed me had not my God supported me by faith. And one remarkable evidence of it was [p. 231] when I was in the most disconsolate condition that could be, in a manner hated of all my friends, having nothing of my own nor no supply from them, and like the unjust steward I could not dig, or work, and to beg I was ashamed;[38] yet even then to one that served and[39] lived with me, who was weeping by me for my sad[40] condition, I said I knew not how, or which way it would come (for in reason I [p. 232] could not expect it, or see any probability of it), and yet I was as confident I should live to be happy in the world, and a contentment to my friends, as if I could chalk out the way to it and visibly see it before my eyes.[41] And so the Lord by faith was pleased to uphold me several times under the greatest of my difficulties and give me a deliverance. As now, to the honor of his name, I must [p. 233] acknowledge he hath made good to me what he made me by faith believe when I was by many years distant from it: even in giving me much content and happiness in a good husband, and many other blessings that attend it. And now, though the greater miracles are ceased, yet I ought to look upon it as the extraordinary power of the infinite God.

[p. 234] For would not they that reproached and made me as the most vile on earth, would not they have looked upon it then as impossible for me ever to have had respect again from any? For with their calumnies[42] they made me below all things but the compassion of my God, who raised me up again to make good in me what he did by his [p. 235] prophet promise: to save her that halted, and to

---

36. See, for example, the Countess of Dunfermline's invitation to Fyvie, *True Account*, 124.

37. Ezekiel 20:37: "And I will cause you to pass under the rod, and I will bring you into the bond of the covenant."

38. Luke 16:1–8; see especially 3: "Then the steward said within himself, what shall I do? for my lord taketh away from me the stewardship: I cannot dig; to beg I am ashamed."

39. "Served and" is an interlineal insertion.

40. "Sad" is an interlineal insertion.

41. See *True Account*, 135n448.

42. "A false charge or imputation, intended to damage another's reputation; a slanderous report," *OED*.

get her praise and fame in every land where she hath been put to shame (Zeph. 3:19).[43]

Since the Lord by faith hath brought me out of the mire that I stood in,[44] oh that now by the same faith I might have power through his name to cast out devils, even those many legions that I find within me: that of pride which sometimes [p. 236] doth possess me and make me think myself better than I am; that of hypocrisy which makes me seem better than I am to others.

Oh, that by faith I might cast out that sullen devil of anger and discontent which too, too often appears upon little or no occasion. And that all the corruption of my heart, which by Satan's wiles are daily increased, might be [p. 237] so ejected as that he nor they might ever find a hiding place; but that my heart and mind, my desires and endeavors might be so wholly taken up with serving of my God that I might so be instrumental in casting out devils, so in others as I had by grace effected in myself.

Then with a new tongue might I magnify my God and, as it was said of the Apostle Paul, I should [p. 238] build up that faith which once I destroyed, and so others that hear of it should glorify God in me.[45]

How often have I vowed new obedience upon new mercies, and to bridle my unruly tongue that it might not speak to the dishonor of its maker, and yet one month, nor week, nor day, nor hour hath hardly passed, without new provocations? And if I have been so faulty in one [p. 239] part when I have been most circumspect, what have I been in the most negligent part of my life?

Taking up of serpents and drinking of deadly things without being hurt by them have I done; for I have often meddled with things dangerous in themselves, and deadly in their consequence, and yet the Lord hath made it not so to me. Though I have drunken iniquity like water,[46] [p. 240] handled things forbidden which hath had the venom of asps,[47] and the deceit of the old serpent, the Devil,[48] who hath laid strong baits to entrap me, but the Lord hath delivered me, so as to let me see there is hope in him, though devils and men should contrive[49] never so much against me.

---

43. Zephaniah 3:19: "Behold, at that time I will undo all that afflict thee: and I will save her that halteth and gather her that was driven out; and I will get them praise and fame in every land where they have been put to shame."

44. Psalm 69:14: "Deliver me out of the mire and let me not sink: let me be delivered from them that hate me, and out of the deep waters."

45. Galatians 1:23–24: "But they had heard only that he which persecuted us in times past now preacheth the faith which once he destroyed. And they glorified God in me."

46. Job 15:16: "How much more abominable, and filthy is man, which drinketh iniquity like water?"

47. Deuteronomy 32:33: "Their wine is the poison of dragons, and the cruel venom of asps."

48. Revelation 12:9: "And the great dragon was cast out, the old serpent, called the Devil, and Satan, which deceiveth the whole world: he was cast out into the earth, and his angels were cast out with him."

49. "To make use of contrivance or ingenuity; to form devices; to plot, conspire," *OED*.

Another evidence of faith is by recovering the sick. How often hath the hand [p. 241] of faith raised me out of my bed of sickness when to all appearance I was liker[50] to die than live?[51] And though I have had troubles enough to make this life a burden to me, yet my desire was neither to wish death, nor life, but to be fit to welcome either that my God saw fittest for me, and hitherto I have been spared. For in my lowest condition, I knew and did believe that God was able to raise me up which [p. 242] to the praise of his great name he hath now done.[52] And often hath he made these hands of mine, which I had made weapons of sins, he hath made instruments of doing good to others who hath been sick and near to death, that the power of his grace might be known.[53] Oh, the infinite power and mercy of God who gives grace and glory, and no good thing doth he withhold [p. 243] from them that do desire to live uprightly;[54] that is all I can say for myself, that my desire is to live to God and die to sin.[55] And he is pleased to reward me as if I did perform what I desire, which only comes from him; for, of myself, I cannot think one good thought but by the help of my God I can do all things through him that strengthens [p. 244] me,[56] and so all things are easy to them that believe.

Upon the Return of His Majesty after His Long Banishment and Variety of Other Troubles.[57]

[p. 366] Hear, oh heavens, and give ear, oh earth,[58] and praise the Lord all the nations[59] of the world: for great in mercy is the God of our salvation, who only

50. I.e., more likely.

51. See illnesses recorded at Naworth, Fyvie, and Balcarres, *True Account*, 95–96, 128–29, 152–53.

52. "He hath now done" is an interlineal insertion.

53. As exemplified in her assistance to wounded soldiers after the Battle of Dunbar, and her treatment of the sick at Fyvie; see *True Account*, 125–26, 129.

54. Psalm 84:11: "For the Lord God is a sun and shield: The Lord will give grace and glory: no good thing will he withhold from them that walk uprightly."

55. Romans 6:11: "Likewise reckon ye also yourselves to be dead indeed unto sin, but alive unto God through Jesus Christ our Lord."

56. Philippians 4:13: "I can do all things through Christ which strengtheneth me."

57. This is the thirty-fifth, and final, meditation in this volume. Although his forthcoming Restoration was announced by the ringing of parish bells, May 8, 1660, Charles II returned to England and rode into the capital in triumph on May 29, 1660. The choice of that date was no accident: not only was it the restored King's birthday, but it also "became known as Royal Oak day (in some places called Oak Apple day) in memory of Charles's escape by hiding in an oak tree after the Battle of Worcester." David Cressy, *Bonfires and Bells: National Memory and the Protestant Calendar in Elizabethan and Stuart England* (Stroud, UK: Sutton, 2004), 64. See also Seaward, "Charles II," *ODNB*.

58. Isaiah 1:2: "Hear, O heavens, and give ear, O earth: for the Lord hath spoken, I have nourished and brought up children, and they have rebelled against me."

59. Psalm 117:1: "O praise the Lord, all ye nations: praise him, all ye people."

can do wonders to make his name glorious that all may know he is the Lord that can raise up, and put down, and that no strength, nor policy can resist his will.[60]

[p. 367] What sad trials hath our King[61] gone through even since the time that he first[62] came to know himself. Had he never been great, his troubles had been less, but every degree that [he] had beyond his meanest subject was but an additional step to aggravate his misfortune.

In his lowest condition ther[e] was plots[63] laid to tak[e] away his life but now they are multiplied since the Lord hath begun to show th[e] light of his countenance upo[n] him.[64] One would think tha[t] [p. 368] the extraordinary preservations that his Majesty had at Worcester[65] might point out he was one dear [t]o the Lord and yet they do not fear to attempt to destroy his anointed.[66] Whereas undoubtedly, since the wonders that the Lord hath done doth not work thankfulness and obedience, therefore they are hardened in their sin, and are but pulling down wrath upon themselves against the day of wrath,[67] and their wickedness shall be manifest to [p. 369] all the world that all may see and fear, and may no more transgress again[st] God and the King.

At the lowest condition I ever had a very grea[t] assurance that the Lord would bring the King home in peace and, as many as I spake it to, I was laughed at for what seemed to them impossible. But since the Lord hath granted my petition, in not only bringing him home but doing it in my days, therefore all the days [p. 370] of my life I will continually praise the Lord for his goodness, and dedicate whatever day the Crown is set upon his head to a weekly commemoration of the mercies of that day,[68] and show my affections to his Majesty most visibly to him that is the King of Kings (to whom I will pray that his throne may be established forever, and his Crown flourish, and that he may be such an example of piety and [p. 371] virtue that may make others afraid to sin when they see how displeasing it is to him). Let not, O Lord, prosperity be a snare to him, nor let anyone prosper

---

60. This entry apparently confirms Halkett's identity as a "prophetess," see *True Account*, 134.

61. I.e., Charles II.

62. "First" is an interlineal insertion.

63. Before "plots," "many" has been deleted.

64. Allegedly, both Bampfield and her brother Will were involved with one of the early plots. See *True Account*, and "Introduction," 119, 29.

65. The Battle of Worcester, September 3, 1651, was a massive defeat for the Royalists that "resulted in the death or capture of virtually the entire royal army"; however, with "incredible good luck," Charles II survived, and escaped to the Continent. Hutton, *Charles II*, 66, 67.

66. 2 Samuel 1:14: "And David said unto him, how wast thou not afraid to stretch forth thine hand to destroy the Lord's anointed?"

67. Romans 2:5: "But after thy hardness and impenitent heart treasurest up unto thyself wrath against the day of wrath and revelation of the righteous judgment of God."

68. See also "Upon His Majesty's Coronation," 207–8.

that cloak their wickedness under the show of godliness to entrap the innocent as too many in these late times hath done.[69] But the Lord tha[t] knows his own will best, put it into the hearts—bot[h] of King and people—to inclin[e] most to that (both in [p. 372] government, discipline, and manners) that is most agreeable to the holy[70] word which ought to be a light [to] our feet and a lantern to our paths.[71]

When the Lord turned back the captivity of his people they were like those that dream,[72] and so am I now when I think of the violent opposition that hath been against the King in all his three dominions; [how] strong his enemies hath been, and how weak his [p. 373] friends; how many h[ave] lost their lives in attempting to serve him; and yet now, without the shedding of one drop of blood (except what must be a sacrifice to justice),[73] the Lord hath brought him in and set him upon his throne, even by the desire of those which formerly were so much against him. Oh, how should this teach all to wait upon God?[74] Who, thou[gh] he seem sometimes to hi[de] [p. 374] his face, yet will show himself gracious in doing above all that we can either ask or think.[75] I believe there is many a person that would have been content to have begged all their life to have had the King established in peace (which I [h]ave often said I wished, [if] I could have so[76] purchased [h]is Majesty's obtaining his [i]nheritance), and now the Lord hath granted this without such penances. [p. 375] But should not this teach me and others t[o] be content if we wa[nt] what we propounded[77] as our own private advantage, since we have obtained what we ha[d] prayed for to the public? And so extraordinary a mercy should make us extraordinarily affected with it, and as many that have formerly bee[n] traitors are now endeavo[ring] to gain the King's fa[ith] again (by doing some [p. 376] remarkable service), so [w]e should all be as careful to become better servants to God than ever we have been ([i]n witness of

69. Charles II did not always live up to Halkett's (and others') expectations; see, for example, "The Widows Mite, Part of It Relating to the King," 241–49.

70. "Holy" is an interlineal insertion.

71. Psalm 119:105: "Thy word is a lamp unto my feet, and a light unto my path."

72. Psalm 126:1: "When the Lord turned again the captivity of Zion, we were like them that dream." See also *True Account*, and "Upon the Fast which by Proclamation Was Kept, January 30, 1660/1," 203–5.

73. Despite the "Act of Free and Generall Pardon, Indempnity, and Oblivion," (August 29, 1660) those who had signed the King's death warrant ("the Regicides") were put on trial in October, 1660, ten of whom were "condemned to death, and publicly hanged, drawn, and quartered at Charing Cross or Tyburn." David Plant, "The Regicides," BCW Project, accessed September 08, 2018, http://bcw-project.org/biography/regicides-index.

74. Psalm 62:5: "My soul, wait thou only upon God; for my expectation is from him."

75. Ephesians 3:20: "Now unto him that is able to do exceeding abundantly above all that we ask or think, according to the power that worketh in us."

76. "So" is an interlineal insertion.

77. "To intend, purpose, design," *OED*.

the sense [o]f our former rebellions [and] to evidence our thankfulness for this never to be enough admired deliverance).

[T]here is none but had a [han]d in the King's sufferings, [whe]ther actively or passively, [and] therefore not anyone [p. 377] can glory of the honor of bringing him back. T[oo] many things concurring ma[de] the General[78] most instrumental in it, yet so as tha[t] it is visible to all it wa[s] the immediate hand of G[od] who was pleased to mak[e] use of some people, and things that by many were despised who thoug[ht] themselves loyal, and even that Covenant[79] (which perhaps[s] at first was invented [for] a combination[80] against his Majesty's father) was the most [ju]stifiable ground they had [p. 378] [no]w for the bringing home himself. For looking upon that, they saw they had [t]aken God to witness th[ey] [i]ntended nothing but good [to] the King and his posterity; for their failing what [w]as then sworn, God had [l]aid many sad strokes [upo]n the whole Three Kingdoms,[81] [and] therefore, upon their reproving, to make good [the]se vows the Lord hath [xxx] returned to them and [wi]ll I hope forever bless [th]ese nations with the bles[ings] [p. 379] [of] peace, righteousness, [and] truth, and make both Ki[ng] and people happy in one [an]other. The Lord hath [xxxxxxx] with scourging and fo[r] [all] that we were [so] [xxxx] against him, and now h[e] is trying us with the gre[at] [te]mporal mercy we could [f]ind; if this doth not bring [xxxx]e, we may justly exp[ect] [e]xemplar wrath which the [Lord's] mercy will I hope de[xxxx] [and] incline us all to be submissive to his will and that [xxxxx]ness may make such [an] [impres]sion upon all; that from [the Ki]ng to his meanest subject [all?] be striving to exceed one[82] another [xxxxxxx] piety and thankful[ness].[83]

---

78. I.e., General Monk. See Ronald Hutton, "Monck [Monk], George, First Duke of Albemarle (1608–1670)," *ODNB*.

79. For an insightful exploration of the changing nature of the use and application of the National Covenant across the seventeenth century, see Bowie, "'A Legal Limited Monarchy,'" 131–54, and John Morrill, ed., *The Scottish National Covenant in Its British Context* (Edinburgh: Edinburgh University Press, 1990).

80. "Agreement, treaty, alliance, compact," *OED*.

81. See "Introduction," 6n21.

82. "One" is an interlineal insertion.

83. The meditation continues onto the next page; however, it is illegible in both the original manuscript and the *Perdita Project* reproduction.

Occasional Meditations, Meditations and Prayers on Every Several Day Ordained to Be Kept Holy in the Church of England *(1660, 1663)*

The first text in this volume is on the inside cover and consists of Halkett's signature "AHalkett," along with the inscription, "all these writ at London, 1660 and 1663."[1] Having celebrated the Restoration of Charles II at the end of her previous volume, Halkett traveled south with her family in the hope of obtaining some recompense for her assistance in the Duke of York's escape and to regain her inheritance; although, as she details below, her activities in this area primarily met with "disappointment."[2] While she was able to enjoy some of the festivities associated with the Coronation,[3] her personal life was marred by mourning: the first entry records the death "of My Dearest Child Betty" from smallpox (Tuesday, November 13, 1660), which was followed (May 12, 1661) by the death of her eldest son, Harry (Henry).[4] However, one of the reasons Halkett remains in London when her husband returns to Scotland (July 19, 1661) is because she is pregnant again, this time with her second daughter, Jane, who was born on October 11, 1661.[5] As in the previous volume, the occasional meditations are numbered, although this time there are only fifteen of them and Halkett also paginates the volume sequentially.[6] Here, the contents are identified on a separate piece of paper that has been tipped into the volume, along with a very brief reflection on "Jacob's Vow, Genesis 28:20," dated January 9, 1660.[7] The occasional entries run from page one to page

---

1. Halkett, *Occasional Meditations, Meditations and Prayers on Every Several Day Ordained to Be Kept Holy in the Church of England*, p. ii. This is volume 7 in Couper's catalogue.

2. See "Upon the Many Disappointments I have Met with in My Business at Court," 205–7.

3. See "Upon His Majesty's Coronation, Tuesday, April 23, 1661" and "*The Widow's Mite*, Part of It Relating to the King," 207–8, 241–49.

4. "Upon the Death of My Dearest Child Betty," in Halkett, *Occasional Meditations, Meditations and Prayers on Every Several Day Ordained to Be Kept Holy in the Church of England*, pp. 1–18, see also Trill, ed., *Halkett*, 15–19; in "Upon the Death of My Dear Son Harry," Halkett observes: "What a sad journey hath this been hitherto to me into England, where I expected greatest satisfaction: first, in seeing the King and royal family restored, and then in seeing my relations and friends. And to mitigate these joys the Lord is pleased daily to find me new afflictions, and to take away al[l or] most [of] the chief comforts of my life which is my dear children." Halkett, *Occasional Meditations, Meditations and Prayers on Every Several Day Ordained to Be Kept Holy in the Church of England*, pp. 52–57, 52.

5. Jane died on February 11, 1665/6. See "Introduction," 17n80, "Upon the Death of My Dearest Sir James Halkett," 226, 226n97.

6. Until page 230, there is agreement between Halkett's own numbering and that of the library cataloguer; at this point, Halkett inadvertently includes two pages with the same number and thus the numbering systems diverge.

7. Halkett, *Occasional Meditations, Meditations and Prayers on Every Several Day Ordained to Be Kept Holy in the Church of England*, pp. iii–iv, v–vi.

ninety-five; however, the bulk of this volume is given over to "Meditations and Prayers upon Every Several Day That Is Ordained to Be Kept Holy in the Church of England."[8] Given the contemporary public debate relating to the organization of the Church, of which Halkett is keenly aware, tackling such a subject could be seen as a form of political intervention.[9] Halkett's nascent consciousness of this is perhaps indicated by an undated "afterword":

> since I ended the meditations upon the festivals of the Church I have since seen another book upon the same subject which yet I have not had time to look over. Those meditations are public which I never intend these; but, if any unexpected occasion should ever bring these to light, all I desire is that as every good motion or desire comes from God, so He may not be dishonored by any reflection upon my incapacity of performing what those of greater parts thought worthy their employment: for though some have ten talents, another but one, yet from the least is expected an improvement. And these endeavors will be, I hope, accepted of my God, who can give more or pardon what I want.[10]

---

8. Halkett, *Occasional Meditations, Meditations and Prayers on Every Several Day Ordained to Be Kept Holy in the Church of England*, pp. 96–257. As Couper records, there are three "select" meditations in this volume. The others are "Meditations upon Isaiah, Chapter Twelve," and "Meditations upon the Four First Verses of the Thirty fourth Psalm," pp. 258–98, 299–319.

9. See "Upon the Meeting That Was to Determine of Church Government, Tuesday, November 3, 1661," in Halkett, *Occasional Meditations, Meditations and Prayers on Every Several Day Ordained to Be Kept Holy in the Church of England*, pp. 76–80; see also Trill, ed., *Halkett*, 23–24.

10. Halkett, *Occasional Meditations, Meditations and Prayers on Every Several Day Ordained to Be Kept Holy in the Church of England*, p. 326. In "Bibliographic data," the *Perdita Project* suggests that the book to which Halkett refers is Edmund Gayton's, *The Religion of a Physician: or, Divine Meditations upon the Grand and Lesser Festivals, Commanded to Be Observed in the Church of England by Act of Parliament* (London: J. G[rismond], 1663). ESTC R7653. Most of Gayton's meditations are poetic; however, his volume concludes with three prose offerings: "A Meditation upon the Churches Pious Observation of Lent," 65–74; " A Meditation on the Passion of Our Savior," 75–92; and "A Meditation upon May 29, Being His Majesty's Birthday and Day of Restoration," 93–99. Ian W. McLellan, "Gayton, Edmund (1608–1666)," *ODNB*.

Selected Meditations 199

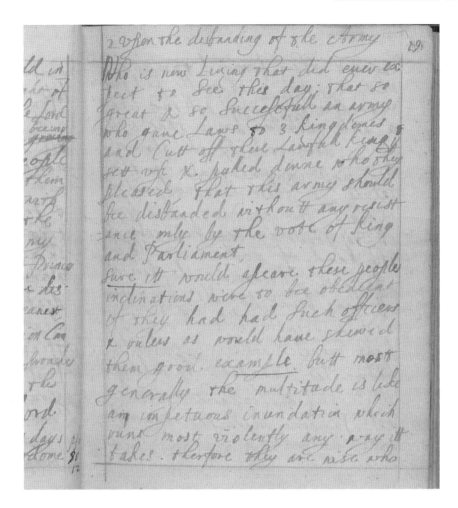

Figure 8. From Anne, Lady Halkett, *Occasional Meditations, Meditations and Prayers on Every Several Day Ordained to Be Kept Holy in the Church of England* (1660, 1663). © National Library of Scotland, NLS, MS 6490, p. 19. Reproduced with permission.

Upon the Disbanding of the Army.[11]

[p. 19] Who is now living that did ever expect to see this day: that so great and so successful an army, who gave laws to Three Kingdoms[12] and cut off their lawful King; that set up and pulled down who they pleased; that this army

---

11. According to Halkett's numbering, this is the second occasional meditation in this volume. See Trill, ed., *Halkett*, 19–22.

12. See "Introduction," 6n21.

should be disbanded, without any resistance, only by the vote of the King and Parliament?[13]

Sure, it would appear these people's inclinations were to be obedient if they had had such officers and rulers as would have showed them good example, but most generally the multitude is like an impetuous inundation which runs most violently anyway it takes. Therefore, they are wise who [p. 20] can set them forward towards what is good and allowable, and then unquestionably they will run like a well biased[14] bowl that way it is directed by the thrower. Men may imagine reasons to themselves for these late, unheard of changes (from good to ill and from ill to good again) but certainly the hand of God is visible in all these alterations. Else how could it have been possible for a good and a greatly beloved King to have been murdered publicly before his own gates by a handful of people (in comparison of the rest) and none made resistance but with sighs and tears?[15] How could [p. 21] this have been done, had not the Lord for a just punishment of our sins taken from us power, strength, and wisdom?

How could the vilest of the people[16] been submitted to, by so many better than themselves who complied with them, had not God taken from them their reason and their honor?

How could so many men have lost their lives, both in England and Scotland, for intending to restore the King and owning of[17] his interest, and then to have him brought home in peace by the unanimous desire of the generality of the people? How could this have [p. 22] been done but by that God who only doth determine of life and death, and times and seasons?

There is a time for all things says the wise man.[18] There was a time for the King to suffer exile and all his subjects to be enslaved, and a time for him to be

---

13. The Convention Parliament met in April 1660 and unanimously voted to restore the monarchy; Hutton, *Charles II*, 131.

14. After "well," "turned" has been deleted and replaced with the interlineal insertion of "biased." Halkett's phraseology suggests an allusion to Jeremiah 18:3-10: "Then I went down to the potter's house, and behold, he wrought a work on the wheels. And the vessel that he made of clay was marred in the hand of the potter: so, he made it again another vessel, as seemed good to the potter to make it. Then the word of the Lord came to me, saying, O house of Israel, cannot I do with you as this potter? saith the Lord. Behold, as the clay is in the potter's hand, so are ye in mine hand, O house of Israel. At what instant I shall speak concerning a nation, and concerning a kingdom, to pluck up, and to pull down, and to destroy it; if that nation, against whom I have pronounced, turn from their evil, I will repent of the evil that I thought to do unto them. And at what instant I shall speak concerning a nation, and concerning a kingdom, to build and to plant it; if it do evil in my sight, that it obey not my voice, then I will repent of the good, wherewith I said I would benefit them."

15. See *True Account*, 88, 88n172.

16. I.e., Cromwell.

17. "Of" is an interlineal insertion.

18. Ecclesiastes 3:1: "To everything there is a season, and a time to every purpose under the heaven."

restored; but until this time came, that God had appointed for it, all industry was fruitless.[19]

Now it seems this was the time, and by this means, that this army was to be disbanded. And from this many expected peace and quiet, which they thought could not be as long as such men were in arms that had done so much against the royal [p. 23] power.

Scatter the people that delight in war was a prayer made long since by the Psalmist.[20] And now we see that prayer made good so many ages after to let us see there never was a prayer put up in faith either from a person or a people, but had a return at some time or other, but to let us see the rules we prescribe ourselves as means to attain our ends proves most times the contrary. (Yet ought none from this, forbear to do what's most agreeable to reason and leave the success to him who makes all things work together for good to them that fear him.)[21]

The disbanding of this army was [p. 24] looked upon as a thing impossible without great mutiny, and the keeping it together seemed very dangerous. And yet how willingly every man went to his own home at their several days of dissipation, with the appearance of joy and acclamation, and praying for the King (who liberally rewarded their last actions though their former had been so rebellious).[22]

From this, which some made a ground to expect peace, others take occasion to raise a disturbance, and are not afraid to entitle God to be[23] the owner of their quarrel and rebellion.[24] But he who sits in heaven will laugh at their folly

19. See *True Account*, 124; see also her account of her response to Lady Anna Erskine at Fyvie, "The Widow's Mite, Part of It Relating to the King," 242.

20. Psalm 68:30: "Rebuke the company of spearmen, the multitude of the bulls, with the calves of the people, till everyone submit himself with pieces of silver: scatter thou the people that delight in war."

21. Romans 8:28: "And we know that all things work together for good to them that love God, to them who are the called according to his purpose." Halkett demonstrates her ability to negotiate "the fine line between fully relying upon providence and presumptuously tempting it"; while "total trust ought to be placed" in providence, "nevertheless, one should not wholly neglect or reject lawful secondary means, feebly surrendering oneself to whatever destiny held in store." Walsham, *Providence in Early Modern England*, 18.

22. On April 25, 1660, the Convention Parliament passed, "An Act for the Speedy Disbanding of the Army and Garrisons of This Kingdome," in Raithby, ed., *Statutes of the Realm*, 5:238–41, BHO. In August 1660, this was followed up by "An Act for the Speedy Provision of Money for Disbanding and Paying Off the Forces of This Kingdome Both by Land and Sea," in Raithby, ed., *Statutes of the Realm*, 5:207–25, BHO.

23. "Be" is an interlineal insertion.

24. As recognition of the part he played in the Restoration of the monarchy, General Monck's regiment was the last section of the New Model Army to be disbanded; however, "in January 1661, the regiment was active in suppressing a sudden insurrection by the Fifth Monarchists in London. The order for disbandment was promptly repealed. On February 14, 1661, the regiment paraded on Tower Hill where the soldiers symbolically laid down their weapons, and with them their association with the New Model Army and the 'Good Old Cause.' They were immediately ordered to take up arms again as

and make them a derision[25] [p. 25] unto all that hate them, because they have blasphemed the name of the most high, and rebelled against the Lord and his anointed.

What disturbance hath these men[26] made these three nights in one of the most populous and best governed cities in the world? And yet they are but a handful in comparison of the multitude that were against them, but a gangrene in the least degree begun hazards the loss of the whole body if not cut off in time. And since the multiplied mercies of a gracious and indulgent King cannot reclaim them, his severity must be made [p. 26] use of, and by letting blood to[27] purge out that corruption which else[28] might be infectious.

There is some people like the nature of the spider that turns that to poison from which others gather honey, which shows the ill quality is in themselves and not in the thing were it not by them empoisoned.[29] How many from the mercy of the King is so convinced that he is truly what he represents (even the great substitute of God) that they now admire and love him with the affections and duty that belongs to faithful subjects, and hate themselves for ever having had a thought that was rebellious against [p. 27] so gracious a Sovereign?

And yet this clemency stirs others up to write and act such treasonable things as might persuade the King to repent his mercy (did it not proceed from that high

---

troops of King Charles II's new standing army." David Plant, "The New Model Army." BCW Project, accessed September 08, 2018, http://bcw-project.org/military/new-model-army. For more detail on "Venner's Rising," see Ronald Hutton, *The Restoration: A Political and Religious History of England and Wales, 1658–1667* (Oxford: Clarendon Press, 1985), 150–52.

25. Psalm 2:4: "He that sitteth in the heavens shall laugh: the Lord shall have them in derision."

26. I.e., the Fifth Monarchists.

27. "To" is an interlineal insertion.

28. "Else" is an interlineal insertion.

29. The opposition between the spider and the bee confirms the constitutive role of the seventeenth-century reader and is not unique to Halkett: see John White, "To All Lovers of Ingenuous and Artificial Conclusions," who encourages his readers to "pick and cull out those flowers which best pleasesth you, and are fittest for your pleasure or profit: For the laborious bee gathereth her cordial honey, and the venomous spider her corroding poison (many times) from the same flower," *A Rich Cabinet, with Variety of Inventions; Unlocked and Opened, for the Recreation of Ingenious Spirits at Their Vacant Hours, Being Receits and Conceits of Severall Natures, and Fit for Those Who Are Lovers of Naturall and Artificiall Conclusions* (London: William Whitwood, 1688), sigs. A4r–v, cited by Dolan, *True Relations*, 13. Although Dolan cites the 1688 edition, White's book was first published in 1651 and had gone through eight editions by 1704. In *The Spiritual Bee or, A Miscellaney of Spiritual, Historical, Natural Observations, and Occasional Occurencyes, Applyed in Divine Meditations* (Oxford: W. H., 1667), attributed to Nicholas Horsman, the writer wishes he "had an antidote against some readers that make it their business . . . like spiders, to gather and by an innate virulency concoct into poison that which of itself was of an innoxious nature," sig. A8r. ESTC R24990. See also Charles H. Hinnant, "The 'Fable of the Spider and the Bee' and Swift's Poetics of Inspiration," *Colby Library Quarterly* 20, no. 3 (1984): 129–36.

principle taught by the[30] Lord of glory, who recommended mercy as part of that perfection which made men like to their heavenly Father, and from that[31] pattern justice is imitable to).[32] And certainly, severity should be used to punish them who, from the miraculous reestablishment of the King, will not be convinced nor by his mercy reclaimed. Though I think they ought to be pitied when we see how Satan [p. 28] leads them captive to his will, and doth so absolutely possess them that he drives them violently upon actions contrary both to sense and reason. And yet they have the confidence to expect help and assistance from that God who daily they blaspheme and dishonor by pretending they are doing him service when they are acting[33] most contrary to his laws?[34] But the Lord will, I hope, make manifest to all that this is not the people he will own, and therefore will destroy their designs,[35] or if not they will be spared only to be as thorns in our sides (and a means to teach such the art of war who by reason of [p. 29] their youth were strangers to it, as it was with the children of Israel and the Canaanites).

Therefore, I will not repine at what the Lord thinks fit to suffer, for he that hath done so much as he hath done for this King and people will still continue to do us good. I will[36] give thanks, therefore, to the God of Gods, for his mercy doth endure forever.[37]

Upon the Fast which by Proclamation Was Kept, January 30, 1660/1.[38]

[p. 30] This is a day on which the greatest murder was committed that ever story mentioned (except the crucifying of our Savior), and many hath lain under

30. "The" is an interlineal insertion.
31. "That" is an interlineal insertion.
32. An allusion to the concluding section of the Sermon on the Mount, Matthew 5:44–45, 48: "But I say unto you, Love your enemies, bless them that curse you, do good to them that hate you, and pray for them which despitefully use you, and persecute you; That ye may be the children of your Father which is in heaven: for He maketh his sun to rise on the evil and on the good, and sendeth rain on the just and on the unjust; Be ye therefore perfect, even as your Father which is in heaven is perfect."
33. "Acting" is an interlineal insertion.
34. "Laws" is an interlineal insertion.
35. "Designs" is an interlineal insertion.
36. "Will" is an interlineal insertion.
37. Psalm 136:2: "O give thanks unto the God of gods: for his mercy endureth forever."
38. This is the third occasional meditation in this volume and is prompted by "A Proclamation, for Observation of the Thirtieth Day of January as a Day of Fast and Humiliation According to the Late Act of Parliament for That Purpose, 1661" (London: John Bill, 1661). ESTC R226600. See also "January 30, 1673/4," "January 30, 1690/1," and "Saturday, January 30, 1696/7," 255–56, 284–85, 304–7. In addition, see also, "January 30, 1687/8," in Halkett, *Meditations on St. Peter*, p. 345; "Wednesday, January 30, 1694/5," in Halkett, *Of Watchfulness*, p. 343; and "Sunday, January 30, 1697/8," in Anne, Lady Halkett, *Select and Occasional Meditations* (1697–1698/9), NLS, MS 6502, p. 256.

the guilt of it these many years who perhaps hath never offered up to God a sigh or tear for pardon of it, and yet it was no less a sin than the public murder of our own lawful and the best of Kings. Some may ask, as the disciples did their master about the man that was born blind, did this [p. 31] man sin or his parents?[39] And the Lord's answer shows that sin is not always the occasion of punishment but that the works of the Lord may be manifest; so, though none can be free from sin in this life, yet it might be neither the King's sins, nor his parents', that pulled down that sad, unexemplary[40] judgment upon him but that the works of the Lord should be made manifest in him. Had not his Majesty come under all those trials and sufferings, how should the world and his own subjects known his piety, patience, his meekness and his charity, [p. 32] his constancy in suffering, and the heavenly ejaculations which upon all occasions he offered up to God in his solitudes, which like monuments are left to future generations to teach them how to follow what was eminent in him?[41]

His virtues made the sin so much the greater and the crime the more enormous. Who could have thought that there had been so much wickedness in this nation, which hath been[42] renowned over all the world for being the best subjects, that they should fall away to commit such great impieties? [p. 33] The Scots are blamed and surely they deserve it, if it were but for being too credulous.[43] But let them that are without this sin of being guilty of the King's murder in the three nations cast the first stone at the other:[44] for[45] either simply, willfully, or passively, all are guilty, and therefore all had need to[46] be humbled greatly for so heinous a transgression.

And since the Lord hath brought back our captivity and restored our lawful King to his throne in peace—notwithstanding all our provocations—oh, that by

39. John 9:1–3: "And as Jesus passed by, he saw a man which was blind from his birth. And his disciples asked him, saying, master, who did sin, this man, or his parents, that he was born blind? Jesus answered, neither hath this man sinned, nor his parents: but that the works of God should be made manifest in him."

40. "Not exemplary; not to be taken as a model," *OED*.

41. Following Charles I's execution, *Eikon Basilike: the Portraiture of His Sacred Majesty in His Solitudes and Sufferings* was released. Otherwise known as "The King's Book" by 1896 it had gone through around seventy-five editions. See Robert Wilcher, "*Eikon Basilike*: The Printing, Composition, Strategy, and Impact of 'The King's Book,'" in *The Oxford Handbook of Literature and the English Revolution*, edited by Laura Lunger Knoppers (Oxford: Oxford University Press, 2012), 289–308, and Lacey, "Texts to Be Read," 4–18. See also "Introduction," 22, 22n104.

42. "Been" is an interlineal insertion.

43. The phrase "if it were but for being too credulous" is an interlineal insertion.

44. An allusion to Jesus's response to how to deal with the woman caught in adultery, John 8:1–11, specifically verse 7: "So when they continued asking him, he lifted up himself, and said unto them, He that is without sin among you, let him first cast a stone at her."

45. "For" is an interlineal insertion.

46. "To" is an interlineal insertion.

our mourning for former rebellions, and thankfulness for undeserved mercies, we might live [p. 34] like a people zealous of good works.[47] Whatever we hear is amiss either in the court, or officers of state, or government in the church, not to exclaim against such who perhaps is innocent and are only blasted by envy or malice, but however to pray to him who can judicially harden the best (and soften the worst) heart to bring glory to himself. For how many hath been accessory to that for which this day we ought all to mourn, who, if some years before had they been foretold it would have said, [p. 35] like Hazael to the prophet, am I a dog that I should do this?[48] And yet so brutish have they been beyond what themselves or any others could imagine them to be? Great sins deserve great humiliation and returning unto God. And if we would give glory unto God, we should, like Achan,[49] confess where the wedge and Babylonish garment was that first allowed us to commit the sin that brought wrath upon the Israel of God, and care not what punishment or shame it brought upon ourselves so that the Lord would turn again [p. 36] in mercy and be reconciled to his people. The sad strokes upon the kingdom in smiting[50] those two branches of the royal stock[51] shows evidently God is displeased, and if judgment begins at the best where shall the sinner and ungodly appear? Oh, that our repentant tears might be such as might be accepted through our mediator, and then we may have hope that what remains[52] shall be blessed, and preserved, and made glorious by their works of piety and virtue.

Upon the Many Disappointments I Have Met with in My Business at Court.[53]

[p. 43] Were there not overruling providence that sets a time and period to everything under heaven, how apt would the frailty of my nature be to repine at the many disappointments that I meet with?

47. Titus 2:14: "Who gave himself for us, that he might redeem us from all iniquity, and purify unto himself a peculiar people, zealous of good works."

48. 2 Kings 8:13: "And Hazael said, but what, is thy servant a dog, that he should do this great thing? And Elisha answered, The Lord hath shewed me that thou shalt be king over Syria."

49. Joshua 7:20–21: "And Achan answered Joshua, and said, Indeed I have sinned against the Lord God of Israel, and thus and thus have I done: When I saw among the spoils a goodly Babylonish garment, and two hundred shekels of silver, and a wedge of gold of fifty shekels weight, then I coveted them, and took them."

50. "To afflict with death or destruction; (also) to punish or afflict in a notable way," *OED*.

51. Prince Henry, Duke of Gloucester, died from smallpox on September 13, 1660; Princess Mary of Orange died, "of a rapid and mysterious fever," on December 24, 1660. Handley, "Henry, Prince," *ODNB*; Hutton, *The Restoration*, 149. Marika Keblusek suggests the illness was either measles or smallpox, "Mary, Princess Royal (1631–1660)," *ODNB*.

52. I.e., King Charles II, and James, Duke of York, later King James VII/II.

53. This is the fifth occasional meditation in this volume.

The court, next heaven, is the greatest place for all beggars to resort to, and there, amongst others, I have given many petitions and requests.[54] But all I receive is civilities that would encourage me to hope that I had a grant, and when it comes to the trial it is but a handsome[55] refusal, and this is all I have met with yet, for many years suffering and expectation of redress.[56] And yet I see others, of as little merit as myself, [p. 44] get all they seek and more than they could expect. I envy no man's happiness but have a share in the satisfaction any person hath in obtaining their desire, yet I cannot but secretly say, "Why cannot I arrive to this degree as to have something, while others want nothing they desire?" But are we not all as clay in the hand of the potter, and may he not do with us what he please?[57] When the Lord sees me fit for to attain that blessing I have so often sought, of having to pay and keep me out of debt, he will put it into the heart of the King not [p. 45] to deny my just requests. And until that time comes, I must be patient, yet to forbear nothing that's rational in pursuance of this end (because I know not but it may be the next petition I give in may put an end to all my former fruitless expectation).

Sometime[s] I am thinking these delays and disappointments are to make trial how I would[58] make good what I have often said, "To see the King brought in, in peace, and established in his just prerogatives, I would be content to beg all my [p. 46] life after." And what I now see as the fruit of many years prayers is come to pass without that conditional penance which I would willingly have undertaken for it. I confess I thought—if ever this day came—I should not have seen others preferred and I forgot; yet myself was the least motive that made me hope or wish for this great blessing which I will still give thanks for (though I should never have more advantage by it but to see peace in our Israel[59] by the King's enjoying of his own). [p. 47] I cannot doubt the having at last something to capacitate[60] me to do what I desire, since I know the end for which I seek it is justifiable both to God and man. But perhaps it is visible to him that knows my heart, which to me may

---

54. Two of Halkett's petitions survive. See Anne, Lady Halkett, "For Forfeited Estates, &c.: Dame Anne, Wife of Sir James Halkett and Daughter of the Late Jane Murray." Volume of Petitions All Addressed to the King, Unless Otherwise Specified, October 1660. TNA, *SP* 29/20, fol.107; and "Petition of Anne Halkett and Thos. Stanley to the King, for the Place of Collectors and Receivers, of the Additional Customs Imposed by Act of Parliament," June 17, 1661. TNA, *SP* 29/37 fol.125. A grant "to Lady Ann Hacket, in consideration of her zeal and sufferings," of £500 was made to her on November 20, 1662. Shaw, *Calendar of Treasury Books, 1660–1667*, 1:452. Loftis, ed., *The Memoirs of Anne, Lady Halkett and Anne, Lady Fanshawe*, 207.

55. "Convenient, handy," *OED*.

56. See Halkett's account of her legal cases in both Scotland and in England, *True Account*, 159, 162–66.

57. Isaiah 64:8: "But now, O Lord, thou art our father; we are the clay, and thou our potter; and we all are the work of thy hand."

58. After "would," "have" has been deleted.

59. England was often referred to as the "new Israel" in early modern writing.

60. "To endow with capacity for or to do (something); to render capable; to qualify, fit," *OED*.

be deceitful, that if I were out of these which is my present troubles I should be forgetful from whence deliverance comes, and therefore to bring me nearer to him I am kept with that allowance which children have from their father that they may every day come[61] to seek their daily bread.[62] For my heavenly Father knoweth what I have need of (Matt. 6:32),[63] and these disappointments [p. 48] may be as necessary and more advantageous than the attaining my desire. Has there not many things I have been crossed in proved a greater mercy to me than if I had enjoyed the thing I sought?[64] Why then should I set limits to the unquestionable goodness of God, who careth more for me than I can for myself, who is wiser than I, and knows what time is best for everything? And if I am but patient, I am confident to see a visible reason why the Lord thinks fit to delay the blessing he intends me (either to make them better, and me fitter for them, and so glory shall be the more ascribed to him).

Upon His Majesty's Coronation, Tuesday, April 23, 1661.[65]

[p. 49] How long have I wished and prayed for this day? And now the Lord is pleased to let me see it.[66] Oh, that it might be a day of joy and rejoicing to the whole earth, that all might sing praises to our God for his goodness to us in crowning of our King. The right of his kingdoms and the obedience of his subjects was as much due to him before, but this day's action is the confirmation of his Majesty's power and our subjection. And so much the more reason have we to be thankful for it because his enemies did give out, for all the preparations that was made, he should never be crowned. But, blessed be the [p. 50] name of the Lord, they are disappointed, and we have seen the desire of our hearts in seeing him now the Lord's anointed, against whom I hope there shall never be no rising up.

It is many months since I made this vow: that if the Lord would be pleased to let me see that mercy, I forever after during my life would[67] make that day, a day of praise every week, and would do something to evidence my thankfulness.[68] What action to fix upon that may express my joy I know not, but I will

61. After "may," "every day come" is an interlineal insertion.
62. An allusion to the Lord's prayer, Matthew 6:9–13, Luke 1:2–4; specifically, Matthew 6:11/Luke 11:3: "Give us this day our daily bread," *BCP*, 247.
63. Matthew 6:32: "(For after all these things do the Gentiles seek): for your heavenly Father knoweth that ye have need of all these things."
64. See also "The Great Conquest, or the Power of Faith," and "What Crosses and Difficulties I Have Met with Myself," 176–84, 307–11.
65. This is the sixth occasional mediation in this volume.
66. See *True Account*, and "The Widow's Mite," 134, 242.
67. "Would" is an interlineal insertion.
68. See "Upon the Return of His Majesty," 193–96.

seek to him who best knows what is most agreeable to his own will, and by his gracious direction, I hope I shall do what may be acceptable [p. 51] unto him and make greatest impression of his goodness on myself. And though I have often dedicated myself to God, yet every renewed mercy deserves new thankfulness, and that is most expressed in living holily in all manner of conversation, and what I have omitted formerly to be more careful now to perform. And so, when my life is such as may glorify my God, he will the more graciously incline to hear and grant my prayers for the King which shall be that the blessings of heaven and earth may crown him with perpetual happiness, that the Lord may direct him in the choosing such a wife as he will bless him with seeing children's children, and peace upon this our Israel.[69]

Upon Making Vows.[70]

[p. 57] Affliction is the time of bringing sins to remembrance, as the widow of Zarephath[71] said to the prophet Elijah when she thought he had slain her son (1 Kings 17:18).[72]

The Lord of that prophet hath been pleased to slay my son,[73] but I hope he hath given him a better resurrection than what that widow begged for her son (so that he shall die no more).

Yet can I not but be afflicted with my own loss which brings me to remember the vows I made at his birth (being upon Sunday, June 13, 1658) being in great extremity, and as some thought past hope of life, yet the Lord was pleased to spare me, and I made this vow that from thenceforth[74] I would be more careful [p. 58] to keep that day holy, which the Lord himself had commanded by a

---

69. A marriage treaty between Charles II and Catherine of Braganza was signed on June 23, 1661, but the wedding did not take place until May 21, 1662. They were married twice: in a secret Catholic ceremony, and in a public Church of England service. Queen Catherine had many miscarriages, and the royal couple did not produce a legitimate heir. Charles II's mistresses were more fertile, among them Lucy Walter, mother of James Crofts Scott, later styled the Duke of Monmouth. S. M. Wynne, "Catherine of Braganza (1638–1705)," *ODNB*; Seaward, "Charles II," *ODNB*; Robin Clifton, "Walter, Lucy (1630?–1658)," *ODNB*; Tim Harris, "Scott [Formerly Crofts], James, Duke of Monmouth and First Duke of Buccleuch (1649–1685)," *ODNB*, 2009.

70. This is the eighth occasional meditation in this volume.

71. "Of Zarephath" is an interlineal insertion.

72. 1 Kings 17:18: "And she said unto Elijah, what have I to do with thee, O thou man of God? art thou come unto me to call my sin to remembrance, and to slay my son?" In the rest of the chapter, 1 Kings 17:19–24, Elijah prays for the son's resurrection and the Lord grants his prayer, much to the widow's contentment.

73. Her second child, Henry.

74. After "thence," "forward" has been deleted and replaced by the interlineal insertion of "forth."

special remembrance should be so.⁷⁵ And though before that time I had vowed to do something extraordinary upon that day, as a perpetual thanksgiving for the mercy I had received, yet until that time—though I had long enjoyed the blessing for which I should have been thankful—yet I had forgot to pay my vows until the Lord was pleased to give me an occasion to renew them by giving me another deliverance from death (as the former had been from trouble). And yet, since that time, how negligent I have been in performing my free will offering my own conscience testifies, which the more accuses me for my transgression because my dear child was taken [p. 59] from me on the night of that day on which I made the vow both for him and for myself.

I never was in any affliction or distress, but I was apt to make vows, and I no sooner was delivered but I forgot them: even lately I have had experience of myself. For having long since vowed that, if I could live to see that day on⁷⁶ which the crown should be set upon the King's head, I would during my life make that a day of particular devotion for blessings upon him; and yet for all there hath been but few Tuesdays past by me, yet half of them I have not remembered until they were past, which makes me now resolve never to vow anything again, but to be humbled that I cannot perform [p. 60] them as I would, and as the benefits require.

Undoubtedly, the breach of a vow makes the committing of that a sin which was none in itself. How wary ought I then to be of ensnaring myself in that which is impossible for me to keep?

I thought myself once so fast tied by a firm vow and resolution that nothing but death could have broke it; yet that proving but a deceit which was the ground of my vow, I was freed from it in the opinion of all to whom I did communicate my trouble when I was earnestly solicited to break it. ⁷⁷ And, Lord pardon me if I sin in saying this which thou art witness of, for truth I did so absolutely resign myself [p. 61] to thy disposal that I could not believe it a sin to do what might cancel the former vow being convinced the sin was greater to continue in it than to change (especially when the Lord was pleased to let all the arguments I used for motives to dissuade to be rather persuasive to that I would have avoided).

---

75. According to Couper, the first—now missing—folio volume of Halkett's *Meditations and Prayers* included "Meditations and Vows upon Psalm 56:12-13, Written on Some Remaining Leaves of This Book, upon Her Deliverance from the Danger of Childbirth, June 13, 1658"; Couper, *The Life of the Lady Halket*, 59. Psalm 56:12-13: "Thy vows are upon me, O God: I will render praises unto thee. For thou hast delivered my soul from death: wilt thou not deliver my feet from falling, that I may walk before God in the light of the living?"
76. "On" is an interlineal insertion.
77. See *True Account*, and "The Great Conquest, or the Power of Faith," 156-57, 176-84.

It was not inclination,[78] but fear to offend and gratitude made me change, and that fear will, I hope, through the mercy of my God ever preserve me from sinning against him who made me what I am. And though rash, unadvised[79] vows, and the breach of them shall be ever an occasion of making me humble before the Lord, yet I do not repent the breach of them except I did offend. And then Lord give me repentance for [p. 62] everything [that] is displeasing unto thee, and punish not others for my offence, but even to me—and all that I have interest in—make good these promises: though your sins be as scarlet, they shall be white like snow; though they be red[80] as crimson, they shall be like wool (Isa 1:18).[81] I am willing to be obedient;[82] oh, let me be partaker of thy grace.[83]

Upon a Dispute with Myself, New Year's Day, 1661.[84]

[p. 85] This is the first day of the new year, and that on which I have several times as a freewill offering given myself to God. And yet the advantage I propounded to receive I am disappointed in. For I find still the same distrust, and pride, and covetousness[85] in my heart that was formerly, and that (which is the ground of all the rest) still I have wandering, sinful thoughts in prayer, and in performing those holy duties God requires from me: so that it hath been a dispute within me this morning whether I had better forbear praying rather than perform it in[86] so ill a manner.

Education and custom hath inured[87] me [p. 86] to say prayers every night and morning, even from my infancy, and the first time that I added one prayer more in the day was upon a sermon Mr. Gale[88] preached, at St. James's (when

---

78. "The action of influencing another's (or one's own) mind, heart, or will," OED.

79. "Unadvised" is an interlineal insertion.

80. "Red" is an interlineal insertion.

81. Isaiah 1:18: "Come now, and let us reason together, saith the Lord: though your sins be as scarlet, they shall be as white as snow; though they be red like crimson, they shall be as wool."

82. Isaiah 1:19: "If ye be willing and obedient, ye shall eat the good of the land."

83. 1 Corinthians 10:30: "For if I by grace be a partaker, why am I evil spoken of for that for which I give thanks?"

84. This is the fourteenth occasional meditation in this volume.

85. "Inordinate and culpable desire of possessing that which belongs to another or to which one has no right," OED.

86. "In" is an interlineal insertion.

87. "To bring (a person, etc.) by use, habit, continual exercise to a certain condition or state of mind, to the endurance of a certain condition, to the following of a certain kind of life, etc.; to accustom, habituate," OED.

88. In the left-hand margin, Halkett identifies Mr. Gale as "Chaplain to the Countess of Devonshire, a good man and an excellent preacher." The spelling of Gale's name is confirmed in Thomas Pomfret,

my mother had the honor to have the care of the Duke of Gloucester[89] and the Princess Elizabeth),[90] wherein, he taxed the sins of the whole kingdom to be the occasion of the breach and distance[91] betwixt the King[92] and his people. And that all should be sensible of it, but particularly his own family and servants who ought most to be sensible of it, but he feared there was none that poured forth a prayer more than ordinary though the judgment was extraordinary [p. 87] that we lay under. Upon this, I was convinced it was a necessary duty, and so dedicated the time immediately after dinner for giving thanks for any mercy I had received that meal, and to pray for a[93] supply to those who wanted what I enjoyed, but the chief of my devotion for that time was for the establishment and preservation of the King in peace and safety.

The next increase in my devotion was at Naworth, where I had been very near death and about five o'clock in the afternoon I began to have a return, as it were, of my spirits.[94] And from that time, I dedicated that hour every day to the remembrance of death, and made it the subject of my prayer to be prepared for it whenever my Lord and master should think [p. 88] fit to call me.

Now one would think me very devout that should know that I spent four half hours in the day (at least) one time with another in prayer, and reading either the Bible, or some other pious book, and possibly my servants (who only can observe my going to my chamber at those times) may think me better than ordinary.[95] But I fear all these times of prayer are but aggravations of my sins, and from thence comes my dispute: whether I had not better leave it off rather than perform it, as I do, with an unprepared heart, and wandering thoughts, and too, too often not thinking what I am speaking nor to whom. So that I am saying prayers when I am not praying, but am like them in Isay,[96] against whom he was [p. 89] to cry

---

The Life of the Right Honorable and Religious Lady Christian[a], Late Countess Dowager of Devonshire (London: William Rawlins, 1685). ESTC R3342.

89. Handley, "Henry, Prince," *ODNB*.

90. Goodwin, "Elizabeth, Princess," *ODNB*.

91. "And distance" is an interlineal insertion.

92. I.e., Charles I.

93. "A" is an interlineal insertion.

94. See *True Account*, 95–96.

95. According to Couper, she regularly spent five hours in devotional activities: "from five to seven in the morning, from one in the afternoon to two, from six to seven, and from nine to ten"; Couper, *The Life of the Lady Halket*, 55. However, "she did not confine her devotion to these stated hours but all day long, however employed, she endeavored to keep up a spiritual frame: And in the night time, when she did awake, she was still with God, and had then her meditations, her songs and prayers"; Couper, *The Life of the Lady Halket*, 56.

96. I.e., Isaiah, especially Isaiah 58:1–2: "Cry aloud, spare not, lift up thy voice like a trumpet, and shew my people their transgression, and the house of Jacob their sins. Yet they seek me daily, and delight to know my ways, as a nation that did righteousness, and forsook not the ordinance of their God: they

aloud, for they sought the Lord daily, and did delight to know his ways as a nation that did righteousness, and did seem to take delight in approaching unto God, but there was so much sin in their performances that they were not acceptable unto God. And so, I fear, it is with me.

Yet one advantage I have found: that my example is a silent remembrancer[97] to them about me to call oftener upon God than other ways perhaps they would do, and so while I can by any means be an occasion of bringing praise to God I ought not to neglect it. For, though my prayers are full of sin, yet perhaps should I omit it altogether I might be more guilty of what I would avoid. And it is a mercy that I am sensible of my sin in that which [p. 90] only God can remedy; for though my conscience hath often checked me that I have not welcomed as I ought the fruits of the spirit (which hath[98] been love to prayer, and joy in it, that hath brought peace and all the rest of that sweet harmony that attends whereever the blessed spirit is), yet the Lord who gives the grace can give improvement by it so as to bring him glory.[99] Therefore, from this day forward, I will make it[100] my particular care, as well as my request, to attain that blessing that I may not only pray with my lips but with my spirit and understanding too.[101]

And if the Lord sees fit he will grant my desire, if not I must submit and be content to want as well as to abound, both [p. 91] in temporal and spiritual gifts;[102] for perhaps the Lord sees in me that natural ground of Popery,[103] that is in all, to think better of myself by my performances, and I cannot but confess when I have prayed with more zeal and fervency than usual I have thought certainly God will bless me this day because I have served him better than ordinary. But I have checked those thoughts as being suggestions from the Devil, and convinced

---

ask of me the ordinances of justice; they take delight in approaching to God;" and 59:1–2: "Behold, the Lord's hand is not shortened, that it cannot save; neither his ear heavy, that it cannot hear: But your iniquities have separated between you and your God, and your sins have hid his face from you, that he will not hear."

97. "A reminder; a memento, souvenir," *OED*.

98. "Hath" is an interlineal insertion and is an archaic form of "have."

99. Galatians 5:22–23: "But the fruit of the Spirit is love, joy, peace, longsuffering, gentleness, goodness, faith, meekness, temperance: against such there is no law."

100. "It" is an interlineal insertion.

101. Here "too" is written over "also." Halkett alludes to Saint Paul's advice to the Corinthians about the use of the gift of "speaking in tongues." 1 Corinthians 14:14–15: "For if I pray in an unknown tongue, my spirit prayeth, but my understanding is unfruitful. What is it then? I will pray with the spirit, and I will pray with the understanding also: I will sing with the spirit, and I will sing with the understanding also."

102. Philippians 4:12: "I know both how to be abased, and I know how to abound: everywhere and in all things, I am instructed both to be full and to be hungry, both to abound and to suffer need."

103. I.e., Roman Catholicism.

myself from those vain thoughts[104] from our Lord's own uncontroverted[105] position, when you have done[106] all those things which are commanded, say, We are unprofitable servants,[107] and as Eliphaz says, can a man be profitable to God as he that [p. 92] is wise may be profitable to himself?[108] Yet for all this I have thought better of myself, and have had more quiet, after one fervent prayer than in a month's time when I have been less careful. And therefore, that I may ascribe nothing to merit or works, perhaps the Lord will still deny me the grace I seek: however, I will still importunately[109] ask since it is the way to have; I will seek and knock until I find the door of mercy opened,[110] which I will quietly expect and hope for (since it is only my desire because I would be acceptable to him with whom it is all one to give a degree of perfection, or to pardon the want of it).

---

104. "Myself from those vain thoughts" is an interlineal insertion.

105. "Undisputed; uncontested," *OED*.

106. "Done" is an interlineal insertion.

107. Luke 17:10: "So likewise ye, when ye shall have done all those things which are commanded you, say, we are unprofitable servants: we have done that which was our duty to do."

108. Job 22:2: "Can a man be profitable unto God, as he that is wise may be profitable unto himself?"

109. "With persistent or pressing solicitation or entreaty; beseechingly, imploringly," *OED*.

110. Matthew 7:7–8: "Ask, and it shall be given you; seek, and ye shall find; knock, and it shall be opened unto you: For everyone that asketh receiveth; and he that seeketh findeth; and to him that knocketh it shall be opened." See also Luke 11:9–10.

Occasional and Select Meditations, including Instructions to My Son *(1667–1670)*

Of all Halkett's extant volumes, this is probably the "messiest," at least so far as its organization is concerned; for example, there are four different dates for when it was started.[1] In this respect, however, the book arguably reflects Halkett's state of mind as it is here that she records not only her husband's death but also her son-in-law's return to Pitfirrane and her own removal to Dunfermline. Indeed, Halkett acknowledges that circumstances altered her intentions for this book's contents:

> When this book was first begun, I intended to have divided it into occasional and select meditations. The last of the occasional having reached where the select meditations began, and being a sad conclusion, I intend the rest of the book to be for instruction to my poor child (who is all the temporal comfort I have left), and praying that they may be useful to him in this I intend to employ the rest of this book, and the remainder of my time.[2]

Halkett paginates the two types of meditation separately: as the occasional meditations are at the front of the book, this means that her pagination and that of the cataloguer diverge when the select meditations begin. The confusion over the volume's start date is mirrored in Halkett's various attempts to produce a list of contents. Here, unusually, there are three different versions: first, on the inside front cover, "The Select Contemplations," of which Halkett identifies six (before her "Instructions to My Son and Only Child Robert Halkett);[3] second, "The Contents of the Occasional Meditations," of which there are twenty-three;[4] and third, "The Subject of the Select Contemplations Are upon These Places Following," near the end of the volume, which have now extended to thirteen in number.[5] While in all cases each entry is numbered, unlike in previous volumes the occasional entries are not identified by number within the main text.

---

1. This is volume 9 in Couper's catalogue, which states that it was begun in 1666; on the volume's first page, Halkett notes, "This book was begun the first Monday in January, 1667/8," *Occasional and Select Meditations*, p. ii; the first occasional meditation describes her illness from December 9 to December 15, 1667, *Occasional and Select Meditations*, pp. 1–15; and the *Perdita Project* notes that another entry, the "Meditation upon the Peace Concluded betwixt the King and the Hollanders," is dated September 1667, *Occasional and Select Meditations*, pp. 30–34. The remains of a piece of paper on the volume's spine also read "Pitfirrane, 1667," so I have adopted 1667 as the most likely start date.

2. Halkett, *Occasional and Select Meditations*, p. iv.

3. Halkett, *Occasional and Select Meditations*, p. i.

4. Halkett, *Occasional and Select Meditations*, pp. iii–iv.

5. Halkett, *Occasional and Select Meditations*, p. 349.

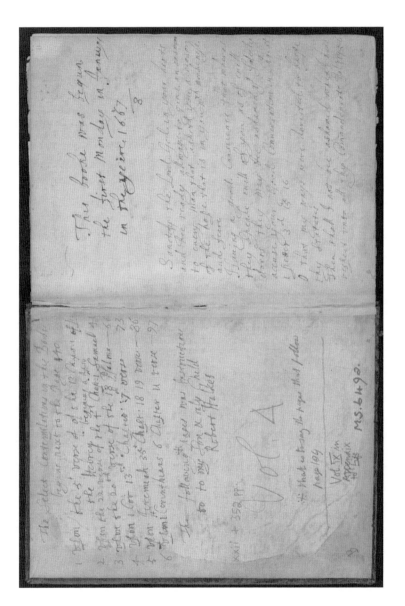

Figure 9. Contents page for "Select Contemplations," from *Occasional and Select Meditations, including Instructions to My Son* (1666–1670). © National Library of Scotland, NLS, MS 6492, pp. i–ii. Reproduced with permission.

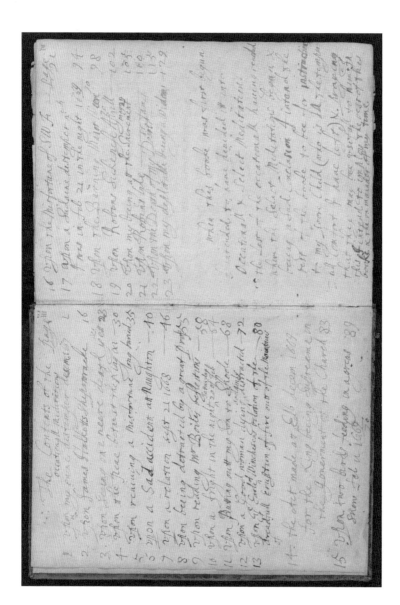

Figure 10. Contents page for "Occasional Meditations," from *Occasional and Select Meditations, including Instructions to My Son* (1666–1670). © National Library of Scotland, NLS, MS 6492, pp. iii–iv. Reproduced with permission.

Despite her initial intention, this volume does not end with "Instructions to My Son," which is perhaps partly why she feels the need to insert the second list of select contemplations. Even that list, however, refers to further materials, including some "Resolutions," which are written after it.[6] Although she declares that these "fill up the remainder of the book," this is still not quite the end, as there is a final two-page entry, "Upon Monday, January 2, 1670/1," in which she dedicates herself, her life, and her child to God.[7] With apparent finality, the inside back cover notes the earlier return of Sir Charles Halkett (December 9, 1670); however, Halkett returns to some blank pages at the beginning of the book to write "Upon My Going to Live at Dunfermline, February 14, 1670/1."[8] At the front of the volume, there are also tipped in four further additions: a note of a report of the eruption of Mount Etna from the London Gazette, dated February 1687/8; a brief note containing her resolution to make "Saturday a day of retirement and devotion" as a mark of respect for Sir James, and with the intention of preparing herself for her own death; a poem, "Grieve No More (Sad Heart) since He's Above";[9] and further "Resolutions Made upon December 9, 1670."[10] All in all, this volume seems curiously resistant to conclusion.

Upon Reading Mr. Boyle's *Occasional Reflections*, January 25, 1668/9.[11]

[p. 58] I have never seen nor heard of this book[12] before, and it hath now given me so much satisfaction that I cannot but bless the spring from which such waters flow, and magnify my God who hath inclined me even from my youth to

---

6. Halkett, *Occasional and Select Meditations*, p. 349. The "Resolutions" occupy the next page, and each one is associated with a specific biblical verse.

7. Halkett, *Occasional and Select Meditations*, pp. 251–352.

8. Halkett, *Occasional and Select Meditations*, pp. v–xii. This entry is not included in any of the lists of contents.

9. This poem has no obvious parallel, although it sounds similar to "Grieve Not Dear Love Although We Often Part," which concludes, "In heavenly joys where we shall no more part," for which there are two sources; one is unattributed within a collection of English poems, "Verse Compilation ("The Skipwith MS")" (1620–1650), BL, Add. MS 25707, fol.14v; the other is attributed to John Digby, first Earl of Bristol, in "Henry Lawes Music Manuscript" (1626–1662), BL, Add. MS 53723, fol.66v; Folger Shakespeare Library, Union First Line Index of English Verse, accessed August 24, 2018, https://firstlines.folger.edu. See also Halkett, *Occasional Meditations*, *Meditations upon Nehemiah*, pp. ii–iii.

10. Halkett, *Occasional and Select Meditations*, pp. xiv–xviii.

11. According to Halkett's list, this is the ninth meditation in this volume, *Occasional and Select Meditations*, p. iii.

12. Dedicated to his sister, Mary, Countess of Warwick, the first edition of Robert Boyle's *Occasional Reflections upon Several Subjects Whereto Is Premis'd a Discourse about Such Kind of Thoughts* was published in 1665 (London: W. Wilson). ESTC R17345. The second edition was published in London by Henry Herringman in 1669. See Anselment, "Robert Boyle and the Art of Occasional Meditation,"

make most of the accidents of my life occasions for to contemplate of them, and from that have found great advantages. For, when I have been in any trouble or discontent, this way of venting[13] it hath been my great consolement,[14] and after many years when I have read them over they have freshly remembered[15] me of their occasion, and served for a new instigation to stir me up to: praise (for being delivered out of that trouble); faith (if I should be under any other); [p. 59] and obedience to him who only deserves all adoration (because his bounty is so great that he turns all things to the advantage of those that serve him, as I desire to do, sincerely).[16]

Though the Lord hath several instruments to praise him and some are more higher[17] tuned than others, yet all being moved by one spirit, and for one end, my mite may be as well accepted as the talent of those that are more rich in spiritual blessings.[18] And since improvement is the chief thing required, I will seek that of him that can give all things and bless him for the good example I see in others. For though I owe not this way to any but (first to bishop Hall's example)[19] the immediate goodness of my God, who by his own most Holy Spirit did vouchsafe to dictate some pious thoughts into my soul (which I have written to be a support to me when I meet with [p. 60] further trials, which I daily expect), yet everything I read or[20] hear of that is good or pious in another I am advantaged by it because it is a new occasion for me to bless my Lord, even for his mercy to another.

And who can tell but even what I have written may, when I am dead, be living monuments of praise to the infinite God of mercy that hath humbled himself

---

73–92. Boyle is best known as a natural philosopher; see Michael Hunter, "Boyle, Robert (1627–1691)," *ODNB*. See also "Introduction," 49.

13. "To relieve or unburden (one's heart or soul) in respect of feelings or emotions," *OED*.

14. "Consolation," *OED*.

15. I.e., reminded.

16. Romans 8:28: "And we know that all things work together for good to them that love God, to them who are the called according to his purpose."

17. I.e., more highly.

18. Luke 21:1–4: "And he looked up, and saw the rich men casting their gifts into the treasury. And he saw also a certain poor widow casting in thither two mites. And he said, 'Of a truth I say unto you, that this poor widow hath cast in more than they all: For all these have of their abundance cast in unto the offerings of God: but she of her penury hath cast in all the living that she had.'"

19. "First to bishop Hall's example" is an interlineal insertion that extends into the margin of the page. *The Art of Divine Meditation* (1606) and *Occasional Meditations* (1633), by bishop Joseph Hall, were highly influential texts; Ian Green, *Print and Protestantism in Early Modern England* (Oxford: Oxford University Press, 2000), 625–26. See also Huntley, *Bishop Joseph Hall and Protestant Meditation in Seventeenth-Century England*, and Richard A. McCabe, "Hall, Joseph (1574–1656)," *ODNB*. See "Introduction," 37–42.

20. Here, "r" has been written over an "f."

to accept of the mean things I can offer: for[21] goat's hair from a willing heart was an acceptable offering as well as gold and onyx stone (Exodus 35),[22] so the meanest capacity may be useful if it were but to excite others. And being even from my infancy accustomed to look upon all events, even of that which crossed me, as being perhaps more for my advantage than the having what [p. 61] I desired. As I remember when my mother used to take me abroad with her sometimes and my inclination would have been to go oftener; yet, when I was restrained, I satisfied myself with this, that perhaps if I had gone I might have said or done something that my mother would have chid[23] me for when I came home, and therefore if I wanted the pleasure I desired, I wanted also the pain I feared.[24] And applications of this nature were very usual with me upon most accidents that I found myself concerned in, even when I was very young.[25] Oh, had these thoughts been improved and increased as my years were, I might have arrived near to the mount of God in holy speculations and practice, but it seems I was like the Israelites: not fit [p. 62] to enter Canaan as soon as I was out of Egypt, and therefore I was suffered to wander in the wilderness many years.[26] But I find it was to let me know what giants I had to fight with besides murmuring and discontent, and yet none of these—though highly aggravated by conviction and continuance in sin—yet none of them were able to separate me[27] from pardon because as the heavens is higher than the earth so is free grace beyond all my transgressions. And this makes me more abhor sin than all the punishments on earth: to think that the infinite God of glory should have love and compassion for me when I had none for him nor for myself! Oh, ever be exalted his most[28] great and glorious name.

[p. 63] What I have written of the traverses[29] of my life hath never yet been seen to any; no, not the nearest of my relations. Nor do I intend they should be

21. "But" has been deleted and replaced with the interlineal insertion of "for" before "goats."

22. Exodus 35:5–6: "Take ye from among you an offering unto the Lord: whosoever is of a willing heart, let him bring it, an offering of the Lord, gold, and silver, and brass, And blue, and purple, and scarlet, and fine linen, and goats' hair."

23. "To scold, rebuke, or find fault with (a thing, an action, etc.)," OED.

24. See *True Account*, 64n30.

25. Couper refers to this instance to exemplify how Halkett "did use herself to this way of pondering things, that what she most earnestly desired became indifferent to her"; Couper, *The Life of the Lady Halket*, 5.

26. After the exodus from Egypt the Israelites spent forty years wandering in the wilderness before they reached the promised land of Canaan. See Numbers 32:13: "And the Lord's anger was kindled against Israel, and he made them wander in the wilderness forty years, until all the generation, that had done evil in the sight of the Lord, was consumed."

27. "Me" is an interlineal insertion.

28. "Most" is written in the right-hand margin.

29. "Traverses" means "something that crosses, thwarts, or obstructs; opposition; an obstacle, impediment; a trouble, vexation; a mishap; misfortune, adversity," OED.

known while I live, and when I am dead, I will leave them wholly to the dispose[30] of the great God for whose praise they were intended. And if they can bring glory to him, or consolation to any that are his, he will give them light; if not, I hope he will bury them in my grave, where I hope will be buried with me all their faults and mine. Our greatest imperfection will be made perfect through him who is our righteousness, and will, I trust, clothe us with his merits that can hide all deformities. In this faith I live, and trust to die, and, until that change comes,[31] be ever waiting for it as the servant of my lord and God.

Upon the Death of My Dearest Sir James Halkett, Who Died upon Saturday Morning, betwixt Eight and Nine o'clock, Being September 24, 1670.[32]

[p. 115] *Where is God my maker who giveth songs in the night?* (Job 35:10.)[33]

If the Lord did not manifest himself under the darkest dispensations,[34] what could support an afflicted soul under so sad a trial as the loss of the best of husbands?

The distemper[35] he hath lain under these eight weeks hath been so treacherous as daily to give me some hopes of his recovery, because there was no visible[36] cause of apprehension[37] to any of the physicians which came to see him. But, by sad experience, I now find the intervals he had was only from mercy, who would not altogether destroy him at one stroke but give him time and leisure to think of death (which had so sure laid on his arrest that there was no shaking it off until he carried his prisoner with him).

[p. 116] But blessed be God, death is swallowed up in victory (1 Cor. 15:54),[38] and when Christ, who is our life, shall appear then will he also appear

---

30. "Power or right to dispose of something, or deal with it at one's will; control," OED.

31. From "be," the rest of this final sentence is written in two lines in the bottom margin.

32. This is meditation number twenty-two according to Halkett's list; *Occasional and Select Meditations*, p. iv. See also Trill, ed., *Halkett*, 30–34.

33. Job 35:10: "But none saith, where is God my maker, who giveth songs in the night."

34. "Ordering, management; especially, the divine administration or conduct of the world; the ordering or arrangement of events by divine providence," OED.

35. "To disorder or derange the physical or bodily condition of; to render unhealthy or diseased; to affect with a distemper; to sicken," OED.

36. "Visible" is an interlineal insertion.

37. "Fear as to what may happen; dread," OED.

38. 1 Corinthians 15:54: "So when this corruptible shall have put on incorruption, and this mortal shall have put on immortality, then shall be brought to pass the saying that is written, Death is swallowed up in victory."

with him in glory. And this consideration sweetens the bitter cup I have now to drink.[39]

For what could be more desolate than my condition, if I had not[40] the promises of mercy from the God of mercy to rely upon?

For I am a stranger, born and bred in another country;[41] a mother-in-law, which always hath a prejudice attending it, and none hath found it more than I (though my Lord knows how I have both prayed and endeavored to take away the reproach which is for the most part laid upon them).[42]

I have the great and holy God to witness for me I had a dear, affectionate [p. 117] husband, and the testimony of my own conscience, and this threefold cord cannot be broken (Eccles. 4:12).[43] And[44] yet for all these I have suffered as much as the evil tongue of men could invent, but I hope they that are my enemies shall be ashamed when the Lord is pleased to manifest to them what he hath imprinted of himself upon[45] my heart of doing justly, of loving mercy, and walking humbly with my God (Mic. 6:8).[46]

I sadly find now what effects grief and discontent may have even upon the strongest and most vigorous spirits. For never did my dearest look better than he did three months before he fell in this distemper, which I fear he brought upon himself with giving too much entertainment to the enemy that did assault him. The long-continued health he had made me often [p. 118] please myself with the hopes that he would live as long as his father, which was eighty-five years, but, alas, I see there is no rules to limit death. For though he[47] could not break in upon him by intemperance, or any gross, scandalous sin, yet he would seize upon him

---

39. An allusion to Christ's prayer in the garden of Gethsemane, Matthew 26:39: "And he went a little further, and fell on his face, and prayed, saying, O my Father, if it be possible, let this cup pass from me: nevertheless, not as I will, but as thou wilt." See also Matthew 26:42; Mark 14:36; and Luke 22:42.

40. "Not" is an interlineal insertion.

41. "One who is not a native of, or who has not long resided in, a country, town, or place. Chiefly, a newcomer, one who has not yet become well acquainted with the place, or one who is not yet well known," *OED*.

42. In early modern English and Scots (and in modern dialectical usage), "mother-in-law" also means "stepmother," *OED*, *DSL*.

43. Ecclesiastes 4:12: "And if one prevail against him, two shall withstand him; and a threefold cord is not quickly broken."

44. After "And," "though" has been deleted and replaced by the interlineal insertion of "yet."

45. "Upon" is an interlineal insertion, following the deletion of five illegible letters.

46. Micah 6:8: "He hath shewed thee, O man, what is good; and what doth the Lord require of thee, but to do justly, and to love mercy, and to walk humbly with thy God?"

47. I.e., Satan.

by that which my dearest had most reason to glory in: even by his most mortified[48] appetite for the most ordinary fare, and even a cup of water was as welcome to him as the greatest rarities to[49] others.

Excess was so much a stranger to him that he never took the least more than ordinary but[50] it disturbed him.

None living had greater inclinations [p. 119] for piety and justice, and the most practical parts of Christianity, and (setting aside that time when the whole kingdom was bemisted[51] with a mistaken zeal) there was not any had more loyal principles, or more wary[52] to do anything that might seem in the least to disrespect authority.[53]

He envied no man's prosperity, nor coveted no man's wealth. And though he had temptations enough to it, yet he could never be persuaded to join with any in what was disputable in the lawfulness of it, as[54] the caping trade[55] which for a time many was enriched by it.

He was a most indulgent father, though unfortunate in being mistaken by his children, and the best of husbands. And when I seriously consider the obligations I had to that dear person I cannot but say I should hate myself [p. 120] if I thought I should ever have an inclination to forget his memory, or be ungrateful to any of his relations. And though (the Lord pardon them) some of them[56] have been very unjust to me, yet the affection I had for my dearest shall I hope swallow up all the former prejudice, and make the future suitable to the impressions that his kindness will ever have upon my heart. And for this I will continually bow my knees unto the Father of our Lord Jesus Christ, of whom the whole family in heaven and earth is named, that he would grant me according to the riches of his glory to be strengthened with might by his spirit in the inner man (Eph. 3:14–16);[57] that Christ may dwell in my heart [p. 121] by faith, that being rooted

---

48. That is "dead to sin or worldly desires; having the appetites and passions in subjection; prompted by a spirit of religious self-mortification; ascetic, unworldly," or abstemious, *OED*.

49. Before "to" an illegible word of four letters has been deleted.

50. I.e., except.

51. "To cover or obscure (a thing) with, or as with, mist; to becloud, dim," *OED*.

52. I.e., warier, or cautious.

53. See *True Account*, and "Introduction," 149–50 and 150n548, 15.

54. "It" and "as" are interlineal insertions.

55. "To take or seize as a privateer; also, to go a privateering," *OED*.

56. After "pardon them)," "they" has been deleted and replaced by the interlineal insertion of "some of them."

57. Ephesians 3:14–16: "For this cause, I bow my knees unto the Father of our Lord Jesus Christ, of whom the whole family in heaven and earth is named, that he would grant you, according to the riches of his glory, to be strengthened with might by his spirit in the inner man."

and grounded in love (Eph. 3:17),[58] I may be able to comprehend with all saints what is the breadth, and length, and depth, and height (Eph. 3:18);[59] and how to know the love of Christ which passes knowledge that I might be filled with all the fullness of God (Eph. 3:19)[60] who is able to do abundantly above all that I can either ask or think (Eph. 3:20).[61] Therefore, to him will I dedicate myself, my child,[62] and all my concerns, and he that is my God will be my guide, I hope, even unto death (Ps. 48:14).[63]

As my dearest was exemplar[64] in many things in health, so in his sickness his patience was remarkable; for though he had great conflicts with death before he yielded up his last, yet "Oh hone,[65] Oh hone," or "Oh sick, sick" was all he said to bemoan himself. It was not without difficulty that he spoke to any, and therefore was [p. 122] but short when he spoke to the ministers that came to see him:[66] only expressed that he relied on the fullness of righteousness in Christ Jesus; and that he had assurance of it being imputed to him, so that he had no fear of death;[67] and only desired exemption from violent pain so that he might die in peace, and he was so far heard that he went out of the world with as much serenity as ever I saw any. And though, three days and nights before, he appeared to be under great oppressions of pain and sickness, yet he was much supported under it. And perhaps the Lord was pleased to give him that [p. 123] trial to let him see it was not so easy a thing to die as he supposed, when too, too often he did wish to die when his serious thoughts represented how difficult it was to make him happy

---

58. Ephesians 3:17: "That Christ may dwell in your hearts by faith; that ye, being rooted and grounded in love."

59. Ephesians 3:18: "May be able to comprehend with all saints what is the breadth, and length, and depth, and height."

60. Ephesians 3:19: "And to know the love of Christ, which passeth knowledge, that ye might be filled with all the fulness of God."

61. Ephesians 3:20: "Now unto him that is able to do exceeding abundantly above all that we ask or think, according to the power that worketh in us."

62. I.e., Robert/Robin.

63. Psalm 48:14: "For this God is our God for ever and ever: he will be our guide even unto death."

64. Archaic form of exemplary.

65. Halkett's spelling of "Ochone," a Scottish Gaelic expression of "grief or sorrow: 'Oh!,' 'alas!,' 'woe!,'" *OED*.

66. The incumbent minister of Dunfermline was William Pierson, January 17, 1666, to September 13, 1676. *FES* 5:28.

67. See Romans 4:20–25: "He staggered not at the promise of God through unbelief; but was strong in faith, giving glory to God; And being fully persuaded that, what he had promised, he was able also to perform. And therefore, it was imputed to him for righteousness. Now it was not written for his sake alone, that it was imputed to him; But for us also, to whom it shall be imputed, if we believe on him that raised up Jesus our Lord from the dead; Who was delivered for our offences and was raised again for our justification."

in that which was his greatest discontent, by the great aversion the other[68] had to satisfy his desires (which the God of mercy pardon and make him sensible of, so that it may produce the effects of a holy life and conversation, and that is all the hurt I wish them.)

Once my dearest, after he had lain quiet sometime, cried out, with a sad tone, "What no more, no more.[69] Oh, no more, no more," as if he had been under some desertion. [p. 124] To which I said, "Remember the promise which the Lord hath made: no more to remember your sins but to blot out all your iniquities for his own name sake" (Heb. 8:12).[70] After which he had no expressions[71] like to that, nor said much only, "Oh,[72] my dear, my dear," when he looked upon me, which looks, and words, and former obligations will, I hope, never be forgot. And as the Lord did graciously hear my prayers, and gave me strength to attend him during his sickness with the care and affection which became a dutiful wife, so I beg still the assistance of my gracious God to support me under this [p. 125] sad stroke; that I may neither faint under it nor forget it, but behave myself like a widow indeed, and desolate, trusting in God, and continuing in supplications and prayers night and day (1 Tim. 5:4).[73]

And since my dearest told me I need not grieve too much, for I should not be long after him, I will therefore beg that my Lord would teach me so to number my days (Ps. 90:12)[74] that I may apply my heart to wisdom (Job 28:28).[75] And though the care that he hath left to me of my poor child is the only and chief thing that ties me to the world, and the desire I have to do good to him and good to this family—in clearing many things that he[76] is ignorant of by his long absence who is to succeed—yet in this, and all [p. 126] things that concerns me in this life, Lord

---

68. This "other" is unidentified; however, on several occasions Halkett refers to ongoing discord between her husband and his eldest son by his first marriage, Sir Charles Halkett.

69. The second "no more" is an interlineal insertion.

70. Hebrews 8:12: "For I will be merciful to their unrighteousness, and their sins and their iniquities will I remember no more."

71. Before "expressions," "more" has been deleted.

72. "Oh" is an insertion in the left-hand margin.

73. 1 Timothy 5:4–5: "But if any widow have children or nephews, let them learn first to shew piety at home, and to requite their parents: for that is good and acceptable before God. Now she that is a widow indeed, and desolate, trusteth in God, and continueth in supplications and prayers night and day."

74. Psalm 90:12: "So teach us to number our days, that we may apply our hearts unto wisdom."

75. Job 28:28: "And unto man he said, Behold, the fear of the Lord, that is wisdom; and to depart from evil is understanding." The reference to Psalm 90:12 is in the left-hand margin and relates directly to "so to number my days"; the reference to Job 28:28 is inserted in the right-hand margin, with a ^ beside it and another ^ being placed by "wisdom" in the main body of the text.

76. I.e., Sir Charles Halkett.

not my will but thine be done.[77] For all my endeavors will be but fruitless without thy blessing, and where thy blessing is everything will prosper. And if thou art pleased to take me away, I will leave my fatherless child to thee,[78] who I trust will preserve him alive[79] and keep him from the paths of sin which lead to death.

Many would make me fear the usage I am to expect from a son-in-law,[80] who hath formerly not been as I could have wished him, to others or myself. But the many prayers I have offered up for him at the throne of grace will, I hope, obtain what I shall still continue instantly to beg: that the [p. 127] Lord will create in[81] him a new heart, and renew a right spirit within him (Ps. 51:10),[82] and where the fear of God is I can apprehend no ill. And if the Lord should yet deny him his grace, yet[83] if he please he can make me say with David: surely the wrath of man shall praise thee and the remainder of it shalt thou restrain (Ps. 76:10).[84] And as long as my Lord is pleased to give me leave to call on him, and to rely on his strength[85] there is in that enough to secure me against all that can oppose me.

Lord, as I have given my heart wholly up to thee, imprint thyself there I beseech thee,[86] so that nothing of this life may have room only those graces which may make me fit for glory: let my conversation be such as becomes the gospel of Christ (Phil. 1:27);[87] [p. 128] let me abstain from all appearance of evil (1 Thess. 5:22);[88] and if it be thy will hide[89] me from the scourge of the tongue,[90] and order my steps in thy word, and let not any iniquity have dominion over me

---

77. Luke 22:42: "Father, if thou be willing, remove this cup from me: nevertheless, not my will, but thine, be done."

78. "To thee" is an interlineal insertion.

79. Jeremiah 49:11: "Leave thy fatherless children, I will preserve them alive; and let thy widows trust in me."

80. Sir Charles Halkett. See also "Resolutions Made upon December 9, 1670," in Halkett, *Occasional and Select Meditations*, pp. xviii–xxi.

81. After "will," "give" has been deleted and replaced by "create in" in an interlineal insertion.

82. Psalm 51:10: "Create in me a clean heart, O God; and renew a right spirit within me."

83. "Yet" is an interlineal insertion.

84. Psalm 76:10: "Surely the wrath of man shall praise thee: the remainder of wrath shalt thou restrain."

85. "And to rely on his strength" is an interlineal insertion.

86. "I beseech thee" is an interlineal insertion.

87. Philippians 1:27: "Only let your conversation be as it becometh the gospel of Christ: that whether I come and see you, or else be absent, I may hear of your affairs, that ye stand fast in one spirit, with one mind striving together for the faith of the gospel."

88. 1 Thessalonians 5:22: "Abstain from all appearance of evil."

89. Here, "preserve" has been deleted and replaced by the interlineal insertion of "hide."

90. Job 5:21: "Thou shalt be hid from the scourge of the tongue: neither shalt thou be afraid of destruction when it cometh."

(Ps. 119:133);[91] so, having a good conscience, they that speak evil of me may be ashamed when they falsely accuse my good conversation in Christ.[92] These mercies I beg, and all things that pertain to life and godliness (2 Pet. 1:3),[93] so shall to the King eternal, immortal, the only wise God, be glory ever more. Amen.[94]

(When my dear child Jane was dying, severals[95] took notice that my dearest Sir James, when he took his leave of her said, "I pray God I may be the first in the family may meet with thee," which request the Lord hath granted and I am confident[96] they are together magnifying the God of mercy.)[97]

Upon My Deplorable Being a Widow.[98]

[p. 129] Widowhood is threatened both by the prophet Isaiah and Jeremiah as one of the greatest temporal crosses that can be inflicted (Isa. 47:9; Jer. 18:21).[99] The Lord is pleased oftentimes to compare his love to his church to that betwixt a man and his wife (Jer. 31:32),[100] as if the Lord thought that the best similitude to represent the great care and affection he had for his people, and when he is

---

91. Psalm 119:133: "Order my steps in thy word: and let not any iniquity have dominion over me."

92. 1 Peter 3:16: "Having a good conscience; that, whereas they speak evil of you, as of evildoers, they may be ashamed that falsely accuse your good conversation in Christ."

93. 2 Peter 1:3: "According as his divine power hath given unto us all things that pertain unto life and godliness, through the knowledge of him that hath called us to glory and virtue."

94. Halkett regularly commemorates her husband's death: see, for example, "Upon September 24, 1673," and "Saturday, February 19, 1697/8," 252–55, 318–21. See also, "Upon Saturday, January 24, 1673/4" and "Upon September 24, 1674," in *The Widow's Mite*, pp. 266–67, 312–15; "Saturday, September 24, 1687," in *Meditations on St. Peter*, pp. 323–24; "Wednesday, September 24, 1690," in *Occasional Meditations, Meditations upon Nehemiah*, pp. 24–25; "Monday, September 24, 1694" and "Saturday, November 24, 1694," in *Of Watchfulness*, pp. 351–52, 355–56; "Saturday, April 24, 1697," "Saturday, July 1697," "Thursday, September 24, 1696," "Saturday, October 24, 1696," in Anne, Lady Halkett, *Select and Occasional Meditations* (1696–1697), NLS, MS 6501, pp. 214–15, 265–66, 324–26, 344.

95. "Several persons or things," *OED*.

96. From "confident" to the end is written in the bottom margin of the page.

97. Their daughter Jane died on February 11, 1665/6. See "Introduction," 17n80.

98. See also Trill, ed., *Halkett*, 34–37.

99. Isaiah 47:9: "But these two things shall come to thee in a moment in one day, the loss of children, and widowhood: they shall come upon thee in their perfection for the multitude of thy sorceries, and for the great abundance of thine enchantments"; Jeremiah 18:21: "Therefore, deliver up their children to the famine, and pour out their blood by the force of the sword; and let their wives be bereaved of their children, and be widows; and let their men be put to death; let their young men be slain by the sword in battle."

100. Jeremiah 31:32: "Not according to the covenant that I made with their fathers in the day that I took them by the hand to bring them out of the land of Egypt; which my covenant they brake, although I was a husband unto them, saith the Lord."

displeased with them he threatens to make them desolate as a wife forsaken.[101] Which shows the strict love and union that ought to be betwixt a man and his wife (and what, I bless the Lord, was betwixt my dearest and me while we were together), and therefore so much the greater is the stroke which makes the separation.

    I will not enquire why the Lord hath taken him from me that was dear [p. 130] to me as my own soul (for nothing did I pray for as a blessing to myself but I did the same for him) because[102] the Lord perhaps hath seen me unworthy of the blessings I enjoyed in him, and therefore hath taken him to glory, and left me desolate. But, my Lord, doth not thou know how I abhorred myself when I have been guilty of a froward[103] word towards him, and how with tears I have begged thy pardon? And hath it not been often a motive whereby I have interceded with thee at the throne of grace for him because he hath been the instrument by which thou hast conveyed great and unspeakable mercies to me? And have not I been instant in praying for a recompense to him and his for the [p. 131] great mercies I enjoyed with him? And since it is thy will, O God, to take him to thyself, let not that which is the greatest joy he can partake be my ground of trouble but rather let me rejoice in his joy, and make it my endeavor to spend the remainder of my days more acceptably to thee than ever; so, when the days of my appointed time is run,[104] I shall have this corruption put on incorruption,[105] and shall with him forever praise the God of our salvation.

    I have many things to discompose me, as: grief, which I desire grace from thee to moderate; fear, for the unkind usage which upon some grounds I have reason to expect (but let the fear of thee, my God, expel all other fear since thou hast promised that whoso hearkeneth[106] unto thee, which I desire ever[107] to do, shall dwell safely and shall be quiet from fear of evil, Prov. 1:33);[108] [p. 132] care

---

101. Isaiah 54:5–6: "For thy maker is thine husband; the Lord of hosts is his name; and thy redeemer the Holy One of Israel; The God of the whole earth shall he be called. For the Lord hath called thee as a woman forsaken and grieved in spirit, and a wife of youth, when thou wast refused, saith thy God."

102. After "him," "God" has been deleted and replaced by the interlineal insertion of "because."

103. "Disposed to go counter to what is demanded or what is reasonable; perverse, difficult to deal with, hard to please; refractory, ungovernable," OED.

104. Job 14:14: "If a man die, shall he live again? all the days of my appointed time will I wait, till my change come."

105. 1 Corinthians 15:42: "So also is the resurrection of the dead. It is sown in corruption; it is raised in incorruption."

106. "To hear with attention, give ear to (a thing); to listen to; to have regard to, heed; to understand, learn by hearing; to hear, perceive by the ear," OED.

107. "Ever" is an insertion in the right-hand margin.

108. Proverbs 1:33: "But whoso hearkeneth unto me shall dwell safely and shall be quiet from fear of evil."

to provide for my poor child is another great divertissement[109] from serving thee (but since Lord thy word hath said, if any provide not for his own, et cetera, he is worse than an infidel (1 Tim. 5:8),[110] I hope thou wilt allow me and instruct me in the care that is necessary, and, what is more, thou wilt restrain and teach me how to cast all my care upon thee since thou carest for me (1 Pet. 5:7);[111] another of my troubles is the great debt this family is involved in, and many[112] things lies upon me to clear (which my God will I hope support me under, that I may be able to help everyone to their own, and then a greater blessing will remain to what is left).

Though my dearest was no prophet yet may not I say with the widow: thy servant, my husband, is dead and thou knowest that thy servant did fear the [p. 133] Lord (2 Kings 4:1).[113] And this, that was an argument for the poor, distressed widow to plead for her with the prophet, I hope I may use to plead with the Lord of prophets, who can by his blessing multiply what is yet left that the creditors may be satisfied, and we may live upon the rest.[114] And this my Lord I do with fervor beg, if it be thy will; if not, give me submission to whatever thou art pleased to do with me or mine, for thou art good and doest good: teach me thy statutes (Ps. 119:68).[115]

I am perplexed when I consider the deceitfulness of my own heart, and when I find still there the same sins which these many years I have been praying against, and using all my endeavors to overcome, and yet I find it unsubdued, and am still subject to wandering [p. 134] thoughts in prayer, and to be more than necessarily angry upon a little provocation. And these are the two sins which this long time I have groaned under, and oft times been afraid thou shouldst say to me, as to the wicked which the Psalmist mentions:[116] what hast thou to do to declare my statutes, or take my covenant in thy mouth? Seeing thou hatest instruction, and castest my word behind thee (Ps. 50:16–17).

---

109. "The action of diverting or fact of being diverted," which is usually associated with entertainment or amusement; here used as an indication of distraction, OED.

110. 1 Timothy 5:8: "But if any provide not for his own, and specially for those of his own house, he hath denied the faith, and is worse than an infidel."

111. 1 Peter 5:7: "Casting all your care upon him; for he careth for you."

112. "Many" is an insertion in the left-hand margin.

113. 2 Kings 4:1: "Now there cried a certain woman of the wives of the sons of the prophets unto Elisha, saying, thy servant my husband is dead; and thou knowest that thy servant did fear the Lord: and the creditor is come to take unto him my two sons to be bondmen."

114. 2 Kings 4:7: "Then she came and told the man of God. And he said, Go, sell the oil, and pay thy debt, and live thou and thy children of the rest."

115. Psalm 119:68: "Thou art good, and doest good; teach me thy statutes."

116. Psalm 50:16–17: "But unto the wicked God saith, what hast thou to do to declare my statutes, or that thou shouldest take my covenant in thy mouth? Seeing thou hatest instruction, and castest my words behind thee."

But Lord, this is my infirmity (Ps. 77:10),[117] and ever blessed be thy name who hath said my grace is sufficient for thee for my strength is made perfect in weakness (2 Cor. 12:9):[118] and what you say to one you say to all (Mark 13:37).[119] Exalted be free grace for giving sinners a claim whereby they may sue out their [p. 135] pardon, and have it confirmed under this great seal: that God is True (John 3:33).[120] And in confidence of this I will look over the promises that is made to the fatherless and widows, on them I will believe.

I will look over what is the duties which belong to me as a widow, a mother, and a Christian (not one only[121] called by the name of Christ but as one that desires to be a true follower of him), and this I will endeavor to practice;[122] for even hereunto were ye called, because Christ also suffered for us, leaving us an example that ye should follow his steps (1 Pet. 2:21).[123]

The first step I desire to begin with is the first lesson as I remember that our Lord bids us learn of him, which is to be meek and lowly in heart, and there is a promise made to it: you shall find rest unto your souls (Matt. 11:29).[124] Oh, that it should be necessary to have [p. 136] blessings promised for the performance of that which is a blessing of itself, but sure our Lord did it because he knows our frame, and remembers that we are but dust (Ps. 103:4).[125]

If any had the experience which I have of a hasty, proud, and choleric[126] nature, and found it in any manner subdued, and made meek and lowly, they would say with me the words of holy David: this is the Lord's doing, it is marvelous in our eyes (Ps. 118:23).[127] And my God who hath begun a good work will perform it, I hope,[128] until the day of our Lord Jesus Christ, for none but himself

---

117. Psalm 77:10: "And I said, this is my infirmity: but I will remember the years of the right hand of the most High."

118. 2 Corinthians 12:9: "And he said unto me, 'My grace is sufficient for thee: for my strength is made perfect in weakness.' Most gladly therefore will I rather glory in my infirmities, that the power of Christ may rest upon me."

119. Mark 13:37: "'And what I say unto you I say unto all, Watch.'"

120. John 3:33: "He that hath received his testimony hath set to his seal that God is true."

121. After "one," "have" has been deleted and replaced by the interlineal insertion of "only."

122. "To practice" is an interlineal insertion.

123. 1 Peter 2:21: "For even hereunto were ye called: because Christ also suffered for us, leaving us an example, that ye should follow his steps."

124. Matthew 11:29: "Take my yoke upon you and learn of me; for I am meek and lowly in heart: and ye shall find rest unto your souls."

125. Psalm 103:14: "For he knoweth our frame; he remembereth that we are dust."

126. "Disposed to anger or easily angered; hot-tempered, fiery; bad-tempered, irascible; irritable, cantankerous," OED.

127. Psalm 118:23: "This is the Lord's doing; it is marvelous in our eyes."

128. "I hope" is an interlineal insertion.

can work that change (Phil. 1:6).[129] I desire to hold fast this profession: for since we have a high priest touched with our infirmity, and was in all points tempted as we are, yet without sin, I will go therefore boldly to the throne of grace that I may obtain mercy, and find grace to help in time of need (Heb. 4:15-16).[130] [p. 137] Whenever[131] I am provoked to anger, or dissention,[132] or anything that may disturb my peace, I desire to remember these words: live in peace, and the God of love and[133] peace shall be with you (2 Cor. 13:11).[134] Finally, whatsoever things are true; whatsoever things are honest; whatsoever things are just; whatsoever things are pure; whatsoever things are lovely; whatsoever things are of good report, if there be any virtue, and if there be any praise, think on these things (Phil. 4:8).[135] Oh, that my thoughts were always thus employed, then out of the abundance of my heart, my mouth would speak to praise the God of my salvation (Luke 6:45).[136]

As a mother my duty is to instruct my child, like Lois and Eunice (as they did Timothy) in the true faith, unfeignedly (2 Tim. 1:5),[137] and to bring him up in the nurture and admonition of the Lord (Eph. 6:4).[138] And to remember his creator in the days of [p. 138] his youth (Eccles. 12:1).[139] As instruction is necessary so is reproof, for the rod and reproof give wisdom but a child left to himself bringeth

---

129. Philippians 1:6: "Being confident of this very thing, that he which hath begun a good work in you will perform it until the day of Jesus Christ."

130. Hebrews 4:15-16: "For we have not an high priest which cannot be touched with the feeling of our infirmities; but was in all points tempted like as we are, yet without sin. Let us therefore come boldly unto the throne of grace, that we may obtain mercy, and find grace to help in time of need."

131. Some illegible text has been deleted before "whenever."

132. "To think differently, disagree, or differ"; or "To be at dissension or variance; to quarrel," *OED*. It can also refer specifically to difference in theological opinion.

133. "Love and" is an interlineal insertion.

134. 2 Corinthians 13:11: "Finally, brethren, farewell. Be perfect, be of good comfort, be of one mind, live in peace; and the God of love and peace shall be with you."

135. Philippians 4:8: "Finally, brethren, whatsoever things are true, whatsoever things are honest, whatsoever things are just, whatsoever things are pure, whatsoever things are lovely, whatsoever things are of good report; if there be any virtue, and if there be any praise, think on these things."

136. Luke 6:45: "A good man out of the good treasure of his heart bringeth forth that which is good; and an evil man out of the evil treasure of his heart bringeth forth that which is evil: for the abundance of the heart his mouth speaketh."

137. 2 Timothy 1:5: "When I call to remembrance the unfeigned faith that is in thee, which dwelt first in thy grandmother Lois, and thy mother Eunice; and I am persuaded that in thee also."

138. Ephesians 6:4: "And, ye fathers, provoke not your children to wrath: but bring them up in the nurture and admonition of the Lord."

139. Ecclesiastes 12:1: "Remember now thy Creator in the days of thy youth, while the evil days come not, nor the years draw nigh, when thou shalt say, I have no pleasure in them."

his mother to shame (Prov. 29:15).[140] Train up a child in the way he should go, and when he is old, he will not depart from it (Prov. 22:6).[141] He was a great and wise King[142] who gave these rules, and the blessings that is promised to it would encourage all that make conscience of their duty to endeavor to perform it.

Now, as a widow, I find my duty to lament my loss is not forbid but rather allowed of, since the Holy Spirit makes it a similitude[143] which sinners[144] should imitate. Lament, says the prophet, like a virgin girded with sackcloth for the husband of her youth (Joel 1:8),[145] and it is mentioned as a judgment that when the priests fell by the sword their widows made no lamentation:[146] next I find there is a garment peculiarly belonging to widows to distinguish them from other women (Gen. 38:14, 19).[147] [p. 139] But whatever my habit is, I desire to have chiefly the ornament of a meek and quiet spirit which is in the sight of God of great price (1 Pet. 3:4).[148]

There is two examples of widows which I desire to follow: one of Anna, and she was a widow, and which departed not from the Temple, but served God with fasting and prayers night and day (Luke 2:36–37).[149] To stay always in the Temple that I cannot do but to live always as in his sight who was figured by the Temple is my desire, and to keep frequently the true fast which is to abstain from all appearance of evil,[150] so shall I be the fitter to offer up the sacrifice of prayers night and day.

---

140. Proverbs 29:15: "The rod and reproof give wisdom: but a child left to himself bringeth his mother to shame."
141. Proverbs 22:6: "Train up a child in the way he should go: and when he is old, he will not depart from it."
142. I.e., Solomon.
143. "A comparison drawn between two things or facts; the expression of such comparison; a simile," *OED*.
144. Some illegible text has been deleted before "sinners."
145. Joel 1:8: "Lament like a virgin girded with sackcloth for the husband of her youth."
146. Psalm 78:64: "Their priests fell by the sword; and their widows made no lamentation."
147. Genesis 38:14, 19: "And she put her widow's garments off from her, and covered her with a vail, and wrapped herself, and sat in an open place, which is by the way to Timnath; for she saw that Shelah was grown, and she was not given unto him to wife"; "And she arose, and went away, and laid by her vail from her, and put on the garments of her widowhood."
148. 1 Peter 3:4: "But let it be the hidden man of the heart, in that which is not corruptible, even the ornament of a meek and quiet spirit, which is in the sight of God of great price."
149. Luke 2:36–37: "And there was one Anna, a prophetess, the daughter of Phanuel, of the tribe of Aser: she was of a great age, and had lived with an husband seven years from her virginity; And she was a widow of about fourscore and four years, which departed not from the temple, but served God with fastings and prayers night and day."
150. 1 Thessalonians 5:22: "Abstain from all appearance of evil."

The other widow is what Saint Paul calls, "a widow indeed" (1 Tim. 5:5).[151] Oh, to be such a one: desolate (which I understand to be alone and retired),[152] trusting in God, and continuing in supplications and prayers, night and day; blameless (1 Tim. 5:7),[153] well reported of, for good works, brought up children, lodged strangers, washed the Saints' feet, relieved the afflicted, diligently followed every good work (1 Tim. 5:10).[154] This Lord, I desire to do; therefore, I beseech thee, admit me into the number of them that are "widows indeed," and then I shall with the more confidence claim an interest in the promises made to them[155] [p. 140] for thou hast promised to establish the border of the widow, and[156] to execute the judgment of the fatherless and widow.[157] A father of the fatherless, and a judge of the widow, is God in his holy habitation;[158] besides many promises, thou hast been pleased at the first giving of thy law to command that they should not afflict any widow or fatherless child, and by the prophet doth pronounce a woe to them that make a prey of widows and rob the fatherless.[159]

Therefore, in confidence that my God in mercy will give me an interest in these promises, and grace to perform the duties belonging to my sad condition, my light may then so shine before men that they[160] may see my good works and glorify my father which is in heaven.[161] Then may I say with Saint Paul to the unmarried and widows, it is good for them if they abide even as I (am now and ever desire to be.[162] Amen, so be it.)[163]

151. 1 Timothy 5:5: "Now she that is a widow indeed, and desolate, trusteth in God, and continueth in supplications and prayers night and day."

152. In glossing "desolate," Halkett stresses its association with being solitary rather than being "destitute of joy or comfort... forlorn, disconsolate; overwhelmed with grief and misery, wretched," OED.

153. 1 Timothy 5:7: "And these things give in charge, that they may be blameless."

154. 1 Timothy 5:10: "Well reported of, for good works; if she have brought up children, if she have lodged strangers, if she have washed the saints' feet, if she have relieved the afflicted, if she have diligently followed every good work."

155. "Then I shall with the more confidence claim an interest in the promises made to them" is written in the bottom margin of the page.

156. "And" is an interlineal insertion.

157. Deuteronomy 10:8: "He doth execute the judgment of the fatherless and widow, and loveth the stranger, in giving him food and raiment."

158. Psalm 68:5: "A father of the fatherless, and a judge of the widows, is God in his holy habitation."

159. Isaiah 10:2: "To turn aside the needy from judgment, and to take away the right from the poor of my people, that widows may be their prey, and that they may rob the fatherless!"

160. "They" is an interlineal insertion.

161. Matthew 5:16: "Let your light so shine before men, that they may see your good works, and glorify your Father which is in heaven."

162. 1 Corinthians 7:8: "I say therefore to the unmarried and widows, it is good for them if they abide even as I."

163. The brackets here are Halkett's own, and the content is written in the bottom margin of the page.

Selected Meditations 233

Upon My Going to Live at Dunfermline, February 14, 1670/1.[164]

[p. v] *Man that is born of a woman is of few days, and full of trouble* (Job 14:1).[165]

Who can wonder if with trouble I leave this place,[166] where I have enjoyed so many blessings, and that I am going where there is so many snares and temptations? It may then be asked, why I make choice of that place to resolve to live, and for ought I know to die in? But chiefly it is because there lies what remains of my dearest Sir James, and where I do intend, if the Lord sees fit, to be buried myself. Another reason is, there is a school that my child hath been accustomed to, and therefore may profit more than with a better master who may alter his course of learning; and next, since what he and I have to subsist on is from this house, therefore[167] it is most convenient to be near it, where frequent conversation [p. vi] may increase that affection and friendship which I shall ever endeavor to have betwixt my son and my own child.

I have long accustomed myself to represent the good and ill of most things of concern to allay either the joy or grief it might occasion.

And from my trouble to leave this sweet place where I have had great satisfaction, I propose the advantages I may have of serving God by being near the church, which ill weather oft times kept me from when health would have allowed me here.

Next, I shall have my child with me, and so a better opportunity of watching all occasions to suppress sin in him, and to be always instructing him in the ways of piety and the virtues that attends it.

Then I shall be free I hope from any dissention[168] with my son; for though I do resolve never willingly to give him occasion for discord myself, yet if we had lived together the indiscretion of servants might have put me to an [p. vii] inconvenience[169] which at this distance may be avoided.[170]

---

164. See also Trill, ed., *Halkett*, 38–41.

165. This entry is unpaginated by Halkett. Although it records events which took place when she was completing this volume, it was been written on some spare pages at its beginning. Here, as elsewhere, Halkett's books show traces of what Gibson has termed "casting off blanks." See Trill, "Critical Categories," 107; Jonathan Gibson, "Casting off Blanks: Hidden Structures in Early Modern Paper Books," in *Material Readings of Early Modern Culture: Texts and Social Practices, 1580–1730*, ed. James Daybell and Peter Hinds (Basingstoke, UK: Palgrave Macmillan, 2010), 208–28.

166. I.e., Pitfirrane.

167. Before "therefore," "and" has been deleted.

168. "To be at dissension or variance; to quarrel," *OED*.

169. "A mischief, an injury; an untoward occurrence, a misfortune," *OED*.

170. In a letter to a Mr. Thomas, presumably her lawyer, dated only December 27, Halkett instructs him to meet with her son's lawyer to "consider of the best way" to draw up "the heads" upon which they

And, lastly, I shall frequently have an opportunity of seeing the place where my dearest Sir James lies buried, and that will I hope be a continual advertisement to me to prepare for death, and to live like one that was once happy in being his wife, and now to resolve ever—while the Lord think fit to continue me upon earth—to live like his widow. With that piety, charity, temperance, and justice that is suitable to one who hath wholly resigned themselves up to live a life of faith and continual dependence upon my God and master, who I hope will accept of me and own me as his devoted servant.

Since I must go from this place, these are the satisfactions that I can most propose to myself, but again the disadvantages are these: the people [p. viii] I am going to live amongst are ill inclined generally, and are under the aspersion of being given to idleness, intemperance, lying, and uncharitableness, and what a list of sin depends upon these I desire not to mention but rather make it my endeavor to suppress it both in myself and others. Oh, that I might be there such an example for the practice of all holy duties, that by my actions I might teach them since by words I dare not (at least at my first coming amongst them) least they say to me as they did to Lot: this one fellow[171] is come to sojourn[172] amongst us, and he[173] will needs be a judge, now will we deal worse with thee than with them (Gen. 19:9).[174]

Therefore, in prudence, I think it not fit for me avowedly[175] to reprove those vices which I detest. But if upon [p. ix] fit occasions, I can insinuate myself into the esteem of the best, and be gently instilling those drops of grace which flows from the fountain of mercy (which, if violently done, might be split and so turn useless) this way I may perhaps do good;[176] but to the poorer sort, my charity (if the Lord please to give me what may make that helpful to them) may invite them to a reformation, since they shall partake of most who I see most careful to serve God and obey him.

I do resolve, since intemperance is so great a sin amongst them, to refrain even from things allowable because I would give no occasion to encourage sin in others or myself. And what I can no other way prevent, I shall be more fervent in [p. x] prayer to the great and powerful God, who can make all things work

---

are agreed, and clearly anticipates that he will think it strange she has "condescended to quit so much." Pitfirrane Papers: Correspondence, NLS, MS 6407, fol. 26r-27v.

171. Here, "person" has been overwritten and turned into "fellow."

172. "To make a temporary stay in a place; to remain or reside for a time," OED.

173. "He" is an interlineal insertion.

174. Genesis 19:9: "And they said, Stand back. And they said again, this one fellow came into sojourn, and he will needs be a judge: now will we deal worse with thee, than with them. And they pressed sore upon the man, even Lot, and came near to break the door."

175. "In an avowed manner; with open declaration or acknowledgement; confessedly, openly," OED.

176. "This way I may perhaps do good" is an insertion written in the right-hand margin.

together for good to them that love him.[177] To him, therefore, I shall with fervor offer up myself, and all mine, and my endeavors, and designs, and if the Lord sees fit he can bless me so that I may be instrumental in doing good even to that place and people[178] who have been very ready to traduce[179] me upon all occasion. But, Lord, pardon them, and protect me from giving them any just occasion; for, if thou wilt be pleased to give me the grace I seek, I shall then live so that if my greatest enemy saw my most secret act, even in my heart, they should find there nothing willingly to offend.

Oh, that I could attain to this degree, for then the very angels should not exceed me[180] in purity and readiness to obey [p. xi] thee, my great and glorious God. And since to obey thee is chiefly my desire, teach me to be content to want as well as to abound,[181] and not to repine when thou art pleased to withdraw that grace which sometime is so fully manifested to me that, even since my late sad condition, I have been twice so highly taken into favor that I was ready to say, "it is too much, O Lord, it is too much." Oh, what is our frame, how frail and weak when even the greatest mercies we can partake of here is dangerous to keep and sad to lose?

I see then, by experience, that a soul may be overwhelmed even with joy as well as grief, and this should teach me humble submission when I want that presence which is too much for me ever to enjoy. And [p. xii] therefore, the Lord, that knows what measure suits everyone's capacity, gives and withholds according to the best way of improvement: for, were it always night, we could not work, and if it were continual day we should not value it so much because even the greatest blessings that are ordinary loses the esteem we should have of them, and we look not upon them as the bounty of the Lord of grace.

But, Lord, what have I but what I have received? And what can I glory in but in thee who hath made this change, so that from a proud and hasty, choleric[182] temper I am become something like (oh, make it more and more) to my Master, meek and lowly in heart. And by that I find in thee more rest than in all the riches of the world without it. How soon thou mayest withdraw this grace I know not, but I do most sincerely beg the continuance of it that my whole life may be to all about me a silent reproof to all sin, and an example of all that is good. Then shall

177. Romans 8:28: "And we know that all things work together for good to them that love God, to them who are the called according to his purpose."

178. "And people" is an interlineal insertion.

179. "To falsely or maliciously speak of as; to slanderously state or affirm (something) to be; to falsely or maliciously blame for, accuse of, charge with," *OED*.

180. "Me" is an interlineal insertion.

181. Philippians 4:12: "I know both how to be abased, and I know how to abound: everywhere and in all things, I am instructed both to be full and to be hungry, both to abound and to suffer need."

182. See "Upon My Deplorable Being a Widow," 229n126.

it be written in the volume of thy book that I delight to do thy will,[183] O my God, and thy law is within my heart (Ps. 40:7–8).[184] Lord say, amen.

---

183. From "will" until "amen" is written in the bottom margin of the page.

184. Psalm 40:7–8: "Then said I, Lo, I come: in the volume of the book it is written of me, I delight to do thy will, O my God: yea, thy law is within my heart."

The Widow's Mite and Occasional Meditations *(1673–1674/5)*

An inscription in Halkett's hand on the inside front cover provides the start date for this volume of June 13, 1673, and the final occasional meditation is dated January 21, 1674/5.[1] It retains its original brown calfskin covers but has been rebound at the spine with some loose papers inserted; in keeping with her new identity as a widow, this and most of the ensuing volumes have black edged paper.[2] As with the previous volumes, Halkett distinguishes between her select and occasional meditations; this time, however, the volume opens with "The Widow's Mite," and the occasional meditations occupy the final third of the volume. The title alludes to the story of the poor widow recounted in Mark 12:41–44;[3] however, according to Halkett's index at the end of the volume, "part of it" relates "to the King."[4] The only other select meditation in this volume is "Meditations and Resolutions upon 1 Corinthians 12:13, Occasioned by the Late Rent in This Church."[5] There follows a title page for the "Occasional Meditations," which begin with "Upon the Death of Sir Robert Moray."[6] This entry includes an inserted leaf that disrupts Halkett's pagination. Apart from "Upon the Peace Proclaimed with the Dutch, February 1673/4," most of the occasional meditations here focus on her own and other people's private lives.[7] In addition to her recurring meditations upon her husband's death, Halkett notes the deaths of Laird of Belboughy,[8] Robert Cunningham,[9] Mrs. Monro,[10] and Lord Preston;[11] her own and her son's

---

1. Halkett, *The Widow's Mite*, pp. i, 334. This is volume 10 in Couper's catalogue.

2. An exception is Halkett, *Meditations on St. Peter*.

3. Halkett, *The Widow's Mite*, 32–154. Mark 12:41–44: "And Jesus sat over against the treasury and beheld how the people cast money into the treasury: and many that were rich cast in much. And there came a certain poor widow, and she threw in two mites, which make a farthing. And he called unto him his disciples, and saith unto them, 'Verily I say unto you, That this poor widow hath cast more in, than all they which have cast into the treasury: for they did cast in of their abundance; but she of her want, did cast in all that she had, even her living.'" See also Luke 21:1–4, 218n18.

4. Halkett, *The Widow's Mite*, p. viii.

5. Halkett, *The Widow's Mite*, pp. 156–212. 1 Corinthians 12:13: "For by one spirit are we all baptized into one body, whether we be Jews or Gentiles, whether we be bond or free; and have been all made to drink into one spirit."

6. Halkett, *The Widow's Mite*, p. 213.

7. Halkett, *The Widow's Mite*, pp. 280–82.

8. Halkett, *The Widow's Mite*, pp. 225–28.

9. Halkett, *The Widow's Mite*, p. 275.

10. Halkett, *The Widow's Mite*, pp. 283–88; see also Trill, ed., *Halkett*, 45–48.

11. Halkett, *The Widow's Mite*, pp. 275, 317–19.

illnesses and accidents;[12] and her attendance at various "Sacraments."[13] When she began this volume, Halkett was taking care of Pitfirrane, while her then unmarried stepson, Sir Charles Halkett, was involved in the third Anglo-Dutch War, 1672–1674.[14] Sir Charles Halkett returned home on April 13, 1674; by Monday, July 6, 1674, Robin had also come home, which suggests Halkett had returned to Dunfermline by that date.[15]

The Widow's Mite.

[p. 1] The great and holy God created all things both in heaven and earth to praise him, and[16] as the greatest of Kings was honored by his acceptation, so the most contemptible was not despised who came with a willing heart to offer though it was but the meanest sacrifice. Thus Lord, I come to offer up myself, and all I am able to give; accept it, I beseech thee, as the widow's mite.[17] For all the faculties, both of soul and body, I humbly present to thee, and desire assistance

---

12. See, for example, "Upon a Bite Robin Got with a Dog on the Inside of His Right Arm, December 27, 1673," in Halkett, *The Widow's Mite*, pp. 258–59.

13. The Sacrament is Holy Communion. Halkett records her attendances at: Aberdour (January 3, 1674/5, *The Widow's Mite*, pp. 327–29; Monday, April 9, 1688; Saturday, April 21, 1688; Tuesday, April 24, 1688, *Meditations on St. Peter*, pp. 374/5, 380–81, 381–84); Carnock (October 26, 1673, *The Widow's Mite*, pp. 229–37; Saturday, August 6, 1687, *Meditations on St. Peter*, pp. 305–7): Dunfermline (August 23, 1674, *The Widow's Mite*, pp. 305–8; August 11 and 12, 1694, *Of Watchfulness*, pp. 237–39, 338–41; August 11, 1695, Halkett, *Meditations upon the Seven Gifts of the Holy Spirit*, 57. ESTC N10709); London (May–July, 1659, *Occasional Meditations*, pp. 96–111); and Torryburn (May 29, 1670, *Occasional and Select Meditations*, pp. 105–9; early 1671, "consecrated her widowhood to the Lord," *The Life of the Lady Halket*, 36; August 9, 1674, *The Widow's Mite*, pp. 302–4; June 4, 1687, *Meditations on St. Peter*, pp. 284–85, 286–87).

14. According to Couper, it was early in 1672 that Sir Charles entrusted his estate to her care, *The Life of the Lady Halket*, 37. An undated letter to the Laird of Sauchie shows Halkett dealing with her stepson's accounts. Pitfirrane Papers: Correspondence. NLS, MS 6407, fol. 145r–45v.

15. Halkett, "Upon My Son's Return, Who Came Here to Me Last Night, Being April 13, 1674," in *The Widow's Mite*, pp. 289–90. The entry recording Robin's return is untitled, *The Widow's Mite*, p. 295.

16. "And" is an interlineal insertion.

17. Luke 21:1–4: "And he looked up, and saw the rich men casting their gifts into the treasury. And he saw also a certain poor widow casting in thither two mites. And he said, "Of a truth I say unto you, that this poor widow hath cast in more than they all: For all these have of their abundance cast in unto the offerings of God: but she of her penury hath cast in all the living that she had." See also Mark 12:42–44. Halkett's self-positioning as a widow bears fruitful comparison with that of Katherine Austen. For her texts, see Pamela S. Hammons, ed., *Book M: A London Widow's Life Writings* (Toronto: Iter Inc. and Centre for Reformation and Renaissance Studies, 2013), and Sarah C. E. Ross, *Katherine Austen's Book M: British Library, Additional Manuscript 4454* (Tempe: Arizona Center for Medieval and Renaissance Studies, 2011). For a discussion of widowhood, see Raymond A. Anselment, "Katherine Austen and the Widow's Might," *Journal for Early Modern Cultural Studies* 5, no. 1 (2005): 5–25.

so to employ them for the setting forth thy praise that my understanding, will, and affections may be raised to the highest point[18] of adoration, and all my senses employed to serve thee in the most perfect way of true obedience. So, shall my faith be evidenced by my works, and my works accepted by my faith, which is the substance of things hoped for, the evidence of things not seen[19] yet believed in because the Lord hath said: Whatsoever you shall ask the father in my name, he will give it you.[20]

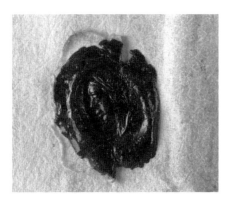

Figure 11. Seal from Anne, Lady Halkett's "Letter to the Laird of Sauchie," (ca. 1673), in Pitfirrane Papers: Correspondence. © National Library of Scotland, NLS, MS 6407, fol.145v. Reproduced with permission.

Then, in confidence of this promise, I seek mercy and expect it from God, the Father; for God, the Son; and by God, the Holy Ghost, to pardon sin, to purchase salvation, and to be sealed with the Holy Spirit of promise[21] [p. 2] who can only lead me in the paths of righteousness.[22] And that is now all my desire, for blessed be the God of my salvation, I have not for the present any doubt of the pardon of my sin. How soon it may return I know not, for the first neglect of duty, or commission of sin may open the floodgates of thy wrath, which mercy for a time hath shut. And then what can be more desolate than my distressed soul, who hath nothing to rely upon but that which is, I confess, sufficient to uphold ages of worlds from condemnation: even the infinite merits of the Lord of glory who can

18. "Point" is an interlineal insertion.
19. Hebrews 11:1: "Now faith is the substance of things hoped for, the evidence of things not seen."
20. John 14:13: "And whatsoever ye shall ask in my name, that will I do, that the Father may be glorified in the Son."
21. Ephesians 1:13: "In whom ye also trusted, after that ye heard the word of truth, the gospel of your salvation: in whom also after that ye believed, ye were sealed with that holy spirit of promise."
22. Psalm 23:3: "He restoreth my soul: he leadeth me in the paths of righteousness for his name's sake."

lose none that the Father hath given him, but they may lose the comfort of this assurance whenever the Lord thinks fit to withdraw his grace, or the light of his countenance from them.

And since the time that this much was written, which was yesterday morning (being June 24),[23] what experience have I had of a perverse, ungrateful heart? For though I heard certain news of my son's, Sir Charles Halkett's,[24] being [p. 3] safe at London, and escaped (as I think, miraculously) eminent danger in the last sea fight,[25] for which I will forever magnify the Lord, yet how froward[26] was I all the day after for the most part, for several sick people's coming to interrupt what I had other ways designed my time for? Which lets me see still there is in me a spirit unsubdued; for should I not rather have employed my time in praising God for his vouchsafing to grant the many prayers I offered up for the preservation of my son, and looked upon the sick people that came (though off my usual day for such employment)[27] as being sent to receive the tribute of my thankfulness even for that mercy? And besides they came not to seek anything that was mine to give: for it is the blessing of the Lord that makes anything prosper, and how should I prize the being honored to be instrumental in doing good to any that may give glory to the Lord that is omnipotent?

Lord, all my follies and my frailties I beg pardon for, and humbly entreat thy favor and acceptance for what I do intend to record here, that it may be to set forth thy praise, and to confirm I am thy Servant. Oh, give me understanding that I may keep thy testimonies.[28] Amen.[29]

---

23. "Being June 24" is an insertion in the left-hand margin.

24. "Sir Charles Halkett's" is an interlineal insertion.

25. This suggests Sir Charles was involved in the "indecisive Anglo-Dutch naval engagements off the Schonveld," which took place in May through June 1673. David L. Smith, *A History of the Modern British Isles, 1603–1707: The Double Crown* (Oxford: Blackwell, 2000), 223. According to the dates provided by J. R. Jones, Sir Charles was probably involved in the "Second Schooneveld action," June 4/14, 1673; J. R. Jones, *The Anglo-Dutch Wars of the Seventeenth Century* (London: Longman, 1996).

26. "Disposed to go counter to what is demanded or what is reasonable; perverse, difficult to deal with, hard to please; refractory, ungovernable," *OED*.

27. Couper records that Halkett was frequently employed in "making preparations of extracted waters, spirits, ointments, conserves, salves, powders, et cetera, which she ministered every Wednesday to a multitude of poor, infirm persons (besides what she daily sent abroad to persons of all ranks who consulted her in their maladies)"; Couper, *The Life of the Lady Halket*, 56. While her volumes provide ample evidence of her assisting the gentry and nobility in various afflictions, I have not found any reference to a weekly "surgery" as implied above.

28. Psalm 119:125: "I am thy servant; give me understanding, that I may know thy testimonies."

29. The final four words here are written in the bottom margin of the page.

Selected Meditations 241

The Widow's Mite, Part of It Relating to the King.[30]

[p. 4] The Temple had a treasury into which the poor as well as rich cast in their gifts, and there it was where a certain poor widow had that testimony of our Lord, that of a truth this poor widow hath cast in more than they all because it was all the living that she had (Luke 21: 3).[31] Then, though my gifts be not so great as others, yet what I have I humbly offer up and hope for acceptation.[32]

I have been some time considering with myself what subject to fix my meditation on and, since I desire my heart should be indicting a good matter, it[33] shall be of the things I have made touching the King (Ps. 45:1).[34] Obligation, gratitude, and education hath been ties upon me ever since I was capable[35] of anything to make me have humble,[36] loyal, and sincere affection, honor, and obedience for the King (as one whose parents and nearest relations had—next to the providence of the Almighty God—their chiefest[37] subsistence from his princely favor).[38] And, during the late troubles, known it is to the hearer of prayer, the supplications and tears that I have offered up for mercy for the late King.[39] And though [p. 5] a temporal deliverance was denied (because the iniquities of Britain, as of the Amorites, was not yet full),[40] yet undoubtedly as his unparalleled murder did fill up the cup of his enemies' wrath, so his Majesty's patient and serene submissive suffering will to after ages be the wonder and astonishment: that subjects could so[41] inflict, and the Sovereign so endure.[42] But both was[43] to accomplish that the Lord had determined: by the sin of the people to bring the Prince sooner to that glory which had been prepared for him from the beginning of the world.

30. The subtitle is provided in Halkett's index to this volume; Halkett, *The Widow's Mite*, p. viii.

31. Luke 21:3: "And he said, 'Of a truth I say unto you, that this poor widow hath cast in more than they all.'"

32. Archaic form of "acceptance."

33. "It" is an interlineal insertion.

34. Psalm 45:1: "My heart is inditing a good matter: I speak of the things which I have made touching the King: my tongue is the pen of a ready writer."

35. "Having general capacity, intelligence, or ability; qualified, gifted, able, competent," *OED*.

36. "An" has been deleted before "humble."

37. I.e., chief.

38. See *True Account*, 60–64, 60n8.

39. I.e., Charles I.

40. Genesis 15:16: "But in the fourth generation they shall come hither again: for the iniquity of the Amorites is not yet full."

41. "So" is an interlineal insertion.

42. The King's experience was widely known through *Eikon Basilike*; see "Upon the Fast which by Proclamation Was Kept, January 30, 1660/1," and "Introduction," 203–5, 22, 22n104.

43. In MS after "both," "what" has been deleted and replaced with the interlineal insertion of "was."

After the murder of that good King, the prayers I daily offered for the present King[44] in his exile, and all the royal family (as it was my duty) so the return of them showed those intercessions were acceptable at the throne of grace. And from thence I had an assured confidence that not by might, nor by power, but by the spirit of the Lord of hosts would his Majesty be restored (Zech. 4:6).[45] And therefore when I heard of the first design that the loyal party had of raising an army for the King after Worcester,[46] I wept being told of it [p. 6] at Fyvie by my Lady Anna Erskine, in the year 1652, which she wondering at I told her my reason was because I grieved to think of the loss of so many brave gentlemen as made any such attempt. For I was very confident it would not be by force of arms but only by the mercy of God that the King should be restored, and to make it the more evident it was only and alone his own work, it would be done in a peaceable manner by the unanimous desire of the people. And to this purpose I spoke my mind freely to Colonel Overton at Fyvie[47] when he pressed to know my opinion of the times, and his answer was that if it should come to pass, he would repent what he had done, and believe I was a prophetess (if he be living he can witness this to be true).[48]

From that time to this, I never thought to make a pen the reporter of it, though severals[49]—many years since—hath heard me relate these passages. But now I hope they may be useful to me to look back upon those sad and cloudy times that was like [p. 7] the storm Saint Paul was in, when neither sun nor stars appeared for many days (Acts 27:20).[50] But blessed be God, even the Father of our Lord Jesus Christ, the Father of mercies and the God of all comfort, who comforts us in all our tribulation that we may be able to comfort them which are in any trouble by the comfort wherewith we ourselves are comforted of God (2 Cor. 1:3–4).[51]

44. I.e., Charles II.

45. Zechariah 4:6: "Then he answered and spake unto me, saying, this is the word of the Lord unto Zerubbabel, saying, Not by might, nor by power, but by my spirit, saith the Lord of hosts."

46. "After Worcester" is an interlineal insertion. "The Battle of Worcester" took place on September 3, 1651. Smith confirms that "the first faint stirrings of a Royalist revival in Scotland did not occur until the end of 1652, over a year after Huntley and Balcarres had surrendered to the victorious forces of George Monck"; Smith, *Royalist Agents, Conspirators, and Spies*, 167.

47. "At Fyvie" is an interlineal insertion.

48. The parentheses here are Halkett's, and the phrase is an interlineal insertion. See *True Account*, 134. Overton did not die until 1678/9. Taft, "Overton, Robert," *ODNB*.

49. "Several persons or things," *OED*.

50. Acts 27:20: "And when neither sun nor stars in many days appeared, and no small tempest lay on us, all hope that we should be saved was then taken away."

51. 2 Corinthians 1:3–4: "Blessed be God, even the Father of our Lord Jesus Christ, the Father of mercies, and the God of all comfort; who comforteth us in all our tribulation, that we may be able to comfort them which are in any trouble, by the comfort wherewith we ourselves are comforted of God."

The times now begin to be very dark and cloudy again, as if some new great storm were hanging over our heads.[52] And I confess when I consider what our former troubles hath been, and the miraculous deliverance out of them (by restoring the church, the King, and the liberties of his people), and yet how unsuitable all our performances hath been, and the ungrateful return we have given for so great and unspeakable mercies, then when I seriously reflect upon this I cannot but have just grounds to fear there is judgments preparing sevenfold worse than the former, because hitherto neither judgments nor mercy hath prevailed to make us humble, thankful, nor obedient. But when I remember: the wonderful power that the Lord hath manifested in the King's preservation, as first in his going from Oxford to Bristol in the beginning of the year, March 1644[53] (I heard my brother Charles Murray,[54] who was of his Highness's [p. 8] bedchamber, relate that they marched in the night through the enemy's army, who had light matches on every side of them, and yet the Lord preserved him so that none of them had power to hurt him); what ill-usage did his Majesty meet with abroad, even from kingly relations; what designs upon his life; what discontents from want, and from the ma[lice] of them that made suspicions, and jealousy, and unkindness betwixt him and his royal brother; how unparalleled was his Majesty's Restoration; how soon was the army dissipated and disbanded who had formerly been most opposite to obedience;[55] and how was the designs of the fanatics[56] disappointed (who had combined, and promised to themselves divine assistance, though they were attempting that which was most contrary to the revealed will of the most High);[57] from all these, I cannot but make the conclusion of Manoah's wife: if the Lord

---

52. This volume was written during the third Anglo-Dutch War, 1672–1674. See Hutton, *Charles II*, chapter 11.

53. "March 1644" is an interlineal insertion. Hutton confirms the then Prince of Wales's movements: "In May 1644 the Privy Council at Oxford debated sending him to take nominal command of Royalist operations in the West Country. When the proposal created great opposition among the Counsellors, and the Prince himself proved hostile, it was shelved. During the following winter the project was revived, and executed in March 1645"; Hutton, *Charles II*, 7.

54. "Murray" is an interlineal insertion.

55. See "Upon the Disbanding of the Army," 199–203.

56. As Alasdair Raffe explains, "across Charles II's kingdoms, the term 'fanatic' was used to stigmatize actual or potential opponents of the Restoration settlements," including "former supporters of the Protectorate, republican ideologues, and demobilized members of the Interregnum regime's armies"; Raffe, *The Culture of Controversy: Religious Arguments in Scotland 1660–1714* (Woodbridge, UK: Boydell, 2012), 121.

57. Here, Halkett is likely referring to Thomas Venner's rising in London, which she also discusses in "Upon the Disbanding of the Army," 201–2, 201n24. As Raffe notes, the Edinburgh diarist John Nichol had referred to the participants in this event as "phanatick rebellis"; Raffe, *Culture of Controversy*, 122.

intended to have destroyed the King, he would never have showed him such mercies and deliverances (Judg. 13:23).[58]

And herein I fortify [p. 9] myself because the gifts of God are without repentance, and who he once loves he loves to the end, and no height, nor depth, nor any other creature shall be able to separate from the love of God, which is in Christ Jesus our Lord (Rom. 8:39).[59] And from this I am confirmed in what I have with confidence often asserted, that I was fully assured the Lord would make the King an instrument of much glory to himself and people, and though of late (June 25)[60] I have heard some reports which would seem very contrary to this expectation, which hath been great disturbance to me. But, in the multitude of my thoughts within me thy comforts, O Lord, delight my soul (Ps. 94:19),[61] and I was much upheld by this promise: in mercy shall the throne be established and he shall sit upon it in truth in the tabernacle of David, judging, and seeking judgment, and hasting righteousness.[62] Lord remember this word unto thy servant upon which thou have caused me to hope (Ps. 119:49):[63] there is none righteous, no, not one.[64] And if the King hath been overtaken with a fault incident to men,[65] possibly the Lord hath permitted it[66] to let him and his people see it was not for [p. 10] his righteousness but the Lord had pity for his holy name (Ezek. 36:21),[67] and is pleased further to add, thus, says the Lord God: I will not do this for your

---

58. Judges 13:23: "But his wife said unto him, If the Lord were pleased to kill us, he would not have received a burnt offering and a meat offering at our hands, neither would he have shewed us all these things, nor would as at this time have told us such things as these."

59. Romans 8:39: "Nor height, nor depth, nor any other creature, shall be able to separate us from the love of God, which is in Christ Jesus our Lord."

60. "June 25" is an insertion in the left-hand margin.

61. Psalm 94:19: "In the multitude of my thoughts within me thy comforts delight my soul."

62. Isaiah 16:5: "And in mercy shall the throne be established: and he shall sit upon it in truth in the tabernacle of David, judging, and seeking judgment, and hasting righteousness."

63. Psalm 119:49: "Remember the word unto thy servant, upon which thou hast caused me to hope."

64. Romans 3:10: "As it is written, there is none righteous, no, not one."

65. I.e., adultery. Although married to Catherine of Braganza in 1662, Charles's first mistress was heavily pregnant when his wife arrived; by 1673/4, he had an extended collection of mistresses, including both Nell Gwynn and Louise de Kérouaille. As Tim Harris observes, "many rhymesters pointed out how Charles's whoring was ruining the country," and one in particular "claimed that the miracle of the King's restoration had now become England's 'curse and punishment'"; Harris, *Restoration: Charles II and His Kingdoms* (London: Penguin, 2006), 73; 80. See also Seaward, "Charles II," *ODNB*; and Wynne, "Catherine [Catherine of Braganza]," *ODNB*.

66. "It" is an interlineal insertion.

67. In the margin, Halkett provides the following reference: "Ezekiel 36:21 to the end." Ezekiel 36:21: "But I had pity for mine holy name, which the house of Israel had profaned among the heathen, whither they went."

sakes, but for mine holy name's sake (Ezek. 36:22).[68] And I hope all the following promises will be made good[69] for this end, that we may know God to be the Lord.

And what can more evidence that than his mercy in pardoning, and his power in cleansing, and giving the new heart? And since it is promised to them that hath gone astray, I will both hope and wait for it, and confidently expect it. For, with the fervor of my soul, I daily make supplication for the King, to the King of Kings and hearer of prayer that he may be blessed with all spiritual and temporal blessings, and that his earthly crown may be so confirmed to him as that it may be a pledge of that eternal crown of glory, which he shall enjoy when he exchanges this life for that which is to come.

And if all within his Majesty's dominions had this faith that I have (of things hoped for [p. 11] though unseen),[70] they would all do as Shem and Japheth, who took a garment and laid it upon both their shoulders, and went backward, and covered the nakedness of their father, and their faces were backwards, and they saw not their father's nakedness (Gen. 9:23).[71]

We all have natural, civil, and spiritual fathers, and disobedience or disrespect to any of these is a breach of the fifth command, which as the Apostle observes is the first command with promise (Eph. 6:2).[72]

And the frailties and infirmities in any of these we should endeavor to cover, and not do as Ham, who not only saw his father's nakedness but he went and told his brethren without, and all he got by it was his father's curse: but the contrary practiced of his brethren[73] made them be blessed, and no doubt so shall all be that

---

68. Ezekiel 36:22: "Therefore say unto the house of Israel, thus saith the Lord God; I do not this for your sakes, O house of Israel, but for mine holy name's sake, which ye have profaned among the heathen, whither ye went."

69. The promises can be found in Ezekiel 36:23–38.

70. Hebrews 11:1 "Now faith is the substance of things hoped for, the evidence of things not seen."

71. In the left-hand margin on this page, there is evidence of some biblical references; however, they have been obscured by pasteboards, with only the end of the book and reference number being visible, "en 3." Genesis 9:23: "And Shem and Japheth took a garment, and laid it upon both their shoulders, and went backward, and covered the nakedness of their father; and their faces were backward, and they saw not their father's nakedness."

72. Ephesians 6:2: "Honor thy father and mother; (which is the first commandment with promise)." The full list of the Ten Commandments can be found in Exodus 20:1–17 and Deuteronomy 5:6–22. For the associated "promises," see Exodus 20:12: "Honor thy father and thy mother: that thy days may be long upon the land which the Lord thy God giveth thee"; and Deuteronomy 5:16: "Honor thy father and thy mother, as the Lord thy God hath commanded thee; that thy days may be prolonged, and that it may go well the thee, in the land which the Lord thy God giveth thee."

73. Genesis 9:22: "And Ham, the father of Canaan, saw the nakedness of his father, and told his two brethren without."

follows their example;[74] for if, when we heard of the nakedness of our civil father (or any other),[75] we went backward and looked upon our own lives, or the lives of many eminent Saints, it would make us the more careful to cover the infirmities of others. And certainly, it was for this end that the Holy Spirit of God recorded the sins of these holy men: not that we [p. 12] should imitate their sin but to teach us to judge charitably of all.[76] And when we see[77] what heinous sins even the chosen of God may fall into and yet not forfeit their right to heaven, oh then, let it be an occasion to magnify the free and unspeakable grace, and boundless love of God: that even sin itself, which is the most contrary to the purity of his essence, yet even that cannot separate them from him because he is God and changes not, therefore is sinners not consumed (Mal. 3:6) . . .[78]

[p. 25] To conclude these meditations concerning the King, I am fully persuaded the Lord hath designed him to be an heir of glory, and an instrument of much praise to himself by being a reformer both by his laws and his practice, and until the time come I will daily pray for the hastening of it. And as his Majesty showed great magnanimity and courage in his undaunted resolution of being crowned the appointed day (though the fanatics[79] both in words and papers flung into the King's court at Whitehall[80] had, with much boldness, affirmed as true some inspiration that [p. 26] the crown should never be set upon his head).

---

74. Genesis 9:24–27: "And Noah awoke from his wine and knew what his younger son had done unto him. And he said, cursed be Canaan; a servant of servants shall he be unto his brethren. And he said, blessed be the Lord God of Shem; and Canaan shall be his servant. God shall enlarge Japheth, and he shall dwell in the tents of Shem; and Canaan shall be his servant."

75. "(Or any other)" is an interlineal insertion.

76. Like Donne and Hall, Halkett characteristically focuses on fallible figures: "They are exemplary not for the Image of God in them, but for the way in which they have worked to rectify that image, not entirely depraved but yet stained, in a fallen world"; see Jeanne M. Shami, "Donne's Protestant Casuistry: Cases of Conscience in the 'Sermons,'" *Studies in Philology* 80, no. 1 (1983): 53–66.

77. "See" is inserted in the left-hand margin.

78. Malachi 3:6: "For I am the Lord, I change not; therefore, ye sons of Jacob are not consumed." Here, Halkett also alludes to Romans 8, especially the final two verses (38–39): "For I am persuaded, that neither death, nor life, nor angels, nor principalities, nor powers, nor things present, nor things to come, nor height, nor depth, nor any other creature, shall be able to separate us from the love of God, which is in Christ Jesus our Lord." Halkett continues by considering the heinous sins of God's chosen leaders and what they teach us before moving to her conclusion.

79. See 243n56.

80. When he returned to London, Charles II took up residence in the royal palace of Whitehall. He lived there "almost continuously for two years, and during every winter thereafter. He was to die in it"; Hutton, *Charles II*, 133. For a detailed description of its layout during this period, see Montagu H. Cox and Philip Norman, eds., "Whitehall Palace: Buildings," in *Survey of London: Volume 13, St Margaret, Westminster, Part II: Whitehall I.* 53 vols. (London: London County Council, 1930), 13:41–115, BHO.

And that from these threats, and more deliberate[81] thoughts, some faithful to his Majesty's interests did endeavor to dissuade from keeping the intended day for Coronation because it fell to be a day on which there was an eclipse of the sun, and that might appear as an ill omen which might confirm some in their thoughts of his Majesty's unhappy reign. But to this the King would not condescend, but with a Christian fortitude replied, he feared neither the threats nor the omen because he knew the Lord overruled all such events, and therefore he would keep his first resolution, and rely upon God for his blessing and preservation.

And that the God of power and glory may be praised, I must record what I was witness of myself when his Majesty rid from the Tower[82] to [p. 27] Whitehall the day before the Coronation, which was one of the greatest solemnities that I believe ever Britain saw. Though the King had great and royal attendance, and faithful servants, yet such was the multitude of beholders that crowded in about the King that his servants were not able to keep about the horse in which his Majesty did ride. And I saw very many mean, ordinary persons laying their hands upon the horse and the rich trappings, which put me into that terror for fear of some attempt upon his Majesty's person that it took away the satisfaction that else I should have had in so glorious a sight. But I turned my fears into prayers, and was heard in that I feared, and the Lord granted[83] my requests, and none had power to hurt him: praised be the God of mercy for it. But while I was thus conflicting with my fears, the King rode on with a serene, undisturbed [p. 28] composure, free either from fear or vanity, and seemed to be pleased with the liberty the rude[84] multitude took to approach him (who certainly was restrained from their ill designs by the same spirit that said: touch not my anointed).[85]

The next day, being Tuesday, his Majesty was crowned notwithstanding all the opposition threatened by the fanatics. And sometime after the Coronation, there was the most terrible tempest of thunder, lightning and rain that ever I saw, so that I feared some danger to his Majesty in his return from Westminster, coming by water to Whitehall, where I waited and had the honor to have the first kiss of his Majesty's hand after coming into the house.[86] And on my knees, with an uplifted heart and soul, I begged[87] that God would crown his Majesty with all the blessings both of heaven and earth; for I was transported to see the King

---

81. "Well weighed or considered; carefully thought out; formed, carried out, etc. with careful consideration and full intention; done of set purpose; studied; not hasty or rash," *OED*.

82. I.e., the Tower of London.

83. "Granted" is an interlineal insertion.

84. "Unmannerly, uncivil, impolite; offensively or deliberately discourteous," *OED*.

85. 1 Chronicles 16:22, Psalm 105:15: "Saying, Touch not mine anointed, and do my prophets no harm."

86. See also her presentation to the King at Dunfermline, *True Account*, 123.

87. After "begged," "a blessing" has been deleted.

come suddenly into the room where [p. 29] I was alone writing and praying for his Majesty's safe arrival, for the storm was such as if his enemies had conspired with the Prince of the power of the air.[88] Yet for that day's mercy to the King I did resolve—and have hitherto kept it—upon every Tuesday[89] to make a solemn acknowledgement of the mercy in giving God thanks for setting the crown that day upon his Majesty's head, and in most humble, fervent intercessions and supplications for his Majesty's long, holy, and prosperous reign.

One remark I must not omit, which was after the crown had been sometime upon the King's head, the weight of it made his Majesty's head to ache, for which he took it off and held it in his hand. And some from that made presages[90] of the short continuance of his Majesty's reign. But, oh, how unreasonable and irreligious is all such observations! Had I been witness of that (which my being great with child[91] made me not venture into such a crowd) I had [p. 30] interpreted rather that his Majesty took off his crown with reverence to adore the King of Kings, who had set it on his head, and in imitation of the four and twenty Elders who cast their crowns before the throne, saying: thou art worthy, O Lord, to receive glory, and honor, and power, for thou hast created all things, and for thy pleasure they are and were created (Rev. 4:10-11).[92] And no doubt, but as the weight of it upon his royal head put him in mind of the great and weighty cares that attend a crown, so the taking it off was with[93] an offering it[94] up and himself to the Lord, and seeking a blessing upon his people and himself, and[95] that that crown might be a pledge to him of that eternal crown that fadeth not,[96] but continueth forever. These and such like I believe was his Majesty's thoughts during that solemnity.[97] Now, if the best interpretations were made of doubtful things, and in[98] things that are really sinful, if they made us the more fervent in begging pardon for them, and

---

88. I.e., the Devil.

89. See "Upon Making Vows," 208-10.

90. "To make a prediction or forecast; to foretell the future," OED.

91. Halkett was pregnant with her fourth child, Jane, who was born on October 11, 1661.

92. Revelation 4:10-11: "The four and twenty elders fall down before him that sat on the throne, and worship him that liveth for ever and ever, and cast their crowns before the throne, saying, Thou art worthy, O Lord, to receive glory and honor and power: for thou hast created all things, and for thy pleasure they are and were created."

93. "With" is an interlineal insertion.

94. "It" is an interlineal insertion.

95. "And" is an interlineal insertion.

96. 1 Peter 5:4: "And when the chief Shepherd shall appear, ye shall receive a crown of glory that fadeth not away."

97. From page 25 to here, in Halkett's pagination, is reproduced in Nichols's "Appendix" to *The Autobiography of Anne Lady Halkett*, 113-15.

98. "In" is an interlineal insertion.

importuning[99] [p. 31] the throne of grace for mercy to restrain sin in ourselves,[100] and give us[101] a renewed heart, then should we sooner see the happy change I expect. And then with horror and detestation will former ways be looked upon, and those shall be best loved who most opposed vice, and were greatest examples of virtue; then shall religion flourish, righteousness and peace shall uphold the throne, for the King trusteth in the Lord, and through the mercy of the most High he shall not be moved (Ps. 21:7).[102]

And when this cometh to pass—lo, it will come—then shall they know that a prophet hath been amongst them.[103]

Now, the God of peace that brought again from the dead our Lord Jesus, that great shepherd of the sheep, through the blood of the everlasting covenant, make the King perfect in every good work to do his will, working in him that which is well pleasing in his sight, through Jesus Christ, to whom be glory forever and ever. Amen (Heb. 13:20–21).[104]

Upon the Death of Sir Robert Moray, Who Died Suddenly in June 1673.[105]

[p. 214] Solomon says, there is no remembrance of the wise more than the fool forever. And how dieth the wise man? Even as the fool (Eccles. 2:16).[106] And that all things come alike to all: there is one event to the righteous, and to the wicked, to the good and to the evil, et cetera (Eccles. 9:2).[107]

---

99. "To make persistent or pressing requests or demands; to ask, or beg for something urgently or repeatedly," OED.

100. "In ourselves" is an interlineal insertion.

101. "Us" is an interlineal insertion.

102. Psalm 21:7: "For the King trusteth in the Lord, and through the mercy of the most High he shall not be moved."

103. Ezekiel 33:33: "And when this cometh to pass, (lo, it will come,) then shall they know that a prophet hath been among them."

104. Hebrews 13:20–21: "Now the God of peace, that brought again from the dead our Lord Jesus, that great shepherd of the sheep, through the blood of the everlasting covenant, Make you perfect in every good work to do his will, working in you that which is well pleasing in his sight, through Jesus Christ; to whom be glory for ever and ever. Amen."

105. Allan dates his death as July 4, 1673, "Moray, Sir Robert," ODNB.

106. Ecclesiastes 2:16: "For there is no remembrance of the wise more than of the fool for ever; seeing that which now is in the days to come shall all be forgotten. And how dieth the wise man? as the fool."

107. Ecclesiastes 9:2: "All things come alike to all: there is one event to the righteous, and to the wicked; to the good and to the clean, and to the unclean; to him that sacrificeth, and to him that sacrificeth not: as is the good, so is the sinner; and he that sweareth, as he that feareth an oath."

And this should make all wary of passing severe censures upon the state of any that dies suddenly or by sad accidents.[108] A fiery chariot was sent to fetch Elijah into heaven, which certainly was a sudden and extraordinary translation (2 Kings 2:11).[109] And if the Lord thought fit to take this excellent person away suddenly, it was that he might not be acquainted with the terrors, and the impatience's, and the doubts, and the failings that attend even the very best when they lie long on the bed languishing. And who knows but he[110] had made it his request to be delivered from some frailties [p. 215] incident to the decays of natural strength, and therefore the Lord has taken him away thus in mercy rather than displeasure; for I am sure his life was a continued preparation for death, and therefore it could at no time surprise him.

I was once a witness of his great submission under the greatest of trials which was when his Lady[111] was dying, who had a most excellent soul lodged within a weak, frail body. I lived some considerable[112] time in the same house with her, where we were constantly together, and I may with much truth aver I never in all that time saw her the least discomposed either with grief, anger, joy, or any passion, but with a cheerful, humble, meek, obliging carriage all her behavior was. She favored me with a particular friendship and that allows freedom of converse, yet I never heard her speak ill of any (only one person she gave me caution not to be too confident of, because from her own experience she had found them not so real as they professed).[113] She had an [p. 216] excellent judgment, much wit (guarded with discretion), and all these were lustered[114] with a religious, devout life, and a real affection to her husband, who knew well how to value such a treasure as she was but thought nothing too dear to him to resign to God when he called for it. And when the time came that the Lord thought fit to take her to himself, though it was through great and the intolerable pains of childbirth of which she never was delivered. But to hear, as I did, how excellently he did exhort her to patience and submission, and though, in health, it was the greatest trouble that either of them

---

108. Although "Protestant preachers did their best to subvert the 'popish' error that a quiet, penitent, and 'lamb-like' death was a guarantee of everlasting happiness and an impatient and uncomfortable one a 'passage to endlesse woe and misery'—a legacy of the medieval *ars moriendi*," there "was a general tendency, by no means confined to narrowly puritan circles, to see sudden death in terms of vengeance visited from above"; Walsham, *Providence*, 104, 99.

109. 2 Kings 2:11: "And it came to pass, as they still went on, and talked, that, behold, there appeared a chariot of fire, and horses of fire, and parted them both asunder; and Elijah went up by a whirlwind into heaven."

110. I.e., Sir Robert Moray.

111. See *True Account*, 147.

112. "Considerable" is an interlineal insertion.

113. Her advice here parallels that of Lady Anne Howard concerning Mr. Nicholls. See *True Account*, 101, 108.

114. "To render illustrious; to render specious or attractive," *OED*.

had to think of a separation, yet such was the great torment she was in that it was her question to him, who constantly held her by the pulse, how near she was to her approaching death; and he, with much cheerfulness, assuring her that every time [p. 217/218][115] she asked that question, she was a step nearer to it. And he had so many excellent arguments to strengthen her faith and increase her confidence in her redeemer that I found more satisfaction in his discourse than in what the ministers said who came to see her, who were the best in Edinburgh, where she died. He saw her breathe her last in his arms, and with a grave, composed behavior left her, and retired himself without the show of any[116] immoderate grief. And he that thus could bear such a stroke could undoubtedly encounter any other affliction or calamity because he had a will wholly subjected to his maker, and therefore knew not how to be discontented at whatever he thought fit to do.

Though he was one of great learning and knowledge, and therefore fit for high employments, yet he never arrived to a greater honor than this testimony that the King[117] gave him when he was dead: that he might have been a companion to any Prince in Christendom.[118] And yet such was his misfortune that his life was rather a struggling with necessity than a partaker of conveniences, yet he was—as Saint Paul said—as having nothing yet possessing all things because he had learned in whatever state he was in to be contented.[119] He was very capable to give advice in any exigent,[120] but even where there[121] was most probability of success he still proposed difficulties to themselves that they might be the better armed for disappointments, and no doubt he found an advantage in it himself which made him practice it to others. And though it was not pleasing, as I know by experience, yet I found it useful. I wish all his other good examples may be

115. Here, Halkett has inserted "to follow two hundred and seventeen page in Sir Robert Moray" in the top margin of the page. From this, and the insertion sign (^) at the end of the next page, along with the blank reverse folio, it is clear that this leaf was intended to be inserted after page 217; however, perhaps because it would interrupt the next meditation, it has been inserted instead between pages 216 and 217, according to Halkett's own pagination. This insertion means that her numbering and that of the library cataloguer diverge from this point.

116. "Any" is an interlineal insertion.

117. I.e., Charles II.

118. The final two lines (from "King" to "Christendom") on this page are written in the bottom margin of the page. The King's respect for Sir Robert was attested to in life by the provision of accommodation at Whitehall and an annual pension of £300, and in death by the holding of a postmortem to investigate the cause of his sudden demise and ordering that he be buried in Westminster Abbey. Stevenson, ed., *Letters of Sir Robert Moray to the Earl of Kincardine, 1657–73*, 26, 57.

119. Philippians 4:11: "Not that I speak in respect of want; for I have learned, in whatsoever state I am, therewith to be content."

120. "A state of pressing need; a time of extreme necessity; a critical occasion, or one that requires immediate action or aid; an emergency, an extremity," *OED*.

121. After "where," "the" has been deleted and replaced by the interlineal insertion of "there."

imitated everywhere, but especially at the court where, if[122] there were many such bulwarks,[123] they might[124] keep off the inundation of that wrath which is provoked to overwhelm us (for righteous lips are the delight of Kings, and they love him that speaketh right).[125]

Upon September 24, 1673.

[p. 219] Upon this day, three year, the Lord was pleased to make me a widow. And though I desire every Saturday, being the day of the week, to have serious reflections upon that sad dispensation,[126] yet this being the day and the month on which my dearest Sir James was taken from me, it doth with more than ordinary grief affect me with the remembrance of that never to be forgotten loss.

I desire not to repine, or mourn as one without hope, but rather to turn my tears to rejoicing for the joy that I am confident he is partaking of and to be fervent in spirit serving the Lord[127] as one that expects salvation from the merits of my redeemer. And when my appointed time is come, I shall then before the throne where angels and the spirits of just men made perfect, and some of[128] all tribes and languages are they[129] shall then[130] hear the praises I shall give[131] for the mercies I enjoyed with him (that I was unworthy of, because I neither valued them as they deserved nor was I thankful for them, and therefore the [p. 220] Lord would not any longer suffer his goodness to be abused). And yet even in judgment the Lord was gracious and merciful unto me, and hath unexpectedly spared me now three years after him, and supported me under that trial (who none can judge of but those that have felt it), and given me hitherto the life of my child,[132] and hopes of his being a comfort to me if we be continued together.

The Lord hath also been pleased to give me great evidences of kindness from my son[133] and all his relations; supplied my wants; withheld creditors from being rigorous; blessed me and my family with a competent measure of health;

122. "If" is an interlineal insertion.
123. "A powerful defense or safeguard," *OED*.
124. "Might" is an interlineal insertion.
125. Proverbs 16:13: "Righteous lips are the delight of kings; and they love him that speaketh right."
126. "Ordering, management: especially the divine administration or conduct of the world; the ordering or arrangement of events by divine providence," *OED*.
127. Romans 12:11: "Not slothful in business; fervent in spirit; serving the Lord."
128. "Some of" is an interlineal insertion.
129. "Are they" is an interlineal insertion.
130. "Then" is an interlineal insertion.
131. Before "give," "then" has been deleted.
132. I.e., Robert/Robin.
133. I.e., Sir Charles Halkett.

all these are great mercies which show forth the bounty of the Lord from whence they come. But all these are as nothing to the peace I have in believing that my redeemer liveth and is ever making intercession for me.[134] And therefore, through him, I hope my praise is accepted for having kept me to this time without the least inclination to marry, and[135] that the longer I live I am the more fortified[136] [p. 221] with reasons against it,[137] and that I daily make it my prayer, Lord lead me not into that temptation but deliver me from the evil of it.[138]

I dare not make vows against marriage, lest the tempter[139] from that should be the more violent in his assaults, for I am not ignorant of his wiles; and if I make vows of widowhood and break it, I then make that a sin by my breach of vows which was no sin in itself.[140] For marriage is honorable in all, as the Apostle says,[141] and therefore I will not condemn any widows that marry, for perhaps they have reasons to justify it which might make them faulty if they did not do it. But my resolution is to be earnest at the throne of grace to be kept from the necessity of marriage, either from without or within, and to bless and magnify the Lord that, with uprightness and sincerity of heart, I[142] can say[143] that since my dearest was taken from me I did never allow my own thoughts to propose any person living to succeed him.[144] And the longer I live, I trust, through the mercy of the Lord, I shall be [p. 222] the more fixedly resolved never to change my condition, nor my life except it be to improve it more and more to all the advantages that holy widowhood is capable of: first, in being[145] wholly devoted to the service of my Lord;

---

134. Job 19:25: "For I know that my redeemer liveth, and that he shall stand at the latter day upon the earth"; Hebrews 7:25: "Wherefore he is able also to save them to the uttermost that come unto God by him, seeing he ever liveth to make intercession for them."

135. "And" is an interlineal insertion.

136. After "fortified," "against" has been deleted.

137. "It" is an interlineal insertion.

138. From "The Lord's Prayer," Matthew 6:9–15: "And lead us not into temptation, but deliver us from evil: For thine is the kingdom, and the power, and the glory, for ever. Amen" (13); Luke 1:2–4: "And forgive us our sins; for we also forgive every one that is indebted to us. And lead us not into temptation; but deliver us from evil" (4).

139. I.e., Satan.

140. See *True Account*, "Upon Making Vows," and "Introduction," 154, 208–10, 36–37.

141. Hebrews 13:4: "Marriage is honorable in all, and the bed undefiled: but whoremongers and adulterers God will judge."

142. After "heart," "and" has been deleted.

143. "Say" is an interlineal insertion.

144. Colonel Joseph Bampfield was alive and living in Holland until 1685. Marshall, "Bampfield, Joseph," *ODNB*.

145. "Being" is an interlineal insertion.

next in doing my duty to my child,[146] and the trust reposed in me by my son,[147] and endeavoring as far as I can that all I converse with may be stirred up to praise the God of my salvation. And this not by an outside merely of profession (though the Lord's livery deserves to be worn, who gives us wages) but by designing all my words and actions to that great end of bringing in all things to evidence I am dedicated to the service of the Lord.

And who more worthy to be praised who giveth songs in the night (Job 35:10).[148] And this I have reason to record from my own experience. For the first time I went into my naked[149] bed after the death of my dearest Sir James (being the same bed in which not long before he had breathed out his soul to him from whom he had received it) while his dead clay[150] lay in [p. 223] the room by me, as soon as I laid me down (with hopes of some rest not having been in a bed in eight nights before) I heard so sweet a harmony of music as if the angels[151] themselves had taken several instruments to praise our God for bringing another son to glory. It was no dream for I was as fully awake as I am now at the writing of it, and I sat up in my bed to try if I could hear it more distinctly; but I found it all alike, when I lay or sat up, it was soft but so ravishing[152] that it made me quite forget my grief. And though I have often heard the most exquisite music that could be composed in England, at masques[153] or other great solemnities, yet all those were nothing to be compared to that sweet, soft harmony that then I heard,

---

146. I.e., Robert/Robin.

147. I.e., Sir Charles Halkett.

148. Job 35:10: "But none saith, where is God my maker, who giveth songs in the night."

149. According to the *OED*, "naked bed" is "one's bed (originally with reference to the practice of sleeping naked)." However, in this context, Halkett is more likely alluding to the extended sense of "naked" as "lacking in something, bare, inadequate," *OED*.

150. I.e., his body.

151. As Joad Raymond states, "angels were very much alive in Protestant Britain"; Raymond, *Milton's Angels: The Early-Modern Imagination* (Oxford: Oxford University Press, 2010), 1. Despite the Reformation, angels retain an important role in relation to the *ars moriendi* (the art of dying well), as demonstrated by Peter Marshall, "Angels around the Deathbed: Variations on a Theme in the English Art of Dying," in *Angels in the Early Modern World*, ed. Peter Marshall and Alexandra Walsham (Cambridge: Cambridge University Press, 2006), 83–103.

152. "That excites ecstasy, strong emotion, or sensuous pleasure; entrancing; overpowering," *OED*.

153. "A form of courtly dramatic entertainment, often richly symbolic, in which music and dancing played a substantial part, costumes and stage machinery tended to be elaborate, and the audience might be invited to contribute to the action or the dancing"; it "became a clearly defined genre during the reigns of James I/VI and Charles I," *OED*. In contrast to the public theatres, women, including queens such as Anna of Denmark and Henrietta Maria, participated fully in these performances; Clare McManus, *Women on the Renaissance Stage: Anna of Denmark and Female Masquing in the Stuart Court, 1590–1619* (Manchester: Manchester University Press, 2002); Karen Britland, *Drama at the Courts of Queen Henrietta Maria* (Cambridge: Cambridge University Press, 2006).

and continued near an hour. What it was I cannot determine, for I desire not to think (of myself) above what is written (1 Cor. 4:6).[154] But this I may conclude that the Lord thought fit by that means, [p. 224] whatever it was, to divert that flood of grief that might without his help have[155] overwhelmed me, and turned my tears into joy; for I could not but with an elevated soul magnify the Lord, who was so greatly to be praised.[156]

For that particular mercy, and for all the supports I have had since; for many evident testimonies of the Lord's spirit in leading me through difficulties; for many good resolutions and intentions of future obedience; for all these, and whatever else I have received, I adore and bless the great, omnipotent God, and supplicate the continuance of all things necessary for life and godliness. And if trouble or sickness, want and distress, or death be thought fit to send me to purge away sin, Lord, let this be the fruits of it: that it may increase faith, and patience, and entire submission to thy will. But whatever way I am tried, oh let not sin be my punishment, but let pure and unspotted widowhood be my guide even unto death. Lord, stablish thy word unto thy servant, who is devoted to thy fear (Ps. 119:8).[157] Amen.

January 30, 1673/4.[158]

[p. 269] As great public mercies should never be forgot, no more should public sins and punishments: the one to excite our praise, and the other, our repentance. And no day in our age deserves more to be remembered with humility, grief, and detestation than this on which was murdered a good King by his own rebellious subjects (which was not only a reproach to all within his Majesty's dominions, but a blot upon all that are called Christians).

That the guilt of that day's sin, and all the procedure to it, and aggravation of it may be pardoned, for this continually I will pray. Lord, enter not into judgment with us but forgive all the sins that relate to that day's judgment, and visit them not on future generations, which we may expect if thou wilt be pleased to

---

154. 1 Corinthians 4:6: "And these things, brethren, I have in a figure transferred to myself and to Apollos for your sakes; that ye might learn in us not to think of men above that which is written, that no one of you be puffed up for one against another."

155. "Have" is an interlineal insertion.

156. An echo of the opening of the Magnificat, Luke 1:46–55, especially verses 46–47: "And Mary said, My soul doth magnify the Lord, and my spirit hath rejoiced in God my Savior."

157. Psalm 119:38: "Stablish thy word unto thy servant, who is devoted to thy fear."

158. See also "Upon the Fast which by Proclamation Was Kept, January 30, 1660/1," "January 30, 1690/1," and "Saturday, January 30, 1696/7," 205–7, 284–85, 304–7.

give us grace to live so as to redeem the time because our former days hath been exceeding evil.[159] Amen.[160]

Upon a Proposal.[161]

[p. 309] Yesterday, being Tuesday, September 1, 1674,[162] a near relation very seriously enquired of me if I intended to marry, to which very freely and frankly I answered that I was as fully resolved as I could be of anything never to marry. But wondering a little how he came to question it, he told me he knew it would be proposed to me by one I highly honored, who, being enquired of by a very near relation of his[163] where to make choice for a wife, had recommended me and, he being satisfied, the next thing was to try me.

I said I could not but think myself infinitely obliged to both persons for their good opinion and the honor they intended me, but I proposed greater satisfaction to myself in this single[164] life than in being a wife to any[165] (having no greater ambition than to serve God, and to endeavor to do that duty to my child[166] as to show I had not forgot the memory of his dear father).[167]

To this he answers, "You will in this have more opportunity to do him good; for he will seek nothing with you and will settle good condition on you if he die before you."

"I entreat you," said I, "leave this discourse," [p. 310] and by my tears he saw how unwelcome it was.[168]

As soon as I could retire alone with bended knees, and sighs, and tears I offered up my supplication to my God (to whom I gave all the interest I had of myself long since to be disposed of by him), and from him I will expect assistance and strength to resist this temptation which may lead me into that snare that may overturn all my resolutions that I thought inflexible.

---

159. Ephesians 5:15–16: "See then that ye walk circumspectly, not as fools, but as wise, redeeming the time, because the days are evil."
160. The last three words are written in the bottom margin of the page.
161. See also Trill, ed., *Halkett*, 48–49.
162. "1674" is an interlineal insertion.
163. "Of his" is an interlineal insertion.
164. "Single" is an interlineal insertion.
165. "Than in being a wife to any" is an interlineal insertion.
166. I.e., Robert/Robin.
167. I.e., Sir James Halkett.
168. Halkett represents herself as tearful on several occasions in the *True Account*; however, the closest analogous situation is when Sir James begins to talk of marriage after the revelation that Bampfield's wife is certainly alive, 154.

I confess it is the only thing that, in my own thoughts, often I laid before me as the greatest motive to tempt me to marry: where I might visibly see a means to be more helpful to my child,[169] and his father's family, and enabled to pay my debts, and be more useful to the poor, if this might be done without wrong to others (for anything that were got by fraud or injustice could not be an acceptable sacrifice to God). And here, in this proposal, all this seems to be for his quality and riches are far beyond what I might expect. And yet when I consider how much I may by such a change be tempted with pride, ambition, sensuality, [p. 311] and many other things that attend such a condition, then I think myself fully fixed and strengthened to resist all assaults, and to place more true content in my quiet retirement than in all the greatness that the other condition promises.

I do not question but if all that wished me well knew what were in my offer, they would condemn me for refusing it. But I am better judges than they of my own happiness. And if the Lord thought fit, by what means he saw best, to give me of my own that I have right to (with which I might help my son to pay his debts, settle my child in a competent provision, and pay everyone that I am indebted to) I should then[170] prefer my present condition before marriage with any person living.

Lord, all my thoughts and desires are before thee, and thou knowest that—with all the sincerity of my heart—I have formerly and do again renew the offering up of myself [p. 312] entirely to the disposal of thy will, and I desire to have no will of my own. But, Lord, order and dispose of this, and all things that concern me, as is most for thy glory and my being serviceable to thee, who I hope will never let me be forgetful of my former resolutions and that I am devoted to thy fear.[171]

---

169. I.e., Robert/Robin.

170. "Then" is an interlineal insertion.

171. Psalm 119:38: "Stablish thy word unto thy servant, who is devoted to thy fear."

The Art of Divine Chemistry and Select Meditations *(1676–1678)*

Although Couper lists a start date of 1677, a note on the first page in Halkett's hand declares this volume was "begun June 20, 1676," and she dates the completion of "The Art of Divine Chemistry" as Saturday, September 2, 1676; another note at the end of the final page confirms this volume was "ended December 5, 1678."[1] As these examples suggest, by this volume Halkett has become more precise in recording both the start and the end dates not only of her volumes but also of the individual meditations within them. It is also this volume that enables us to date the composition of *A True Account of My Life* as between September 11, 1677, and April 21, 1678.[2]

There is no extant table of contents for this volume, although with the exception of the date, Couper's catalogue is accurate: after the titular entry, the other select meditations comprise: "The Rule for Thoughts, Begun Monday, September 4, 1676",[3] "The Rule for Action What We Are to Do";[4] "The Rule for Words, Ended September 10, 1677";[5] "Meditations upon Psalm 106:4–5, Begun Monday, April 22, 1678";[6] and "Meditations and Prayers Concerning the King, Begun Tuesday, November 26, 1678."[7] Not included in Halkett's list is the only entry within this volume that might be characterized as "occasional"; "finding [perhaps having inadvertently turned over two pages] an empty place here and a loose paper writ by me, (Saturday, September 30, 1676) in which there is something fit for me to remember, I have inserted it as a memorial of what I then thought and desired" (which was to be released from sin throughout her widowhood by God's grace).[8] Here, then, we have both some insight into the time of writing particular entries and a confirmation that her "books" were only part of Halkett's textual output. Couper's list notes the existence of several "stitched books" that have not survived, but here, and elsewhere, Halkett reminds us that she also wrote on loose papers. A further scrap of paper, inserted at the end of this volume, simply reads: "The Popish Plot; the Phanatical Plot; the Pharisaical Plot, from which Good Lord deliver us."[9] In her "Meditations and Prayers Concerning the King," Halkett views "The Popish Plot" in particular as a justification for her continual prayers for the King:

1. Halkett, *The Art of Divine Chemistry*, pp. i, 56, iii. This is volume 12 in Couper's catalogue.
2. See "Meditations upon Psalm 106:4–5," 264–65.
3. Halkett, *The Art of Divine Chemistry*, pp. 57–201.
4. Halkett, *The Art of Divine Chemistry*, pp. 202–58.
5. Halkett, *The Art of Divine Chemistry*, pp. 259–91.
6. Halkett, *The Art of Divine Chemistry*, pp. 294–370.
7. Halkett, *The Art of Divine Chemistry*, pp. 371–80.
8. Halkett, *The Art of Divine Chemistry*, pp. 292–93.
9. Halkett, *The Art of Divine Chemistry*, p. ii.

When I consider what wonders God hath done in preserving the King, both abroad and at home, and particularly this late deliverance from that horrid conspiracy (which hath been of so long a contrivance and so secretly carried on, though many were involved in it, and yet never discovered until the moment it should have been performed) in which disappointment of their designs the hand of God was so visibly seen that by the remorse of one of the conspirators others were detected, and daily more and more light is given to discover that detestable work of darkness. What an encouragement is this to persist in the duty of making prayers for the King continually, when such a return of prayer is granted as not only the King's life is spared, but with it our lives and laws preserved, and what is the greatest mercy of all, our religion which should be, and undoubtedly is, dearer to all true Protestants than all things else besides.[10]

The Art of Divine Chemistry.

[p. 1] It is natural for all persons to please themselves in pursuing what is most suitable to their inclination,[11] and to aim at an eminency in whatever profession their genius[12] leads them to from which many hath arrived to great knowledge in several arts and sciences.

Now, I, being by profession[13] a Christian, and my inclination through grace leading me to a calm, serene temper of soul, I now resolve by the divine assistance to extract good out of all the cross occurrences I have met withal of late. And not only out of them but from whatever else shall arrive to me, or others within my knowledge, I shall endeavor to make useful for the increase of patience, humility, charity, and contentedness that in all things God may be glorified.[14]

And this will I do, if God permit (Heb. 6:3).[15] Now the God of hope, patience, and consolation fill me with all joy and peace in believing that I[16] may

---

10. Halkett, *The Art of Divine Chemistry*, pp. 378–79.
11. "The overall or innate disposition of a person or animal; nature, character," *OED*.
12. "Natural ability or capacity; quality of mind; attributes which suit a person for his or her peculiar work," *OED*.
13. "The declaration of belief in and obedience to religion, or of acceptance of and conformity to the faith and principles of any religious community; (hence) the faith or religion which a person professes," *OED*.
14. See also, "What Crosses and Difficulties I Have Met with Myself," 307–11.
15. Hebrews 6:3: "And this will I do, if God permit."
16. Romans 15:13: "Now the God of hope fill you with all joy and peace in believing, that ye may abound in hope, through the power of the Holy Ghost."

abound in hope, and be assisted in what now I design through the power of the Holy Ghost (Rom. 15:13). Amen.[17]

[p. 2] Although affliction cometh not forth of the dust, neither doth trouble spring out of the ground, yet man is born to trouble as the sparks fly upward (Job 5:6–7).[18]

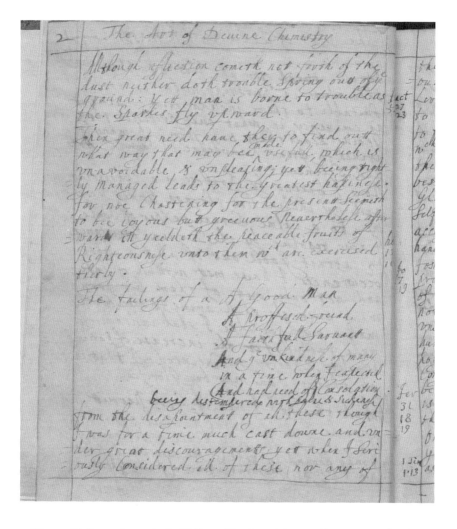

Figure 12. From Anne, Lady Halkett, *The Art of Divine Chemistry and Select Meditations* (1676–1678). © National Library of Scotland, NLS, MS 6494, p. 2. Reproduced with permission.

17. "Amen" is in the bottom margin as ruled by Halkett.

18. Job 5:6–7: "Although affliction cometh not forth of the dust, neither doth trouble spring out of the ground; Yet man is born unto trouble, as the sparks fly upward."

Then great need have they to find out what way that may be made[19] useful which is unavoidable and unpleasing, yet, being rightly managed, leads to the greatest happiness. For no chastening for the present seemeth to be joyous, but grievous: nevertheless, afterward[20] it yieldeth the peaceable fruits of righteousness unto them which are exercised thereby (Heb. 12:11).[21]

> The failings of: a good man; a professed friend; a faithful servant; and the unkindness of many in a time when I expected and had need of consolation, being distempered with palsy[22] and sickness:

from the disappointment of all these, though I was for a time much cast down and under great discouragements, yet, when I seriously considered all of these—nor any of [p. 3] them—could not have arrived to me without the permission and appointment of the Lord (whose I am and who I desire in all things to obey), and therefore my business must be to find out what my sin hath been for which the Lord hath thought fit to give me these trials, and what is[23] the best use of them to make them bring most glory to God, and most advantage to myself. And if these be the fruits, the Lord will accept of them, I hope, as the work of his own hands.

Joshua, by the affectionate compellation[24] of my[25] son, prayed Achan to give glory to the Lord God of Israel by making confession of sin to him (Jos. 7:19).[26] Not that confession informs him of anything unknown unto him, but as it is a means of humbling the sinner and exalting the great and holy God, who vouchsafes to have pity and compassion upon those who, like Ephraim,[27] bemoans themselves, and confesses, and repents, and is ashamed, and confounded for the sins of their youth (Jer. 31:18–19).[28]

---

19. "Made" is an interlineal insertion.

20. Here, Halkett has crossed through a final "s."

21. Hebrews 12:11: "Now no chastening for the present seemeth to be joyous, but grievous: nevertheless, afterward it yieldeth the peaceable fruit of righteousness unto them which are exercised thereby."

22. "Paralysis or paresis (weakness) of all or part of the body, sometimes with tremor," OED.

23. After "is," "the use of" has been deleted.

24. "Addressing by a particular name or title," OED.

25. "My" is an interlineal insertion.

26. Joshua 7:19: "And Joshua said unto Achan, my son, give, I pray thee, glory to the Lord God of Israel, and make confession unto him; and tell me now what thou hast done; hide it not from me."

27. After "Ephraim," "who" has been deleted.

28. Jeremiah 31:18–19: "I have surely heard Ephraim bemoaning himself thus; Thou hast chastised me, and I was chastised, as a bullock unaccustomed to the yoke: turn thou me, and I shall be turned; for thou art the Lord my God. Surely after that I was turned, I repented; and after that I was instructed, I smote upon my thigh: I was ashamed, yea, even confounded, because I did bear the reproach of my youth."

Oh, that my sins had been confined only to youth, then I might have pleaded ignorance, as Saint Paul did for which he obtained mercy (1 Tim. 1:13).[29] [p. 4] But now, in my old age, after fifty years' experience of the infinite mercy of God, of the deceitfulness of my own heart, of the imperfection that is in all mankind, and the vigilency[30] of Satan to make use of all these to the utmost of his power for my destruction: oh, why was I not then more watchful to restrain my thoughts, and words, and actions from being too much placed upon any earthly satisfaction?

I confess, I thought my designs so innocent and allowable that I gave way to entertain myself with the advantages that I might have by the converse of a pious man, from whom I expected more of his care and conduct while I lived. And I had not the fear of having any suspect me guilty of my breach of resolution (I dare not call it vow) of holy widowhood because all that saw or knew my converse with him believed, as I did, that his affections were placed upon another. And even in that I had a satisfaction because I had a kindness for her, and therefore did from both expect their care of my dear child if they survived me, [p. 5] and of whatever else I intended to have recommended to their care.[31]

But the event hath shown what Solomon affirms: the lot is cast into the lap, but the disposing thereof is from the Lord.[32]

Shall I then blame him or any other[33] for all the disquiet, both at home and abroad, that I have met with from the unjust scandals of lying and malicious tongues?[34] No, my Lord God, I will complain to none but unto thee, my God, nor of none but myself.

For had I not offended thee, none of these troubles had arrived to me, and what reason have I to magnify thy name: who will rather deliver up those who I thought more than ordinary of to do things displeasing unto thee, rather than I should want a rod to drive me nearer to thee?

Known to thee, O God, are all the troubles of my life and what of late hath encompassed me about so that I have no refuge but to fly to thee to whom I do lift up my soul.[35] Oh, save me and deliver me, and hold up my goings in thy paths that my footsteps slip not (Ps. 17:5) [36] [p. 6] wherein I have failed, though it was but in thinking better of some than they deserved. I beg pardon for his sake who hath

---

29. 1 Timothy 1:13: "Who was before a blasphemer, and a persecutor, and injurious: but I obtained mercy, because I did it ignorantly in unbelief."

30. "Watchfulness; alertness or closeness of observation," *OED*.

31. See Trill, "Critical Categories," 113–15.

32. Proverbs 16:33: "The lot is cast into the lap; but the whole disposing thereof is of the Lord."

33. After "other," "than" has been added as an interlineal insertion but is also crossed out.

34. See also "The Great Conquest, or the Power of Faith," 176–84.

35. There are echoes of the Psalms in "refuge" (eighteen references in the book of Psalms), and "lift up my soul" (25:1, 86:4, 143:8).

36. Psalm 17:5: "Hold up my goings in thy paths, that my footsteps slip not."

said: whatsoever you shall ask the father in my name, that will I do (John 14:13).[37] And for his intercession I seek grace to prevent what I might do if not assisted by thee, and that the remainder of my days may be wholly spent in the study of this art of divine chemistry: so shall I extract such cordials as may be useful to myself or others if, when I am dead, my Lord thinks fit to make them visible.

The Rule for Action.

[p. 233] And here I cannot but insert the satisfaction which this last night's dream afforded me though I use not much to observe them. Yet since it was prophesied that old men should dream dreams,[38] by which certainly is meant dreams that should be correspondent[39] with visions that young men should see, this may be some ground [p. 234] for me (that am an old woman) not to seclude[40] myself from what that dream may, I hope, promise.[41]

It was this: I thought the person (whose kindnesses I have endeavored to obtain with all the performances of love and respect that I was capable to express) who of late hath—by some mistake—been very unkind, and to justify their unkindness hath endeavored to cast an odium[42] upon me to severals[43] where it might do me prejudices, I thought this person came to me in a riding habit, and told me he was to go a great journey, and had ridden[44] six miles of it, and his heart had smote[45] him for going away without acknowledging he had injured me. And being now convinced of his error, he had rid back again to beg my pardon, and

---

37. John 14:13: "And whatsoever ye shall ask in my name, that will I do, that the Father may be glorified in the Son."

38. Joel 2:28: "And it shall come to pass afterward, that I will pour out my spirit upon all flesh; and your sons and your daughters shall prophesy, your old men shall dream dreams, your young men shall see visions." Joel's prophecy is also cited in Acts 2:16–21, specifically verse 17: "And it shall come to pass in the last days, saith God, I will pour out of my spirit upon all flesh: and your sons and your daughters shall prophesy, and your young men shall see visions, and your old men shall dream dreams."

39. "Answering to or agreeing with something else in the way of likeness of relation or analogy; analogous, or having an analogous relation to," *OED*.

40. "To debar from a privilege, advantage, dignity, succession, etc.; to prevent from doing something," *OED*.

41. On the problematic nature of dreams in early modern England, see S. J. Wiseman, "Introduction: Reading the Early Modern Dream," in *Reading the Early Modern Dream: The Terrors of the Night*, ed. Katharine Hodgkin, Michelle O'Callaghan, and S. J. Wiseman (New York; London: Routledge, 2008), 1–13.

42. "The reproach or shame attached to or incurred by a particular act or fact; opprobrium; disgrace. Also: an instance of this; a taint, slur," *OED*.

43. "Several persons or things," *OED*.

44. "Ride" in original MS.

45. "To punish or afflict in a notable way," *OED*.

be reconciled to me before he went away. I thought he spoke [p. 235] this with so great a sense[46] that tears was in his eyes, and by sympathy drew tears from mine (though from different reasons, for my tears proceeded from joy that he was convinced of his error). And I gave him all the testimonies of it by assuring him, though it was a very great trouble to me to find his unkindness, and the effects of it, yet it had no way lessened my affection which should be ever to him and my own.

And with this I wakened with contentment and hope that by this dream God will give me an answer of peace. He that is the God of peace hath said (and I will hope I may apply it to myself): I know the thoughts that I think towards you, says the Lord, thoughts of peace, and not of evil, to give you an expected end.[47] This was not spoken to them that were without sin but to those who for their transgression was carried captive to Babylon. And though sin hath brought me under captivity, and that the Lord in [p. 236] his justice hath thought fit to punish me, yet I will hope for deliverance and an expected end.[48]

Meditations upon Psalm 106:4–5, Begun Monday, April 22, 1678.

[p. 294] Though it be long since I left off what is hitherto writ here,[49] yet the occasion of it may be of some advantage to me, if the Lord sees fit to give a seasonable opportunity to divulge it: by representing my unparalleled misfortunes, and the wonderful power and mercy of God in supporting me under them, which, being an evidence of the Lord's compassion, may incline others to the greater charity, whose severe censure of me occasioned an interruption to the conclusion of this book to relate a true account of my life. What effects it may produce I leave to him to whom I resign the entire disposal of all that concerns me.

I have been this long time considering what to fix my meditation upon and no place of Holy Scripture can I find more proper now than what, I hope, I am directed to by the dictates of the blessed [p. 295] spirit of God, who first inspired his servant to record it seasonably, having been for some time under a cloud in my private condition (by the Sun of Righteousness withdrawing of himself) and the public divisions (both in church and state threatens much wrath and ruin);[50] that

---

46. "Capacity for mental sensitivity or responsiveness; sensibility," *OED*.

47. Jeremiah 29:11: "For I know the thoughts that I think toward you, saith the Lord, thoughts of peace, and not of evil, to give you an expected end."

48. On interpreting early modern dreams, see Katharine Hodgkin, "Dreaming Meanings: Some Early Modern Dream Thoughts," in *Reading the Early Modern Dream*, ed. Katharine Hodgkin et al., 109–24.

49. The previous substantive entry is noted by Halkett to have been "ended September 10, 1677"; Halkett, *The Art of Divine Chemistry*, p. 291.

50. At the time of writing, there were rivalries between the powerful Earls in Scotland (Hamilton and Lauderdale), and the Popish Plot was about to emerge; Hutton, *Charles II*, 350–54, 357–64; Harris,

from both these considerations I shall make use of the Psalmist's words, and[51] to the same God of mercy to whom he addressed himself will I make supplication, and say, as he:

Remember me, O Lord, with the favor that thou bearest unto thy people: O visit me with thy salvation:

That I may see the goodness of thy chosen, that I may rejoice in the gladness of thy nation, that I may glory with thy inheritance (Ps. 106:4–5).[52]

Restoration, 136–37.

51. After "and," "from" has been deleted and replaced by "to" in an interlineal insertion.

52. Psalm 106:4–5. Apart from changing "good" to "goodness" in verse 6, Halkett's text follows the KJV. Psalm 106 is to be read during evening prayer on the twenty-first day of the month, *BCP*, 569. According to Calvin, this Psalm is "a confession of [Israel's] sins, in order to the obtaining the pardon of them. For the prophet commences with the praises of God, with the design of encouraging both himself and others to cherish good hope in him. Then he prays that God would continue his blessing to the seed of Abraham. But because the people, after so frequently revolting from God, were unworthy of the continuation of his kindness, he asks pardon to be extended to them, and this after he had confessed that from first to last, they had provoked God's wrath by their malice, ingratitude, pride, perfidy, and other vices," *Calvin's Commentaries*, vol. 11, *Psalms, Part IV*, trans. John King (1847–1850), accessed July 23, 2018, http://www.sacred-texts.com/chr/calvin/cc11/cc11014.htm.

Meditations on St. Peter, the Passion, and Occasional Meditations (1686/7–1688)

Although Halkett does not provide a start date for this volume on the inside cover, a note in Halkett's hand on the remains of some paper glued to the spine indicates the volume was "begun January 8[x], ended 18 M[ay] 1688." The opening meditation is dated January 24, 1686/7, and the end date is inscribed in Halkett's hand on the inside of the volume's back cover.[1] The volume opens with a preparatory deliberation on the meaning of meditation: "Meditation is the life of action," which reflects Halkett's concern that if she does not perform this activity properly she may "profane a holy duty."[2] There follow two, very small, inserted items: the first, "Observation Monday, February 6, 1687/8, upon reading Leviticus 8:22–24," concludes with a reference to Psalm 26:12;[3] the second contains a short quotation from *The Godly Man's Sanctuary* and a reference.[4] Halkett's list of this volume's contents separates her select meditations from her occasional entries;[5] however, in the main body of her text, there are no title pages, and the materials are identified primarily by date rather than by subject matter. There are two select meditations: first, "Meditations on What Is Recorded of St. Peter in the Gospels," which were "ended July 28, 1687";[6] the second, "Meditations on the Passion of Our Lord, Divided into Seven Periods, According to the Days of the Week," was begun "Monday, August 15, 1687," and "ended Wednesday, January 25, 1687/8."[7]

---

1. Halkett, *Meditations on St. Peter*, p. i, vii. This is volume 16 in Couper's catalogue.

2. Halkett, *Meditations on St. Peter*, p. i.

3. Halkett, *Meditations on St. Peter*, pp. iii–iv. Leviticus 8:22–24: "And he brought the other ram, the ram of consecration: and Aaron and his sons laid their hands upon the head of the ram. And he slew it; and Moses took the blood of it upon the tip of Aaron's right ear, and upon the thumb of his right hand, and upon the great toe of his right foot. And he brought Aaron's sons, and Moses put of the blood upon the tip of their right ear, and upon the thumbs of their right hand, and upon the great toes of their right feet: and Moses sprinkled the blood upon the altar round about"; Psalm 26:12: "My foot standeth in an even place: in the congregations will I bless the Lord."

4. Halkett, *Meditations on St. Peter*, p. v. Halkett abbreviates the title of a book by R[ichard] A[lleine], *The Godly Mans Portion and Sanctuary Opened, in Two Sermons, Preached August 17, 1662* (London: [s.n.], 1664?). ESTC R214832. The passage she cites is "Come not together to strengthen parties or propagate opinions: Let all matters of controversy be waved; and hereof let there be such mutual assurance given aforehand, that you may be together, without fear of becoming thorns or snares one to another," 143. The page reference, however, relates to a longer exhortation against divisions within the church that calls for "peace and union" instead, 138.

5. Halkett, *Meditations on St. Peter*, p. vii.

6. Halkett, *Meditations on St. Peter*, pp. 1–122.

7. Halkett, *Meditations on St. Peter*, pp. 123–273. Halkett's meticulous dating of her entries reveals that she actually started writing these entries on successive days of the week: "Monday, August 15," Gethsemane, pp. 123–36; "Tuesday, September 6, 1687," Judas and kiss, pp. 137–51; "Wednesday,

Although not included in her index, on the next page Halkett writes what looks like an occasional meditation in layout but in content provides a reflection on the previous meditation with the request that God help her be "the body of Christ."[8] The occasional meditations begin with an entry dated Tuesday, May 3, 1687, and conclude with one dated May 15, 1688.[9] In this volume, there is no separate list of the occasional meditations' contents, nor are they given titles; instead, they are identified solely by their date of composition.

Sunday, May 29, 1687.

[p. 283] This day was ordained twenty-seven years since to be ever remembered with solemn thanksgiving for the goodness of God in returning to us our King and Princes in peace and safety, and establishing the church and state according to the former government, which was a thing so wonderful when the Lord turned our captivity that we were like them that dream (Ps. 126:1).[10] And it is to be feared with too, too many, it is passed away as a dream and remembered no more.[11] But, whatever others do, while I live I will—as daily as this day recurs—bless and exalt thy name, holy Lord God, for this day's mercies and all the blessings which by it we have enjoyed. And will continually pray that as thou hast the heart of Kings in thy hands, and can turn it as the rivers of water whither-soever thou wilt so be pleased (Pro. 21:1),[12] I beseech thee to turn the King's[13] heart so entirely to thy self that thy honor and glory may be his chief delight; and then thou wilt honor him, and bless him with long life, and show him thy salvation. Amen, and amen.

September 28, 1687," appearance before Caiaphas and false witnesses, pp. 152–68; "Thursday, October 20, 1687," delivery to Pontius Pilate, pp. 169–88; "Friday, November 11, 1687," Simon of Cyrene and carrying of cross, pp. 189–227; "Saturday, December 10, 1687," Joseph of Arimathea and request for Christ's body, pp. 228–39; "Sunday, December 18, 1687," the two Marys visit the sepulcher, pp. 240–73, "ended Wednesday, January 25, 1687/8."

8. Halkett, *Meditations on St. Peter*, p. 274.

9. Halkett, *Meditations on St. Peter*, pp. 275, 390–92.

10. Psalm 126:1: "When the Lord turned again the captivity of Zion, we were like them that dream." See *True Account*, and "Upon the Return of His Majesty," 88, 195. See also Anne, Lady Halkett, *Joseph's Trial and Triumph* (1678/9–1681), NLS, MS 6495, p. 70, and "Saturday, May 29, 1697," in Halkett, *Select and Occasional Meditations* (1696–1697), pp. 235–37. Halkett also includes two entries celebrating King James VII/II's birthday. See "October 14, 1687" and "Wednesday, October 14, 1696," 269–70, 302–304.

11. Cressy, *Bonfires and Bells*, 171–89. See *True Account*, and "January 30, 1690/1," 88, 284.

12. Proverbs 21:1: "The King's heart is in the hand of the Lord as the rivers of water: he turneth it whithersoever he will."

13. By this date, King "James [who] came to the throne following the death of Charles II on 6 February 1685," Speck, "James II and VII," *ODNB*.

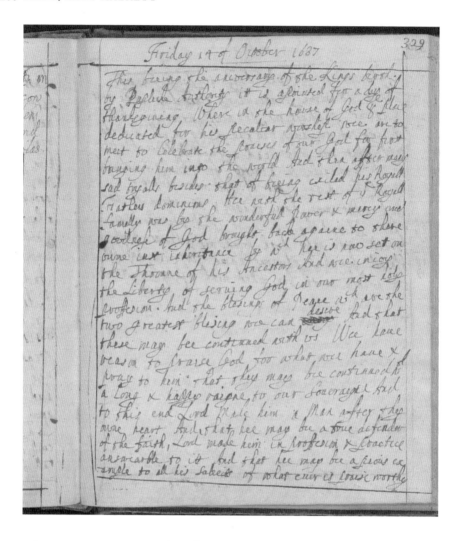

Figure 13. From Anne, Lady Halkett, *Meditations on St. Peter, the Passion, and Occasional Meditations* (1686/7–1688). © National Library of Scotland, NLS, MS 6497, p. 329. Reproduced with permission.

Friday, October 14, 1687.

[p. 329] This being the anniversary of the King's birth,[14] by public authority it is appointed for a day of thanksgiving.[15] Where—in the house of God, the place dedicated for his peculiar[16] worship—we are to meet to celebrate the praises of our God; for, first, bringing him into the world; and then (after many sad trials, besides that of being exiled his royal father's dominions) he, with the rest of the royal family, was by the wonderful power, and mercy, and goodness of God brought back again to their own just inheritance by which he is now set on the throne of his ancestors. And we enjoy the liberty of serving God in our most holy profession[17] and the blessings of peace, which are the two greatest blessings we can desire.[18] And that these may be continued with us, we have reason to praise God for what we have, and pray to him that they may be continued with a long and happy reign to our Sovereign. And to this end, Lord make him a man after thy own heart,[19] and that he may be a true defender of the faith, Lord make him in profession and practice answerable to it, and that he may be a pious example to all his subjects of whatever is praiseworthy.

[p. 330] Thus, as we ought daily to pray for the King, so more particularly this day we must present supplications, prayers, intercession, and giving of thanks for the King and all in authority that we may lead a quiet and peaceable life in all godliness and honesty; for this is good and acceptable in the sight of God our Savior (1 Tim. 2:1–3).[20]

And that we have reason and occasion to do this, blessed be the Lord God, the God of Israel, who only doth wondrous things. And blessed be his glorious

---

14. I.e., James VII/II.

15. King James VII/II, "A Proclamation, for an Anniversary Thanksgiving, in Commemoration of His Majesties Happy Birthday, Being the Fourteenth Day of October" (Edinburgh: Andrew Anderson, 1685). ESTC R18754. Halkett explores the biblical authority for celebrating monarch's birthdays in *Meditations upon the Book of Jonah* (1683/4–1685), NLS, MS 6496, pp. 88–89.

16. "Distinguished in nature, character, or attributes; unlike others; special, remarkable; distinctive," *OED*.

17. "The declaration of belief in and obedience to religion, or of acceptance of and conformity to the faith and principles of any religious community; (hence) the faith or religion which a person professes," *OED*.

18. "Desire" is an interlineal insertion, replacing the deleted "enjoy."

19. Acts 13:22: "And when he had removed him, he raised up unto them David to be their king; to whom also he gave testimony, and said, I have found David the son of Jesse, a man after mine own heart, which shall fulfil all my will."

20. 1 Timothy 2:1–3: "I exhort therefore, that, first of all, supplications, prayers, intercessions, and giving of thanks, be made for all men; For kings, and for all that are in authority; that we may lead a quiet and peaceable life in all godliness and honesty. For this is good and acceptable in the sight of God our Savior."

name for ever, and let the whole earth be filled with his glory. Amen, and amen (Ps. 72:18–19).[21]

Friday, March 30, 1688.

[p. 365] What day is there passes over my head wherein I have not great manifestation of the goodness of God in pardoning my transgressions or dealing with me as if I had never transgressed? Which should more humble me than all that can be inflicted to punish me,[22] for the one were but justly what I do deserve, and the other flows merely from the bounty and beneficence[23] of my most gracious God, to whom praise and adoration doth belong.

Yesterday, very early, there came an express to me from my Lady Marquess of Atholl[24] with much earnestness desiring me to come and see her daughter (who had been long disordered with a sore breast),[25] offering any accommodation either of horse or coach to transport me, which I would willingly have complied with if my health and strength would have allowed me; for though they were both more than I deserve considering my age, yet it were not rational to undertake the journey considering the charge under my care, and the debt I am still in which obliges me to be the more careful of myself lest others suffer by my death.

While [p. 366] I was writing my excuse, and preparing more of the same things to send that my Lady writ had done good, the Lady Pittencrieff[26] and her husband came to me (having been desired by my Lady Atholl to persuade me to the journey, who I convinced of my unfitness for it). But, by their being here, I took occasion to tell them of one who, the night before, had been recommended to my endeavors to assist her to employment, which my own inclination would prompt me enough to (being both a stranger and a widow which are such as the

---

21. Psalm 72:18–19: "Blessed be the Lord God, the God of Israel, who only doeth wondrous things. And blessed be his glorious name for ever: and let the whole earth be filled with his glory; Amen, and amen."

22. "To punish me" is an interlineal insertion.

23. "Doing good, the manifestation of benevolence or kindly feeling, active kindness," *OED*.

24. Lady Amelia Sophia (1633–1703), daughter of James Stanley, seventh earl of Derby, married John Murray, second Earl and First Marquess of Atholl, on May 5, 1659. See David Stevenson, "Murray, John, First Marquess of Atholl (1631–1703)," *ODNB*.

25. Lady Amelia Murray, who married Hugh Fraser, ninth Lord Fraser of Lovat, in 1685. The couple had at least five children, *BP* 1:134; *TCP* 8:191, 3:546; *TCB* 4:292.

26. Pittencrieff was a property of Dunfermline Abbey, and passed to the Earls of Dunfermline, and then to the Wemyss family after the Reformation. The property went to the Clerks in the seventeenth century, and Sir Alexander Clerk of Pittencrieff built the house. "Pittencrieff House," The Castles of Scotland, accessed August 08, 2016, https://www.thecastlesofscotland.co.uk/the-best-castles/stately-homes-and-mansions/pittencrieff-house.

Lord compassionates,[27] and provides for, and commands to love by the consideration of having been a stranger myself [Deut. 10:18–19]).[28] As I had charity in my design for her, so as a reward for my intention, whatever the success be, I received a satisfactory letter last night from my dear child confirming me of his continuing steadfast in the truth[29] for all the changes of others. Blessed be the Lord for his goodness to him and me in [p. 367] this.

And another letter I received, with a proposal for another young gentlewoman to come and board with me as being the most earnest desire of her friends.[30] But, Lord, what am I that any should desire to be with me? Did they see what thou, O God, hath beheld in me, and what I confess I have been guilty of, all persons would abhor and abandon me rather than desire to converse with me. When I reflect upon my by past[31] life, how may it humble me even to the lowest hell, the place where I ought deservedly to be condemned to all eternity.

How, then, should I adore, and magnify, and exalt the praises of my God who hath made good that promise unto me: I will save her that halteth, and gather her that was driven out, and I will get them praise and fame in every land where they have been put to shame (Zeph. 3:19).[32] Blessed be God for the consolation that I had from those words, many years since, when I was in a sad condition.[33] What I believed then of the power of God, I have found in the performance to the glory of his name. Another evidence of the Lord's favor [p. 368] to me in blessing my endeavors was[34] the being the instrument by which the Lord was pleased to give life again to a newborn child that appeared to be dead; and with wetting my finger in cinnamon water, and frequently wetting the mouth, and rubbing the temples, and touching the nostrils with it, it began to move and cry, and (when I left it) very hopeful of being a lively[35] child.

For this, and all thy mercies to me (in giving me a heart desirous to do good to the whole world if it were in my power, and for thy blessing several things

27. "To regard or treat with compassion; to pity, commiserate," *OED*.

28. Deuteronomy 10:18–19: "He doth execute the judgment of the fatherless and widow, and loveth the stranger, in giving him food and raiment. Love ye therefore the stranger: for ye were strangers in the land of Egypt."

29. "In the truth" is an interlineal insertion.

30. For more information on Halkett's boarders, see Trill, ed., *Halkett*, xxvn52.

31. "That has passed or gone by, (of time) elapsed; that has happened or existed in past time; former," *OED*.

32. Zephaniah 3:19: "Behold, at that time I will undo all that afflict thee: and I will save her that halteth, and gather her that was driven out, and I will get them praise and fame in every land where they have been put to shame."

33. See "The Power of Faith, upon Mark 16:17–18," 189–93.

34. After "was," I have deleted an unnecessary "the."

35. "Animated, vivacious; jolly, cheerful," *OED*.

which by thy providence thou hast directed me to give others); for this, forever may thy name be magnified. And though I find by my dear child's letter I am not like to see him in haste, yet I hope we meet daily in our prayers to God for one another. And if we never meet here[36] again upon earth, yet, Lord, direct us so as that we may be sure to meet in heaven, where we shall join together in singing everlasting praise to thee, our God. Amen.

---

36. "Here" is an interlineal insertion.

Meditations on Moses and Samuel *(1688–1689/90)*

Although Couper's list attributes the date of 1689 to this volume, Halkett's annotations tell a different story. The prefatory material, reproduced below, was written Monday, May 21, 1688, and a note on the inside back cover states that the volume was "ended March 17, 1689/90."[1] These dates are confirmed by the remains of the first of two pieces of paper glued to its spine: the second attachment reads "Moses and S," so presumably it was intended to provide a "title" or short indication of the book's contents when on the shelf or when handed over to other readers.[2] Perhaps because of this, there is no list of contents: Halkett has announced her intention to study the lives of these two great Old Testament figures and no more detail is necessary. Despite the shared billing, Moses's life takes up three-quarters of the book.[3] On the next page, Halkett reaffirms her initial stated intention, and begins her analysis of the first book of Samuel on Wednesday, November 27, 1689, but her commentary has run only to chapter 28 by the end of the volume.[4] As its title suggests, this volume is primarily exegetical, and Halkett reads these figures' lives as exemplars for her, and other Christians, to imitate.

The preface is reproduced below for two reasons: first, because it is typical of the way in which Halkett introduces her select meditations across her volumes; second, because it gestures toward another mysterious event in Halkett's life that has so far gone unnoticed: what happened on Monday, May 21, 1649?[5]

Monday, May 21, 1688.

[p. i] Having so often mentioned the advantage I have found by fixing my morning thoughts upon some pious meditation I need not insist further upon that, only reflect upon the reason I had to make this day the date for beginning this book.

For it was the evening of Monday, May 21, 1649 that I was under the greatest trial that ever any now living I believe[6] hath met with.[7] The particulars,

---

1. Halkett, *Meditations on Moses and Samuel*, pp. i, v. This is volume 17 in Couper's catalogue.

2. This is not an isolated occurrence, although it is not consistent even across the volumes that retain their original covers.

3. Halkett, *Meditations on Moses and Samuel*, pp. 1–308.

4. Halkett, *Meditations on Moses and Samuel*, pp. 309–72. The first book of Samuel runs to thirty-one chapters.

5. See "Introduction," 26.

6. "I believe" is an interlineal insertion.

7. After the execution of King Charles I (January 30, 1648/9) and before her journey north (September 1649) Halkett refers to the unexpected revelation that Bampfield's wife might still be living as a "trial," see *True Account*, 89. However, in another entry in a later volume, she indicates that this specific trial

and the person that occasioned it, I desire ever to conceal. But while I live, and as[8] ever since, so I intend to continue with the Lord's assistance every Monday to commemorate the deliverance with praise, adoration, and thanksgiving to my gracious God, who did vouchsafe to hear me when none but himself could save me, and he was pleased to deliver me from all my fears (Ps. 34:4).[9] This day it is forty-eight year since that time, [p. ii] and yet it is as fresh in my memory (with the help of a reflection that I writ the next day)[10] as if it were but yesterday performed.

Oh, how great is the long, patient suffering of my God who hath spared me thus many years; in which time, millions have gone to eternity, and many of them (as is much to be feared) snatched away in the midst of their sins. And yet I am spared. Lord, let it be in mercy, and not for my greater condemnation that thou hast given me this space for to repent. I confess my works hath not been perfect before thee (Rev. 3:2),[11] but my desire is to follow thy counsel, and to buy of thee gold tried in the fire, that I may be rich; and white raiment, that I may be clothed, and that the shame of my nakedness do not appear; and [p. iii] anoint my eyes with eye salve, that I may see (Rev. 3:18).[12] And then, blessed Lord, stand not at the door to knock, but open the door of my heart, and come in, and make it an everlasting habitation for thyself (Rev. 3:20).[13] And then, thou wilt be pleased so to assist me in what I am now designing to write, that if it should ever come to be seen of others they may say God is in her of a truth (1 Cor. 14:25).[14]

Before I had finished my last book, I was several times considering where to fix my thoughts for a new employment. And having found personal examples[15] in Holy Scripture very useful to meditate upon, I determined to make Moses and

---

involved a physical attack on her person: "What Crosses and Difficulties I Have Met with Myself," and alludes to this event again, "Saturday, May 21, 1698," 308, 322–23.

8. "As" is an interlineal insertion.

9. Psalm 34:4: "I sought the Lord, and he heard me, and delivered me from all my fears."

10. According to Couper's catalogue, this reflection would have been contained within the now missing second volume.

11. Revelation 3:2: "Be watchful, and strengthen the things which remain, that are ready to die: for I have not found thy works perfect before God."

12. Revelation 3:18: "I counsel thee to buy of me gold tried in the fire, that thou mayest be rich; and white raiment, that thou mayest be clothed, and that the shame of thy nakedness do not appear; and anoint thine eyes with eye salve, that thou mayest see."

13. Revelation 3:20: "Behold, I stand at the door, and knock: if any man hear my voice, and open the door, I will come in to him, and will sup with him, and he with me."

14. 1 Corinthians 14:25: "And thus are the secrets of his heart made manifest; and so, falling down on his face he will worship God, and report that God is in you of a truth."

15. Halkett does this at length in two other extant volumes: *Joseph's Trial and Triumph* and *Meditations on the Book of Jonah*.

Samuel the subject of this treatise:[16] they being joined together by the Lord himself, it shall now be my task to trace what's most considerable in both their lives to make them practicable in my own. And [p. iv] the good hand of God be with me to enable me to perform it (Neh. 2:8).[17] And as thou wert pleased to accept what the women that were wise hearted did spin with their hands for the service of the Tabernacle (Exod. 35:25),[18] as well as the gold and silver (Exod. 35:5),[19] and the onyx stones (Exod. 35:9)[20] that were offered by others,[21] and that thou art pleased with whosoever brings an offering with a willing heart;[22] therefore, since the desire comes from thyself—from thy blessed self—I beg assistance to perform what may bring glory to thee, and endless consolation to my own soul, whose desire above all things is to be acceptable in thy sight, O Lord, my strength, and my redeemer (Ps. 19:14).[23]

---

16. "A book or writing which treats of some particular subject; commonly (in modern use always), one containing a formal or methodical discussion or exposition of the principles of the subject; formerly more widely used for a literary work in general," *OED*.

17. Nehemiah 2:8: "And a letter unto Asaph the keeper of the King's forest, that he may give me timber to make beams for the gates of the palace which appertained to the house, and for the wall of the city, and for the house that I shall enter into. And the King granted me, according to the good hand of my God upon me."

18. Exodus 35:25: "And all the women that were wise hearted did spin with their hands, and brought that which they had spun, both of blue, and of purple, an of scarlet, and of fine linen."

19. Exodus 35:5: "Take ye from among you an offering unto the Lord: whosoever is of a willing heart, let him bring it, an offering of the Lord; gold, and silver, and brass."

20. Exodus 35:9: "And onyx stones, and stones to be set for the ephod, and for the breastplate."

21. "By others" is an interlineal insertion.

22. Exodus 35:29: "The children of Israel brought a willing offering unto the Lord, every man and woman, whose heart made them willing to bring for all manner of work, which the Lord had commanded to be made by the hand of Moses."

23. Psalm 19:14: "Let the words of my mouth, and the meditation of my heart, be acceptable in thy sight, O Lord, my strength, and my redeemer.

Occasional Meditations, Meditations upon Nehemiah, and Observations of Several Good Women Mentioned in Scripture (1690–1692)

In her opening list of "the contents of this book," Halkett notes that this volume was begun on June 24, 1690, and on the inside back cover that it was "ended May 22, 1692."[1] According to the contents list, this volume opens with occasional meditations "concerning the public and my own private concerns."[2] As in *Meditations on St. Peter*, Halkett does not provide a comprehensive list of all of the individual entries in this section, and the entries themselves are simply dated (rather than being "upon" a particular occasion). Nevertheless, the contents list provides another indication of the way in which Halkett used her books, as she draws attention to three specific entries that rereading has made her recall. The first relates to a resolution she had made ("August 16, 1690") to address her debts: rereading that entry ("Saturday, May 28, 1692") Halkett laments her lack of progress in this area; a note at its end, indicates that she reread it again ("Saturday, June 2, 1694") and that there has still been little improvement.[3] The second attests to her ongoing interest in dreams, despite frequent disavowals;[4] and the third, "of one put to the rack," recalls the torture of a Catholic Englishman in December 1690.[5] According to Halkett's dating, the occasional mediations were begun on Tuesday, June 24, 1690 and all except the final two relate to 1690.[6] The meditations on Nehemiah were "begun Monday, July 22, 1690," and the "Observations of Several Good Women Mentioned in Scripture" on Monday, June 29, 1691.[7] One item that is missing from Halkett's list is a poem inserted at the beginning of the volume, "Praise God, My Soul, Who from Death's Gate," written "Thursday Morning, early when I could

---

1. Halkett, *Occasional Meditations, Meditations upon Nehemiah*, pp. i, iv. This is volume 18 in Couper's catalogue.

2. Halkett, *Occasional Meditations, Meditations upon Nehemiah*, p. i.

3. Halkett, *Occasional Meditations, Meditations upon Nehemiah*, pp. i, 13–14, 14.

4. Halkett, *Occasional Meditations, Meditations upon Nehemiah*, pp. i, 36–37. This entry, "Monday, November 3, 1690," opens with such a disavowal: "though I never allowed myself (nor approved of in others) to take notice of dreams, yet, last night, having had one so extraordinary, I cannot but write it down and observe what follows upon it," p. 36. See also Trill, ed., *Halkett*, 160.

5. Halkett, *Occasional Meditations, Meditations upon Nehemiah*, pp. i, 48–51. See also Trill, ed., *Halkett*, 161–62.

6. Halkett, *Occasional Meditations, Meditations upon Nehemiah*, pp. 1–3. The exceptions are "Sunday, March 29, 1691," and Sunday, April 11, 1691," pp. 78–79.

7. Halkett, *Occasional Meditations, Meditations upon Nehemiah*, pp. 80–253, 254–370. Couper's catalogue identifies all the women Halkett discusses.

not sleep, being February 11, 1691/2, after my recovery beyond expectation" (pp. ii–iii).[8]

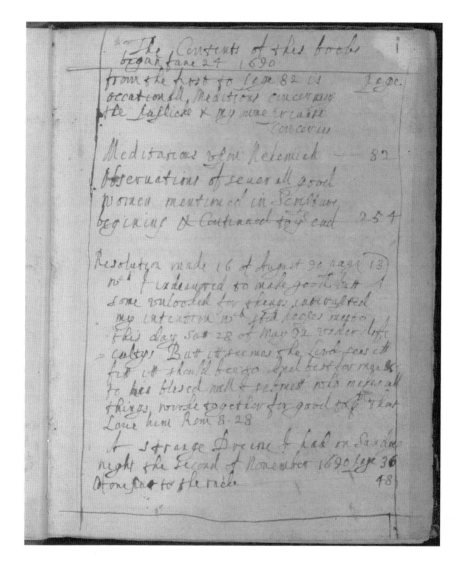

Figure 14. Contents page for "Occasional Meditations," from *Occasional Meditations, Meditations upon Nehemiah, and Observations of Several Good Women Mentioned in Scripture* (1690–1692). © National Library of Scotland, NLS, MS 6499, p. i. Reproduced with permission.

8. Halkett, *Occasional Meditations, Meditations upon Nehemiah*, pp. ii–iii. Again, this seems to be an original composition, and consists of nine stanzas of four lines each, with an abab rhyme scheme. See also *Occasional and Select Meditations*, pp. xiv–xviii.

Tuesday, June 24, 1690.

[p. 1] I was for some time without the conveniency[9] of having a book wherein I might transmit my thoughts and meditations to be a memorial of mercies and judgments, of which David did sing unto the Lord (Ps. 101:1).[10] (And, oh, that my soul were as well tuned as his was, that I might behave myself wisely in a perfect way. And, O Lord, if thou wilt come unto me, I will walk within my house with a perfect heart [Ps. 101:2].)[11] And great need have I it, this day, to be directed by thee how to offer up an acceptable sacrifice unto thee, who hath no pleasure in wickedness, neither shall evil dwell with thee (Ps. 5:4).[12]

For this being a day appointed by those in authority to make it a day of fasting and humiliation[13] for the good success of their new made King[14] in Ireland,[15] which should I pray for, or wish, or desire I were unjust to our own lawful King,[16] ungrate[17] for all the benefits I, and my parents, and relations, had to the royal family;[18] and, in short, it were to wish that the cup of the Lord's indignation against him (for whom they fast)[19] might be filled by making him the instrument of destroying the Lord's anointed, and to be guilty of ruin[20] to his uncle[21] and his father-in-law.[22]

---

9. I.e., convenience.

10. Psalm 101:1: "I will sing of mercy and judgment: unto thee, O Lord, will I sing."

11. Psalm 101:2: "I will behave myself wisely in a perfect way. O when wilt thou come unto me? I will walk within my house with a perfect heart."

12. Psalm 5:4: "For thou art not a God that hath pleasure in wickedness: neither shall evil dwell with thee."

13. In the right-hand margin, a reference has been crossed out, although it is still legible. Leviticus 10:19: "And Aaron said unto Moses, Behold, this day have they offered their sin offering and their burnt offering before the Lord; and such things have befallen me: and if I had eaten the sin offering today, should it have been accepted in the sight of the Lord?"

14. I.e., William of Orange.

15. See "June 13. Act, for a Public Fast" (Edinburgh: Andrew Anderson, 1690), ESTC R183890; see also "April 11. A Proclamation, Declaring William and Mary King and Queen of England to Be King and Queen of Scotland." (London: G. Croom, 1689), R225323.

16. I.e., King James VII/II.

17. "An ungrateful person; an ingrate," *OED*.

18. See *True Account*, 60–64.

19. "(For whom they fast)" is an interlineal insertion, enclosed within brackets.

20. "Ruin" is an interlineal insertion.

21. William's mother was Mary, Princess Royal, sister to Charles II and James VII/II. Keblusek, "Mary, Princess Royal," *ODNB*.

22. William was married to Queen Mary, James VII/II's daughter.

Selected Meditations 279

And if I should go to church upon these considerations should I be accepted in the sight of the Lord? (Lev. 10:19)[23] For if it be a fault to handle the word of God deceitfully, it cannot [p. 2] but be a fault to hear the word of God deceitfully.[24] For as to this,[25] I can neither pray with the spirit, nor with the understanding so as to say "amen" to that for which this day is set apart to pray.[26] And therefore, I forbear going to church rather than to go and not[27] with sincerity of heart. For though I could go and hear the word of God with joy and rejoicing that I have health and liberty[28] to go unto the house of God (and it is not without trouble that I do at this time withdraw from it), yet I must take heed by any means[29] that this liberty of mine (should I use it) become not a stumbling block to them[30] that are weak (1 Cor. 8:9).[31] And they think all things are lawful, though I think this not expedient (1 Cor. 6:12).[32]

But if any mourn this day for sin, who hath more reason than myself? And in that I will bear a share with them, and pray for mercy to the distressed, divided church, and upon our unjustly used King. Lord, give him victory over all his enemies, spiritual and temporal; first over sin, which is his greatest enemy; and then over those which thou hast made his enemies because he hath sinned.[33] And since all hath sinned and come short of the glory [p. 3] of God, let us all, O Lord, be justified freely by thy grace through the Redemption that is in Christ Jesus (Rom. 3:23–24).[34] Amen.

---

23. The reference crossed out above has been inserted here, 278n13.

24. 2 Corinthians 4:2: "But have renounced the hidden things of dishonesty, not walking in craftiness, nor handling the word of God deceitfully; but by manifestation of the truth commending ourselves to every man's conscience in the sight of God."

25. I.e., the proclamation.

26. 1 Corinthians 14:15–16: "What is it then? I will pray with the spirit, and I will pray with the understanding also: I will sing with the spirit, and I will sing with the understanding also. Else when thou shalt bless with the spirit, how shall he that occupieth the room of the unlearned say Amen at thy giving of thanks, seeing he understandeth not what thou sayest?"

27. "Not" is an interlineal insertion.

28. "Freedom to do a specified thing; permission, leave," OED.

29. "By any means" is an interlineal insertion.

30. Here, "those" has been overwritten to form "them."

31. 1 Corinthians 8:9: "But take heed lest by any means this liberty of yours become a stumbling block to them that are weak."

32. 1 Corinthians 6:12: "All things are lawful unto me, but all things are not expedient: all things are lawful for me, but I will not be brought under the power of any."

33. I.e., his being a Catholic.

34. Romans 3:23–24: "For all have sinned and come short of the glory of God; Being justified freely by his grace through the redemption that is in Christ Jesus."

Christmas Day, Thursday, December 25, 1690.[35]

[p. 52] Since ever I came into this kingdom[36] it hath been my regret that so few commemorates this day with that religious solemnity usual in other churches, not only in that best reformed Church of England but even among the Protestants of France when allowed the exercise of their religion. And yet they were not Episcopal, no more than these here who now governs and set up so high for Presbytery.

Have we not all one Creed?[37] And is it not an Article of it that Jesus Christ was born of the Virgin Mary?[38] And had he not been born, he could neither have died for our sins, nor rose for our justification (Rom. 4:25), and then had we been of all creatures most miserable.[39]

The opposers of this festivity object that the very day of the Lord's nativity is uncertain, and that there is no express command in Scripture for it.[40] Should no day therefore be kept because the particular [p. 53] day is not known? Sure, it had never been the practice of so many ages before us if they had not believed they either knew the day, or that the day set by them apart for that commemoration was as acceptable as if they had known the particular day? And being so determined by them the Apostle says expressly, obey them that have the rule over you and submit yourselves: for they watch for your souls, as they that must give an account, that they may do it with joy, and not with grief: for that is profitable for you (Heb. 13:17).[41]

Now though too, too many others neglect this day altogether; others remember it, but not in a right way; my endeavor, with the Lord's assistance, shall be to take all good opportunity to improve this day's mercy both to myself and others, begging of God that I may be enabled to go into his house this day, being

---

35. Christmas had once again been banned in Scotland by William of Orange, or at least courts were still to sit. *RPS* 1690/4/113.

36. I.e., Scotland.

37. "A form of words setting forth authoritatively and concisely the general belief of the Christian Church, or those articles of belief which are regarded as essential; a brief summary of Christian doctrine: usually and properly applied to the three statements of belief known as the Apostles', Nicene, and Athanasian Creeds ('the Creed,' without qualification, usually = the Apostles' Creed)," *OED*. See also, "Wednesday, December 1, 1697," 314–16.

38. This is the Third Article of the Apostle's Creed: see "Wednesday, December 1, 1697," 316. See also "Morning Prayer," *BCP*, 247.

39. Romans 4:25: "Who was delivered for our offences and was raised again for our justification."

40. "For it" is an interlineal insertion.

41. Hebrews 13:17: "Obey them that have the rule over you and submit yourselves: for they watch for your souls, as they that must give account, that they may do it with joy, and not with grief: for that is unprofitable for you." Although she is clearly using the *KJV*, Halkett writes "profitable" rather than "unprofitable."

the weekly sermon day.[42] Where, I hope, without offence to others, the Lord will direct Mr. Graeme, who is to preach, that [p. 54] he may say something to justify them who desire always, in all things to bless God (who sent his beloved Son to seek and to save those which were lost). And none more under that bondage of corruption than myself; therefore, none hath more reason than I to say, glory to God in the highest, and on earth, peace and good will towards men (Luke 2:14).[43]

There is some this day who partake of the blessed Sacrament of the Lord's Supper in which is commemorated the whole mystery of our Redemption. Lord, as[44] I pray for them that they may not receive that grace in vain, so I beseech thee let me have the benefit of their prayers; though not personally with them, yet let me spiritually receive of the fruits,[45] and benefit of that holy Sacrament by having my sins pardoned, and my soul strengthened that I may spend all the days of my [p. 55] appointed time as one[46] that sincerely desires to be devoted to thy fear (Ps. 119:38).[47]

Then, since I desire to keep this day holy to the Lord, my God (Neh. 8:9),[48] having prepared to eat the fat, and drink the sweet, and sent portions unto them for whom nothing is prepared, Lord accept what I have done, and intend to do; for the joy of the Lord[49] is my strength (Neh. 8:10).[50] And let our meeting together, either in the church or at home, be for thy glory and the mutual edification of one another that whether we eat, or drink, or whatever we do,[51] it may all may be to thy glory (1 Cor. 10:31). Amen.

---

42. As in Dunfermline, most parishes offered only one weekday sermon in addition to "multiple Sunday sermons"; however, in the 1580s, Perth was an exception, as it provided "Monday, Tuesday and Thursday morning sermons in addition to the Wednesday presbytery exercise," Todd, *The Culture of Protestantism in Early Modern Scotland*, 30.

43. Luke 2:14: "Glory to God in the highest, and on earth peace, good will toward men."

44. "As" is an interlineal insertion.

45. From François de Sales, Halkett learned that you need not be physically present to receive spiritual benefit from others' participation in the Lord's Supper, see Trill, ed., *Halkett*, xxvii.

46. "One" is an interlineal insertion.

47. Psalm 119:38: "Stablish thy word unto thy servant, who is devoted to thy fear."

48. Nehemiah 8:9: "And Nehemiah, which is the Tirshatha, and Ezra the priest the scribe, and the Levites that taught the people, said unto all the people, this day is holy unto the Lord your God; mourn not, nor weep. For all the people wept when they heard the words of the law."

49. After "joy," "of the joy" has been deleted and replaced by "of the Lord" in an interlineal insertion.

50. Nehemiah 8:10: "Then he said unto them, go your way, eat the fat, and drink the sweet, and send portions unto them for whom nothing is prepared: for this day is holy unto our Lord: neither be ye sorry; for the joy of the Lord is your strength."

51. 1 Corinthians 10:31: "Whether therefore ye eat, or drink, or whatsoever ye do, do all to the glory of God."

Thursday, January 8, 1690/1.[52]

[p. 63] This being the day of our weekly sermon here,[53] it is not without some trouble that I absent myself from it, but, being appointed by them who call themselves the General Assembly (though very improperly, the generality of the ministers being unjustly put from their ministry) to have this day kept for a fast[54] for such reasons as I cannot join with them, I think I had much better stay at home than go to hear that made a crime, which I believe a duty. And whatsoever is not of faith is sin (Rom. 14:23).[55]

For all they can say (though Mr. Graeme puts the best gloss[56] that such things will admit of) shall never convince me that it is a sin to be Episcopal; for I esteem it the greatest honor I have, that I have been educated in the Church of England in the time in[57] which it had greatest encouragements.[58] And whoever hath failed in their duty (either a bishop, or any under their charge) shall be my regret. And for any defection[59] in the royal family. But, Lord, forgive, for thy mercy's sake, whatever hath been amiss either in church [p. 64] or state, for there is none

---

52. See also Trill, ed., *Halkett*, 162–63.

53. See "Christmas Day, Thursday, December 25, 1690," 281n42.

54. See the "Act of the General Assembly, anent a Solemn National Fast and Humiliation, with the Causes Thereof. At Edinburgh, November 12, 1690." (Edinburgh: Andrew Anderson, 1690). ESTC R173923. A copy of this Act is included in John Cockburn, *An Historical Relation of the Pretended General Assembly, Held at Edinburgh, from Oct. 16 to Nov. 13 in the Year 1690. In a Letter from a Person in Edinburgh, to His Friend in London* (London: J. Hindmarsh, 1691). ESTC R175777. Halkett would have agreed with Cockburn's account of Couper and Graeme's citation: "The libels were generally so frivolous and impertinent that they ought to have been rejected with scorn; but whatever was offered by the bigots was admitted, and all care and caution used not to discourage them. The great scandals of Mr. Couper and Mr. Graeme, ministers at Dunfermline, were the admitting persons promiscuously to the Sacrament; the profaning the Lord's Day in suffering people to bring in kale and fan barley for the pot that day; and allowing their children to play with others, though they were very much under that age, which even in the opinion of Jewish doctors, was obliged to the strict observance of the Sabbath," 10. Halkett certainly later read Cockburn's, *Bourignianism Detected; or, The Delusions and Errors of Antonia Bourignon, and Her Growing Sect. Which May Also Serve for a Discovery of All Other Enthusiastical Impostures* (London: C. Brome, W. Keblewhite, and H. Hindmarsh, 1698), ESTC R17688, see Trill, ed., *Halkett*, 195–96. Tristram Clarke, "Cockburn, John (1652–1729)," *ODNB*. See also Raffe, *Culture of Controversy*, 114–15.

55. Romans 14:23: "And he that doubteth is damned if he eat, because he eateth not of faith: for whatsoever is not of faith is sin."

56. "To make glozes or glosses upon; to discourse upon, expound, interpret. Also, to interpret (a thing) to be (so and so)," *OED*.

57. "In" is an interlineal insertion.

58. See *True Account*, 64.

59. "The action or an act of abandoning one's faith, religion, or moral duty; backsliding; apostasy," *OED*.

that sinneth not.[60] And if it be the glory of a man to pass over transgressions (Pro. 19:11),[61] how much greater glory is it to thee, our God, to blot out as a thick cloud their transgressions, and as a cloud their sins, and make them so return to thee that it may be visible to the whole world that thou hast redeemed them (Isa. 44:22),[62] as the two anointed ones (magistracy and ministry) that stand by the Lord of the whole earth (Zec. 4:14).[63] That the throne may be established in righteousness and truth in this church, Lord grant,[64] and then say unto them as of old, fear thou not; for I am with thee: be not dismayed; for I am thy God: I will strengthen thee; yea, I will uphold thee with the right hand of my righteousness (Isa. 41:10).[65] Amen (Jer. 28:6).[66] So be it (Jer. 11:5).[67]

I now intend part of this day to employ myself in writing out what the Lord shall direct me to say in answer to one I never saw, who sent to me yesterday to inform me of her trouble which she hath lain in since April last in a great trouble of mind. Lord, who art the comfort of[68] all that art cast down, assist me that I may be able to comfort her with the comforts wherewith I have been comforted of God (2 Cor. 1:4).[69]

---

60. See 1 Kings 8:46: "If they sin against thee, (for there is no man that sinneth not,) and thou be angry with them, and deliver them to the enemy, so that they carry them away captives unto the land of the enemy, far or near"; 2 Chronicles 6:36: "If they sin against thee, (for there is no man which sinneth not,) and thou be angry with them, and deliver them over before their enemies, and they carry them away captives unto a land far off or near"; Ecclesiastes 7:20: "For there is not a just man upon earth, that doeth good, and sinneth not."

61. Proverbs 19:11: "The discretion of a man deferreth his anger; and it is his glory to pass over a transgression."

62. Isaiah 44:22: "I have blotted out, as a thick cloud, thy transgressions, and, as a cloud, thy sins: return unto me; for I have redeemed thee."

63. Zechariah 4:14: "Then said he, these are the two anointed ones, that stand by the Lord of the whole earth."

64. "Lord grant" is an interlineal insertion.

65. Isaiah 41:10: "Fear thou not; for I am with thee: be not dismayed; for I am thy God: I will strengthen thee; yea, I will help thee; yea, I will uphold thee with the right hand of my righteousness."

66. Jeremiah 28:6: "Even the prophet Jeremiah said, amen: The Lord do so: The Lord perform thy words which thou hast prophesied, to bring again the vessels of the Lord's house, and all that is carried away captive, from Babylon into this place."

67. Jeremiah 11:5: "That I may perform the oath which I have sworn unto your fathers, to give them a land flowing with milk and honey, as it is this day. Then answered I, and said, so be it, O Lord."

68. After "of," the rest of this sentence is written in the bottom margin of the page.

69. 2 Corinthians 1:4: "Who comforteth us in all our tribulation, that we may be able to comfort them which are in any trouble, by the comfort wherewith we ourselves are comforted of God."

January 30, 1690/1.[70]

[66] How truly doth our own experience verify what David says: verily every man at his best estate is altogether vanity (Ps. 39:5).[71] And he puts a "Selah" to it as a mark of observation.

And what can more confirm this, than to reflect upon what was acted upon this day of the month, 1648? Whereon the best King of Europe was murdered by his rebellious subjects and, by the shedding of his innocent blood, filled up the cup of their own iniquity which to this day is still visited upon these Three Kingdoms,[72] for their actual or passive concurrence[73] in so horrid a guilt. The sense that some had both in church and state of that execrable[74] crime made it enacted to be an Anniversary Fast upon this day: to confess the sin and bewail the guilt that brought our Sovereign—the best of Kings, the anointed of the Lord, the breath of our nostrils—to be taken in their pits (Lam. 4:20).[75] But now all that is laid aside, and now in these times no sin hath public allowance to be mourned for but such as others think their duty to comply, as far as was just, [67] both with what by authority was settled both in the church and state. And whatever hath been of late done by either, we have reason to mourn for being laid upon an ill foundation.[76] But the accession[77] of their guilt cannot make void former sins but rather increase them, and therefore as I desire yearly while I live to be humbled for the sins of this day, either in myself or others, so also for whatever hath provoked God to deliver us up to the scourge[78] we now lie under by such men who hold the truth in unrighteousness (Rom. 1:18).[79]

---

70. See also "Upon the Fast which by Proclamation Was Kept, January 30, 1660/1," "January 30, 1673/4," and "Saturday, January 30, 1696/7," 203–5, 255–56, 304–7.

71. Psalm 39:5: "Behold, thou hast made my days as an handbreadth; and mine age is as nothing before thee: verily every man at his best state is altogether vanity. Selah."

72. See "Introduction," 6n21.

73. "Accordance, agreement; assent, consent," OED.

74. "Deserving to be execrated or cursed; abominable, detestable," OED.

75. Lamentations 4:20: "The breath of our nostrils, the anointed of the Lord, was taken in their pits, of whom we said, under his shadow we shall live among the heathen."

76. Halkett was not only hostile to William and Mary's accession because they had "usurped" the throne from James VII/II, but also disagreed with the 1689 Toleration Act, and the abolition of prelacy and establishment of Presbyterian Church government in Scotland. See Raffe, "Presbyterians and Episcopalians," and Trill, "Royalism and Resistance."

77. "The action or an act of acceding or agreeing to a decision, plan, proceeding, etc.; adherence, assent," OED.

78. "A thing or person that is an instrument of divine chastisement," OED.

79. Romans 1:18: "For the wrath of God is revealed from heaven against all ungodliness and unrighteousness of men, who hold the truth in unrighteousness."

O, Lord, arise with healing in thy wings (Mal. 4:2),[80] and whatever hath been amiss in our ways, Lord heal them. Lead us also, and restore comforts to our church, and our King, and to his mourners, and create peace unto them: for thou only art the Lord that can heal them (Isa. 57:18–19).[81]

---

80. Malachi 4:2: "But unto you that fear my name shall the Sun of righteousness arise with healing in his wings; and ye shall go forth and grow up as calves of the stall."

81. Isaiah 57:18–19: "I have seen his ways and will heal him: I will lead him also and restore comforts unto him and to his mourners. I create the fruit of the lips; Peace, peace to him that is far off, and to him that is near, saith the Lord; and I will heal him."

Of Watchfulness, Select, and Occasional Meditations (1693/4–1695)

Like *Occasional and Select Meditations*, *Of Watchfulness* is uncharacteristically "messy" in its organization. Although there is the customary note on the inside front cover informing us that this volume was "begun Sunday, January 28, 1693/4," there is no end date provided.[1] While the book closes with an entry titled "February 6, Being Ash Wednesday, 1694/5," the final entry chronologically is "Monday, December 16, 1695";[2] and whereas Halkett's table of contents attempts to maintain the usual division between select and occasional meditations,[3] in practice the distinction appears to be breaking down. For once, Couper's list of this volume's contents is clearer than Halkett's and its organization indicates the crossover between genres that takes place.[4] While Couper identifies two groups of occasional meditations, according to Halkett's list, everything in the volume after page 160 is occasional (whereas Couper identifies a further six select meditations within these pages).[5] The overlap is made more complicated by Halkett's identification of some "personal" moments within the materials she has defined as select meditations; for example, she draws attention to her reference to "the fire at the Rhodes" in "Of Watchfulness."[6] There is also some inconsistency between titles and dates: for example, whereas the second select meditation is defined as "Of Restraining the Tongue, upon Psalm 39:1–4" in her table of contents, within the main text it is headed only with the date "Wednesday, March 21, 1693/4."[7] This lack of distinction is mirrored in the occasional meditations insofar as they include a number of materials that elsewhere would be defined as select meditations, such as "Meditations of the Man of God who came to Jeroboam," on 1 Kings 13.[8] Among the occasional meditations to which she draws attention in her table, one is described there as "Upon Beating Sugar"; in the main text, it is identified

---

1. Halkett, *Of Watchfulness*, p. i.

2. Halkett, *Of Watchfulness*, pp. 377, 283–97.

3. Halkett, *Of Watchfulness*, pp. ii–iii.

4. See "Appendix 4.2," 348–49. See also "Figure 15," 288.

5. According to Couper, the final six select meditations are: "Upon the Man of God, 1 Kings 13"; "Serious Thoughts upon the By Past Years since 1688"; "Upon Contentment Phil. 4:11"; "God's Husbandry, 1 Cor. 3:9"; "Upon Psalm 139:23–24: "Search Me"; and "Upon Matt. 11:29–30: "Take my Yoke." See "Appendix 4.3," 356.

6. Halkett, *Of Watchfulness*, pp. iii, 18.

7. Halkett, *Of Watchfulness*, pp. ii, 34.

8. Halkett, *Of Watchfulness*, pp. ii, 189–218. This is one of the other six select meditations identified in Couper's catalogue. For a discussion of the political typology involved in alluding to Jeroboam, see Killeen, "Chastising with Scorpions," 498–506.

only by date, "Monday, April 22, 1695."[9] Another is listed as "a hazard I was in" but is located earlier in the book than Halkett says her occasional meditations begin.[10] While Halkett's occasional meditations never straightforwardly imitated bishop Hall's models, by this point in her writing career, the distinction between her meditative modes seems to be dissolving.

---

9. Halkett, *Of Watchfulness*, pp. ii, 187. Couper summarizes this entry as an example of Halkett's practice: "Beating sugar, her reflection was, 'How happy I, if the many strokes I have met with, did refine me, subdue every gross part, and make me wholly fit for my master's use"; Couper, *The Life of the Lady Halkett*, 57.
10. Halkett, *Of Watchfulness*, pp. iii, 158–59.

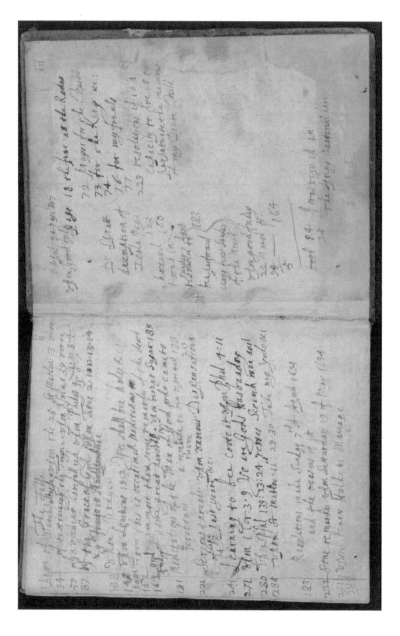

Figure 15. "The Table," from *Of Watchfulness, Select, and Occasional Meditations* (1693/4–1695). © National Library of Scotland, NLS, MS 6500, pp. ii–iii. Reproduced with permission.

Saturday, June 23, 1694.[11]

[p. 325] Great reason have I to say with the Psalmist, it is good for me to draw near to God: I have put my trust in the Lord God, that I may declare all thy works (Ps. 73:28).[12] I have of late been under great despondency, both in my spiritual and temporal condition, finding great deadness of heart under the one, and many difficulties in the other. But, fixing my morning thoughts and mediations upon what Saint Paul instructs the Philippians in whatever trouble came inwardly, or outwardly, I suppressed it by these words: Be careful for nothing, but in everything by prayer, et cetera (Phil. 4:6–7).[13] So, endeavoring to make this my daily practice, I have within these few days found so great advantage by it that I cannot but declare: it is good for me to draw near unto God,[14] who, though he hath been pleased to blast the expectation I had from those I had most confidence in, yet, where I least expected help, I have found it. Blessed be the Lord God, the God of Israel,[15] who doth wondrous things (Ps. 72:18–19).[16]

And blessed be his glorious name, by whose good providence, I hope, it was ordered that the Countess of[17] Argyll[18] sent me a letter yesterday [p. 326] with the greatest pressing arguments that could be that I would take her grandchild, the Earl of Balcarres's son,[19] to stay in the house, and go to the school.[20] And though I was in a manner fully determined not to take any more charge of this kind upon me, yet I could not refuse a person to whom I was so much obliged to at

---

11. See also Trill, ed., *Halkett*, 168–69.

12. Psalm 73:28: "But it is good for me to draw near to God: I have put my trust in the Lord God, that I may declare all thy works." Halkett's original reference is to Psalm 73:26: "My flesh and my heart faileth: but God is the strength of my heart, and my portion forever."

13. Philippians 4:6–7: "Be careful for nothing; but in everything by prayer and supplication with thanksgiving let your requests be made known unto God. And the peace of God, which passeth all understanding, shall keep your hearts and minds through Christ Jesus."

14. Psalm 73:28: "But it is good for me to draw near to God: I have put my trust in the Lord God, that I may declare all thy works."

15. The phrase "God, the God of Israel" is an interlineal insertion.

16. Psalm 72:18–19: "Blessed be the Lord God, the God of Israel, who only doeth wondrous things. And blessed be his glorious name for ever: and let the whole earth be filled with his glory; Amen, and amen." Halkett's original reference to Psalm 62 is erroneous.

17. After "of," "her" has been deleted.

18. Anna MacKenzie, who was formerly Countess of Balcarres but married the ninth Earl of Argyll in 1670. Marshall, "MacKenzie, Anna," *ODNB*.

19. Colin Lindsay, son of Colin Lindsay, third Earl of Balcarres, and Lady Jean Kerr, later Captain Lindsay, and Lord Cummerland; he would have been somewhere between five and fourteen in 1694, *TCP* 1:378; *BP* 1:952.

20. There had been a grammar school in Dunfermline since 1625. Henderson, *The Annals of Dunfermline and Vicinity*, 290.

my first return from Fyvie,[21] and besides knowing how great an advantage it is to the reputation of this place[22] that there is such a schoolmaster[23] here (though the benefit I make by it is little considering the trouble and care it brings me). Yet, I have condescended to that little Lord's coming, with his page and governor (who is an Episcopal minister that hath the character of a very good man, who left his church rather than wound his conscience). Now holy God, who knows all things and knows that above all things I desire to obey thee, let nothing exalt me, nor cast me down, but in all things so to behave myself as one that is devoted to thy fear (Ps. 119:38).[24]

Besides the satisfaction I had yesterday to have [p. 327] an unlooked for opportunity to serve the heir of Balcarres, where many years since I received great civilities, at the same time I heard that my son[25] was come into the town here, with the Laird of Gosford,[26] who gave up[27] his name for proclamation with Janet Halkett,[28] with whom he is shortly to be married.[29] I pray[30] that the Lord may give his blessing to them. Now, he that ministreth seed to the sower both minister bread for our food, and multiply the seed (of grace) sown, and increase in me (and all mine) the fruits of righteousness (2 Cor. 9:10),[31] being enriched in everything to all bountifulness, which causeth through us thanksgiving unto God.[32] Amen.

---

21. Lady Balcarres helped Halkett to obtain furniture for herself and her waiting woman when she moved into the Earl of Tweeddale's house in Edinburgh; see *True Account*, 139–40.

22. Either the town of Dunfermline, or specifically Halkett's place of residence (Abbot House).

23. David Dobson identifies numerous schoolmasters across Scotland, including Fife. However, while there are several names for Culross and Cupar, the only name associated with Dunfermline Grammar School is Peter Kennedy in 1705; David Dobson, *Scottish Schoolmasters of the Seventeenth Century* (St. Andrews: D. Dobson, 1995), 19. Henderson notes "money paid to the Teachers, April 9, 1682," of ten and five merks, respectively, for the previous year for William Hay and Peter Kennedy in *The Annals of Dunfermline and Vicinity*, 351. A "merk" was a Scottish silver coin that was roughly equivalent to an English shilling in worth.

24. Psalm 119:38: "Stablish thy word unto thy servant, who is devoted to thy fear."

25. I.e., Sir Charles Halkett.

26. Peter Wedderburn, son of Sir Peter Wedderburn, Lord Gosford and Agnes Dickson. A. H. Millar, "Wedderburn, Sir Peter, Lord Gosford (ca. 1616–1679)," *ODNB*.

27. After "up," "there" has been deleted.

28. Daughter of Sir Charles Halkett and his wife, Janet Murray.

29. A contract of marriage between Peter Wedderburn of Gosford and Janet Halkett was signed on July 12, 1694. Angus, ed., *Inventory of Pitfirrane Writs, 1230–1740*, no. 554, 30.

30. "I pray" is an interlineal insertion.

31. 2 Corinthians 9:10: "Now he that ministereth seed to the sower both minister bread for your food, and multiply your seed sown, and increase the fruits of your righteousness."

32. 2 Corinthians 9:11: "Being enriched in everything to all bountifulness, which causeth through us thanksgiving to God."

Tuesday, January 15, 1694/5.

[p. 370] I cannot omit to make some remarks upon the fast that is kept here this day by Proclamation upon the Queen's death[33] as they called her (who died upon Friday, December 28, 1694, and is to be kept as a national humiliation).[34] It seems by the Proclamation that the ministers and brethren of the Commission of the Late General Assembly[35] have addressed the Lords of the Privy Council that a day may be solemnly set apart for that effect, with intimation that all such who shall contemn,[36] or[37] neglect, et cetera, shall be proceeded against, and punished as contemners[38] of the authority and highly disaffected to the person and government of him who now reigns.[39] Of which number I acknowledge myself to be one, and therefore will not dissemble, either with God or man, so as to go[40] into their assembly.

Had our Episcopal ministers supplicated for anything like this, they had been accused as tending to Popery; for it is ordinary in the Romish church to say masses for the dead to help them out of purgatory. Or, if they did [p. 371] it out of the consideration on which the Act of Parliament was grounded—for an anniversary fast for the King's murder, that by repentance and humiliation the wrath of God for the guilt of that excellent King's murder might be turned away, and our sins washed away in the blood of Christ which cleanseth from all sin—this had been justifiable.[41] And, indeed, to consider how the church hath been harassed, divided, and the servants of the Lord exposed to great extremities, our lawful King exiled, and his throne usurped by these of his own loins. For it was not an enemy but those that professed friendship to him and zeal for the Protestant Religion that hath brought this oppression upon all (except those whose hands have been instrumental in procuring all these evils unto us); though, I confess, sin is the chief cause for had we not sinned none of these had ever been armed for

---

33. I.e., Queen Mary II. W. A. Speck, "Mary II (1662–1694), Queen of England, Scotland, and Ireland," *ODNB*.

34. Privy Council Scotland, "A Proclamation for a National Humiliation upon the Account of the Queens Death" (Edinburgh: Andrew Anderson, 1695). ESTC R183465.

35. The national organizing body of the Scottish Presbyterian Kirk.

36. "To treat (law, orders, etc.) with contemptuous disregard," *OED*.

37. "Shall contemn, or" is an interlineal insertion.

38. "One who contemns; a despiser, scorner," *OED*.

39. The Proclamation concludes: "Certifying all such who shall contemn or neglect so religious and important a duty, as the Humiliation hereby appointed is, they shall be proceeded against, and punished as contemners of Our Authority, and as highly disaffected to Our Person and Government."

40. "Go" is an interlineal insertion.

41. "This had been justifiable" is an interlineal insertion. See "Upon the Fast which by Proclamation Was Kept, January 30, 1660/1," 203–5.

our destruction. Oh Lord, look down from heaven, and pity the sad calamities of thy people; [p. 372] for from the crown of the head to the sole of the foot, there is nothing but wounds, and bruises, and putrefied sores (Isa. 1:6).[42]

I will not say but that Princess, if she had that natural affection which became a child, could not but have great debates with herself betwixt performing the duty she owed her Father and her husband.[43] It is true wives are commanded to submit to their own husbands (Eph. 5:22),[44] but it is in the Lord, and certainly in things contrary to the will and established law of the Lord they should not be submitted to.[45] For if the wife of one's bosom shall not be consented to when they entice to sin, no more should a husband be consented to in such acts as is an evident breach of the fifth and tenth Command (Deut. 13:6, 8).[46] Had the fifth been observed, the promise of long life had perhaps been continued to her.[47] It is

---

42. Isaiah 1:6: "From the sole of the foot even unto the head there is no soundness in it; but wounds, and bruises, and putrifying sores: they have not been closed, neither bound up, neither mollified with ointment."

43. Whereas in the *True Account*, Halkett suffers a conflict "betwixt love and honor," Princess Mary exhibits the conflict between obedience to the twin figures of patriarchy: father and husband. See Desdemona, "My most noble father, / I do perceive here a divided duty," as "You are the lord of duty; / I am, hitherto, your daughter"; however, as Othello is now her husband "so much duty as my mother showed / To you, preferring her before her father, / So much I challenge that I may profess / Due to the Moor my lord"; William Shakespeare, *Othello*, 1.3: 179–80, 183–84, 185–88.

44. Ephesians 5:22: "Wives, submit yourselves unto your own husbands, as unto the Lord."

45. Here, Halkett echoes the rhetoric used by sectarian women, itself influenced by Milton's *The Doctrine and Discipline of Divorce* (London: T[homas] P[aine] and M[atthew] S[immons], 1643, ESTC R12932), which "'justified . . . repudiating and even abandoning' their husbands if they felt themselves to be enmeshed within an 'anti-Christian yoke.'" Katharine Gillespie, "Cure for a Diseased Head: Divorce and Contract in the Prophecies of Elizabeth Poole," in *Domesticity and Dissent in the Seventeenth Century: English Women Writers and the Public Sphere* (Cambridge: Cambridge University Press, 2004), 151. See also 2 Corinthians 6:14: "Be ye not unequally yoked together with unbelievers: for what fellowship hath righteousness with unrighteousness? and what communion hath light with darkness?"

46. Deuteronomy 13:6: "If thy brother, the son of thy mother, or thy son, or thy daughter, or the wife of thy bosom, or thy friend, which is as thine own soul, entice thee secretly, saying, Let us go and serve other gods, which thou hast not known, thou, nor thy fathers"; Deuteronomy 13:8: "Thou shalt not consent unto him, nor hearken unto him; neither shall thine eye pity him, neither shalt thou spare, neither shalt thou conceal him."

47. The fifth commandment is "Honor your mother and your father"; the tenth commandment is "You shall not covet." Exodus 20:12, 17: "Honor your mother and your father; that thy days may be long upon the land which the Lord thy God giveth thee"; "Thou shalt not covet thy neighbor's house, thou shalt not covet thy neighbor's wife, nor his manservant, nor his maidservant, nor his ox, nor his ass, nor any thing that is thy neighbor's." Deuteronomy 5:16, 21: "Honor thy father and thy mother, as the Lord thy God hath commanded thee; that thy days may be prolonged, and that it may go well with thee, in the land which the Lord thy God giveth thee"; "Neither shalt thou desire thy neighbor's wife,

to be hoped she[48] repented, and I wish repentance to him[49] she hath left behind, and that there may be such evidence of it that others may hear, and fear, and do no more presumptuously (Deut. 17:13).[50] Amen.[51]

Friday, April 5, 1695.

[p. 176] The continuance of my distemper being sometimes so well as if, at this time, the bitterness of death were past, another time such a damp upon my spirits as if the God of the spirits of all flesh had summoned me[52] to appear before him (Num. 16:22):[53] then what can be more suitable to my daily meditations than to fix them upon death, who gives an universal arrest upon all flesh, and where he lays on his hands there is no shaking him off until he carry his prisoner with him.

How many great persons died the last year? Duke Hamilton[54] began the scene and others followed him. I will make no ill reflections upon any, but happy are they that make so good use of their reason, judgements, and other worldly advantages that, when they are deprived of them at their death, it may not be thought a judgement but a mercy to be kept from the terror that sometimes attends death, even to the very best: that we may see all things come alike to all, there is one event to the righteous, and to the wicked, et cetera (Eccles. 9:2).[55]

[p. 177] The next considerable person of this kingdom, though at distance, was my Lord James Seton,[56] Earl of Dunfermline, Knight of the ancient order

---

neither shalt thou covet thy neighbor's house, his field, or his manservant, or his maidservant, his ox, or his ass, or anything that is thy neighbor's."

48. Here "she" has been written over "her."

49. I.e., William of Orange.

50. Deuteronomy 17:13: "And all the people shall hear, and fear, and do no more presumptuously."

51. The final two words are in the bottom margin.

52. "Me" is an interlineal insertion.

53. Numbers 16:22: "And they fell upon their faces, and said, O God, the God of the spirits of all flesh, shall one-man sin, and wilt thou be wroth with all the congregation?"

54. "Hambleton" in MS, but Halkett means William, third Duke of Hamilton, who died in April 1694. Rosalind K. Marshall, "Hamilton [Formerly Douglas], William, Third Duke of Hamilton (1634–1694)," *ODNB*. Although Hamilton supported the settling of the succession upon James VII/II, and was rewarded for doing so, when he "heard that James had fled for France he went to Sion house, where William was staying, and received a warm welcome," *ODNB*.

55. Ecclesiastes 9:2: "All things come alike to all: there is one event to the righteous, and to the wicked; to the good and to the clean, and to the unclean; to him that sacrificeth, and to him that sacrificeth not: as is the good, so is the sinner; and he that sweareth, as he that feareth an oath."

56. James Seton, fourth Earl of Dunfermline, was the third son of Charles Seton, second Earl of Dunfermline. In "Seton, Charles," Henderson and Furgol confirm that he died in France but give the date as 1699, *ODNB*.

of Saint Andrews who died at Saint Germaine, December 26, there still[57] being always distinguished by his inviolable fidelity to his lawful Sovereign, and by his singular valor which was suitable to his noble birth. This was the character given him in the Public Gazette,[58] and none could contradict it, but such as perhaps may live to see they were enemies to themselves in being enemies to him. But as for me, I will never be unmindful of the favor I received from his noble parents in the time of my retreat when I came as a stranger here to Scotland,[59] and was treated at Fyvie as a daughter of the family.[60]

Therefore, I will pray that the Lord may preserve him a posterity in the earth[61] and that his memory with the just may be blessed.[62]

The next great person that Death triumphed over was a Princess who, had she kept her first station, might have deserved all the praises that the height of flattery itself [p. 178] gave her after she was dead.[63] Naaman was a great man with his master, and honorable, because by him the Lord had given deliverance unto Syria; he was also a mighty man of valor, but he was a leper, which conclusion lessened all the high attributes he had before (2 Kings 5:1).[64] So, when all the high attributes was given that Princess, when it is added she usurped her Father's throne, and wore the royal diadem on her own head, what a dimness doth that cast up on the luster of the brightest actions of her life? But it is to be hoped that repentance for her great transgression, and belief in the meritorious death and suffering of the Lord Jesus, whose blood cleanseth from all sin, hath purchased pardon for her

---

57. "There still" is an interlineal insertion.

58. This is not the only time Halkett refers to information she has gleaned from a contemporary newspaper. While I have not been able to trace this specific edition, it, along with Halkett's response to public Proclamations for Feasts and Fasts, suggests that she actively participated in the emergent public sphere. See Joad Raymond, "The Newspaper, Public Opinion, and the Public Sphere in the Seventeenth Century," *Prose Studies* 21, no. 2 (1998): 109–37. See also, Trill, "Royalism and Resistance."

59. "To Scotland" is an interlineal insertion.

60. See *True Account*, 120–36.

61. Genesis 45:7: "And God sent me before you to preserve you a posterity in the earth, and to save your lives by a great deliverance."

62. Proverbs 10:7: "The memory of the just is blessed: but the name of the wicked shall rot."

63. Halkett's skepticism demonstrates her Jacobite loyalties; however, she was in the minority as an unprecedented "number of sermons, elegies, and medals appeared to memorialize Mary's death," Lois G. Schwoerer, "Images of Queen Mary II, 1689–95," *Renaissance Quarterly* 42, no. 4 (1989): 717–48. While this was partly the result of the Williamite propaganda machine, Queen Mary's popularity is attested to by Ralph Hyde, "Romeyn de Hooghe and the Funeral of the People's Queen," *Print Quarterly* 15, no. 2 (1998): 150–72.

64. 2 Kings 5:1: "Now Naaman, captain of the host of the King of Syria, was a great man with his master, and honorable, because by him the Lord had given deliverance unto Syria: he was also a mighty man in valor, but he was a leper."

(1 John 1:7).[65] And I pray God that he,[66] by[67] whose example and authority she was ensnared, may in time be humbled for all his offences, and bring forth fruit meet for repentance that so iniquity may not be his ruin (Matt. 3:8; Ezek. 18:13).[68]

The next great person that lately died here [181/79] was the Duke of Queensbury,[69] whose opulent fortune was such that if riches would have redeemed from the grave he might have still lived and not seen corruption (Ps. 49:9).[70] But we see that wise men die, likewise the fool and the brutish person, and leave their wealth to others (Ps. 49:10),[71] as is said he hath left abundantly to several charitable uses. For whoever dieth can carry nothing away, his glory shall not descend after him (Ps. 49:17).[72]

Therefore, Solomon's advice is good: whatsoever thy hand findeth to do, do it with thy might; for there is no work, nor device, nor knowledge, nor wisdom,[73] in the grave whither thou goest (Eccles. 9:10),[74] which should excite all that hath power and opportunity to do all the charitable and bountiful acts in their life; for death oft times comes so suddenly that it prevents many good intentions. Therefore, none should delay until their death that which might make it most welcome in life. This is[75] to remember their work of faith and labor of love (1 Thess.

---

65. 1 John 1:7: "But if we walk in the light, as he is in the light, we have fellowship one with another, and the blood of Jesus Christ his Son cleanseth us from all sin."

66. I.e., William of Orange.

67. "By" is an interlineal insertion.

68. Matthew 3:8: "Bring forth therefore fruits meet for repentance"; Ezekiel 18:13: "Hath given forth upon usury, and hath taken increase: shall he then live? he shall not live: he hath done all these abominations; he shall surely die; his blood shall be upon him." Despite her in-text reference, Halkett's phraseology here resonates with Ezekiel 18:30: "Therefore I will judge you, O house of Israel, everyone according to his ways, saith the Lord God. Repent, and turn yourselves from all your transgressions; so, iniquity shall not be your ruin."

69. William Douglas, first duke of Queensbury, became high treasurer of Scotland under Charles II in 1682. Although he remained in office at the accession of James VII/II, his refusal to convert to Catholicism and his antipathy toward the Earl of Aberdeen led to his removal from office. J. D. Ford, "Douglas, William, First Duke of Queensberry (1637–1695)," *ODNB*.

70. Psalm 49:9: "That he should still live forever, and not see corruption."

71. Psalm 49:10: "For he seeth that wise men die, likewise the fool and the brutish person perish, and leave their wealth to others."

72. Psalm 49:17: "For when he dieth he shall carry nothing away: his glory shall not descend after him."

73. "Nor wisdom" is an interlineal insertion.

74. Ecclesiastes 9:10: "Whatsoever thy hand findeth to do, do it with thy might; for there is no work, nor device, nor knowledge, nor wisdom, in the grave, whither thou goest."

75. "This is" is an interlineal insertion.

1:3),[76] so becoming examples to all that believe[77] that man shall be blessed in his deed (James 1:25).[78]

It is appointed unto me once to die, but after this the judgment (Heb. 9:27).[79] It may be a suitable subject for my [p. 180] thoughts now to be employed on death, when I am daily, and have been a considerable time, under such indisposition as hath made me often think it was sent as the harbinger of death to prepare for his coming. Had not sin been the first introduction of death, none could have feared it; but the consequences of that first disobedience hath, by sin, given such a sting to death (1 Cor. 15)[80] as it hath passed upon all men for that all have sinned (Rom. 5:12).[81] But, as by one man's disobedience many were made sinners, so by the obedience of one shall many be made righteous (Rom. 5:19);[82] that as sin reigneth unto death, even so might grace reign through righteousness unto eternal life by Jesus Christ, our Lord (Rom. 5:21),[83] who his own self bore our sins on his own body on the tree, that we, being dead unto sin, should live unto righteousness: by whose stripes we are healed (1 Pet. 2:24).[84] And that he died for all that they which live should not henceforth live unto themselves, but unto him (Gal. 2:20)[85] which

---

76. 1 Thessalonians 1:3: "Remembering without ceasing your work of faith, and labor of love, and patience of hope in our Lord Jesus Christ, in the sight of God and our Father."

77. 1 Thessalonians 1:7: "So that ye were ensamples to all that believe in Macedonia and Achaia."

78. James 1:25: "But whoso looketh into the perfect law of liberty, and continueth therein, he being not a forgetful hearer, but a doer of the work, this man shall be blessed in his deed."

79. Hebrews 9:27: "And as it is appointed unto men once to die, but after this the judgment."

80. Unusually, here Halkett provides a reference to a whole chapter, 1 Corinthians 15, in which Saint Paul exhorts his audience to stay true to the Gospel, at the heart of which is Christ's death and resurrection by which all are saved. Toward the end of this chapter, Paul addresses the "sting of death," which is conquered through Christ, see 1 Corinthians 15:54–57: "So when this corruptible shall have put on incorruption, and this mortal shall have put on immortality, then shall be brought to pass the saying that is written, death is swallowed up in victory. O death, where is thy sting? O grave, where is thy victory? The sting of death is sin; and the strength of sin is the law. But thanks be to God, which giveth us the victory through our Lord Jesus Christ."

81. Romans 5:12: "Wherefore, as by one man, sin entered into the world, and death by sin; and so, death passed upon all men, for that all have sinned."

82. Romans 5:19: "For as by one man's disobedience many were made sinners, so by the obedience of one shall many be made righteous."

83. Romans 5:21: "That as sin hath reigned unto death, even so might grace reign through righteousness unto eternal life by Jesus Christ our Lord."

84. 1 Peter 2:24: "Who his own self bare our sins in his own body on the tree, that we, being dead to sins, should live unto righteousness: by whose stripes ye were healed."

85. Galatians 2:20: "I am crucified with Christ: nevertheless, I live; yet not I, but Christ liveth in me: and the life which I now live in the flesh I live by the faith of the Son of God, who loved me, and gave himself for me."

died for them, and rose again (2 Cor. 5:15).[86] Oh, that Christ would vouchsafe to live in me, that the life[87] which I now live in the flesh may be by faith in the son of God, who loved me, and gave himself for me: so shall Christ be to me both in life and[88] death advantage. Amen.

---

86. 2 Corinthians 5:15: "And that he died for all, that they which live should not henceforth live unto themselves, but unto him which died for them, and rose again."
87. After "life," the rest of the meditation is written in the bottom margin of the page.
88. "And" is an interlineal insertion.

Select and Occasional Meditations *(1696–1697)*

Halkett began this volume on May 21, 1696, and it was completed on July 24, 1697.[1] Introducing her list of its contents, Halkett draws attention to its organization: "At first I designed to write upon select and occasional observations. And to that end began the first part of it the date above mentioned (May 21, 1696). And the other part, May 26, 1696 (page 265). But the occasional observations ended, when I thought there might be something worth remembering I began them then again, page 201."[2] Although this may seem complicated, it results in this volume being almost equally divided between select and occasional meditations.[3] Following an extended list of the volume's contents, there are two insertions:[4] the first is a scrap of paper, identifying the start pages for each section of occasional meditations;[5] the second, another scrap of paper, records her response to reading "The Mischief of Faction," by bishop Joseph Hall, where he provides examples of popes involved in "schism," after which Halkett inquires: "Where was infallibility then?"[6] As in the previous volume, the predominant way of identifying different meditations within the main volume is by date; however, the list of contents primarily identifies entries by their subject matter.[7] While she specifies the individual titles of all of her select meditations, Halkett's listing of her occasional meditations is more selective than in other volumes: there are eighty-two individually dated entries in this manuscript, but Halkett draws attention to only twenty-four of them in her table of contents.[8] As in the previous volume, there is some slippage between categories of meditation, with some "occasional" moments being

---

1. Halkett, *Select and Occasional Meditations* (1696–1697), pp. i, 263–64. This is volume 20 in Couper's catalogue.

2. Halkett, *Select and Occasional Meditations* (1696–1697), p. i. Halkett's pagination omits pages 256–57; thus, after page 255, her numbering diverges from that of the library cataloguer. I have therefore changed Halkett's reference from "267" to "265." Two later errors (364/363, and 369) bring the numbering systems back into accordance.

3. The select meditations run from vii to 200, and the occasional from 201 to 373.

4. Halkett, *Select and Occasional Meditations* (1696–1697), pp. i–iv.

5. Halkett, *Select and Occasional Meditations* (1696–1697), p. v.

6. Halkett, *Select and Occasional Meditations* (1696–1697), p. vi. Given the short title and page reference Halkett provides, she was reading "The Mischief of Faction, and the Remedy of It, Laid Forth in a Sermon before His Majesty, in the Courtyard at Whitehall, on the Second Sunday in Lent, 1641," in Joseph Hall, *The Shaking of the Olive-Tree: The Remaining Works of That Incomparable Prelate Joseph Hall D. D., Late Lord Bishop of Norwich. With Some Specialties of Divine Providence in His Life, Noted by His Own Hand. Together with His Hard Measure, Written Also by Himself* (London: J. Cadwell,1660), 72. ESTC R10352.

7. For example, the entry dated "Monday, May 9, 1697," p. 139, is listed as "Meditations upon Deuteronomy," p. ii.

8. One of those she lists, "Concerning My Son, Thursday, July 1, 1697," is now missing.

highlighted in those identified as select items.[9] Generally, both the select and the occasional meditations here are, individually, shorter than those in previous volumes. The detailed contents of the select meditations are provided by Couper, but it is worth noting that Halkett is consciously extending her repertoire while recognizing practical constraints:

> Having ended the forgoing meditations, and having looked over briefly the contents of all the books that I have formerly written, and finding nothing in them on the book of Esther; nor having read of any upon that subject, and having no more room than to the two hundred and first page; therefore, I do intend, with the Lord's assistance to make such observations upon that historical part of Scripture as may be useful to me, edifying to others (if ever it should come to be known), and bring praise and glory to God.[10]

The occasional meditations continue to record the conflict between Presbyterianism and Episcopalianism in Scotland and reiterate Halkett's objections to William of Orange while also frequently reflecting on the poor state of her health.[11]

Monday, June 8, 1696.[12]

[p. 273] Upon Saturday night, late, Mr. Couper came home, whose business was not heard on the Tuesday, according to his citation; for his enemies knew that on that day he would have more for him than against him, and therefore they got it delayed to another day, being Thursday. And then, though it was debated two hours in the Council, and then put to the vote, it was only carried by one vote that he should have a charge of horning[13] to remove within fifteen days from the church and manse[14] but not out of the parish, which was the only thing in

---

9. This practice is illustrated below in a dated interjection within a meditation upon John 14:6: "Jesus saith unto him, I am the way, the truth, and the life: no man cometh unto the Father, but by me." See "Saturday, January 30, 1696/7," 304–307.
10. Halkett, *Select and Occasional Meditations* (1696–1697), p. 186.
11. See Trill, ed., *Halkett*, 175.
12. See also Trill, ed., *Halkett*, 178–79.
13. Letters of horning: "Letters in the Sovereign's name charging the persons named in them to make the payment or performance ordered under the penalty of being put to the horn for disobedience. 'They are directed to messengers-at-arms . . . who are ordered to charge the person, against whom the letters are directed, to pay or perform in terms of the will of the letters, which must be consistent with the warrant on which the letters proceed' (Bell)," *DSL*.
14. "The dwelling house provided for the minister of a particular church, the parsonage; sometimes the minister's household," *DSL*.

the petition that was not granted. The charge not being yet come, he preached yesterday to the satisfaction of his friends and the rancor of his enemies. And I wish the charge may be so long in coming that the Lord, by his good providence, may put such a stop to their proceedings as may secure him from the power of his adversaries.

This puts me in mind of what in some way may be applicable to this. The [p. 274] same night that the Duke of York made his escape from Saint James's (April 20, 1648),[15] after he was missed there was order sent to Lenthall,[16] who was Speaker to the House of Commons, to send orders to all the ports to stop all ships, boats, or barges, and there were severals[17] employed to write them about midnight. And the Lord put such a trembling in the hands of those that were to write that not one of them could write one order as it should be until morning, and before that time his Highness was safely out of their hands. (This account I had from Mr. Norfolk, who was Macebearer to the Speaker.)[18]

So, it may please God to put some stop to the writing of the charge of horning until more mature thoughts may be taken to prevent the execution of that sentence which was sinistrously[19] gained. And whatever the event may be, one person hath reason to repent who, upon a private pick,[20] would not go to the Council nor concern himself so much as either to write or speak when the doing either might have kept that worthy man in his place. Is this a time [p. 275] to silence good men? When there is so much reason rather to continue them to cry aloud, spare not to lift up their voice like a trumpet, and show the people their transgressions, and the house of Jacob their sin (Isa. 58:1).[21] Did ever Atheism, Popery, and Schism[22] more prevail? And is this a time to take pastors from us who, according to God's heart,[23] feeds us with knowledge and understanding?[24]

---

15. "1648" is an interlineal insertion.

16. Roberts, "Lenthall, William," *ODNB*. See *True Account*, 85, 85n146.

17. "Several persons or things," *OED*.

18. See *True Account*, 85, 85n150. See also Trill, "Royalism and Resistance."

19. "In an erroneous manner; incorrectly, wrongly, perversely; awkwardly," *OED*.

20. "To seek and find an opportunity for (a quarrel, fight, argument, etc.). Formerly also: to seek and find (a pretext for hostile action, a fault, occasion for a grievance, etc.)," *OED*.

21. Isaiah 58:1: "Cry aloud, spare not, lift up thy voice like a trumpet, and shew my people their transgression, and the house of Jacob their sins."

22. "A breach of the unity of the visible church; the division, either of the whole church or of some portion of it, into separate and mutually hostile organizations; the condition of being so divided, or an instance of this," *OED*.

23. After "heart," the interlineal insertion of "who" has been deleted.

24. Jeremiah 3:15: "And I will give you pastors according to mine heart, which shall feed you with knowledge and understanding."

They hate him without a cause and devise deceitful matters against them that are quiet in the land (Ps. 35:19–20).[25] This thou hast seen, O Lord, be not far from him, stir up thy self and awake for his help, and all thy servants that suffer, and are like to suffer hard things, and plead their cause, my Lord and my God (Ps. 35:22–23).[26] But, if their enemies prevail, it seems the iniquity of the Amorites is not yet full (Gen. 15:16).[27] And their putting out such as may truly say to their flock, we preach not ourselves, but Christ Jesus the[28] Lord, and ourselves your servants for Jesus' sake (2 Cor. 4:5);[29] their putting out such may fill up the cup of the Lord's indignation against them, who can justly lay nothing to any of our ministers' charge [p. 276] but forbid them to preach because, as[30] the Disciples said, they followed not with us (Mark 9:38).[31] This mistaken zeal was even amongst the Disciples of our Lord, to whom he said: forbid them not; for he that is not against us is on our part (Mark 9:39–40).[32]

Had they had that to say, which may as a fault be laid to the charge of the minister of Culross,[33] whose style is Brays[34] (that until yesterday, being Sunday, June 7, 1696, never administered the Sacrament of the Lord's Supper since he came to that place, in[35] which he[36] hath been seven years, and as it's said never

25. Psalm 35:19–20: "Let not them that are mine enemies wrongfully rejoice over me: neither let them wink with the eye that hate me without a cause. For they speak not peace: but they devise deceitful matters against them that are quiet in the land."

26. Psalm 35:22–23: "This thou hast seen, O Lord: keep not silence: O Lord, be not far from me. Stir up thyself, and awake to my judgment, even unto my cause, my God and my Lord."

27. Genesis 15:16: "But in the fourth generation they shall come hither again: for the iniquity of the Amorites is not yet full."

28. Here, Halkett has written both "the" and "our"; unusually, it is unclear which is her preference, although "the" is used in the *KJV*, as below.

29. 2 Corinthians 4:5: "For we preach not ourselves, but Christ Jesus the Lord; and ourselves your servants for Jesus' sake."

30. Before "as," "they" has been deleted.

31. Mark 9:38: "And John answered him, saying, master, we saw one casting out devils in thy name, and he followeth not us: and we forbad him, because he followeth not us."

32. Mark 9:39–40: "But Jesus said, 'Forbid him not: for there is no man which shall do a miracle in my name, that can lightly speak evil of me. For he that is not against us is on our part.'"

33. The royal burgh and parish of Culross lies about ten miles east of Dunfermline.

34. The minister of Culross was James Fraser of Brae, who was appointed in early 1689 and preached in a meeting house until the Committee of Estates "sanctioned his use of the church, May 13, 1689." Although called to Inverness, his ministry there was never settled. A committed Presbyterian, he died in Edinburgh on September 13, 1699. *FES* 5:15–16, 6.461. His memoirs were posthumously published as *Memoirs of the Life of the Very Reverend James Fraser of Brea, Minister of the Gospel at Culross. Written by Himself* (Edinburgh: Thomas Lumisden and John Robertson, 1738). ESTC T127427.

35. "In" is an interlineal insertion.

36. "He" is an interlineal insertion.

catechized[37] any of the parishioners), what exclamations had they made against our ministers had they neglected so great a duty! But they are like to them our Lord speaks of which strain at a gnat and swallow a camel (Matt. 23:24);[38] who behold the mote that is in their brother's eye but considers not the beam that is in their own eye (Matt. 7:3).[39] Be merciful to us, O God, be merciful unto us: for our soul trusteth in thee, et cetera. I will cry unto God most high who performeth all things for us (Ps. 57:1–2).[40] He will send from heaven and save us from the reproach of them that would swallow us up. God will send forth his mercy and his truth (Ps. 57:3).[41] Be then exalted, O God, above the heavens; let thy glory be above all the earth (Ps. 57:5).[42] Amen, and amen.

Wednesday, October 14, 1696.

[p. 338] Solomon says: to everything there is a season, and a time to every purpose under heaven (Eccles. 3:1).[43]

This day was once a season when all the Three Kingdoms[44] gave thanks to God, and showed good will to one another, in cheerful commemorating the birthday of their lawful Sovereign, King James; but, for some late years, they

---

37. "An elementary treatise for instruction in the principles of the Christian religion, in the form of question and answer; such a book accepted and issued by a church as an authoritative exposition of its teaching, as the *Longer Catechism* and *Shorter Catechism*, of the Westminster Assembly of Divines, used by the Presbyterian churches," *OED*. However, as Ian Green points out: "In the early modern period the term 'catechism' was applied by authors to a bewildering variety of works: statements of principles in continuous prose as well as in (what to us today may be the more familiar) question-and-answer form; very short forms . . . right up to a thousand-page or multi-volume exposition of catechetical material clearly intended to be studied rather than memorized; works designed for use in church or school and works intended for domestic catechizing . . . works with a political message or a point to make about church government as well as works which, more conventionally, were focused on the Apostles' Creed, the Ten Commandments, and the Lord's Prayer. The term 'catechism' was also used to describe a form of preparation, either for confirmation or holy communion." Ian Green, *The Christian's ABC: Catechisms and Catechizing in England c.1530–1740* (Oxford: Oxford University Press, 1996), 4–5. See also "A Catechism," *BCP*, 426–31.
38. Matthew 23:24: "Ye blind guides, which strain at a gnat, and swallow a camel."
39. Matthew 7:3: "And why beholdest thou the mote that is in thy brother's eye, but considerest not the beam that is in thine own eye?"
40. Psalm 57:1–2: "Be merciful unto me, O God, be merciful unto me: for my soul trusteth in thee: yea, in the shadow of thy wings will I make my refuge, until these calamities be overpast. I will cry unto God most high; unto God that performeth all things for me."
41. Psalm 57:3: "He shall send from heaven and save me from the reproach of him that would swallow me up. Selah. God shall send forth his mercy and his truth."
42. Psalm 57:5: "Be thou exalted, O God, above the heavens; let thy glory be above all the earth."
43. Ecclesiastes 3:1: "To everything there is a season, and a time to every purpose under the heaven."
44. See "Introduction," 6n21.

have turned many of them their hosannas into crucify.⁴⁵ Yet some, whose heart God had touched, continues in their loyalty by offering up prayers to God for his Majesty, and as far as they can, or dare, they eat the fat, and drink the sweet, and send portions to them for whom nothing is provided (Neh. 8:10).⁴⁶ The first part I have endeavored to perform with my private family, offering up prayers and supplication for the King (for all things that may make him acceptable to God, bring peace to his own conscience, and make him a blessing to his people by his Restoration). As for the other part of the usual custom, in feasting with friends and neighbors, and sending relief to those in want, which I usually did when I had wherewithal; now, having neither money, meat, meal, nor little of [p. 339] anything for myself or servants to eat, I bless God, I am now as much contented to sit down with a piece of bread and cheese alone as I had been formerly in the time that corn and wine increased (Ps. 4:7),⁴⁷ and had a full table with friends and neighbors praying for the good of thy chosen, and rejoicing in the gladness of the nation (Ps. 106:5).⁴⁸

As I have reason to acknowledge that was⁴⁹ a time of mercy, so it is no less mercy to be upheld under the cross dispensations⁵⁰ that I am now under. What sweet repose had I this last night in sleep. And though unallowed of thoughts came into my mind at my first waking, reflecting on my wants, yet remembering these words of the Apostle (be content with such things as you have; for He, even the omnipotent God, hath said I will never leave thee, nor forsake thee [Heb. 13:5]),⁵¹ I hope the Lord hath thoughts of peace towards me, and not of evil, to

---

45. Here, Halkett draws an analogy between King James's experiences and the people's changing attitude to Jesus, from his triumphal entry into Jerusalem to his judgment and crucifixion. John 12:12–13: "On the next day much people that were come to the feast, when they heard that Jesus was coming to Jerusalem, took branches of palm trees, and went forth to meet him, and cried, Hosanna: Blessed is the King of Israel that cometh in the name of the Lord," and John 19:14–15: "And it was the preparation of the Passover, and about the sixth hour: and he [Pilate] saith unto the Jews, behold your king! But they cried out, away with him, away with him, crucify him. Pilate saith unto them, shall I crucify your king? The chief priests answered, we have no king but Caesar."
46. Nehemiah 8:10: "Then he said unto them, go your way, eat the fat, and drink the sweet, and send portions unto them for whom nothing is prepared: for this day is holy unto our Lord: neither be ye sorry; for the joy of the Lord is your strength."
47. Psalm 4:7: "Thou hast put gladness in my heart, more than in the time that their corn and their wine increased."
48. Psalm 106:5: "That I may see the good of thy chosen, that I may rejoice in the gladness of thy nation, that I may glory with thine inheritance."
49. "Was" is an interlineal insertion.
50. "Ordering, management; especially, the divine administration or conduct of the world; the ordering or arrangement of events by divine providence," *OED*.
51. Hebrews 13:5: "Let your conversation be without covetousness; and be content with such things as ye have: for he hath said, I will never leave thee, nor forsake thee."

give me an expected end (Jer. 29:11).[52] And to his holy will do I resign myself: let him do with me what he please, so that he will vouchsafe to keep me from doing anything to displease him. Amen.

Saturday, January 30, 1696/7.[53]

[p. 109] Where can I look or in what station can I consider any in within these Three Kingdoms[54] on who thy judgments are not? Oh, that by them the inhabitants might learn righteousness (Isa. 26:9).[55] The church, which is the ground and pillar of truth (1 Tim. 3:15),[56] how is that divided, rent, and torn[57] by Atheism, Popery, and Schism?[58] The throne, how is that usurped,[59] and the lawful, righteous heir of it exiled,[60] and the people oppressed and ensnared [p. 110] as is usual when a hypocrite reigns (Job 34:30)?[61] There is neither mercy nor truth. And should not the land mourn when the Lord's judgments are upon us by pestilential diseases and scarcity, and yet few or none lay it to heart?

And it is to be feared that the innocent blood of our Sovereign, King Charles the first, who was martyred this day (January 30, 1648) is still crying for vengeance. And yet few, or none, considers it with that grief and remorse due for so horrid a crime. When the Lord maketh inquisition for blood he remembereth

---

52. Jeremiah 29:11: "For I know the thoughts that I think toward you, saith the Lord, thoughts of peace, and not of evil, to give you an expected end."

53. This entry is an excerpt from a meditation on John 14:6: "Jesus saith unto him, I am the way, the truth, and the life: no man cometh unto the Father, but by me." The date is written in the left-hand margin of the page, and in her index, she draws attention to it as "January 30, 1696/7: sad calamities." See also "Upon the Fast which by Proclamation Was Kept, January 30, 1660/1," "January 30, 1673/4," and "January 30, 1690/1," 203–5, 255–56, 284–85.

54. See "Introduction," 6n21.

55. Isaiah 26:9: "With my soul have I desired thee in the night; yea, with my spirit within me will I seek thee early: for when thy judgments are in the earth, the inhabitants of the world will learn righteousness."

56. 1 Timothy 3:15: "But if I tarry long, that thou mayest know how thou oughtest to behave thyself in the house of God, which is the church of the living God, the pillar and ground of the truth."

57. "Torn" is an insertion in the left-hand margin.

58. "A breach of the unity of the visible church; the division, either of the whole church or of some portion of it, into separate and mutually hostile organizations; the condition of being so divided, or an instance of this," *OED*.

59. I.e., by William of Orange.

60. I.e., James VII/II, who returned to France after his defeat at the Battle of the Boyne (1690). Speck, "James II and VII," *ODNB*.

61. Job 34:30: "That the hypocrite reign not, lest the people be ensnared."

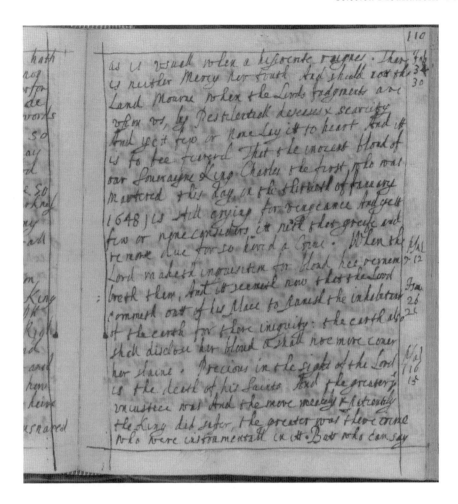

Figure 16. From Anne, Lady Halkett, *Select and Occasional Meditations* (1696–1697). © National Library of Scotland, NLS, MS 6501, p. 110. Reproduced with permission.

them (Ps. 9:12),[62] and it seemeth now that the Lord commeth out of his place to punish the inhabitants of the earth for their iniquity: the earth also shall disclose her blood and shall no more cover her slain (Isa. 26:21).[63] Precious in the sight of the Lord is the death of his Saints (Ps. 116:15).[64] And the greater the injustice was,

62. Psalm 9:12: "When he maketh inquisition for blood, he remembereth them: he forgetteth not the cry of the humble."
63. Isaiah 26:21: "For, behold, the Lord cometh out of his place to punish the inhabitants of the earth for their iniquity: the earth also shall disclose her blood, and shall no more cover her slain."
64. Psalm 116:15: "Precious in the sight of the Lord is the death of his saints."

and the more meekly, and patiently the King did suffer, the greater was their crime who were instrumental in it. But who can say [p. 111] in the Three Kingdoms: our hands have not shed this blood, nor our eyes[65] seen it (Deut. 21:7).[66] But is anyone free of sin, for which they who were actually guilty of it were strengthened by them who were passively guilty? And therefore, all have need to say be merciful, O Lord, unto thy people whom thou hast redeemed, and lay not innocent blood onto thy people's charge (Deut. 21:8).[67] O shut not up our souls with sinners, nor our life with bloodthirsty men (Ps. 26:9).[68] Deliver us from blood guiltiness, O God, the God of our salvation.[69]

O remember not against us former iniquities: let thy tender mercies speedily prevent us, for we are brought very low (Ps. 79:8).[70] Help us, O God of our salvation, for the glory of thy name: and deliver us, and purge away our sins for thy name's sake (Ps. 79:9).[71] O merciful Father, let the blood of Jesus Christ, thy Son, cleanse us from all sin[72] (1 John 1:7), and all unrighteousness (1 John 1:9)[73] that so we may be partakers of the heavenly calling (Heb. 3:1).[74] And then when Christ, who is our life, shall appear we shall also appear with him in glory.[75]

But until that [p. 112] time comes, we must not expect to be free of trials and temptations, but if we are so blessed as to endure them as we should do we shall receive the crown of life, which the Lord hath promised to them that love

---

65. "Eyes" is an interlineal insertion.

66. Deuteronomy 21:7: "And they shall answer and say, our hands have not shed this blood, neither have our eyes seen it."

67. Deuteronomy 21:8: "Be merciful, O Lord, unto thy people Israel, whom thou hast redeemed, and lay not innocent blood unto thy people of Israel's charge. And the blood shall be forgiven them."

68. Psalm 26:9: "Gather not my soul with sinners, nor my life with bloody men." In the *BCP*, this verse reads: "O shut not up my soul with the sinners: nor my life with the blood-thirsty."

69. Psalm 51:14: "Deliver me from blood-guiltiness, O God, thou God of my salvation: and my tongue shall sing aloud of thy righteousness."

70. Psalm 79:8: "O remember not against us former iniquities: let thy tender mercies speedily prevent us: for we are brought very low."

71. Psalm 79:9: "Help us, O God of our salvation, for the glory of thy name: and deliver us, and purge away our sins, for thy name's sake."

72. 1 John 1:7: "But if we walk in the light, as he is in the light, we have fellowship one with another, and the blood of Jesus Christ his Son cleanseth us from all sin."

73. 1 John 1:9: "If we confess our sins, he is faithful and just to forgive us our sins, and to cleanse us from all unrighteousness."

74. Hebrews 3:1: "Wherefore, holy brethren, partakers of the heavenly calling, consider the apostle and high priest of our profession, Christ Jesus."

75. Colossians 3:4: "When Christ, who is our life, shall appear, then shall ye also appear with him in glory."

him (James 1:12).[76] For what is this temporal life? It is even a vapor that appeareth for a little time, and vanisheth away (James 4:14).[77] Therefore, we have reason to pass the time of our sojourning here in fear (1 Pet. 1:17),[78] redeeming the time because never was any time more evil (Eph. 5:16).[79] But if we be dead to sin and live unto righteousness (1 Pet. 2:24),[80] our life will then be hid with Christ in God (Col. 3:3).[81] And then nothing shall be able to separate us from the love of God which is in Christ Jesus our Lord (Rom. 8:39).[82] And this is the record, that God hath given to us eternal life, and this life is in his Son (1 John 5:11).[83] Now unto him that is able to keep us from falling, and to present us faultless before the presence of his glory with exceeding joy, to the only wise God, our Savior, be glory and majesty, dominion and power, both now and ever. Amen.[84]

What Crosses and Difficulties I Have Met with Myself, and Deliverances out of Them, ever to Be Remembered with Thankfulness and Praise.[85]

[p. 151] What straits and difficulties have I been plunged in as seemed ever to overwhelm me, and the Lord said to them as to the sea, hitherto shalt thou come, but no further (Job 38:11)[86] when they had accomplished the end for which they were sent (which was to humble and prove me that I might know my own heart, which the Lord knows better than myself whether I would keep his Commandments or no).[87] [p. 152] Saint Paul, by mentioning the many trials

---

76. James 1:12: "Blessed is the man that endureth temptation: for when he is tried, he shall receive the crown of life, which the Lord hath promised to them that love him."
77. James 4:14: "Whereas ye know not what shall be on the morrow. For what is your life? It is even a vapor, that appeareth for a little time, and then vanisheth away."
78. 1 Peter 1:17: "And if ye call on the Father, who without respect of persons judgeth according to every man's work, pass the time of your sojourning here in fear."
79. The original marginal reference reads "Ephesians 1:16"; however, the reference should be Ephesians 5:16: "Redeeming the time, because the days are evil."
80. 1 Peter 2:24: "Who his own self bare our sins in his own body on the tree, that we, being dead to sins, should live unto righteousness: by whose stripes ye were healed."
81. Colossians 3:3: "For ye are dead, and your life is hid with Christ in God."
82. Romans 8:39: "Nor height, nor depth, nor any other creature, shall be able to separate us from the love of God, which is in Christ Jesus our Lord."
83. 1 John 5:11: "And this is the record, that God hath given to us eternal life, and this life is in his Son."
84. "Now and ever. Amen." is written in the bottom margin of the page.
85. Here, Halkett interrupts her exegetical discussion of Deuteronomy 8:2 to reflect on her own experiences. The title here is how the passage is identified in Halkett's index to this book.
86. Job 38:11: "And said, hitherto shalt thou come, but no further: and here shall thy proud waves be stayed?"
87. "Or no" is a subscript insertion.

he met with, glorified God for upholding him under them, and delivering him from them; not only from deceitful works, which I have also met with, but with many other severities (2 Cor. 11:13).[88] Though I have not been beaten with rods as he was, yet I have been suffered much by the scourge[89] of the tongue, and my fame hath suffered shipwreck, many a night and a day have I been in the deep of sorrow and affliction (2 Cor. 11:25).[90] In perils of my life being once threatened to be killed with a sword; another time to be brained with a pair of tongs (being the readiest instrument that one in the rage of fury had to make use of); another time with a dirk.[91] The God and Father of our Lord Jesus Christ, which is blessed for evermore knoweth that I lie not (2 Cor. 11:31).[92] The deliverance I had from these trials I weekly remember every Monday, being the day on which in the evening two of them arrived to me,[93] with all the thanksgiving, praise, and adoration I am capable to give to the most high, who humbled himself to behold the things that are in heaven and earth (Ps. 113:5–6).[94] [p. 153] For the Lord delivered my soul from death, my eyes from tears, my feet from falling (Ps. 116:8)[95] into the snares that was laid for me; forever may the God of my salvation be exalted. Have I not often found the Lord, my God, to enlighten me in darkness, and by him I have run through a troop?[96]

For at that time, 1649/50,[97] that, upon a Friday, I was expecting nothing but death at Naworth Castle,[98] and having taken my leave of all about me,[99] and resolved to speak no more to any but to compose myself for dying, while I was

---

88. 2 Corinthians 11:13: "For such are false apostles, deceitful workers, transforming themselves into the apostles of Christ."

89. Above "scourge," there is an interlineal insertion of "Job." This is an incomplete reference to Job 5:21: "Thou shalt be hid from the scourge of the tongue: neither shalt thou be afraid of destruction when it cometh."

90. 2 Corinthians 11:25: "Thrice was I beaten with rods, once was I stoned, thrice I suffered shipwreck, a night and a day I have been in the deep."

91. "A kind of dagger or poniard: specifically, the dagger of a Highlander," *OED*.

92. 2 Corinthians 11:31: "The God and Father of our Lord Jesus Christ, which is blessed for evermore, knoweth that I lie not."

93. See also "Monday, May 21, 1688," and "Saturday, May 21, 1698," and "Introduction," 273–75, 322–23.

94. Psalm 113:5–6: "Who is like unto the Lord our God, who dwelleth on high, who humbleth himself to behold the things that are in heaven, and in the earth!"

95. Psalm 116:8: "For thou hast delivered my soul from death, mine eyes from tears, and my feet from falling."

96. Psalm 18:28–29: "For thou wilt light my candle: The Lord my God will enlighten my darkness. For by thee I have run through a troop; and by my God have I leaped over a wall."

97. "1649/50" is an insertion in the left-hand margin.

98. See *True Account*, 95–96.

99. "About me" is an interlineal insertion.

meditating upon the transcendent goodness of God, and the meritorious sufferings of the Lord Jesus, Satan did, in a manner, draw up as it had been a troop of my sins, and beset them on every side, and asked me how I could hope to escape through all them, and come to heaven? To whom I replied, I would not trouble myself with looking over them, my sins being more than could be numbered, but I would look to him that [p. 154] was the Captain of my salvation, and through his strength I run through that troop. They thrust sore at me that I might fall, but the Lord helped me (Ps. 118:13).[100] As he was graciously pleased also to do at Fyvie, when I thought I was dying there (under great discouragements, being at a great distance from all my relations, and having had no opportunity to vindicate myself from some aspersions that by misfortune more than intention I was fallen under).[101] This, and the want of that great cordial for a fainting soul drawing near the gates of death (the Sacrament of the Lord's Supper, which at that time of Presbytery they would give to none); but under both these wants the Lord supported me, and supplied by the consolations of his Holy Spirit by which I was so far exalted as to triumph over all discouragements through Christ[102] who had given me victory through his meritorious death and powerful intercession.

At which the Devil, [p. 155] though not visibly seen, did powerfully assault me with questioning how I could believe that the eternal and only Son of God would leave heaven and be incarnate only to redeem such a sinner as I was? At the first this put a damp upon my spirits. But I did, as it were, hold him fast, and would not let him go without an answer, which I begged the Lord would instruct me how to give as that it might evidence my faith, and foil him. I lay some time without knowing what to say. At last, the Lord asked me why I called upon Him; to whom I replied, "because thou art a God hearing prayer."[103]

The whole particular of this trial and deliverance is mentioned in the parchment book in folio, part written at Fyvie, in which that[104] is writ and many other things entitled *The Soul's Remembrancer*.[105] Should I record all the trials and mercies I have met with, even since my coming out of Egypt that the Lord my God

---

100. Psalm 118:13: "Thou hast thrust sore at me that I might fall: but the Lord helped me."
101. See *True Account*, 128.
102. "Christ" is an interlineal insertion.
103. Psalm 65:2: "O thou that hearest prayer, unto thee shall all flesh come." Within the psalms, David frequently asks God to hear his prayers: see, for example, Psalm 54:2: "Hear my prayer, O God; give ear to the words of my mouth," and Psalm 61:1: "Hear my cry, O God; attend unto my prayer."
104. "That" is an interlineal insertion.
105. This text is listed in Couper's catalogue as the final section of volume 2, which is now missing.

[p. 156] hath led me in these forty years,[106] time would fail me (Heb. 11:32)[107] for to tell[108] all the steps and traverses[109] of my life. Where have I lived without provoking the most High? And yet no time nor place can I name wherein I have not received manifest evidence of the Lord's favor. And after all this, should I break the Commandments of my God (Ezra 9:13–14)[110] and continue in[111] sin because grace abounds? (Rom. 6:1)[112] God forbid![113] Though I was conceived in sin, brought forth in iniquity, and a transgressor from the very womb, yet Lord, if thou wilt, thou canst make me clean (Matt. 8:2).[114] Oh, gracious, merciful, and faithful high priest, wherein things pertaining to God can make reconciliation for the sins of the people (Heb. 2:17).[115] Let my leprosy of sin be cleansed (Lev. 14:14)[116] by thy precious blood (which typically was represented, under the Law, when the priest put some of the blood of the trespass offering upon the tip of the

---

106. Typologically, Halkett identifies herself with the disobedient Israelites, whose punishment for not believing in God's promises led to them wandering in the wilderness for forty years. Numbers 14:34: "After the number of the days in which ye searched the land, even forty days, each day for a year, shall ye bear your iniquities, even forty years, and ye shall know my breach of promise." In the New Testament this is paralleled by Christ's temptation in the desert, Mark 1:13: "And he was there in the wilderness forty days, tempted of Satan; and was with the wild beasts; and the angels ministered unto him." See also Matthew 4:2 and Luke 4:2. The timing suggests that Halkett saw her marriage to Sir James as her escape from Egypt.

107. Hebrews 11:32: "And what shall I more say? for the time would fail me to tell of Gedeon, and of Barak, and of Samson, and of Jephthae; of David also, and Samuel, and of the prophets."

108. "To tell" is an interlineal insertion.

109. "The action of traversing, passing across, or going through (a region, etc.); passage, crossing: orig. from side to side, but soon also from end to end, or in any course," *OED*.

110. Ezra 9:13–14: "And after all that is come upon us for our evil deeds, and for our great trespass, seeing that thou our God hast punished us less than our iniquities deserve, and hast given us such deliverance as this; Should we again break thy commandments, and join in affinity with the people of these abominations? wouldst not thou be angry with us till thou hadst consumed us, so that there should be no remnant nor escaping?"

111. "Continue in" is an interlineal insertion.

112. Romans 6:1: "What shall we say then? Shall we continue in sin, that grace may abound?"

113. Romans 6:2: "God forbid. How shall we, that are dead to sin, live any longer therein?"

114. Matthew 8:2: "And, behold, there came a leper and worshipped him, saying, Lord, if thou wilt, thou canst make me clean."

115. Hebrews 2:17: "Wherefore in all things it behoved him to be made like unto his brethren, that he might be a merciful and faithful high priest in things pertaining to God, to make reconciliation for the sins of the people."

116. Leviticus 14:14: "And the priest shall take some of the blood of the trespass offering, and the priest shall put it upon the tip of the right ear of him that is to be cleansed, and upon the thumb of his right hand, and upon the great toe of his right foot."

right ear of him that was to be cleansed, and upon the thumb of his right hand, and upon the great toes of his right foot).[117]

Friday, May 14, 1697.

[p. 231] The kingly prophet, and sweet Psalmist, said: I am as a wonder unto many (Ps. 71:7).[118] But I am as a wonder to myself: for when I was upon my knees this morning, enumerating the wonderful mercies of my God, which I daily endeavor to do every Friday to commemorate the greatness of the Lord's compassion in raising me from the gates of death at Naworth, 1649/50, when I thought the sentence had been past and no hope of recovery;[119] from that time, I, weekly, on this day, praise and magnify the Lord for all his mercies to me from the first moment of my birth to that time; and from that time to this day, admiring the infinite wisdom, power, and goodness of God, that notwithstanding he, by his[120] omnisciency,[121] foresaw all the sins of my life that I should be guilty of, yet it did not withhold him from bringing me into the world, born of Christian parents, within the visible church,[122] where, by early baptism, I had my original sin washed away in the laver[123] of regeneration.

But, alas, and woe is me, I was [p. 232] no sooner capable of actual sin than I transgressed in early discovering the corruption of ungoverned nature: so that for my sister's taking away a baby from me, I bit her hand while it bled, and her meek carriage to me in it was a greater conviction to me of my passionate folly than if I had been severely whipped, which I justly deserved.[124] To consider from that time to this, how manifoldly[125] and heinously I have transgressed against the mighty and eternal God, my wonder is that ever he should vouchsafe a favorable regard to

---

117. The rest of the meditation continues in this vein, with Halkett making an extended application to her own life under the title, "Applying the Cleansing of the Leper by Way of Prayer to Myself," 156–62.
118. Psalm 71:7: "I am as a wonder unto many; but thou art my strong refuge."
119. See *True Account*, 95–96.
120. "His" is an interlineal insertion.
121. Archaic form of "omniscience," *OED*.
122. "Within the visible church" is an interlineal insertion.
123. "The baptismal font; the spiritual 'washing' of baptism; in wider sense, any spiritually cleansing agency," *OED*.
124. This may be the source for Couper's observation that "in one of her childish plays, being angered by her sister, in her passion, she bit her sister's hand; but upon her Sister's gentle reproof, saying only, 'look what you have done,' she retired and wept most bitterly"; Couper, *The Life of the Lady Halket*, 4. However, Couper provides further details that suggest there may have been a longer reflection on this topic elsewhere in Halkett's writings. See also, Sir James's response to Halkett's anger, "Monday, April 23, 1694," in *Of Watchfulness*, pp. 314–18.
125. An archaic adverbial form of "manifold."

one so unworthy of mercy; or how I should ever be so wretchedly ingrate[126] as[127] to sin against my God, who is so transcendent in goodness as not to be provoked to cast me off, though millions in hell hath never offended as I have done? Oh, who is able to comprehend what is the breadth, and length, and depth, and all height, and to know the love of Christ which passeth knowledge? (Eph. 3:18–19.)[128] For of him, and through him, and to him are all things: to whom be glory for ever and ever, amen (Rom. 11:36).[129] Oh, that the remainder of my life might evidence my abhorrence of sin and my sincere desire to perform all acts of obedience suitable to one that[130] desires to adorn the doctrine of God, our Savior, in all things (Titus 2:10).[131]

---

126. "An ungrateful person; one who does not feel or show gratitude," *OED*.

127. "As" is an interlineal insertion.

128. Halkett's original citation reads Ephesians 4:18–19; however, she clearly means Ephesians 3:18–19: "May be able to comprehend with all saints what is the breadth, and length, and depth, and height; And to know the love of Christ, which passeth knowledge, that ye might be filled with all the fulness of God."

129. Romans 11:36: "For of him, and through him, and to him, are all things: to whom be glory forever. Amen."

130. After "that," the rest of the meditation is written in the bottom margin of the page.

131. Titus 2:10: "Not purloining but shewing all good fidelity; that they may adorn the doctrine of God our Savior in all things."

Select and Occasional Meditations *(1697–1698/9)*

This is the final volume of Halkett's meditations, in which she was writing until two months before her death, Saturday, April 22, 1699.[1] This volume is, therefore, unfinished, which is perhaps why there is no note inside of the covers of the dates of composition and conclusion, even though this volume retains its original covers and binding (along, uniquely, with its metal clasps). However, the opening entry is dated "Wednesday, December 1, 1697," and the final date provided is Wednesday, February 22, 1698/9.[2] In the main text, Halkett notes that this fell to be Ash Wednesday:

> This then being the first day of Lent, as is observed in the Church of England where I was born and educated, to show I desire ever to preserve as far as I am able—both in profession and practice—what I learnt there, I intend to place these meditations upon that place which is the ground of this institution: *then was Jesus led up of the spirit into the Wilderness to be tempted*[3] *of the devil. And when he had fasted forty days and forty nights, he was afterward an hungred*[4] (Matt. 4:1–2).[5]

Although she initially cites only the first two verses of Matthew 4, in the pages that follow, she also explicates verse 3 and begins to comment on verse 4. This, and the fact that the full story of Christ's temptation extends to Matthew 4:10, confirms Couper's suggestion that this meditation is unfinished.[6] Additionally, the meditation does not reach the end of the page and, more significantly, at this point many pages are missing, apparently having been cut out of the volume.[7]

---

1. This is volume 21 in Couper's catalogue. In his account of her death, Couper notes: "On Saturday, April 22, 1699, between seven and eight o'clock at night, she finished her warfare, and entered into the joy of her Lord. That was the Day which for twenty-nine years preceding, she had weekly set apart for abstinence, meditation and preparation for death, on which she wished (if it might so please God) to die.... And her body was on April 24, honorably convoyed and laid in the same grave in which her husband Sir James had been laid"; Couper, *The Life of the Lady Halket*, 54.
2. Halkett, *Select and Occasional Meditations* (1697–1698/9), pp. i, 1, 202.
3. After "tempted," "and" has been deleted.
4. Adjectival form of "hungry; famished, starved," *OED*.
5. Halkett, *Select and Occasional Meditations* (1697–1698/9), p. 203. Halkett's quotation above accords exactly with the *KJV*.
6. See "Appendix 4.2," 349n58.
7. According to Halkett's pagination, there are about thirty-five pages missing (pp. 214–49). Consequently, in addition to the one-page discrepancy between Halkett's own calculation and that of the cataloguer (occasioned by the mis-numbering of page 104), there is a much larger discrepancy in pagination within the occasional meditation section of this volume.

Whatever their contents might have been, their removal reveals that, in this volume at least, Halkett paginated her book before she started writing.

While this volume is more rigidly divided into select and occasional mediations than its immediate predecessors, Halkett's listing of its contents suggests a continued awareness of overlap: for example, she highlights "some experiences of myself," in "Upon Probable Conjectures about the Calling of the Jews."[8] Couper provides a full list of the select meditations in this volume; however, neither he nor Halkett indexes the full contents of the occasional meditations. As in *Select and Occasional Meditations* (1696–1697), Halkett draws attention to only a selection of her occasional meditations: whereas there are fifty-seven individually dated entries, only twenty-one are identified in her list. Again, as in the previous volume, those registered are provided with titles that identify their main concern, such as "My Charity for Them Who Hath Little Charity for Me";[9] "Upon My Daughter Going the Bath";[10] and "Upon the Account I Heard of Three New Sects."[11] As demonstrated below, the final occasional entry quite self-consciously concludes the volume.[12] Chronologically, however, her writing career closes with her meditation upon Lent; tellingly, she once again entertains the prospect that her work may reach an audience beyond herself and God:

> Having yesterday finished the foregoing meditation, and resolving while I live, and that the Lord is pleased to continue with me the use of my senses to employ them upon meditations on[13] such places of Holy Scripture for some time after my usual devotion of prayer and reading, both in private and in the family, as may daily increase in me, more and more, a fervent desire to advance the glory of God, the good of my own soul, and be an example to others to follow, if ever the Lord thought fit to have them made known.[14]

Wednesday, December 1, 1697.

[p. 1] Having by the merciful goodness of God and the assistance of his Holy Spirit lived to write above seventeen books,[15] and lately ended one of three

---

8. Halkett, *Select and Occasional Meditations* (1697–1698/9), pp. i, 185–86; 178–202.

9. Halkett, *Select and Occasional Meditations* (1697–1698/9), p. 217.

10. Halkett, *Select and Occasional Meditations* (1697–1698/9), pp. 241–43.

11. Halkett, *Select and Occasional Meditations* (1697–1698/9), pp. 249–53.

12. See "Saturday, November 26, 1698," 324–25.

13. "Meditations on" is an interlineal insertion.

14. "Wednesday, February 22, being Ash Wednesday, 1698/9," in Halkett, *Select and Occasional Meditations* (1697–1698/9), p. 202.

15. "Books" is an insertion in the right-hand margin.

hundred and seventy three pages,[16] and having looked over the contents of them all, wherein is nothing writ particularly of the Apostle's Creed (though, I hope, nothing in them unsuitable to what is believed in the church of the living God, the pillar and ground of truth [1 Tim. 3:15]);[17] therefore,[18] I intend now to fix my meditations upon these Articles, which we are taught to believe were made[19] by the Apostles after the Resurrection of our Lord, when they were met together and like to be dispersed in obedience to our Lord who commanded them to go and teach all nations.[20] They, therefore, that at whatever distance they were at from one another might all agree, they made these the principles of the doctrine of Christ and of faith towards God.[21] And since I have hitherto professed and endeavored (though very weakly) to live in that faith, so I desire to die in it. And that I may be the more influenced and enabled to perform this my purpose, blessed Jesus (who hath said our heavenly Father will give the Holy Spirit to them that ask him [Luke 11:13]),[22] [p. 2] I will ask him of the Father through the promise of the Son. And having access by faith unto this grace (Rom. 5:1),[23] I hope the spirit of truth will in this guide me into all truth that so glory may be to the Father, and the Son, and to the Holy Ghost in what I am now intended to begin. And may praise forever be ascribed to the whole Trinity,[24] world without end, amen.

16. Halkett, *Select and Occasional Meditations* (1696–1697) is indeed 373 pages; however, the last entry chronologically, "Saturday, July 24, 1697," can be found about two-thirds of the way through the volume, pp. 263-64.

17. 1 Timothy 3:15: "But if I tarry long, that thou mayest know how thou oughtest to behave thyself in the house of God, which is the church of the living God, the pillar and ground of the truth."

18. "Therefore" is an interlineal insertion.

19. "Made" is an interlineal insertion.

20. Matthew 28:18–20: "And Jesus came and spake unto them, saying, all power is given unto me in heaven and in earth. Go ye therefore, and teach all nations, baptizing them in the name of the Father, and of the Son, and of the Holy Ghost: Teaching them to observe all things whatsoever I have commanded you: and, lo, I am with you always, even unto the end of the world. Amen."

21. Hebrews 6:1: "Therefore leaving the principles of the doctrine of Christ, let us go on unto perfection; not laying again the foundation of repentance from dead works, and of faith toward God."

22. "That ask him" is a subscript insertion. Luke 11:13: "If ye then, being evil, know how to give good gifts unto your children: how much more shall your heavenly Father give the Holy Spirit to them that ask him?"

23. Romans 5:1: "Therefore being justified by faith, we have peace with God through our Lord Jesus Christ."

24. The Trinity is the belief that God is one being made of three persons: the Father, the Son, and the Holy Ghost. Here, Halkett reiterates the Trinitarian doxology from the *BCP*, which she expressed fully in the previous sentence ("Glory be to the Father, and to the Son, and to the Holy Ghost"). As Ryrie explains, "a Trinitarian doxology rounded off a prayer with appropriate solemnity," *Being Protestant in Reformation Britain*, 237. Halkett's usage here is particularly appropriate as she prepares to confess her faith through her meditation on the Apostle's Creed.

This being the day that I, weekly, make confessions of all the sins of my life, as far as I can remember, as they have been committed either in thought, word, or deed against every particular of the Ten Commandments (which, though given in the time of the law, was not abrogated[25] by the Gospel but more fully established, as appears by our Lord's most excellent Sermon upon the Mount [Matt. 5:17]);[26] and after confession of sin, what more sovereign antidote against it than to look up to him who took away the sting and, by faith in him, can give me victory over him who had the[27] power of death (Heb. 2:14)? And this being the first day of the last month in the year (and may perhaps be the last month that may put a period to all my years), therefore no way can I better end it than both with my heart and hand, after confession of my sins, to [p. 3] make confession of my Faith, according to the Apostle's Creed (as they are divided into twelve Articles):

1. *I believe in God the Father Almighty, Maker of heaven and earth,*
2. *And in Jesus Christ his only Son our Lord,*
3. *Who was conceived by the Holy Ghost, born of the Virgin Mary,*
4. *He suffered under Pontius Pilate, was crucified, dead and buried,*
5. *He descended into hell: the third day, He arose again from the dead,*
6. *He ascended into Heaven and sitteth on the right hand of God the Father Almighty,*
7. *From thence He can come to judge the quick and the dead,*
8. *I believe in the Holy Ghost,*
9. *The Holy Catholic*[28] *church, the communion of saints,*
10. *The forgiveness of sins,*
11. *The Resurrection of the body,*
12. *And the Life everlasting, amen.*[29]

---

25. "To repeal (a law, established usage, etc.); to abolish authoritatively or formally; to annul, to cancel," *OED*.

26. Matthew 5:17: "Think not that I am come to destroy the law, or the prophets: I am not come to destroy, but to fulfil."

27. Hebrews 2:14: "Forasmuch then as the children are partakers of flesh and blood, he also himself likewise took part of the same; that through death he might destroy him that had the power of death, that is, the devil."

28. In this context, Catholic does not mean Roman Catholic but instead refers to "the church universal, the whole body of Christians," *OED*.

29. With four minor exceptions, Halkett's wording suggests that she is using the 1662 version of the *BCP*: in 4, there is no initial "He"; in 5, "arose" is "rose"; in 6, "on" is "at"; and in 7, "can" is "shall," 426–27.

1 Corinthians 15:58.[30]

[p. 120] For my God thou hast been a strength to me when I was poor and needy. Not as to outward things: for, blessed be thy name, hitherto the Lord hath helped me (1 Sam. 7:12)[31] so that I never knew what it was to want food, and raiment, and therewith I[32] ought to be content (1 Tim. 6:8).[33] But my greatest poverty and need was of spiritual supplies, and never was I reduced to that so as I knew not what to do but my eyes were upon thee (2 Chron. 20:12),[34] and then thou wert pleased to strengthen me with might by the spirit in the inward man (Eph. 3:16).[35]

Have I not found my God a refuge from the storm,[36] when I was thirteen months under my mother's [p. 121] displeasure, so that in all that time she never gave me her blessing (though I sought it morning and evening upon my knees, as was the custom in England for all children to their parents). But, by patient continuing in all dutiful observance to her, I obtained the greatest testimony she could give me of her affection: before her death, saying she had greater contentment in me than in all her children.[37]

Was not my God a shadow to me from the heat, when the blast of the terrible ones, as a storm against the wall,[38] imprisoned and had put to death (if they had not ventured their life by escaping by a window out of the prison) one,[39] who with myself and others, had evidenced our duty and loyalty in obeying what the best King[40] (though the most unjustly used by his rebellious subjects) had

---

30. In concluding her extended meditation on 1 Corinthians 15:58 ("Therefore, my beloved brethren, be ye steadfast, unmovable, always abounding in the work of the Lord, forasmuch as ye know that your labor is not in vain in the Lord"), Halkett characteristically applies the text to her experience and confidently anticipates a continuation of the same.

31. 1 Samuel 7:12: "Then Samuel took a stone, and set it between Mizpeh and Shen, and called the name of it, Ebenezer, saying, hitherto hath the Lord helped us."

32. After "I," "am" has been deleted.

33. I Timothy 6:8: "And having food and raiment let us be therewith content."

34. 2 Chronicles 20:12: "O our God, wilt thou not judge them? for we have no might against this great company that cometh against us; neither know we what to do: but our eyes are upon thee."

35. Ephesians 3:16: "That he would grant you, according to the riches of his glory, to be strengthened with might by his spirit in the inner man."

36. Isaiah 25:4: "For thou hast been a strength to the poor, a strength to the needy in his distress, a refuge from the storm, a shadow from the heat, when the blast of the terrible ones is as a storm against the wall."

37. See *True Account*, 77.

38. Isaiah 25:4; see 317n36.

39. I.e., Colonel Joseph Bampfield. See *True Account*, 97–98.

40. I.e., Charles I.

desired, under his Majesty's own hand, to contrive the Duke of York's[41] escape: for he[42] writ he looked upon James's[43] escape as Charles's[44] preservation, and nothing could be greater satisfaction to him.[45] Known to thee, my God, are all the troubles and trials I have met with since that time. And being supported under them, and delivered from them, to this present day (September 2, 1698)[46] with that measure of health that few of my age enjoys (being near seventy-seven, and hath the use of my reason, memory, hearing, and seeing) so as to record [p. 122] these wonders of thy power. Oh, that I could sufficiently praise the Lord for his goodness and for his wonderful works to me, the most unworthy of the children of men (Ps. 107:8).[47]

But what I want of perfection let me endeavor to supply with sincerity, always approving things that are excellent and to be sincere without offence until the day of Christ (Phil. 1:10).[48] This would prove the sincerity of my love (2 Cor. 8:8)[49] and that my labor hath not been in vain in the Lord. For it is He only that can keep me steadfast, and immoveable, and strengthen me that I may be always abounding in the work of the Lord. Now, to him that is able to keep me from falling, and to present me faultless before the presence of his glory with exceeding joy, to the only wise God, our Savior, be glory and majesty, dominion and power, now and forever, amen (Jude 1:24–25).[50]

Saturday, February 19, 1697/8.[51]

[p. 225] Though the occasion of this day's retirement, which I have weekly performed ever since the death of my dear Sir James, who died this day of the week[52] (and therefore, I set it apart to endeavor as far as I am enabled to be

---

41. Later James VII/II.

42. I.e., Charles I. After "he," "said" has been deleted and replaced by "writ" as an interlineal insertion.

43. I.e., the then Duke of York, later James VII/II.

44. I.e., Prince Charles, later Charles II.

45. See *True Account*, 81.

46. The specific date is inserted in the right-hand margin.

47. Psalm 107:8: "Oh that men would praise the Lord for his goodness, and for his wonderful works to the children of men!"

48. Philippians 1:10: "That ye may approve things that are excellent; that ye may be sincere and without offence till the day of Christ."

49. 2 Corinthians 8:8: "I speak not by commandment, but by occasion of the forwardness of others, and to prove the sincerity of your love."

50. Jude 1:24–25: "Now unto him that is able to keep you from falling, and to present you faultless before the presence of his glory with exceeding joy, to the only wise God our Savior, be glory and majesty, dominion and power, both now and ever. Amen."

51. See also Trill, ed., *Halkett*, 188–90.

52. "Of the week" is an interlineal insertion.

humbled for the sins of my whole life past, and to be fervent at the throne of grace that my life for the future may be so spent as looking for that blessed hope, and the glorious appearing of the great God and our Savior Jesus Christ [Titus 2.13]).[53] Yet, to quicken me the more to this duty, hearing that a gentleman of good esteem that lives about Brigton,[54] having some occasion to go to Edinburgh this week, crossed the water well enough as he seemed, and as soon as ever he came out of the boat fell down dead upon the sands, and was taken in to the Haws's, being the nearest house, where he still lies until his friends come to take order for his interment. The suddenness of this gentleman's death is a fresh excitement[55] to me to prepare for my own and made me resolve on that which before I was undetermined of (though solicited to do it by Mr. Couper, for whom I have a great respect as [p. 226] he very worthily deserves).

Some years since, looking over the books which by the assistance of God I had been enabled to write, and never intending they should be seen to any as long as I lived but fearing when I was dead, if undisposed of, they might fall into such hands as might make ill use of them; therefore, I writ the contents of every one of them, and enclosed them in a sheet of paper, sealed up, and directed them to Mr. Couper and Mr. Graeme,[56] with a letter acquainting them that as I had formerly acquainted them with the *Account of My Life* [sic] and the occasion that made me put it in writing,[57] so now I thought none so fit as themselves to make known the effects which my misfortunes through the blessing of God had wrought in me; that, if after I was dead, if they thought fit then to make them known perhaps it might excite some to have charity to my memory, and others of greater capacity employ them to the honor of God (when they see what an unworthy person, like myself, hath endeavored [p. 227] from most of the sad dispensations[58] of my life to arrive at the setting forth the praise of my never enough to be admired, who is the God of my salvation). Something to this purpose I writ them, desiring that if my dear child, Robin Halkett, lived to come home, who was then abroad,[59] they would advise with him before they divulged any of them.

53. Titus 2:13: "Looking for that blessed hope, and the glorious appearing of the great God and our Savior Jesus Christ."

54. Originally "Brighon." Possibly Brigton in the parish of Cameron on the outskirts of St. Andrews. "Brigton," Scotland's Places, accessed July 23, 2018, https://scotlandsplaces.gov.uk/search/place/Brigton?id=2338.

55. "A motive or incentive to action; an exhortation, encouragement," *OED*.

56. See Trill, ed., *Halkett*, xxxi–xxxiv.

57. See "Meditations upon Psalm 106: 4–5," 264–65.

58. "Ordering, management; especially, the divine administration or conduct of the world; the ordering or arrangement of events by divine providence," *OED*.

59. Against her advice in "Instructions to My Son," Robert/Robin joined the army and was away in France and Ireland for much of the 1680s. He fought for King James, but by August 1690 he was a

After it pleased God to bring him home, after much hardship and imprisonment, Mr. Couper gave me back the paper, sealed as I delivered it, but it seems kept the letter, which coming accidentally lately to his hands, he came to me and very earnestly desired me that I would continue my former resolutions of letting him and Mr. Graeme have those books and paper books I had written committed to their trust (and that Mr. Marshall[60] might be joined with them to look them over, and said[61] they being both out of employment they would have the more leisure to consider them). Though I willingly condescended that Mr. Marshall should be entrusted with them and that I had fully resolved to send the sealed paper, having opened one end and inserted what I writ since I had first sent it (for since my dear child's death none but themselves could I think fit to communicate it to), and resolved to seal it up again, and send it with all the books but not to be opened as long as I was alive. This I was [p. 228] positive in until very lately that I heard of several considerable merchants' broke[62] and all that they had in their houses exposed to the view of strangers. This, with the gentleman's sudden death, made me resolve not to expose the greatest treasure of my soul to such as perhaps may laugh at my trial (Job 9:23),[63] who though not innocent, yet I hope I am innocent of the great transgression (Ps. 19:13).[64] And then the words of my mouth and the meditation of my heart, which there are fully expressed, will be acceptable in the sight of my Lord, who is my strength and my redeemer.[65]

And these being the motives that were very persuasive with me, having for several days before being very sincere in seeking direction from the Almighty to determine me in it, yesterday, Mr. Couper coming in, without his speaking to me further in it, I began the discourse to him and offered to send the trunk to him with as many of them as it[66] would hold. But he was against that, only desired one book at a time; and, promising secrecy, I delivered him the parchment book, with

---

prisoner in London. Couper records that he returned to Dunfermline on December 17, 1692. He left again only a month later and died two days after arriving at Brielle in the Netherlands on October 5, 1693. Couper, *The Life of the Lady Halket*, 49. Halkett records the anniversary of his death on "Friday, October 5, 1694," in *Of Watchfulness*, pp. 351–52; see also Trill, ed., *Halkett*, 171–72.

60. Mr. Marshall was admitted to ministry at Carnock on August 27, 1679. Like Couper and Graeme, he was deprived of his ministry for "not reading the Proclamation of the Estates, and not praying for William and Mary, but for King James, and 'hoping to see him in his throne before Lammas,'" *FES* 5:8–9.

61. "And said" is an interlineal insertion.

62. "To enter (a house, an enclosed place, etc.) . . . by force or violence," *OED*.

63. Job 9:23: "If the scourge slay suddenly, he will laugh at the trial of the innocent."

64. Psalm 19:13: "Keep back thy servant also from presumptuous sins; let them not have dominion over me: then shall I be upright, and I shall be innocent from the great transgression."

65. Psalm 19:14: "Let the words of my mouth, and the meditation of my heart, be acceptable in thy sight, O Lord, my strength, and my redeemer."

66. "It" is an interlineal insertion.

pink and ash ribbon, where the most considerable of my troubles are [p. 229] registered.[67] The disorder I was in at the giving[68] it, and what disquiet of mind I had about it for several hours after it, had any known they would have freed me from thinking that vanity had any prevalency[69] in it. For I hate vain thoughts, but, Lord, thy law do I love (Ps. 119:113).[70] And I have nothing to glory in but the things which concern my infirmities by[71] which the God and Father of our Lord Jesus Christ, blessed for evermore, hath made the means to bring glory to himself (2 Cor. 11:30–31).[72] According to the working whereby he is able to subdue all things unto himself (Phil. 3:19).[73] O my God, which hath hitherto held my soul in life, suffer not my feet to be moved (Ps. 66:9).[74] But let me so ponder the[75] path of my feet that all my ways may be established (Prov. 4:26).[76] Then will I say, blessed be God, which hath not turned away my prayer nor his mercy from me (Ps. 66:20).[77] Amen.

Tuesday, March 2, 1697/8.

[p. 232] Upon Sunday, in the evening at Charlton (my sister's house), I was married by Mr. Gale (an excellent divine, chaplain to the old Countess of Devonshire,[78] who was one of my Godmothers) in the year 1655/6 which is now forty-eight year.[79] When I reflect upon the many misfortunes of my life to that time, and that then I looked upon myself as a brand plucked out of the fire

---

67. As the only other book identified as parchment is "The Soul's Remembrancer," which has green strings ("Saturday, May 21, 1698," 322–23), it is most likely that this volume, "with pink and ash ribbon," was the *True Account*.

68. "Given" in the MS.

69. "Prevailing or effective power or influence; weight, persuasiveness," *OED*.

70. Psalm 119:113: "I hate vain thoughts: but thy law do I love."

71. "By" is an interlineal insertion.

72. 2 Corinthians 11:30–31: "If I must needs glory, I will glory of the things which concern mine infirmities. The God and Father of our Lord Jesus Christ, which is blessed for evermore, knoweth that I lie not."

73. The correct reference here is Philippians 3:21: "Who shall change our vile body, that it may be fashioned like unto his glorious body, according to the working whereby he is able even to subdue all things unto himself." Philippians 3:19 reads: "Whose end is destruction, whose God is their belly, and whose glory is in their shame, who mind earthly things."

74. Psalm 66:9: "Which holdeth our soul in life, and suffereth not our feet to be moved."

75. After "the," "way" has been deleted and replaced with the interlineal insertion of "path."

76. Proverbs 4:26: "Ponder the path of thy feet and let all thy ways be established."

77. Psalm 66:20: "Blessed be God, which hath not turned away my prayer, nor his mercy from me."

78. Stater, "Cavendish [née Bruce], Christian [Christiana]," *ODNB*.

79. See *True Account*, 167.

(Zech. 3:2),[80] how did I then resolve to live holy in all manner of conversation (1 Pet. 1:15);[81] with perpetual thankfulness to my God; a sincere affection and due observance to my dear Sir James; and with a motherly love and care to all his children; and to live towards all in all well pleasing in the sight of God. I will not mention what trials I met with in my married life from all except him that was the best of husbands (for had I been more studious to perform what I was convinced was my duty, the Lord perhaps might have restrained that in others which occasioned the chief disquiet I had in my married state or else supported me better to bear it). But by all this I came to know the [p. 233] perverseness of corrupt nature, and how far the grace of God evidences itself in strengthening me, so as that I heartily forgave them before they died and prayed for them that most despitefully did use me. And since my widowhood, which hath been now above twenty-seven years, Oh, what sadness and sorrow, trouble and grief have I met with in these years! And am yet spared in mercy, I hope, to the praise of the glory of his grace, whereby I hope I am accepted in the beloved (Eph. 1:6).[82] Whatever I have been guilty of either in thought, word, or deed I beg pardon for, through the merits and intercession of our Lord Jesus Christ, who is the advocate of sinners, who will plead for me when I can plead nothing for myself. But, Lord, thou knowest all things, and knowest that above all things that[83] I love and desire[84] to obey thee. Therefore, I beseech thee, order my steps in thy word, and let not any iniquity have dominion over me (Ps. 119:133).[85]

Saturday, May 21, 1698.

[p. 266] As it is the day of the week, since September 24, 1670, I have weekly made it a day to call my sins to remembrance with sincere repentance and unfeigned resolutions, strengthened by earnest prayer for pardon and grace that I may live the remainder of my days like one looking for that blessed hope, and the glorious appearing of the great God and our Savior Jesus Christ (Titus 2:13);[86] so, to increase in me admiration in me at the power and goodness of God and compassion for the depravedness of human nature, accidentally there came to my

---

80. Zechariah 3:2: "And the Lord said unto Satan, The Lord rebuke thee, O Satan; even the Lord that hath chosen Jerusalem rebuke thee: is not this a brand plucked out of the fire?"
81. 1 Peter 1:15: "But as he which hath called you is holy, so be ye holy in all manner of conversation."
82. Ephesians 1:6: "To the praise of the glory of his grace, wherein he hath made us accepted in the beloved."
83. An ink blot obscures part of this word.
84. "Desire" is an interlineal insertion.
85. Psalm 119:133: "Order my steps in thy word: and let not any iniquity have dominion over me."
86. Titus 2:13: "Looking for that blessed hope, and the glorious appearing of the great God and our Savior Jesus Christ."

memory what had like to have been a sad tragedy, May 21, 1649, falling then to be a Monday.[87] The particular account of it I did then write in a parchment book in folio with green strings, which I desire never to forget:[88] to give God praise for his wonderful deliverance to her that was under the trial, and pray for him (if he be yet living) who was the occasion of it[89] that he may with great remorse bewail his great weakness in relying so much upon his own strength as to expose himself [p. 267] into the territories of Satan. And that he may be the more circumspect hereafter not to provoke God to deliver him up to vain imaginations whereby the foolish heart was darkened (Rom. 1:21).[90] When at any time I think upon this sad story, but especially when upon this same day it comes into my mind, I cannot but as the Apostle says: Remember them that are in bonds, as bound with them; and them which suffer adversity, as being myself also in the body (Heb. 13:3).[91]

Lord, redeem Israel, thy people, from all their iniquities.[92] And grant that, that beam of light that darted upon me this morning (when in my private devotion I was with earnestness praying for the King)[93] may be as a pledge to confirm that thou art a God hearing prayer. Lord, let the paths of the just lead them to him, and him to them that they may be as the shining light[94] that showeth more and more unto the perfect day (Prov. 4:18).[95] Lord, give strength unto the King[96] and exalt the horn of thy anointed (1 Sam. 2:10),[97] so will I ever praise thee while I have any being, amen.

---

87. See "What Crosses and Difficulties I Have Met with Myself," and "Introduction," 308, 26.

88. According to Couper's catalogue, volume 2, which contained "The Soul's Remembrancer," was written between 1649 and 1650, "Appendix 4.2," 341–42.

89. See "Monday, May 21, 1688," 273–75. Bampfield was already dead by the time Halkett wrote the former entry.

90. Romans 1:21: "Because that, when they knew God, they glorified him not as God, neither were thankful; but became vain in their imaginations, and their foolish heart was darkened."

91. Hebrews 13:3: "Remember them that are in bonds, as bound with them; and them which suffer adversity, as being yourselves also in the body."

92. Psalm 130:8: "And he shall redeem Israel from all his iniquities."

93. I.e., James VII/II.

94. "Light" is an interlineal insertion.

95. Proverbs 4:18: "But the path of the just is as the shining light, that shineth more and more unto the perfect day."

96. I.e., James VII/II.

97. 1 Samuel 2:10: "The adversaries of the Lord shall be broken to pieces; out of heaven shall he thunder upon them: The Lord shall judge the ends of the earth; and he shall give strength unto his king and exalt the horn of his anointed."

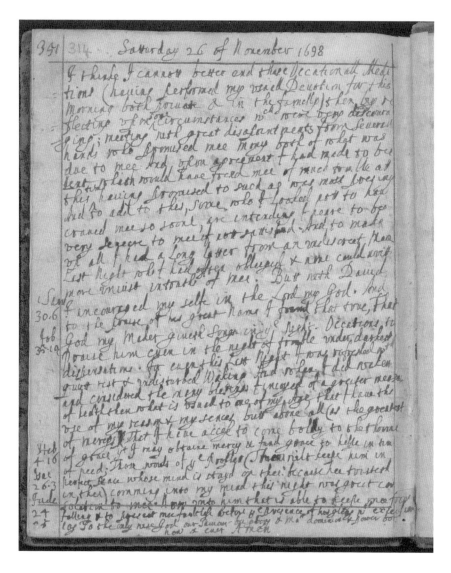

Figure 17. From Anne, Lady Halkett, *Select and Occasional Meditations* (1697–1698/9). © National Library of Scotland, NLS, MS 6502, p. 314. Reproduced with permission.

Saturday, November 26, 1698.

[p. 314] I think I cannot better end these *Occasional Meditations* (having performed my usual devotion for this morning both private and in the family) than by reflecting upon some[98] circumstances which were very discouraging: meeting with great disappointments from several hands who promised me money (both of what was due to me and upon agreement I had made to be lent) which would have freed me of much trouble at this time,[99] having promised to such as was most pressing; and to add to this, some who I looked not to have craved me so soon are intending, I hear, to be very severe to me if not satisfied; and to make up all, I had a long letter from an undiscreet[100] man last night, who I had often obliged, and none could writ more unjust untruths of me.[101] But, with David, I encouraged myself in the Lord my God (1 Sam. 30:6).[102] And to the praise of his great name I found that true, that God, my maker, giveth songs in the night (Job 35:10),[103] occasions to praise him even in the night of trouble under darkest dispensations.[104] For even this last night I was refreshed with quiet rest and undisturbed waking. And when I did waken and considered the many blessings I enjoyed (of a greater measure of health than what is usual to one of my age; that I have the use of my reason, and my senses; but above all, as the greatest of mercies, that I have access to come boldly to that house of grace that I may obtain mercy and find grace to help in time of need [Heb. 4:16]),[105] those words of the prophet (thou wilt keep him in perfect peace, whose mind is stayed on thee: because he trusted in thee [Isa. 26:3])[106] coming into my mind this night was great consolation to me. Now unto him that is able to keep me from[107] falling, and to present me faultless before the presence of his glory with exceeding joy, to the only wise God, our Savior, be glory and majesty, dominion and power, both now and ever. Amen (Jude 1:24–25).[108]

98. "Some" is an interlineal insertion.

99. "Time" is an interlineal insertion.

100. I.e., indiscreet.

101. See "Introduction," 42.

102. 1 Samuel 30:6: "And David was greatly distressed; for the people spake of stoning him, because the soul of all the people was grieved, every man for his sons and for his daughters: but David encouraged himself in the Lord his God."

103. Job 35:10: "But none saith, where is God my maker, who giveth songs in the night."

104. "Ordering, management; especially, the divine administration or conduct of the world; the ordering or arrangement of events by divine providence," *OED*.

105. Hebrews 4:16: "Let us therefore come boldly unto the throne of grace, that we may obtain mercy, and find grace to help in time of need."

106. Isaiah 26:3: "Thou wilt keep him in perfect peace, whose mind is stayed on thee: because he trusteth in thee."

107. After "from," the rest of the entry is squeezed into the bottom margin of the page.

108. Jude 1:24–25: "Now unto him that is able to keep you from falling, and to present you faultless before the presence of his glory with exceeding joy, to the only wise God our Savior, be glory and majesty, dominion and power, both now and ever. Amen."

Appendix 1:
Anne, Lady Halkett, "Letter to the Earl of Lauderdale"
(n.d.)[1]

[fol. 1r]

My Lord,[2]

having so good a hand to make my address as the Earl of Dunfermline,[3] who hath promised me the favor of delivering this to your Lordship, I will take the liberty of representing the long expectation I have had of finding something to propose that might be answerable to what his Majesty was pleased to give me hopes that I might obtain, which now I despair ever to find, and can[4] have nothing to fix a request upon except it be upon some part of the fines which I hear is not yet all disposed of; and therefore, if your Lordship would be pleased to mediate for me to the King,[5] to grant me such a sum as his Majesty thinks fit to bestow upon me to be a livelihood to my poor children,[6] they and I shall ever [fol. 1v] pray for a perpetuity of blessings ever[7] to attend the King. And I am confident your Lordship will be a sharer in them for contributing to so good and charitable an action: for my Lord, though I bless God I am as happy as any woman can be in the best of husbands,[8] yet that must not make me think of prejudicing the children he

---

1. NLS, Acc. 6112 contains seven miscellaneous items that were acquired by the NLS in 1974. Halkett's letter is addressed "For the Earle of Lauderdale" and bears the remnants of a red seal. Halkett's use of space here indicates her awareness of social distinction: she leaves a two-line gap between the address and the opening of her letter, and her subscription is spread over approximately fourteen lines (i.e., the entirety of fol. 2r).

2. Hutton, "Maitland, John," *ODNB*.

3. Assuming this is Charles Seton, second Earl of Dunfermline, with whom Halkett was most closely linked in the 1650s, this letter must have been written before his death, on May 11, 1672. Henderson and Furgol, "Seton, Charles," *ODNB*.

4. "Can" is an interlineal insertion.

5. I.e., Charles II.

6. Although she uses the plural, her only biological child known to be alive at this date was Robert (Robin); for Sir James's children from his first marriage, see "Introduction," 16.

7. "Ever" is an interlineal insertion.

8. I.e., Sir James Halkett. She describes him in this exact phrase on several occasions; see, for example, "Upon the Death of My Dearest Sir James," 222; "Saturday, July 9, 1687," in Halkett, *Meditations on St. Peter*, p. 301; "Wednesday, September 24, 1690," in Halkett, *Occasional Meditations*, p. 24; "Monday, April 23, 1694" and "Saturday, November 24, 1694," in Halkett, *Of Watchfulness*, pp. 316, 353; "Saturday, April 24, 1697," "Saturday, July 24, 1697," "Thursday, September 24, 1696," and "Saturday, October 24, 1696," in Halkett, *Select and Occasional Meditations* (1696–1697), pp. 214, 265, 324, 344; and "Tuesday,

had formerly by a more deserving wife.[9] And to think what want my poor babies may be exposed to, if I should die and no provision made for them, cannot but be an affliction to me; for it were unreasonable for me to seek anything from their father for them until I could contribute something myself, which I could never yet do, but rather much the contrary in pursuit of it.[10] And therefore, if your Lordship will be assistant in what I shall have humbly recommended to your favor, it will be such an obligation as I cannot express, nor how much I am,

[fol. 2r] My Lord, your Lordship's most humble and obedient servant,
AHalkett.[11]

March 2, 1697/8," 322. As Halkett refers to her husband in the present tense, and the remnants of the letter's seal is red, this letter must have been written before Sir James's death, September 24, 1670.

9. Sir James Halkett's first wife was Margaret Montgomery; see "Introduction," 15–16.

10. See *True Account*, and "Introduction," 140, 16–17.

11. This is an example of Halkett's characteristic signature, in which the initials "AH" are combined, that can also be found in most of her "books."

Appendix 2:
Anne, Lady Halkett, "Letter to Her Stepson, Sir Charles Halkett" (n.d.)[1]

Dunfermline
Dear son,[2] February 3

your letter was so obliging that I want words to express my sense of it, but if I live I hope my actions will confirm that it is one of the things in the world I desire most to do you some effectual service; and I shall be the more capable of doing it if I can be successful in obtaining what I might expect, if I were not still what I have been hitherto—as to that part—very unfortunate. You have twice writ to me to give you some employment, and as the greatest concern I have to look after, except what your dear father left me, I have in this enclosed paper given you an account of.[3]

I believe you as many others will think [it] strange I did not endeavor to gain the Duchess of Lauderdale's[4] to favor me in it. But, though I found her Grace very civil and kind, yet I found an unwillingness to hear of any particular from me, and I never offered to speak (for I thought it much better to say nothing than not have a good answer).[5] And therefore all I did was to give Mr. Forester[6] information of the right I had to the plantation called the Spring in the Barbados[7] to try what might be done in that, and, at your leisure, I hope you will do me the favor

---

1. Pitfirrane Papers: Correspondence. NLS, MS 6409, no. 40. Unlike the letter to Lauderdale, there is here no deferential use of space, which is telling given the uneasy relationship between Halkett and her stepson: there is a one-line gap between the address and the opening of the letter, but the subscription is squeezed into the bottom of the leaf, with Halkett's signature in the gap left on the right-hand side of the leaf between the last line of the letter and the subscription. The letter is addressed "For Sir Charles Halkett of Pitfirrane" and has the remains of a black seal.

2. Her stepson, Sir Charles Halkett.

3. See "Appendix 3," 333–35.

4. Lauderdale's first wife, Lady Anne Home, died in 1671; on February 17, 1672, he married Elizabeth Murray, Countess of Dysart, daughter of William Murray, first Earl of Dysart, and Halkett's cousin on her father's side. Hutton, "Maitland, John," *ODNB*; Rosalind K. Marshall, "Murray [Married Names Tollemache, Maitland], Elizabeth, Duchess of Lauderdale and Suo Jure Countess of Dysart (bap. 1626, d. 1698)," *ODNB*.

5. Couper records that "she went to Edinburgh, partly in civility, to pay a visit to the Duchess of Lauderdale her near kinswoman; partly on design to procure some advantage to her child and the family she was so much obliged to," August 19, 1672, and remained in Edinburgh for "some time... where she found great civilities, favorable looks, and good words, but nothing more," Couper, *The Life of the Lady Halkett*, 38.

6. Mr. Forester. Identified as the Duke of Lauderdale's secretary, "Appendix 3," 335.

7. See "Introduction," 18–19.

to speak with him and my brother Newton[8] (who now will be at London, and he and Sir Robert Moray[9] have both so much friendship for me as I believe they will both advise and assist you in any thing is to be done for me).

This which I have sent to you is a copy of the information [fol. 1v] which three year since I sent to my Lord Lauderdale but yet nothing ever done in it (though I had his Majesty's[10] promise of something here in Scotland).[11] Perhaps it hath been delayed to this time to make it the more welcome, and to make my obligation the more to you if you will concern yourself in it. I only now acquaint you with it, and leave it to you, and them I have already mentioned to consider of the time and way how to move in it. And if it be thought necessary to move the Duke of York[12] to speak for me, I do believe Colonel Villiers[13] will be my friend in it. But at this distance none can judge what is fit to be done, since I know it is usual for some to cross even what they approve of, if it be not done their own way. And therefore, I leave it to[14] you, and the great over ruler of all things,[15] to dispose of me in that and all things else as He sees fit.

And now I must give you an account of all your friends and neighbors here: Pitreavie,[16] and Balbougie,[17] and Dunfermline town[18] was all very well pleased with your remembrance of them; and I believe James Greenhorn and Will Smith will live seven year longer with the joy they had for your care of them; Garioch[19] is your humblest servant; and, for Robin, it is one of the greatest satisfaction I have to find he hath that respect, value, and[20] love for you that he ought to have for his father, brother, and friend. And what he most desires from you is to haste home that he may have the benefit of these relations to you which would be an

8. I.e., her brother-in-law, Sir Henry Newton-Puckering.

9. Sir Robert Moray. As he died June/July 1673, the letter must have been written before then. Allan, "Sir Robert Moray," *ODNB*.

10. I.e., Charles II.

11. See *True Account*, 123.

12. Duke of York, later James VII/II.

13. The Duke of York had been educated alongside the First Duke of Buckingham's children, so this is probably a reference to George Villiers. Bruce Yardley, "Villiers, George, Second Duke of Buckingham (1628–1687)," *ODNB*.

14. "To" is an interlineal insertion.

15. I.e., God.

16. "Pitravey" in MS, see figure 4, map of Fife, 121.

17. "Belbougy" in MS, see figure 4, map of Fife, 121.

18. "Town" is an interlineal insertion.

19. In *Meditations on St. Peter*, Halkett recalls looking over the entries she wrote in 1666 and 1677, and notes "upon Friday, June 29, 1677 Garioch died, a faithful servant and the only one of my family that hath died in it since I came to this town [Dunfermline] which is going on eighteen years," p. 378.

20. After "and," "friendship" has been deleted.

advantage to him and, dear son, your most affectionate mother and humble servant, AHalkett.

Appendix 3:
Anne, Lady Halkett, "An Information of What Was Left Me by My Mother" (n.d.)[1]

[fol. 170r] My mother had by Indenture under the Great Seal (dated the March 14, in the third year of his Majesty's reign of ever blessed memory)[2] the herbage[3] and panage[4] of Berkhamsted Park in the county of Hertford; then reduced to three hundred and seventy three acres, and the residue of the same Park (then disparked with mills), and other parcels of land and meadows thereto belonging for thirty one year.[5] Five hundred and fifty pound fine being paid by my Mother into the exchequer,[6] and the yearly rent of £45, 6d. At her death there was twelve years of the lease to run;[7] of which there was left to my brother Will Murray[8] and me so much of the lease as came to £412 yearly. My brother Will sold his interest to me to get money to carry him abroad to attend his Highness, the Duke of York. A little while after it being publicly discovered what I had done to assist his Highness escape,[9] I was forced—for my own preservation—to leave London and all I was concerned in, and after some time came to Scotland, where I heard that (several persons having been possessed of the house and manor of Berkhamsted) it was at last given by the (then) pretended power to Colonel Axtell (and was hanged, drawn & quartered for the King's murder).[10]

1. The Pitfirrane Papers, NLS, MS 6481, contains miscellaneous legal papers relating to the Halkett family and Pitfirrane that are mostly undated. From folds on the paper, this item (fols. 170r–71v) was clearly once an enclosure, and the heading "Information" in Halkett's hand remains visible, fol. 171v.

2. I.e., Charles I, and therefore 1628/9.

3. "Herbs collectively; herbaceous growth or vegetation; usually applied to grass and other low growing plants covering a large extent of ground, esp. as used for pasture," OED.

4. "The right or privilege to pasture pigs (or other animals) in a forest; payment made to the owner of a tract of woodland for this right or privilege; the right to collect such payment; the income accruing from this," OED.

5. "Grant to Jane Murray, Widow, for Thirty-One Years, of the Herbage and Westminster Pannage of the Park of Berkhampstead, Co. Herts," March 3, 1628, *CSP(Dom)*, vol. 3, March 1628–June 1629.

6. Despite Halkett's claim there is a "Warrant to the Exchequer, that no Process Be Issued against Mrs. Jane Murray for £550 Paid by Her to Sir Adam Newton, Receiver of His Majesty's Revenue When Prince of Wales, for a Lease of Thirty-One Years of the Herbage of the Park of Berkhamstead, co. Herts, Whereas the Same Ought to Have Been Paid into the Exchequer," May 27, 1628, *CSP(Dom)*, vol. 3, March 1628–June 1629.

7. Halkett's mother died on August 28, 1647.

8. See *True Account*, 89–92.

9. See *True Account*, 93.

10. Alan Thomson, "Axtell, Daniel (bap. 1622, d. 1660)," *ODNB*.

My mother also left me twelve hundred pound that was due of her pension out of the exchequer in England, and seven hundred [fol.170v] pound sterling that was due out of the exchequer of Scotland (two hundred pound being paid to her yearly out of each of them).

There was also due to me by bond from the late Earl of Kinnoull[11] and Archibald Hay[12] two-thousand-pound sterling, and the interest of it since June 1641. In Hilary term of 1647, I recovered a judgment against Archibald Hay for £40,000 debt, and costs of suit. He dies, and leaves Andrew Hay Executor (who I pursued in Scotland, but had no favor nor hardly justice from the English judges).[13] Yet, after much pains and expense, I obtained a Decreet[14] that Andrew Hay should assign me over his right of Executory, with full power to recover anything I could find belonging to Archibald Hay. And amongst other papers give me right to a debt due by James, Earl of[15] Carlisle[16] to Archibald Hay for £212, 6s. 8d, and secured to him out of the profits of the Barbados, and a lease that he had of the manor of Westcote and rectory of Barrow in the county of Lincoln (part of the late Queen's[17] jointure) of which there was some years to run. For that lease of Westcote, I petitioned her Majesty's Council when I was at London[18] and had the grant of being preferred before any other. And I was so far in possession that the tenant there paid me part of the rent due at that term, but my Lord St. Albans[19] got an order from the Queen to have that lease let to his Lordship's nephew,[20]

11. Probably George, third Earl of Kinnoull, who died November 20, 1649; William, the fourth Earl of Kinnoull was still alive in 1677, so after the possible date range for this letter and its enclosure, *BP* 2.2189.

12. See "Introduction," 17–19.

13. See *True Account*, 140.

14. "A judicial judgment or pronouncement; a decree of a court or competent judge or arbiter," *DSL*.

15. "Of" is an interlineal insertion.

16. According to Roy E. Schreiber, "the Caribbean islands, despite early difficulties, ... became [the Earl of Carlisle's] own highly valuable domain. He managed to outmaneuver the Earls of Marlborough and Montgomery and take possession of all the islands from Barbados and St Kitts. By the time he died the customs revenue alone reached £9000 per annum and from all sources on the island closer to £12,000"; "Hay, James, First Earl of Carlisle (ca. 1580–1636)," *ODNB*. See also Roy E. Schreiber, *The First Carlisle: Sir James Hay, First Earl of Carlisle as Courtier, Diplomat, and Entrepreneur, 1580–1636* (Philadelphia: American Philosophical Society, 1984).

17. I.e., Henrietta Maria, the wife of Charles I, who died in 1669; Hibbard, "Henrietta Maria," *ODNB*.

18. Halkett's *Occasional Meditations, Meditations and Prayers on Every Several Day Ordained to Be Kept Holy in the Church of England* indicate that she was in London from 1660 to 1661, and in 1663. As Charles did not marry Catherine of Braganza until May 21, 1662, this must refer to her later visit. Wynne, "Catherine [Catherine of Braganza]," *ODNB*.

19. Anthony R. J. S. Adolph, "Jermyn [Germain], Henry, Earl of St Albans (bap. 1605, d. 1684)," *ODNB*.

20. Either Thomas Jermyn (1633–1703) or Henry Jermyn, earl of Dover, who inherited their uncle's barony; Adolph, "Jermyn, Henry," *ODNB*.

and so I was disappointed of it. As for what relates to the debt secured out of the Barbados [fol. 171r] I often petitioned his Majesty, and, there being other creditors engaged in the same security, upon the June 13, 1663, his Majesty—in Council having heard the several pretensions—ordered that a moiety[21] of the profits of the Barbados should be for the payment of the said debts. But I do not hear that anything hath yet been received of it.

What I had right to would come to about £10,844, and I never received anything but £500 sterling which his Majesty was graciously pleased to give me when I was at London.[22] But if my sufferings were truly represented, I could not but hope for something for my poor child[23] to secure him from many wants and troubles I have met with myself.

This debt secured out of the Barbados, my brother Newton[24] had a letter of Attorney from your father to take care of,[25] and when you meet with him he will tell you of anything hath or may be done that way.[26]

Archibald Hay had a plantation in the Barbados called the Spring,[27] and a full information of that I sent to Mr. Forester, secretary to the Duke of Lauderdale,[28] of whom you may have an account; for I fear this will give you a surfeit[29] if you read it all at one time, and therefore I did not send a copy of that.

---

21. "Either of two (occasionally more) parts (not necessarily equal) into which something is divided; one's share or portion," *OED*.
22. See *True Account*, and "Upon the Many Disappointments I Have Met with in My Business at Court," 7n27, 206n54.
23. I.e., Robert/Robin.
24. Sir Henry Newton-Puckering, Halkett's brother-in-law.
25. Halkett, "Copy Resignation of a Factory by Sir James Halkett of Pitfirren [sic]."
26. There is a one-line space between these two paragraphs.
27. See "Introduction," 18.
28. See "Appendix 2," 329.
29. "Illness attributed to excessive eating or drinking. Also, in figurative contexts," *OED*.

Appendix 4:
Items from Simon Couper,
The Life of the Lady Halket *(1701)*

1. "Experiences in Fyvie."

[p. 23] The misfortune of the King's affairs put the loyal party from acting anything and forced them to suffer what they could not prevent, and to retire from the enemy so long as there was any place of retreat. And, at length, to capitulate and make the best conditions they could everyone for himself: for Cromwell marched whither he pleased and gave laws to the whole kingdom.

When the English army came to Aberdeen, some troopers came to Fyvie who were very rude: beating the men, frightening the women, and threatening to pistol them. My Lady Dunfermline, big with child and much disordered with fear of their insolence, entreated Mrs. Murray to go and see if she could pacify them, being their country woman. She, committing herself to God, went with her maid: so soon as she appeared, they asked if she was the English whore that came to meet the King, bending their pistols against her. She, without any fear, owned herself [p. 24] to be an Englishwoman, and to honor the King, but that she abhorred the name they gave her; that she was sorry to hear that the English nation (generally esteemed the most civil people in the world) should give occasion to be thought barbarously rude; that they could propose to themselves no advantage in frightening a person of honor, big with child, and a few children and women; that if any misfortune happened to my Lady Dunfermline or any in the family, they might expect to be called to account for it; that she was confident they had no allowance from their officers to be uncivil to any; that it would be more their interest to oblige all than disoblige any (the one would procure them love, the other hatred). They heard her with patience and, throwing down their pistols, promised that no disturbance should be given to the meanest of the family. They kept their word so far that my Lady Dunfermline was, by their staying in the house, secured from many insolences that were practiced in other places.

A little after there came three regiments to Fyvie, commanded by Colonels Lillburn, Fitch, and Overton. With this last, she was engaged in a pleasant communing. He had said to her, according to the cant[1] of that time, that God had wonderfully evidenced his power in the great things he had done. She replied, "No doubt but God would evidence his power in the great things he designed to do."

---

1. "The special phraseology of a particular class of persons or belonging to a particular subject," or "the peculiar phraseology of a religious sect or class," *OED*.

This she spake with some ardor, which made him reply, "You speak much my words but not, I think, my sense."

"When I know your sense," said she, "then I will tell you, whither it be mine or not."

"I mean," said he, "what God hath done by his servants in the late times, which could not be brought about without the immediate assistance and direction of God. It's in this I would know your mind."

She answered, "Sir, if you had not begun this discourse, I had said nothing to you but, since you desire my opinion of the times, I shall freely give it on condition that you make not use of what I say to the prejudice of the noble family I live in; for I can hold my tongue but I cannot speak anything contrary to what I think. I confess you have had great success in [p. 25] your undertakings, but it's no good rule by that to justify ill actions. You pretend to great zeal in religion and obedience to God's word; but, if you can shew me from it a warrant for murdering your lawful King and banishing his children, I will then say, all you have done is well and shall be of your opinion. But, since I am sure that cannot be done, I must condemn that horrid act and whatever has been done in prosecution or vindication of it."

He replied, "that they who have wrote on the prophecy of Daniel say that he foretold the destruction of monarchy and that it was a tyrannical government, fit to be destroyed."

"But how comes it," said she, "that you have taken the power from the Parliament, and those successive models that have governed since you wanted a King?"

"Because," said he, "we found in a little time, they began to be as bad as he."

"And so," replied she, "you will ever find reason to change whatever government you try until you come to beg the King to come home again and govern you. And this I am as confident of, as that I am speaking to you."

"If," said he, "I thought that would be true, I would repent all that I have done."

"It will come to that I dare assure you," said she, "and the greatest hindrance will be that you think your crimes such as it is impossible he should forgive you, but, to encourage you, I can assure you there was never any Prince more easy to be entreated or more inclined to pardon."

"Well," says he, "if this should come to pass, I will say you are a prophetess."

So, they broke off, and she found afterwards that he was not unsatisfied with her discourse.

2. "Books by the Lady Halket."

Drawing *The Life of the Lady Halket* to a close, Simon Couper emphasizes his subject's godly and virtuous disposition and adds: "As a confirmation of the preceding account and character, there is added a catalogue of some books writ by her, the bare contents of which will show how well she was employed and how much conversant with spiritual things."[2] He stresses that her "books" were written secretly, in private, after she had fulfilled her public devotional duties, and that they came to light only because the sudden deaths of "several persons" encouraged her to share them with "some, in whom she reposed great confidence"; even then, "she imparted this secret with bashfulness and reluctancy, occasioned by her modesty and great humility."[3] Couper's depiction of Halkett as shy and retiring is unlikely to have been believed by those who knew her, but Couper's biography was not aimed primarily at them; as discussed above, he had his own political agenda, which that image suited perfectly.[4] It is, however, somewhat at odds with the number of books that Couper attributes to her, and with her frequent references to potential readers within the extant volumes.

For over the next six pages, Couper provides varying degrees of detail about the contents of twenty-one books by Halkett, and concludes that list with the admission that, in addition, there are "about thirty stitched books" containing further occasional meditations. For a seventeenth-century woman, that is unusually prolific, especially as, although Couper calls them "books," none were published in her lifetime.[5] This material alone testifies to her "immense literary output";[6] however, Couper's catalogue is apparently incomplete.[7] Most obviously, it does not include *A True Account of My Life*, although as "Appendix 4.1" clearly demonstrates, he undoubtedly had access to it.[8] Less obvious is the fact that not all

---

2. Couper, *The Life of the Lady Halket*, 58.

3. Couper, *The Life of the Lady Halket*, 58. For Halkett's own account of this transaction, see "Saturday, February 19, 1697/8," 318–21. See also Trill, ed., *Halkett*, 188–90.

4. See "Living Monuments of Praise," 42–54.

5. While research has demonstrated that there were many more women writers in the early modern period than had previously been thought, most of them are represented by either only one or a small number of texts. A few, perhaps most notably Aphra Behn and Margaret Cavendish, published prolifically in the second part of the seventeenth century, but, with the possible exception of Lady Anne Clifford, it is difficult to think of any other British woman who produced so much in manuscript at this time. Margaret J. M. Ezell, "The Myth of Judith Shakespeare: Creating the Canon of Women's Literature in the Twentieth Century," in *Writing Women's Literary History* (Baltimore: Johns Hopkins University Press, 1993), 39–65. See also Trill, "Critical Categories," 119.

6. Jill S. Millman, "Introduction to the Perdita Project Catalogue, 1997–2007," Perdita Manuscripts, Adam Matthew (2007).

7. Trill, "Critical Categories," 104.

8. See *True Account*, and "Appendix 4.1," 337–38.

of the meditations that Couper chooses to publish in 1701 and 1702 are included there either. Strikingly, those that are all come from volumes that are now missing (for example, *Meditations upon the Twenty-fifth Psalm*). Therefore, it is possible that Couper simply omitted some parts of a volume's contents: after all, his list is not always exhaustive. Indeed, some of the materials he publishes include dates of writing that do not correspond with the list he has provided. While some of these materials may have been among the "stitched books," they are unlikely to include for example *Meditations upon Jabez's Request* (1686) as Couper states that "most" were "only ten or twelve sheets" long and contained only occasional meditations. It therefore seems possible that Halkett's "immense output" was once even larger.

The list below of Anne, Lady Halkett's works thus both draws upon and adds to the list provided by Couper at the end of his biography. For ease of cross reference, I have retained his numbering of the volumes but have inserted the titles of missing materials at the point they should appear chronologically. Couper identifies each volume by number, size, binding, number of pages, and date of composition, before providing a title and describing their contents. The detail with which he describes the contents decreases as his list increases; however, where the volumes remain extant, his list is generally verified. That said, as discussed in the headnotes to each volume, Couper makes some changes to Halkett's own designations of her texts.[9] So, while I take Couper's catalogue as a base text, where the extant volumes provide conflicting information, I use that to update Couper's claims. I explain what I have done and why in an accompanying footnote. Where appropriate, further information is also provided in the headnote to the individual volume. Rather than providing the biblical quotations in footnotes, I have instead produced a separate list of "Biblical References in the 'Books by the Lady Halkett'" in "Appendix 4.3." These references are perhaps particularly useful for the information they provide about the contents of the volumes that are currently missing, especially volume 2. A full list of Halkett's biblical references would require a separate concordance; therefore, the list below focuses only those references included in the titles of volumes or individual meditations.

---

9. See also Trill, "Critical Categories," 105–11.

Volume 1.[10] *Meditations, Prayers, and Vows in Childbirth.*
(1644–1658)

    1. Meditations and Prayers, upon the Miracles Wrought by Our Lord Jesus Christ Recorded by St. John.
    2. Of Meditation, Prayer, and Practice.
    3. Meditations upon one Verse of Every Psalm, Continued to the Fiftieth Psalm.
    4. A Short Meditation on the Lord's Supper.
    5. Meditations and Vows upon Psalm 56:12–13, Written on Some Remaining Leaves of This Book, upon Her Deliverance from the Danger of Childbirth.

Volume 2.[11] *Meditations, Contemplations, and the Soul's Remembrancer.*
(1649–1650)

    1. Meditations and Resolutions, Fit to Be Put in Practice, in Twenty Chapters.
    2. Meditations on the Lord's Supper and Private Prayers.
    3. Select Contemplations on Several Texts of Scripture, with These Following Titles:

1. The New Year's Gift, upon,	Rev. 2:17.
2. The Pattern of Patience	Job 1:22.
3. The Guilty Acquitted	John 8:11.
4. The Satisfaction of Mercy	Gen. 18:21.
5. The Proclamation	Isa. 55:7.
6. The Assurance of the Faithfull	Ps. 71:20.
7. The Reward of Charity	Ps. 41:1.
8. The Tempter's Assault	Matt. 4:8.
9. The Directory for Salvation	Rom. 10:9.
10. The Soul's Injunction	Ps. 103:2.
11. The Comfort of the Afflicted	Rom. 8:28.
12. The Assurance of What Is Necessary	Matt. 6:32.
13. The Way to Attain Perfection	Matt. 7:7.
14. The Power of Love	Luke 7:47.
15. The Benefit of Confession	1 John 1:9.
16. The Fiery Trial	Zech. 13:9.

---

10. Missing. Bound folio, 152 pages. Couper's date range is 1644–1648; however, he notes that the final meditation refers to "June 13, 1658," which is when her first son, Henry (Harry) Halkett, was born.

11. Missing. Bound folio, 376 pages.

17. The Precedent[12] for Youth	Ps. 119:9.
18. The Christian's Daily Exercise	Acts 24:16.
19. The Humble Expostulation	Jer. 12:9.
20. The Way to Heaven.	2 Pet. 1:10
21. The Comfortable Persuasion	Rom. 8:28–39.
22. The Best Oculist	Matt. 7:5.
23. The True Peace	John 16:3.
24. The Promise of Mercy	Ps. 91:15.
25. The Triumph of Affliction	2 Cor. 4:8–9.
26. The Humble Submission	1 Sam. 3:18.
27. The Request	Judges 6:17.
28. The Needful Exhortation	Isa. 26:4.
29. The Extent of the Law	Gal. 5:22–23.
30. The Evidence of Grace	2 Chron. 33:12–13.

4.[13] The Soul's Progress.
5. The Original and Use of Scripture.
6. The Soul's Remembrancer.[14]

Volume 3.[15] (1651)[16]   *Meditations upon the Twenty-Fifth Psalm.*

Volume 4.[17] (1652)   *Meditations on Death, from Heb. 9:27.*

Volume 5.[18] (1653–1657)[19]   *A Short Expostulation about Prayer, Meditations, and the Mother's Will to Her Unborn Child.*

1. A Short Expostulation about Prayer.
2. The Great Conquest and Power of Faith, 1 John 5:4.

---

12. Originally "president."
13. Wrongly numbered "5" in original.
14. In *Select and Occasional Meditations* (1696–1697), Halkett says that she wrote "The Soul's Remembrancer" while living in Fyvie, which suggests it was written sometime between September 27, 1650, and June 1652. See *True Account*, 127–36.
15. Missing. Bound folio, 59 pages. Published as Halkett, *Meditations upon the Twentieth and Fifth Psalm*, and reprinted in Halkett, *Meditations upon the Twenty-fifth Psalm*.
16. In Couper's original list, this reads "1561." A note on the final page of Couper's edition of this meditation informs us that it was completed "at Fyvie, January 1, 1651/2," 48.
17. Missing. Bound folio, 73 pages.
18. NLS, MS 6489. Bound folio, 150 pages.
19. In the printed edition, the date range reads 1653–1675; however, the contents suggest this is a typographical error that should read 1657. The entries in this volume are undated, apart from "The

3. Meditations on Psalm 143.
4. Elisha's Request Granted.
5. The Mother's Will to the Unborn Child.

Volume 6.[20] *Occasional Meditations.*
(1658/9–1660)[21]

The Select Meditations Are:

1. On Hypocrisy.
2. Upon the Sacrament.
3. Upon Riches.
4. Upon 2 Chron. 28:10.
5. Upon Beauty.
6. Upon Poverty.
7. Upon Imagination.
8. The Power of Faith, upon Mark 16:17–18.[22]
9. Upon Covetousness.
10. Upon the Failings of Great Professors.

The Occasional Meditations Are upon Several Public and Private Occurrences: Whereof the Two Last Are upon the Late Change of Public Affairs, and upon the Return of the King, May 1660.

Volume 7.[23] *Occasional Meditations, Meditations and Prayers on Every Sev-*
(1660, 1663)[24] *eral Day Ordained to Be Kept Holy in the Church of England.*

1. Part One, Contains Fifteen Meditations, on Public and Private Occurrences.
2. Part Two, Contains Select Meditations on the Following Subjects:

Mother's Will to Her Unborn Child, 1656," pp. 198–256. See also "Headnote" to this volume, 173–74.

20. NLS, MS 6490. Although Couper notes this volume is a bound octavo, he does not provide the number of pages and has redefined the volume's contents as *Select and Occasional Meditations*. As far as Halkett is concerned, this volume contains only occasional meditations; see Trill, "Critical Categories," 106–7. According to the library cataloguer, this volume has 380 pages.

21. Couper's date range was 1657–1660, but Halkett's annotations confirm the dating above; see "Headnote," 185.

22. Couper changes the title to "Upon the Power of Faith, from Mark 16: 17–18."

23. NLS, MS 6491. Bound in quarto, 326 pages, according to the library cataloguer. In *The Life of the Lady Halkett*, Couper substitutes "the Festival Days" for Halkett's original "Every Several Day."

24. On the inside front cover, Halkett confirms that these meditations were written in 1660 and 1663; however, the occasional meditations appear to date from 1660–1661, and no date is provided in text for the select meditations.

1. Meditations and Prayers on Every Several Day Observed in the Church of England.
2. Meditations on Isaiah 12.
3. Meditations on Psalm 34:1–5, after Childbirth.

Volume 8.[25]
(1663–1665)

Meditations and Prayers upon the First Week, and Occasional Meditations.

1. Part One, Containing Select Meditations and Prayers upon the First Week, with Observations on Each Day's Creation, and Considerations on the Seven Capital Vices, to Be Opposed, and Their Opposite Virtues to Be Studied and Practiced:

Vices to Be Subdued,		*Virtues to Be Learned,*
Pride	*Sunday*	Humility
Covetousness	*Monday*	Contentation[26]
Lust	*Tuesday*	Chastity
Envy	*Wednesday*	Charity
Gluttony	*Thursday*	Temperance
Anger	*Friday*	Patience
Sloth	*Saturday*	Diligence

2. Part Two, Fifteen Occasional Meditations on Public and Private Occurrences.

Volume 9.[27]
(1667–1670)[28]

Occasional and Select Meditations, including Instructions to My Son.

1. Part One, Twenty-One Occasional Meditations on Public and Private Occurrences.
2. Part Two, Select Meditations:
   1. On Heb. 13:5: "Let Your Conversation."
   2. On 1 Sam. 4:22: "The Glory Is Departed."
   3. On Ps. 18:20: "The Lord Rewarded Me."
   4. On 1 Cor. 13:7: "Beareth All Things."

---

25. Missing. Bound in quarto, 315 pages. The first part is published as Halkett, *Meditations and Prayers, upon the First Week*, and reprinted in Halkett, *Meditations upon the Twenty-Fifth Psalm*.

26. "The contenting oneself or one's mind with what one has; acquiescence in or acceptance of the situation," *OED*.

27. NLS, MS 6492. Bound in quarto, 452 pages.

28. Couper states the volume was started in 1666, this is contradicted by Halkett's dating, see "Headnote," 214–17.

5. On Jer. 35:18–19: "Jeremiah Said to the Rechabites."
6. On 1 Cor. 6:11: "Such Were Some of You."
7. Instructions to My[29] Son.
8. Confessions, Prayers, and Supplications; Promises and Duties; Characters and Blessings of the Righteous; Thanksgivings and Praise, and Resolutions, All in Scripture Terms.

Volume 10.[30]   *The Widow's Mite and Occasional Meditations.*
(1673–1674/5)

    1. Part One, Select Meditations, on These Subjects:
        1. The Widows Mite, Relating Partly to the King.
        2. Meditations and Resolutions upon the Devout Widow, Anna, Luke 2:36–38; In Which Are Observations on the Lord's Prayer,[31] Creed[32] and Decalogue.[33]
        3. Meditations and Resolutions, 1 Cor. 1:12–13, Occasioned by the Great Rent in This Church.
    2. Part Two, Thirty-Two Occasional Meditations on Public and Private Occurrences.

Volume 11.[34]   *The True Balm and Select Meditations.*
(1675–1676)

    1. The True Balm.
    2. Meditations and Observations on the Book of Judges.
    3. Upon the Sacrament of the Lord's Supper, Luke 22:18.

---

29. "Her" in Couper's catalogue.

30. NLS, MS 6493. Bound in quarto, 336 pages. Couper provides an end date of 1674; however, the final occasional meditation in this volume is dated January 21, 1674/5, 334.

31. The Lord's Prayer. Matthew 6:9–13; Luke 11:2–4.

32. "A form of words setting forth authoritatively and concisely the general belief of the Christian Church, or those articles of belief which are regarded as essential; a brief summary of Christian doctrine: usually and properly applied to the three statements of belief known as the Apostles', Nicene, and Athanasian Creeds. ('The Creed,' without qualification, usually = the Apostles' Creed)," *OED*. The Apostle's Creed forms part of daily "Morning Prayer," in the *BCP*, 247; Halkett returns to the Creed in her final volume, *Select and Occasional Meditations* (1697–1698/9), pp. 1–74; see also "Wednesday, December 1, 1697," 314–16; the Nicene Creed is repeated in "The Order for the Administration of the Lords Supper or Holy Communion," *BCP*, 392; the Athanasian Creed is used in "Morning Prayer" on Feast days, *BCP*, 257–59.

33. Decalogue, or the Ten Commandments. Exodus 20:1–17; Deuteronomy 5:6–22.

34. Missing. Book in quarto, 371 pages.

346 Appendix 4

Volume 12.[35] *The Art of Divine Chemistry and Select Meditations.*
(1676–1678)[36]

                    1. The Art of Divine Chemistry.
                    2. The Rule for Thoughts, Words and Actions.
                    3. Meditations on Psalm 106:4–5.
                    4. Meditations and Prayers Concerning the King.

                  A True Account of My Life.
(1677–1678)[37]

Volume 13.[38] *Joseph's Trial and Triumph.*
(1678/9–1681)[39]

                  Observations on the Whole History of Joseph, with Particular Applications to Her Own Case.

                  Meditations upon the Seven Gifts of the Holy Spirit.
(1679–1680)[40]

Volume 14.[41] *The Fruits of the Spirit, Reflections, and Occasional Meditations.*
(1682–1683)

                  1. The Fruits of the Spirit, Compared with the Fruits of the Tree of Life.

35. NLS, MS 6494. Quarto, of 380 pages.

36. Couper lists the date range as 1677–1678; however, Halkett notes it was "begun, June 20, 1676," and that she finished this volume on Saturday, September 2, 1676. Halkett, *The Art of Divine Chemistry*, pp.i, 56.

37. Not included in Couper's catalogue, although he clearly had access to it; compare, for example, *True Account* and "Appendix 4.1," 133–34.

38. NLS, MS 6495. Quarto, 505 pages.

39. Couper gives the dates as 1678–1679; however, annotations in Halkett's own hand confirm the dates indicated above: "begun Monday, February 10, 1678/9," and "ended Saturday, November 5, 1681," *Joseph's Trial and Triumph*, pp. i, v. At the book's close, Halkett adds the note: "To the praise of my most gracious God, who hath brought me through many difficulties and trials since the book was first begun, and until he please to end them will, I hope, support me with his grace so as that I may do nothing unsuitable to a widow indeed, that is, O Lord, devoted to they fear," *Joseph's Trial and Triumph*, p. v.

40. Not included in Couper's catalogue but published as Halkett, *Meditations upon the Seven Gifts of the Holy Spirit*, ESTC T200617. The date of writing is included at the end of this section of the printed volume: "Written at Edinburgh, in the month of January 1679/80," 22. This text was also published alongside Halkett, *Meditations upon Jabez's Request*, ESTC N10709, see figure 2, 51.

41. Missing. Book in quarto, 556 pages.

	2. Reflections and Meditations on 2 Chron. 28; upon 1 Kings 17; on the Blessed Virgin; on Jer. 50:15; on Jeroboam's Sin; on Psalm 27:9; upon Jer. 30:21–22; on John 13:15.
	3. Occasional Meditations.
Volume 15.[42] (1683/4–1685)[43]	*Meditations on the Book of Jonah, and Other Select Meditations.*
	1. Meditations on the Book of Jonah.
	2. Meditations on the Times of David's Prayers, et cetera.
	3. Meditations on Paul's Conversion, and What Is Recorded of Him in Acts, Chapters 1–23.
(1686)[44]	Continuation of the same.
	Meditations upon Jabez's Request.
(1686)[45]	
Volume 16.[46] (1686/7–1688)[47]	*Meditations on St. Peter, the Passion, and Occasional Meditations.*
	1. Meditations on What Is Recorded of St. Peter in the Gospels.
	2. Meditations on the Passion of Our Lord, Divided into Seven Periods, According to the Days of the Week.
	3. Occasional Meditations.

---

42. NLS, MS 6496. Book in quarto, 378 pages.

43. Couper's dates for this volume are 1684–1685; however, Halkett gives the date "Monday, January 21, 1683/4" as the start date for these meditations, *Meditations on the Book of Jonah*, p. ii. On the inside back cover, she notes that the volume was "ended Saturday, June 27, 1685," *Meditations on the Book of Jonah*, p. iii.

44. Missing. Stitched book in quarto, 136 pages.

45. Not included in Couper's catalogue but published alongside Halkett, *Meditations upon the Seven Gifts of the Holy Spirit*, ESTC N10709. The date of writing is included in a separate title page for this section of the book: "Written by the Lady Halkett, begun October 24, ended November 30, 1686," 23. This volume also includes *Sacramental Meditations upon the Lord's Supper, and Prayers, Pious Reflections and Observations*. These materials have clearly been selected by Couper from different volumes, or, perhaps, from the stitched books, as the dates provided range from February 7, 1678/9, to August 11, 1695, *Meditations upon the Seven Gifts of the Holy Spirit*, 68, 57. ESTC N10709.

46. NLS, MS 6497. Book in quarto, of 392 pages.

47. Couper gives the date 1687, but Halkett's first entry is dated January 24, 1686/7, *Meditations on St. Peter*, p. i.

Volume 17.[48] *Meditations on Moses and Samuel.*
(1688–1689/90)[49]

                Instructions for Youth.

(n.d.)[50]

Volume 18.[51] *Occasional Meditations, Meditations upon Nehemiah, and Ob-*
(1690–1692)   *servations of Several Good Women Mentioned in Scripture.*

1. Occasional Meditations.
2. Meditations on the Book of Nehemiah.
3. Observations on Several Good Women Mentioned in Scripture: Eve; Sarah; Rebecca; Rachel and Leah; Miriam; The Daughters of Zelophehad; Ruth; Hannah; Bathsheba; Deborah; Huldah; The Woman of Canaan, Matt. 15; Mary Magdalen; Mary and Martha; Elisabeth; the Virgin Mary.[52]

Volume 19.[53] *Of Watchfulness, Select, and Occasional Meditations.*
(1693/4–1695)

1. Upon Watchfulness, Matt. 25:13.
2. Restraining the Tongue, Ps. 39.
3. Avoiding Carefulness, Phil. 4:6–7.
4. The Grace of God, and its effects, Titus 2:11–13.
5. Upon Prayer.
6. Upon Leviticus 19:2: "Ye shall be Holy . . ."
7. Occasional Meditations.
8. Upon the Man of God, 1 Kings 13.
9. Serious Thoughts upon the By-past Years since 1688.
10. Upon Contentment Phil. 4:11.

---

48. NLS, MS 6498. Book in quarto, 372 pages.

49. Couper gives the date as simply 1689; however, Halkett's dating of her materials indicates she started writing this volume on Monday, May 21, 1688, and completed it on March 17, 1689/90, *Meditations on Moses and Samuel*, pp. i, v.

50. Not included in Couper's catalogue but published as Halkett, *Instructions for Youth* and reprinted in Halkett, *Meditations upon the Twenty-Fifth Psalm*. Although Halkett does not provide an exhaustive list of her boarders, separate entries provide evidence that she was involved in this activity circa 1687–1694, see Trill, ed., *Halkett*, xxvn52.

51. NLS, MS 6499. Book in quarto, 370 pages.

52. Although Couper does not provide details here, I have recovered them from the manuscript and they are included in the list of biblical references, see "Appendix 4.3," 355.

53. NLS, MS 6500. Book in quarto, 377 pages.

11. God's Husbandry, 1 Cor. 3:9.
12. Upon Psalm 139:23–24: "Search Me . . ."
13. Upon Matt. 11:29–30: "Take My Yoke . . ."
14. Occasional Meditations.

Volume 20.[54]   *Select and Occasional Meditations.*
(1696–1697)

1. Some Reflections Concerning Them That Are Reduced.
2. Meditations on Exodus 3:14. I Am That I Am; I Am the Bread of Life; The Light of the World; The Door of the Sheep; The Good Shepherd; The Resurrection; The Way, Truth, and Life; The True Vine, with Prayers Accommodated.[55]
3. Meditations on Deut. 8:2: "Thou Shalt Remember all the Way . . ."
4. Upon Rom. 13:8: "Owe No Man . . . ," and Isa. 40:31: "But They That Wait."
5. Meditations on the Book of Esther.
6. Occasional Meditations.

Volume 21.[56]   *Select and Occasional Meditations.*
(1697–1698/9)[57]

1. Meditations on the Articles of the Creed.
2. Meditation on Ephes. 4:30–32; Upon Hos. 14:1–4; Upon 1 Cor. 15:58; Upon Naaman, 2 Kings 5.
3. A Probable Conjecture, Concerning the Calling of the Jews.
4. Upon Christ's Forty Days Fasting, Matt. 4.[58]
5. Occasional Meditations.[59]

There are, besides the aforementioned, about thirty stitched books, some in folio, some in quarto, most of them of ten or twelve sheets, all containing occasional meditations.

54. NLS, MS 6501. Book in quarto, 373 pages.

55. Although Couper does not provide details here, I have recovered them from the manuscript and they are included in the list of biblical references, see "Appendix 4.3," 356–57.

56. NLS, MS 6502. Book in quarto, 351 pages.

57. Couper dates this volume 1698–1699, but dates provided by Halkett confirm the dates given above.

58. According to Couper, this Meditation was "begun February 22, being Ash Wednesday, but not finished," which is confirmed by Halkett, *Select and Occasional Meditations*, (1697–1698/9), p. i.

59. Dated "from January 1698 to November 1698" by Couper and erroneously identified as item "4" rather than "5;" see "Headnote," 313–314.

3. Biblical References in the "Books by the Lady Halket."

Volume 1. Psalm 56:12–13: "Thy vows are upon me, O God: I will render praises unto thee. For thou hast delivered my soul from death: wilt not thou deliver my feet from falling, that I may walk before God in the light of the living?"

Volume 2. Revelation 2:17: "He that hath an ear, let him hear what the spirit saith unto the churches: To him that overcometh will I give to eat of the hidden manna, and will give him a white stone, and in the stone a new name written, which no man knoweth saving he that receiveth it."
Job 1:22: "In all this Job sinned not, nor charged God foolishly."
John 8:11: "She said, No man, Lord. And Jesus said unto her, neither do I condemn thee: go and sin no more."
Genesis 18:21: "I will go down now and see whether they have done altogether according to the cry of it, which is come unto me; and if not, I will know."
Isaiah 55:7: "Let the wicked forsake his way, and the unrighteous man his thoughts: and let him return unto the Lord, and he will have mercy upon him; and to our God, for he will abundantly pardon."
Psalm 71:20: "Thou, which hast shewed me great and sore troubles, shalt quicken me again, and shalt bring me up again from the depths of the earth."
Psalm 41:1: "Blessed is he that considereth the poor: the Lord will deliver him in time of trouble."
Matthew 4:8: "Again, the devil taketh him up into an exceeding high mountain, and sheweth him all the kingdoms of the world, and the glory of them."
Romans 10:9: "That if thou shalt confess with thy mouth the Lord Jesus, and shalt believe in thine heart that God hath raised him from the dead, thou shalt be saved."
Psalm 103:2: "Bless the Lord, O my soul, and forget not all his benefits."
Romans 8:28: "And we know that all things work together for good to them that love God, to them who are the called according to his purpose."
Matthew 6:32: "For after all these things do the Gentiles seek: for your heavenly Father knoweth that ye have need of all these things."
Matthew 7:7: "Ask, and it shall be given you; seek, and ye shall find; knock, and it shall be opened unto you."

Luke 7:47: "Wherefore I say unto thee, her sins, which are many, are forgiven; for she loved much: but to whom little is forgiven, the same loveth little."

John 1:9: "If we confess our sins, he is faithful and just to forgive us our sins, and to cleanse us from all unrighteousness."

Zechariah 13:9: "And I will bring the third part through the fire, and will refine them as silver is refined and will try them as gold is tried: they shall call on my name, and I will hear them: I will say, it is my people: and they shall say, The Lord is my God."

Psalm 119:9: "Wherewithal shall a young man cleanse his way? by taking heed thereto according to thy word."

Acts 24:16: "And herein do I exercise myself, to have always a conscience void of offence toward God, and toward men."

Jeremiah 12:9: "Mine heritage is unto me as a speckled bird, the birds round about are against her; come ye, assemble all the beasts of the field, come to devour."

2 Peter 1:10: "Wherefore the rather, brethren, give diligence to make your calling and election sure: for if ye do these things, ye shall never fall."

Romans 8:28, 38–39: "And we know that all things work together for good to them that love God, to them who are the called according to his purpose"; "For I am persuaded, that neither death, nor life, nor angels, nor principalities, nor powers, nor things present, nor things to come, nor height, nor depth, nor any other creature, shall be able to separate us from the love of God, which is in Christ Jesus our Lord."

Matthew 7:5: "Thou hypocrite, first cast out the beam out of thine own eye, and then shalt thou see clearly to cast out the mote out of thy brother's eye."

John 16:3: "And these things will they do unto you, because they have not known the Father, nor me."

Psalm 91:15: "He shall call upon me, and I will answer him: I will be with him in trouble: I will deliver him and honor him."

2 Corinthians 4:8–9: "We are troubled on every side, yet not distressed; we are perplexed, but not in despair; persecuted, but not forsaken; cast down, but not destroyed."

Isaiah 26:4: "Trust ye in the Lord forever: for in the Lord Jehovah is everlasting strength."

Galatians 5:22–23: "But the fruit of the spirit is love, joy, peace, longsuffering, gentleness, goodness, faith, meekness, temperance: against such there is no law."

2 Chronicles 33:12–13: "And when he was in affliction, he besought the Lord his God and humbled himself greatly before the God of his fathers and prayed unto him: and he was intreated of him, and heard his supplication, and brought him again to Jerusalem into his kingdom. Then Manasseh knew that the Lord, he was God.

Volume 3. Psalm 25.

Volume 4. Hebrews 9:27: "And as it is appointed unto men once to die, but after this the judgment."

Volume 5. 1 John 5:4: "For whatsoever is born of God overcometh the world: and this is the victory that overcometh the world, even our faith." Psalm 143.

Volume 6. 2 Chronicles 28:10: "And now ye purpose to keep under the children of Judah and Jerusalem for bondmen and bondwomen unto you: but are there not with you, even with you, sins against the Lord your God?"
Mark 16:17–18: "And these signs shall follow them that believe; in my name shall they cast out devils; they shall speak with new tongues; they shall take up serpents; and if they drink any deadly thing, it shall not hurt them; they shall lay hands on the sick, and they shall recover."

Volume 7. Isaiah 12:1–6: "And in that day thou shalt say, O Lord, I will praise thee: though thou wast angry with me, thine anger is turned away, and thou comfortedst me. Behold, God is my salvation; I will trust, and not be afraid: for the Lord Jehovah is my strength and my song; he also is become my salvation. Therefore, with joy shall ye draw water out of the wells of salvation. And in that day shall ye say, Praise the Lord, call upon his name, declare his doings among the people, make mention that his name is exalted. Sing unto the Lord; for he hath done excellent things: this is known in all the earth. Cry out and shout, thou inhabitant of Zion: for great is the Holy One of Israel in the midst of thee."
Psalm 34:1–5: "I will bless the Lord at all times: his praise shall continually be in my mouth. My soul shall make her boast in the Lord: the humble shall hear thereof and be glad. O magnify the Lord with me and let us exalt his name together. I sought the Lord, and he heard me, and delivered me from all my fears. They looked unto him and were lightened: and their faces were not ashamed."

Volume 8.   Genesis 1–2:3.

Volume 9.   Hebrews 13:5: "Let your conversation be without covetousness; and be content with such things as ye have: for he hath said, I will never leave thee, nor forsake thee."
1 Samuel 4:22: "And she said, the glory is departed from Israel: for the ark of God is taken."
Psalm 18:20: "The Lord rewarded me according to my righteousness: according to the cleanness of my hands hath he recompensed me."
1 Corinthians 13:7: "[Charity] beareth all things, believeth all things, hopeth all things, endureth all things."
Jeremiah 35:18–19: "And Jeremiah said unto the house of the Rechabites, thussaith the Lord of hosts, the God of Israel; Because ye have obeyed the commandment of Jonadab your father, and kept all his precepts, and done according unto all that he hath commanded you: therefore, thus saith the Lord of hosts, the God of Israel; Jonadab the son of Rechab shall not want a man to stand before me forever."
1 Corinthians 6:11: "And such were some of you: but ye are washed, but ye are sanctified, but ye are justified in the name of the Lord Jesus, and by the spirit of our God."

Volume 10. Luke 2:36–38: "And there was one Anna, a prophetess, the daughter of Phanuel, of the tribe of Aser: she was of a great age, and had lived with an husband seven years from her virginity; And she was a widow of about fourscore and four years, which departed not from the temple, but served God with fastings and prayers night and day. And she coming in that instant gave thanks likewise unto the Lord, and spake of him to all them that looked for redemption in Jerusalem."
1 Corinthians 1:12–13: "Now this I say, that every one of you saith, I am of Paul; and I of Apollos; and I of Cephas; and I of Christ. Is Christ divided? was Paul crucified for you? or were ye baptized in the name of Paul?"

Volume 11. Judges.
Luke 22:18: "For I say unto you, I will not drink of the fruit of the vine, until the kingdom of God shall come."

Volume 12.   Psalm 106:4–5: "Remember me, O Lord, with the favor that thou bearest unto thy people: O visit me with thy salvation; That I may see the good of thy chosen, that I may rejoice in the gladness of thy nation, that I may glory with thine inheritance."

Volume 13.   Genesis 37–50.

Meditations upon the Seven Gifts of the Holy Spirit.
    Isaiah 11: 2–3: "And the spirit of the Lord shall rest upon him, the spirit of wisdom and understanding, the spirit of counsel and might, the spirit of knowledge and of the fear of the Lord; and shall make him of quick understanding in the fear of the Lord: and he shall not judge after the sight of his eyes, neither reprove after the hearing of his ears."

Volume 14.   2 Chronicles 28.
    1 Kings 17.
    Jeremiah 50:15: "Shout against her [Babylon] round about: she hath given her hand: her foundations are fallen, her walls are thrown down: for it is the vengeance of the Lord: take vengeance upon her; as she hath done, do unto her.
    1 Kings 12.
    Psalm 27:9: "Hide not thy face far from me; put not thy servant away in anger: thou hast been my help; leave me not, neither forsake me, O God of my salvation."
    Jeremiah 30:21–22: "And their nobles shall be of themselves, and their governor shall proceed from the midst of them; and I will cause him to draw near, and he shall approach unto me: for who is this that engaged his heart to approach unto me? saith the Lord. And ye shall be my people, and I will be your God."
    John 13:15: "For I have given you an example, that ye should do as I have done to you."

Volume 15.   Jonah.
    Acts 1–23.

Meditations upon Jabez's Request.
        1 Chronicles 4:10: "And Jabez called on the God if Israel, saying, Oh that thou wouldest bless me indeed, and enlarge my coast, and that thine hand might be with me, and that thou wouldest keep me from evil, that it may not grieve me! And God granted him that which he requested."

Volume 16. The Gospels (Matthew, Mark, Luke and John).

Volume 17. 1 Samuel 1–28.

Volume 18. Nehemiah.
    Genesis.
    Numbers 27.
    Ruth.
    1 Samuel 1–2.
    2 Samuel 11:2–3: "And it came to pass in an evening tide, that David arose from off his bed and walked upon the roof of the King's house: and from the roof he saw a woman washing herself; and the woman was very beautiful to look upon. And David sent and enquired after the woman. And one said, Is not this Bathsheba, the daughter of Eliam, the wife of Uriah the Hittite?"
    Proverbs 31.
    Judges 4–5.
    2 Kings 22:14–20: "So Hilkiah the priest, and Ahikam, and Achbor, and Shaphan, and Asahiah, went unto Huldah the prophetess, the wife of Shallum the son of Tikvah, the son of Harhas, keeper of the wardrobe; (now she dwelt in Jerusalem in the college;) and they communed with her."
    Matthew 15:22: "And, behold, a woman of Canaan came out of the same coasts, and cried unto him, saying, have mercy on me, O Lord, thou Son of David; my daughter is grievously vexed with a devil."
    Matthew 26:6–7: "Now when Jesus was in Bethany, in the house of Simon the leper, there came unto him a woman having an alabaster box of very precious ointment, and poured it on his head, as he sat at meat."
    Luke 1:13: "But the angel said unto him, Fear not, Zacharias: for thy prayer is heard; and thy wife Elisabeth shall bear thee a son, and thou shalt call his name John."
    Luke 1–2.

Volume 19. Matthew 25:13: "Watch therefore, for ye know neither the day nor the hour wherein the Son of man cometh."

Psalm 39.

Philippians 4:6-7: "Be careful for nothing; but in everything by prayer and supplication with thanksgiving let your requests be made known unto God. And the peace of God, which passeth all understanding, shall keep your hearts and minds through Christ Jesus."

Titus 2:11-13: "For the grace of God that bringeth salvation hath appeared to all men, teaching us that, denying ungodliness and worldly lusts, we should live soberly, righteously, and godly, in this present world; looking for that blessed hope, and the glorious appearing of the great God and our Savior Jesus Christ."

Leviticus 19:2: "Speak unto all the congregation of the children of Israel, and say unto them, Ye shall be holy: for I the Lord your God am holy."

1 Kings 13.

Philippians 4:11: "Not that I speak in respect of want: for I have learned, in whatsoever state I am, therewith to be content."

1 Corinthians 3:9: "For we are laborers together with God: ye are God's husbandry, ye are God's building."

Psalm 139:23-24: "Search me, O God, and know my heart: try me, and know my thoughts: And see if there be any wicked way in me and lead me in the way everlasting."

Matthew 11:29-30: "Take my yoke upon you and learn of me; for I am meek and lowly in heart: and ye shall find rest unto your souls. For my yoke is easy, and my burden is light."

Volume 20. Exodus 3:14: "And God said unto Moses, I am that I am: and he said, thus shalt thou say unto the children of Israel, I am hath sent me unto you."

John 6:35: "And Jesus said unto them, I am the bread of life: he that cometh to me shall never hunger; and he that believeth on me shall never thirst."

John 8:12: "Then spake Jesus again unto them, saying, I am the light of the world: he that followeth me shall not walk in darkness but shall have the light of life."

John 10:7: "Then said Jesus unto them again, Verily, verily, I say unto you, I am the door of the sheep."

John 10:14: "I am the good shepherd, and know my sheep, and am known of mine."

John 11:25: "Jesus said unto her, I am the resurrection, and the life: he that believeth in me, though he were dead, yet shall he live."

John 14:6: "Jesus saith unto him, I am the way, the truth, and the life: no man cometh unto the Father, but by me."

John 15:1: "I am the true vine, and my Father is the husbandman."

Deuteronomy 8:2: "And thou shalt remember all the way which the Lord thy God led thee these forty years in the wilderness, to humble thee, and to prove thee, to know what was in thine heart, whether thou wouldst keep his commandments, or no."

Romans 13:8: "Owe no man anything, but to love one another: for he that loveth another hath fulfilled the law."

Isaiah 40:31: "But they that wait upon the Lord shall renew their strength; they shall mount up with wings as eagles; they shall run, and not be weary; and they shall walk, and not faint."

Esther.

Volume 21. Ephesians 4:30–32: "And grieve not the holy spirit of God, whereby ye are sealed unto the day of redemption. Let all bitterness, and wrath, and anger, and clamor, and evil speaking, be put away from you, with all malice: And be ye kind one to another, tenderhearted, forgiving one another, even as God for Christ's sake hath forgiven you."

Hosea 14:1–4: "O Israel, return unto the Lord thy God; for thou hast fallen by thine iniquity. Take with you words and turn to the Lord: say unto him, Take away all iniquity, and receive us graciously: so will we render the calves of our lips. Asshur shall not save us; we will not ride upon horses: neither will we say any more to the work of our hands, Ye are our gods: for in thee the fatherless findeth mercy. I will heal their backsliding, I will love them freely: for mine anger is turned away from him."

1 Cor. 15:58: "Therefore, my beloved brethren, be ye steadfast, unmovable, always abounding in the work of the Lord, forasmuch as ye know that your labor is not in vain in the Lord."

2 Kings 5.

Matthew 4:1–11: "Then was Jesus led up of the spirit into the wilderness to be tempted of the devil. And when he had fasted forty days and forty nights, he was afterward an hungred. And when the tempter came to him, he said, if thou be the Son of God, command that these stones be made bread. But he answered and said, 'It is written, man shall not live by bread alone, but by every word that proceedeth out of the mouth of God.' Then the devil taketh him up into the holy city, and setteth him on a pinnacle of the temple, And saith unto him, If thou be the Son of God, cast thyself down: for it is written, He shall give his angels charge concerning thee: and in their hands they shall bear thee up, lest at any time thou dash thy foot against a stone. Jesus said unto him, 'It is written again, thou shalt not tempt the Lord thy God.' Again, the devil taketh him up into an exceeding high mountain, and sheweth him all the kingdoms of the world, and the glory of them; And saith unto him, all these things will I give thee, if thou wilt fall down and worship me. Then saith Jesus unto him, 'Get thee hence, Satan: for it is written, thou shalt worship the Lord thy God, and him only shalt thou serve.' Then the devil leaveth him, and behold, angels came and ministered unto him."

Bibliography

Primary Sources

Manuscript Sources

Anon. "Grieve Not Dear Love Although We Often Part." In "Verse Compilation ("The Skipwith MS")." 1620–1650. BL, Add. MS 25707, fol.14v.

Digby, John, Earl of Bristol. "Grieve Not Dear Love Although We Often Part." In "Henry Lawes Music Manuscript." 1626–1662. BL, Add. MS 53723. Fol. 66v.

Douglas, Anne, Countess of Morton. "Letters to Sir James Halkett." 1648/9. Pitfirrane Papers: Correspondence. NLS, MS 6409, nos. 19–26.

Douglas, Lady Anne. "Letters to Sir James Halkett." 1654. Pitfirrane Papers: Correspondence, NLS, MS 6409, nos. 27–37.

Evelyn, John. "Evelyn Papers. Vol. CXXXI. Letters from Evelyn to Various Correspondents." 1644–1679. BL, Add. MS 78298.

———. "Evelyn Papers. Vol. CXLIX. General Correspondence." 1637–1706. BL, Add. MS 78316.

Halkett, Anne, Lady. *The Art of Divine Chemistry and Select Meditations*. 1676–1678. NLS, MS 6494.

———. "For Forfeited Estates, &c.: Dame Anne, Wife of Sir James Halkett and Daughter of the Late Jane Murray." Volume of Petitions All Addressed to the King, Unless Otherwise Specified, October 1660. TNA, SP 29/20, fol.107.

———. *An Information of What Was Left Me by My Mother*. N.d. Pitfirrane Papers. NLS, MS 6481, fols.170r–71v.

———. *Joseph's Trial and Triumph*. 1678/9–1681. NLS, MS 6495.

———. "Letter to Her Stepson, Sir Charles Halkett." N.d. Pitfirrane Papers: Correspondence. NLS, MS 6409, no. 40.

———. "Letter to Mr. Thomas." December 27, 1670. Pitfirrane Papers: Correspondence. NLS, MS 6407, fols. 26r–27v.

———. "Letter to the Earl of Lauderdale." N.d. NLS, Acc. 6112.

———. "Letter to the Laird of Sauchie." N.d. Pitfirrane Papers: Correspondence. NLS, MS 6407, fol. 145r–145v.

———. *Meditations on Moses and Samuel*. 1688–1689/90. NLS, MS 6498.

———. *Meditations on St. Peter, the Passion, and Occasional Meditations*. 1686/7–1688. NLS, MS 6497.

———. *Meditations on the Book of Jonah, and Other Select Meditations*. 1683/4–1685. NLS, MS 6496.

———. *Occasional and Select Meditations, including Instructions to My Son*. 1667–1670. NLS, MS 6492.

———. *Occasional Meditations.* 1658/9–1660. NLS, MS 6490.

———. *Occasional Meditations, Meditations and Prayers on Every Several Day Ordained to Be Kept Holy in the Church of England.* 1660–1663. NLS, MS 6491.

———. *Occasional Meditations, Meditations upon Nehemiah, and Observations of Several Good Women Mentioned in Scripture.* 1690–1692. NLS, MS 6499.

———. *Of Watchfulness, Select, and Occasional Meditations.* 1693/4–1695. NLS, MS 6500.

———. "Petition of Anne Halkett and Thos. Stanley to the King, for the Place of Collectors and Receivers, of the Additional Customs Imposed by Act of Parliament," June 17, 1661. TNA, SP 29/37, fol.125.

———. *Select and Occasional Meditations.* 1696–1697. NLS, MS 6501.

———. *Select and Occasional Meditations.* 1697–1698/9. NLS, MS 6502.

———. *A Short Expostulation about Prayer, Meditations, and the Mother's Will to Her Unborn Child.* 1653–1657. NLS, MS 6489.

———. *A True Account of My Life.* 1677–1678. BL, Add. MS 32376.

———. *The Widow's Mite and Occasional Meditations.* 1673–1674/5. NLS, MS 6493.

Halkett, Sir James. "Copy Resignation of a Factory by Sir James Halkett of Pitfirren, Commissioner for Anna Murray before the Commissioners for the Administration of Justice in Scotland against Mr. Andrew Hay as Executor of Archibald Hay at the Instance of Anna Murray, Assignee of a Bond for £4000." April 27, 1655. NRS, GD34/843/3/23.

Printed Sources

Proclamations and Acts of Parliament

"An Act Enabling the Lords Commissioners for Custody of the Great Seal of England, to Issue Commissions of Delegates in Cases of Pretended Marriages (January 1651)." In *Acts and Ordinances of the Interregnum, 1642–1660*, edited by C. H. Firth and R. S. Rait, 496–97. London: HMSO, 1911.

"An Act for the Speedy Provision of Money for Disbanding and Paying Off the Forces of This Kingdome Both by Land and Sea." In *Statutes of the Realm: Volume 5, 1628–80*, edited by John Raithby, 207–25. s.l: Great Britain Record Commission:1819, *BHO*.

"Act of the General Assembly, anent a Solemn National Fast and Humiliation, with the Causes Thereof. At Edinburgh, November 12, 1690." Edinburgh: Andrew Anderson, 1690. ESTC R173923.

"An Act Touching Marriages and the Registering Thereof; and Also Touching Births and Burials, August 1653." In *Acts and Ordinances of the Interregnum, 1642–1660*, edited by C. H. Firth and R. S. Rait. London: HMSO, 1911.

Charles II (King). "An Act of Free and Generall Pardon, Indempnity, and Oblivion, 1660." In *Statutes of the Realm: Volume 5, 1628–80*, edited by John Raithby, 226–34. s.l: Great Britain Record Commission:1819, BHO.

———. "April 25, 1660. An Act for the Speedy Disbanding of the Army and Garrisons of This Kingdome." In *Statutes of the Realm: Volume 5, 1628–80*, edited by John Raithby, 238–41. s.l: Great Britain Record Commission, 1819, BHO.

———. "A Proclamation for a General Fast throughout the Realm of England." London: John Bill and Christopher Barker, 1661. ESTC R39168.

———. "A Proclamation, for Observation of the Thirtieth Day of January as a Day of Fast and Humiliation According to the Late Act of Parliament for That Purpose." London: John Bill, 1661. ESTC R226600.

James VII/II (King). "A Proclamation, for an Anniversary Thanksgiving, in Commemoration of His Majesties Happy Birthday, Being the Fourteenth Day of October." Edinburgh: Andrew Anderson, 1685. ESTC R18754.

Parliament, England and Wales. "Die Sabbathi, 2 Septemb. 1648. Ordered by the Lords and Commons Assembled in Parliament, That Tuesday-Come-Seven-Night, the Twelfth [sic] of This Instant September, Be Appointed and Observed as a Day of Publique Humiliation, by the Members of Both Houses, and in All the Churches and Chappells within the Late Lines of Communication and Weekly Bills of Mortalitie, to Seeke God Earnestly for a Blessing upon the Treaty [of Newport]." London: John Wright, 1648. ESTC R221344.

Protector, Lord. "An Ordinance against Challenges, Duels, and All Provocations Thereunto. Thursday, June 29." London: William du-Gard and Henry Hills, 1654. ESTC R210257.

Scotland. Convention of Estates. "June 13. Act, for a Publick Fast." Edinburgh: Andrew Anderson, 1690. ESTC R183890.

Scotland, Parliament; Committee of Estates. "April 11. A Proclamation, Declaring William and Mary King and Queen of England to Be King and Queen of Scotland." London: G. Croom, 1689. ESTC R225323.

Scotland, Privy Council. "A Proclamation for a National Humiliation upon the Account of the Queens Death." Edinburgh: Andrew Anderson, 1695. ESTC R183465.

Other Printed Sources

A[lleine], R[ichard]. *The Godly Man's Portion and Sanctuary Opened in Two Sermons, Preached August 17, 1662*. London: [s.n.], 1664? ESTC R214832.

Anon. *A Brief Narrative of a Strange and Wonderful Old Woman That Hath a Pair of Horns Growing upon Her Head. Giving a True Account How They Have Several Times after Being Shed, Grown Again. Declaring the Place of Her Birth, Her Education and Conversation; with the First Occasion of Their Growth, the Time of Their Continuance; and Where She Is Now to Be*

Seen, Viz. at the Sign of the Swan near Charing Cross. London: T[homas] J[ohnson], 1676. ESTC R29132.

———. *A Directory for the Publicke Worship of God throughout the Three Kingdoms of Scotland, England, and Ireland*. Edinburgh: Evan Tyler, 1645. ESTC R31329.

———. "Grant to Jane Murray, Widow, for Thirty-One Years, of the Herbage and Westminster Pannage of the Park of Berkhampsted, Co. Herts." March 3, 1628. In *Calendar of State Papers, Domestic Series, of the Reign of Charles I*, edited by John Bruce. Vol. 3, *March 1628–June 1629*. London: Longman, 1859.

———. *A Myraculous, and Monstrous, but yet Most True, and Certayne Discourse, of a Woman (Now to Be Seene in London) of the Age of Threescore Yeares, or There Abouts, in the Midst of Whose Fore-Head (by the Wonderfull Worke of God) There Groweth out a Crooked Horne, of Foure Ynches Long*. London: Thomas Orwin, 1588. ESTC S105391.

———. *The Prince of Orange His Declaration: Shewing the Reasons Why He Invades England. With a Short Preface, and Some Modest Remarks on It*. London: Randall Taylor, 1688. ESTC R3225.

———. *Strange Newes from the North. Containing a True and Exact Relation of a Great and Terrible Earthquake in Cumberland and Westmoreland. With the Miraculous Apparition of Three Glorious Suns That Appeared at Once*. London: J. Clowes, 1650. ESTC R205789.

———. "Warrant to the Exchequer, that no Process Be Issued against Mrs. Jane Murray for £550 Paid by Her to Sir Adam Newton, Receiver of His Majesty's Revenue When Prince of Wales, for a Lease of Thirty-One Years of the Herbage of the Park of Berkhamstead, co. Herts, Whereas the Same Ought to Have Been Paid into the Exchequer." May 27, 1628. In *Calendar of State Papers, Domestic Series, of the Reign of Charles I*, edited by John Bruce. Vol. 3, *March 1628–June 1629*. London: Longman, 1859.

Bampfield, Joseph. *Colonel Joseph Bamfield's Apologie, Written by Himselfe and Printed at His Desire*. The Hague?: [s. n.], 1685. ESTC R16264.

Berkeley, George. *Historical Applications and Occasional Meditations upon Several Subjects. Written by a Person of Honor*. London: J. Flesher, 1667. ESTC R235194.

Birch, Thomas, ed. *A Collection of the State Papers of John Thurloe*. Vol. 3, *December 1654–August 1655*. London: Fletcher Gyles, 1742.

Boyle, Robert. *Occasional Reflections upon Several Subjects. Whereto Is Premis'd a Discourse about Such Kind of Thoughts*. London: W. Wilson, 1665. ESTC R17345.

Bury, Edward. *The Husbandman's Companion: Containing One Hundred Occasional Meditations, Reflections, and Ejaculations: Especially Suited to Men of That Employment. Directing Them How They May Be Heavenly-Minded*

While about Their Ordinary Calling. London: Thomas Parkhurst, 1677. ESTC R23865.

Calvin, Jean. *Calvin's Commentaries*. Vol. 11, *Psalms, Part IV*, translated by John King (1847–50). http://www.sacred-texts.com/chr/calvin/cc11/cc11014.htm.

Cary, Mary. *The Little Horn's Doom and Downfall; or, A Scripture-prophesie of King James, and King Charles, and of this Present Parliament, Unfolded*. London: [s. n.], 1651. ESTC R210569.

Chambers, Douglas D. C. and David Galbraith, eds. *The Letterbooks of John Evelyn*. 2 vols. Toronto, ON: University of Toronto Press, 2014.

Charles II (King). *A Declaration by the King's Majesty, to His Subjects of the Kingdoms of Scotland, England, and Ireland*. Edinburgh: [s.n.], 1650. ESTC R35923.

———. *His Majesties Declaration to All His Loving Subjects, March 15, 1672. Published by the Advice of His Privy Council*. Edinburgh: Evan Tyler, 1672. ESTC R171213.

Cockburn, John. *Bourignianism Detected; or, The Delusions and Errors of Antonia Bourignon, and Her Growing Sect. Which May Also Serve for a Discovery of All Other Enthusiastical Impostures*. London: C. Brome, W. Keblewhite, and H. Hindmarsh, 1698. ESTC R17688.

———. *An Historical Relation of the Pretended General Assembly, Held at Edinburgh, from Oct. 16. to Nov. 13. in the Year 1690. In a Letter from a Person in Edinburgh, to His Friend in London*. London: J. Hindmarsh, 1691. ESTC R175777.

Couper, Simon. *Four Essays Concerning Church Government: Viz. I. An Impartial Inquiry into the Order and Government Settled by Christ and His Apostles, in the Church. II. An Inquiry into the Divine Right of Presbytery. III. The Phoenix; or, Prelacy Revived from the Ashes of Its Funeral, and Established upon the Same Principles and Arguments Which Are Made Use of against It, by the Author of the Funeral of Prelacy. IV. The Moral of the Phoenix Justified; or, the Reflections on the Funeral of Prelacy Vindicated*. Edinburgh: Andrew Symson, 1705. ESTC T183203.

———. *The Life of the Lady Halket*. Edinburgh: Andrew Symson and Henry Knox, 1701. ESTC T72803.

Daems, Jim, and Holly Faith Nelson, eds. *Eikon Basilike with Selections from Eikonoklastes by John Milton*. Ontario: Broadview Press, 2006.

Dickson, David. *A Brief Explication of the First Fifty Psalms*. London: T. M., 1655. ESTC R175951.

———. *Therapeutica Sacra; Shewing Briefly the Method of Healing the Diseases of the Conscience, Concerning Regeneration: Written First in Latin by David Dickson, Professor of Divinity in the Colledge of Edinburgh, and Thereafter Translated by Him*. Edinburgh: Evan Tyler, 1664. ESTC R24294.

Dod, John, and Robert Cleaver. *A Godly Form of Houshold Government, for the Ordering of Private Families, According to the Direction of God's Word.* London: Thomas Man, 1630. ESTC S117160.

Dyke, Jeremiah. *A Worthy Communicant; or, A Treatise, Showing the Due Order of Receiving the Sacrament of the Lord's Supper.* London: R. B[ishop], 1636. ESTC S100166.

Espagne, Jean d'. *The Abridgement of a Sermon Preached on the Fast-Day Appointed to Be Held for the Good Successe of the Treatie That Was Shortly to Ensue between the King and the Parliament, September 12, 1648.* Translated by William Umfrevile. London: Ruth Raworth, 1648. ESTC R20881.

Firth, C. H., and R. S. Rait, eds. *Acts and Ordinances of the Interregnum, 1642–1660.* London: Her Majesty's Stationary Office, 1911.

Flavell, John. *Husbandry Spiritualized; or, The Heavenly Use of Earthly Things. Consisting of Many Pleasant Observations, Pertinent Applications, and Serious Reflections.* London: Robert Boulter, 1669. ESTC R7793.

Fraser, James. *Memoirs of the Life of the Very Reverend Mr. James Fraser of Brea, Minister of the Gospel at Culross. Written by Himself.* Edinburgh: Thomas Lumisden and John Robertson, 1738. ESTC T127427.

Fuller, Thomas. *Good Thoughts in Bad Times, Consisting of Personall Meditations, Scripture Observations, Historicall Applications, Mixt Contemplations.* Exeter: Thomas Hunt, 1645. ESTC R7287.

———. *Good Thoughts in Worse Times. Consisting of Personall Meditations, Scripture Observations, Meditations on the Times, Meditations on All Kind of Prayers, Occasionall Meditations.* London: W. W., 1647. ESTC R7345.

———. *Mixt Contemplations in Better Times.* London: R. D., 1660. ESTC R7395.

Gayton, Edmund. *The Religion of a Physician; or, Divine Meditations upon the Grand and Lesser Festivals, Commanded to Be Observed in the Church of England by Act of Parliament.* London: J. G[rismond], 1663. ESTC R7653.

Gordon, James. *Plan de la Ville d'Edenbourg, Capitale d'Ecosse.* Leiden: P. van der Aa, ca. 1729. NLS, EMS.s.53. https://maps.nls.uk/towns/rec/2705.

Gordon, James, and Joan Blaeu. *Fifae Vicecomitatus, The Sherifdome of Fyfe.* Amsterdam: Blaeu, 1654. NLS, EMW.X.015 (formerly WD.3B). https://maps.nls.uk/view/00000444.

Gouge, William. *The Right Way; or, A Direction for Obtaining Good Successe in a Weighty Enterprise. Set out in a Sermon Preached on the 12th of September 1648 before the Lords on a Day of Humiliation for a Blessing on a Treaty between His Majesties and the Parliaments Commissioners.* London: A. Miller, 1648. ESTC R202327.

Halkett, Anne, Lady. *Instructions for Youth. Written by the Lady Halket, for the Use of Those Young Noblemen and Gentlemen, Whose Education Was Committed to Her Care.* Edited by Simon Couper. Edinburgh: Andrew Symson, 1701. ESTC T72792.

———. *Meditations and Prayers, upon the First Week; With Observations on Each Day's Creation: And Considerations on the Seven Capital Vices, to Be Opposed: And Their Opposit Virtues to Be Studied and Practiced*. Edited by Simon Couper. Edinburgh, Andrew Symson, 1701. ESTC T72793.

———. *Meditations upon the Seven Gifts of the Holy Spirit, Mentioned Isaiah 11:2–3*. Edited by Simon Couper. Edinburgh: Andrew Symson, 1702. ESTC T200617.

———. *Meditations upon the Seven Gifts of the Holy Spirit, Mentioned Isaiah 11:2–3. As Also, Meditations upon Jabez His Request, 1 Chron. 4:10. Together with Sacramental Meditations on the Lord's Supper; and Prayers, Pious Reflections, and Observations*. Edited by Simon Couper. Edinburgh: Andrew Symson, 1702. ESTC N10709.

———. *Meditations upon the Twentieth and Fifth Psalm*. Edited by Simon Couper. Edinburgh: Andrew Symson and Henry Knox, 1701. ESTC T72797.

———. *Meditations upon the Twenty-Fifth Psalm. Also, Meditations and Prayers upon the First Week: With Observations on Each Day's Creation. Likewise, Instructions for Youth. By Lady Halket. To Which Is Prefixed, an Account of Her Life*. Edinburgh: Bayne and Mennons, 1778. ESTC T106403.

Hall, Joseph. *Resolutions and Decisions of Divers Practicall Cases of Conscience in Continuall Use amongst Men, Very Necessary for Their Information and Direction: In Foure Decades*. London: M. F., 1649. ESTC R202349.

———. *The Shaking of the Olive-Tree. The Remaining Works of That Incomparable Prelate Joseph Hall, D. D., Late Lord Bishop of Norwich. With Some Specialties of Divine Providence in His Life, Noted by His Own Hand. Together with His Hard Measure, Written Also by Himself*. London: J. Cadwell, 1660. ESTC R10352.

Hammons, Pamela S., ed. *Book M: A London Widow's Life Writings*. Toronto: Iter Inc. and Centre for Reformation and Renaissance Studies, 2013.

Horsman, Nicholas. *The Spiritual Bee; or, A Miscellaney of Spiritual, Historical, Natural Observations, and Occasional Occurencyes, Applyed in Divine Meditations*. Oxford: W. H., 1667. ESTC R24990.

Huntley, Frank Livingstone. *Bishop Joseph Hall and Protestant Meditation in Seventeenth-Century England: A Study, with the Texts of The Art of Divine Meditation (1606) and Occasional Meditations (1633)*. Binghamton, NY: Center for Medieval and Early Renaissance Studies, 1981.

James VII/II (King). *By the King, a Declaration as We Cannot Consider This Invasion of Our Kingdoms by the Prince of Orange without Horror*. London: Charles Bill, Henry Hills, and Thomas Newcomb, 1688. ESTC R37010.

Milton, John. *The Doctrine and Discipline of Divorce*. London: T[homas] P[aine] and M[atthew] S[immons], 1643. ESTC R12932.

Pitcher, John, ed., *Francis Bacon: The Essays*. Harmondsworth, UK: Penguin, 1985.

Pomfret, Thomas. *The Life of the Right Honorable and Religious Lady Christian[a], Late Countess Dowager of Devonshire.* London: William Rawlins, 1685. ESTC R3342.

Ross, Sarah C. E., ed. *Katherine Austen's Book M: British Library, Additional Manuscript 4454.* Tempe: Arizona Center for Medieval and Renaissance Studies, 2011.

Speed, John. *The Kingdome of Scotland.* London: Roger Rea, 1662. NLS, EMS.s.9B. https://maps.nls.uk/view/00000601.

Trapnel, Anna. *The Cry of a Stone; or, A Relation of Something Spoken in Whitehall.* London: [s.n.], 1654. ESTC R203788.

———. *Strange and Wonderful Newes from White-Hall.* London: Robert Sele, 1654. ESTC R3949.

White, John. *A Rich Cabinet, with Variety of Inventions; Unlocked and Opened, for the Recreation of Ingenious Spirits at Their Vacant Hours, Being Receits and Conceits of Severall Natures, and Fit for Those Who Are Lovers of Naturall and Artificiall Conclusions.* London: William Whitwood, 1688. ESTC R232211.

W[ilkins], J[ohn]. *Mercury; or, The Secret and Swift Messenger; Shewing, How a Man May with Privacy and Speed Communicate His Thoughts to a Friend at any Distance.* London: J. Norton, 1641. ESTC R1665.

William III (King). *The Declaration of His Highnes William Henry, by the Grace of God Prince of Orange, &c. of the Reasons Inducing Him, to Appear in Armes in the Kingdome of England, for Preserving of the Protestant Religion, and for Restoring the Lawes and Liberties of England, Scotland, and Ireland.* The Hague: Arnold Leers, 1688. ESTC R187748.

Secondary Sources

Abbot House—The Reawakening of Dunfermline's Oldest Building, accessed May 5, 2020, https://www.abbothouse.org/.

Adams, Sharon, and Julian Goodare, eds. *Scotland in the Age of Two Revolutions.* Woodbridge, UK: Boydell Press, 2014.

Adolph, Anthony R. J. S. "Jermyn [Germain], Henry, Earl of St Albans (bap. 1605, d. 1684)." In *Oxford Dictionary of National Biography*, edited by Lawrence Goldman. Oxford: Oxford University Press, 2004–. Article published May 2015. http://www.oxforddnb.com.

Akkerman, Nadine. *Invisible Agents: Women and Espionage in Seventeenth-Century Britain.* Oxford: Oxford University Press, 2018.

Allan, David. "Moray, Sir Robert (1608/9?–1673)." In *Oxford Dictionary of National Biography*, edited by Lawrence Goldman. Oxford: Oxford University Press, 2004–. Article published October 2007. http://www.oxforddnb.com.

Alnwick Castle website. Accessed August 10, 2016. https://www.alnwickcastle.com.

Ancestry.com, Ancestry®: Genealogy, Family Trees & Family History Records. https://www.ancestry.co.uk.

———. *England, Select Births and Christenings, 1538–1975.* [database on-line]. Provo, UT, USA: Ancestry.com Operations, Inc., 2014.

———. *Scotland, Select Births and Baptisms, 1564–1950* [database on-line]. Provo, UT, USA: Ancestry.com Operations, Inc., 2014.

———. *Scotland: Select Marriages, 1561–1910* [database on-line]. Provo, UT, USA: Ancestry.com Operations, Inc., 2014.

Angus, William, ed. *Inventory of Pitfirrane Writs, 1230–1740.* Edinburgh: J. Skinner & Co., 1932.

Anselment, Raymond A. "Anthony Walker, Mary Rich, and Seventeenth-Century Funeral Sermons of Women." *Prose Studies* 37, no. 3 (2015): 200–24.

———. "Feminine Self-Reflection and the Seventeenth-Century Occasional Meditation." *Seventeenth Century* 26, no. 1 (2011): 69–93.

———. "Katherine Austen and the Widow's Might." *Journal for Early Modern Cultural Studies* 5, no. 1 (2005): 5–25.

———. "Robert Boyle and the Art of Occasional Meditation." *Renaissance and Reformation* 32, no. 4 (2009): 73–92.

———, ed. *The Occasional Meditations of Mary Rich, Countess of Warwick.* Tempe: Arizona Center for Medieval and Renaissance Studies, 2009.

Apted, M. R. *Aberdour Castle.* 2nd ed. Edinburgh: Historic Scotland, 1985.

Ashley, Maurice. *Charles II: The Man and the Statesman.* St. Albans, UK: Panther, 1973.

Bagwell, Richard, and Rev. Jason McElligott. "Wild, George (1610–1665)." In *Oxford Dictionary of National Biography*, edited by Lawrence Goldman. Oxford: Oxford University Press, 2004–. Article published September 2004. http://www.oxforddnb.com.

Balfour, Sir James. *The Historical Works of Sir James Balfour: Annals of the History of Scotland.* 4 vols. Edinburgh: W. Aitchison, 1824.

———. *The Scots Peerage Founded on Wood's Edition of Sir Robert Douglas's Peerage of Scotland.* 9 vols. Edinburgh: David Douglas, 1904–1914.

Barclay, Andrew. "Mary [Mary of Modena] (1658–1718), Queen of England, Scotland, and Ireland, Consort of James II and VII." In *Oxford Dictionary of National Biography*, edited by Lawrence Goldman. Oxford: Oxford University Press, 2004–. Article published January 2008. http://www.oxforddnb.com.

Barnard, Toby. "Boyle, Roger, First Earl of Orrery (1621–1679)." In *Oxford Dictionary of National Biography*, edited by Lawrence Goldman. Oxford: Oxford University Press, 2004–. Article published May 2012. http://www.oxforddnb.com.

Bedford, Ronald, Lloyd Davis, and Philippa Kelly, eds. *Early Modern Autobiography: Theories, Genres, Practices.* Ann Arbor: University of Michigan Press, 2006.

Bennett, Harry J. "Peter Hay: Proprietary Agent in Barbados, 1636–1641." *Jamaican Historical Review* 5, no. 2 (1965): 9–29.

Bennitt, F. W. "The Diary of Isabella, Wife of Sir Roger Twysden, Baronet, of Roydon Hall, East Peckham, 1645–1651." *Archaeologia Cantiana* 51 (1939): 113–36.

Botonaki, Effie. *Seventeenth-Century English Women's Autobiographical Writing: Disclosing Enclosures*. Lewiston, NY: Edwin Mellen Press, 2004.

Bowie, Karin. "'A Legal Limited Monarchy': Scottish Constitutionalism in the Union of the Crowns, 1603–1707." *Journal of Scottish Historical Studies* 35, no. 2 (2015): 131–54.

"Brigton." Scotland's Places. Accessed July 23, 2018. https://scotlandsplaces.gov.uk/search/place/Brigton?id=2338.

Britland, Karen. *Drama at the Courts of Queen Henrietta Maria*. Cambridge: Cambridge University Press, 2006.

Broadway, Jan. "Puckering [Newton], Sir Henry, Third Baronet (bap. 1618, d. 1701)." In *Oxford Dictionary of National Biography*, edited by Lawrence Goldman. Oxford: Oxford University Press, 2004–. Article published September 2004. http://www.oxforddnb.com.

Bryson, Anna. *From Courtesy to Civility: Changing Codes of Conduct in Early Modern England*. Oxford: Oxford University Press, 1998.

Burke, Victoria E. "Bibliographic Data for BL, Add. MS. 32,376." Perdita Manuscripts. Adam Matthew Digital, 2007. Accessed, July 10, 2018. http://www.perditamanuscripts.amdigital.co.uk.

Butler, Todd. "Equivocation, Cognition, and Political Authority in Early Modern England." *Texas Studies in Literature and Language* 54, no. 1 (2012): 132–54.

Cambers, Andrew. *Godly Reading: Print, Manuscript, and Puritanism in England, 1580–1720*. Cambridge: Cambridge University Press, 2011.

Capp, Bernard. *The Fifth Monarchy Men: A Study in Seventeenth-Century Millenarianism*. London: Faber, 1972.

Card, Tim. *Eton Established: A History from 1440 to 1860*. London: John Murray, 2001.

Carnell, Rachel. "Slipping from Secret History to Novel." *Eighteenth-Century Fiction* 28, no. 1 (2015): 1–24.

Castle Howard. "The Building of Castle Howard." Accessed July 17, 2020. https://www.castlehoward.co.uk/visit-us/the-house/history-of-castle-howard#.

Christensen, Paul. "Charles Seton, Second Earl of Dunfermline: The Reluctant Rebel." *History Scotland* 17, no. 6 (Nov./Dec. 2017): 32–36.

Clarke, J. S., ed. *The Life of James the Second, King of England, &c. Collected Out of Memoirs Writ of His Own Hand. Together with the King's Advice to His Son, and His Majesty's Will*. 2 vols. London: Longman, 1816.

Clarke, Tristram. "Cockburn, John (1652–1729)." In *Oxford Dictionary of National Biography*, edited by Lawrence Goldman. Oxford: Oxford University Press, 2004–. Article published January 2008. http://www.oxforddnb.com.

Clifton, Robin. "Walter, Lucy (1630?–1658)." In *Oxford Dictionary of National Biography*, edited by Lawrence Goldman. Oxford: Oxford University Press, 2004–. Article published September 2006. http://www.oxforddnb.com.

Coffey, John. "Elphinstone, John, Second Lord Balmerino (d. 1649)." In *Oxford Dictionary of National Biography*, edited by Lawrence Goldman. Oxford: Oxford University Press, 2004–. Article published May 2007. http://www.oxforddnb.com.

Cokayne, George E. *Complete Baronetage*. 6 vols. Exeter: W. Pollard & Co., 1900–1909.

———. *The Complete Peerage of England, Scotland, Ireland, Great Britain, and the United Kingdom, Extant, Extinct, or Dormant*. 13 vols. London: St. Catherine, 1825–1911.

Coolahan, Marie-Louise. "Redeeming Parcels of Time: Aesthetics and Practice of Occasional Meditation." *Seventeenth Century* 22, no. 1 (2007): 124–43.

Corthell, Ronald J. "Joseph Hall and Protestant Meditation." *Texas Studies in Literature and Language* 20, no. 3 (1978): 356–85.

Coward, Barry. "Lilburne, Robert (bap. 1614, d. 1665)." In *Oxford Dictionary of National Biography*, edited by Lawrence Goldman. Oxford: Oxford University Press, 2004–. Article published January 2008. http://www.oxforddnb.com.

Cowie, L. W. "Whitefriars in London." *History Today* 25, no. 6 (June 1975): 436–41.

Cox, Montagu H., and Philip Norman, eds. "Whitehall Palace: Buildings." In *Survey of London: Volume 13, St Margaret, Westminster, Part II: Whitehall I*, 41–115. London: London County Council, 1930.

Crane, Mary Thomas. "Illicit Privacy and Outdoor Spaces in Early Modern England." *Journal for Early Modern Cultural Studies* 9, no. 1 (2009): 4–22.

Cressy, David. *Birth, Marriage, and Death: Ritual, Religion, and the Lifecycle in Tudor and Stuart England*. Oxford: Oxford University Press, 1997.

———. *Bonfires and Bells: National Memory and the Protestant Calendar in Elizabethan and Stuart England*. 2nd ed. Stroud, UK: Sutton, 2004.

Cruickshanks, Eveline. "Sir Thomas Allen (1603–1681)." In *The History of Parliament: The House of Commons, 1660–1690*, edited by B. D. Henning. London: Boydell and Brewer, 1983.

Cummings, Brian, ed. *The Book of Common Prayer: The Texts of 1549, 1559, and 1662*. Oxford: Oxford University Press, 2011.

Delany, Paul. *British Autobiography in the Seventeenth Century*. London: Routledge & Kegan Paul, 1969.

Dobson, David. *Barbados and Scotland Links, 1627–1877*. Baltimore, MD: Clearfield, 2005.

———. *Scottish Emigration to Colonial America, 1607–1785*. Athens; London: University of Georgia Press, 1994.

———. *Scottish Schoolmasters of the Seventeenth Century. Part 1*. St Andrews: D. Dobson, 1995.

Dolan, Frances E. *True Relations: Reading, Literature, and Evidence in Seventeenth-Century England*. Philadelphia: University of Pennsylvania Press, 2013.

Donagan, Barbara. "Varieties of Royalism." In *Royalists and Royalism during the English Civil Wars*, edited by Jason McElligott and David L. Smith, 66–88. Cambridge: Cambridge University Press, 2007.

"Douglas, Archibald, Tenth Laird of Mains." Macfarlane Families and Connected Clans Genealogies, accessed September 08, 2018, https://www.clanmacfarlanegenealogy.info/genealogy/TNGWebsite/getperson.php?personID=I22363&tree=CC.

Dowd, Michelle M., and Julie A. Eckerle, eds. *Genre and Women's Life Writing in Early Modern England*. Aldershot, UK: Ashgate, 2007.

Drake, George A. "Percy, Algernon, Tenth Earl of Northumberland (1602–1668)." In *Oxford Dictionary of National Biography*, edited by Lawrence Goldman. Oxford: Oxford University Press, 2004–. Article published January 2008. http://www.oxforddnb.com.

Drummond, William. *The Genealogy of the Most Noble and Ancient House of Drummond by the Honorable William Drummond*. Edinburgh: A. Balfour & Co., 1831.

Dunn, Richard Minta. "Howard, James, Third Earl of Suffolk, Nobleman (1619–1689)." In *Oxford Dictionary of National Biography*, edited by Lawrence Goldman. Oxford: Oxford University Press, 2004–. Article published September 2004. http://www.oxforddnb.com.

Durston, Christopher. "Lords of Misrule: The Puritan War on Christmas, 1642–60." *History Today* 35, no. 12 (1985): 7–14.

Eckerle, Julie A. *Romancing the Self in Early Modern Englishwomen's Life Writing*. Aldershot, UK: Ashgate, 2013.

Ezell, Margaret J. M. "Ann Halkett's Morning Devotions: Posthumous Publication and the Culture of Writing in Late Seventeenth-Century Britain." In *Print, Manuscript, Performance: The Changing Relations of the Media in Early Modern England*, edited by Arthur Marotti and Michael D. Bristol, 215–31. Columbus: Ohio State University Press, 2000.

———. "The Myth of Judith Shakespeare: Creating the Canon of Women's Literature in the Twentieth Century." In *Writing Women's Literary History*, 39–65. Baltimore: Johns Hopkins University Press, 1993.

———. "The Posthumous Publication of Women's Manuscripts and the History of Authorship." In *Women's Writing and the Circulation of Ideas: Manuscript Publication in England, 1550–1800*, edited by George L. Justice and Nathan Tinker, 121–36. Cambridge: Cambridge University Press, 2002.

"Families Database." Stirnet.com. Accessed November 10, 2015. http://www.stirnet.com/genie/index.php.

Fincham, Kenneth. "The Roles and Influence of Household Chaplains, ca. 1600–ca. 1660." In *Chaplains in Early Modern England: Patronage, Literature, and Religion*, edited by Hugh Adlington, Tom Lockwood, and Gillian Wright, 11–35. Manchester: Manchester University Press, 2013.

Findley, Sandra, and Elaine Hobby. "Seventeenth Century Women's Autobiography." In *1642: Literature and Power in the Seventeenth Century*, edited by Francis Barker et al., 11–36. Essex: University of Essex, 1981.

Firth, Charles, and Godfrey Davies. *The Regimental History of Cromwell's Army*. 2 vols. Oxford: Clarendon Press, 1940.

Folger Shakespeare Library. Union First Line Index of English Verse. Accessed August 24, 2018. https://firstlines.folger.edu.

Ford, J. D. "Douglas, William, First Duke of Queensberry (1637–1695)." In *Oxford Dictionary of National Biography*, edited by Lawrence Goldman. Oxford: Oxford University Press, 2004–. Article published September 2004. http://www.oxforddnb.com.

"Fraser of Muchall." The Baronage. The Baronage Press Ltd and Pegasus Associated Ltd. Accessed August 3, 2016. http://www.baronage.co.uk/bphtm-03/fraser04.html.

French, Michael. "Sir Francis Dodington (1604–1670): A Prominent Somerset Royalist in the English Civil War." *Somerset Archaeology and Natural History Proceedings* 156 (2013): 112–26.

Furgol, Edward M. *A Regimental History of the Covenanting Armies, 1639–1651*. Edinburgh: John Donald, 1990.

Gater, G. H., and F. R. Hiorns, eds. *Survey of London: Volume 20, St. Martin-in-The-Fields, Pt. III: Trafalgar Square and Neighborhood*. London: London County Council, 1940.

Gibson, Jonathan. "Casting off Blanks: Hidden Structures in Early Modern Paper Books." In *Material Readings of Early Modern Culture: Texts and Social Practices, 1580–1730*, edited by James Daybell and Peter Hinds, 208–28. Basingstoke, UK: Palgrave Macmillan, 2010.

Gibson, William. *A Social History of the Domestic Chaplain, 1530–1840*. London: Leicester University Press, 1997.

Gillespie, Katharine. "Cure for a Diseased Head: Divorce and Contract in the Prophecies of Elizabeth Poole." In *Domesticity and Dissent in the Seventeenth Century: English Women Writers and the Public Sphere*, 116–65. Cambridge: Cambridge University Press, 2004.

Goodwin, Gordon. "Elizabeth, Princess (1635–1650)." In *Oxford Dictionary of National Biography*, edited by Lawrence Goldman. Oxford: Oxford University Press, 2004–. Article published September 2004. http://www.oxforddnb.com.

———. "Howard, Charles, First Earl of Carlisle (1628–1685)." In *Oxford Dictionary of National Biography*, edited by Lawrence Goldman. Oxford: Oxford University Press, 2004–. Article published October 2009. http://www.oxforddnb.com.

Graham, Elspeth. "Women's Writing and the Self." In *Women and Literature in Britain, 1500–1700*, edited by Helen Wilcox, 209–33. Cambridge: Cambridge University Press, 1996.

Greaves, Richard L. "Howard, William, Third Baron Howard of Escrick (ca. 1630–1694)." In *Oxford Dictionary of National Biography*, edited by Lawrence Goldman. Oxford: Oxford University Press, 2004–. Article published May 2009. http://www.oxforddnb.com.

Green, Ian. *Print and Protestantism in Early Modern England*. Oxford: Oxford University Press, 2000.

———. *The Christian's ABC: Catechisms and Catechizing in England ca. 1530–1740*. Oxford: Oxford University Press, 1996.

Gregg, Edward. "James Francis Edward [James Francis Edward Stuart; Styled James; Known as Chevalier de St George, the Pretender, the Old Pretender] (1688–1766)." In *Oxford Dictionary of National Biography*, edited by Lawrence Goldman. Oxford: Oxford University Press, 2004–. Article published May 2012. http://www.oxforddnb.com.

Hamilton, J. A. "Gilmour, Sir John, of Craigmillar (bap. 1605, d. 1671)." In *Oxford Dictionary of National Biography*, edited by Lawrence Goldman. Oxford: Oxford University Press, 2004–. Article published September 2004. http://www.oxforddnb.com.

Handley, Stuart. "Baird, Sir John, Lord Newbyth (bap. 1620, d. 1698)." In *Oxford Dictionary of National Biography*, edited by Lawrence Goldman. Oxford: Oxford University Press, 2004–. Article published September 2004. http://www.oxforddnb.com.

———. "Henry, Prince, Duke of Gloucester (1640–1660)." In *Oxford Dictionary of National Biography*, edited by Lawrence Goldman. Oxford: Oxford University Press, 2004–. Article published September 2004. http://www.oxforddnb.com.

———. "Kennedy, John, Sixth Earl of Cassillis (1601x7–1668)." In *Oxford Dictionary of National Biography*, edited by Lawrence Goldman. Oxford: Oxford University Press, 2004–. Article published October 2009. http://www.oxforddnb.com.

Harris, Frances. "Lady Sophia's Visions: Sir Robert Moray, the Earl of Lauderdale, and the Restoration Government of Scotland." *Seventeenth Century* 24, no. 1 (2006): 129–55.

Harris, Tim. *Restoration: Charles II and His Kingdoms*. London: Penguin, 2006.

———. *Revolution: The Great Crisis of the British Monarchy, 1685–1720*. London: Penguin, 2007.

———. "Scott [Formerly Crofts], James, Duke of Monmouth and First Duke of Buccleuch (1649–1685)." In *Oxford Dictionary of National Biography*, edited by Lawrence Goldman. Oxford: Oxford University Press, 2004–. Article published October 2009. http://www.oxforddnb.com.

Heller, Jennifer. *The Mother's Legacy in Early Modern England*. Farnham, UK: Ashgate, 2011.

Henderson, Ebenezer. *The Annals of Dunfermline and Vicinity, from the Earliest Authentic Period to the Present Time, A.D. 1069–1878*. Glasgow: J. Tweed, 1879.

Henderson, T. F. "Baber, Sir John (1625–1704)." In *Oxford Dictionary of National Biography*, edited by Lawrence Goldman. Oxford: Oxford University Press, 2004–. Article published September 2004. http://www.oxforddnb.com.

———. "Seton, Charles, Second Earl of Dunfermline (1615–1672)." In *Oxford Dictionary of National Biography*, edited by Lawrence Goldman. Oxford: Oxford University Press, 2004–. Article published September 2004. http://www.oxforddnb.com.

Hibbard, Caroline M. "Henrietta Maria [Princess Henrietta Maria of France] (1609–1669), Queen of England, Scotland, and Ireland, Consort of Charles I." In *Oxford Dictionary of National Biography*, edited by Lawrence Goldman. Oxford: Oxford University Press, 2004–. Article published January 2008. http://www.oxforddnb.com.

Hill, Christopher. *The World Turned Upside Down: Radical Ideas during the English Revolution*. Harmondsworth, UK: Penguin, 1975.

Hindson, Edward E. *The King James Study Bible*. 2nd ed. Nashville, TN: Thomas Nelson, 1988.

Hinnant, Charles H. "The 'Fable of the Spider and the Bee' and Swift's Poetics of Inspiration." *Colby Quarterly* 20, no. 3 (1984): 129–36.

Hodgkin, Katharine. "Dreaming Meanings: Some Early Modern Dream Thoughts." In *Reading the Early Modern Dream: The Terrors of the Night*, edited by Katharine Hodgkin, Michelle O'Callaghan, and S. J. Wiseman, 109–24. New York; London: Routledge, 2008.

Holfelder, K. D. "Dickson, David (ca. 1583–1662)." In *Oxford Dictionary of National Biography*, edited by Lawrence Goldman. Oxford: Oxford University Press, 2004–. Article published September 2004. http://www.oxforddnb.com.

Holstun, James. *Ehud's Dagger: Class Struggle in the English Revolution*. London: Verso, 2000.

Hunter, Michael. "Boyle, Robert (1627–1691)." In *Oxford Dictionary of National Biography*, edited by Lawrence Goldman. Oxford: Oxford University Press, 2004–. Article published May 2015. http://www.oxforddnb.com.

Hutton, Ronald. *Charles II: King of England, Scotland, and Ireland*. Oxford: Oxford University Press, 1989.

———. "Maitland, John, Duke of Lauderdale (1616–1682)." In *Oxford Dictionary of National Biography*, edited by Lawrence Goldman. Oxford: Oxford University Press, 2004–. Article published May 2006. http://www.oxforddnb.com.

———. "Monck [Monk], George, First Duke of Albemarle (1608–1670)." In *Oxford Dictionary of National Biography*, edited by Lawrence Goldman. Oxford: Oxford University Press, 2004–. Article published October 2012. http://www.oxforddnb.com.

———. *The Restoration: A Political and Religious History of England and Wales, 1658–1667*. Oxford: Clarendon Press, 1985.

Hyde, Ralph. "Romeyn de Hooghe and the Funeral of the People's Queen." *Print Quarterly* 15, no. 2 (1998): 150–72.

Jenstad, Janelle, ed. "The Agas Map." *The Map of Early Modern London*, Edition 6.6. Victoria, BC: University of Victoria. Accessed June 30, 2021, https://mapoflondon.uvic.ca/edition/6.6/map.htm.

Jones, J. R. *The Anglo-Dutch Wars of the Seventeenth Century*. London: Longman, 1996.

Jones, N. G. "Puckering, Sir John (1543/4–1596)." In *Oxford Dictionary of National Biography*, edited by Lawrence Goldman. Oxford: Oxford University Press, 2004–. Article published May 2007. http://www.oxforddnb.com.

Kearns, Judith. "Fashioning Innocence: Rhetorical Construction of Character in the Memoirs of Anne, Lady Halkett." *Texas Studies in Literature and Language* 46, no. 3 (2004): 340–62.

Keblusek, Marika. "Mary, Princess Royal (1631–1660)." In *Oxford Dictionary of National Biography*, edited by Lawrence Goldman. Oxford: Oxford University Press, 2004–. Article published January 2008. http://www.oxforddnb.com.

Keeble, Neil H. "Obedient Subjects? The Loyal Self in Some Later Seventeenth-Century Royalist Women's Memoirs." In *Culture and Society in the Stuart Restoration: Literature, Drama, History*, edited by Gerald Maclean, 201–18. Cambridge: Cambridge University Press, 1995.

Kidd, Colin. "Mackenzie, George, First Earl of Cromarty (1630–1714)." In *Oxford Dictionary of National Biography*, edited by Lawrence Goldman. Oxford: Oxford University Press, 2004–. Article published May 2006. http://www.oxforddnb.com.

Killeen, Kevin. "Chastising with Scorpions: Reading the Old Testament in Early Modern England." *Huntington Library Quarterly* 73, no. 3 (2010): 491–506.

Kishlansky, Mark A., and John Morrill. "Charles I (1600–1649)." In *Oxford Dictionary of National Biography*, edited by Lawrence Goldman. Oxford: Oxford University Press, 2004–. Article published October 2008. http://www.oxforddnb.com.

Lacey, Andrew. "Texts to Be Read: Charles I and the *Eikon Basilike*." *Prose Studies* 29, no. 1 (2007): 4–18.
Lamb, Mary Ellen. "Merging the Secular and the Spiritual in Lady Anne Halkett's Memoirs." In *Genre and Women's Life Writing in Early Modern England*, edited by Michelle M. Dowd and Julie A. Eckerle, 81–96. Aldershot, UK: Ashgate, 2007.
Landry, Donna. "Eroticizing the Subject, or Royals in Drag: Reading the Memoirs of Anne, Lady Halkett." *Prose Studies* 18, no. 3 (1995): 134–49.
Lee, Maurice, Jr. *The "Inevitable" Union and Other Essays on Early Modern Scotland*. East Linton, UK: Tuckwell, 2003.
Lejeune, Philippe. "The Autobiographical Pact." In *On Autobiography*, edited by Paul John Eakin, translated by Katherine M. Leary, 3–30. Minneapolis: University of Minnesota Press, 1989.
Lindsay, Lord Alexander. *A Memoir of Lady Anna Mackenzie, Countess of Balcarres and Afterwards of Argyll, 1621–1706*. Edinburgh: Edmonston and Douglas, 1868.
Little, Patrick. *Lord Broghill and the Cromwellian Union with Ireland and Scotland*. Woodbridge, UK: Boydell Press, 2004.
Loftis, John. *Bampfield's Later Career: A Biographical Supplement*. London: Associated University Presses, 1993.
———, ed. *The Memoirs of Anne, Lady Halkett and Anne, Lady Fanshawe*. Oxford: Clarendon Press, 1979.
Loftis, John, and Paul H. Hardacre, eds. *Colonel Joseph Bampfield's Apology: "Written By Himself and Printed at His Desire," 1685*. London: Associated University Presses, 1993.
Lowrey, John. "Bruce, Sir William, First Baronet (ca. 1625–1710)." In *Oxford Dictionary of National Biography*, edited by Lawrence Goldman. Oxford: Oxford University Press, 2004–. Article published May 2006. http://www.oxforddnb.com.
Lynch, Kathleen. *Protestant Autobiography in the Seventeenth-Century Anglophone World*. Oxford: Oxford University Press, 2012.
Lysons, Daniel. "Putney." In *The Environs of London*. Vol. 1, *County of Surrey*, 404–35. London: T. Cadell and W. Davies, 1792.
MacDonald, Alan R. "Ker, Robert, First Earl of Roxburghe (1569/70–1650)." In *Oxford Dictionary of National Biography*, edited by Lawrence Goldman. Oxford: Oxford University Press, 2004–. Article published September 2004. http://www.oxforddnb.com.
Macray, Rev. W. Dunn, and Rev. H. O. Coxe, eds. *Calendar of the Clarendon State Papers Preserved in the Bodleian Library*. Vol. 2. Oxford: Clarendon Press, 1872.
Mann, Alastair J. *The Scottish Book Trade, 1500–1720: Print Commerce and Print Control in Early Modern Scotland*. East Linton, UK: Tuckwell, 2000.

Marshall, Alan. "Bampfield, Joseph (1622–1685)." In *Oxford Dictionary of National Biography*, edited by Lawrence Goldman. Oxford: Oxford University Press, 2004–. Article published January 2008. http://www.oxforddnb.com.

Marshall, Peter. "Angels around the Deathbed: Variations on a Theme in the English Art of Dying." In *Angels in the Early Modern World*, edited by Peter Marshall and Alexandra Walsham, 83–103. Cambridge: Cambridge University Press, 2006.

Marshall, Rosalind K. "Hamilton [Formerly Douglas], William, Third Duke of Hamilton (1634–1694)." In *Oxford Dictionary of National Biography*, edited by Lawrence Goldman. Oxford: Oxford University Press, 2004–. Article published September 2004. http://www.oxforddnb.com.

———. "Mackenzie, Anna [Known as Lady Anna Mackenzie], Countess of Balcarres and Countess of Argyll (ca. 1621–1707)." In *Oxford Dictionary of National Biography*, edited by Lawrence Goldman. Oxford: Oxford University Press, 2004–. Article published September 2006. http://www.oxforddnb.com.

———. "Murray [Married Names Tollemache, Maitland], Elizabeth, Duchess of Lauderdale and Suo Jure Countess of Dysart (bap. 1626, d. 1698)." In *Oxford Dictionary of National Biography*, edited by Lawrence Goldman. Oxford: Oxford University Press, 2004–. Article published September 2004. http://www.oxforddnb.com.

Maxwell-Lyte, H. C. *A History of Eton College, 1440–1910*. London: Macmillan, 1911.

McCabe, Richard A. "Hall, Joseph (1574–1656)." In *Oxford Dictionary of National Biography*, edited by Lawrence Goldman. Oxford: Oxford University Press, 2004–. Article published January 2008. http://www.oxforddnb.com.

McElligott, Jason, and David L. Smith, eds. *Royalists and Royalism during the English Civil Wars*. Cambridge: Cambridge University Press, 2007.

———, eds. *Royalists and Royalism during the Interregnum*. Manchester, UK: Manchester University Press, 2010.

McGrigor, Mary. *Anna, Countess of the Covenant*. Edinburgh: Birlinn, 2008.

McKitterick, David. "Women and Their Books in Seventeenth-Century England: The Case of Elizabeth Puckering." *Library* 1, no. 4 (2000): 359–80.

McLellan, Ian W. "Gayton, Edmund (1608–1666)." In *Oxford Dictionary of National Biography*, edited by Lawrence Goldman. Oxford: Oxford University Press, 2004–. Article published September 2004. http://www.oxforddnb.com.

McManus, Clare. *Women on the Renaissance Stage: Anna of Denmark and Female Masquing in the Stuart Court, 1590–1619*. Manchester: Manchester University Press, 2002.

McMullan, Gordon. "Fletcher, John (1579–1625)." In *Oxford Dictionary of National Biography*, edited by Lawrence Goldman. Oxford: Oxford University

Press, 2004–. Article published September 2006. http://www.oxforddnb.com.

Mendelson, Sara, and Patricia Crawford. *Women in Early Modern England.* Oxford: Clarendon Press, 1998.

Millar, A. H. "Wedderburn, Sir Peter, Lord Gosford (ca. 1616–1679)." In *Oxford Dictionary of National Biography*, edited by Lawrence Goldman. Oxford: Oxford University Press, 2004–. Article published September 2004. http://www.oxforddnb.com.

Millman, Jill S. "Introduction to the Perdita Project Catalogue, 1997–2007," Perdita Manuscripts. Adam Matthew Digital, 2007. Accessed, July 10, 2018. http://www.perditamanuscripts.amdigital.co.uk.

Moody, Ellen. "'Cast Out from Respectability a While': Anne Murray Halkett's Life in the Manuscripts." 2006. http://www.jimandellen.org/halkett/CastOut.html.

Morrill, John, ed. *The Scottish National Covenant in Its British Context.* Edinburgh: Edinburgh University Press, 1990.

Mosley, Charles, ed. *Burke's Peerage, Baronetage, & Knightage.* 107th ed. 3 vols. Wilmington, DE: Burke's Peerage, 2003.

Mullan, David G. *Narratives of the Religious Self in Early-Modern Scotland.* Farnham, UK: Ashgate, 2010.

———. *Women's Life Writing in Early Modern Scotland: Writing the Evangelical Self, ca. 1670–ca. 1730.* Aldershot, UK: Ashgate, 2003.

Musson, Roger M. W. "Early Seismicity of the Scottish Borders Region." *Annals of Geophysics* 47, no. 6 (2004): 1827–47.

Narveson, Kate. "Godly Gentility as Spiritual Capital: The Appeal of Hall's *Meditations* in Early Stuart England." *Explorations in Renaissance Culture* 30, no. 2 (2004): 149–70.

Naworth Castle. Accessed 07 July 2018. http://www.naworth.co.uk.

Nevitt, Marcus. "Agency in Crisis: Women Write the Regicide." In *Women and the Pamphlet Culture of Revolutionary England*, 49–84. Aldershot, UK: Ashgate, 2006.

Nichols, John G., ed., *The Autobiography of Anne Lady Halkett.* London: Camden Society, 1875.

Ogle, Rev. O., and W. H. Bliss, eds. *Calendar of the Clarendon State Papers Preserved in the Bodleian Library.* Vol. 1. Oxford: Clarendon Press, 1872.

O'Hara, Diana. *Courtship and Constraint: Rethinking the Making of Marriage in Tudor England.* Manchester: Manchester University Press, 2000.

Ottway, Sheila. "They Only Lived Twice: Public and Private Selfhood in the Autobiographies of Anne, Lady Halkett and Colonel Joseph Bampfield." In *Betraying Our Selves: Forms of Self-Representation in Early Modern English Texts*, edited by Henk Dragsta, Sheila Ottway, and Helen Wilcox, 136–47. Basingstoke, UK: Macmillan, 2000.

"Ouse Bridge." History of York. Accessed August 8, 2016. http://www.historyofyork.org.uk/themes/tudor-stuart/ouse-bridge.

Page, William. ed., "Berkhamsted St. Peter: Introduction, Honor, Manor, and Castle." In *A History of the County of Hertford*, 4 vols. London: Westminster, 1908.

Patterson, W. B. "Fuller, Thomas (1607/8–1661)." In *Oxford Dictionary of National Biography*, edited by Lawrence Goldman. Oxford: Oxford University Press, 2004–. Article published January 2008. http://www.oxforddnb.com.

Payne, Helen. "Ker [Kerr; née Drummond], Jane [Jean], Countess of Roxburghe (b. in or before 1585, d. 1643)." In *Oxford Dictionary of National Biography*, edited by Lawrence Goldman. Oxford: Oxford University Press, 2004–. Article published May 2008. http://www.oxforddnb.com.

Peltonen, Markku. *The Duel in Early Modern England: Civility, Politeness, and Honor*. Cambridge: Cambridge University Press, 2003.

Pitcairn, Sheila. "Descendants of Sir James Halkett." Unpublished genealogy, n.d.

"Pittencrieff House." The Castles of Scotland. Accessed August 08, 2016. https://www.thecastlesofscotland.co.uk/the-best-castles/stately-homes-and-mansions/pittencrieff-house.

Plant, David. "The Battle of Dunbar, September 3, 1650." BCW Project: British Civil Wars, Commonwealth & Protectorate, 1638–1660. Accessed September 08, 2018. http://bcw-project.org/military/third-civil-war/dunbar.

———. "Cromwell in Scotland, 1650–1651." BCW Project: British Civil Wars, Commonwealth & Protectorate, 1638–1660. Accessed August 02, 2018. http://bcw-project.org/military/third-civil-war/cromwell-in-scotland.

———. "The New Model Army." BCW Project: British Civil Wars, Commonwealth & Protectorate, 1638–1660. Accessed September 08, 2018. http://bcw-project.org/military/new-model-army.

———. "The Regicides." BCW Project: British Civil Wars, Commonwealth & Protectorate, 1638–1660. Accessed September 08, 2018. http://bcw-project.org/biography/regicides-index.

Potter, Louis. *Secret Rites and Secret Writing: Royalist Literature, 1641–1660*. Cambridge: Cambridge University Press, 1989.

Raffe, Alasdair. *The Culture of Controversy: Religious Arguments in Scotland, 1660–1714*. Woodbridge, UK: Boydell Press, 2012.

———. "Presbyterians and Episcopalians: The Formation of Confessional Cultures in Scotland, 1660–1715." *English Historical Review* 125, no. 514 (2010): 570–98.

Raymond, Joad. *Milton's Angels: The Early-Modern Imagination*. Oxford: Oxford University Press, 2010.

———. "The Newspaper, Public Opinion, and the Public Sphere in the Seventeenth Century." *Prose Studies* 21, no. 2 (1998): 109–37.

Richardson, R. C. "Social Engineering in Early Modern England: Masters, Servants, and the Godly Discipline." *Clio* 33, no. 2 (2004): 163–87.

Rippl, Gabriele. "'The Conflict Betwixt Love and Honor': The Autobiography of Anne, Lady Halkett." In *Feminist Contributions to the Literary Canon: Setting Standards of Taste*, edited by Susanne Fendler, 7–29. Lewiston, NY: Edwin Mellen Press, 1997.

Roberts, Stephen K. "Lenthall, William, Appointed Lord Lenthall under the Protectorate (1591–1662)." In *Oxford Dictionary of National Biography*, edited by Lawrence Goldman. Oxford: Oxford University Press, 2004–. Article published May 2005. http://www.oxforddnb.com.

Royal Greenwich Trust. "Charlton House." Accessed August 8, 2018. https://www.greenwichheritage.org/visit/charlton-house.

Ryrie, Alec. *Being Protestant in Reformation Britain*. Oxford: Oxford University Press, 2013.

Scally, John J. "Seton, Alexander, First Viscount Kingston (1621–1691)." In *Oxford Dictionary of National Biography*, edited by Lawrence Goldman. Oxford: Oxford University Press, 2004–. Article published September 2004. http://www.oxforddnb.com.

Schmitt, Arnaud. "From Autobiographical Act to Autobiography." *Life Writing* 15, no. 4 (2018): 469–86.

Schreiber, Roy E. *The First Carlisle: Sir James Hay, First Earl of Carlisle as Courtier, Diplomat, and Entrepreneur, 1580–1636*. Philadelphia, PA: American Philosophical Society, 1984.

———. "Hay [née Percy], Lucy, Countess of Carlisle (1599–1660)." In *Oxford Dictionary of National Biography*, edited by Lawrence Goldman. Oxford: Oxford University Press, 2004–. Article published September 2004. http://www.oxforddnb.com.

———. "Hay, James, First Earl of Carlisle (ca. 1580–1636)." In *Oxford Dictionary of National Biography*, edited by Lawrence Goldman. Oxford: Oxford University Press, 2004–. Article published January 2008. http://www.oxforddnb.com.

Schwoerer, Lois G. "Images of Queen Mary II, 1689–95." *Renaissance Quarterly* 42, no. 4 (1989): 717–48.

Scott, Hew. *Fasti Ecclesiae Scoticanæ: The Succession of Ministers in the Church of Scotland from the Reformation*. 7 vols. Edinburgh: Oliver and Boyd, 1915–1928.

Seaward, Paul. "Charles II (1630–1685), King of England, Scotland, and Ireland." In *Oxford Dictionary of National Biography*, edited by Lawrence Goldman. Oxford: Oxford University Press, 2004–. Article published May 2011. http://www.oxforddnb.com.

Seelig, Sharon C. "Review of *Lady Anne Halkett: Selected Self-Writings*, and *Witchcraft, Exorcism and the Politics of Possession in a Seventeenth-Century Convent: 'How Sister Ursula Was Once Bewitched and Sister Margaret Twice.'*" *Renaissance Quarterly* 61, no. 2 (2008): 680–82.

———. "Romance and Respectability: The Autobiography of Anne Halkett." In *Autobiography and Gender in Early Modern Literature: Reading Women's Lives, 1600–1690*, 110–30. Cambridge: Cambridge University Press, 2006.

Shakespeare, William. *Othello*. In *The Norton Shakespeare*, edited by Stephen Greenblatt, Walter Cohen, Suzanne Gossett, Jean E. Howard, Katharine Eisaman Maus, and Gordon McMullan. 3rd ed. 2073–158. W.W. Norton & Company: New York, 2016.

Shami, Jeanne M. "Donne's Protestant Casuistry: Cases of Conscience in the 'Sermons.'" *Studies in Philology* 80, no. 1 (1983): 53–66.

Shaw, William A. *Calendar of Treasury Books, 1660–1667*. 4 vols. London: Mackie & Co., 1904.

———. "Seymour, Henry (bap. 1612, d. 1687)." In *Oxford Dictionary of National Biography*, edited by Lawrence Goldman. Oxford: Oxford University Press, 2004–. January 2008. http://www.oxforddnb.com.

Sizer, J. R. M. "Douglas, William, Seventh Earl of Morton (1582–1648)." In *Oxford Dictionary of National Biography*, edited by Lawrence Goldman. Oxford: Oxford University Press, 2004–. Article published September 2004. http://www.oxforddnb.com.

Smith, David L. *A History of the Modern British Isles, 1603–1707: The Double Crown*. Oxford: Blackwell, 2000.

———. "Stuart, James, Fourth Duke of Lennox and First Duke of Richmond (1612–1655)." In *Oxford Dictionary of National Biography*, edited by Lawrence Goldman. Oxford: Oxford University Press, 2004–. Article published January 2008. http://www.oxforddnb.com.

Smith, Geoffrey. *Royalist Agents, Conspirators, and Spies: Their Role in the British Civil Wars, 1640–1660*. Farnham, UK: Ashgate, 2011.

Smuts, R. Malcolm. "Murray, Thomas (1564–1623)." In *Oxford Dictionary of National Biography*, edited by Lawrence Goldman. Oxford: Oxford University Press, 2004–. Article published September 2004. http://www.oxforddnb.com.

———. "Murray, William, First Earl of Dysart (d. 1655)." In *Oxford Dictionary of National Biography*, edited by Lawrence Goldman. Oxford: Oxford University Press, 2004–. Article published January 2008. http://www.oxforddnb.com.

Smyth, Adam. ed., *Autobiography in Early Modern England*. Cambridge: Cambridge University Press, 2010.

———. *A History of English Autobiography*. Cambridge: Cambridge University Press, 2016.

———. "Money, Accounting, and Life-Writing, 1600–1700: Balancing a Life." In *A History of English Autobiography*, edited by Adam Smyth, 86–99. Cambridge: Cambridge University Press, 2016.

The Society of Scottish Armigers. "The Lord Lyon Court of Arms." Accessed August 03, 2016. http://www.scotarmigers.net/lordlyon.htm.

Somerville, Robert. *The Savoy: Manor, Hospital, Chapel.* London: Chancellor and Council of the Duchy of Lancaster, 1960.

Speck, W. A. "James II and VII (1633–1701), King of England, Scotland, and Ireland." In *Oxford Dictionary of National Biography*, edited by Lawrence Goldman. Oxford: Oxford University Press, 2004–. Article published October 2009. http://www.oxforddnb.com.

———. "Mary II (1662–1694), Queen of England, Scotland, and Ireland." In *Oxford Dictionary of National Biography*, edited by Lawrence Goldman. Oxford: Oxford University Press, 2004–. Article published May 2012. http://www.oxforddnb.com.

Stachniewski, John. *The Persecutory Imagination: English Puritanism and the Literature of Religious Despair.* Oxford: Clarendon Press, 1991.

Stater, Victor. "Cavendish [née Bruce], Christian [Christiana], Countess of Devonshire (1595–1675)." In *Oxford Dictionary of National Biography*, edited by Lawrence Goldman. Oxford: Oxford University Press, 2004–. Article published September 2004. http://www.oxforddnb.com.

———. "Cavendish, William, Third Earl of Devonshire (1617–1684)." In *Oxford Dictionary of National Biography*, edited by Lawrence Goldman. Oxford: Oxford University Press, 2004–. Article published May 2006. http://www.oxforddnb.com.

———. "Howard, Edward, First Baron Howard of Escrick (d. 1675)." In *Oxford Dictionary of National Biography*, edited by Lawrence Goldman. Oxford: Oxford University Press, 2004–. Article published January 2008. http://www.oxforddnb.com.

———. "Howard, Theophilus, Second Earl of Suffolk (1584–1640)." In *Oxford Dictionary of National Biography*, edited by Lawrence Goldman. Oxford: Oxford University Press, 2004–. Article published September 2004. http://www.oxforddnb.com.

———. "Knollys, William, First Earl of Banbury (ca. 1545–1632)." In *Oxford Dictionary of National Biography*, edited by Lawrence Goldman. Oxford: Oxford University Press, 2004–. Article published October 2007. http://www.oxforddnb.com.

———. "Mordaunt, Henry, Second Earl of Peterborough (bap. 1623, d. 1697)." In *Oxford Dictionary of National Biography*, edited by Lawrence Goldman. Oxford: Oxford University Press, 2004–. Article published September 2004. http://www.oxforddnb.com.

Stevenson, David. "Campbell, Archibald, Marquess of Argyll (1605x7–1661)." In *Oxford Dictionary of National Biography*, edited by Lawrence Goldman. Oxford: Oxford University Press, 2004–. Article published May 2006. http://www.oxforddnb.com.

———. "Campbell, Archibald, Ninth Earl of Argyll (1629–1685)." In *Oxford Dictionary of National Biography*, edited by Lawrence Goldman. Oxford: Oxford University Press, 2004–. Article published September 2005. http://www.oxforddnb.com.

———. *The Covenanters: The National Covenant and Scotland*. Edinburgh: Saltire Society, 1988.

———. "Halkett [née Murray], Anne [Anna], Lady Halkett (1623–1699)." In *Oxford Dictionary of National Biography*, edited by Lawrence Goldman. Oxford: Oxford University Press, 2004–. Article published September 2004. http://www.oxforddnb.com.

———. "A Lady and Her Lovers: Anne, Lady Halkett." In *King or Covenant: Voices from Civil War*, 189–206. East Linton, UK: Tuckwell, 1996.

———, ed. *Letters of Sir Robert Moray to the Earl of Kincardine, 1657–73*. Aldershot, UK: Ashgate, 2007.

———. "Lindsay, Alexander, First Earl of Balcarres (1618–1659)." In *Oxford Dictionary of National Biography*, edited by Lawrence Goldman. Oxford: Oxford University Press, 2004–. Article published September 2006. http://www.oxforddnb.com.

———. "Livingston, James, First Earl of Callendar (d. 1674)." In *Oxford Dictionary of National Biography*, edited by Lawrence Goldman. Oxford: Oxford University Press, 2004–. Article published September 2004. http://www.oxforddnb.com.

———. "Murray, John, First Marquess of Atholl (1631–1703)." In *Oxford Dictionary of National Biography*, edited by Lawrence Goldman. Oxford: Oxford University Press, 2004–. Article published September 2004. http://www.oxforddnb.com.

Stewart, Alan. *Early Modern*. Vol. 2: *The Oxford History of Life-Writing*. Oxford: Oxford University Press, 2018.

Stirling, A.M.W. *Fyvie Castle: Its Lairds and Their Times*. London: John Murray, 1928.

Taft, Barbara. "Overton, Robert (1608/9–1678/9)." In *Oxford Dictionary of National Biography*, edited by Lawrence Goldman. Oxford: Oxford University Press, 2004–. Article published January 2008. http://www.oxforddnb.com.

Thomson, Alan. "Axtell, Daniel (bap. 1622, d. 1660)." In *Oxford Dictionary of National Biography*, edited by Lawrence Goldman. Oxford: Oxford University Press, 2004–. Article published January 2008. http://www.oxforddnb.com.

Thornbury, Walter, ed. "Whitefriars." In *Old and New London*. 6 vols. London: Cassell, 1878.

Todd, Margo. *The Culture of Protestantism in Early Modern Scotland*. New Haven: Yale University Press, 2002.

———. "Profane Pastimes and the Reformed Community: The Persistence of

Popular Festivities in Early Modern Scotland." *Journal of British Studies* 39, no. 2 (2000): 123–56.

Trill, Suzanne. "Beyond Romance? Re-Reading the 'Lives' of Anne, Lady Halkett (1621/2?–1699)." *Literature Compass* 6, no. 2 (2009): 446–59.

———. "Critical Categories: Toward an Archaeology of Anne, Lady Halkett's Archive." In *Editing Early Modern Women*, edited by Sarah C. E. Ross and Paul Salzman, 97–120. Cambridge: Cambridge University Press, 2016.

———, ed. *Lady Anne Halkett: Selected Self-Writings*. Aldershot, UK: Ashgate, 2007.

———. "Life-writing: Encountering Selves." In *Handbook of English Renaissance Literature*, edited by Ingo Berensmeyer, 108–35. Berlin; Boston: De Gruyter, 2019.

———. "'Refreshment,' 'Intertainment,' and 'Imployment': Anne, Lady Halkett's *Meditations* and the Practice of Daily Devotion." Paper presented for the London Renaissance Seminar. Birkbeck College, London, February 2002.

———. "Re-Writing Revolution: Life-Writing in the Civil Wars." In *A History of English Autobiography*, edited by Adam Smyth, 70–85. Cambridge: Cambridge University Press, 2016.

———. "Royalism and Resistance: The Personal and the Political in Anne, Lady Halkett's *Meditations*, 1660–1699." In *Worldmaking Women: New Perspectives on the Centrality of Women in Sixteenth- and Seventeenth-Century Culture*, edited by Pamela Hammons & Brandie Siegfried, 153–67. Cambridge: Cambridge University Press, 2021.

Vallance, Edward. "The Kingdom's Case: The Use of Casuistry as a Political Language, 1640–1692." *Albion* 34, no. 4 (2002): 557–83.

Wagner, Erica. "The Greater British Bake-Off." *Financial Times*, November 29, 2013. Accessed September 08, 2018. https://www.ft.com/content/68926c64-56f3-11e3-8cca-00144feabdc0.

Walker, Kim. "'Divine Chymistry' and Dramatic Character: The Lives of Lady Anne Halkett." In *Women Writing, 1550–1750*, edited by Jo Wallwork and Paul Salzman, 133–49. Bundoora, Australia: Meridian, 2001.

Walsham, Alexandra. *Providence in Early Modern England*. Oxford: Oxford University Press, 1999.

Watt, Ian P. "The Naming of Characters in Defoe, Richardson, and Fielding." *Review of English Studies* 25, no. 100 (1949): 322–38.

Wilcher, Robert. "*Eikon Basilike*: The Printing, Composition, Strategy, and Impact of 'The King's Book.'" In *The Oxford Handbook of Literature and the English Revolution*, edited by Laura Lunger Knoppers, 289–308. Oxford: Oxford University Press, 2012.

Wiseman, S. J. "Introduction: Reading the Early Modern Dream." In *Reading the Early Modern Dream: The Terrors of the Night*, edited by Katharine Hodgkin,

Michelle O'Callaghan, and S. J. Wiseman, 1–13. New York; London: Routledge, 2008.

Wiseman, Susan. "Legitimizing Conspiracy: Anne Halkett, Rachel Russell, Aphra Behn." In *Conspiracy and Virtue: Women, Writing, and Politics in Seventeenth-Century England*, 313–59. Oxford: Oxford University Press, 2006.

———. "'The Most Considerable of My Troubles': Anne Halkett and the Writing of Civil War Conspiracy." In *Women Writing, 1550–1750*, edited by Jo Wallwork and Paul Salzman, 25–45. Bundoora, Australia: Meridian, 2001.

Wisker, Richard. "Gower, Sir Thomas, Second Baronet (1604/5–1672)." In *Oxford Dictionary of National Biography*, edited by Lawrence Goldman. Oxford: Oxford University Press, 2004–. Article published September 2004. http://www.oxforddnb.com.

Wormald, Jenny. "James VI and I (1566–1625), King of Scotland, England, and Ireland." In *Oxford Dictionary of National Biography*, edited by Lawrence Goldman. Oxford: Oxford University Press, 2004–. Article published September 2014. http://www.oxforddnb.com.

Wynne, S. M. "Catherine [Catherine of Braganza, Catarina Henriqueta de Bragança] (1638–1705), Queen of England, Scotland, and Ireland, Consort of Charles II." In *Oxford Dictionary of National Biography*, edited by Lawrence Goldman. Oxford: Oxford University Press, 2004–. Article published January 2008. http://www.oxforddnb.com.

Yardley, Bruce. "Villiers, George, Second Duke of Buckingham (1628–1687)." In *Oxford Dictionary of National Biography*, edited by Lawrence Goldman. Oxford: Oxford University Press, 2004–. Article published May 2009. http://www.oxforddnb.com.

Young, John R. "Hay, John, First Marquess of Tweeddale (1626–1697)." In *Oxford Dictionary of National Biography*, edited by Lawrence Goldman. Oxford: Oxford University Press, 2004–. Article published September 2004. http://www.oxforddnb.com.

Zie, Qin. "Meet the 87-year-old Woman Who Has a Five Inch Horn Growing Out of Her Head." *MailOnline*. August 28, 2015, 8:42 a.m. BST, http://www.dailymail.co.uk/news/peoplesdaily/article-3212536/Meet-87-year-old-woman-five-inch-HORN-growing-head.html.

Index of Names and Subjects

Note: Anne, Lady Halkett is referred to as "ALH" everywhere except for the main entry for her name. All other Annes are referred to by name and/or title. Colonel Joseph Bampfield is likewise referred to as JB with the exception of his main entry. Numbers in italics indicate figures.

Abbot House, 10, 46, 47, 214, 217, 233–236, 238, 289, 290n22
Aberdour Castle, 119–120
angels, 26, 37, 94, 169, 177, 235, 252, 254; in biblical citations, 192n48, 246n78, 310n106, 351, 355, 358
Anglo-Dutch War, third, 10, 238, 240n25, 243
Anne (queen), 6, 7n26
anti-Catholicism, 46–47, 250n108, 295n69; ALH's, 61, 101, 161, 212, 291, 298. See also Catholicism
Apostle's Creed. See Creed, Apostle's
Ardross, Lady, 34, 153
Argyll, Countess of (Anna MacKenzie, earlier Countess of Balcarres), 9, 34, 126n399, 139–140, 152, 289–290
Argyll, Marquess of (Archibald Campbell, also Lord Lorne and Earl of Argyll), 13–14, 16, 29, 118, 122, 126–127, 150
Arington, Mr., 160
ars moriendi, 48, 250n108, 254n151
The Art of Divine Chemistry and Select Meditations, 46, 258–265, *260*, 346; "The Art of Divine Chemistry," 19–20, 38, 39n186, 127, 259–263, *260*, 346; "Meditations upon Psalm 106:4–5, Begun Monday, April 22, 1678," 264–265; "The Rule for Action," 263–264

Atholl, Marquess of (Lady Amelia Sophia Stanley Murray), 270
autobiography, 1, 3, 4–5, 21, 22, 41, 54
"The Autobiography of Anne, Lady Halkett," 1n1, 54
Axtell, Colonel (Daniel), 333

Baber, John (physician), 165n638
Balcarres, Countess of (Lady Anna MacKenzie, later Countess of Argyll), 9, 34, 126n399, 139–140, 289–290
Balcarres, Earl of (Lord Alexander Lindsay, first Earl of Balcarres), 14, 15, 33, 34, 137, 145, 149, 150–153
Balcarres, Earl of (Lord Colin Lindsay, third Earl of Balcarres), 289
Balcarres, Lady (Sophia Seton), 146
Bampfield, Colonel Joseph: and ALH's marriage to Sir James Halkett, 15, 35–36, 146, 163–164; and the Earl of Balcarres, 15, 33, 145; and Charles I, 11–12, 13, 14, 24, 81–82, 86, 87; and Charles II, 12–13, 14, 25, 29, 33, 44, 86, 128, 143; *Colonel Joseph Bamfield's Apologie Written by Himself and Printed at His Desire*, 12, 13nn57–58, 25, 54, 81n124, 94n214; Simon Couper's characterization of, 44; and the Earl

385

of Cromartie, 33, 145, 146, 147; duel with Sir Henry Newton, 28, 114–115, 128; and the Earl of Dunfermline, 14, 33, 116, 128, 143, 145; in Europe, 24, 25, 44, 114; in Flanders, 28, 116; and Sir James Halkett, 33, 144, 145, 146; in Holland, 13, 35, 44, 164, 253n144; imprisonment and escape, 13, 15, 92n196, 94, 97–98, 114–115, 317–318; and James VII/II (Duke of York), 12, 24, 25, 29, 81–84, 86, 318; and Sir Robert Moray, 33, 142–143; and Will Murray, 12, 24, 25, 80, 88, 89, 91, 92, 194n64; and the Parliamentarians, 14–15, 24, 81; political duplicity of, 11, 14–15, 54; and Presbyterianism, 12, 13; as Royalist, 12, 24, 29, 81–85, 86, 88, 93; as questionable Royalist, 11–12, 13, 14–15, 25, 194n64; trouble with authorities, 82, 92, 119, 128, 142–143, 145; and the Earl of Tweeddale, 145; wife (Catherine Sydenham), 11, 22, 27, 33, 35, 50, 80, 98, 109, 115, 119, 151, 174, 273n7; alleged death of, 24, 25–26, 29, 87, 89, 95, 96, 97, 128–129, 144; political affiliations of, 81, 96. *See also* marriage of JB to ALH; relationship of JB with ALH

Banbury, Countess of (Lady Elizabeth Howard), 77, 78, 80

Barbados, 18–19, 329, 334–335

Bayning, Anne (wife of Henry Murray), 8, 162n622

bees, 49, 202n29

Lord Belmerinoth (John Elphinstone, third Lord Balmerino and second Lord Cupar), 149

Berkhamsted, 9, 333

Book of Common Prayer, 64n25, 189n23, 315n24, 316n29; and marriage, 36n172, 37; and psalm readings, 97n234, 265n52

Boyle, Robert, 49, 217–220

Braganza, Catherine of (queen), 208n69, 224n65, 334

Broghill, Lady (Margaret Howard), 170–171

Broghill, Lord (Roger Boyle), 3, 37, 170, 171

Bruce, Sir William of Kinross, 16, 155n577

Bryson, Anna, 115n338

Callendar, Earl of (James Livingston, first Earl of Callendar), 159n606, 160n609, 162

Campbell, Lady Anne Douglas (daughter of the Marquess of Argyll), 9, 34n161, 118

Campbell, Lady Mary, 16

Carlisle, Earl of. *See* Howard, Sir Charles

Carlisle, Earl of (Sir James Hay, second Earl of Carlisle, second creation), 18, 334

casuistry, 4, 21–22, 35. *See also* equivocation

Catholicism, 47, 63n19, 101, 103, 276, 279; ALH's anti-Catholicism, 61, 101, 161, 212, 291, 298; and Thomas Howard, 22, 66, 67; and James VII/II, 46; and social/political turmoil, 300, 304; and Charles II, 208n69; Thomas Howard and, 22, 66, 67; and James VII/II, 46, 295n69; and William of Orange, 279

Cavers, the, 160, 170

charity, ALH's, 43, 148–149, 234, 259, 341; and healing skill, 127, 129; and Nehemiah 8:10, 281, 303
Charles I (king), 22, 60, 76n92, 91n189, 136n458, 162n624, 211, 337; and Joseph Bampfield, 11, 12–13, 14, 24, 33, 81, 86, 87, 317–318; execution of, 3, 6, 22, 25, 88, 90n186, 118n348, 133, 273n7, 333, 338; and God's providence, 41, 200, 204; as a sin, 181, 203–205, 241–242, 255, 284, 291, 304–306; and Thomas Murray, 61; and Will Murray, 25. See also *Eikon Basilike: The Portraiture of His Sacred Majesty in His Solitudes and Sufferings*
Charles II (king), 9n38, 10, 134, 168, 205, 243–244, 246, 249, 259, 295, 318; ALH meeting with, 29, 119–120, 122–124, 127, 131, 247; arrival in Scotland, 29, 119; and Joseph Bampfield, 12–13, 14, 25, 29, 33, 44, 86, 128, 143; and Lord Belmerinoth, 149; cabal communication with, 33, 145–146; coronation of, 3, 15, 41, 128n405, 197, 207–208, 246–247; death of, 267n13; and the Earl of Dunfermline, 3, 14, 34, 122, 130, 137, 147, 151; at Dunfermline, 122–124; in exile, 14, 181, 200–201, 242, 243, 338; and financial support of ALH, 123, 127, 168, 327, 330, 335; and Sir James Halkett, 15, 143, 145–146, 149–150; marriage and potential wives, 118n351, 208; and Sir Robert Moray, 251; and Will Murray, 29, 89–90, 194n64; and the New Model Army, 201–203; physicians of, 153, 165n638; Restoration of, 2, 3, 6, 13, 15, 140n481, 185, 193–196, 197, 199–201, 203, 204, 243, 244n65, 267, 303; ALH's vow regarding, 194, 209, 248; as time marker, 37, 59, 81n121, 91n189, 153n564, 181n40; at Whitehall, 246–247, 298n6
Charlton House, 9, 15, 36, 65, 78, 162, 165, 167, 321. See also Newton, Lady Elizabeth Murray; Newton, Sir Henry
children, ALH and: miscarriage, 17, 185; motherhood, 17, 38, 173, *175*, 229, 230–231, 232, 322, 331, 343; sons (*see* Halkett, Henry; Halkett, Robert); stepdaughters, 9, 16, 34, 48, 80n111, 155, 160, 170; stepmotherhood, 1, 9, 17, 45, 221, 322, 331; stepson (*see* Halkett, Sir Charles)
Christmas, 147n530, 280–281
Church of England (Episcopalianism), 5n19, 21, 91n189, 103n264, 208n69, 290, 291; ALH's support of, 1, 57, 64, 197, 198, *199*, 280, 282, 313, 343–344; conflict with Presbyterians, 53, 284n76, 299; Simon Couper's promotion of, 7, 48, 53
Civil Wars/Wars of the Three Kingdoms, 2, 6, 11, 18, 57, 72, 103n265. See also Cromwell, Oliver; Dunbar, Battle of; New Model Army, the; Overton, Colonel (Robert); Parliamentarians; Worcester, Battle of
Cole, Mrs., 163, 168
Commandment, Fifth, 182, 245, 292
Commandment, Tenth, 292
Commandments, Ten, 182n44, 245n72, 302n37, 310, 316, 345

Communion, Holy. *See* Sacrament, the
confession, religious, 25, 261, 306n73, 316, 341, 345, 351
conscience, 25, 226, 279n24, 290; ALH's, 4, 178, 209, 212, 231; David Dickson and, 34–35; and the Fifth Commandment, 182; and kings, 22, 303; and marriage, 35, 164, 221; of Mr. Nicholls, 28, 116; and sin, 180, 183
conscience, cases of, 3, 4, 5, 21, 22, 35; and ALH's marriage to Sir James Halkett, 32, 34, 35, 36, 37, 156–157; and ALH's relationship with Joseph Bampfield, 24–25, 30, 33, 35, 37; and ALH's relationship with Thomas Howard, 23–24; and Charles II, 29, 120; and Sir James Halkett's appointment as Justice of the Peace, 4, 37, 171; and the Nicholls affair, 27–28; and personal reputation, 21, 65
Couper, Simon, 2, 41–53, *51*, 63n21, 311n124, 319–321; and ALH's charity, 43, 46–47; and ALH's children, 45, 47; and ALH's death, 47–48, 313n1; and ALH's devotional practice, 43, 44, 47, 48–49, 50–52, 183n56, 211n95, 287n9, 339; and ALH's finances, 45, 46, 47, 49, 329n5; and ALH's marriage to Sir James Halkett, 44, 45; and ALH's mother, 80n111; and ALH's piety, 7, 42, 45, 48–49, 52; and ALH's politics, 44–45, 46–47, 52, 53, 88n172; and ALH's relationship to Sir Charles Halkett, 45, 238n14; and ALH's romantic entanglements, 25, 44; and ALH's widowhood, 45–46, 47; and ALH's writing catalogue, 41, 59, 173, 313, 314, 339–349, 347n45; described as "books," 3n11, 49, 258; designation of select/occasional meditations, 42, 50, 52, 53, 185, 258, 286, 343n20; and missing writings, 44, 47, 52, 59, 128n409, 209n75, 258; and ALH's writing timeline, 41, 44–45, 128n409, 173, 341n10, 342n16; contradicting her dual dating system, 347n43, 347n47; inaccurate, 258, 273, 342n19, 343n21, 344n28, 345n30, 346n39, 348n49, 349n57; and Joseph Bampfield, 44; characterization of ALH, 6–7, 52, 53, 219n25, 240n240, 339; charges against, 282n54, 299–301; Church of England motivations, 6–7, 48, 53, 339; and Sir James Halkett, 45, 155n577; and Henry Murray, 84n142. *See also Life of the Lady Halket*
Covenanters, 1, 12, 140n481, 196. *See also* Presbyterianism
covenants: in Bible verses, 191n37, 226n100, 228, 249; as sacramental, 5, 23, 35. *See also* oaths; vows
creditors, 46, 228, 252, 335
Creed, Apostle's, 280, 315, 316, 345
Crew (ALH's maid), 9, 73, 143, 147, 153, 160, 162, 169; in Edinburgh, 125, 137, 139, 148, 152; at Fyvie, 131, 135, 136, 191, 337; at Naworth, 95, 116
Cromwell, Oliver, 15, 18, 65n31, 118n348, 133n438, 134; military activity and soldiers of, 29, 32, 34, 116, 124, 130, 137, 199–200, 337; and religious practice, 91n189, 146n530, 164. *See also* Dunbar, Battle of; New Model Army, the; Parliamentarians; Worcester, Battle of

Culcheth, Mr., 99, 111
Culcheth, Mrs., 95, 99, 111
Culross, minister of. *See* Fraser, James (clergy)
Cunningham, Dr. Robert (physician), 153, 159, 237

Daniel (biblical person), 133, 338
David (biblical person), 225, 228, 269n19, 284, 289, 311, 325, 355; and ALH's relationship with Joseph Bampfield, 50; and God's works, 229; and judgment, 244, 278; and prayer, 201, 309n103, 347
Devil, the. *See* Satan
Devonshire, Countess of (Lady Elizabeth Cecil), 9, 36, 165–166, 167
Devonshire, Dowager Countess of (Lady Christian(a) Bruce Cavendish), 165n640, 167, 321
Dickson, Mr. David (clergy), 32, 50; counseling ALH, 34–35, 36, 141, 156–157, 166
A Directory for the Publicke Worship of God, 37, 64n25, 167
Dobson, David, 290n23
Dolan, Frances, 4, 202n13
Douglas, Sir James, 119, 120
dreams, 88nn172–173, 195, 267; ALH's, 173, 254, 263–264, 276
Drummond, Sir Patrick, 76–77
Dunbar, Battle of, 18, 29, 30, 32, 124, 125–126, 127
Dunfermline, 6n22, 10, 120, 223n66, 282n54, 320n59, 330; Abbot House, 10, 46, 47, 214, 217, 233–236, 238, 289, 290n22
Dunfermline, Countess of (Lady Mary Douglas Seton, Countess of Dunfermline), 9, 28, 30, 128, 135, 136; and Charles II, 29, 120, 122, 123, 126, 127; and the English soldiers, 130, 131–132, 337; inviting ALH to Fyvie, 124–125
Dunfermline, Dowager Countess of (Lady Margaret Douglas Hay), 142, 159–160
Dunfermline, Earl of (Lord Charles Seton, second Earl of Dunfermline), 127, 134, 136, 293n56, 327; and Joseph Bampfield, 14, 33, 116, 128, 143, 144, 145; and Charles II, 116, 120, 122, 130; and Sir James Halkett, 140–141; invitation to ALH, 29, 116; and the Marquess of Argyll, 14; as Royalist, 14, 33, 34, 120, 121–123, 124, 130, 132, 137, 140, 143, 145, 147–148, 151
Dunfermline, Earl of (Lord James Seton, fourth Earl of Dunfermline), 293–294
Dysart, Countess of (Lady Elizabeth Murray, also Duchess of Lauderdale), 18, 19, 329
Dysart, Earl of (Lord William Murray), 10, 12, 61n9, 125, 329n4

earthquake, 106
Edinburgh, ALH in, 33–34, 35, 116, 117–119, 134–142, *138*, 143–152, 153–159, 170–171; and the Marquess of Argyll, 13, 29, 118, 150; and Joseph Bampfield, 143, 144, 145, 146, 147, 148; and Sir James Halkett, 16, 34, 37, 141–142, 144–145, 146–147, 149–151, 153–156, 157–159, 170–171; and Royalist planning, 24, 32–33, 143, 145–146, 148, 151–152

Edinburgh Castle, 37, 162n624, 170, 171
Eikon Basilike: The Portraiture of His Sacred Majesty in His Solitudes and Sufferings, 22, 204n41, 241n42. *See also* Charles I
Elizabeth, Princess (Elizabeth Stuart), 63, 81, 211
Elkonhead, Justice, 37, 167
equivocation, 21, 25, 35; by ALH, 21–22, 23, 35, 36, 68, 164; by Joseph Bampfield, 24, 81; by Sir James Halkett, 33, 34, 149. *See also* casuistry
Erskine, Lady Anna, 9, 30, 126, 127, 132, 134, 136, 242; and Charles II, 122, 123
Esther (biblical person), 299, 349, 357
Eton College, 60, 61
Evelyn, John, 8, 65n31
Ezell, Margaret, 19, 339n5

faith, 230, 234, 245, 269, 282, 316; ALH's exploration of, 39, 178–182; ALH's request for, 182, 184; and Christ's indwelling, 222, 297; and grace, 177, 315; and perfection, 40, 182n50, 184, 220; power of, 39, 189–193, 316, 342, 343; and prayer, 181, 201; signs and evidence of, 189–190, 192–193, 239, 309, 352; strengthening of, 39, 50, 218, 251, 255; and temptation, 39, 173, 176; and trials of misfortune, 20, 50, 60, 97, 129, 178–180, 187, 190–192, 255 (*see also* trials, personal/spiritual); and works, 212, 239, 295. See also *A Short Expostulation about Prayer, Meditations, and the Mother's Will to Her Unborn Child*
Fallowfield, Mr. (clergy), 161

Fanshawe, Lady Ann, 14, 54
Fifth Monarchists, 133n438, 201n24, 202
finances, ALH's, 47, 187, 205–207, 252, 271, 317, 325, 329n5; borrowing money, 10, 29–30, 125, 127, 142, 159–160, 165–166, 325; debts, 52, 127, 157, 161, 162–163, 206, 228, 257, 270, 276; and fraud, 162–163, 168; inheritance (*see* inheritance, ALH's); precarity of, 10, 32, 46, 105, 135, 148, 256–257, 303; support from Charles II, 123, 127, 206n54, 327, 330, 335; support from Lady Dunfermline, 124–125; support from Sir James Halkett, 17–18, 33, 35, 147, 149, 160, 335; support from Lady Anne and Sir Charles Howard, 116; support from James VII/II, 46; support from Sir Henry Newton, 9, 19; support from sister, 9, 149, 162
Fitch, Colonel (Thomas), 132, 337
Flanders, 28, 113, 116, 160
Floors Castle, 142–143
Forester, Mr. (Duke of Lauderdale's secretary), 329, 335
Forret, David, 152n563, 153
Fraser, James (clergy), 301–302
The Fruits of the Spirit, Reflections, and Occasional Meditations, 346–347
Fyvie Castle, 10, 29, 30, 50, 127–136, 137, 193n53, 290, 294, 309; incident with the English soldiers at, 31–32, 131–134, 242, 337–338

Gale, Mr. Robert (clergy), 165n640, 167, 210, 321
Garioch (servant), 330
Gilmour, Sir John, 141

Gloucester, Duke of (Henry Stuart), 63n17, 63n19, 81, 205n51, 211
Gosford, Laird of (Peter Wedderburn), 290
Gower, Sir Thomas (second Baronet), 93–94
grace, divine, 57, 212, 219, 234, 259, 281, 290, 342, 348; denial of, 183, 213, 225, 235, 240; desire for, 60, 210, 227, 232, 235, 256, 263, 325; and faith, 177, 192, 315; and forgiveness, 181n37, 322; and sin, 166, 180, 193, 229, 246, 258, 279, 296, 310; throne of, 225, 227, 230, 242, 249, 253, 319
Graeme, Mr. (clergy), 281, 282, 319, 320
Greenhorn, James, 330

Halkett, Anne, Lady, at Abbot House, 10, 46, 47, 214, 217, 233–236, 238, 289, 290n22; at Aberdour Castle, 119–120; and Archibald Hay, 18, 140, 334, 335; and the Marquess of Argyll, 13–14, 29, 118, 122, 126–127, 150; arrest of, 162–163, 168; and Lady Balcarres, 9, 126n399, 139–140, 151–153, 152n558, 289–290; and Lord Balcarres, 15, 33, 34, 137, 145, 149, 150, 151–153; brother (Charles Murray), 7, 29, 120, 243; brother (Henry Murray), 7, 8, 9n38, 84, 144, 158, 162, 165; brother (Will Murray) (*see* Murray, William (Will)); and Charles II, meeting with, 29, 123, 247–248; danger to, 26, 37, 130–131, 138–139, 169–170, 209, 274n7, 337; death and anticipated death, 10, 47, 128n409, 217, 224, 234, 313, 319, 342; and David Dickson, 34–35, 36, 141, 156–157, 166; education, 21, 63–64; and Lord Edward Howard (father of Thomas), 10, 66, 67, 72, 74, 77, 95; communication with ALH's mother, 70–71, 73, 75, 79; willingness to have ALH marry Thomas, 69; family history, 60–61, 63; in Fife, 119–120, 121–127; at Floors Castle, 142–143; in Fyvie, 29–30, 32, 50, 127–136, 290, 294, 309; incident with the English soldiers, 131–134, 242, 337–338; writings, 342n14, 342n16; as healer/midwife, 30, 95, 161, 193, 270, 271; healing as charity, 43, 46, 125–126, 127, 129, 240; interest in dreams, 173, 263–264, 276; and Sir James Douglas (tenth Earl of Morton), 119, 120; in London and surrounds, 60–93, 161–168, 197, 333, 335; marriage to Sir James Halkett, 9, 10, 15, 17, 32, 36–37, 44, 60, 163–164, 166–168, 169–171, 217, 309–310, 321–322, 327–328 (*see also* widowhood; widows); and Lady Moray, 143–144, 147; and Lady Morton, 141, 158, 159; mother (*see* Murray, Jane Drummond); at Naworth Castle, 26–29, 94–116, 132, 211; and Sir Henry Newton, 15, 159, 167; duel with Joseph Bampfield, 28, 114–115, 128; regarding ALH's finances, 165, 330, 335; as Royalist, 66, 72; and Mr. Nicholls (*see* Nicholls, Mr.); at Pitfirrane, 233, 238; sister (*see* Newton, Lady Elizabeth Murray); and Thomas Howard, 23–24, 27, 65–71, 72–75, 77–80; and Lord Tweeddale, 10, 32, 139–140, 143, 148, 290n21; and William of Orange, 278–279,

284n76; youth, 63–65, 262, 311. *See also* charity, ALH's; Charles, Sir Howard; children, ALH and; Dunfermline, Lady; Dunfermline, Lord; Edinburgh, ALH in; finances, ALH's; Halkett, Sir James; manuscript characteristics, ALH's; marriage of JB to ALH; Moray, Sir Robert; politics, ALH's; relationship of JB with ALH

Halkett, Anne/Anna (daughter of Sir James), 16, 155n577

Halkett, Sir Charles (son of Sir James), 6n22, 16, 217, 224, 290; letter from ALH, 329–331; relationship with ALH, 17, 19, 45, 225, 233, 238n14, 240, 252, 254, 329–331; in the third Anglo-Dutch War, 238, 240

Halkett, Elizabeth (Betty, daughter of ALH and Sir James), 17, 36, 173, 188, 197

Halkett, Henry (Harry, son of ALH and Sir James), 197, 208–209

Halkett, James (son of Sir James), 16

Halkett, Sir James: as Royalist, 14, 33, 141, 143, 144, 145, 150, 171, 222

Halkett, Sir James, 21, 160, 161, 191, 197, 256; and ALH's finances, 17–18, 33, 35, 147, 149, 165, 335; and Joseph Bampfield, 36, 146, 164–165, 174; as "best of husbands," 17, 220, 222, 322, 327; as cabal member, 33, 143, 144, 145; and Charles II, 149–150; and the Countess of Morton, 158, 159; courting of ALH, 16, 17, 33, 34, 35, 144, 146–147, 153, 155, 156, 157, 158, 163, 165, 166; daughters, 9, 16, 34, 48, 80n111, 155, 160, 170; death of, 45, 55, 214, 217, 220–226, 234, 237, 252, 254–255, 256, 318; first meeting with ALH, 32, 141; grave of, 48, 227, 233, 234, 313n1; Justice of the Peace appointment, 37, 170–171; marriage to ALH, 9, 10, 15, 17, 32, 36–37, 44, 60, 163–164, 166–168, 169–171, 217, 309–310, 321–322, 327–328; marriage to Margaret Montgomery, 14n62, 15–16, 155n577, 328; military service, 141n492, 149–150; political views, 14, 15, 32–33, 143, 145, 150, 161; sons (*see* Halkett, Sir Charles; Halkett, Robert)

Halkett, Jane (daughter of ALH and Sir James), 17, 197, 226, 248n91

Halkett, Janet (daughter of Sir Charles), 290

Halkett, Mary (daughter of Sir James), 16, 155n577

Halkett, Robert (Robin, son of ALH and Sir James), 17, 223, 237–238, 252, 262; ALH's financial concerns for, 228, 257, 327, 335; ALH's sense of duty to, 224, 230–231, 254, 256; birth, 185; death, 320; education, 45; "Instructions to My Son," 19, 38n179, 214, *215–216*, 217, 344, 345; and James VII/II, 47, 319–320; letters to ALH, 271, 272; relationship with Sir Charles Halkett, 233, 330–331

Halkett, Sir Robert (Sir James's father), 15

Hall, Joseph, 22–23, 37, 53, 218, 246n76, 287, 298; *The Art of Divine Meditation*, 37, 218n19; method for meditation, 38–39, 40; *Resolutions and Decisions of Divers Practicall Cases of Conscience in Continuall Use amongst Men*,

22–23, 24n113, 25n113, 35, 35n166
Hambleton, Jane, 147, 148
Hamilton, Duke of, 139n471, 293
Harding, Mr. (Richard), 29, 122
Hay, Archibald, 18, 140, 334, 335
Hay, Peter, 18
healing/midwifery, ALH's avocation of, 30, 95, 161, 193, 240n27, 270, 271; as charity, 43, 46, 125–126, 127, 129, 240
Henrietta Maria (queen), 12, 60, 63n19, 90, 90n184, 120n361, 254n153, 334
Holland, 63, 76, 114n327; ALH in, 25, 43; Joseph Bampfield in, 13, 35, 164, 253n144
Holy Spirit, the, 57, 181, 231, 239, 246, 309, 315, 357; ALH's sense of connection to, 218, 314; *Meditations upon the Seven Gifts of the Holy Spirit*, 50, *51*, 346, 354
Howard, Lady Anne (Countess of Carlisle), 9, 10–11, 93, 95, 116, 117, 142; and Thomas Howard, 65, 66, 67, 75, 79; and the Nicholls affair, 26, 27–28, 98–100, 102–103, 104–105, 106–112
Howard, Sir Charles (Lord Charles Howard, first Earl of Carlisle, third creation), 11, 93, 94, 95, 97, 101, 102, 104, 113, 116, 117, 118; and the Nicholls affair, 27–28, 99–100, 105, 106–108, 109–112; as Royalist, 11, 103n265, 161n616
Howard, Lord Edward (first Baron of Escrick, Lady Anne and Thomas's father), 10, 66, 67, 69, 77, 95, 108; communication with ALH's mother, 70–71, 73, 75, 79
Howard, George, 12, 82n128

Howard, Thomas (Lady Anne's brother), 8, 9, 21, 22, 23, 27, 30, 65–75, 77–79, 317; and ALH's equivocation, 22, 68, 74
humility, 184, 205, 255, 259, 339, 344

illness, of ALH, 159, 193, 238, 255, 276, 293, 296; at Balcarres, 34, 152, 153; at Fyvie, 20, 30, 128, 261; at Naworth Castle, 95–96, 211, 308–309, 311
"An Information of What Was Left Me by My Mother," 333–335
inheritance, ALH's, 17–19, 45, 69, 116, 197, 329–330, 333–335; and Barbados, 18–19, 329–330, 334–335; and legal action, 35, 136, 140, 157, 158, 334
Instructions for Youth, 49, 348
"Instructions to My Son," 19, 38n179, 214, *215–216*, 217, 344, 345
Israel (biblical people), 200, 203, 227n101, 275n22, 306n67, 353, 356; ALH's self-comparison to, 219, 310; England as, 206, 208, 323; failings of, 179, 205, 244n67, 245n68, 265n52, 295n68, 357; God of, 205n49, 261, 269, 270n21, 289, 352, 353, 355; Jesus as king of, 303n45

Jacobitism, ALH's, 46–47, 278–279, 291–293, 294–295, 299, 302–303, 322
James VI/I, 6, 61
James VII/II (king, Duke of York), 2, 46–47, 205, 330, 333; ALH's prayers for, 267, 269, 323; and Joseph Bampfield, 25, 29; and Catholicism, 46, 295n69; deposition of (Glorious Revolution), 47, 278, 284, 292, 293n54, 294,

302–303, 304, 320n60; escape from St. James's Palace, 1, 2, 3, 6, 12, 24, 26, 44, 81–85, 123, 197, 300, 318, 333; exile of, 47, 181, 269, 293n54, 338; and Robin Halkett, 47, 319; rumors of Scottish preference for, 12–13, 89–90

John, Saint ("Apostle"), 176

Joseph's Trial and Triumph, 274n15, 346

justification, 20, 113, 139, 253, 258; and accusations against ALH, 111, 263; to God, 7, 25, 79, 205, 279, 280, 281; and intentions, 88, 89, 291; Parliamentarian, 133, 338; *A True Account of My Life* as, 1, 11

Kinnoull, Countess of (Landy Anne Douglas Hay), 126

Kinnoull, Earl of (Lord George Hay, third Earl of Kinnoull), 126n398, 334

Kinnoull, Earl of (Lord William Hay, fourth Earl of Kinnoull), 140, 334n11

Kinross, 16, 125–126, 129

Knox, Henry, *51*, 53

Lady Anne Halkett: Selected Self-Writings, 56

Lamb, Mary Ellen, 3, 21n98, 22, 74n82

Lauderdale, Duchess of (Lady Elizabeth Murray, also Countess of Dysart), 18, 19, 329

Lauderdale, Earl of (Lord John Maitland, also Duke of Lauderdale), 18, 264n50, 327–328, 329n4, 330, 335

"Letter to Her Stepson, Sir Charles Halkett," 329–331

"Letter to the Earl of Lauderdale," 327–328

The Life of the Lady Halket, 6–7, 42–49, 53, 337–358; ALH's finances in, 46, 52, 329n5; ALH's healing avocation in, 43, 46, 240n27; ALH's meditative practice in, 43, 287n9; ALH's missing writings and, 44, 45, 47, 49, 128n409, 340; ALH's piety in, 7, 43, 44, 47, 48–49, 211n95, 219n25, 339; ALH's political views in, 44, 46–47, 52, 337–338; ALH's siblings in, 23n110, 49, 84n142, 311n124, 319n59; ALH's widowhood in, 45, 48, 52, 238n13; and Joseph Bampfield, 44; Biblical References in the "Books by the Lady Halket," 350–358; "Books by the Lady Halket," 339–349; and Charles I's execution, 88n172, 337; "Experiences in Fyvie," 337–338; and Robin Halkett, 45, 47; and Sir Charles Halkett, 45–46, 238n14; and Sir James Halkett, 44, 45, 48, 52; and Thomas Howard, 44

Lilburn, Colonel (Robert), 132, 337

Loftis, John, 65n33, 84n141, 91n189, 92n199, 93n206, 96n227, 124n381, 139n471, 153n564, 155n580; and ALH's finances, 116n340, 206n54; and Joseph Bampfield, 11n42, 14–15, 54, 87n163, 97n235, 115n336; and Sir James Halkett, 150n548; and Mr. Nicholls, 94n213

Lord's Supper. See Sacrament, the

Lorne, Lord. See Argyll, Marquess of

Lowe, Colonel (Hercules), 115

Lord Lyon, 136

Mackenzie, Sir George (first Earl of Cromarty), 33, 145, 146, 147

Mains, Laird of (Sir Archibald Douglas, tenth Laird), 119
Maitland, Mr., 162–163, 168
manuscript characteristics, ALH's, 33, 55, 56–58, 60n8, 80, 151, 173, 185, 237, 313; additions, 197, 217, 251n115, 258, 298; bound folios, 341nn10–11, 342n15, 342nn17–18; bound in quarto, 343n23, 344n25, 344n27, 345n30; bound octavos, 343n20; damage, 58, 59, 60, 185; missing elements, 2, 59, 80, 151; pagination, 20, 55, 58, 59, 173, 185, 197, 214, 233n165, 237, 251n115, 298n2, 313n7, 314; stitched books, 44, 258, 339, 340, 347nn44–45, 349; writing and orthographic style, 56–58
maps, *31, 121, 138*; and occasional meditations, 41, 49
marriage, of JB to ALH: declared, 104, 113; possible, 25, 26, 27, 35, 37, 44, 50, 156, 209; proposed, 24–25, 26, 40, 44, 87, 92, 98, 144, 151, 156–157, 177, 180, 209
Marshall, Mr. (clergy), 320
Mary II (queen, Princess Royal), 63, 90, 320n60; accession of, 47, 278n21, 284n76 294–295; death of, 6, 205, 291, 292–293, 294–295
meditation and meditations, 20–21, 54, 58, 173, 258, 273, 278, 289, 320; ALH's definitions of, 37, 38, 39, 42, 55, 185, 214, 237, 266–287, 298–299; ALH's expectations of an audience for, 4, 7, 42, 49, 50, 198, 273, 278, 314, 319; and ALH's interest in dates, 33, 273; and ALH's life experience, 18, 19, 38, 45, 47, 50, 52, 185, 237, 241, 276, 299; and ALH's sense of identity, 5, 11; ALH's topic selection for, 267, 293, 298–299, 315; Bible passages, 41, 45, 49, 55–56, 241, 274–275, 286, 313; everyday life, 41, 49, 53, 286–287, 314; and ALH's trials, 26; ALH's use as memory aid, 3, 42, 258, 274, 276, 278, 298; and kings, 41, 45, 47, 237, 241–249, 258; method of, 22, 38–39, 40, 43, 48, 49, 266; relation to prayer, 39, 50, 198, 258–259; and temptation, 39–40, 309, 313. *See also* Boyle, Robert; Hall, Joseph; meditations, occasional; meditations, select; individual meditations and volumes
Meditations, Contemplations, and the Soul's Remembrancer, 26, 341–342; "The Soul's Remembrancer," 26n126, 128n409, 309, 321n67, 323n88, 342
meditations, occasional, 5, 37–42, 50, 54, 56, 339–340; bases for, 41, 42, 237; Robert Boyle and, 217–220; and Simon Couper, 52, 53, 286, 314; as defined by ALH, 42, 50, 55, 185, 214, 237, 258, 266–267, 286–287, 298–299, 314; definition, 38. *See also* individual meditations and volumes
Meditations, Prayers, and Vows in Childbirth, 44, 341
meditations, select, 5, 21, 37–42, 50, 54, 55–56, 173, 273; and Simon Couper, 42, 50, 185, 286; as defined by ALH, 38, 41, 42, 55, 237, 266, 286, 298–299, 314; definition, 38. *See also* individual meditations and volumes
Meditations and Prayers upon the First Week, and Occasional Meditations, 344; "Part One, Containing Select Meditations and Prayers upon the First Week,

396 *Index of Names and Subjects*

with Observations on Each Day's Creation, and Considerations on the Seven Capital Vices, to Be Opposed, and Their Opposite Virtues to Be Studied and Practiced," 49, 53n259, 344; "Part Two, Fifteen Occasional Meditations on Public and Private Occurrences," 344

Meditations on Death, from Heb. 9:27, 128n409, 342

Meditations on Moses and Samuel, 26, 38, 39n186, 58n271, 273–275, 348; "Monday, May 21, 1688," 273–275

Meditations on St. Peter, the Passion, and Occasional Meditations (1686/7–1688), 266–272, *268,* 347; "Friday, March 30, 1688," 270–272; "Friday, October 14, 1687," 269–270; "Sunday, May 29, 1687," 267

Meditations on the Book of Jonah, and Other Select Meditations, 269n15, 274n15, 347

Meditations upon Jabez His Request, 1 Chron. 4:10, 50, *51,* 340, 347, 355

Meditations upon the Seven Gifts of the Holy Spirit, 50, *51,* 52nn252–256, 346, 347n45, 354

Meditations upon the Twenty-Fifth Psalm, 49–50, 53n259, 340, 342, 344n25, 348n50

miscarriage, 17, 79, 185, 208n69

modernity, early, 4, 67n44, 206; English pronunciation in, 7n26, 56; English writing in, 56, 57; women in, 6, 54, 339; word meanings in, 67n46, 76n94, 78n104, 81n118, 83n138, 221n42, 302n37

Monck, General (George, first Duke of Albemarle), 196, 201n24, 242n46

Monmouth, Duke of (James Scott, first Duke of Monmouth), 46, 208n69

Montgomery, Margaret (first wife of Sir James), 14n62, 15–16, 155n577, 328

Montgomery, Sir Robert (of Haselhead), 155

Montgomery, Sir Robert (third Baronet of Skelmorlie), 15, 41, 183

Moray, Lady (Sophia Lindsay), 9, 33, 137n462, 143–144, 147, 250–251

Moray, Sir Robert, 9, 137, 144, 330; and Joseph Bampfield, 142–143; as cabal member, 33, 143, 145–146; death of, 33, 237, 249–252; and Sir James Halkett, 33, 141–142, 143, 149; wife's death, 33, 147, 250–251

Mordaunt, Elizabeth, 24, 78–79

Morton, Countess of (Lady Anne Douglas), 140–141, 158

Morton, Earl of (Lord James Douglas, tenth Earl of Morton), 119, 120

Murray, Charles (ALH's brother), 7, 29, 120, 243

Murray, Elizabeth (ALH's sister). *See* Newton, Lady Elizabeth Murray

Murray, Henry (ALH's brother), 7, 8, 9n38, 84, 144, 158, 159, 162, 165; and ALH's relationship with Joseph Bampfield, 92, 94–95, 96, 105

Murray, Jane Drummond (ALH's mother), 60–64, 78, 80, 117–118, 161, 162, 219; ALH's inheritance from (*see* inheritance, ALH's); and ALH's youth and education, 21, 63–64, 70–71, 72; alleged royal service of, 63, 211, 241; communication with Lord Edward Howard, 70–71, 73, 75, 79; death of, 80n111, 84n142, 92, 333; and

Thomas Howard, 23, 24, 65, 66, 68–69, 73–74, 75–76, 77, 317; importance to ALH, 8–9, 76–77, 79, 317
Murray, Margaret (Sir James's mother), 15
Murray, Thomas (ALH's father), 6n21, 7, 9n38, 61, 63, 92
Murray, William (of Hermiston), 139
Murray, William (Will, ALH's brother), 7, 12–13, 24, 30, 65, 89–92, 118, 162, 333; and Joseph Bampfield, 12, 24, 25, 80, 88, 89, 91, 92, 194n64; and Charles I, 25; and Charles II, 29, 89–90, 194n64; death, 25, 92

National Library of Scotland, *31, 51*, 54, *121, 138, 175, 186, 199, 215–216, 239, 260, 268, 277, 288, 305, 324*
Naworth, 10, 29
Naworth Castle, 9, 23, 26–27, 29, 132, 142–143, 161; ALH at, 94–117, 211, 308, 311
Neal, Mr., 166, 167, 168
Netherlands, 44, 115n336, 320n59
Newbyth, Lord (John Baird), 140
New Model Army, the, 116, 130, 199–203, 243
Newton, Lady Elizabeth Murray (ALH's sister), 7, 8, 49, 65, 72, 93, 113–114; and ALH's relationship with Sir James Halkett, 158–159, 160, 161–162, 165, 167, 168; and ALH's relationship with Joseph Bampfield, 92, 94–95, 96, 105, 114, 144; and ALH's relationship with Thomas Howard, 69–70, 71, 73, 75, 78, 79; childhood, 64n27, 311; financial support of ALH, 9, 149, 162. *See also* Charlton House

Newton, Sir Henry (later Puckering, third Baronet), 8, 15, 65n38, 128, 161, 162; and ALH's finances, 9, 19, 165, 330, 335; and ALH's relationship with Sir James Halkett, 159, 167; duel with Joseph Bampfield, 28, 114–115, 128; sequestration of estate, 66n42, 72. *See also* Charlton House
Nicholls, Mr. (clergy), 23, 94, 95, 98, 106, 112, 116–117; ALH's forgiveness of, 28, 112, 113, 132; confrontation by ALH and Lady Howard, 110–111; letter to ALH, 28, 109; misbehavior of, 25, 26–27, 101, 102–103, 104, 132; speaking against ALH, 27–28, 100, 101, 102, 105, 107–108; speaking against Lady Howard, 99–100, 104, 107, 108
Nichols, John Gough, 53–54
Norfolk, Mr., 85, 300
Northumberland, Earl of (Lord Algernon Perry, tenth Earl of Northumberland), 81, 83, 85

oaths: in Bible verses, 186n7, 249n107, 283n67, 293n55; and Thomas Howard, 23, 69, 74, 78; and Jane Murray, 23, 71; as sacramental, 5, 23, 28, 111. *See also* covenants; vows
Occasional and Select Meditations, including Instructions to My Son, 19, 214, *215–216*, 217–233, 319n59, 344–345; "Upon My Deplorable Being a Widow," 226–232; "Upon My Going to Live at Dunfermline, February 14, 1670/1," 233–236; "Upon Reading Mr. Boyle's *Occasional Reflections*, January 25, 1668/9," 217–220;

"Upon the Death of My Dearest Sir James Halkett, Who Died upon Saturday Morning, betwixt Eight and Nine o'clock, Being September 24, 1670," 220–226

Occasional Meditations, 41, 185–196, *186*, 343; "Upon Riches," 185–188, *186*; "Upon the Return of His Majesty after His Long Banishment and Variety of Other Troubles," 185, 193–196

Occasional Meditations, Meditations and Prayers on Every Several Day Ordained to Be Kept Holy in the Church of England, 197–213, *199*, 343–344; "Upon a Dispute with Myself, New Year's Day, 1661," 210–213; "Upon His Majesty's Coronation, Tuesday, April 23, 1661," 207–208; "Upon Making Vows," 208–210; "Upon the Disbanding of the Army," 199–203; "Upon the Fast which by Proclamation Was Kept, January 30, 1660/1," 203–205; "Upon the Many Disappointments I Have Met with in My Business at Court," 205–207

Occasional Meditations, Meditations upon Nehemiah, and Observations of Several Good Women Mentioned in Scripture, 276–285, *277*, 348; "Christmas Day, Thursday, December 25, 1690," 280–281; "January 30, 1690/1," 284–285; "Thursday, January 8, 1690/1," 282–283; "Tuesday, June 24, 1690," 278–279

Of Watchfulness, Select, and Occasional Meditations, 286–297, *288*, 348–349; "Friday, April 5, 1695," 293–297; "Saturday, June 23, 1694," 289–290; "Tuesday, January 15, 1694/5," 291–293

Overton, Colonel (Robert), 32, 132, 133, 242, 337–338

Parliamentarians, 72, 82, 93, 97, 103n265, 140, 141, 162; Marquess of Argyll as, 13–14, 150; Joseph Bampfield as, 11–12, 14, 15, 33, 54, 194n64; Lord Broghill as, 170, 171; Earl of Dunfermline as possible, 14; Lord Edward Howard as, 10; Sir Charles Howard as, 11; Will Murray accused of being, 194n64; Robert Overton as, 32, 132, 133, 242, 337–338; ships of, 12, 29; Sydenham family as, 24, 81, 96

Paul, Saint ("Apostle"), 166, 192, 253, 262, 303, 323; ALH's self-comparison to, 26, 44, 179, 192, 242, 308; and keeping faith, 192, 289, 296n80; and kings, 181–182, 245, 280; "Meditations on Paul's Conversion, and What Is Recorded of Him in Acts, Chapters 1–23," 347; and the signs of belief, 189–190, 212n101; trials of, 190, 242, 251, 307–308; and widows, 232

Perdita Manuscripts, 55
Perkins, William, 22
Peter, Saint, 190, 266–272
Pitfirrane, 15, 18, 47, 48, 60, 119
Pitfirrane House, 10, 37, 46, 173, 214, 233, 238
Pitfirrane Papers, 54–55, 233n170, 238n14, *239*, 329, 333
Pittencrieff, Lady, 270
politics, ALH's, 22, 94, 96, 133–134, 199–203; Couper's disconnection from, 52; and covert activity,

24, 26, 32–33, 34, 44, 86, 142, 145–146, 148, 151–153; Jacobitism of, 46–47, 278–279, 291–293, 294–295, 299, 302–303, 322; and Parliamentarians, 14, 30, 32; religious foundations of, 41, 198, 242–249, 278–279, 291–293, 294–295, 299, 302–303; rescue of the Duke of York (James VII/II), 81–85, 93, 105, 123, 300, 318, 333. *See also under* Royalists

Popish Plot, the, 258, 264n50

"The Power of Faith, upon Mark 16:17–18," 42, 189–193, 343

prayer, 180, 225, 234, 272, 315n24, 321, 322; ALH's daily practice of, 64, 210, 224, 231–232, 246, 253, 269, 289, 311, 314, 325; ALH's leading of, 48, 325; ALH's struggle with, 210, 211–212, 228; ALH's writing of, 48, 50, 52 (*see also* individual writings and volumes); and benefit of the Lord's Supper (Holy Communion/Sacrament), 281; and divine providence, 27, 105, 178n15, 201, 206, 224, 240, 247, 259; with fasting, 36, 166, 231; God as hearing, 20, 105, 241, 245, 309, 323; and Will Murray, 91, 115; and Mr. Nicholls, 94, 98, 109, 117; relation to meditation, 39, 43, 50, 198, 258–259; in remembrance of death, 211; and spiritual ease, 213; and trials/misfortune, 20; as written preface, 20, 39n186

prayer, for kings, 181–182, 269, 328; Charles I, 88n172, 211, 241; Charles II, 206, 208, 209, 242, 245, 246, 248, 258–259, 327; James VII/II, 267, 303, 323; and rejection of William of Orange, 278–279

Prayers, Pious Reflections, and Observations, 50, *51*, 52, 347n23

Presbyterianism, 13, 57, 291, 301n34, 302n37, 309; and the Earl of Balcarres, 151n557; Joseph Bampfield's support of, 12, 92n196; conflict with the Church of England (Episcopalianism), 48, 53, 284n76, 299. *See also* Covenanters

Preston, Battle of, 18, 162n624

primary sources, 54–58

prophecy, 32, 133, 263n38, 338

prophets, 50, 191, 205, 228, 249, 265n52, 311; ALH as, 32, 134, 194n60, 242, 338; Daniel, 133, 338; Elijah, 208; Isaiah, 226, 232, 325; Jeremiah, 283n66; Joel, 231, 263n38

prosperity, 188, 222; as blessing, 225, 240, 248; pitfalls of, 177, 190, 194, 222

Protestantism, 5, 57, 76, 254n151, 259, 280. *See also* anti-Catholicism; Church of England; Presbyterianism

providence, divine, 25, 41, 48, 183, 191, 201n21, 241, 272; and ALH's relationship with Bampfield, 28, 40; and cases of conscience, 21, 29; and escape from danger, 37, 169–170; and financial support, 9, 29, 32, 46, 187–188, 289, 317; and financial trouble, 205, 206–207, 300; and marriage to Sir James Halkett, 36, 166, 220, 252; and providential imagination, 5, 29, 32, 34; and social trouble, 27, 34

Puckering, Henry. *See* Newton, Sir Henry

Puritanism, 38, 64n26, 250n108

400 Index of Names and Subjects

Queensbury, Duke of (William Douglas), 295
queens of England. *See* Anne (queen); Braganza, Catherine of; Henrietta Maria; Mary II

redemption, 57, 105, 253, 275, 307, 320, 353, 357; and communion, 281; and grace, 279; "redeemed one of Christ," 39, 176; of the Three Kingdoms, 323; and transgression, 256, 283, 306, 309; trust in, 180n32, 251, 252
relationship of JB with ALH, 17, 21, 28, 80, 86–88, 92, 93, 95, 104, 105, 113, 116, 144–145, 253; ALH's misgivings and regrets, 20, 39–40, 127–129, 163, 309, 323; marital status issues, 22, 29, 30, 50, 89, 96, 98, 109, 128–129, 151, 156, 261, 273n7
repentance, 79, 205, 244, 255, 274, 300; and confession, 261; desire for, 210; lack of, 163, 184; and memory, 60, 322; and Mr. Nicholls, 112, 117; for regicide, 30, 129, 134, 291, 338; royal, 293, 294, 295
Restoration, the, 2, 3, 6, 13, 15, 140n481, 185, 193–196, 197, 199–201, 203, 204, 243, 244n65, 267, 303; ALH's vow regarding, 194, 209, 248; as time marker, 37, 59, 81n121, 91n189, 153n564, 181n40
Richmond, Duchess of (Mary Villiers), 90
Richmond, Duke of (James Stuart, first Duke of Richmond), 90
Roxburghe, Countess of (Lady Jane [Jean] Drummond Ker[r]), 9, 19, 63

Roxburghe, Dowager Countess of (Lady Isabel Douglas Ker), 142
Roxburghe, Earl of (Lord Robert Ker, first Earl of Roxburghe), 63n19, 142n502, 149n544
Roxburghe, Earl of (Lord William Ker [born Drummond], second Earl of Roxburghe), 149
Royalists, 1, 11, 14, 21, 162, 168, 170, 194n65, 242, 243n53; ALH as, 6, 11, 15, 18, 55, 63n22, 88–89, 116, 122–123, 131, 140, 161, 162, 168, 170, 206, 207–208, 209, 267, 337–338 (*see also* politics, ALH's); ALH's milieu as, 10–11, 13, 14, 32; Lady Balcarres as, 151–153; Lord Balcarres as, 14, 33, 34, 145, 151–153; Joseph Bampfield as, 12, 24, 29, 81–85, 86, 88, 93; Joseph Bampfield as questionable, 11–12, 13, 14–15, 25, 194n64; Lady Broghill as, 170; Lord Broghill as, 170, 171; Earl of Callendar as, 162n624; Christian(a) Cavendish as, 165n640; Francis Dodington as, 96n225; Lord Dunfermline as, 14, 33, 34, 120, 121–123, 124, 130, 132, 137, 140, 143, 145, 147–148, 151; and the escape of the Duke of York, 1, 2, 3, 6, 12, 24, 26, 44, 81–85, 123, 197, 300, 318, 333; Sir John Gilmour as, 141; Thomas Gower as, 93; Sir James Halkett as, 14, 33, 141, 143, 144, 145, 150, 171, 222; Margaret Hay as, 142; Sir Charles Howard as, 11, 103n265, 161n616; George Mackenzie of Tarbat as, 14, 33, 145, 147; Sir Robert Moray as, 14, 33, 143, 145–146; William Murray (of Hermiston) as, 139; Sir Henry Newton as, 66n42, 72; Sydenham

family as, 24; Lord Tweeddale as, 32
"The Rule for Words," 19, 258
Rymere, Henry, 153
Ryrie, Alec, 5n20, 36n174, 37–38, 39, 315n24

Sacrament, the (Holy Communion, Lord's Supper), 36, 57, 282, 301–302; ALH's meditations on, 50, *51*, 341, 343, 345; and ALH's piety, 3, 43, 47, 52, 238, 309; and Joseph Bampfield, 30, 128; at a distance, 52, 281; kneeling and, 52; by Will Murray, 30, 91; and Mr. Nicholls, 28, 112, 113
Satan, 248, 309, 316n27, 322n80, 358; and corruption, 192, 323; and Sir James Halkett, 221; and politics, 203; and temptation, 176, 182, 192, 212, 253, 262, 313, 350, 357–358
Seaton, Mr., 141
Select and Occasional Meditations (1696–1697), 298–312, *305*, 311–312, 314, 342n14, 349; "Friday, May 14, 1697," 237–257; "Monday, June 8, 1696," 299–302; "Saturday, January 30, 1696/7," 304–307; "Wednesday, October 14, 1696," 302–304; "What Crosses and Difficulties I Have Met with Myself, and Deliverances out of Them, ever to Be Remembered with Thankfulness and Praise," 307–311
Select and Occasional Meditations (1697–1698/9), 313–325, *324*, 349; "1 Corinthians 15:58," 317–318; "Saturday, February 19, 1697/8," 318–321; "Saturday, May 21, 1698," 322–324; "Saturday, November 26, 1698," 324–325; "Tuesday, March 2, 1697/8," 321–322; "Wednesday, December 1, 1697," 314–316
Sermon on the Mount, the, 108n296, 203n32, 316
Seymour, Mr. (Henry), 29, 120, 127
Sharpe, Mr. George (clergy), 136
sheep, 41, 49, 53, 183, 249, 349, 356
A Short Expostulation about Prayer, Meditations, and the Mother's Will to Her Unborn Child, 38, 59, 115n338, 173–184, *174*, *175*, 176–184, 342–343; "The Great Conquest and Power of Faith, 1 John 5:4," 3, 33, 39–41, 173, 176–184, 342
sin, 42n200, 57, 115n338, 178, 194, 221, 230, 235, 246, 274, 278n13, 282–283, 293n53, 300, 347, 350, 352; and ALH's children, 208, 225, 233; ALH's desire to be free of, 40, 179, 181, 184, 193, 228, 234, 249, 255, 262, 307, 312, 320n64; and conscience, 183, 309; forgiveness of, 177, 179, 180, 209, 210, 219, 224, 239, 253n138, 265n52, 281, 351; and Joseph Bampfield, 40, 129, 180, 209; and marriage, 157, 166, 253, 292; and Mr. Nichols, 113, 132; and prayer, 50, 211, 212; of rebellion against kings, 30, 129, 181, 194, 200, 204, 205, 211, 241, 255, 279, 284, 291–292, 294, 306; redemption from, 59n4, 239, 258, 280, 291, 294, 295n65, 296, 306, 310, 311; repentance of, 60, 132, 205, 210, 261, 311, 319, 322; trials as punishment for, 181, 204, 261, 264, 284. *See also* confession, religious
Smith, Will, 330
Smyth, Adam, 4–5

soldiers, 150n548; in Edinburgh, 92, 137, 140; English, 30–31, 34, 129, 130–131, 135, 163, 201n24; wounded, 30, 125–127, 196n53
Solomon (biblical person), 115n338, 185, 231, 249, 262, 295, 302
"The Soul's Remembrancer," 26, 128n409, 309, 321n67, 323n88, 342
spiders, 41, 202
St. Albans, Earl of (Lord Anthony R. J. S. Adolph), 334
St. James's Palace, 2, 3, 6, 24, 81, 85, 210. See also James VII/II (King, Duke of York)
St. Martin's Lane, 9, 80
Strafford, Earl of, 22
submission, 40, 128, 180, 188, 228, 235, 250, 255, 342
Symson, Andrew, 51, 53

temptation, 44, 61, 113, 190, 222, 230, 306, 307n76; of Satan, 182, 253, 310n106, 313, 341, 357–358; of the world, 39, 173, 176–177, 184, 233, 256, 257
Tindall, Mr. (John F.), 72, 73, 74
trials, judicial, 22, 45, 90, 97, 163, 168
trials, personal/spiritual ("cross occurrences"), 40, 43–44, 179–180, 207, 219, 255, 259, 264, 273–274, 303, 306, 307–311, 320, 323, 341; and Joseph Bampfield, 44, 50, 89, 151, 156, 159, 179–180, 273n7, 323; of Charles II, 194, 204; and finances, 187–188, 228; of friendship, 117; and Sir James Halkett's death, 220, 223, 252; and illness, 128, 153, 308–309, 311; of James VII/II, 269; of Joseph (biblical person), 346; of Sir Robert Moray, 250–251; of Mr. Nicholls, 104, 113; as punishment for sin, 187, 261, 262; of Saint Paul, 307–308; and scandal, 20; and spiritual growth, 46, 188, 218, 259–260, 262, 289, 303, 307–308, 309, 318, 322, 325; and submission, 129, 187; of threatened violence, 26, 274n7, 308; "What Crosses and Difficulties I Have Met with Myself, and Deliverances out of Them, ever to Be Remembered with Thankfulness and Praise," 26, 128n409, 307–311; of widowhood, 226–232
A True Account of My Life: audience for, 4, 7, 19, 30, 42, 219–220, 319; and cases of conscience, 3, 4, 21–23, 29, 34–35, 37; Simon Couper's summary of, 43–44, 45, 46; devotion in, 21, 30, 36, 55; earthquake in, 106; equivocation in, 68, 73–74, 149, 164; incompleteness of, 2, 45, 59; and literary convention, 4–5, 21, 22, 38, 56, 57–58; motivations for, 19–21, 25, 27, 42; primary sources of, 54–58; relationship to her meditations, 3, 5, 20, 42, 54; timeline of, 2, 41, 173; writing and orthographic style in, 56–58. *See also* Bampfield, Joseph; Charles II; Halkett, Anne, Lady ; Halkett, Sir James; Howard, Lady Anne; James VII/II; *The Life of the Lady Halkett*; Murray, William (brother)
The True Balm and Select Meditations, 345
Tweeddale, Countess of (Lady Jean Scott Hay), 9, 139
Tweeddale, Earl of (Lord John Hay, first Marquess and second Earl of Tweeddale), 10, 32, 139–140, 143, 148, 290n21

Vallance, Edward, 4n13
Venner, Thomas, 243n57
Villiers, Colonel, 330
violence, threats of against ALH, 26, 131, 308, 337
virtue, 194, 204, 230, 249; ALH's, 43, 95, 117, 157; of ALH's family, 21; ALH's interest in, 24, 41, 80, 88, 183, 233; and works, 205
vows: and Joseph Bampfield, 35; in Bible verses, 197, 350; and Sir James Halkett, 34; *Meditations, Prayers, and Vows in Childbirth*, 44, 341; misuse of, 25, 34, 36, 154, 192, 209–210, 253, 262; and Jane Murray, 70; as sacramental, 5, 23, 35, 43, 196, 207, 209–210, 262; "Upon Making Vows," 208–210; violation of, 23, 27, 209, 210. *See also* covenants; oaths

Walsingham, Lady Anne, 78
"What Crosses and Difficulties I Have Met with Myself, and Deliverances out of Them, ever to Be Remembered with Thankfulness and Praise," 26, 39n186, 128n409, 274n7, 307–312
Whitefriars, 9, 35, 80n111, 84n142, 161
widowhood, 9, 149, 208, 228, 231, 237, 241, 253, 258, 270–271; ALH's, 45, 55, 217, 234, 237, 252, 256, 258, 270, 322, 346n39; consecrated to God, 27, 224, 234–236, 238–239, 253–254, 255, 257, 262; duties of, 229, 231; exemplars of, 231–232; and financial hardship, 160, 228, 252, 256–257; and God's promises, 229, 232; and piety, 7, 48, 224, 253; and prayer, 20; as trial, 226, 227, 228, 322; "Upon My Deplorable Being a Widow," 226–232; vows/resolutions of, 27, 253, 262; "The Widow's Mite," 39, 41, 238–241, 345; "The Widow's Mite, Part of It Relating to the King," 39, 41, 241–249, 345
The Widow's Mite and Occasional Meditations, 38, 39, 41, 64n24, 237–257, 345; "January 30, 1673/4," 255–256; "Upon a Proposal," 256–257; "Upon September 24, 1673," 252–255; "Upon the Death of Sir Robert Moray, Who Died Suddenly in June 1673," 249–252; "The Widow's Mite," 238–240; "The Widow's Mite, Part of It Relating to the King," 39, 41, 241–249, 345
Wild, Doctor George, 91
William of Orange (king), 6, 63n20, 278, 280n35, 320n60; ALH's antipathy toward, 47, 278, 284n76, 292–293, 295, 299, 304; ALH's questionable support for, 46–47
Wiseman, Susan, 19
Witherington, Sir, 160
Worcester, Battle of, 11, 103n265, 130n419, 153n564, 193n57, 194, 242

York, Duke of. *See* James VII/II

Index of Biblical References

Acts: 1–23, 347; 5:15, 190; 9:15, 181n37; 14:22, 182; 16:16–18, 189; 18:3, 181n37; 24:16, 342; 27:20, 242; 28:3–6, 190

1 Chronicles: 4:10, 355; 16:22, 247n85
2 Chronicles: 6:2, 179n21; 6:36, 283n60; 20:12, 317; 28, 347, 354; 28:10, 42, 343, 352; 33:12–13, 342, 352
1 Corinthians: 1:12–13, 345, 353; 3:9, 349, 356; 4:6, 255; 6:11, 345, 353; 6:12, 279; 7:8, 232n162; 8:9, 279; 10:30, 210n83; 10:31, 281; 11:27–29, 36n174; 12:12–13, 345, 353; 12:13, 237; 13:7, 344, 353; 14:14–15, 212n101; 14:15–16, 279n26; 14:25, 274; 15, 296, 296n80; 15:42, 227n105; 15:54, 220; 15:54–57, 296n80; 15:58, 317–318, 349, 357
2 Corinthians: 1:3–4, 242; 1:4, 283; 4:2, 279n24; 4:5, 301; 4:8, 179n20; 4:8–9, 342, 351; 5:15, 297; 6:14, 292; 8:8, 318; 9:10, 290; 9:11, 290n32; 11:13, 308; 11:25, 44n211, 308; 11:30–31, 321; 11:31, 36, 166, 308; 12:9, 229; 13:11, 230
Colossians: 3:3, 307; 3:4, 306n75

Deuteronomy: 5:6–22, 345; 5:16, 245n72; 5:16, 21, 292n47; 8:2, 307n85, 349, 357; 10:8, 232n157; 10:18–19, 271; 13:6, 292, 292n46; 13:8, 292, 292n46; 17:13, 293, 293n50; 21:7, 306; 21:8, 306; 32:33, 192n47

Ecclesiastes: 2:16, 249; 3:1, 200n18, 302; 4:12, 221; 7:20, 283n60; 9:1, 185; 9:2, 186n7, 249, 293; 9:10, 295; 12:1, 230
Ephesians: 1:6, 322; 1:13, 239n21; 3:12, 60; 3:13, 60n6; 3:14–16, 222; 3:16, 317; 3:17, 223; 3:18, 223; 3:18–19, 312; 3:19, 223; 3:20, 195n75, 223; 4:30–32, 357; 5:15–16, 256n159; 5:16, 307; 5:22, 292; 6:2, 245; 6:4, 230; 6:16, 176n12
Esther, 299, 349, 357
Exodus: 3:14, 349, 356; 20:1–17, 345n33; 20:12, 182n44, 245n72, 292n47; 22:22–23, 20; 35, 219; 35:5, 275; 35:5–6, 219, 275n19; 35:9, 275; 35:25, 275; 35:29, 275n22
Ezekiel: 18:13, 295; 18:30, 295n68; 20:37, 191n37; 33:33, 249n103; 36:21, 244n67; 36:22, 245
Ezra: 9:13–14, 310

Galatians: 1:23–24, 192n45; 2:20, 296; 3:27, 189n23; 5:22–23, 212n99, 351
Genesis, 355; 1, 49; 1–2:3, 353; 2:1–3, 49; 9:22, 245n73; 9:23, 245; 9:24–27, 246n74; 15:16, 241n40, 301; 18:21, 341, 350; 19:9, 234; 28:20, 197; 37–50, 354; 38:14, 231; 38:19, 231n147; 45:7, 294n61

Habakkuk: 3:16, 180
Hebrews: 2:14, 316; 2:17, 310; 3:1, 306; 4:15–16, 230; 4:16, 325; 6:1, 315n21; 6:3, 259; 7:25, 253n134; 8:12, 224; 9:27, 342, 352; 11:1,

405

178n15, 239n19, 245n70; 11:32, 310; 12:11, 261; 13:3, 323; 13:4, 253n141; 13:5, 55n269, 105n286, 303, 344, 353; 13:17, 280; 13:20–21, 249; 19:27, 296
Hosea: 2:6, 166n643, 179; 9:14, 79n108; 14:1–4, 349, 357

Isaiah: 1:6, 292; 1:18, 210; 1:19, 210n18; 10:2, 232n159; 11:2–3, 354; 12, 344; 12:1–6, 352; 16:5, 244n62; 25:4, 317n36; 26:3, 325; 26:4, 342, 351; 26:9, 304; 26:21, 305; 40:31, 349, 357; 41:2, 193n58; 41:10, 283; 44:22, 283; 47:9, 226; 48:10, 60; 54:5–6, 227n101; 55:7, 341, 350; 57:18–19, 285; 58:1, 300; 58:1–2, 211n96; 64:8, 206n57

James: 1:12, 307; 1:17, 188n14; 1:25, 296; 4:14, 307
Jeremiah: 3:15, 300n24; 11:5, 283; 12:9, 342, 351; 18:3–10, 200n14; 18:21, 226; 28:6, 283; 29:11, 264n47, 304; 30:21–22, 347, 354; 31:18–19, 261; 31:32, 226; 35:18–19, 345, 353; 49:11, 225n79; 50:15, 347, 354
Job: 1:22, 341, 350; 5:6–7, 260; 5:21, 88n171, 225n90, 308n89; 9:23, 320; 14:1, 233; 14:14, 227n104; 15:16, 192n46; 19:25, 253n134; 22:2, 213n108; 28:28, 224; 33:6, 173n3; 34:30, 164n635, 304; 35:10, 220, 254, 325; 38:11, 307
Joel: 1:8, 231
1: John 1:7, 295, 306; John 1:9, 306, 341; John 2:1, 59
1 John 3:1, 176
1 John 5:4, 39, 176, 342, 352
1 John 5:11, 307

John, 354; 1:9, 351; 3:17, 60; 3:33, 229; 6:35, 356; 8:1–11, 204n39; 8:11, 341, 350; 8:12, 356; 9:1–3, 204n39; 10:7, 356; 10:14, 356; 11:25, 357; 12:12–13, 303n45; 13:15, 347, 354; 14:3, 239n20, 263; 14:6, 299n9, 304n53, 357; 15:1, 357; 15:5, 178n15; 16:3, 342, 351; 16:33, 176; 19:14–15, 303n45
Jonah, 55n269, 347, 354
Joshua: 7:19, 261; 7:20–21, 205n49
Jude: 1:24–25, 318, 325
Judges, 345, 353; 4–5, 355; 6:17, 342; 13:23, 244

1 Kings: 8:46, 283n60; 12, 354; 13, 286, 348, 356; 17, 347, 354; 17:18, 208; 18:21, 179
2 Kings: 2:11, 250; 4:1, 228; 4:7, 228n114; 5, 349, 357; 5:1, 294; 8:13, 205n48; 22:14–20, 355

Lamentations: 4:20, 284
Leviticus: 5:17, 178; 8:22–24, 266; 10:19, 278n13, 279; 14:14, 310; 19:2, 348, 356
Luke, 355; 1–2, 355; 1:13, 355; 1:46–55, 255n156; 2:14, 281; 2:36–37, 231; 2:36–38, 345, 353; 4:2, 310n106; 6:45, 230; 7:47, 341, 351; 11:2–4, 207n62, 253n138, 345n31; 11:9–10, 213n109; 11:13, 315; 16:1–8, 191n38; 17:10, 213n107; 18:18–25, 188n19; 19:43, 105n288; 21:1–4, 41, 218n18, 238n17; 21:3, 241; 22:18, 345, 353; 22:42, 221n39, 225n77

Malachi: 3:6, 246; 4:2, 285
Mark, 355; 1:13, 310; 9:38, 301; 9:39–40, 301; 10:17–25, 188n19; 12:41–44, 237; 13:37, 229; 14:36,

Index of Biblical References 407

221n39; 16:17–18, 42, 189–193, 343, 352
Matthew, 355; 3:8, 295; 4, 313, 349; 4:1–2, 313; 4:1–11, 357; 4:2, 310n106; 4:8, 341, 350; 4:10, 313; 5:16, 232n161; 5:17, 316; 5:44–45, 48, 203n32; 6:9–13, 207n62, 345n31; 6:9–15, 253n138; 6:11, 207n62; 6:32, 207, 207n63, 341, 350; 7:3, 302; 7:5, 342, 351; 7:7, 341, 350; 7:7–8, 213n110; 8:2, 310; 11:29, 229; 11:29–30, 349, 356; 15, 348; 15:22, 355; 16:18, 184; 19:16–24, 188n19; 23:24, 302; 25:13, 348, 356; 26:6–7, 355; 26:39, 221n39; 26:42, 221n39; 28:18–20, 315n20
Micah: 6:8, 221

Nehemiah, 348, 355; 2:8, 275; 8:9, 281; 8:10, 281, 303
Numbers: 14:34, 310n106; 16:22, 293; 27, 355; 32:13, 219n26

1 Peter: 1:15, 322; 1:17, 307; 2:21, 228; 2:24, 296, 307; 3:4, 231; 3:16, 226n92; 5:4, 248n96; 5:7, 228
2 Peter: 1:3, 226; 1:10, 342, 351
Philippians: 4:6–7, 289, 348; 4:11, 251; 4:12, 190
Proverbs: 1:33, 227; 4:18, 323; 4:26, 321; 10:7, 294n62; 14:9, 115n338; 15:19, 166n643; 16:13, 252n125; 16:33, 262n32; 19:11, 283n61; 21:1, 267n12; 22:6, 231; 29:15, 179, 231; 31, 355
Psalms: 2:4, 202n25; 4:7, 303n47; 5:4, 278n12; 7:9, 44; 9:12, 305n62; 9:13, 153n566; 16:5, 187n11; 17:5, 262n36; 18:20, 55n269, 344, 353; 18:28–29, 308n96; 19:13, 320n64; 19:14, 275n23, 320n65; 21:7, 249n102; 22:8, 106n290; 23:3, 239n22; 24, 45; 25, 49–50, 352 (*see also* main index: *Meditations upon the Twentieth and Fifth Psalm*); 25:1, 262n35; 26:9, 306n68; 26:12, 266; 27:9, 347, 354; 27:14, 135n449; 31:24, 135n449; 34:1–5, 344, 352; 34:4, 274n9; 35:19–20, 301n25; 35:22–23, 301n26; 39, 348; 39:1–4, 286; 39:5, 284n71; 40:7–8, 236n184; 41:1, 341, 350; 45:1, 241n34; 48:14, 223n63; 49:9, 295n70; 49:10, 295n71; 49:17, 295n72; 50:16–17, 228n116; 51:6, 96n232; 51:10, 225n82; 51:14, 306n69; 54:2, 309n103; 56:12–13, 209n75, 341, 350; 57:1, 95n1, 179n21; 57:1–2, 302n40; 57:3, 302n41; 57:5, 302n42; 61:1, 309n103; 65:2, 309n103; 66:9, 321n74; 66:20, 321n77; 68:5, 232n158; 68:30, 201n20; 69:14, 192n44; 71:7, 311n118; 71:20, 341, 350; 72:18–19, 270n21, 289n16; 73:26, 289n12; 73:28, 289n12, 289n14; 76:10, 225n84; 77:10, 229n117; 78n.64, 231n146; 79:8, 306n70; 79:9, 306n71; 84:11, 193n54; 86:4, 262n35; 90:12, 224nn74–75; 91:15, 342, 351; 94:19, 244n61; 101:1, 278n10; 101:2, 278n11; 102:19–20, 97; 103:2, 341, 350; 103:14, 187n9, 229n125; 105:15, 247n85; 106:4–5, 258, 264–265, 346, 354; 106:5, 303n48; 107:8, 318n47; 113:5–6, 308n94; 116:8, 308n95; 116:15, 305n64; 117:1, 193n59; 118:13, 309n100; 118:23, 229n127; 119:9, 342, 351; 119:38, 255n157, 257n171, 281n47, 290n24; 119:49, 244n63; 119:68, 228n115; 119:105,

195n71; 119:113, 321n70; 119:125, 240n28; 119:133, 226n91, 322n85; 126:1, 88n173, 195n72, 267n10; 130:83, 323n92; 136:2, 203n37; 139:23–24, 349, 356; 142:2, 105n287; 143, 343, 352; 143:8, 262n35; 162:5, 195n74

Revelation: 2:1–7, 178n18; 2:8–11, 178n18; 2:12–17, 178n18; 2:17, 341, 350; 2:18–29, 178n18; 3:1–6, 178n18; 3:2, 274n11; 3:7–13, 178n18; 3:14–22, 178n18; 3:18, 274n11; 3:20, 274n11; 4:10–11, 248n92; 12:9, 192n9; 13:10, 182n47; 21:7, 178n18; 22:2, 178n18

Romans: 1:18, 284; 1:21, 323; 2:5, 194n67; 3:10, 244n64; 3:23–24, 279; 4:25, 280; 5:1, 315; 5:12, 296; 5:19, 296; 5:21, 296; 6:1, 310; 6:2, 310; 6:11, 193n55; 8:17, 176n9; 8:28, 201n21, 218n16, 235n177, 341, 350, 351; 8:28–39, 342; 8:38–39, 246n78, 350, 351; 8:39, 244, 307; 10:9, 341, 350; 11:36, 312; 12:11, 252n127; 13:7, 182; 14:23, 178, 282; 15:13, 259n16

Ruth, 355

1 Samuel, 50n248; 1, 50n248; 1–2, 355; 1–28, 355; 2:10, 323; 3:18, 342; 4:22, 344, 353; 7:12, 317; 30:6, 325

2 Samuel: 1:14, 194n66; 11:2–3, 355

1 Thessalonians: 1:3, 295–296; 1:7, 296, 296n77; 5:22, 225, 231n150

1 Timothy: 1:13, 262; 2:1–2, 182; 2:1–3, 269; 2:3, 182n43; 3:15, 304, 315; 5:4, 224; 5:4–5, 224n73; 5:5, 232; 5:7, 232; 5:8, 228n110; 5:10, 232; 6:8, 317

2 Timothy: 1:5, 230

Titus: 2:10, 312; 2:11–13, 348, 356; 2:13, 319, 322; 2:14, 205n47

Zechariah: 4:6, 242; 4:14, 283; 13:9, 341, 351; 43:2, 322

Zephaniah: 3:19, 192, 271

The Other Voice in Early Modern Europe: The Toronto Series

Series Titles

Madre María Rosa
Journey of Five Capuchin Nuns
Edited and translated by Sarah E. Owens
Volume 1, 2009

Giovan Battista Andreini
Love in the Mirror: *A Bilingual Edition*
Edited and translated by Jon R. Snyder
Volume 2, 2009

Raymond de Sabanac and Simone Zanacchi
Two Women of the Great Schism: The Revelations *of Constance de Rabastens by Raymond de Sabanac and* Life of the Blessed Ursulina of Parma *by Simone Zanacchi*
Edited and translated by Renate Blumenfeld-Kosinski and Bruce L. Venarde
Volume 3, 2010

Oliva Sabuco de Nantes Barrera
The True Medicine
Edited and translated by Gianna Pomata
Volume 4, 2010

Louise-Geneviève Gillot de Sainctonge
Dramatizing Dido, Circe, and Griselda
Edited and translated by Janet Levarie Smarr
Volume 5, 2010

Pernette du Guillet
Complete Poems: A Bilingual Edition
Edited with introduction and notes by Karen Simroth James
Poems translated by Marta Rijn Finch
Volume 6, 2010

Antonia Pulci
Saints' Lives and Bible Stories for the Stage: A Bilingual Edition
Edited by Elissa B. Weaver
Translated by James Wyatt Cook
Volume 7, 2010

Valeria Miani
Celinda, A Tragedy: *A Bilingual Edition*
Edited with an introduction by Valeria Finucci
Translated by Julia Kisacky
Annotated by Valeria Finucci and Julia Kisacky
Volume 8, 2010

Enchanted Eloquence: Fairy Tales by Seventeenth-Century French Women Writers
Edited and translated by Lewis C. Seifert and Domna C. Stanton
Volume 9, 2010

Gottfried Wilhelm Leibniz, Sophie, Electress of Hanover and Queen Sophie Charlotte of Prussia
Leibniz and the Two Sophies: The Philosophical Correspondence
Edited and translated by Lloyd Strickland
Volume 10, 2011

In Dialogue with the Other Voice in Sixteenth-Century Italy: Literary and Social Contexts for Women's Writing
Edited by Julie D. Campbell and Maria Galli Stampino
Volume 11, 2011

SISTER GIUSTINA NICCOLINI
The Chronicle of Le Murate
Edited and translated by Saundra Weddle
Volume 12, 2011

LIUBOV KRICHEVSKAYA
No Good without Reward: Selected Writings: A Bilingual Edition
Edited and translated by Brian James Baer
Volume 13, 2011

ELIZABETH COOKE HOBY RUSSELL
The Writings of an English Sappho
Edited by Patricia Phillippy
With translations from Greek and Latin by Jaime Goodrich
Volume 14, 2011

LUCREZIA MARINELLA
Exhortations to Women and to Others If They Please
Edited and translated by Laura Benedetti
Volume 15, 2012

MARGHERITA DATINI
Letters to Francesco Datini
Translated by Carolyn James and Antonio Pagliaro
Volume 16, 2012

DELARIVIER MANLEY AND MARY PIX
English Women Staging Islam, 1696–1707
Edited and introduced by Bernadette Andrea
Volume 17, 2012

CECILIA DEL NACIMIENTO
Journeys of a Mystic Soul in Poetry and Prose
Introduction and prose translations by Kevin Donnelly
Poetry translations by Sandra Sider
Volume 18, 2012

LADY MARGARET DOUGLAS AND OTHERS
The Devonshire Manuscript: A Women's Book of Courtly Poetry
Edited and introduced by Elizabeth Heale
Volume 19, 2012

ARCANGELA TARABOTTI
Letters Familiar and Formal
Edited and translated by Meredith K. Ray and Lynn Lara Westwater
Volume 20, 2012

PERE TORRELLAS AND JUAN DE FLORES
Three Spanish Querelle *Texts: Grisel and Mirabella, The Slander against Women, and The Defense of Ladies against Slanderers: A Bilingual Edition and Study*
Edited and translated by Emily C. Francomano
Volume 21, 2013

BARBARA TORELLI BENEDETTI
Partenia, a Pastoral Play: A Bilingual Edition
Edited and translated by Lisa Sampson and Barbara Burgess-Van Aken
Volume 22, 2013

FRANÇOIS ROUSSET, JEAN LIEBAULT, JACQUES GUILLEMEAU, JACQUES DUVAL AND LOUIS DE SERRES
Pregnancy and Birth in Early Modern France: Treatises by Caring Physicians and Surgeons (1581–1625)
Edited and translated by Valerie Worth-Stylianou
Volume 23, 2013

MARY ASTELL
The Christian Religion, as Professed by a Daughter of the Church of England
Edited by Jacqueline Broad
Volume 24, 2013

SOPHIA OF HANOVER
Memoirs (1630–1680)
Edited and translated by Sean Ward
Volume 25, 2013

KATHERINE AUSTEN
Book M: *A London Widow's Life Writings*
Edited by Pamela S. Hammons
Volume 26, 2013

ANNE KILLIGREW
"My Rare Wit Killing Sin": Poems of a Restoration Courtier
Edited by Margaret J. M. Ezell
Volume 27, 2013

TULLIA D'ARAGONA AND OTHERS
The Poems and Letters of Tullia d'Aragona and Others: A Bilingual Edition
Edited and translated by Julia L. Hairston
Volume 28, 2014

LUISA DE CARVAJAL Y MENDOZA
The Life and Writings of Luisa de Carvajal y Mendoza
Edited and translated by Anne J. Cruz
Volume 29, 2014

Russian Women Poets of the Eighteenth and Early Nineteenth Centuries: A Bilingual Edition
Edited and translated by Amanda Ewington
Volume 30, 2014

JACQUES DU BOSC
L'Honnête Femme: *The Respectable Woman in Society and the* New Collection of Letters and Responses by Contemporary Women
Edited and translated by Sharon Diane Nell and Aurora Wolfgang
Volume 31, 2014

LADY HESTER PULTER
Poems, Emblems, *and* The Unfortunate Florinda
Edited by Alice Eardley
Volume 32, 2014

JEANNE FLORE
Tales and Trials of Love, Concerning Venus's Punishment of Those Who Scorn True Love and Denounce Cupid's Sovereignity: *A Bilingual Edition and Study*
Edited and translated by Kelly Digby Peebles
Poems translated by Marta Rijn Finch
Volume 33, 2014

VERONICA GAMBARA
Complete Poems: A Bilingual Edition
Critical introduction by Molly M. Martin
Edited and translated by Molly M. Martin and Paola Ugolini
Volume 34, 2014

CATHERINE DE MÉDICIS AND OTHERS
Portraits of the Queen Mother: Polemics, Panegyrics, Letters
Translation and study by Leah L. Chang and Katherine Kong
Volume 35, 2014

FRANÇOISE PASCAL, MARIE-CATHERINE DESJARDINS, ANTOINETTE DESHOULIÈRES, AND CATHERINE DURAND
Challenges to Traditional Authority: Plays by French Women Authors, 1650–1700
Edited and translated by Perry Gethner
Volume 36, 2015

FRANCISZKA URSZULA RADZIWIŁŁOWA
Selected Drama and Verse
Edited by Patrick John Corness and
Barbara Judkowiak
Translated by Patrick John Corness
Translation Editor Aldona
Zwierzyńska-Coldicott
Introduction by Barbara Judkowiak
Volume 37, 2015

DIODATA MALVASIA
*Writings on the Sisters of San Luca and
Their Miraculous Madonna*
Edited and translated by Danielle Callegari
and Shannon McHugh
Volume 38, 2015

MARGARET VAN NOORT
*Spiritual Writings of Sister Margaret of the
Mother of God (1635–1643)*
Edited by Cordula van Wyhe
Translated by Susan M. Smith
Volume 39, 2015

GIOVAN FRANCESCO STRAPAROLA
The Pleasant Nights
Edited and translated by Suzanne
Magnanini
Volume 40, 2015

ANGÉLIQUE DE SAINT-JEAN ARNAULD
D'ANDILLY
Writings of Resistance
Edited and translated by John J. Conley, S.J.
Volume 41, 2015

FRANCESCO BARBARO
*The Wealth of Wives: A Fifteenth-Century
Marriage Manual*
Edited and translated by Margaret L. King
Volume 42, 2015

JEANNE D'ALBRET
*Letters from the Queen of Navarre with an
Ample Declaration*
Edited and translated by Kathleen M.
Llewellyn, Emily E. Thompson, and
Colette H. Winn
Volume 43, 2016

BATHSUA MAKIN AND MARY MORE
WITH A REPLY TO MORE BY ROBERT
WHITEHALL
*Educating English Daughters: Late
Seventeenth-Century Debates*
Edited by Frances Teague and Margaret
J. M. Ezell
Associate Editor Jessica Walker
Volume 44, 2016

ANNA STANISŁAWSKA
*Orphan Girl: A Transaction, or an Account
of the Entire Life of an Orphan Girl by way
of Plaintful Threnodies in the Year 1685:
The Aesop Episode*
Verse translation, introduction, and
commentary by Barry Keane
Volume 45, 2016

ALESSANDRA MACINGHI STROZZI
Letters to Her Sons, 1447–1470
Edited and translated by Judith Bryce
Volume 46, 2016

MOTHER JUANA DE LA CRUZ
*Mother Juana de la Cruz, 1481–1534:
Visionary Sermons*
Edited by Jessica A. Boon and Ronald E.
Surtz
Introductory material and notes by Jessica
A. Boon
Translated by Ronald E. Surtz and Nora
Weinerth
Volume 47, 2016

CLAUDINE-ALEXANDRINE GUÉRIN DE TENCIN
Memoirs of the Count of Comminge and The Misfortunes of Love
Edited and translated by Jonathan Walsh
Foreword by Michel Delon
Volume 48, 2016

FELICIANA ENRÍQUEZ DE GUZMÁN, ANA CARO MALLÉN, AND SOR MARCELA DE SAN FÉLIX
Women Playwrights of Early Modern Spain
Edited by Nieves Romero-Díaz and Lisa Vollendorf
Translated and annotated by Harley Erdman
Volume 49, 2016

ANNA TRAPNEL
Anna Trapnel's Report and Plea; or, A Narrative of Her Journey from London into Cornwall
Edited by Hilary Hinds
Volume 50, 2016

MARÍA VELA Y CUETO
Autobiography and Letters of a Spanish Nun
Edited by Susan Diane Laningham
Translated by Jane Tar
Volume 51, 2016

CHRISTINE DE PIZAN
The Book of the Mutability of Fortune
Edited and translated by Geri L. Smith
Volume 52, 2017

MARGUERITE D'AUGE, RENÉE BURLAMACCHI, AND JEANNE DU LAURENS
Sin and Salvation in Early Modern France: Three Women's Stories
Edited, and with an introduction by Colette H. Winn
Translated by Nicholas Van Handel and Colette H. Winn
Volume 53, 2017

ISABELLA D'ESTE
Selected Letters
Edited and translated by Deanna Shemek
Volume 54, 2017

IPPOLITA MARIA SFORZA
Duchess and Hostage in Renaissance Naples: Letters and Orations
Edited and translated by Diana Robin and Lynn Lara Westwater
Volume 55, 2017

LOUISE BOURGEOIS
Midwife to the Queen of France: Diverse Observations
Translated by Stephanie O'Hara
Edited by Alison Klairmont Lingo
Volume 56, 2017

CHRISTINE DE PIZAN
Othea's Letter to Hector
Edited and translated by Renate Blumenfeld-Kosinski and Earl Jeffrey Richards
Volume 57, 2017

MARIE-GENEVIÈVE-CHARLOTTE THIROUX D'ARCONVILLE
Selected Philosophical, Scientific, and Autobiographical Writings
Edited and translated by Julie Candler Hayes
Volume 58, 2018

LADY MARY WROTH
Pamphilia to Amphilanthus *in Manuscript and Print*
Edited by Ilona Bell
Texts by Steven W. May and Ilona Bell
Volume 59, 2017

Witness, Warning, and Prophecy: Quaker Women's Writing, 1655–1700
Edited by Teresa Feroli and Margaret Olofson Thickstun
Volume 60, 2018

SYMPHORIEN CHAMPIER
The Ship of Virtuous Ladies
Edited and translated by Todd W. Reeser
Volume 61, 2018

ISABELLA ANDREINI
Mirtilla, A Pastoral: *A Bilingual Edition*
Edited by Valeria Finucci
Translated by Julia Kisacky
Volume 62, 2018

MARGHERITA COSTA
The Buffoons, A Ridiculous Comedy:
A Bilingual Edition
Edited and translated by Sara E. Díaz and Jessica Goethals
Volume 63, 2018

MARGARET CAVENDISH, DUCHESS OF NEWCASTLE
Poems and Fancies *with* The Animal Parliament
Edited by Brandie R. Siegfried
Volume 64, 2018

MARGARET FELL
Women's Speaking Justified *and Other Pamphlets*
Edited by Jane Donawerth and Rebecca M. Lush
Volume 65, 2018

MARY WROTH, JANE CAVENDISH, AND ELIZABETH BRACKLEY
Women's Household Drama:
Loves Victorie, A Pastorall, *and* The concealed Fansyes
Edited by Marta Straznicky and Sara Mueller
Volume 66, 2018

ELEONORA FONSECA PIMENTEL
From Arcadia to Revolution: The Neapolitan Monitor *and Other Writings*
Edited and translated by Verina R. Jones
Volume 67, 2019

CHARLOTTE ARBALESTE DUPLESSIS-MORNAY, ANNE DE CHAUFEPIÉ, AND ANNE MARGUERITE PETIT DU NOYER
The Huguenot Experience of Persecution and Exile: Three Women's Stories
Edited by Colette H. Winn
Translated by Lauren King and Colette H. Winn
Volume 68, 2019

ANNE BRADSTREET
Poems and Meditations
Edited by Margaret Olofson Thickstun
Volume 69, 2019

ARCANGELA TARABOTTI
Antisatire: *In Defense of Women, against Francesco Buoninsegni*
Edited and translated by Elissa B. Weaver
Volume 70, 2020

MARY FRANKLIN AND HANNAH BURTON
She Being Dead Yet Speaketh: The Franklin Family Papers
Edited by Vera J. Camden
Volume 71, 2020

LUCREZIA MARINELLA
Love Enamored and Driven Mad
Edited and translated by Janet E. Gomez and Maria Galli Stampino
Volume 72, 2020

ARCANGELA TARABOTTI
Convent Paradise
Edited and translated by Meredith K. Ray and Lynn Lara Westwater
Volume 73, 2020

GABRIELLE-SUZANNE BARBOT DE VILLENEUVE
Beauty and the Beast: *The Original Story*
Edited and translated by Aurora Wolfgang
Volume 74, 2020

FLAMINIO SCALA
The Fake Husband, A Comedy
Edited and translated by Rosalind Kerr
Volume 75, 2020

ANNE VAUGHAN LOCK
Selected Poetry, Prose, and Translations,
with Contextual Materials
Edited by Susan M. Felch
Volume 76, 2021

CAMILLA ERCULIANI
Letters on Natural Philosophy: The
Scientific Correspondence of a Sixteenth-
Century Pharmacist, with Related Texts
Edited by Eleonora Carinci
Translated by Hannah Marcus
Foreword by Paula Findlen
Volume 77, 2021

REGINA SALOMEA PILSZTYNOWA
My Life's Travels and Adventures: An
Eighteenth-Century Oculist in the Ottoman
Empire and the European Hinterland
Edited and translated by Władysław Roczniak
Volume 78, 2021

CHRISTINE DE PIZAN
The God of Love's Letter and The Tale of
the Rose: A Bilingual Edition
Edited and translated by Thelma S. Fenster
and Christine Reno
With Jean Gerson, "A Poem on Man and Woman." Translated from the Latin by Thomas O'Donnell
Foreword by Jocelyn Wogan-Browne
Volume 79, 2021

MARIE GIGAULT DE BELLEFONDS, MARQUISE DE VILLARS
Letters from Spain: A Seventeenth-Century
French Noblewoman at the Spanish Royal
Court
Edited and translated by Nathalie Hester
Volume 80, 2021

ANNA MARIA VAN SCHURMAN
Letters and Poems to and from Her Mentor
and Other Members of Her Circle
Edited and translated by Anne R. Larsen
and Steve Maiullo
Volume 81, 2021

VITTORIA COLONNA
Poems of Widowhood: A Bilingual Edition
of the 1538 Rime
Translation and introduction by Ramie Targoff
Edited by Ramie Targoff and Troy Tower
Volume 82, 2021

VALERIA MIANI
Amorous Hope, A Pastoral Play: A Bilingual Edition
Edited and translated by Alexandra Coller
Volume 83, 2020

MADELEINE DE SCUDÉRY
Lucrece and Brutus: Glory in the Land of
Tender
Edited and translated by Sharon Diane Nell
Volume 84, 2021

ANNA STANISŁAWSKA
One Body with Two Souls Entwined:
An Epic Tale of Married Love in
Seventeenth-Century Poland
Orphan Girl: The Oleśnicki Episode
Verse translation, introduction, and commentary by Barry Keane
Volume 85, 2021

CHRISTINE DE PIZAN
Book of the Body Politic
Edited and translated by Angus J. Kennedy
Volume 86, 2021